Advance Praise for
Readings on the Ultimate Questions: An Introduction to Philosophy

"This is an excellent anthology for introducing today's students to contemporary philosophical problems debated within the analytic tradition, with large sections on epistemology and the philosophy of mind. The selections are clearly written and appropriately related to create an internal dialogue among the texts."

Mark Strawser
University of Central Florida

"The major strengths of this text are the many lucid, well written, yet very contemporary readings. . . . It is important to present to students what is currently happening in philosophy, but be able to do so in a way that they will find intelligible!"

Mark Price
Columbia College

"The first section is maybe the most brilliant compilation of readings about the nature of philosophy I've encountered in an Intro text. . . . [O]verall, they are a wonderful way to start a semester."

Joseph P. Porter
St. Louis Community College

"Part One and its contents are a definite strength as . . . [the readings] . . . the student will first encounter. The selections are intriguing and interesting, and accessible enough as not to be discouraging."

Susanne D. Claxton
Oklahoma State University

"The overall selection of readings provides the instructor with a solid base from which to select assignments. . . . The major strength of this text is the choice of readings over the range of philosophical history. As I have said, it provides the reader with a true sense of continuity and life to philosophy."

Alan B. Clark
Del Mar College

Also look for this anthology's companion text, **Ultimate Questions: Thinking About Philosophy** (ISBN: 0-321-10893-0) by Nils Ch. Rauhut. These two volumes—text and anthology—can be ordered together (ISBN: 0-321-28127-6) at a special package discount.

D0162311

About the Authors

Nils Ch. Rauhut studied philosophy and history at the University of Regensburg (Germany). He received an M.A. degree in philosophy from the University of Colorado at Boulder, and a Ph.D. in philosophy from the University of Washington in Seattle. He taught at Weber State University in Ogden, Utah, and he is currently teaching at Coastal Carolina University in Conway, South Carolina.

Renée Smith earned her M.A. and Ph.D. in Philosophy from the University of Colorado, Boulder. She teaches at Coastal Carolina University in Conway, South Carolina.

Readings on the Ultimate Questions

An Introduction to Philosophy

Edited by

Nils Ch. Rauhut
Coastal Carolina University

Renée Smith
Coastal Carolina University

PENGUIN ACADEMICS

PEARSON
Longman

New York Boston San Francisco
London Toronto Sydney Tokyo Singapore Madrid
Mexico City Munich Paris Cape Town Hong Kong Montreal

Vice President and Publisher: Priscilla McGeehon
Executive Marketing Manager: Ann Stypuloski
Production Manager: Ellen MacElree
Project Coordination, Text Design, and Electronic Page Makeup:
    Nesbitt Graphics, Inc.
Cover Designer/Manager: Nancy Danahy
Cover Photo: Burstein Collection/CORBIS
Senior Manufacturing Buyer: Dennis J. Para
Printer and Binder: R. R. Donelley and Sons Company
Cover Printer: Phoenix Color Corps.

For permission to use copyrighted material, grateful acknowledgment is made
to the copyright holders on pp. 643–645, which are hereby made part of this
copyright page.

Library of Congress Cataloging-in-Publication Data
Readings on the ultimate questions: an introduction to philosophy /
[compiled by] Nils Ch. Rauhut, Renée Smith.—1st ed.
    p. cm.
  Includes bibliographical references
  ISBN 0-321-19549-3 (student)
  1. Philosophy. I. Rauhut, Nils Ch. II. Smith, Renée.
B74.R39 2004
100—dc22

                                                                2004013233

Copyright © 2005 by Pearson Education, Inc.

All rights reserved. No part of this publication may be reproduced, stored in a
retrieval system, or transmitted, in any form or by any means, electronic,
mechanical, photocopying, recording, or otherwise, without the prior written
permission of the publisher. Printed in the United States.

Please visit us at http://www.ablongman.com

ISBN 0-321-19549-3

  2 3 4 5 6 7 8 9 10—DOH—07 06 05

Contents

PART 7   What Is Moral?   511

Preface

Readings on the Ultimate Questions: An Introduction to Philosophy, is a collection of philosophical essays that complements the topics and approach of *Ultimate Questions: Thinking About Philosophy*. In selecting its contents, we have been guided by three overarching goals.

First, we hope to entice introductory students to actively read and think about philosophical issues and problems. Toward this end, we selected papers that engagingly and creatively present the central topics of an introductory philosophy course. For example, John Perry's paper presents the problem of personal identity in a conversation between a priest and a dying philosopher, and Aeon J. Skoble, in "Virtue Ethics in TV's *Seinfeld*," discusses moral theory in the context of characters from the TV sitcom *Seinfeld*. We also include a piece by Christopher Grau that introduces Cartesian skepticism within the framework of the popular movie *The Matrix*, and in the autobiographical essay "Philosophy, a Bus Ride, and Dumb Luck," Alfred Mele shares the story of how he came to philosophy. These are just a few of the papers we selected because they are enjoyable to read, they encourage philosophical thought, and they lend themselves to lively discussion.

Second, we want to introduce students to excellent, and accessible, contemporary philosophy. Therefore, the second most important feature of this anthology is its focus on clearly written and well-argued papers by outstanding contemporary philosophers. We include work by Daniel Dennett on genetic determinism, David Lewis on functionalism, Richard Taylor on the cosmological argument, and van Inwagen on Free Will. These articles introduce beginning students to the way contemporary philosophers approach philosophical problems, and they complement the topics and questions discussed in the text *Ultimate Questions: Thinking About Philosophy*.

Third, we want to acquaint introductory students with the work of important figures in the history of philosophy. Although our anthology predominantely focuses on contemporary philosophy, we also include many of the classic works essential to an introductory course in philosophy, specifically, Descartes' *Meditations*, Plato's *Apology*, William James' *The Will to Believe*, John Stuart Mill's discussion of utilitarianism, selections from Kant's *Groundwork for the Metaphysics of Morals* and selections from Aristotle's *Nicomachean Ethics*.

It is our hope that *Readings on the Ultimate Questions: An Introduction to Philosophy*, together with *Ultimate Questions: Thinking About Philosophy*, will awaken students' philosophical curiosity by providing them with both contemporary and classical work in philosophy that is accessible, engaging, and thought-provoking.

Nils Ch. Rauhut

Renée Smith

PART ONE

WHAT IS PHILOSOPHY?

Philosophy—the love of wisdom—seeks to find rationally plausible answers to the most fundamental questions. Philosophers want to know, for instance, whether God exists or whether humans have souls. At first glance, these questions appear very intimidating. Can everyone participate in the attempt to find solutions to these questions? Might it not be easier to let a small group of professional thinkers wrestle with these questions and accept whatever answers they devise?

In his essay "What Is Enlightenment?" Immanuel Kant argues that each and every human being has the duty to use his own understanding without the guidance of another person. We must have the courage to find answers to fundamental questions on our own. If we avoid this duty, we live in a self-imposed immaturity that is incompatible with the dignity and freedom of humankind.

The seventeenth-century philosopher Baruch Spinoza came to philosophy in a different way. In his *Treatise on the Emendation of the Intellect*, Spinoza writes that it was his desire to find a *true good* that would bring him continuous and supreme joy to all eternity that turned him toward the study of philosophy. Spinoza discovered that those goods that are normally considered to be of extreme importance—money, fame, and sensual pleasure—are intrinsically uncertain and stand in the way of true happiness. He thus followed a new path of thinking and living that made him understand that the human mind forms a union with the whole of Nature.

A contemporary perspective on the value of the philosophical life is offered by Alfred Mele. In the essay "Philosophy, a Bus Ride, and Dumb Luck," Mele describes his first foray into philosophical thinking when, as a child, he wondered whether it is possible to love God more than one's own parents. Although he eventually decided to major in philosophy, he did not set out to become a philosopher. It was a chance meeting with his teacher, Robert Baker, on a bus that prompted him to think seriously about attending graduate school in philosophy. While writing his dissertation on Aristotle, he realized that he had fallen in love with philosophy and that he could not imagine a better way to spend his life.

These three selections show that philosophers are often convinced that the philosophical life is very rewarding. The general public, on the other hand, is often afraid that philosophy has a negative influence on young people. Socrates, for example, was accused by his fellow citizens of introducing new religious beliefs and of corrupting the young men of Athens who enjoyed listening to him. We include Socrates' famous defense against these charges. In Plato's *Apology*, Socrates argues that he is not ashamed to have followed a philosophical way of life and that his questioning of prominent Athenian men has provided a great service to all Athenians, for "life without such examination is not worth living."

Bertrand Russell, too, provides a defense of the philosophical life. In "The Value of Philosophy," Russell writes that it is often held that philosophy is nothing but useless trifling about matters concerning which knowledge is impossible. In response, Russell argues that philosophy is not to be studied for the sake of any definite answers to its questions, but rather "for the sake of the questions themselves." Philosophical questions "enlarge our conception of what is possible . . . and prepare our mind for the union with the universe which constitutes its highest good."

We finish our introductory section with Dennis Earl's discussion of classical conceptual analysis. In order to answer central philosophical questions like "What is justice?" or "Do we know anything?" one invariably needs to clarify the meaning of terms like *justice* or *knowledge*. In the essay "Classical Conceptual Analysis," Earl presents a clear description of how an analysis that involves the development of necessary and jointly sufficient conditions can clarify the meanings of such complex terms. He concludes by arguing that classical conceptual analysis can be defended against some frequently voiced objections.

What Is Enlightenment?[1]

Immanuel Kant   *(Translated by Ted Humphrey)*

Enlightenment is man's emergence from his self-imposed immaturity.[2]
Immaturity is the inability to use one's understanding without guidance
from another. This immaturity is *self-imposed* when its cause lies not
in lack of understanding, but in lack of resolve and courage to use it without guidance from another. *Sapere Aude!*[3] "Have courage to use your
own understanding!"—that is the motto of enlightenment.

Laziness and cowardice are the reasons why so great a proportion
of men, long after nature has released them from alien guidance
(*naturaliter maiorennes*),[4] nonetheless gladly remain in lifelong immaturity, and why it is so easy for others to establish themselves as their
guardians. It is so easy to be immature. If I have a book to serve as my
understanding, a pastor to serve as my conscience, a physician to determine my diet for me, and so on, I need not exert myself at all. I need
not think, if only I can pay: others will readily undertake the irksome
work for me. The guardians who have so benevolently taken over the
supervision of men have carefully seen to it that the far greatest part of
them (including the entire fair sex) regard taking the step to maturity
as very dangerous, not to mention difficult. Having first made their
domestic livestock dumb, and having carefully made sure that these
docile creatures will not take a single step without the go-cart to which
they are harnessed, these guardians then show them the danger that
threatens them, should they attempt to walk alone. Now this danger is
not actually so great, for after falling a few times they would in the end
certainly learn to walk; but an example of this kind makes men timid and
usually frightens them out of all further attempts.

Thus, it is difficult for any individual man to work himself out of
the immaturity that has all but become his nature. He has even become
fond of this state and for the time being is actually incapable of using
his own understanding, for no one has ever allowed him to attempt it.
Rules and formulas, those mechanical aids to the rational use, or rather
misuse, of his natural gifts, are the shackles of a permanent immaturity. Whoever threw them off would still make only an uncertain leap over
the smallest ditch, since he is unaccustomed to this kind of free movement. Consequently, only a few have succeeded, by cultivating their own
minds, in freeing themselves from immaturity and pursuing a secure
course.

But that the public should enlighten itself is more likely; indeed, if it is only allowed freedom, enlightenment is almost inevitable. For even among the entrenched guardians of the great masses a few will always think for themselves, a few who, after having themselves thrown off the yoke of immaturity, will spread the spirit of a rational appreciation for both their own worth and for each person's calling to think for himself. But it should be particularly noted that if a public that was first placed in this yoke by the guardians is suitably aroused by some of those who are altogether incapable of enlightenment, it may force the guardians themselves to remain under the yoke—so pernicious is it to instill prejudices, for they finally take revenge upon their originators, or on their descendants. Thus a public can only attain enlightenment slowly. Perhaps a revolution can overthrow autocratic despotism and profiteering or power-grabbing oppression, but it can never truly reform a manner of thinking;[5] instead, new prejudices, just like the old ones they replace, will serve as a leash for the great unthinking mass.

Nothing is required for this enlightenment, however, except *freedom;* and the freedom in question is the least harmful of all, namely, the freedom to use reason *publicly* in all matters. But on all sides I hear: *"Do not argue!"* The officer says, "Do not argue, drill!" The taxman says, "Do not argue, pay!" The pastor says, "Do not argue, believe!" (Only one ruler in the world[6] says, *"Argue* as much as you want and about what you want, *but obey!"*) In this we have [examples of] pervasive restrictions on freedom. But which restriction hinders enlightenment and which does not, but instead actually advances it? I reply: The *public* use of one's reason must always be free, and it alone can bring about enlightenment among mankind; the *private use* of reason may, however, often be very narrowly restricted, without otherwise hindering the progress of enlightenment. By the public use of one's own reason I understand the use that anyone as a *scholar* makes of reason before the entire *literate world.* I call the private use of reason that which a person may make in a *civic post* or office that has been entrusted to him.[7] Now in many affairs conducted in the interests of a community, a certain mechanism is required by means of which some of its members must conduct themselves in an entirely passive manner so that through an artificial unanimity the government may guide them toward public ends, or at least prevent them from destroying such ends. Here one certainly must not argue, instead one must obey. However, insofar as this part of the machine also regards himself as a member of the community as a whole, or even of the world community, and as a consequence addresses the public in the role of a scholar, in the proper sense of that term, he can most certainly argue, without thereby harming the affairs for which as a passive member he is partly responsible. Thus it would be disastrous if an officer on duty who was given a command by his superior were to question the appropriateness or utility of the order. He must obey. But as a scholar he cannot be justly constrained from making comments about errors in military service, or from placing them before the public for its judgment. The citizen cannot refuse to pay the taxes imposed on him; indeed, impertinent criticism of such levies, when they should be paid by him, can be punished as a scandal (since it can lead to widespread insubordination). But the same person does not act contrary to civic duty when, as a scholar, he publicly expresses his thoughts regarding the impropriety or even injustice of such taxes. Likewise a pastor is bound to instruct his catecumens and congregation in accordance with the symbol of the church he serves, for he was appointed on that condition. But as a scholar he has complete freedom, indeed even the calling, to impart to the public all of his carefully considered and well-intentioned thoughts concerning mistaken aspects of that symbol,[8] as well as his suggestions for the better arrangement of religious and church matters. Nothing in this can weigh on his conscience. What he teaches in consequence of his office as a servant of the church he sets out as something with regard to which he has no discretion to teach in accord with his own lights; rather, he offers it under the direction and in the name of another. He will say, "Our church teaches this or that and these are the demonstrations it uses." He thereby extracts for his congregation all practical uses from precepts to which he would not himself subscribe with complete conviction, but whose presentation he can nonetheless undertake, since it is not entirely impossible that truth lies hidden in them, and, in any case, nothing contrary to the very nature of religion is to be found in them. If he believed he could find anything of the latter sort in them, he could not in good conscience serve in his position; he would have to resign. Thus an appointed teacher's use of his reason for the sake of his congregation is merely *private*, because, however large the congregation is, this use is always only domestic; in this regard, as a priest, he is not free and cannot be such because he is acting under instructions from someone else. By contrast, the cleric—as a scholar who speaks through his writings to the public as such, i.e., the world—enjoys in this *public use* of reason an unrestricted freedom to use his own rational capacities and to speak his own mind. For that the (spiritual) guardians of a people should themselves be immature is an absurdity that would insure the perpetuation of absurdities.

But would a society of pastors, perhaps a church assembly or venerable presbytery (as those among the Dutch call themselves), not be justified in binding itself by oath to a certain unalterable symbol in order to secure a constant guardianship over each of its members and through them over the people, and this for all time: I say that this is wholly impossible. Such a contract, whose intention is to preclude forever all further enlightenment of the human race, is absolutely null and void, even if it should be ratified by the supreme power, by parliaments, and by the most solemn peace treaties. One age cannot bind itself, and thus conspire, to place a succeeding one in a condition whereby it would be impossible for the later age to expand its knowledge (particularly where it is so very important), to rid itself of errors, and generally to increase its enlightenment. That would be a crime against human nature, whose essential destiny lies precisely in such progress; subsequent generations are thus completely justified in dismissing such agreements as unauthorized and criminal. The criterion of everything that can be agreed upon as a law by a people lies in this question: Can a people impose such a law on itself?[9] Now it might be possible, in anticipation of a better state of affairs, to introduce a provisional order for a specific, short time, all the while giving all citizens, especially clergy, in their role as scholars, the freedom to comment publicly, i.e., in writing, on the present institution's shortcomings. The provisional order might last until insight into the nature of these matters had become so widespread and obvious that the combined (if not unanimous) voices of the populace could propose to the crown that it take under its protection those congregations that, in accord with their newly gained insight, had organized themselves under altered religious institutions, but without interfering with those wishing to allow matters to remain as before. However, it is absolutely forbidden that they unite into a religious organization that nobody may for the duration of a man's lifetime publicly question, for so doing would deny, render fruitless, and make detrimental to succeeding generations an era in man's progress toward improvement. A man may put off enlightenment with regard to what he ought to know, though only for a short time and for his own person; but to renounce it for himself, or, even more, for subsequent generations, is to violate and trample man's divine rights underfoot. And what a people may not decree for itself may still less be imposed on it by a monarch, for his lawgiving authority rests on his unification of the people's collective will in his own. If he only sees to it that all genuine or purported improvement is consonant with civil order, he can allow his subjects to do what they find necessary to their spiritual well-being, which is not his affair. However, he must prevent anyone from forcibly interfering with another's working as best he can to determine and promote his well-being. It detracts from his own majesty when he interferes in these matters, since the writings in which his subjects attempt to clarify their insights lend value to his conception of governance. This holds whether he acts from his own highest insight—whereby he calls upon himself the reproach, *"Caesar non est supra grammaticos."*[10]—as well as, indeed even more, when he despoils his highest authority by supporting the spiritual despotism of some tyrants in his state over his other subjects.

If it is now asked, "Do we presently live in an *enlightened* age?" the answer is, "No, but we do live in an age of *enlightenment.*" As matters now stand, a great deal is still lacking in order for men as a whole to be, or even to put themselves into a position to be able without external guidance to apply understanding confidently to religious issues. But we do have clear indications that the way is now being opened for men to proceed freely in this direction and that the obstacles to general enlightenment—to their release from their self-imposed immaturity—are gradually diminishing. In this regard, this age is the age of enlightenment, the century of Frederick.[11]

A prince who does not find it beneath him to say that he takes it to be his *duty* to prescribe nothing, but rather to allow men complete freedom in religious matters—who thereby renounces the arrogant title of *tolerance*—is himself enlightened and deserves to be praised by a grateful present and by posterity as the first, at least where the government is concerned, to release the human race from immaturity and to leave everyone free to use his own reason in all matters of conscience. Under his rule, venerable pastors, in their role as scholars and without prejudice to their official duties, may freely and openly set out for the world's scrutiny their judgments and views, even where these occasionally differ from the accepted symbol. Still greater freedom is afforded to those who are not restricted by an official post. This spirit of freedom is expanding even where it must struggle against the external obstacles of governments that misunderstand their own function. Such governments are illuminated by the example that the existence of freedom need not give cause for the least concern regarding public order and harmony in the commonwealth. If only they refrain from inventing artifices to keep themselves in it, men will gradually raise themselves from barbarism.

I have focused on religious matters in setting out my main point concerning enlightenment, i.e., man's emergence from self-imposed immaturity, first because our rulers have no interest in assuming the role of their subjects' guardians with respect to the arts and sciences, and secondly because that form of immaturity is both the most pernicious and disgraceful of all. But the manner of thinking of a head of state who favors religious enlightenment goes even further, for he realizes that there is no danger to his *legislation* in allowing his subjects to use reason *publicly* and to set before the world their thoughts concerning better formulations of his laws, even if this involves frank criticism of legislation currently in effect. We have before us a shining example, with respect to which no monarch surpasses the one whom we honor.

But only a ruler who is himself enlightened and has no dread of shadows, yet who likewise has a well-disciplined, numerous army to guarantee public peace, can say what no republic[12] may dare, namely: *"Argue as much as you want and about what you want, but obey!"* Here as elsewhere, when things are considered in broad perspective, a strange, unexpected pattern in human affairs reveals itself, one in which almost everything is paradoxical. A greater degree of civil freedom seems advantageous to a people's *spiritual* freedom; yet the former established impassable boundaries for the latter; conversely, a lesser degree of civil freedom provides enough room for all fully to expand their abilities. Thus, once nature has removed the hard shell from this kernel for which she has most fondly cared, namely, the inclination to and vocation for free *thinking*, the kernel gradually reacts on a people's mentality (whereby they become increasingly able to *act freely*), and it finally even influences the principles of *government*, which finds that it can profit by treating men, *who are now more than machines*, in accord with their dignity.*

Königsberg in Prussia, 30 September 1784
I. Kant

---

*Today I read in Büsching's *Wöchentliche Nachtrichten* for September 13th a notice concerning this month's *Berlinischen Monatsschift* that mentions *Mendelssohn's* answer to this same question. I have not yet seen this journal, otherwise I would have withheld the foregoing reflections, which I now set out in order to see to what extent two person's thoughts may coincidentally agree.

Notes

1. A. A., VIII, 33–42. This essay first appeared in the *Berlinische Monatsschrift*, December, 1784.
2. The German is *Unmündigkeit*, which quite literally means "minority," where one is referring to the inability to make decisions for oneself. Kant's point in the essay is that by virtue of understanding and reason men have the inherent right and ability to make all intellectual, political and religious decisions for themselves. That they do not is a function of certain, perhaps implicit, choices they make in regard to exercising rights and developing capacities.
3. "Dare to know!" (Horace, *Epodes*, 1, 2, 40.) This motto was adopted by the Society of the Friends of Truth, an important circle of the German Enlightenment.
4. "Those who have come of age by virtue of nature."
5. The term Kant uses here and later, on p. 41, is *Denkungsart*; it occurs in the second edition preface to the *Critique of Pure Reason*, where he works out his famous analogy of the Copernican Revolution in philosophy, which he refers to as a revolution in the method of thought. (B vii–xxiv) The term refers to one's characteristic pattern of thought, whether it is marked by systematic, rational procedures or by prejudice and superstition, criticism or dogmatism.
6. Frederick II (the Great) of Prussia.
7. See *Theory and Practice*, 304.
8. Kant distinguishes between two classes of concepts, those that we can schematize, i.e., directly represent in experience (intuition), and those that we must symbolize, i.e., indirectly represent in experience (intuition). Symbolized concepts, such as the one we have of God, are those for which no experience can provide adequate content; consequently, experience can only be used to indicate the content we intend. All religious concepts have this character. By symbol in this context, then, Kant means those beliefs and practices in which a group expresses the content of its concept of the divine. (*Crit. Judgment*, 351–54)
9. This would seem a peculiarly political expression of the Categorical Imperative, particularly as it is expressed in *Groundings*, 428–29.
10. "Caesar is not above the grammarians." See *Perpetual Peace*, 368 f.
11. Frederick II (the Great), King of Prussia.
12. The term Kant uses here is *Freistaat*, which is idiomatically translated "republic." However, Kant never again uses this Germanic rooted word in the essays included in this volume. In all the other essays he uses the Latin loan word *Republic*. I point this out because what Kant says here about a *Freistaat* is inconsistent with what he says elsewhere about a *Republic*.

Treatise on the Emendation of the Intellect

Baruch Spinoza   *(Translated by Samuel Shirley)*

After experience had taught me the hollowness and futility of every-thing that is ordinarily encountered in daily life, and I realized that all the things which were the source and object of my anxiety held nothing of good or evil in themselves save in so far as the mind was influenced by them, I resolved at length to enquire whether there existed a true good, one which was capable of communicating itself and could alone affect the mind to the exclusion of all else, whether, in fact, there was something whose discovery and acquisition would afford me a continuous and supreme joy to all eternity.

I say 'I resolved at length,' for at first sight it seemed ill-advised to risk the loss of what was certain in the hope of something at that time uncertain. I could well see the advantages that derive from honor and wealth, and that I would be forced to abandon their quest if I were to devote myself to some new and different objective. And if in fact supreme happiness were to be found in the former, I must inevitably fail to attain it, whereas if it did not lie in these objectives and I devoted myself entirely to them, then once again I would lose that highest happiness.

I therefore debated whether it might be possible to arrive at a new guiding principle—or at least the sure hope of its attainment—without changing the manner and normal routine of my life. This I frequently attempted, but in vain. For the things which for the most part offer them-selves in life, and which, to judge from their actions, men regard as the highest good, can be reduced to these three headings: riches, honor, and sensual pleasure. With these three the mind is so distracted that it is quite incapable of thinking of any other good. With regard to sensual pleasure, the mind is so utterly obsessed by it that it seems as if it were absorbed in some good, and so is quite prevented from thinking of anything else. But after the enjoyment of this pleasure there ensues a profound depres-sion which, if it does not completely inhibit the mind, leads to its con-fusion and enervation. The pursuit of honor and wealth, too, engrosses the mind to no small degree, especially when the latter is sought exclu-sively for its own sake,[1] for it is then regarded as the highest good. Even

---

[1]This could be explained more fully and clearly by making a distinction between wealth that is sought for its own sake, for the sake of honor, for sensual pleasure, for health, or for the advancement of the sciences and the arts. But this is reserved for its proper place, such a detailed investigation being inappropriate here.

more so is the mind obsessed with honor, for this is always regarded as a good in itself and the ultimate end to which everything is directed. Then again, in both these cases, there is no repentance as in the case of sensual pleasure. The more each of them is possessed, the more our joy is enhanced, and we are therefore more and more induced to increase them both. But if it should come about that our hopes are disappointed, there ensues a profound depression. And finally, honor has this great drawback, that to attain it we must conduct our lives to suit other men, avoiding what the masses avoid and seeking what the masses seek.

So when I saw that all these things stood in the way of my embarking on a new course, and were indeed so opposed to it that I must necessarily choose between the one alternative and the other, I was forced to ask what was to my greater advantage; for, as I have said, I seemed set on losing a certain good for the sake of an uncertain good. But after a little reflection, I first of all realized that if I abandoned the old ways and embarked on a new way of life, I should be abandoning a good that was by its very nature uncertain—as we can clearly gather from what has been said—in favour of one that was uncertain not of its own nature (for I was seeking a permanent good) but only in respect of its attainment. Then persistent meditation enabled me to see that, if only I could be thoroughly resolute, I should be abandoning certain evils for the sake of a certain good. For I saw that my situation was one of great peril and that I was obliged to seek a remedy with all my might, however uncertain it might be, like a sick man suffering from a fatal malady who, foreseeing certain death unless a remedy is forthcoming, is forced to seek it, however uncertain it be, with all his might, for therein lies all his hope. Now all those objectives that are commonly pursued not only contribute nothing to the preservation of our being but even hinder it, being frequently the cause of the destruction of those who gain possession of them, and invariably the cause of the destruction of those who are possessed by them.[2] For there are numerous examples of men who have suffered persecution unto death because of their wealth, and also of men who have exposed themselves to so many dangers to acquire riches that they have finally paid for their folly with their lives. Nor are there less numerous examples of men who, to gain or preserve honor, have suffered a most wretched fate. Finally, there are innumerable examples of men who have hastened their death by reason of excessive sensual pleasure.

These evils, moreover, seemed to arise from this, that all happiness or unhappiness depends solely on the quality of the object to which we are bound by love. For strife will never arise on account of that which is

[2]This is to be demonstrated at greater length.

not loved; there will be no sorrow if it is lost, no envy if it is possessed by another, no fear, no hatred—in a word, no emotional agitation, all of which, however, occur in the case of the love of perishable things, such as all those of which we have been speaking. But love towards a thing eternal and infinite feeds the mind with joy alone, unmixed with any sadness. This is greatly to be desired, and to be sought with all our might. However, it was not without reason that I used these words, 'If only I could be earnestly resolute,' for although I perceived these things quite clearly in my mind, I could not on that account put aside all greed, sensual pleasure, and desire for esteem.

This one thing I could see, that as long as my mind was occupied with these thoughts, it turned away from those other objectives and earnestly applied itself to the quest for a new guiding principle. This was a great comfort to me, for I saw that those evils were not so persistent as to refuse to yield to remedies. And although at first these intermissions were rare and of very brief duration, nevertheless, as the true good became more and more discernible to me, these intermissions became more frequent and longer, especially when I realised that the acquisition of money, sensual pleasure, and esteem is a hindrance only as long as they are sought on their own account, and not as a means to other things. If they are sought as means, they will then be under some restriction, and far from being hindrances, they will do much to further the end for which they are sought, as I shall demonstrate in its proper place.

At this point I shall only state briefly what I understand by the true good, and at the same time what is the supreme good. In order that this may be rightly understood, it must be borne in mind that good and bad are only relative terms, so that one and the same thing may be said to be good or bad in different respects, just like the terms perfect and imperfect. Nothing, when regarded in its own nature, can be called perfect or imperfect, especially when we realize that all things that come into being do so in accordance with an eternal order and Nature's fixed laws.

But human weakness fails to comprehend that order in its thought, and meanwhile man conceives a human nature much stronger than his own, and sees no reason why he cannot acquire such a nature. Thus he is urged to seek the means that will bring him to such a perfection, and all that can be the means of his attaining this objective is called a true good, while the supreme good is to arrive at the enjoyment of such a nature, together with other individuals, if possible. What that nature is we shall show in its proper place; namely, the knowledge of the union which the mind has with the whole of Nature.[3]

---

[3]This is explained more fully in its proper place.

This, then, is the end for which I strive, to acquire the nature I have described and to endeavour that many should acquire it along with me. That is to say, my own happiness involves my making an effort to persuade many others to think as I do, so that their understanding and their desire should entirely accord with my understanding and my desire. To bring this about, it is necessary[4] (1) to understand as much about Nature as suffices for acquiring such a nature, and (2) to establish such a social order as will enable as many as possible to reach this goal with the greatest possible ease and assurance. Furthermore, (3) attention must be paid to moral philosophy and likewise the theory of the education of children; and since health is of no little importance in attaining this end, (4) the whole science of medicine must be elaborated. And since many difficult tasks are rendered easy by contrivance, and we can thereby gain much time and convenience in our daily lives, (5) the science of mechanics is in no way to be despised. . . .

Philosophy, a Bus Ride, and Dumb Luck
Alfred Mele

It is easy enough for philosophers to find signs of a philosophical disposition in their childhood. However, if, as I suspect, most children entertain philosophical questions and thoughts, these signs probably count for little. Children strike me as being by nature small athletes, scientists, and artists as well. Perhaps some of us, for some reason or other, never shed our childlike curiosity about things philosophical and our associated appetite for explanation.

I remember pondering as a child questions that I now know to be philosophical: when I was eight or nine, for example, my catechism teacher told the class that we must love God more than we love our parents. I worried about that all day. I knew that I loved my parents most, and I didn't see any way to change that. Furthermore, I did not understand how children *could* love God more than their parents, since we knew our parents but didn't know God. I decided that the catechism

---

[4]Note that here I am only concerned to enumerate the sciences necessary to our purpose, without regard to their order.

teacher had to be wrong, that God could not make impossible demands on people; and I felt OK. The next day, after church, I asked my brother Ron whom he loved more. He said "God," and I started to worry again. But I suspect that many of the kids in my catechism class had similar worries—or worse ones: the venial/mortal sin distinction was a real puzzler, for example; and if one couldn't get straight on that, how was one to avoid hell? In any case, I (and they) thought just as hard about issues that we later learned fell under the heading "physics," or "biology." Once, at about the same time, after learning that the earth rotates, I tried to figure out how anything on the earth could move in the direction of the earth's rotation unless it moved faster than the earth rotates. I spun my globe and raced one of my toy cars along its surface, over and over again, but I don't recall coming to a conclusion.

So much for my childhood. It was intellectually uninspiring, as you can see. Besides, I spent most of my free time playing baseball and football.

I first heard of philosophy, I think, in high school—a Catholic high school in Detroit. I was doing some research for an essay on religion when I came across Tolstoy's *My Religion.* That was my first encounter with what I regarded as rational reflection on religion. It struck me as brilliant, and when I finished it I wanted to read more. A search of the card catalogue, however, turned up only Tolstoy's fiction; so, I decided that I would just wait for college and take a philosophy course there. (We did read Paul Tillich in high school, but I recall thinking that Tillich sounded a lot like the nuns, and I was already fed up with them. Understandably, the feeling was mutual. I was expelled a month or so before graduation in 1969 for radical behavior—refusing to cut my collar-length hair, as I recall. My mother tried to persuade the good sisters to let me back in, using a dozen homemade pizzas to soften them up. That failed, and so did I.)

Eventually, I got to college by being recruited by the football coach of the Kalamazoo College Fighting Hornets: The conjunction of my SAT scores and All-State football honors outweighed all those *F*s in my final term of high school. I took a class in philosophy of religion in my first term. The reading material (which undoubtedly was first-rate) seemed to me to pale by comparison with Tolstoy. So I turned to mathematics for a time before transferring, at the end of my freshman year, to Wayne State University—back in Detroit. In the meantime, I married Connie, who transformed me into a serious student.

At Wayne State, I gave philosophy another try. At the same time, however, I re-discovered literature. After a year or so, I had to make a choice between English and philosophy. Surprisingly, in retrospect, it wasn't an easy choice to make. I stayed up all night—first trying to decide on a decision procedure, and then, after I settled that issue, making the actual decision. What it came down to, as I recall, was this: Both philosophy and literature were enormously enjoyable (this was in the pre-deconstruction days, of course), but philosophy, in addition, was challenging; and, I thought, enjoyment plus challenge defeats mere enjoyment.

I had no thought at the time of actually becoming a philosopher myself, which wasn't surprising, since I rarely thought more than a month ahead back then. In fact, I'm not sure that I would even have gone to graduate school if I hadn't run into Robert Baker (another teacher of mine) on the bus one day on my way home from school. He asked what I was planning to do after graduation. I replied that I hadn't given it much thought. He mentioned graduate school as a possibility, which struck me as interesting, so I asked him where I might apply. He recommended the University of Michigan, which was pretty much in the neighborhood, and after a thoroughly enjoyable year laying bricks and painting HUD houses, I went there.

That is where I fell in love with philosophy, though it took several years. It was twelve to fifteen hours a day in the company of absolute brilliance that did it—Aristotle, that is, whose theory of motivation was my dissertation topic. Prior to that time, my main philosophical interest was in solving philosophical puzzles. That is how I approached interpreting Aristotle as well. How can virtuous actions uniformly be products of choice, and therefore of deliberation, if, as Aristotle also said, there are instances of "sudden" virtuous action, as on the battlefield? How can it be true that virtuous agents uniformly perform virtuous actions for the sake of the actions themselves, or as ends, if virtuous actions issue from deliberation, and the function of deliberation is to identify means to ends? And so on. To feel confident that one understands Aristotle well enough to see how textual tensions are to be resolved, one needs to read a lot of Aristotle, which I did. That was my first real exposure to systematic philosophy. Everything in Aristotle, I came to believe, was importantly related to everything else—metaphysics, ethics, philosophy of mind, physics, logic, political theory, epistemology, philosophy of biology, and so on. I finally had a glimpse of philosophy writ large, and I was hooked.

Only when my dissertation was nearly complete—by then I was thinking about two months ahead—did it become clear to me that I wanted to stay in this line of work. Fortunately, I found a teaching job that year—at Davidson College. I enjoyed teaching and had ample time to continue exploring Aristotle and some of the philosophical issues that he addressed. I could think of no better way to spend my remaining years.

Like most philosophers, I now find it hard to imagine myself doing anything else for a living. If catechism and high school religion classes made a contribution to my now being a philosopher, I am grateful for them. It is a good thing, too, that I ran into Robert Baker on the bus.

Apology

Plato   *(Translated by Hugh Tredennick and Harold Tarrant)*

What effect my accusers have had upon you, gentlemen, I do not know, but for my own part I was almost carried away by them; their arguments were so convincing. On the other hand, scarcely a word of what they said was true. I was especially astonished at one of their many misrepresentations: the point where they told you that you must be careful not to let me deceive you, implying that I am a skilful speaker. I thought that it was peculiarly brazen of them to have the nerve to tell you this, only just before events must prove them wrong, when it becomes obvious that I have not the slightest skill as a speaker—unless, of course, by a skilful speaker they mean one who speaks the truth. If that is what they mean, I would agree that I am an orator, and quite out of their class. . . .

Very well, then; I must begin my defence, gentlemen, and I must try, in the short time that I have,[1] to rid your minds of a false impression which is the work of many years. I should like this to be the result, gentlemen, assuming it to be for your advantage and my own; and I should like to be successful in my defence; but I think that it will be difficult, and I am quite aware of the nature of my task. However, let that turn out as God wills; I must obey the law and make my defence.[2]

Let us go back to the beginning and consider what the charge is that has made people so critical of me, and has encouraged Meletus to draw up this indictment. Very well; what did my critics say in attacking my character? I must read out their affidavit, so to speak, as though they were my legal accusers. 'Socrates is committing an injustice, in that he inquires into things below the earth and in the sky, and makes the weaker argument defeat the stronger, and teaches others to follow his example.[3] It runs something like that. You have seen it for yourselves in the play by Aristophanes, where Socrates is lifted around, proclaiming that he is walking on air, and uttering a great deal of other nonsense about things of which I know nothing whatsoever.[4] I mean no disrespect for such knowledge, if anyone really is versed in it—I do not want any more lawsuits brought against me by Meletus[5]—but the fact is, gentlemen, that I take no interest in these things. What is more, I call upon the greater part of you as witnesses to my statement, and I appeal to all of you who have ever listened to me talking (and there are a great many to whom this applies) to reassure one another on this point. Tell one another whether any one of you has ever heard me discuss such questions briefly or at length; and then you will realize that the other popular reports about me are equally unreliable.[6] . . .

Here perhaps one of you might interrupt me and say, 'But what is it that you do, Socrates? How is it that you have been misrepresented like this? Surely all this talk and gossip about you would never have arisen if you had confined yourself to ordinary activities, but only if your behaviour was abnormal. Give us the explanation, if you do not want us to draw our own conclusions.' This seems to me to be a reasonable request, and I will try to explain to you what it is that has given me this false notoriety; so please give me your attention. Perhaps some of you will think that I am not being serious; but I assure you that I am going to tell you the whole truth.

I have gained this reputation, gentlemen, from nothing more or less than a kind of wisdom. What kind of wisdom do I mean? Human wisdom, I suppose. It seems that I really am wise in this limited sense. Presumably the geniuses whom I mentioned just now are wise in a wisdom that is more than human—I do not know how else to account for it, because I certainly do not have this knowledge, and anyone who says that I have is lying and just saying it to slander me. Now, gentlemen, please do not interrupt me even if I seem to make an extravagant claim; for what I am going to tell you is not a tale of my own; I am going to refer you to an unimpeachable authority. I shall call as witness to my wisdom (such as it is) the god at Delphi.[7]

You know Chaerephon,[8] I presume. He was a friend of mine from boyhood, and a good democrat who played his part with the rest of you in the recent expulsion and restoration.[9] And you know what he was like; how enthusiastic he was over anything that he had once undertaken. Well, one day he actually went to Delphi and asked this question of the god—as I said before, gentlemen, please do not interrupt—what he asked was whether there was anyone wiser than myself. The Pythian priestess replied that there was no one. As Chaerephon is dead, the evidence for my statement will be supplied by his brother here.[10]

Please consider my object in telling you this. I want to explain to you how the attack on my reputation first started.[11] When I heard about the oracle's answer, I said to myself, 'What is the god saying, and what is his hidden meaning? I am only too conscious that I have no claim to wisdom, great or small; so what can he mean by asserting that I am the wisest man in the world? He cannot be telling a lie; that would not be right for him.[12]

After puzzling about it for some time, I set myself at last with considerable reluctance to check the truth of it in the following way. I went to interview a man with a high reputation for wisdom, because I felt that here if anywhere I should succeed in disproving the oracle and pointing out to my divine authority, 'You said that I was the wisest of men, but here is a man who is wiser than I am.'

Well, I gave a thorough examination to this person—I need not mention his name, but it was one of our politicians that I was studying when I had this experience—and in conversation with him I formed the impression that although in many people's opinion, and especially in his own, he appeared to be wise, in fact he was not. Then when I began to try to show him that he only thought he was wise and was not really so, my efforts were resented both by him and by many of the other people present. However, I reflected as I walked away: 'Well, I am certainly wiser than this man. It is only too likely that neither of us has any knowledge to boast of; but he thinks that he knows something which he does not know, whereas I am quite conscious of my ignorance. At any rate it seems that I am wiser than he is to this small extent, that I do not think that I know what I do not know.'

After this I went on to interview a man with an even greater reputation for wisdom, and I formed the same impression again; and here too I incurred the resentment of the man himself and a number of others.

From that time on I interviewed one person after another. I realized with distress and alarm that I was making myself unpopular, but I felt compelled to put the god's business first; since I was trying to find out the meaning of the oracle, I was bound to interview everyone who had a reputation for knowledge. And by Dog,[13] gentlemen (for I must be frank with you), my honest impression was thus: it seemed to me, as I pursued my investigation at the god's command, that the people with the greatest reputations were almost entirely deficient, while others who were supposed to be their inferiors were much more noteworthy for their general good sense.

I want you to think of my adventures as a cycle of labors[14] undertaken to establish the truth of the oracle once for all. After I had finished with the politicians I turned to the poets, dramatic, lyric, and all the rest, in the belief that here I should expose myself as a comparative ignoramus.[15] I used to pick up what I thought were some of their most polished works and question them closely about the meaning of what they had written, in the hope of incidentally enlarging my own knowledge. Well, gentlemen, I hesitate to tell you the truth, but it must be told. It is hardly an exaggeration to say that any of the bystanders could have explained those poems better than their actual authors. So I soon made up my mind about the poets too: I decided that it was not wisdom that enabled them to write their poetry, but a kind of instinct or inspiration, such as you find in seers and prophets who deliver all their sublime messages without knowing in the least what they mean.[16] It seemed clear to me that the poets were in much the same case; and I also observed that the very fact that they were poets made them think that they had a perfect understanding of all other subjects, of which they were totally ignorant. So I left that line of inquiry too with the same sense of advantage that I had felt in the case of the politicians.

Last of all I turned to the skilled craftsmen.[17] I knew quite well that I had practically no understanding myself, and I was sure that I should find them full of impressive knowledge. In this I was not disappointed; they understood things which I did not, and to that extent they were wiser than I was. However, gentlemen, these professional experts seemed to share the same failing which I had noticed in the poets; I mean that on the strength of their technical proficiency they claimed a perfect understanding of every other subject, however important; and I felt that this error eclipsed their positive wisdom. So I made myself spokesman for the oracle, and asked myself whether I would rather be as I was—neither wise with their wisdom nor ignorant with their ignorance—or posses both qualities as they did. I replied through myself to the oracle that it was best for me to be as I was.

The effect of these investigations of mine, gentlemen, has been to arouse against me a great deal of hostility, and hostility of a particularly bitter and persistent kind, which has resulted in various malicious suggestions, and in having that term 'wise' applied to me. This is due to the fact that whenever I succeed in disproving another person's claim to wisdom in a given subject, the bystanders assume that I know everything about that subject myself.[18] But the truth of the matter, gentlemen, is likely to be this: that real wisdom is the property of the god, and this oracle is his way of telling us that human wisdom has little or no value. It seems to me that he is not referring literally to Socrates, but has merely taken my name as an example, as if he would say to us, 'The wisest of you men is he who has realized, like Socrates, that in respect of wisdom he is really worthless.'

That is why I still go about seeking and searching in obedience to the divine command, if I think that anyone is wise, whether citizen or stranger; and when I decide that he is not wise, I try to assist the god[19] by proving that he is not. This occupation has kept me too busy to do much either in politics or in my own affairs; in fact, my service to God has reduced me to extreme poverty.

Furthermore the young men—those with wealthy fathers and plenty of leisure—have of their own accord[20] attached themselves to me because they enjoy hearing other people cross-questioned. These often take me as their model, and go on to try to question other persons; whereupon, I suppose, they find an unlimited number of people who think that they know something, but really know little or nothing. Consequently their victims become annoyed, not with themselves but with me; and they complain that there is a pestilential busybody called Socrates who fills young people's heads with wrong ideas. If you ask them what he does, and what he teaches that has this effect, they have no answer, not knowing what to say; but as they do not want to admit their confusion, they fall back on the stock charges against any seeker after wisdom: that he teaches his pupils about things in the heavens and below the earth, and to disbelieve in gods, and to make the weaker argument defeat the stronger. They would be very loath, I fancy, to admit the truth: which is that they are being convicted of pretending to knowledge when they are entirely ignorant. They were so jealous, I suppose, for their own reputation, and also energetic and numerically strong, and spoke about me with such vigour and persuasiveness, that their harsh criticisms have for a long time now been monopolizing your ears. . . .

As a matter of fact, gentlemen, I do not feel that it requires much defence to clear myself of Meletus's accusation; what I have said already is enough. But you know very well the truth of what I said in an earlier part of my speech, that I have incurred a great deal of bitter hostility; and this is what will bring about my destruction, if anything does; not Meletus or Anytus, but the slander and jealousy of a very large section of the people. They have been fatal to a great many other innocent men, and I suppose will continue to be so; there is no likelihood that they will stop at me. But perhaps someone will say, 'Do you feel no compunction, Socrates, at having pursued an activity which puts you in danger of the death penalty?' I might fairly reply to him, 'You are mistaken, my friend, if you think that a man who is worth anything ought to spend his time weighing up the prospects of life and death. He has only one thing to consider in performing any action; that is, whether he is acting justly or unjustly, like a good man or a bad one. On your view the heroes who died at Troy would be poor creatures, especially the son of Thetis.[21] He, if you remember, made so light of danger in comparison with incurring dishonour that when his goddess mother warned him, eager as he was to kill

Hector, in some such words as these, I fancy, "My son, if you avenge your comrade Patroclus's death and kill Hector, you will die yourself;

Next after Hector is thy fate prepared."[22]

—when he heard this warning, he made light of his death and danger, being much more afraid of an ignoble life and of failing to avenge his friends. "Let me die forthwith," said he, "when I have requited the villain, rather than remain here by the beaked ships to be mocked, a burden on the ground." Do you suppose that he gave a thought to death and danger?'

The truth of the matter is this, gentlemen. Where a man has once taken up his stand, either because it seems best to him or in obedience to his orders, there I believe he is bound to remain and face the danger, taking no account of death or anything else before dishonour.

This being so, it would be shocking inconsistency on my part, gentlemen, if when the officers whom you chose to command me assigned me my position at Potidaea and Amphipolis and Delium,[23] I remained at my post like anyone else and faced death, and yet afterwards, when God appointed me, as I supposed and believed, to the duty of leading the philosophic life, examining myself and others, I were then through fear of death or of any other danger to desert my post. That would indeed be shocking, and then I might really with justice be summoned to court for not believing in the gods, and disobeying the oracle, and being afraid of death, and thinking that I am wise when I am not. For let me tell you, gentlemen, that to be afraid of death is only another form of thinking that one is wise when one is not; it is to think that one knows what one does not know. No one knows with regard to death whether it is not really the greatest blessing that can happen to a man; but people dread it as though they were certain that it is the greatest evil; and this ignorance, which thinks that it knows what it does not, must surely be ignorance most culpable. This, I take it, gentlemen, is the extent, and this the nature of my superiority over the rest of mankind; and if I were to claim to be wiser than my neighbour in any respect, it would be in this: that not possessing any real knowledge of what awaits us in Hades, I am also conscious that I do not possess it. But I do know that to do wrong and to disobey my superior, whether god or man, is bad and dishonourable; and so I shall never feel more fear or aversion for something which, for all I know, may really be a blessing than for those evils which I know to be evils.

Suppose, then, that you acquit me, and pay no attention to Anytus, who has said that either I should not have appeared before this court at all, or, since I have appeared here, I must be put to death, because if I once escaped your sons would all immediately become utterly corrupted by putting the teaching of Socrates into practice. Suppose that, in view of this, you said to me, 'Socrates, on this occasion we shall disregard Anytus and acquit you, but only on one condition: that you give up spending your time on this quest and stop philosophizing.[24] If we catch you going on in the same way, you shall be put to death.' Well, supposing, as I said, that you should offer to acquit me on these terms, I should reply, 'Gentlemen, I am your very grateful and devoted servant, but I owe a greater obedience to God than to you; and so long as I draw breath and have my faculties, I shall never stop practising philosophy and exhorting you and indicating the truth for everyone that I meet. I shall go on saying, in my usual way, "My very good friend, you are an Athenian and belong to a city which is the greatest and most famous in the world for its wisdom and strength. Are you not ashamed that you give your attention to acquiring as much money as possible, and similarly with reputation and honor, and give no attention or thought to truth and understanding and the perfection of your soul?" And if any of you disputes this and professes to care about these things, I shall not at once let him go or leave him; no, I shall question him and examine him and put him to the test; and if it appears that in spite of his profession he has made no real progress towards goodness, I shall reprove him for neglecting what is of supreme importance, and giving his attention to trivialities. I shall do this to everyone that I meet, young or old, foreigner or fellow-citizen; but especially to you my fellow-citizens, inasmuch as you are closer to me in kinship. This, I do assure you, is what my god commands; and it is my belief that no greater good has ever befallen you in this city than my service to my god; for I spend all my time going about trying to persuade you, young and old, to make your first and chief concern not for your bodies or for your possessions, but for the highest welfare of your souls, proclaiming as I go, "Wealth does not bring goodness, but goodness brings wealth and every other blessing, both to the individual and to the state." Now if I corrupt the young by this message, the message would seem to be harmful; but if anyone says that my message is different from this he is talking nonsense. And so, gentlemen,' I would say, 'You can please yourselves whether you listen to Anytus or not, and whether you acquit me or not; you know that I am not going to alter my conduct, not even if I have to die a hundred deaths.'

Order, please, gentlemen! Abide by my request to give me a hearing without interruption; besides, I believe that it will be to your advantage to listen. I am going to tell you something else which may provoke a clamour; but please restrain yourselves. I assure you that if I am what I claim to be, and you put me to death, you will harm yourselves more than me. Neither Meletus nor Anytus can do me any harm at all; they would not have the power, because I do not believe that the law of God permits a better man to be harmed by a worse.[25] No doubt my accuser might put me to death or have me banished or deprived of civic rights; but even if he thinks, as he probably does (and others too, I dare say), that these are great calamities, I do not think so; I believe that it is far worse to do what he is doing now, trying to put a man to death unjustly. For this reason, gentlemen, far from pleading on my own behalf, as might be supposed, I am really pleading on yours, to save you from misusing the gift of God by condemning me. If you put me to death, you will not easily find anyone to take my place. To put it bluntly (even if it sounds rather comical) God has assigned me to this city, as if to a large thoroughbred horse which because of its great size is inclined to be lazy and needs the stimulation of some stinging fly. It seems to me that God has attached me to this city to perform the office of such a fly; and all day long I never cease to settle here, there, and everywhere, rousing, persuading, reproving every one of you. You will not easily find another like me, gentlemen, and if you take my advice you will spare my life. But perhaps before long you may awake from your drowsing, and in your annoyance take Anytus's advice and finish me off thoughtlessly with a single slap; and then you could go on sleeping till the end of your days, unless God in his care for you sends someone to take my place.

If you doubt whether I am really the sort of person who would have been sent to this city as a gift from God, you can convince yourselves by looking at it in this way. Does it seem human that I should have neglected my own affairs and endured the humiliation of allowing my family to be neglected for all these years, while I busied myself all the time on your behalf, going like a father or an elder brother to see each one of you privately, and urging you to set your thoughts on goodness? If I had got any enjoyment from it, or if I had been paid for my good advice, there would have been some explanation for my conduct; but as it is you can see for yourselves that although my accusers unblushingly charge me with all sorts of other crimes, there is one thing that they have not had the impudence to pretend on any testimony, and that is that I have ever exacted or asked a fee from anyone. The witness that I can offer to prove the truth of my statement is good enough, I think—my poverty.

It may seem curious that I should go round giving advice like this and busying myself in people's private affairs, and yet never venture publicly to address you as a whole and advise on matters of state. The reason for this is what you have often heard me say before on many other occasions: that I am subject to a divine or supernatural experience, which Meletus saw fit to travesty in his indictment. It began in my early childhood—a sort of voice which comes to me; and when it comes it always dissuades me from what I am proposing to do, and never urges me on. It is this that debars me from entering public life, and a very good thing too, in my opinion; because you may be quite sure, gentlemen, that if I had tried long ago to engage in politics, I should long ago have lost my life, without doing any good either to you or to myself. Please do not be offended if I tell you the truth. No man on earth who conscientiously opposes either you or any other organized democracy, and flatly prevents a great many wrongs and illegalities from taking place in the state to which he belongs, can possibly escape with his life. The true champion of justice, if he intends to survive even for a short time, must necessarily confine himself to private life and leave politics alone.

I will offer you substantial proofs of what I have said; not theories, but what you better appreciate, facts. Listen while I describe my actual experiences, so that you may know that I would never submit wrongly to any authority through fear of death, but would refuse at any cost—even that of my life. It will be a commonplace story, such as you often hear in the courts;[26] but it is true.

The only office which I have ever held in our city, gentlemen, was when I served on the Council. It so happened that our tribe Antiochis was presiding[27] when you decided that the ten commanders who had failed to rescue the men who were lost in the naval engagement[28] should be tried *en bloc;* which was illegal, as you all recognized later. On this occasion I was the only member of the executive who opposed your acting in any way unconstitutionally, and voted against the proposal; and although the public speakers were all ready to denounce and arrest me, and you were all urging them on at the top of your voices, I thought that it was my duty to face it out on the side of law and justice rather than support you, through fear of prison or death, in your wrong decision.

This happened while we were still under a democracy. When the oligarchy came into power, the Thirty Commissioners in their turn summoned me and four others to the Round Chamber[29] and instructed us to go and fetch Leon of Salamis from his home for execution. This was of course only one of many instances in which they issued such instructions, their object being to implicate as many people as possible in their crimes. On this occasion, however, I again made it clear, not by my words but by my actions, that the attention[30] I paid to death was zero (if that is not too unrefined a claim); but that I gave all my attention to avoiding doing anything unjust or unholy. Powerful as it was, that government did not terrify me into doing a wrong action; when we came out of the Round Chamber the other four went off to Salamis and arrested Leon,[31] and I went home. I should probably have been put to death for this, if the government had not fallen soon afterwards. There are plenty of people who will testify to these statements.

Do you suppose that I should have lived as long as I have if I had moved in the sphere of public life, and conducting myself in that sphere like an honourable man, had always upheld the cause of right, and conscientiously set this end above all other things? Not by a very long way, gentlemen; neither would any other man. You will find that throughout my life I have been consistent in any public duties that I have performed, and the same also in my personal dealings: I have never countenanced any action that was incompatible with justice on the part of any person, including those whom some people maliciously call my pupils. I have never set up as any man's teacher; but if anyone, young or old, is eager to hear me conversing and carrying out my private mission, I never grudge him the opportunity; nor do I charge a fee for talking to him, and refuse to talk without one; I am ready to answer questions for rich and poor alike, and I am equally ready if anyone prefers to listen to what I have to say and answer my questions. If any given one of these people becomes a good citizen or a bad one, I cannot with justice be held responsible, since I have never promised or imparted any teaching to anybody; and if anyone asserts that he has ever learned or heard from me privately anything which was not open to everyone else, you may be quite sure that he is not telling the truth.

But how is it that some people enjoy spending a great deal of time in my company? You have heard the reason, gentlemen; I told you quite frankly. It is because they enjoy hearing me examine those who think that they are wise when they are not; an experience which has its amusing side. This duty I have accepted, as I said, in obedience to God's commands given in oracles and dreams and in every way that any other divine dispensation has ever impressed a duty upon man.[32] This is a true statement, gentlemen, and easy to verify.

If it is a fact that I am in process of corrupting some of the young, and have succeeded already in corrupting others; and if it were a fact that some of the latter, being now grown up, had discovered that I had ever given them bad advice when they were young, surely they ought now to be coming forward to denounce and punish me; and if they did not like to do it themselves, you would expect some of their families—their fathers and brothers and other near relations—to remember it now, if their own flesh and blood had suffered any harm from me. Certainly a great many of them have found their way into this court, as I can see for myself: first Crito[33] over there, my contemporary and near neighbor, the father of this young man Critoboulos; and then Lysanias of Sphettus, the father of Aeschines[34] here; and next Antiphon of Cephisian, over there, the father of Epigenes. Then besides there are all those whose brothers have been members of our circle: Nicostratus the son of Theozotides, the brother of Theodotus—but Theodotus is dead, so he cannot appeal to his brother—and Paralius here, the son of Demodocus; his brother was Theages.[35] And here is Adeimantus[36] the son of Ariston, whose brother Plato is over there; and Acautidorus, whose brother Apollodorus[37] is here on this side. I can name many more besides, some of whom Meletus most certainly ought to have produced as witnesses in the course of his speech. If he forgot to do so then, let him do it now—I'll make a concession; let him state whether he has any such evidence to offer. On the contrary, gentlemen, you will find that they are all prepared to help me—the corrupter and evil genius of their nearest and dearest relatives, as Meletus and Anytus say. The actual victims of my corrupting influence might perhaps be excused for helping me; but as for the uncorrupted, their relations of mature age, what other reason can they have for helping me except the just and proper one, that they know Meletus is lying and I am telling the truth? . . .

But apart from all question of appearances, gentlemen, I do not think that it is *just* for a man to appeal to the jury or to get himself acquitted by doing so; he ought to inform them of the facts and convince them by argument. The jury does not sit to dispense justice as a favour, but to decide where justice lies; and the oath which they have sworn is not to show favour at their own discretion, but to return a just and lawful verdict. It follows that we must not develop in you, nor you allow to grow in yourselves, the habit of perjury; that would be impious[38] for us both. Therefore you must not expect me, gentlemen, to behave towards you in a way which I consider neither reputable nor just nor consistent with my religious duty; and above all you must not expect it when I stand charged with impiety by Meletus here. Surely it is obvious that if I tried to persuade you and prevail upon you by my entreaties to go against your solemn oath, I should be teaching you contempt for religion; and by my very defence I should be virtually accusing myself of having no religious belief. But that is very far from the truth. I have a more sincere belief, gentlemen, than any of my accusers; and I leave it to you and to God to judge me in whatever way shall be best for me and for yourselves.

[*At this point the jury gives the verdict of guilty, and Meletus asks for the penalty of death.*]

There are a great many reasons, gentlemen, why I am not distressed by this result—I mean your condemnation of me—but the chief reason is that the result was not unexpected. What does surprise me is the number of votes cast on the two sides. I should never have believed that it would be such a close thing; but now it seems that if a mere thirty votes[39] had gone the other way, I should have been acquitted. Even as it is, I feel that so far as Meletus's part is concerned I have been acquitted; and not only that, but anyone can see that if Anytus and Lycon had not come forward to accuse me, Meletus would actually have lost a thousand drachmae for not having obtained one fifth of the votes.[40]

However, we must face the fact that he demands the death penalty. Very good. What alternative penalty shall I propose to you, gentlemen? Obviously it must be what's deserved. Well, what penalty do I deserve to pay or suffer, in view of what I have done?

I have never lived an ordinary quiet life. I did not care for the things that most people care about: making money, having a comfortable home, high military or civil rank, and all the other activities—political appointments, secret societies, party organizations—which go on in our city; I thought that I was really too fair-minded to survive if I went in for this sort of thing. So instead of taking a course which would have done no good either to you or to me, I set myself to do you individually in private what I hold to be the greatest possible service: I tried to persuade each one of you not to think more of practical advantages than of his mental and moral well-being, or in general to think more of advantage than of well-being, in the case of the state or of anything else. What do I deserve for behaving in this way? Some reward, gentlemen, if I am bound to suggest what I really deserve; and what is more, a reward which would be appropriate for myself. Well, what is appropriate for a poor man who is a public benefactor and who requires leisure for the purpose of giving you moral encouragement? Nothing could be more appropriate for such a person than free dining in the Prytaneum.[41] He deserves it much more than any victor in the races at Olympia, whether he wins with a single horse or a pair or a team of four. These people give you the semblance of success, but I give you the reality; they do not need maintenance, but I do. So if I am to suggest an appropriate penalty which is strictly in accordance with justice, I suggest free maintenance by the state.

Perhaps when I say this I may give you the impression, as I did in my remarks about exciting sympathy and making passionate appeals, that I am showing a stubborn perversity. That is not so, gentlemen; the real position is this. I am convinced that I never wrong anyone intentionally, but I cannot convince you of this, because we have had so little time for discussion. If it was your practice, as it is with other nations, to give not one day but several to the hearing of capital trials, I believe that you might have been convinced; but under present conditions it is not easy to dispose of grave allegations in a short space of time. So being convinced that I do no wrong to anybody, I can hardly be expected to wrong myself by asserting that I deserve something bad, or by proposing a corresponding penalty.[42] Why should I? For fear of suffering this penalty proposed by Meletus, when, as I said, I do not know whether it is a good thing or a bad? Do you expect me to choose something which I know very well is bad by making my counterproposal? Imprisonment? Why should I spend my days in prison, in subjection to whichever Eleven hold office?[43] A fine, with imprisonment until it is paid? In my case the effect would be just the same, because I have no money to pay a fine. Or shall I suggest banishment? You would very likely accept the suggestion.[44]

I should have to be desperately in love with life to do that, gentlemen. I am not so blind that I cannot see that you, my fellow-citizens, have come to the end of your patience with my discussions and conversations; you have found them too irksome and irritating, and now you are trying to get rid of them. Will any other people find them easy to put up with? That is most unlikely, gentlemen. A fine life I should have if I left this country at my age and spent the rest of my days trying one city after another and being turned out every time! I know very well that wherever I go the young people will listen to my conversation just as they do here; and if I try to keep them off, they themselves will prevail upon their elders and have me thrown out, while if I do not, the fathers and other relatives will drive me out of their own accord for the sake of the young.

Perhaps someone may say, 'But surely, Socrates, after you have left us you can spend the rest of your life in quietly minding your own business.' This is the hardest thing of all to make some of you understand. If I say that this would be disobedience to God, and that is why I cannot 'mind my own business', you will not believe me—you'll think I'm pulling your leg.[45] If on the other hand I tell you that to let no day pass without discussing goodness and all the other subjects about which you hear me talking and examining both myself and others is really the very best thing that a man can do, and that life without this sort of examination is not worth living, you will be even less inclined to believe me. Nevertheless that is how it is, gentlemen, as I maintain; though it is not easy to convince you of it. Besides, I am not accustomed to think of myself as deserving punishment. If I had money, I would have suggested a fine that I could afford, because that would not have done me any harm. As it is, I cannot, because I have none; unless of course you like to fix the penalty at what I could pay. I suppose I could probably afford a hundred drachmae and I suggest a fine of that amount.[46]

One moment, gentlemen. Plato here, and Crito and Critobulus and Apollodorus, want me to propose three thousand drachmae on their security. Very well, I agree to this sum, and you can rely upon these gentlemen for its payment.[47]

[*The jury votes again and sentences Socrates to death.*]

Well, gentlemen, for the sake of a very small gain in time you are going to earn the reputation—and the blame from those who wish to disparage our city—of having put Socrates to death, 'that wise man', because they will say I am wise even if I am not, these people who want to find fault with you. If you had waited just a little while, you would have had your way in the course of nature. You can see that I am well on in life and near to death. I am saying this not to all of you but to those who voted for my execution, and I have something else to say to them as well.

No doubt you think, gentlemen, that I have been condemned for lack of the arguments which I could have used if I had thought it right to leave nothing unsaid or undone to secure my acquittal. But that is very far from the truth. It is not a lack of arguments that has caused my condemnation, but a lack of effrontery and impudence,[48] and the fact that I have refused to address you in the way which would give you most pleasure. You would have liked to hear me weep and wail, doing and saying all sorts of things which I declare to be unworthy of myself, but which you are used to hearing from other people. But I did not think then that I ought to stoop to servility because I was in danger, and I do not regret now the way in which I pleaded my case; I would much rather die as the result of this defence than live as the result of the other sort. In a court of law, just as in warfare, neither I nor any other ought to use his wits to escape death by any means. In battle it is often obvious that you could escape being killed by giving up your arms and throwing yourself upon the mercy of your pursuers; and in every kind of danger there are plenty of devices for avoiding death if you are unscrupulous enough to stop at nothing. But I suggest, gentlemen, that the difficulty is not so much to escape death; the real difficulty is to escape from wickedness, which is far more fleet of foot. In this present instance I, the slow old man, have been overtaken by the slower of the two, but my accusers, who are clever and quick, have been overtaken by the faster: by iniquity. When I leave this court I shall go away condemned by you to death, but they will go away convicted by Truth herself of depravity and injustice. And they accept their sentence even as I accept mine. No doubt it was bound to be so, and I think that the result is fair enough.

Having said so much, I feel moved to prophesy to you who have given your vote against me; for I am now at that point where the gift of prophecy comes most readily to men: at the point of death. I tell you, my executioners, that as soon as I am dead, vengeance shall fall upon you with a punishment far more painful than your killing of me. You have brought about my death in the belief that through it you will be delivered from submitting the conduct of your lives to criticism; but I say that the result will be just the opposite. You will have more critics, whom up till now I have restrained without your knowing it; and being younger they will be harsher to you and will cause you more annoyance.

If you expect to stop denunciation of your wrong way of life by putting people to death, there is something amiss with your reasoning. This way of escape is neither possible nor creditable; the best and easiest way is not to stop the mouths of others, but to make yourselves as well behaved as possible. This is my last message to you who voted for my condemnation.

As for you who voted for my acquittal, I should very much like to say a few words to reconcile you to this result, while the officials are busy and I am not yet on my way to the place where I must die. I ask you, gentlemen, to spare me these few moments; there is no reason why we should not exchange a few words while the law permits. I look upon you as my friends, and I want to show you the meaning of what has now happened to me.

Gentlemen of the jury[49]—for you deserve to be so called—I have had a remarkable experience. In the past the prophetic voice to which I have become accustomed has always been my constant companion, opposing me even in quite trivial things if I was going to take the wrong course. Now something has happened to me, as you can see, which might be thought and is commonly considered to be a supreme calamity; yet neither when I left home this morning, nor when I was taking my place here in the court, nor at any point in any part of my speech, did the divine sign oppose me. In other discussions it has often checked me in the middle of a sentence; but this time it has never opposed me in any part of this business in anything that I have said or done. What do I suppose to be the explanation? I will tell you. I suspect that this thing that has happened to me is a blessing, and we are quite mistaken in supposing death to be an evil. I have good grounds for thinking this, because my accustomed sign could not have failed to oppose me if what I was doing had not been sure to bring some good result.

We should reflect that there is much reason to hope for a good result on other grounds as well. Death is one of two things. Either it is annihilation, and the dead have no consciousness of anything; or, as we are told,[50] it is really a change: a migration of the soul from this place to another. Now if there is no consciousness but only a dreamless sleep, death must be a marvellous gain. I suppose that if anyone were told to pick out the night on which he slept so soundly as not even to dream, and then to compare it with all the other nights and days of his life, and then were told to say, after due consideration, how many better and happier days and nights than this he had spent in the course of his life—well, I think that the Great King himself,[51] to say nothing of any private person, would find these days and nights easy to count in comparison with the rest. If death is like this, then, I call it gain; because the whole of time, if you look at it in this way, can be regarded as no more than one single night. If on the other hand death is a removal from here to some other place, and if what we are told is true, that all the dead are there, what greater blessing could there be than this, gentlemen of the jury? If on arrival in the other world, beyond the reach of these so-called jurors here, one will find there the true jurors who are said to preside in those courts, Minos and Rhadamanthus and Aeacus[52] and Triptolemus[53] and all those other demi-gods who were upright in their earthly life, would that be an unrewarding place to settle? Put it in this way: how much would one of you give to meet Orpheus and Musaeus, Hesiod and Homer?[54] I am willing to die ten times over if this account is true. For me at least it would be a wonderful personal experience to join them there, to meet Palamedes and Ajax the son of Telamon[55] and any other heroes of the old days who met their death through an unjust trial, and to compare my fortunes with theirs—it would be rather amusing, I think—and above all I should like to spend my time there, as here, in examining and searching people's minds, to find out who is really wise among them, and who only thinks that he is. What would one not give, gentlemen, to be able to scrutinize the leader of that great host against Troy, or Odysseus, or Sisyphus,[56] or the thousands of other men and women whom one could mention, their company and conversation—like the chance to examine them— would be unimaginable happiness? At any rate I presume that they do not put one to death there for such conduct; because apart from the other happiness in which their world surpasses ours, they are now immortal for the rest of time, if what we are told is true.

You too, gentlemen of the jury, must look forward to death with confidence, and fix your minds on this one belief, which is certain: that nothing can harm a good man either in life or after death, and his fortunes are not a matter of indifference to the gods. This present experience of mine does not result from mere earthly causes; I am quite clear that the time had come when it was better for me to die and be released from my distractions. That is why my sign never turned me back. For my own part I bear no grudge at all against those who condemned me and accused me, although it was not with this kind intention that they did so, but because they thought that they were hurting me; and that is culpable of them. However, I ask them to grant me one favour. When my sons grow up, gentlemen, if you think that they are putting money or anything else before goodness, take your revenge by plaguing them as I plagued you; and if they fancy themselves for no reason, you must scold them just as I scolded you, for neglecting the important things and thinking that they are good for something when they are good for nothing. If you do this, I shall have had justice at your hands—I *and* my children.

Well, now it is time to be off, I to die and you to live; but which of us has the happier prospect is unknown to anyone but God.

Notes

1. It is important to note that the speeches in many important Athenian trials were timed by the water-clock (*clepsydra*), equal time being allotted to defence and prosecution. It seems difficult to reconcile Socrates' attitude here with the notion that there may have been further speakers who spoke for the defence, though Plato's version of Socrates' speech is not so very long when one bears in mind that there were three speakers for the prosecution (23e).

2. The tone of this paragraph is hesitant, and the repeated verbals (translated 'must') suggest tasks that Socrates might prefer to have avoided.

3. A comic touch which many would find inappropriate, satirizing the old prejudices by casting them in the solemn form of a legal charge. In this 'charge' we see three mistaken views of Socrates: that he is a physical philosopher, that he is a sophist and that he is a professional teacher.

4. Aristophanes' *Clouds* introduces a Socrates who is swung out above the set suspended from the crane (218). His first full line (225) has him proclaim that he is treading the air and looking askance at the sun. In lines 227–234 he gives an absurd biological explanation of why he needs to be up high.

5. Another jest, with the serious purpose of depicting Meletus as one who would prosecute somebody at the drop of a hat.

6. The *Phaedo* speaks of a period in which Socrates *was* interested in Presocratic philosophy (96a–98b), and it is uncertain how early this would have been. Surely not all the jury could have been too young to have experienced this side of Socrates? The reason why Socrates is able to make this appeal is because such theories had never been discussed publicly as this was too dangerous. For this very reason it was easy enough for Athenians to suspect Socrates of engaging in such things privately. Notice that he does not *deny* that he had discussed them; he denies that he has any expertise in them, something of which he was certainly convinced.

7. To call a god as witness is a grotesque idea that is unlikely to have found favour. The Delphic oracle, sacred to Pythian Apollo, god of prophecy among other things, was the supreme authority in the Greek world. However, it had fallen out of favour at Athens by its apparent bias towards the other side during the Peloponnesian War, and it is very doubtful whether the Athenians would have been so impressed by the oracle's reply as Socrates is. Its advice could be sought on all matters, great and small. It is not known when Chaerephon visited it, and Xenophon's account (*Apology* 14) says that the oracle made Socrates supreme in the moral virtues instead of in wisdom.

8. Chaerephon features as a kind of apprentice of Socrates in the *Gorgias*, and is mentioned several times in Aristophanes' *Clouds* as being the other leader of Socrates' school. He is mocked there for his feeble appearance and his interest in entomology, and may have played an even greater role in the version originally staged (fr. 139 *Poetae Comici Graeci*). He occurs also in *Wasps* and *Birds*. Elsewhere in comedy he appears as a cheat and/or thief. It is unlikely that a mention of this favorite butt of comic humor (democrat or not) would have done anything to raise the tone of Socrates' case.

9. Socrates refers to the establishment and overthrow of the rule of the Thirty Tyrants (404 B.C.), when the democratic party was banned, but returned after capturing the Piraeus.

10. We meet this brother, Chaerecrates, in Xenophon's *Memorabilia* 2.3.

11. We may deduce from this that the oracular response preceded Socrates' investigations, which in turn preceded his unpopularity. He is unpopular by 423 B.C., something which Aristophanes capitalizes on rather than causes.

12. Socrates' unorthodox beliefs are now in evidence. He cannot accept that the gods will engage in any dishonourable conduct, such as lies. Yet deception among the gods is frequent in Greek myth. Moreover Socrates appears to be laying down rules for divine conduct in much the same way as he will impose moral rules upon the jury.

13. A favourite oath of Socrates; at *Phaedrus* 236e he offers to swear by the plane-tree he sits under. It is doubtful whether his use of pseudo-oaths would have been perceived as having any bearing on the question of his impiety.

14. With these words Socrates manages to compare his superficially meddlesome tasks with the Labours of Heracles; a jury might have seen this as either mockery or arrogance or both.

15. It is important to note that the poet traditionally had the role of teacher in Greece, and Greeks expected to learn from them. Greek education gave great weight to the study of Homer and other poets.

16. Plato's *Ion* shows Socrates exposing a rhapsode's reliance upon such inspiration (as opposed to knowledge); the *Phaedrus* sees it as characteristic of lover, faith-healer, true prophet and true poet (244a ff.); and the *Meno* explains political virtue too as dependent upon correct opinion derived from quasi-divine inspiration akin to that of the seer.

17. A much-respected class of person among the democrats of Athens.

18. Compare Charicles at Xenophon, *Memorabilia* 1.2.36 and Thrasymachus at *Republic* 337a.

19. Helping the gods is another odd idea, as *Euthyphro* 15a shows.

20. It is important to Socrates' case that he should not have been seeking such followers.

21. Achilles, hero of the *Iliad*, from which Socrates now gives a paraphrase of 18.94–106.

22. *Iliad* 18.96.

23. The three campaigns at which Socrates is known to have served as a hoplite. The fighting around Potidaea in 432 B.C., just before the outbreak of the Peloponnesian War, was intense, and Socrates' friends are surprised to see him back (*Charmides* 153b); he saved Alcibiades there, and again showed great gallantry at Delium in the disaster of 424 B.C. (*Symposium* 220d). Plato does not refer elsewhere to Socrates fighting at Amphipolis. A battle at Amphipolis, like Potidaea a Thracian settlement, took place in 422 B.C., but Burnet doubts whether an elderly Socrates could have served in a small select force then. Fighting also took place there in 437 B.C.

24. Note that this is not a real option for the court—the notion is introduced so that Socrates can make his priorities clear.

25. A radical idea, unlikely to convince the jury, and likely to be taken as a gesture of defiance. Socrates sometimes believes that the only significant way of helping or harming a man is to give or take away knowledge (*Euthydemus* 292b, *Protagoras* 345b). As we see from the *Phaedo* (97d), Socrates believes in a rationally governed universe, in which evil will not triumph over good.

26. It was normal for a defendant to insert a catalogue of his own and his family's services to the city.

27. Members of each tribe were selected for duty by lot, and each tribe took its turn to serve as presidents (or *prytaneis*) for one month. At this time they had a great deal of extra executive power.

28. The Athenians fought a sea-battle at Arginusae in 406 B.C., where victory was marred by the failure (owing to a storm) to recover the bodies. It was decided illegally to try all the generals responsible for this calamity (only eight in fact, of whom two were not present, having fled Athens) by a single vote.

29. The Tholos, where the Thirty had their headquarters, but which was generally used by the *prytaneis*.

30. There may once again be a play on the name of Meletus here; it has been argued that Socrates may be alluding to the fact that Meletus had himself taken part in the arrest of Leon; see H. Blumenthal, *Philologus* 117 (1973), 169–78, and J.J. Kearney, *Classical Quarterly* 30 (1980), 296–98. See also note 60, below.

31. It is interesting that one of their names was Meletus (Andocides, *On the Mysteries* 94), a man who took part in the prosecution of Andocides for religious crimes. Scholars have often thought that this Meletus could not possibly have been the prosecutor of Socrates, but see previous note.

32. The effect of this passage is to liken Socrates to the soothsayers, who were held in very little honor during the Peloponnesian War, being satirized mercilessly in comedy, and suffering from a mood of general scepticism as to the efficacy of trying to keep the gods on one's side. Compare the treatment Euthyphro had experienced (*Euthyphro* 3b–c).

33. The interlocutor in *Crito*.

34. A prominent Socratic who wrote dialogues of which significant fragments remain. See Saunders (1987).

35. Demodocus and Theages appear in Plato's (?) *Theages*.

36. Prominent in the *Republic*, along with Plato's other brother Glaucon.

37. Narrator of the *Symposium*; he also appears in the *Phaedo*.

38. i.e. a crime against the gods, as contravening an oath.

39. If the number of the jury was the reputed 500 or 501 and 30 is not a round figure, then the vote was 280 to 220 or 221.

40. Socrates is mocking Meletus still. The total of votes cast against Socrates was less than three fifths, and he divides the number by three, attributing just over ninety votes to each speaker.

41. As provided for victors at the Olympic and perhaps other games, and for certain representatives of eminent families, etc. Socrates is clearly being most provocative in proposing a considerable state honor as his punishment.

42. Socrates' belief that nobody does wrong willingly does not elsewhere lead to the view that nobody deserves to be punished: indeed *Gorgias* 474–481 argues that it is better for a man who has erred to submit to punishment.

43. A reference to the eleven magistrates in charge of prisons, etc.

44. This is confirmed by the *Crito* (52c), and the accusers would almost certainly have been satisfied with it.

45. i.e. they will think Socrates is using his 'irony': I have tried to translate in such a way as to suggest both evasion and playfulness.

46. Said by Xenophon (*Oeconomicus* 2.3) to have been about a fifth of his entire property.

47. The fine proposed is finally a large one, but the jury now know that he will not be bearing the brunt of it himself. What kind of punishment will it be?

48. How paradoxical this would have sounded to a jury who had no doubt felt Socrates to be the most impudent offender they had come across and the least willing to bow to the authority of the court.

49. One should remember during this section that the *dikasts* were both jury and judges, so a true juryman will also be a true judge, judging truly.

50. It is generally assumed that Socrates has Orphic and/or Pythagorean ideas in mind here; the belief in some kind of after-life was of course common, but the more orthodox Greek view made this a dismal half-life which could not be welcomed. One may compare ideas on the after-life which emerge in the *Phaedo*. *Gorgias* 493a–d certainly has an Orphic/Pythagorean myth of the after-life in mind; *Meno* 81a–b thinks of a specific type of person as holding relevant beliefs in the after-life, though it is to be emphasized that their views also allow for the return of souls to this world. No such provision is made in the *Apology*.

51. The King of Persia was seen by the Greeks as a paradigm of wordly happiness.

52. A traditional triad of just men who were rewarded with the role of underworld judges, and who feature in the myth of judgement at the end of the *Gorgias* (523c ff.). There is an implication that Socrates will find much in common with these traditionally just figures!

53. An agricultural divinity, associated with the cult of Demeter and Kore. He may take the place of Minos in Athenian representations of the underworld judges, for Minoan Crete had been considered an unjust enemy of Athens.

54. Musaeus and Orpheus were seen as the supreme bards of the Orphic religion; Hesiod and Homer were of course the two supremely influential Greek epic poets, who also had considerable influence on the shape of religious beliefs. Note the somewhat immodest assumption that Socrates will readily be able to mix with the great figures who shaped Greek religion.

55. Both in a sense victims of the wily Odysseus. Palamedes was supposed to have been tried and executed on false treason charges (a story from the *Cypria*), while Ajax committed suicide after losing the 'trial' for the arms of Achilles. Socrates is now succeeding in comparing himself with two heroes of the Trojan War period!

56. Agamemnon (Greek leader in the Trojan War, who had to sacrifice his daughter in order to sail), Odysseus (famed for worldly cunning) and Sisyphus (a Corinthian king famed for unscrupulous cleverness, and subsequently doomed to eternal punishment in Hades) were all figures in whom Socrates might expect to find character defects and unsound moral reasoning.

The Value of Philosophy
Bertrand Russell

Having now come to the end of our brief and very incomplete review of the problems of philosophy, it will be well to consider, in conclusion, what is the value of philosophy and why it ought to be studied. It is the more necessary to consider this question, in view of the fact that many men, under the influence of science or of practical affairs, are inclined to doubt whether philosophy is anything better than innocent but useless trifling, hair-splitting distinctions, and controversies on matters concerning which knowledge is impossible.

This view of philosophy appears to result, partly from a wrong conception of the ends of life, partly from a wrong conception of the kind of goods which philosophy strives to achieve. Physical science, through the medium of inventions, is useful to innumerable people who are wholly ignorant of it; thus the study of physical science is to be recommended, not only, or primarily, because of the effect on the student, but rather because of the effect on mankind in general. This utility does not belong to philosophy. If the study of philosophy has any value at all for others than students of philosophy, it must be only indirectly, through its effects upon the lives of those who study it. It is in these effects, therefore, if anywhere, that the value of philosophy must be primarily sought.

Source: From Bertrand Russell, *The Problems of Philosophy* (Oxford University Press, 1969). Reprinted by permission of Oxford University Press.

But further, if we are not to fail in our endeavour to determine the value of philosophy, we must first free our minds from the prejudices of what are wrongly called 'practical' men. The 'practical' man, as this word is often used, is one who recognizes only material needs, who realizes that men must have food for the body, but is oblivious of the necessity of providing food for the mind. If all men were well off, if poverty and disease had been reduced to their lowest possible point, there would still remain much to be done to produce a valuable society; and even in the existing world the goods of the mind are at least as important as the goods of the body. It is exclusively among the goods of the mind that the value of philosophy is to be found; and only those who are not indifferent to these goods can be persuaded that the study of philosophy is not a waste of time.

Philosophy, like all other studies, aims primarily at knowledge. The knowledge it aims at is the kind of knowledge which gives unity and system to the body of the sciences, and the kind which results from a critical examination of the grounds of our convictions, prejudices, and beliefs. But it cannot be maintained that philosophy has had any very great measure of success in its attempts to provide definite answers to its questions. If you ask a mathematician, a mineralogist, a historian, or any other man of learning, what definite body of truths has been ascertained by his science, his answer will last as long as you are willing to listen. But if you put the same question to a philosopher, he will, if he is candid, have to confess that his study has not achieved positive results such as have been achieved by other sciences. It is true that this is partly accounted for by the fact that, as soon as definite knowledge concerning any subject becomes possible, this subject ceases to be called philosophy, and becomes a separate science. The whole study of the heavens, which now belongs to astronomy, was once included in philosophy; Newton's great work was called 'the mathematical principles of natural philosophy'. Similarly, the study of the human mind, which was a part of philosophy, has now been separated from philosophy and has become the science of psychology. Thus, to a great extent, the uncertainty of philosophy is more apparent than real: those questions which are already capable of definite answers are placed in the sciences, while those only to which, at present, no definite answer can be given, remain to form the residue which is called philosophy.

This is, however, only a part of the truth concerning the uncertainty of philosophy. There are many questions—and among them those that are of the profoundest interest to our spiritual life—which, so far as we can see, must remain insoluble to the human intellect unless its powers become of quite a different order from what they are now. Has the universe any unity of plan or purpose, or is it a fortuitous concourse of atoms? Is consciousness a permanent part of the universe, giving hope of indefinite growth in wisdom, or is it a transitory accident on a small planet on which life must ultimately become impossible? Are good and evil of importance to the universe or only to man? Such questions are asked by philosophy, and variously answered by various philosophers. But it would seem that, whether answers be otherwise discoverable or not, the answers suggested by philosophy are none of them demonstrably true. Yet, however slight may be the hope of discovering an answer, it is part of the business of philosophy to continue the consideration of such questions, to make us aware of their importance, to examine all the approaches to them, and to keep alive that speculative interest in the universe which is apt to be killed by confining ourselves to definitely ascertainable knowledge.

Many philosophers, it is true, have held that philosophy could establish the truth of certain answers to such fundamental questions. They have supposed that what is of most importance in religious beliefs could be proved by strict demonstration to be true. In order to judge of such attempts, it is necessary to take a survey of human knowledge, and to form an opinion as to its methods and its limitations. On such a subject it would be unwise to pronounce dogmatically; but if the investigations of our previous chapters have not led us astray, we shall be compelled to renounce the hope of finding philosophical proofs of religious beliefs. We cannot, therefore, include as part of the value of philosophy any definite set of answers to such questions. Hence, once more, the value of philosophy must not depend upon any supposed body of definitely ascertainable knowledge to be acquired by those who study it.

The value of philosophy is, in fact, to be sought largely in its very uncertainty. The man who has no tincture of philosophy goes through life imprisoned in the prejudices derived from common sense, from the habitual beliefs of his age or his nation, and from convictions which have grown up in his mind without the co-operation or consent of his deliberate reason. To such a man the world tends to become definite, finite, obvious; common objects rouse no questions, and unfamiliar possibilities are contemptuously rejected. As soon as we begin to philosophize, on the contrary, we find, as we saw in our opening chapters, that even the most everyday things lead to problems to which only very incomplete answers can be given. Philosophy, though unable to tell us with certainty what is the true answer to the doubts which it raises, is able to suggest many possibilities which enlarge our thoughts and free them from the tyranny of custom. Thus, while diminishing our feeling of certainty as to what things are, it greatly increases our knowledge as to what they may be; it removes the somewhat arrogant dogmatism of those who have never travelled into the region of liberating doubt, and it keeps alive our sense of wonder by showing familiar things in an unfamiliar aspect.

Apart from its utility in showing unsuspected possibilities, philosophy has a value—perhaps its chief value—through the greatness of the objects which it contemplates, and the freedom from narrow and personal aims resulting from this contemplation. The life of the instinctive man is shut up within the circle of his private interests: family and friends may be included, but the outer world is not regarded except as it may help or hinder what comes within the circle of instinctive wishes. In such a life there is something feverish and confined, in comparison with which the philosophic life is calm and free. The private world of instinctive interests is a small one, set in the midst of a great and powerful world which must, sooner or later, lay our private world in ruins. Unless we can so enlarge our interests as to include the whole outer world, we remain like a garrison in a beleagured fortress, knowing that the enemy prevents escape and that ultimate surrender is inevitable. In such a life there is no peace, but a constant strife between the insistence of desire and the powerlessness of will. In one way or another, if our life is to be great and free, we must escape this prison and this strife.

One way of escape is by philosophic contemplation. Philosophic contemplation does not, in its widest survey, divide the universe into two hostile camps—friends and foes, helpful and hostile, good and bad—it views the whole impartially. Philosophic contemplation, when it is unalloyed, does not aim at proving that the rest of the universe is akin to man. All acquisition of knowledge is an enlargement of the Self, but this enlargement is best attained when it is not directly sought. It is obtained when the desire for knowledge is alone operative, by a study which does not wish in advance that its objects should have this or that character, but adapts the Self to the characters which it finds in its objects. This enlargement of Self is not obtained when, taking the Self as it is, we try to show that the world is so similar to this Self that knowledge of it is possible without any admission of what seems alien. The desire to prove this is a form of self-assertion and, like all self-assertion, it is an obstacle to the growth of Self which it desires, and of which the Self knows that it is capable. Self-assertion, in philosophic speculation as elsewhere, views the world as a means to its own ends; thus it makes the world of less account than Self, and the Self sets bounds to the greatness of its goods. In contemplation, on the contrary, we start from the not-Self, and through its greatness the boundaries of Self are enlarged; through the infinity of the universe the mind which contemplates it achieves some share in infinity.

For this reason greatness of soul is not fostered by those philosophies which assimilate the universe to Man. Knowledge is a form of union of Self and not-Self; like all unions, it is impaired by dominion, and therefore by any attempt to force the universe into conformity with what we find in ourselves. There is a widespread philosophical tendency towards the view which tells us that Man is the measure of all things, that truth is man-made, that space and time and the world of universals are properties of the mind, and that, if there be anything not created by the mind, it is unknowable and of no account for us. This view, if our previous discussions were correct, is untrue; but in addition to being untrue, it has the effect of robbing philosophic contemplation of all that gives it value, since it fetters contemplation to Self. What it calls knowledge is not a union with the not-Self, but a set of prejudices, habits, and desires, making an impenetrable veil between us and the world beyond. The man who finds pleasure in such a theory of knowledge is like the man who never leaves the domestic circle for fear his word might not be law.

The true philosophic contemplation, on the contrary, finds its satisfaction in every enlargement of the not-Self, in everything that magnifies the objects contemplated, and thereby the subject contemplating. Everything, in contemplation, that is personal or private, everything that depends upon habit, self-interest, or desire, distorts the object, and hence impairs the union which the intellect seeks. By thus making a barrier between subject and object, such personal and private things become a prison to the intellect. The free intellect will see as God might see, without a *here* and *now*, without hopes and fears, without the trammels of customary beliefs and traditional prejudices, calmly, dispassionately, in the sole and exclusive desire of knowledge—knowledge as impersonal, as purely contemplative, as it is possible for man to attain. Hence also the free intellect will value more the abstract and universal knowledge into which the accidents of private history do not enter, than the knowledge brought by the senses, and dependent, as such knowledge must be, upon an exclusive and personal point of view and a body whose sense-organs distort as much as they reveal.

The mind which has become accustomed to the freedom and impartiality of philosophic contemplation will preserve something of the same freedom and impartiality in the world of action and emotion. It will view its purposes and desires as parts of the whole, with the absence of insistence that results from seeing them as infinitesimal fragments in a world of which all the rest is unaffected by any one man's deeds. The impartiality which, in contemplation, is the unalloyed desire for truth, is the very same quality of mind which, in action, is justice, and in emotion is that universal love which can be given to all, and not only to those who are judged useful or admirable. Thus contemplation enlarges not only the objects of our thoughts, but also the objects of our actions and our affections: it makes us citizens of the universe, not only of one walled city at war with all the rest. In this citizenship of the universe consists man's true freedom, and his liberation from the thraldom of narrow hopes and fears.

Thus, to sum up our discussion of the value of philosophy; Philosophy is to be studied, not for the sake of any definite answers to its questions, since no definite answers can, as a rule, be known to be true, but rather for the sake of the questions themselves; because these questions enlarge our conception of what is possible, enrich our intellectual imagination and diminish the dogmatic assurance which closes the mind against speculation; but above all because, through the greatness of the universe which philosophy contemplates, the mind also is rendered great, and becomes capable of that union with the universe which constitutes its highest good.

Classical Conceptual Analysis

Dennis Earl

Philosophy involves the exercise of one's rational capacities in seeking correct answers to the most fundamental questions there are. That capacity includes at least two components: One is the ability to grasp various logical relationships that may exist between premises and conclusions, and another is the ability to engage in *analysis*. But what is analysis? In one sense, analysis is an *activity:* For instance, when Socrates asks a question like "What is justice?" he wants to know more clearly what is *meant* by the term 'justice', which is just a desire to know what the nature of justice really is. The activity of analysis seeks to answer such Socratic questions. Now, the *product* of such an activity will be a proposition that says what justice is, or what piety is, or what knowledge is, etc. and such a proposition can also be said to give the *meaning* of the terms 'justice', 'piety', 'knowledge', etc. Such a proposition is also called an analysis. So there are at least two different senses of the term 'analysis': One sense refers to an activity, and another refers to the product of that activity.

But why does analysis matter to doing philosophy? Consider the following argument:

(P1) Killing a person is morally wrong.
(P2) A fetus is a person.
(P3) Abortion is the act of killing a fetus.

(C) Abortion is morally wrong.

The argument is valid: The conclusion is guaranteed to be true if the premises are all true. So whether the argument is sound or not is a matter of the truth of the premises. But what is meant by 'person', 'killing', and 'morally wrong' here? What an analysis of the meanings of those terms would do is provide some correct account of what a person really *is*, what killing *is*, and what it is for something to be morally wrong. For instance, what will decide premise (P2)'s truth or falsity will be the rather significant matter of what characteristics all persons have in virtue of *being* persons, and whether fetuses have those characteristics or not. In other words, a correct analysis of what is meant by 'person' will be essential to whether the argument is sound or unsound. It is in this way that analysis is an essential component of philosophy itself.

My topic in this short essay is conceptual analysis in its classical or traditional sense, and my primary goal here is to give as clear a statement as possible of the nature of classical analysis. I occupy myself with that task in §1. Although my main focus here is exegetical, it should be pointed out that the classical notion of analysis has been exposed to a great deal of criticism over the years, and a few of the more common objections to the classical notion of analysis are considered in §2. Some alternatives to the classical view of analysis are noted in §3.

1. CLASSICAL ANALYSIS

I begin with the question of the nature of those propositions that themselves *are* analyses. According to the picture of analysis under consideration here, an analysis is an analysis of a *concept:* Just as a proposition is what is meant by a complete declarative sentence, a concept is what is meant by, or what is expressed by, linguistic items such as predicates, adjectives, and the like. For instance, the concept of *being green* is what is meant by the predicate 'is green', and the concept of *being a star* is what is meant by the predicate 'is a star'. What an analysis is *of* is a concept, and an analysis is a proposition that gives the meaning of those expressions of the concept being analyzed.[1]

A *classical conceptual analysis*[2] specifies such meanings in the following way. Take the concept of *being a square*. A classical analysis of that concept takes the form of a set of necessary and jointly sufficient conditions that specifies, among other things, what it is *to be* a square. Such an analysis gives a list of *necessary conditions*, each of which is a condition that has to be satisfied in order for something to be a square. The conjunction of that list of necessary conditions is itself a *sufficient condition* for being a square, in that if a thing satisfies all of those conditions, then that thing must be a square. Put more formally,

> A necessary condition for being an *F* is a condition that something must satisfy in order for it to be an *F*.
>
> A sufficient condition for being an *F* is a condition such that if something satisfies that condition, then it must be an *F*.
>
> Necessary and jointly sufficient conditions for being an *F* are a set of necessary conditions such that satisfying all of them is sufficient for being an *F*.

For the concept of *being a square*, the following serves as a correct analysis: A square is a four-sided, closed plane figure with sides all the same length, and with neighboring sides meeting at right angles. This might be put more formally as follows:

x is a square if and only if: (1) *x* is four-sided,
(2) *x* is a closed plane figure,
(3) *x* has sides that are all the same length, and
(4) *x*'s neighboring sides meet at right angles.

---

[1] For the purposes of elucidation of the nature of classical conceptual analysis, this is all that needs to be said concerning the question of what a concept itself is. On deeper investigation of the issue, there are of course some competing views on the subject: On one view, concepts are identical to the words or phrases used to express them; on another, they are a sort of idea or mental category that one has in one's head; on still another view, they are abstract entities. There are other views as well. While I take no stand on this issue here, it *does* seem as if the right view of the nature of concepts themselves will have bearing on whether *every* concept has a classical conceptual analysis. To consider one kind of example, suppose that concepts really are identical to a sort of mental category by which we sort things as being in that category or not, and suppose further that concepts construed that way can include categories of things that only have *typical features*, rather than features describable in terms of necessary conditions (to be discussed shortly). If this is what concepts are, then not every concept will have a classical analysis, since analyses in terms of typical features are not classical analyses.

[2] Some would call such a proposition a *definition*. However, one might use a more refined term and call them *classical definitions*, since there seem to be many sorts of definitions (partial definitions, ostensive definitions, procedural definitions, etc.). This alternate terminology is agreeable enough, but I will use the term *classical analysis* to speak of such propositions.

Each of conditions (1)–(4) are necessary conditions for being a square, and the conjunction of all of them counts as a sufficient condition for being a square. Moreover, being a square is itself a sufficient condition for satisfying each of conditions (1)–(4).[3]

I should add that there are several other conditions[4] that a proposition must meet in order to *count* as a classical analysis. First, an analysis cannot be circular: The concept being analyzed cannot appear in the necessary conditions put forth as an analysis of that concept. The concept of *being a square* cannot be analyzed in terms of the concept of *being a square*, for instance. Second, an analysis of a given concept cannot be in terms of concepts that are more complex than the concept being analyzed. While it is true that the notion of conceptual complexity is a bit murky, an example should make the condition clearer: The concept of *being a square* can be analyzed in terms of *being four-sided, being a closed plane figure*, etc., but the concept of *being a four-sided, closed plane figure with sides all the same length and having sides meeting at right angles* cannot be analyzed in terms of the concept of *being a square*. This is in keeping with the idea that analyses give at least some of the "components" or "constituents" of the concept being analyzed.[5]

One other point needs to be emphasized. Analyses are put forth as necessary truths: In other words, the preceding analysis of the concept of *being a square* does not just claim that squares are four-sided, closed plane figures, with sides all the same length, and with neighboring sides meeting at right angles, but that squares *must* have those characteristics. So for condition (1), for instance, that necessary condition is not just

---

[3]Another correct analysis for the concept of *being a square* is:

x is a square if and only if: (1) x is four-sided, and
                                (2) x is a regular figure.

This suggests that there may be *many* correct analyses for a given concept, and no one of them is *the* analysis of that concept. Is this a problem for the philosophical view that every complex concept has a classical analysis? One way it would be a problem is if one held that concepts are literally *composed* (as a whole is composed of its proper parts) only of those simpler concepts that appear in the necessary conditions given in an analysis of that concept. In that case, it would seem impossible for the concept of *being a square* to have *being four-sided* and *being a regular figure* as its only proper parts and also have *being four-sided, being a closed plane figure, having sides all the same length*, and *having sides that meet at right angles* as its only proper parts. But there is little reason for thinking that this is the only sort of internal structure that concepts can have.

[4]See also Ackerman 1986, 1992, 1995.

[5]There are at least two senses of 'constituent' that could be in play here. To say that the concept of *being an F* is a constituent of the concept of *being a G* might be to say that the concept of *being an F* is literally part of the concept of *being a G*. Such *literal* constituency is distinct from what one might call *logical* constituency: On this other sense of 'constituent', *being an F* is a constituent of *being a G* if something's being a G logically entails its being an F, and nothing more.

the claim that squares have four sides, but the stronger claim that it *must* be that squares have four sides. In other words, it simply *cannot be* that there is a square that fails to have four sides.

Counterexamples and Testing Candidate Analyses

What is it that makes a given analysis a *correct* analysis, and how does one figure this out? Suppose that instead of the preceding analysis, one instead thought that the concept of *being a square* has the following analysis:

x is a square if and only if: (1) x is four-sided,
(2) x is a closed plane figure, and
(3) x has sides that are all the same length.

For this *candidate analysis*, which one might consider as part of one's investigation into the concept of *being a square*, the claim is that conditions (1)–(3) are each necessary conditions for being a square, and satisfying all of them would be sufficient for being a square. In other words, part of what is being claimed here is that it must be that everything that is a four-sided, closed plane figure with sides all the same length is a square. But this would be a false claim if there could be something that has those three characteristics (i.e., meets those three necessary conditions) yet is *not* a square. And indeed there could: A rhombus is a four-sided, closed plane figure with sides all the same length, and any rhombus without neighboring sides meeting at right angles would count as a *counterexample* to the candidate analysis given above. This kind of counterexample shows the candidate analysis to have a certain kind of flaw: It is *too broad*, since it includes things as squares that are not squares, and any candidate analysis that has counterexamples to it is not a correct analysis.

There is another sort of counterexample of note: a counterexample that shows an analysis to be *too narrow*. Suppose that the following candidate analysis is under consideration:

x is a square if and only if: (1) x is four-sided,
(2) x is a closed plane figure,
(3) x has sides that are all the same length,
(4) x's neighboring sides meet at right angles, and
(5) x is red.

There are no counterexamples to this analysis of the previous sort—that is, it is impossible for there to be anything that satisfies conditions (1)–(5) yet not be a square. But there is another sort of counterexample to consider here, namely something that *is* a square, yet fails to satisfy all of conditions (1)–(5). Supposing for a moment that squares are the sorts of things that can be colored at all, a blue square is indeed a square, yet fails to satisfy condition (5). Since the candidate analysis under consideration leaves out some things that are squares, this is enough to show that the analysis is too narrow.

For other concepts, the classical view of analysis holds that one can follow the very same sort of strategy of offering a candidate analysis, testing it by means of seeking counterexamples, and revising that candidate analysis until it is free of counterexamples. For instance, the candidate analysis *that a bachelor is an unmarried male* seems to be too broad, since any dog counts as a counterexample. The candidate analysis *that a bachelor is an unmarried male under age 90* seems too narrow, as it seems at least possible for there to be a 92-year-old bachelor. However difficult it might actually be to discover a correct analysis for the concept of *being a bachelor* (as well as such more philosophically interesting concepts as *being a person, being morally good, being conscious*, etc.), the classical view holds that there is at least one such correct analysis for that concept.[6]

2. OBJECTIONS TO THE CLASSICAL VIEW OF ANALYSIS

The classical view faces a number of important objections, but it is not my aim in this essay to defend the classical view in any kind of comprehensive way. So I hold my discussion here to just two difficulties: *Plato's problem* and *the problem of typicality effects*.[7] Again, my primary aim here is exegetical—a complete discussion of even these two objections would require considerably more space.

---

[6]So long as that concept is a *complex* concept, that is. If a concept is analyzed in terms of some other concepts, and those other concepts themselves have analyses in terms of still other concepts, it would seem that there has to be some collection of *primitive* concepts that themselves have no analyses. It is beyond the scope of this paper to delve into the nature of primitive concepts further, but suffice it to say that views of concepts friendly to classical analysis would seem committed to the thesis that there *are* such primitive concepts, whatever their nature would be. Otherwise, such views would have to allow for there to be circular analyses, or allow for the process of analyzing concepts in terms of simpler concepts to go on *ad infinitum*, or allow for there to be analyses in terms of concepts that are *more* complex.

[7]The names of these two objections are from Laurence and Margolis 1999; and see the same work for a longer list of objections and replies as well.

Plato's problem is this: Given that with millennia of efforts to find classical analyses for concepts such as the concept of *being a person*, the concept of *being a mind*, the concept of *being a case of knowledge*, the concept of *being morally good*, the concept of *being beautiful*, and so forth, one would think that some correct classical analyses for these concepts would have been discovered by now if the classical view were true. But since few such analyses have been uncovered outside of the realm of logic and mathematics, it is tempting to infer that the classical view cannot be correct for *all* complex concepts. The reason the objection is termed *Plato's problem* is that in Plato's dialogues, often enough Socrates seeks an answer to some question such as "What is piety?" or "What is justice?" and never seems to receive a complete answer. As it is evident that Socrates is after something much like a classical analysis as described previously, the ongoing failure to uncover complete answers to "What is F?"-type questions might be taken as evidence that there are no such classical analyses to be discovered at all.

The most immediate response to the objection is straightforward enough: The lack of universally (or even widely) agreed-upon correct classical analyses for a wide range of philosophically significant concepts hardly *shows* that there are some complex concepts that cannot be analyzed classically. But this will hardly satisfy the critics of classical analysis, since it is not as if philosophers have been halfhearted in their efforts in seeking classical analyses—after all, philosophers have sought such analyses for over two thousand years, and one might have expected a much greater rate of success if the classical view were true for all complex concepts. The objection might not be intended to give a deductive *proof* that the classical view is false, after all, but merely to point out that there seems to be overwhelming inductive evidence that the classical view is mistaken.

Perhaps a better reply to Plato's problem is a version of a *tu quoque* argument: Plato's problem is really a general problem for those who seek *any* sort of analysis, whether one seeks analyses along classical lines or not. The success rate for other views of analysis seems to be about the same as that for classical analysis, where success is measured here in terms of *widespread* agreement that a candidate analysis of a given concept is really a correct analysis. So the reply is that one cannot reject the classical view based on the lack of universal agreement unless one is prepared to reject all views of analysis where there is no universal agreement. As this includes the competitors to the classical view, then those views are no better off.

Another objection raised against the classical view is the problem of typicality effects. The problem arises from experimental results concerning how people sort things into various categories. The evidence shows that people sort things into various categories at different rates; for instance, people tend to sort sparrows into the *bird* category more quickly than they do eagles, and they tend to sort eagles into the *bird* category more quickly than they do ostriches.[8] It is as if people sort "more typical" birds into the *bird* category more quickly than "less typical" birds. How is this experimental evidence a problem for the classical view of conceptual analysis? The critics charge that these differences in sorting behavior show something about the nature of concepts, namely that if they are to be analyzed at all, they should be analyzed in terms of "typical" features rather than in terms of necessary conditions. For when someone sorts a sparrow into the *bird* category, the critics say, this is a case of applying the concept of *being a bird* to that individual sparrow. But the critics claim that if concepts really *did* have classical analyses, then one would expect everyone who understands a given concept to apply that concept in exactly the same way, and at exactly the same rate. But since such behavior is not observed at all, the critics infer that it cannot be that the classical view of conceptual analysis applies to every concept.

There are a number of responses to consider with respect to this objection, but perhaps the strongest is this: Quite simply, the experimental evidence concerning our sorting behavior has little or no bearing on the question of whether concepts have classical analyses. For there is a difference between how someone *figures out* whether to apply a concept to a particular thing, or how fast one does it, and whether that concept *really does* apply to that particular thing. Sparrows, eagles, and ostriches are all equally birds, even if we might recognize sparrows as birds a bit more quickly than we recognize ostriches as birds. What it is *to be* a bird is one thing, while what set of characteristics we look for in *identifying* something as a bird is another. But given this distinction, one can now see where the objection goes astray: An analysis of the concept of *being a bird* gives the conditions necessary for *being* a bird, not the conditions under which someone identifies something as a bird or not. The objection having to do with typicality effects takes the differences in sorting things into a given category and makes an inference to an explanation. Part of the best explanation for the categorization differences, the critics say, is that the classical view of conceptual analysis is false. But since that inference to an explanation falsely presumes that a

---

[8]The evidence mentioned here is reviewed in Rey 1983 and Laurence and Margolis 1999.

conceptual analysis gives the conditions under which an agent identifies something as an instance[9] of that concept, the objection fails.[10]

3. ALTERNATIVE FORMS OF ANALYSIS

As indicated earlier, my purpose here is not to give a full-blown defense
of the classical view of conceptual analysis. But even so, one might wonder what view of analysis might be substituted for the classical view
should it turn out not to hold for all concepts. For one might hold that
the classical view holds for some concepts (like the concept of *being a
square*, for instance) but not for others (like the concept of *being a bird*).
But how might those other concepts be analyzed if not in terms of necessary and jointly sufficient conditions?

One option would be to allow for analyses that include lists of necessary conditions, but that the conjunction of those conditions fails to
constitute a sufficient condition. For instance, the proposition *that a
bachelor is an unmarried male* seems to specify at least some of the conditions necessary for being a bachelor, even if it fails to specify everything
necessary for being a bachelor. Such *partial analyses* would preserve
some features of the classical view and still provide a great deal of information concerning the logical relationships between the concept being
analyzed and other concepts. Partial analyses could well be decisive in
evaluating arguments. For example, consider once again the argument
against abortion mentioned at the outset of this paper. If the proposition *that a person is a rational, self-conscious being* is a correct partial
analysis of the concept of *being a person*, then premise (P2) of the argument is false if fetuses fail to be self-conscious.

Another sort of analysis is inspired by the experimental evidence
(mentioned previously) having to do with sorting things into various cat-

---

[9]An instance of a concept is something to which that concept applies: For instance, an individual sparrow
is an instance of the concept of *being a sparrow*. An individual sparrow is also an instance of some other
concepts, like the concepts of *being a bird* and *being an animal*.

[10]This reply to the problem of typicality effects is essentially that of Rey 1983. It should be noted that
even though Rey draws the distinction given above, there are even more distinctions to consider here
than at first sight. For the concept of *being a bird*, there is the distinction (from above) between what
one might call the *satisfaction conditions* (or what it is to *be* a bird) and what one might call the
identification conditions (or what one uses in identifying something as a bird). But other sets of
conditions could well be relevant to explaining the differences in categorization: For instance, there
is a difference between the satisfaction conditions for *being a bird* and what one *believes* the satisfaction
conditions for *being a bird* to be. There is also a difference between those conditions one typically
uses in sorting things into the *bird* category and those conditions one *believes* could be used for successful
sorting of things into the *bird* category. The point is that classical analyses give the satisfaction conditions
for a concept, and the experimental evidence pointed to by the critics would seem to be more readily
explained in terms of these other sets of conditions. As such, there is no reason to give up the classical
view on the basis of that evidence.

egories by means of *typical features*. One might analyze the concept of *being a bird*, say, not in terms of necessary and sufficient conditions, but in terms of those features common to birds. Such an analysis might be expressed as "a bird is something (typically) with wings, beak, feathers, and claws and is capable of flight." Some types of flying dinosaurs might fit this description as well, but this is beside the point. An analysis of *being a bird* in terms of typical features does not aim to give an analysis completely free of any counterexamples—such an analysis is only intended to describe what birds are typically like.

Concepts might also be analyzed in terms of the *functions* had by their instances. The concept of *being a carburetor* might be analyzed in terms of the purpose of such devices. This might be done in terms of the role a carburetor plays in the overall mechanical system of which it is a part, and this role might be described in terms of a carburetor's inputs, outputs, and relations to other states of that system. As another example, such a functional analysis might be attempted for concepts having to do with mental states (like the concept of *being in pain*), and this is the basic idea behind some versions of functionalism in philosophy of mind.

Still another possibility would be to analyze concepts in terms of how instances of that concept *come to be*. For instance, one might analyze the concept of *being an artwork* not in terms of necessary conditions or typical features, or in terms of what art is for, but instead in terms of the procedure one uses in *producing* an artwork. On this sort of analysis, the question "What is art?" would just be answered in terms of how art is made, and nothing more.

Finally, one might analyze a concept in terms of the *composition* of instances of that concept. For instance, "Granite is an igneous rock consisting mostly of quartz, microcline, and mica" seems to express some sort of analysis of the concept of *being granite*, even though it is just in terms of the physical composition of granite and not in terms of how granite comes to be, what it is for, etc.[11]

In summary, an analysis of a concept is a proposition that gives the meaning of all expressions of that concept. For a classical conceptual analysis, this is done in terms of a set of necessary and jointly sufficient conditions for something to be an instance of that concept. According to the classical view of the *activity* of seeking analyses, one determines whether a candidate analysis is correct by seeking counterexamples to

---

[11]On further reflection, this example might well be a *classical* analysis at heart, since it looks like being an igneous rock is necessary for being granite, as well as being composed mostly of quartz, microcline, and mica. However, this was meant only as an illustration: One can surely imagine other cases in which a concept seems to be analyzed in terms of the composition of its instances, yet that analysis is not a classical analysis.

that analysis. If there are no counterexamples, then that analysis is a correct analysis. Other sorts of propositions might count as analyses, too, such as analyses in terms of typical features, functional analyses, procedural analyses, and analyses in terms of physical constitution. At the very least, analysis is essential to the practice of philosophy as a whole: As long as there are arguments that stand or fall depending on the meanings of the terms employed in them, what will decide such matters is the correct analyses of those terms.

Bibliography

Ackerman, D. F. 1986. "Essential Properties and Philosophical Analysis." In P. French et al. (Eds.), *Midwest Studies in Philosophy*, vol. 11. Minneapolis, MN: University of Minnesota Press, 304–313.

———. 1992. "Analysis and Its Paradoxes." In E. Ullman-Margalit (Ed.), *The Scientific Enterprise: The Israel Colloquium Studies in History, Philosophy, and Sociology of Science*, vol. 4. Norwell, MA: Kluwer, 169–178.

———. 1995. "Analysis." In J. Kim and E. Sosa (Eds.), *A Companion to Metaphysics*, Oxford: Blackwell, 9–11.

Laurence, Stephen and Margolis, Eric. 1999. "Concepts and Cognitive Science." In Eric Margolis and Stephen Laurence (Eds.), *Concepts: Core Readings*. Cambridge: MIT Press, 3–81.

Rey, Georges. 1983. "Concepts and Stereotypes." *Cognition* 15, 237–262.

PART TWO

WHAT IS KNOWLEDGE?

The readings in this section address the nature and scope of human knowledge—that area of philosophy called *epistemology*. This area of philosophical inquiry dates back at least as far as Plato's time (circa 400 B.C.) when, in the *Meno*, he describes Socrates' inquiry into the difference between mere *belief* (doxa) and *knowledge* (episteme). There is, it seems, something real knowledge has that mere belief lacks. One goal of philosophy is to discover what this difference is. The classical analysis of knowledge, which is usually attributed to Plato, is that knowledge is justified true belief. This definition of knowledge can be seen as giving rise to the central questions of epistemology: Is knowledge even possible? That is, can we ever satisfy these criteria? What does it take for a belief to be justified? Are these criteria sufficient for knowledge? What are the limits of knowledge? And, how do we acquire knowledge?

In the first reading, sections I and II of the *Meditations*, René Descartes states that what distinguishes real knowledge from mere belief is the added feature of *indubitability*. That is, while one may have many beliefs, only those whose truth cannot be doubted, those of which one is certain, will count as knowledge. Thus, Descartes introduces a *criterion of certainty*. In the two meditations included here, Descartes subjects his formerly held opinions, his beliefs, to doubt in an attempt to discover which, if any, meet the criterion of certainty. If Descartes is working with the correct criteria for knowledge, and nothing can satisfy that criteria, then the result would be an extreme form of skepticism—the view that knowledge is not possible. However, even though Descartes employs a skeptical approach to knowledge, in the end he rejects skepticism. Ultimately, he defends a rationalist epistemology—he argues that beliefs justified *a priori*, or on the basis of reason, satisfy the criterion of certainty.

In "Brain in a Vat Skepticism," Christopher Grau reminds us that Descartes' worries are not so foreign or outdated; instead, they are the stuff of contemporary science fiction. Like the character Neo in *The Matrix*, we might wonder if this so-called life is only a very convincing dream. Grau expresses this familiar Cartesian skeptical worry by asking, "How can any of us be sure that we have ever *genuinely* woken up? Perhaps . . . our dreams thus far have in fact been dreams *within* dreams." Still, to most of us, it seems rather far-fetched to think that we, like Neo, are being deceived on such a grand scale; however, to know that this is true, we need a sound argument to justify our belief that things are as they seem. In the second part of Grau's paper, he explores a contemporary version of Cartesian skepticism called brain-in-a-vat skepticism. Like Descartes' character wondering whether he is dreaming, and Neo wondering whether he is or is not in the Matrix, we might ask ourselves how we know that we are not disembodied brains "plugged in" to a supercomputer that stimulates our brains in such a way for it to seem to us that we are "normal" people with "normal" lives. Grau sketches philosopher Hilary Putnam's argument that we are not brains in vats, according to which, if we were brains in vats, then we could not coherently think that we are brains in vats.

In "Knowing as Having the Right to Be Sure," a section from his book, *The Problem of Knowledge*, A. J. Ayer offers an analysis of knowledge along the lines of the classical "justified true belief" analysis. His task is to spell out the so-called "justification condition" for knowledge. He rejects Descartes' indubitability requirement, and he questions the claim that knowing something entails that one cannot possibly be wrong. This is an outright rejection of Descartes' criterion of certainty. Ayer's take on the justification condition is much more lenient than Descartes' because he does not think that knowledge requires certainty. Instead, to say that one knows that so-and-so, Ayer argues, is just to say that one has *the right to be sure* of one's true belief.

Edmund Gettier's influential paper, "Is Justified True Belief Knowledge?" challenges the sufficiency of the classical "justified true belief" analysis of knowledge. Gettier offers a counterexample to this analysis; that is, he describes a case in which a person has a *justified true belief* that *P* and yet does not *know* that *P*. If having a justified true belief were sufficient for knowledge, then the person would know that *P*. So, having a justified true belief is not sufficient for knowledge.

One obvious response to Gettier's objection is to question whether or not his subjects' beliefs are really justified given that they are based on a false intermediate belief. Richard Feldman, in his paper, "An Alleged Defect in Gettier Counter-examples," responds to the charge that Gettier has relied on a false principle in challenging the sufficiency of the classical analysis of knowledge. He offers a revised "Gettier-style" counterexample to the justified true belief analysis that, unlike Gettier's, does not depend on the subject having a false intermediate belief. Thus, proponents of the classical analysis of knowledge are left with the burden of providing a satisfactory response to Gettier-style counterexamples that do not depend on a false intermediary belief.

While Descartes' inquiry begins with what might be called a skeptical descent by stripping away more and more of what we think we know, in the end Descartes makes an epistemological ascent. He defends a view called *rationalism* according to which *a priori* (reason-based) beliefs are self-evident, or self-justifying, and provide the foundation upon which all other knowledge is built. A similar answer to skepticism is a view called *empiricism*. An empiricist holds that *a posteriori* (experience-based) beliefs form the foundation of all other knowledge. Empiricists argue that we have *immediate* knowledge of our own experiences and that we have only *inferential* knowledge of the external causes of experience, namely, objects in the world. For example, while one can know that it seems as if one is seeing a red tomato, it is only inferred that the red tomato really exists and is the cause of this experience. These sorts of worries point to a skeptical concern inherent to empiricism. While we can know our immediate sensations, if empiricism is correct, then we should be skeptical about the existence of the physical world because we do not have immediate epistemic access to it. In "Science and the Physical World," W. T. Stace explains that empirical science can operate despite this sort of skepticism concerning the existence of material objects.

In response to the sort of skepticism about the existence of material objects suggested by empiricism, one might simply look at one's own hands and argue "I see my hands, so they must exist." It is this sort of response that G. E. Moore considers in "Proof of an External World." The problem he is addressing is this: If one's experience of seeing one's hands is meant to be *reason* for believing those hands exist, that is, if seeing in some way *justifies* the belief that hands exist, then one must *know* that one is seeing one's hands (rather than it merely *seeming* to one that one sees one's hands) or have proof that the proposition expressed by 'I am seeing my hands' is true. This idea hinges on what is called an *evidentialist* view of justification. Evidentialists treat the justification required for knowledge as a certain sort of evidence. Something unknown cannot count as evidence, so justification must be known to the subject. That is, if P is reason for believing that Q, that is, P is justification for Q, then, according to the evidentialist, P must be *known*. Moore rejects this understanding of justification. He thinks sensations (and experiences) and unknown propositions *can* justify beliefs even if they are not epistemically accessible to the subject.

Many philosophers agree that knowledge requires justification and that justification for believing something amounts to having reasons for believing it—having an argument for it. There are two types of arguments—*inductive* arguments and *deductive* arguments. Deductive arguments are those whose premises, if true, guarantee the truth of their conclusion (i.e., they have that feature called *validity*). Inductive arguments are those whose premises, if true, make it highly probable that their conclusion is true (i.e., they have that feature called *strength*). If being justified in believing that P means that there is an argument that P is true, and an argument is either deductive or inductive, then justification is either deductive or inductive.

It would seem that most of what we believe about the world is justified inductively. If induction is going to provide the sort of justification required for knowledge, then induction itself must be justified. However, if all justification is either inductive or deductive, then, if induction is justified, it must be justified either inductively or deductively. The Problem of Induction is that it seems that we cannot justify induction either inductively or deductively; thus, induction is not justified, and our inductively justified true beliefs do not count as knowledge. John Hospers offers what is called a pragmatic solution to the problem of induction. In short, he argues that we are justified in justifying our beliefs inductively because, practically speaking, induction works.

In the final selection in this section, "The Problem of Induction—Old and New," Howard Kahane and Paul Tidman offer a concise statement of the problem of induction and explain why several standard sorts of responses to the problem, including a pragmatic solution like Hospers', are unsatisfactory. In the second section of this reading, Kahane and Tidman explain what has been coined "The New Riddle of Induction." This problem concerns the nature of confirming evidence itself. In science, certain observations count as *evidence* in support of certain hypotheses. The "old" riddle of induction (the Problem of Induction) is the problem of justifying the *inductive inference* from some bit of evidence to some conclusion or hypothesis. The new riddle of induction, however, focuses on the *nature of the confirming evidence* itself. What exactly should count as confirming evidence?

Meditations 1 and 2

René Descartes   *(Translated by F. E. Sutcliffe)*

First Meditation

About the Things We May Doubt

It is some time ago now since I perceived that, from my earliest years, I had accepted many false opinions as being true, and that what I had since based on such insecure principles could only be most doubtful and uncertain; so that I had to undertake seriously once in my life to rid myself of all the opinions I had adopted up to then, and to begin afresh from the foundations, if I wished to establish something firm and constant in the sciences. But as this undertaking seemed to me very great, I waited until I had attained an age sufficiently mature that I could not hope, at a later stage in life, to be more fit to execute my plan; and this has made me delay so long that I should henceforth consider that I was committing a fault if I were still to use in deliberation the time which remains to me for action.

Now therefore, that my mind is free from all cares, and that I have obtained for myself assured leisure in peaceful solitude, I shall apply myself seriously and freely to the general destruction of all my former opinions. Now it will not be necessary, in order to accomplish this aim, to prove that they are all false, a point which perhaps I would never reach; but inasmuch as reason persuades me already that I must avoid believing things which are not entirely certain and indubitable, no less carefully than those things which seem manifestly false, the slightest ground for doubt that I find in any, will suffice for me to reject all of them. And to this end there will be no need for me to examine each one individually, which would be an endless task; but because the destruction of the foundations necessarily brings down with it the rest of the edifice, I shall make an assault first on the principles on which all my former opinions were based.

Everything I have accepted up to now as being absolutely true and assured, I have learned from or through the senses. But I have sometimes found that these senses played me false, and it is prudent never to trust entirely those who have once deceived us.

But, although the senses sometimes deceive us, concerning things which are barely perceptible or at a great distance, there are perhaps many other things about which one cannot reasonably doubt, although we know them through the medium of the senses, for example, that I am here, sitting by the fire, wearing a dressing-gown, with this paper in my hands, and other things of this nature. And how could I deny that these hands and this body belong to me, unless perhaps I were to assimilate myself to those insane persons whose minds are so troubled and clouded by the black vapours of the bile that they constantly assert that they are kings, when they are very poor; that they are wearing gold and purple, when they are quite naked; or who imagine that they are pitchers or that they have a body of glass. But these are madmen, and I would not be less extravagant if I were to follow their example.

However, I must here consider that I am a man, and consequently that I am in the habit of sleeping and of representing to myself in my dreams those same things, or sometimes even less likely things, which insane people do when they are awake. How many times have I dreamt at night that I was in this place, dressed, by the fire, although I was quite naked in my bed? It certainly seems to me at the moment that I am not looking at this paper with my eyes closed; that this head that I shake is not asleep; that I hold out this hand intentionally and deliberately, and that I am aware of it. What happens in sleep does not seem as clear and distinct as all this. But in thinking about it carefully, I recall having often been deceived in sleep by similar illusions, and, reflecting on this circumstance more closely, I see so clearly that there are no conclusive signs by means of which one can distinguish clearly between being awake and being asleep, that I am quite astonished by it; and my astonishment is such that it is almost capable of persuading me that I am asleep now.

Let us suppose, then, that we are now asleep, and that all these particulars, namely, that we open our eyes, move our heads, hold out our hands, and such like actions, are only false illusions; and let us think that perhaps our hands and all our body are not as we see them. Nevertheless, we must at least admit that the things which appear to us in sleep are, as it were, pictures and paintings which can only be formed in the likeness of something real and true; and that therefore these general things at least, namely, eyes, head, hands and all the rest of the body are not imaginary things but are real and existent. For indeed painters, even when they study with the utmost skill to represent Sirens and Satyrs by strange and extraordinary shapes, cannot attribute to them entirely new forms and natures, but only make a certain mixture and compound of the limbs of various animals; or if perhaps their imagination is extravagant enough to invent something so new that we have never seen the like of it, and that, in this way, their work presents us with something purely fictitious and absolutely false, at least the colours of which they have composed it are real. And by the same reasoning, although these general things, viz. eyes, head, hands and the like, may be imaginary, we have to admit that there are even simpler and more universal things which are true and exist, from the mixture of which, no more or less than from the mixture of certain real colours, all the images of things, whether true and real or fictitious and fantastic, which dwell in our thoughts, are formed. Corporeal nature in general, and its extension, are of this class of things: together with the figure of extended things, their quantity or size, and their number, as also the place where they are, the time during which they exist, and such like.

This is why perhaps that, from this, we shall not be wrong in concluding that physics, astronomy, medicine, and all the other sciences which depend on the consideration of composite things, are most doubtful and uncertain, but that arithmetic, geometry and the other sciences of this nature, which deal only with very simple and general things, without bothering about their existence or non-existence, contain something certain and indubitable. For whether I am awake or sleeping, two and three added together always make five, and a square never has more than four sides; and it does not seem possible that truths so apparent can be suspected of any falsity or uncertainty.

Nevertheless, I have for a long time had in my mind the belief that there is a God who is all-powerful and by whom I was created and made as I am. And who can give me the assurance that this God has not arranged that there should be no earth, no heaven, no extended body, no figure, no magnitude, or place, and that nevertheless I should have the perception of all these things, and the persuasion that they do not exist other than as I see them? And, further, as I sometimes think that others are mistaken, even in the things they think they know most certainly, it is possible that God has wished that I should be deceived every time I add two and three or count the sides of a square, or form some judgement even simpler, if anything simpler than that can be imagined. But perhaps God has not wished me to be deceived in this way, for he is said to be supremely good. However, if it were in contradiction to his goodness to have made me in such a way that I always deceived myself, it would seem also to be contrary to his goodness to allow me to be wrong sometimes, and nevertheless it is beyond doubt that he permits it.

There will be some perhaps who would prefer to deny the existence of a God so powerful than to believe that all other things are uncertain.

But let us not oppose them for the moment, and let us suppose in their favour that everything said here about a God is a fable. Nevertheless, however they suppose that I reached the state and being which I possess, whether they attribute it to some destiny or fate, or to chance or to a continuous sequence and conjunction of events, it is certain that, because fallibility and error are a kind of imperfection, the less powerful the author to whom they attribute my origin, the more probable it will be that I am so imperfect as to be deceived all the time. I have certainly nothing to say in reply to such reasonings, but am constrained to avow that, of all the opinions that I once accepted as true, there is not one which is not now legitimately open to doubt, not through any lack of reflection or lightness of judgement, but for very strong and deeply considered reasons; so that if I wish to find anything certain and assured in the sciences, I must from now on check and suspend judgement on these opinions and refrain from giving them more credence than I would do to things which appeared to me manifestly false.

But it is not enough to have made these observations; I must also take care to remember them; for those old and customary opinions still recur often in my mind, long and familiar usage giving them the right to occupy my mind against my will and, as it were, to dominate my mind. And I shall never rid myself of the habit of acquiescing in them and of having confidence in them so long as I look upon them as what in fact they are, that is to say, in some degree doubtful, as I have just shown, and yet highly probable, so that it is more reasonable to believe than to deny them. This is why I think I shall proceed more prudently if, taking an opposite course, I endeavour to deceive myself, pretending that all these opinions are false and imaginary, until, having so balanced my prejudices that they may not make my judgement incline more to one side than to another, my judgement may no longer be overpowered as hitherto by bad usage and turned from the right path which can lead it to the knowledge of truth. For I am assured that, meanwhile, there can be no danger or error in this course, and that, for the present, it would be impossible to press my distrust too far, for it is not now action I seek as my end but simply meditation and knowledge.

I shall suppose, therefore, that there is, not a true God, who is the sovereign source of truth, but some evil demon, no less cunning and deceiving than powerful, who has used all his artifice to deceive me. I will suppose that the heavens, the air, the earth, colours, shapes, sounds and all external things that we see, are only illusions and deceptions which he uses to take me in. I will consider myself as having no hands, eyes, flesh, blood or senses, but as believing wrongly that I have all these things. I shall cling obstinately to this notion; and if, by this means, it is not in my power to arrive at the knowledge of any truth, at the very least it is in my power to suspend my judgement. This is why I shall take great care not to accept into my belief anything false, and shall so well prepare my mind against all the tricks of this great deceiver that, however powerful and cunning he may be, he will never be able to impose on me.

But this undertaking is arduous, and a certain indolence leads me back imperceptibly into the ordinary course of life. And just as a slave who was enjoying in his sleep an imaginary freedom, fears to be awakened when he begins to suspect that his liberty is only a dream, and conspires with these pleasant illusions to be deceived by them longer, so I fall back of my own accord into my former opinions, and fear to awake from this slumber lest the laborious wakeful hours which would follow this peaceful rest, instead of bringing me any light of day into the knowledge of truth, would not be sufficient to disperse the shadows caused by the difficulties which have just been raised.

Second Meditation

Of the Nature of the Human Mind; and That It Is Easier to Know Than the Body

The Meditation of yesterday has filled my mind with so many doubts that it is no longer in my power to forget them. And yet I do not see how I shall be able to resolve them; and, as though I had suddenly fallen into very deep water, I am so taken unawares that I can neither put my feet firmly down on the bottom nor swim to keep myself on the surface. I make an effort, nevertheless, and follow afresh the same path upon which I entered yesterday, in keeping away from everything of which I can conceive the slightest doubt, just as if I knew that it was absolutely false; and I shall continue always in this path until I have encountered something which is certain, or at least, if I can do nothing else, until I have learned with certainty that there is nothing certain in the world.

Archimedes, in order to take the terrestrial globe from its place and move it to another, asked only for a point which was fixed and assured. So also, I shall have the right to entertain high hopes, if I am fortunate enough to find only one thing which is certain and indubitable.

I suppose therefore that all the things I see are false; I persuade myself
that none of those things ever existed that my deceptive memory represents to me; I suppose I have no senses; I believe that body, figure, extension, movement and place are only fictions of my mind. What, then, shall
be considered true? Perhaps only this, that there is nothing certain in the
world.

But how do I know there is not some other thing, different from those
I have just judged to be uncertain, about which one could not have the
slightest doubt? Is there not a God, or some other power, which puts these
thoughts into my mind? But that is unnecessary, for perhaps I am capable of producing them myself. Myself, then, at least am I not something?
But I have already denied that I have any senses or any body. I hesitate, however, for what follows from that? Am I so dependent on body
and senses that I cannot exist without them? But I had persuaded myself
that there was nothing at all in the world: no sky, no earth, no minds
or bodies; was I not, therefore, also persuaded that I did not exist? No
indeed; I existed without doubt, by the fact that I was persuaded, or
indeed by the mere fact that I thought at all. But there is some deceiver
both very powerful and very cunning, who constantly uses all his wiles
to deceive me. There is therefore no doubt that I exist, if he deceives
me; and let him deceive me as much as he likes, he can never cause me
to be nothing, so long as I think I am something. So that, after having
thought carefully about it, and having scrupulously examined everything,
one must then, in conclusion, take as assured that the proposition: *I am,
I exist,* is necessarily true, every time I express it or conceive of it in my
mind.

But I, who am certain that I am, do not yet know clearly enough what
I am; so that henceforth I must take great care not imprudently to take
some other object for myself, and thus avoid going astray in this knowledge which I maintain to be more certain and evident than all I have
had hitherto.

For this reason, I shall now consider afresh what I thought I was
before I entered into these last thoughts; and I shall retrench from my former opinions everything that can be invalidated by the reasons I have
already put forward, so that absolutely nothing remains except that which
is entirely indubitable. What, then, did I formerly think I was? I thought
I was a man. But what is a man? Shall I say rational animal? No indeed:
for it would be necessary next to inquire what is meant by animal, and
what by rational, and, in this way, from one single question, we would
fall unwittingly into an infinite number of others, more difficult and awkward than the first, and I would not wish to waste the little time and

leisure remaining to me by using it to unravel subtleties of this kind. But I shall rather stop to consider here the thoughts which sprang up hitherto spontaneously in my mind, and which were inspired by my own nature alone, when I applied myself to the consideration of my being. I considered myself, firstly, as having a face, hands, arms, and the whole machine made up of flesh and bones, such as it appears in a corpse and which I designated by the name of body. I thought, furthermore, that I ate, walked, had feelings and thought, and I referred all these actions to the soul; but I did not stop to consider what this soul was, or at least, if I did, I imagined it was something extremely rare and subtle, like a wind, flame or vapour, which permeated and spread through my most substantial parts. As far as the body was concerned, I was in no doubt as to its nature, for I thought I knew it quite distinctly, and, if I had wished to explain it according to the notions I had of it, I would have described it in this way: by body, I understand all that can be terminated by some figure; that can be contained in some place and fill a space in such a way that any other body is excluded from it; that can be perceived, either by touch, sight, hearing, taste or smell; that can be moved in many ways, not of itself, but by something foreign to it by which it is touched and from which it receives the impulse. For as to having in itself the power to move, to feel and to think, I did not believe in any way that these advantages might be attributed to corporeal nature; on the contrary, I was somewhat astonished to see that such faculties were to be found in certain bodies.

But as to myself, who am I, now that I suppose there is someone who is extremely powerful and, if I may so say, malicious and cunning, who employs all his efforts and industry to deceive me? Can I be sure of having the least of all the characteristics that I have attributed above to the nature of bodies? I pause to think about it carefully, I turn over all these things in my mind, and I cannot find one of which I can say that it is in me. There is no need for me to stop and enumerate them. Let us pass, then, to the attributes of the soul, and see if there are any of these in me. The first are eating and walking; but if it is true that I have no body, it is true also that I cannot walk or eat. Sensing is another attribute, but again this is impossible without the body; besides, I have frequently believed that I perceived in my sleep many things which I observed, on awakening, I had not in reality perceived. Another attribute is thinking, and I here discover an attribute which does belong to me; this alone cannot be detached from me. *I am, I exist*: this is certain; but for how long? For as long as I think, for it might perhaps happen, if I ceased to think, that I would at the same time cease to be or to exist. I now admit nothing which is not necessarily true: I am therefore, precisely speaking, only a thing which thinks, that is to say, a mind, understanding, or reason, terms whose significance was hitherto unknown to me. I am, however, a real thing, and really existing; but what thing? I have already said it: a thing which thinks. And what else? I will stir up my imagination in order to discover if I am not something more. I am not this assemblage of limbs called the human body; I am not a thin and penetrating air spread through all these members; I am not a wind, a breath of air, a vapour, or anything at all that I can invent or imagine, since I have supposed that all those things were nothing, and yet, without changing this supposition, I find I am nevertheless certain that I am something.

But also, it may be that these same things that I suppose do not exist, because they are unknown to me, are not in truth different from me whom I know. I do not know; I am not debating this point now. I can judge only of things which are known to me: I have recognized that I exist, and I, who recognize I exist, seek to discover what I am. It is most certain, however, that this notion and knowledge of myself, thus precisely taken, do not depend on things the existence of which is not yet known to me; neither, consequently, and *a fortiori*, do they depend on any of those which are feigned and invented by the imagination. And even these terms feigning and imagining, warn me of my error; for I should be feigning, in truth, if I were to imagine that I am anything, since imagining is nothing other than contemplating the figure or image of a corporeal object. Now I know already for certain that I exist, and at the same time that it is possible that all those images, and, in general, all the things one relates to the nature of body, are nothing but dreams or chimera. From this I see clearly that it is as unreasonable for me to say: I shall stir up my imagination in order to know more distinctly what I am, as to say: I am now awake, and I perceive something real and true; but, because I do not perceive it clearly enough, I shall go to sleep expressly so that my dreams may show this object to me with greater truth and clearness. And in this way, I recognize certainly that nothing of all that I can understand by means of imagination belongs to this knowledge that I have of myself, and that it is necessary to call one's mind back and turn it away from this mode of thinking, so that it can itself recognize its own nature very distinctly.

But what, then, am I? A thing that thinks. What is a thing that thinks? That is to say, a thing that doubts, perceives, affirms, denies, wills, does not will, that imagines also, and which feels. Indeed this is not a little, if all these properties belong to my nature. But why should they not so belong? Am I not still this same being who doubts of almost everything; who nevertheless understands and conceives certain things; who affirms those alone to be true; who denies all the rest; who wishes and desires to know more of them and does not wish to be deceived; who imagines many things, even sometimes in spite of himself; and who also perceives many, as if through the intermediary of the organs of the body? Is there nothing in all this which is as true as it is certain that I am, and that I exist, even though I were always to be sleeping, and though he who has given me my being should use all his power to deceive me? Is there also any one of these attributes which may be distinguished from my thought, or that one could say was separate from me? For it is so self evident that it is I who doubt, who understand and who wish, that there is no need here to add anything to explain it. And I have equally certainly the power to imagine, for even though it may be (as I have supposed above) that the things I imagine are not true, nevertheless, this capacity for imagining does not cease to be really in me, and forms part of my thinking. Finally, I am the same being who senses, that is to say who apprehends and knows things, as by the sense-organs, since, in truth, I see light, hear noise and feel heat. But it will be said that these appearances are false and that I am dreaming. Let it be so; all the same, at least, it is very certain that it seems to me that I see light, hear a noise and feel heat; and this is properly what in me is called perceiving and this, taken in this precise sense, is nothing other than thinking. From this I begin to know what I am, a little more clearly and distinctly than hitherto.

But I cannot help believing that corporeal objects, whose images are formed by my thoughts, and which come under the senses, are more distinctly known to me than that, I know not what, part of me which does not fall within the grasp of the imagination; although in truth it may seem very strange that things I find doubtful and distant, are more clearly and easily known to me than those which are true and certain, and which belong to my own nature. But I see very well how it is: my mind likes to wander, and cannot yet contain itself within the precise limits of truth. Let us therefore give it its head once more, so that, later on, tightening the rein gently and opportunely, we shall the more easily be able to govern and control it.

Let us begin by considering the most common things, those which we believe we understand the most distinctly, namely, the bodies we touch and see. I am not speaking of bodies in general, for these general notions are usually more confused, but of one body in particular. Let us take, for example, this piece of wax which has just been taken from the hive; it has not yet lost the sweetness of the honey it contained; it still retains something of the smell of the flowers from which it was gathered; its colour, shape and size, are apparent; it is hard, cold, it is tangible; and if you tap it, it will emit a sound. So, all the things by which a body can be known distinctly are to be found together in this one.

But, as I am speaking, it is placed near a flame: what remained of its taste is dispelled, the smell disappears, its colour changes, it loses its shape, it grows bigger, becomes liquid, warms up, one can hardly touch it, and although one taps it, it will no longer make any sound. Does the same wax remain after this change? One must admit that it does remain, and no one can deny it. What, then, was it that I knew in this piece of wax with such distinctness? Certainly it could be nothing of all the things which I perceived by means of the senses, for everything which fell under taste, smell, sight, touch or hearing, is changed, and yet the same wax remains. Perhaps it was what I now think, namely, that the wax was not the sweetness of honey, or the pleasant smell of flowers, the whiteness, or the shape, nor the sound, but only a body which a little earlier appeared to me in these forms, and which is now to be perceived in other forms. But to speak precisely, what is it that I imagine when I conceive it in this way? Let us consider it attentively, and setting aside everything that does not belong to the wax, let us see what remains. Indeed nothing remains, except something extended, flexible and malleable. Now, what does that mean: flexible and malleable? Is it not that I imagine that this wax, being round, is capable of becoming square, and of passing from a square to a triangular figure? No indeed, it is not that, for I conceive of it as capable of undergoing an infinity of similar changes, and as I could not embrace this infinity by my imagination, consequently this conception I have of the wax is not the product of the faculty of imagination.

What, now, is this extension? Is it not also unknown, since it increases as the wax melts, is greater when the wax is completely melted, and very much greater still when the heat is intensified; and I should not conceive clearly and according to truth what the wax is, if I did not remember that it is capable of taking on more variations in extension that I have ever imagined. I must therefore agree that I could not even conceive by means of the imagination what this wax is, and that it is my understanding alone which conceives it. I say this piece of wax in particular, for, as to wax in general, this is still more evident. Now, what is this wax, which cannot be conceived except by the understanding or mind? Indeed it is the same which I see, touch, imagine, and which I knew from the start. But, and this is to be noted, the perception of it, or the action by which one perceives it, is not an act of sight, or touch, or of imagination, and has never been, although it seemed so hitherto, but only an intuition of the mind, which may be imperfect and confused, as it was formerly, or else clear and distinct, as it is at present according as my attention directs itself more or less to the elements which it contains and of which it is composed.

However, I am greatly astonished when I consider the weakness of my mind, and its proneness to error. For although, without speaking, I consider all this in my own mind, yet words stop me, and I am almost led into error by the terms of ordinary language. For we say we see the same wax if it is put before us, and not that we judge it to be the same, because it has the same colour and shape: whence I would almost conclude that one knows the wax by the eyesight, and not by the intuition of the mind alone. If I chance to look out of a window on to men passing in the street, I do not fail to say, on seeing them, that I see men, just as I say that I see the wax; and yet, what do I see from this window, other than hats and cloaks, which can cover ghosts or dummies who move only by means of springs? But I judge them to be really men, and thus I understand, by the sole power of judgement which resides in my mind, what I believed I saw with my eyes.

A man who wishes to lift his knowledge above the common, must feel ashamed to seek occasions for doubting from the forms and terms of common speech. I prefer to avoid this and to go on to consider whether I conceived more evidently and perfectly what the wax is when I first saw it, and believed I knew it by means of my external senses, or at the very least by the common sense, as it is called, that is to say by the imaginative faculty, than I conceive it at present, after having more carefully examined what it is and by what means it can be known. Indeed, it would be ridiculous to have any doubt on this point. For what was there in that first perception that was distinct and evident, and which could not be perceived in the same way by the senses of the least of animals? But when I distinguish the wax from its external forms, and, just as if I had removed its garments, I consider it quite naked, it is certain that, although some error in my judgement may still be encountered, I cannot conceive of it in this way without possessing a human mind.

But finally, what shall I say of this mind, that is to say of myself? For so far I admit in myself nothing other than a mind. What shall I say of myself, I ask, I who seem to conceive so clearly and distinctly this piece of wax? Do I not know myself, not only with much more truth and certainty, but also more distinctly and clearly? For if I judge that the wax is, or exists, because I see it, certainly it follows much more evidently from the same fact that I myself am, or exist. For it may well be that what I see is not in effect wax; it may also be that I do not even have eyes with which to see anything; but it cannot be that, when I see or (which I no longer distinguish) think I see, I, who think, am nothing. Similarly, if I judge that the wax exists because I touch it, the same conclusion follows, namely, that I am. And if I judge thus because my imagination persuades me that it is so, or on account of any other cause whatever, I shall still draw the same conclusion. And what I have said here about the wax can apply to all the other things external to me.

Now, if my notion and knowledge of the wax seems to be more precise and distinct after it has become known to me not only by sight or touch, but also in many other ways, with how much greater distinctness, clarity and precision must I know myself, since all the means which help me to know and perceive the nature of wax, or of any other body, prove much more easily and evidently the nature of my mind? And so many other things besides are to be found in the mind itself, which can contribute to the clarification of its nature, that those which depend on the body, such as these mentioned here, scarcely deserve to be taken into account.

But now I have come back imperceptibly to the point I sought; for, since it is now known to me that, properly speaking, we perceive bodies only by the understanding which is in us, and not by the imagination, or the senses, and that we do not perceive them through seeing them or touching them, but only because we conceive them in thought, I know clearly that there is nothing more easy for me to know than my own mind. But, because it is almost impossible to rid oneself so quickly of a long-held opinion, I should do well to pause at this point, so that, by long meditation, I may imprint this new knowledge more deeply in my memory.

Brain in a Vat Skepticism

Christopher Grau

Dream Skepticism

MORPHEUS: *Have you ever had a dream, Neo, that you were so sure was real?*

MORPHEUS: *What if you were unable to wake from that dream, Neo? How would you know the difference between the dreamworld and the real world?*

Neo has woken up from a hell of a dream—the dream that was his life. How was he to know? The cliché is that if you are dreaming and you pinch yourself, you will wake up. Unfortunately, things aren't quite that simple. It is the nature of most dreams that we take them for reality—

while dreaming we are unaware that we are in fact in a dreamworld. Of course, we eventually wake up, and when we do we realize that our experience was all in our mind. Neo's predicament makes one wonder, though: how can any of us be sure that we have ever *genuinely* woken up? Perhaps, like Neo prior to his downing the red pill, our dreams thus far have in fact been dreams *within* a dream.

The idea that what we take to be the real world could all be just a dream is familiar to many students of philosophy, poetry, and literature. Most of us, at one time or another, have been struck with the thought that we might mistake a dream for reality, or reality for a dream. Arguably the most famous exponent of this worry in the Western philosophical tradition is the seventeenth-century French philosopher René Descartes. In an attempt to provide a firm foundation for knowledge, he began his *Meditations* by clearing the philosophical ground through doubting all that could be doubted. This was done, in part, in order to determine if anything that could count as certain knowledge could survive such rigorous and systematic skepticism. Descartes takes the first step towards this goal by raising (through his fictional narrator) the possibility that we might be dreaming:

> How often, asleep at night, am I convinced of just such familiar events —that I am here in my dressing gown, sitting by the fire—when in fact I am lying undressed in bed! Yet at the moment my eyes are certainly wide awake when I look at this piece of paper; I shake my head and it is not asleep; as I stretch out and feel my hand I do so deliberately, and I know what I am doing. All this would not happen with such distinctness to someone asleep. Indeed! As if I did not remember other occasions when I have been tricked by exactly similar thoughts while asleep! As I think about this more carefully, I see plainly that there are never any sure signs by means of which being awake can be distinguished from being asleep. The result is that I begin to feel dazed, and this very feeling only reinforces the notion that I may be asleep. (Descartes, 13)

When we dream we are often blissfully ignorant that we are dreaming. Given this, and the fact that dreams often seem as vivid and "realistic" as real life, how can you rule out the possibility that you might be dreaming even now, as you sit and read this? This is the kind of perplexing thought Descartes forces us to confront. It seems we have no justification for the belief that we are not dreaming. If so, then it seems we similarly have no justification in thinking that the world we experience is the real world. Indeed, it becomes questionable whether we are justified in thinking that *any* of our beliefs are true.

The narrator of Descartes' *Meditations* worries about this, but he ultimately maintains that the possibility that one might be dreaming cannot by itself cast doubt on all we think we know; he points out that even if all our sensory experience is but a dream, we can still conclude that we have *some* knowledge of the nature of reality. Just as a painter cannot create *ex nihilo* but must rely on pigments with which to create her image, certain elements of our thought must exist prior to our imaginings. Among the items of knowledge that Descartes thought survived dream skepticism are truths arrived at through the use of reason, such as the truths of mathematics: "For whether I am awake or asleep, two and three added together are five, and a square has no more than four sides." (Descartes, 14)

While such an insight offers little comfort to someone wondering whether the people and objects she confronts are genuine, it served Descartes' larger philosophical project: he sought, among other things, to provide a foundation for knowledge in which truths arrived at through reason are given priority over knowledge gained from the senses. (This bias shouldn't surprise those who remember that Descartes was a brilliant mathematician in addition to being a philosopher.) Descartes was not himself a skeptic—he employs this skeptical argument so as to help remind the reader that the truths of mathematics (and other truths of reason) are on firmer ground than the data provided to us by our senses.

Despite the fact that Descartes' ultimate goal was to demonstrate how genuine knowledge is possible, he proceeds in *The Meditations* to utilize a much more radical skeptical argument, one that casts doubt on even his beloved mathematical truths. In the next section we will see that, many years before the Wachowskis dreamed up *The Matrix*, Descartes had imagined an equally terrifying possibility.

Brains In Vats and the Evil Demon

MORPHEUS: What is the Matrix? Control.
MORPHEUS: The Matrix is a computer-generated dreamworld built to keep us under control in order to change a human being into this. (Holds up a battery)
NEO: No! I don't believe it! It's not possible!

Before breaking out of the Matrix, Neo's life was not what he thought it was. It was a lie. Morpheus described it as a "dreamworld," but unlike a dream, this world was not the creation of Neo's mind. The truth is more sinister: the world was a creation of the artificially intelligent computers that have taken over the Earth and have subjugated mankind in the process. These creatures have fed Neo a simulation that he couldn't possibly help but take as the real thing. What's worse, it isn't clear how any of us can know with certainty that we are not in a position similar to Neo before his "rebirth." Our ordinary confidence in our ability to reason and our natural tendency to trust the deliverances of our senses can both come to seem rather naïve once we confront this possibility of deception.

A viewer of *The Matrix* is naturally led to wonder: How do I know I am not in the Matrix? How do I know for sure that my world is not also a sophisticated charade, put forward by some super-human intelligence in such a way that I cannot possibly detect the ruse? The philosopher René Descartes suggested a similar worry: the frightening possibility that all of one's experiences might be the result of a powerful outside force, a "malicious demon."

> And yet firmly implanted in my mind is the long-standing opinion that there is an omnipotent God who made me the kind of creature that I am. How do I know that he has not brought it about that there is no earth, no sky, no extended thing, no shape, no size, no place, while at the same time ensuring that all these things appear to me to exist just as they do now? What is more, just as I consider that others sometimes go astray in cases where they think they have the most perfect knowledge, how do I know that God has not brought it about that I too go wrong every time I add two and three or count the sides of a square, or in some even simpler matter, if that is imaginable? But perhaps God would not have allowed me to be deceived in this way, since he is said to be supremely good; [. . .] I will suppose therefore that not God, who is supremely good and the source of truth, but rather some malicious demon of the utmost power and cunning has employed all his energies in order to deceive me. I shall think that the sky, the air, the earth, colours, shapes, sounds and all external things are merely the delusions of dreams which he has devised to ensnare my judgment. (Descartes, 15)

The narrator of Descartes' *Meditations* concludes that none of his former opinions are safe. Such a demon could not only deceive him about his perceptions, it could conceivably cause him to go wrong when performing even the simplest acts of reasoning.

This radical worry seems inescapable. How could you possibly prove to yourself that you are not in the kind of nightmarish situation Descartes describes? It would seem that any argument, evidence, or proof you might put forward could easily be yet another trick played by the demon. As ludicrous as the idea of the evil demon may sound at first, it is hard, upon reflection, not to share Descartes' worry: for all you know, you may well be a mere plaything of such a malevolent intelligence. More to the point of our general discussion: for all you know, you may well be trapped in the Matrix.

Many contemporary philosophers have discussed a similar skeptical dilemma that is a bit closer to the scenario described in *The Matrix*. It has come to be known as the "brain in a vat" hypothesis, and one powerful formulation of the idea is presented by the philosopher Jonathan Dancy:

> You do not know that you are not a brain, suspended in a vat full of liquid in a laboratory, and wired to a computer which is feeding you your current experiences under the control of some ingenious technician scientist (benevolent or malevolent according to taste). For if you were such a brain, then, provided that the scientist is successful, nothing in your experience could possibly reveal that you were; for your experience is *ex hypothesi* identical with that of something which is not a brain in a vat. Since you have only your own experience to appeal to, and that experience is the same in either situation, nothing can reveal to you which situation is the actual one. (Dancy, 10)

If you cannot know whether you are in the real world or in the world of a computer simulation, you cannot be sure that your beliefs about the world are true. And, what was even more frightening to Descartes, in this kind of scenario it seems that your ability to reason is no safer than the deliverances of the senses: the evil demon or malicious scientist could be ensuring that your reasoning is just as flawed as your perceptions.

As you have probably already guessed, there is no easy way out of this philosophical problem (or at least there is no easy *philosophical* way out!). Philosophers have proposed a dizzying variety of "solutions" to this kind of skepticism but, as with many philosophical problems, there is nothing close to unanimous agreement regarding how the puzzle should be solved.

Descartes' own way out of his evil demon skepticism was to first argue that one cannot genuinely doubt the existence of oneself. He pointed out that all thinking presupposes a thinker: even in doubting, you realize that there must at least be a self which is doing the doubting. (Thus Descartes' most famous line: "I think, therefore I am.") He then went on to claim that, in addition to our innate idea of self, each of us has an idea of God as an all-powerful, all-good, and infinite being implanted in our minds, and that this idea could only have come *from* God. Since this shows us that an all-good God does exist, we can have confidence that he would not allow us to be so drastically deceived about the nature of our perceptions and their relationship to reality. While Descartes' argument for the existence of the self has been tremendously influential and is still actively debated, few philosophers have followed him in accepting his particular theistic solution to skepticism about the external world.

One of the more interesting contemporary challenges to this kind of skeptical scenario has come from the philosopher Hilary Putnam. His point is not so much to defend our ordinary claims to knowledge as to question whether the "brain in a vat" hypothesis is coherent, given certain plausible assumptions about how our language refers to objects in the world. He asks us to consider a variation on the standard "brain in a vat" story that is uncannily similar to the situation described in *The Matrix*:

> Instead of having just one brain in a vat, we could imagine that all human beings (perhaps all sentient beings) are brains in a vat (or nervous systems in a vat in case some beings with just nervous systems count as 'sentient'). Of course, the evil scientist would have to be outside? or would he? Perhaps there is no evil scientist, perhaps (though this is absurd) the universe just happens to consist of automatic machinery tending a vat full of brains and nervous systems. This time let us suppose that the automatic machinery is programmed to give us all a *collective* hallucination, rather than a number of separate unrelated hallucinations. Thus, when I seem to myself to be talking to you, you seem to yourself to be hearing my words. . . . I want now to ask a question which will seem very silly and obvious (at least to some people, including some very sophisticated philosophers), but which will take us to real philosophical depths rather quickly. Suppose this whole story were actually true. Could we, if we were brains in a vat in this way, say or think that we were? (Putnam, 7)

Putnam's surprising answer is that we cannot coherently think that we are brains in vats, and so skepticism of that kind can never really get off the ground. While it is difficult to do justice to Putnam's ingenious argument in a short summary, his point is roughly as follows: Not everything that goes through our heads is a genuine thought, and far from everything we say is a meaningful utterance.

Sometimes we get confused or think in an incoherent manner—sometimes we say things that are simply nonsense. Of course, we don't always realize at the time that we aren't making sense—sometimes we earnestly believe we are saying (or thinking) something meaningful. High on Nitrous Oxide, the philosopher William James was convinced he was having profound insights into the nature of reality—he was convinced that his thoughts were both sensical and important. Upon sobering up and looking at the notebook in which he had written his drug-addled thoughts, he saw only gibberish.

Just as I might say a sentence that is nonsense, I might also use a name or a general term which is meaningless in the sense that it fails to hook up to the world. Philosophers talk of such a term as "failing to refer" to an object. In order to successfully refer when we use language, there must be an appropriate relationship between the speaker and the object referred to. If a dog playing on the beach manages to scrawl the word "Ed" in the sand with a stick, few would want to claim that the dog actually meant to refer to someone named Ed. Presumably the dog doesn't know anyone named Ed, and even if he did, he wouldn't be capable of intending to write Ed's name in the sand. The point of such an example is that words do not refer to objects "magically" or intrinsically: certain conditions must be met in the world in order for us to accept that a given written or spoken word has any meaning and whether it actually refers to anything at all.

Putnam claims that one condition which is crucial for successful reference is that there be an appropriate causal connection between the object referred to and the speaker referring. Specifying exactly what should count as "appropriate" here is a notoriously difficult task, but we can get some idea of the kind of thing required by considering cases in which reference fails through an inappropriate connection: if someone unfamiliar with the film *The Matrix* manages to blurt out the word "Neo" while sneezing, few would be inclined to think that this person has actually *referred* to the character Neo. The kind of causal connection between the speaker and the object referred to (Neo) is just not in place. For reference to succeed, it can't be simply accidental that the name was uttered. (Another way to think about it: the sneezer would have uttered "Neo" even if the film *The Matrix* had never been made.)

The difficulty, according to Putnam, in coherently supposing the brain in a vat story to be true is that brains raised in such an environment could not successfully refer to genuine brains, or vats, or anything else in the real world. Consider the example of someone who has lived their entire life in the Matrix: when they talk of "chickens," they don't actually refer to real *chickens*; at best they refer to the computer representations of chickens that have been sent to their brain. Similarly, when they talk of human bodies being trapped in pods and fed data by the Matrix, they don't successfully refer to real bodies or pods—they can't refer to physical bodies in the real world because they cannot have the appropriate causal connection to such objects. Thus, if someone were to utter the sentence "I am simply a body stuck in a pod somewhere being fed sensory information by a computer" that sentence would itself be necessarily false. If the person is in fact not trapped in the Matrix, then the sentence is straightforwardly false. If the person is trapped in the Matrix, then he can't successfully refer to real human bodies when he utters the word "human body," and so it appears that his statement must also be false. Such a person seems thus doubly trapped: incapable of knowing that he is in the Matrix, and even incapable of successfully expressing the thought that he might be in the Matrix! (Could this be why at one point Morpheus tells Neo that "no one can be told what the Matrix is"?)

Putnam's argument is controversial, but it is noteworthy because it shows that the kind of situation described in *The Matrix* raises not just the expected philosophical issues about knowledge and skepticism, but more general issues regarding meaning, language, and the relationship between the mind and the world.

The Value of Reality: Cypher & the Experience Machine

CYPHER: *You know, I know that this steak doesn't exist. I know when I put it in my mouth, the Matrix is telling my brain that it is juicy and delicious. After nine years, do you know what I've realized?*
CYPHER: *Ignorance is bliss.*
AGENT SMITH: *Then we have a deal?*
CYPHER: *I don't want to remember nothing. Nothing! You understand? And I want to be rich. Someone important. Like an actor. You can do that, right?*
AGENT SMITH: *Whatever you want, Mr. Reagan.*

Cypher is not a nice guy, but is he an unreasonable guy? Is he right to want to get re-inserted into the Matrix? Many want to say no, but giving reasons for why his choice is a bad one is not an easy task. After all, so long as his experiences will be pleasant, how can his situation be worse than the inevitably crappy life he would lead outside of the Matrix?

What could matter beyond the quality of his experience? Remember, once he's back in, living his fantasy life, he won't even know he made the deal. What he doesn't know can't hurt him, right?

Is feeling good the only thing that has value in itself? The question of whether only conscious experience can ultimately matter is one that has been explored in depth by several contemporary philosophers. In the course of discussing this issue in his 1971 book, *Anarchy, State, and Utopia*, Robert Nozick introduced a "thought experiment" that has become a staple of introductory philosophy classes everywhere. It is known as "the experience machine":

> Suppose there were an experience machine that would give you any experience you desired. Superduper neuropsychologists could stimulate your brain so that you would think and feel you were writing a great novel, or making a friend, or reading an interesting book. All the time you would be floating in a tank, with electrodes attached to your brain. Should you plug into this machine for life, preprogramming your life's desires? . . . Of course, while in the tank you won't know that you're there; you'll think it's all actually happening. Others can also plug in to have the experiences they want, so there's no need to stay unplugged to serve them. (Ignore problems such as who will service the machines if everyone plugs in.) Would you plug in? What else can matter to us, other than how our lives feel from the inside? (Nozick, 43)

Nozick goes on to argue that other things do matter to us: For instance, that we actually do certain things, as opposed to simply have the experience of doing them. Also, he points out that we value being (and becoming) certain kinds of people. I don't just want to have the experience of being a decent person, I want to actually be a decent person. Finally, Nozick argues that we value contact with reality in itself, independent of any benefits such contact may bring through pleasant experience: we want to know we are experiencing the real thing. In sum, Nozick thinks that it matters to most of us, often in a rather deep way, that we be the authors of our lives and that our lives involve interacting with the world, and he thinks that the fact that most people would not choose to enter into such an experience machine demonstrates that they do value these other things. As he puts it: "We learn that something matters to us in addition to experience by imagining an experience machine and then realizing that we would not use it" (Nozick, 44).

While Nozick's description of his machine is vague, it appears that there is at least one important difference between it and the simulated world of the Matrix. Nozick implies that someone hooked up to the experience machine will not be able to exercise their agency—they become the passive recipients of preprogrammed experiences. This apparent loss of free will is disturbing to many people, and it might be distorting people's reactions to the case and clouding the issue of whether they value contact with reality per se. The Matrix seems to be set up in such a way that one can enter it and retain one's free will and capacity for decision making, and perhaps this makes it a significantly more attractive option than the experience machine Nozick describes.

Nonetheless, a loss of freedom is not the only disturbing aspect of Nozick's story. As he points out, we seem to mourn the loss of contact with the real world as well. Even if a modified experience machine is presented to us, one which allows us to keep our free will but enter into an entirely virtual world, many would still object that permanently going into such a machine involves the loss of something valuable.

Cypher and his philosophical comrades are likely to be unmoved by such observations. So what if most people are hung-up on "reality" and would turn down the offer to permanently enter an experience machine? Most people might be wrong. All their responses might show is that such people are superstitious, or irrational, or otherwise confused. Maybe they think something could go wrong with the machines, or maybe they keep forgetting that while in the machine they will no longer be aware of their choice to enter the machine.

Perhaps those hesitant to plug-in don't realize that they value being active in the real world only because normally that is the most reliable way for them to acquire the pleasant experience that they value in itself. In other words, perhaps our free will and our capacity to interact with reality are means to a further end—they matter to us because they allow us access to what really matters: pleasant conscious experience. To think the reverse, that reality and freedom have value in themselves (or what philosophers sometimes call nonderivative or intrinsic value), is simply to put the cart before the horse. After all, Cypher could reply, what would be so great about the capacity to freely make decisions or the ability to be in the real world if neither of these things allowed us to feel good?

Peter Unger has taken on these kinds of objections in his own discussion of "experience inducers." He acknowledges that there is a strong temptation when in a certain frame of mind to agree with this kind of Cypher-esque reasoning, but he argues that this is a temptation we ought to try and resist. Cypher's vision of value is too easy and too simplistic. We are inclined to think that only conscious experience can really matter in part because we fall into the grip of a particular picture of what values must be like, and this in turn leads us to stop paying attention to our actual values. We make ourselves blind to the subtlety and complexity of our values, and we then find it hard to understand how something that doesn't affect our consciousness could sensibly matter to us. If we stop and reflect on what we really do care about, however, we come across some surprisingly everyday examples that don't sit easily with Cypher's claims:

> Consider life insurance. To be sure, some among the insured may strongly believe that, if they die before their dependents do, they will still observe their beloved dependents, perhaps from a heaven on high. But others among the insured have no significant belief to that effect. . . . Still, we all pay our premiums. In my case, this is because, even if I will never experience anything that happens to them, I still want things to go better, rather than worse, for my dependents. No doubt, I am rational in having this concern. (Unger, 301)

As Unger goes on to point out, it seems contrived to chalk up all examples of people purchasing life insurance to cases in which someone is simply trying to benefit (while alive) from the favorable impression such a purchase might make on the dependents. In many cases it seems ludicrous to deny that "what motivates us, of course, is our great concern for our dependents' future, whether we experience their future or not" (Unger, 302). This is not a proof that such concern is rational, but it does show that incidents in which we intrinsically value things other than our own conscious experience might be more widespread than we are at first liable to think. (Other examples include the value we place on not being deceived or lied to—the importance of this value doesn't seem to be completely exhausted by our concern that we might one day become aware of the lies and deception.)

Most of us care about a lot of things independently of the experiences that those things provide for us. The realization that we value things other than pleasant conscious experience should lead us to at least wonder if the legitimacy of this kind of value hasn't been too hastily dismissed by Cypher and his ilk. After all, once we see how widespread and commonplace our other nonderivative concerns are, the insistence that conscious experience is the only thing that has value in itself can come to seem downright peculiar. If purchasing life insurance seems like a rational thing to do, why shouldn't the desire that I experience reality (rather than some illusory simulation) be similarly rational? Perhaps the best test of the rationality of our most basic values is actually whether they, taken together, form a consistent and coherent network of attachments and concerns. (Do they make sense in light of each other and in light of our beliefs about the world and ourselves?) It isn't obvious that valuing interaction with the real world fails this kind of test.

Of course, pointing out that the value I place on living in the real world coheres well with my other values and beliefs will not quiet the defender of Cypher, as he will be quick to respond that the fact that my values all cohere doesn't show that they are all justified. Maybe I hold a bunch of exquisitely consistent but thoroughly irrational values!

The quest for some further justification of my basic values might be misguided, however. Explanations have to come to an end somewhere, as Ludwig Wittgenstein once famously remarked. Maybe the right response to a demand for justification here is to point out that the same demand can be made to Cypher: "Just what justifies your exclusive concern with pleasant conscious experience?" It seems as though nothing does—if such concern is justified it must be somehow self-justifying, but if that is possible, why shouldn't our concerns for other people and our desire to live in the real world also be self-justifying? If those can also be self-justifying, then maybe what we don't experience should matter to us, and perhaps what we don't know *can* hurt us. . . .

Bibliography

Dancy, Jonathan (1985). *Introduction to Contemporary Epistemology*, Cambridge, MA: Blackwell.

Descartes. (1984). *The Philosophical Writings of Descartes*, trans. John Cottingham, Robert Stoothoff, Dugald Murdoch, Cambridge: Cambridge University Press.

Johnston, Mark (1992). "Reasons and Reductionism," *Philosophical Review*.

Nagel, Thomas (1970). "Death," *Nous*.

Nagel, Thomas (1986). *The View from Nowhere*, New York: Oxford University Press.

Nozick, Robert (1971). *Anarchy, State, and Utopia*, New York: Basic Books.

Putnam, Hilary (1981). *Reason, Truth, and History*, Cambridge: Cambridge University Press.

Strawson, P. F. (1983), *Skepticism and Naturalism: Some Varieties*, New York: Columbia University Press.

Stroud, Barry (1984). *The Significance of Philosophical Scepticism*, New York: Oxford University Press.

Unger, Peter (1990). *Identity, Consciousness, and Value*, New York: Oxford University Press.

Knowing as Having the Right to Be Sure

A. J. Ayer

. . . The mistaken doctrine that knowing is an infallible state of mind may
have contributed to the view, which is sometimes held, that the only statements that it is possible to know are those that are themselves in some
way infallible. The ground for this opinion is that if one knows something
to be true one cannot be mistaken. As we remarked when contrasting
knowledge with belief, it is inconsistent to say 'I know but I may be
wrong'. But the reason why this is inconsistent is that saying 'I know'
offers a guarantee which saying 'I may be wrong' withdraws. It does
not follow that for a fact to be known it must be such that no one could
be mistaken about it or such that it could not have been otherwise. It is
doubtful if there are any facts about which no one could be mistaken,
and while there are facts which could not be otherwise, they are not the
only ones that can be known. But how can this second point be reconciled with the fact that what is known must be true? The answer is that
the statement that what is known must be true is ambiguous. It may
mean that it is necessary that if something is known it is true; or it may
mean that if something is known, then it is a necessary truth. The first
of these propositions is correct; it re-states the linguistic fact that what
is not true cannot properly be said to be known. But the second is in general false. It would follow from the first only if all truths were necessary, which is not the case. To put it another way, there is a necessary
transition from being known to being true; but that is not to say that what
is true, and known to be true, is necessary or certain in itself.

 If we are not to be bound by ordinary usage, it is still open to us to
make it a rule that only what is certain can be known. That is, we could
decide, at least for the purposes of philosophical discourse, not to use the
word 'know' except with the implication that what was known was necessarily true, or, perhaps, certain in some other sense. The consequence
would be that we could still speak of knowing the truth of *a priori* statements, such as those of logic and pure mathematics; and if there were any
empirical statements, such as those describing the content of one's present experience, that were certain in themselves, they too might be
included: but most of what we now correctly claim to know would not be
knowable, in this allegedly strict sense. This proposal is feasible, but it

does not appear to have anything much to recommend it. It is not as if a statement by being necessary became incapable of being doubted. Every schoolboy knows that it is possible to be unsure about a mathematical truth. Whether there are any empirical statements which are in any important sense indubitable is, as we shall see, a matter of dispute: if there are any they belong to a very narrow class. It is, indeed, important philosophically to distinguish between necessary and empirical statements, and in dealing with empirical statements to distinguish between different types and degrees of evidence. But there are better ways of bringing out these distinctions than by tampering with the meaning, or the application, of the verb 'to know'.

Discussion of Method: Philosophy and Language

We have now answered some of the questions which are raised by a philosophical enquiry into the nature of knowledge. It has been found that there is no very close resemblance between the different instances which are correctly described as instances of knowing, and in particular that to know something does not consist in being in some special state of mind. There are facts which we can be said to know intuitively, but these intuitions cannot be infallible. It has further been shown that the conception of objects of knowledge can be philosophically misleading, and that while there is a sense in which one cannot be mistaken if one knows that something is so, this does not imply that what one knows is itself necessary or indubitable. The whole discussion was introduced as an example of philosophic method. Let us therefore consider, for a moment, how these conclusions have in fact been reached.

An important part of our procedure has been to put these general questions about knowledge to the test of particular instances. Thus the proof that one can know an object, in the sense of being able to recognize it, without making any conscious judgement about it, is that it is possible to find examples of such recognition where there is no evidence that any judgement is made. The proof that knowing how to do something need not include the ability to give an account of the way in which it is done is just that there are many things which people know how to do without their being able to give any such accounts. To discover that there need be no difference, in respect of being sure, between knowing and believing, we need only look at cases in which it turns out that someone does not know what he thought he knew. Very often the reason for this is that what he thought he knew was false. Consequently, he could not have known it, he only believed it. But there is no suggestion that his mental state was different from what it was supposed to be. Had what he claimed to know been true he would, in these circumstances, have known it. In such cases we show that what might be thought to be a necessary factor in a given type of situation is really not necessary, by finding examples in which it does not occur. This is essentially a method of disproof: we cannot so decisively show that a certain factor is necessary, merely by finding examples in which it does occur; we have to be able to see that its presence is logically required by the fact that the situation is of the given type. At the same time we may test the view that it is so required by searching for counter-examples. That none are forthcoming is at least an indication that it is correct. There is a certain analogy here with scientific reasoning, except that it is not so much a matter, as in the scientific case, of discovering whether there are any counter-examples as of deciding whether there could be. The question is whether there is anything that we should be prepared to count as an exception to the suggested rule. Thus the proof that knowing, in the sense of 'knowing that', is always knowledge of some truth is that it would not otherwise be reckoned as knowledge. But it is not always so clear whether or not we should be prepared to admit exceptions. And one way to finding out is to examine carefully whatever might appear to be a doubtful case.

It does not matter whether the examples taken are actual or imaginary. In either case we describe a situation in order to see how it should be classified. Or if there be no doubt as to its classification, we may redescribe it in such a way as to bring to light certain features of it which might otherwise be overlooked. The argument therefore depends upon considerations of language; in the present instance upon the ways in which we use, or propose to use, the verb 'to know'. But this does not mean that it is an argument about words, in any trivial sense, or that it is especially tied to the English language. We are concerned with the work that the word 'know' does, not with the fact that it is this particular word that does it. It is for this reason that we can spare ourselves a sociological investigation into the ways in which people actually do use words. For it would not matter if the popular practice were different from what we took it to be, so long as we were clear about the uses that we ourselves were ascribing to the word in question. And in talking about these uses we are talking about the uses of any words in any language that are, or may be, used in the same way. It is therefore indifferent whether, in this manner of philosophizing, we represent ourselves as dealing with words or as dealing with facts. For our enquiry into the use of words can equally be regarded as an enquiry into the nature of the facts which they describe.

Although we have not been in any way concerned with setting up a formal system, the argument has also been developed by means of deductive logic. Thus the proof that no cognitive state of mind could be infallible depends upon the logical truism that if two states of affairs are distinct a statement which refers to only one of them does not entail anything about the other. If the statement that someone is apprehending, or intuiting, something is to be regarded purely as a description of his state of mind it cannot follow from it that what he apprehends is true. A similar argument was used by Hume to prove that knowledge of causal relations 'is not, in any instance, attained by reasonings *a priori*'.[1] 'The effect', he says, 'is totally different from the cause, and consequently can never be discovered in it.'[2] Or again, 'there is no object, which implies the existence of any other if we consider these objects in themselves, and never look beyond the idea which we form of them.'[3] As Hume puts them these statements are not obviously tautological; but they become so when it is seen that what he is saying is that when two objects are distinct, they are distinct; and consequently that to assert the existence of either one of them is not necessarily to assert the existence of the other.

When they are formulated in this way such statements may seem too trivial to be worth making. But their consequences are important and easily overlooked. The proof of this is that many philosophers have in fact maintained that causality is a logical relation and that there can be infallible acts of knowing. To refute them satisfactorily, we may need to do more than merely point out the logical mistake. We may have to consider how they could have come to be misled, what are the arguments which seem to support their view, how these arguments are to be met. In general, it will be found that the points of logic on which philosophical theories turn are simple. How much of moral theory, for example, is centred upon the truism, again remarked by Hume, that 'ought' is not implied by 'is', that there can be no deductive step from saying how things are to saying how they ought to be. What is difficult is to make the consequences of such truisms palatable, to discover and neutralize the motives which lead to their being denied. It is the fact that much philosophizing consists in persuasive work of this sort, the fact also that in

[1]D. Hume, *An Enquiry Concerning Human Understanding*, section IV, part I, para. 23.
[2]*Ibid.* section IV, part I, para. 25.
[3]D. Hume, *A Treatise of Human Nature*, Book I, part III, section vi.

all philosophy so much depends upon the way in which things are put, that gives point to the saying that philosophy is an exercise in rhetoric. But if this is to be said, it must be understood that the word 'rhetoric' is not to be taken, as it now very often is, in a pejorative sense.

It is not my purpose to give an exhaustive list of philosophical procedures. Those that I have described are typical and important, but they are not the only ones that will come within our notice. In particular, it will be seen that philosophers do not limit themselves to uncovering the criteria which we actually use in assessing different types of statement. They also question these criteria; they may even go so far as to deny their validity. In this way they come to put forward paradoxes, such as that matter is unreal or that no one can ever really know what goes on in the mind of another. In themselves such statements may seem merely perverse: their philosophical importance comes out in the discussion of what lies behind them.

Knowing as Having the Right to Be Sure

The answers which we have found for the questions we have so far been discussing have not yet put us in a position to give a complete account of what it is to know that something is the case. The first requirement is that what is known should be true, but this is not sufficient; not even if we add to it the further condition that one must be completely sure of what one knows. For it is possible to be completely sure of something which is in fact true, but yet not to know it. The circumstances may be such that one is not entitled to be sure. For instance, a superstitious person who had inadvertently walked under a ladder might be convinced as a result that he was about to suffer some misfortune; and he might in fact be right. But it would not be correct to say that he knew that this was going to be so. He arrived at his belief by a process of reasoning which would not be generally reliable; so, although his prediction came true, it was not a case of knowledge. Again, if someone were fully persuaded of a mathematical proposition by a proof which could be shown to be invalid, he would not, without further evidence, be said to know the proposition, even though it was true. But while it is not hard to find examples of true and fully confident beliefs which in some ways fail to meet the standards required for knowledge, it is not at all easy to determine exactly what these standards are.

One way of trying to discover them would be to consider what would count as satisfactory answers to the question How do you know? Thus people may be credited with knowing truths of mathematics or logic if they are able to give a valid proof of them, or even if, without themselves being able to set out such a proof, they have obtained this information from someone who can. Claims to know empirical statements may be upheld by a reference to perception, or to memory, or to testimony, or to historical records, or to scientific laws. But such backing is not always strong enough for knowledge. Whether it is so or not depends upon the circumstances of the particular case. If I were asked how I knew that a physical object of a certain sort was in such and such a place, it would, in general, be a sufficient answer for me to say that I could see it; but if my eyesight were bad and the light were dim, this answer might not be sufficient. Even though I was right, it might still be said that I did not really know that the object was there. If I have a poor memory and the event which I claim to remember is remote, my memory of it may still not amount to knowledge, even though in this instance it does not fail me. If a witness is unreliable, his unsupported evidence may not enable us to know that what he says is true, even in a case where we completely trust him and he is not in fact deceiving us. In a given instance it is possible to decide whether the backing is strong enough to justify a claim to knowledge. But to say in general how strong it has to be would require our drawing up a list of the conditions under which perception, or memory, or testimony, or other forms of evidence are reliable. And this would be a very complicated matter, if indeed it could be done at all.

Moreover, we cannot assume that, even in particular instances, an answer to the question How do you know? will always be forthcoming. There may very well be cases in which one knows that something is so without its being possible to say how one knows it. I am not so much thinking now of claims to know facts of immediate experience, statements like 'I know that I feel pain', which raise problems of their own into which we shall enter later on.[4] In cases of this sort it may be argued that the question how one knows does not arise. But even when it clearly does arise, it may not find an answer. Suppose that someone were consistently successful in predicting events of a certain kind, events, let us say, which are not ordinarily thought to be predictable, like the results of a lottery. If his run of successes were sufficiently impressive, we might very well come to say that he knew which number would win, even though he did not reach this conclusion by any rational method, or indeed by any method at all. We might say that he knew it by intuition, but this would

---

[4]*Vide* ch. 2, section iv.

be to assert no more than that he did know it but that we could not say how. In the same way, if someone were consistently successful in reading the minds of others without having any of the usual sort of evidence, we might say that he knew these things telepathically. But in default of any further explanation this would come down to saying merely that he did know them, but not by an ordinary means. Words like 'intuition' and 'telepathy' are brought in just to disguise the fact that no explanation has been found.

But if we allow this sort of knowledge to be even theoretically possible, what becomes of the distinction between knowledge and true belief? How does our man who knows what the results of the lottery will be differ from one who only makes a series of lucky guesses? The answer is that, so far as the man himself is concerned, there need not be any difference. His procedure and his state of mind, when he is said to know what will happen, may be exactly the same as when it is said that he is only guessing. The difference is that to say that he knows is to concede to him the right to be sure, while to say that he is only guessing is to withhold it. Whether we make this concession will depend upon the view which we take of his performance. Normally we do not say that people know things unless they have followed one of the accredited routes to knowledge. If someone reaches a true conclusion without appearing to have any adequate basis for it, we are likely to say that he does not really know it. But if he were repeatedly successful in a given domain, we might very well come to say that he knew the facts in question, even though we could not explain how he knew them. We should grant him the right to be sure, simply on the basis of his success. This is, indeed, a point on which people's views might be expected to differ. Not everyone would regard a successful run of predictions, however long sustained, as being by itself a sufficient backing for a claim to knowledge. And here there can be no question of proving that this attitude is mistaken. Where there are recognized criteria for deciding when one has the right to be sure, anyone who insists that their being satisfied is still not enough for knowledge may be accused, for what the charge is worth, of misusing the verb 'to know'. But it is possible to find, or at any rate to devise, examples which are not covered in this respect by any established rule of usage. Whether they are to count as instances of knowledge is then a question which we are left free to decide.

It does not, however, matter very greatly which decision we take. The main problem is to state and assess the grounds on which these claims to knowledge are made, to settle, as it were, the candidate's marks. It is a relatively unimportant question what titles we then bestow upon them.

So long as we agree about the marking, it is of no great consequence where we draw the line between pass and failure, or between the different levels of distinction. If we choose to set a very high standard, we may find ourselves committed to saying that some of what ordinarily passes for knowledge ought rather to be described as probable opinion. And some critics will then take us to task for flouting ordinary usage. But the question is purely one of terminology. It is to be decided, if at all, on grounds of practical convenience.

One must not confuse this case, where the markings are agreed upon, and what is in dispute is only the bestowal of honours, with the case where it is the markings themselves that are put in question. For this second case is philosophically important, in a way in which the other is not. The sceptic who asserts that we do not know all that we think we know, or even perhaps that we do not strictly know anything at all, is not suggesting that we are mistaken when we conclude that the recognized criteria for knowing have been satisfied. Nor is he primarily concerned with getting us to revise our usage of the verb 'to know', any more than one who challenges our standards of value is trying to make us revise our usage of the word 'good'. The disagreement is about the application of the word, rather than its meaning. What the sceptic contends is that our markings are too high; that the grounds on which we are normally ready to concede the right to be sure are worth less than we think; he may even go so far as to say that they are not worth anything at all. The attack is directed, not against the way in which we apply our standards of proof, but against these standards themselves. It has, as we shall see, to be taken seriously because of the arguments by which it is supported.

I conclude then that the necessary and sufficient conditions for knowing that something is the case are first that what one is said to know be true, secondly that one be sure of it, and thirdly that one should have the right to be sure. This right may be earned in various ways; but even if one could give a complete description of them it would be a mistake to try to build it into the definition of knowledge, just as it would be a mistake to try to incorporate our actual standards of goodness into a definition of good. And this being so, it turns out that the questions which philosophers raise about the possibility of knowledge are not all to be settled by discovering what knowledge is. For many of them reappear as questions about the legitimacy of the title to be sure. They need to be severally examined; and this is the main concern of what is called the theory of knowledge.

Is Justified True Belief Knowledge?

Edmund L. Gettier

Various attempts have been made in recent years to state necessary and sufficient conditions for someone's knowing a given proposition. The attempts have often been such that they can be stated in a form similar to the following:[1]

(a) S knows that P   *IFF*   (i)   P is true,
                               (ii) S believes that P, and
                               (iii) S is justified in believing that P.

For example, Chisholm has held that the following gives the necessary and sufficient conditions for knowledge:[2]

(b) S knows that P   *IFF*   (i)   S accepts P,
                               (ii) S has adequate evidence for P, and
                               (iii) P is true.

Ayer has stated the necessary and sufficient conditions for knowledge as follows:[3]

(c) S knows that P   *IFF*   (i)   P is true,
                               (ii) S is sure that P is true, and
                               (iii) S has the right to be sure that P is true.

I shall argue that (a) is false in that the conditions stated therein do not constitute a *sufficient* condition for the truth of the proposition that S knows that P. The same argument will show that (b) and (c) fail if 'has adequate evidence for' or 'has the right to be sure that' is substituted for 'is justified in believing that' throughout.

I shall begin by noting two points. First, in that sense of 'justified' in which S's being justified in believing P is a necessary condition of S's knowing that P, it is possible for a person to be justified in believing a proposition that is in fact false. Secondly, for any proposition P, if S is justified

[1]Plato seems to be considering some such definition at *Theaetetus* 201, and perhaps accepting one at *Meno* 98.

[2]Roderick M. Chisholm, *Perceiving: a Philosophical Study*; Cornell University Press (Ithaca, New York, 1957), p. 16.

[3]A. J. Ayer, *The Problem of Knowledge*, Macmillan (London, 1956), p. 34.

in believing P, and P entails Q, and S deduces Q from P and accepts Q as a result of this deduction, then S is justified in believing Q. Keeping these two points in mind, I shall now present two cases in which the conditions stated in (a) are true for some proposition, though it is at the same time false that the person in question knows that proposition.

Case I:

Suppose that Smith and Jones have applied for a certain job. And suppose that Smith has strong evidence for the following conjunctive proposition:

> (d) Jones is the man who will get the job, and Jones has ten coins in his pocket.

Smith's evidence for (d) might be that the president of the company assured him that Jones would in the end be selected, and that he, Smith, had counted the coins in Jones's pocket ten minutes ago. Proposition (d) entails:

> (e) The man who will get the job has ten coins in his pocket.

Let us suppose that Smith sees the entailment from (d) to (e), and accepts (e) on the grounds of (d), for which he has strong evidence. In this case, Smith is clearly justified in believing that (e) is true.

But imagine, further, that unknown to Smith, he himself, not Jones, will get the job. And, also, unknown to Smith, he himself has ten coins in his pocket. Proposition (e) is then true, though proposition (d), from which Smith inferred (e), is false. In our example, then, all of the following are true: (*i*) (e) is true, (*ii*) Smith believes that (e) is true, and (*iii*) Smith is justified in believing that (e) is true. But it is equally clear that Smith does not *know* that (e) is true; for (e) is true in virtue of the number of coins in Smith's pocket, while Smith does not know how many coins are in Smith's pocket, and bases his belief in (e) on a count of the coins in Jones's pocket, whom he falsely believes to be the man who will get the job.

Case II:

Let us suppose that Smith has strong evidence for the following proposition:

> (f) Jones owns a Ford.

Smith's evidence might be that Jones has at all times in the past within Smith's memory owned a car, and always a Ford, and that Jones has just offered Smith a ride while driving a Ford. Let us imagine, now, that

Smith has another friend, Brown, of whose whereabouts he is totally igno-rant. Smith selects three place-names quite at random, and constructs the following three propositions:

(g) Either Jones owns a Ford, or Brown is in Boston;
(h) Either Jones owns a Ford, or Brown is in Barcelona;
(i) Either Jones owns a Ford, or Brown is in Brest-Litovsk.

Each of these propositions is entailed by (f). Imagine that Smith real-izes the entailment of each of these propositions he has constructed by (f), and proceeds to accept (g), (h), and (i) on the basis of (f). Smith has correctly inferred (g), (h), and (i) from a proposition for which he has strong evidence. Smith is therefore completely justified in believing each of these three propositions. Smith, of course, has no idea where Brown is.

But imagine now that two further conditions hold. First, Jones does *not* own a Ford, but is at present driving a rented car. And secondly, by the sheerest coincidence, and entirely unknown to Smith, the place men-tioned in proposition (h) happens really to be the place where Brown is. If these two conditions hold then Smith does *not* know that (h) is true, even though (*i*) (h) *is* true, (*ii*) Smith does believe that (h) is true, and (*iii*) Smith is justified in believing that (h) is true.

These two examples show that definition (a) does not state a *sufficient* condition for someone's knowing a given proposition. The same cases, with appropriate changes, will suffice to show that neither definition (b) nor definition (c) do so either.

An Alleged Defect in Gettier Counter-Examples

Richard Feldman

A number of philosophers have contended that Gettier counter-examples to the justified true belief analysis of knowledge all rely on a certain false principle. For example, in their recent paper, 'Knowledge Without Para-dox',[1] Robert G. Meyers and Kenneth Stern argue that 'counter-exam-

Source: From Richard Feldman, *The Australasian Journal of Philosophy*, vol. 52 (Oxford University Press, 1974): 68–69. Reprinted by permission of Oxford University Press.
[1]*The Journal of Philosophy* 6 (March 22, 1973) pp. 147–60.

ples of the Gettier sort all turn on the principle that someone can be justified in accepting a certain proposition h on evidence p even though p is false'.[2] They contend that this principle is false, and hence that the counter-examples fail. Their view is that one proposition, p, can justify another, h, only if p is true. With this in mind, they accept the justified true belief analysis.

D. M. Armstrong defends a similar view in *Belief, Truth and Knowledge*.[3] He writes:

> This simple consideration seems to make redundant the ingenious argument of . . . Gettier's . . . article . . . Gettier produces counter-examples to the thesis that justified true belief is knowledge by producing true beliefs based on justifiably believed grounds, . . . but where these grounds are in fact *false*. But because possession of such grounds could not constitute possession of *knowledge*, I should have thought it obvious that they are too weak to serve as suitable grounds.[4]

Thus he concludes that Gettier's examples are defective because they rely on the false principle that false propositions can justify one's belief in other propositions. Armstrong's view seems to be that one proposition, p, can justify another, h, only if p is known to be true (unlike Meyers and Stern who demand only that p in fact be true).[5]

I think, though, that there are examples very much like Gettier's that do not rely on this allegedly false principle. To see this, let us first consider one example in the form in which Meyers and Stern discuss it, and then consider a slight modification of it.

> Suppose Mr. Nogot tells Smith that he owns a Ford and even shows him a certificate to that effect. Suppose, further, that up till now Nogot has always been reliable and honest in his dealings with Smith. Let us call the conjunction of all this evidence m. Smith is thus justified in believing that Mr. Nogot who is in his office owns a Ford (r) and, consequently, is justified in believing that someone in his office owns a Ford (h).[6]

As it turns out, though, m and h are true but r is false. So, the Gettier example runs, Smith has a justified true belief in h, but he clearly does not know h.

---

[2]*Ibid.*, p. 147.
[3](1973).
[4]*Ibid.*, p. 152.
[5]Armstrong ultimately goes on to defend a rather different analysis.
[6]Meyers and Stern, *op. cit.*, p. 151.

What is supposed to justify *h* in this example is *r*. But since *r* is false, the example runs afoul of the disputed principle. Since *r* is false, it justifies nothing. Hence, if the principle is false, the counter-example fails.

We can alter the example slightly, however, so that what justifies *h* for Smith is true and he knows that it is. Suppose he deduces from *m* its existential generalization:

> (*n*) There is someone in the office who told Smith that he owns a Ford and even showed him a certificate to that effect, and who up till now has always been reliable and honest in his dealings with Smith.

(*n*), we should note, is true and Smith knows that it is, since he has correctly deduced it from *m*, which he knows to be true. On the basis of *n* Smith believes *h*—someone in the office owns a Ford. Just as the Nogot evidence, *m*, justified *r*—Nogot owns a Ford—in the original example, *n* justifies *h* in this example. Thus Smith has a justified true belief in *h*, knows his evidence to be true, but still does not know *h*.

I conclude that even if a proposition can be justified for a person only if his evidence is true, or only if he knows it to be true, there are still counter-examples to the justified true belief analysis of knowledge of the Gettier sort. In the above example, Smith reasoned from the proposition *m*, which he knew to be true, to the proposition *n*, which he also knew, to the truth *h*; yet he still did not know *h*. So some examples, similar to Gettier's, do not 'turn on the principle that someone can be justified in accepting a certain proposition . . . even though (his evidence) . . . is false'.[7]

Science and the Physical World

W. T. Stace

So far as I know scientists still talk about electrons, protons, neutrons, and so on. We never directly perceive these, hence if we ask how we know of their existence the only possible answer seems to be that they are an inference from what we do directly perceive. What sort of an inference? Apparently a causal inference. The atomic entities in some way impinge

[7]*Ibid.*, p. 147.

upon the sense of the animal organism and cause that organism to perceive the familiar world of tables, chairs, and the rest.

But is it not clear that such a concept of causation, however interpreted, is invalid? The only reason we have for believing in the law of causation is that we *observe* certain regularities or sequences. We observe that, in certain conditions, *A* is always followed by *B*. We call *A* the cause, *B* the effect. And the sequence *A-B* becomes a causal law. It follows that all *observed* causal sequences are between sensed objects in the familiar world of perception, and that all known causal laws apply solely to the world of sense and not to anything beyond or behind it. And this in turn means that we have not got, and never could have, one jot of evidence for believing that the law of causation can be applied *outside* the realm of perception, or that that realm can have any causes (such as the supposed physical objects) which are not themselves perceived.

Put the same thing in another way. Suppose there is an observed sequence *A-B-C*, represented by the vertical lines in the following diagram.

The observer X sees, and can see, nothing except things in the familiar world of perception. What *right* has he, and what *reason* has he, to assert causes of *A*, *B*, and *C*, such as *a′*, *b′*, *c′*, which he can never observe, behind the perceived world? He has no *right*, because the law of causation on which he is relying has never been observed to operate outside the series of perceptions, and he can have, therefore, no evidence that it does so. And he has no *reason* because the phenomenon *C* is *sufficiently* accounted for by the cause *B*, *B* by *A*, and so on. It is unnecessary and superfluous to introduce a *second* cause *b′* for *B*, *c′* for *C*, and so forth. To give two causes for each phenomenon, one in one world and one in another, is unnecessary, and perhaps even self-contradictory.

Is it denied, then, it will be asked, that the star causes light waves, that the waves cause retinal changes, that these cause changes in the optic nerve, which in turn causes movement in the brain cells, and so on? No,

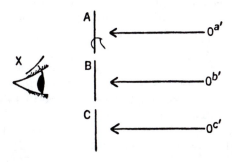

it is not denied. But the observed causes and effects are all in the world of perception. And no sequences of sense-data can possibly justify going outside that world. If you admit that we never observe anything except sensed objects and their relations, regularities, and sequences, then it is obvious that we are completely shut in by our sensations and can never get outside them. Not only causal relations, but all other observed relations, upon which *any* kind of inferences might be founded, will lead only to further sensible objects and their relations. No inference, therefore, can pass from what is sensible to what is not sensible.

The fact is that atoms are *not* inferences from sensations. No one denies, of course, that a vast amount of perfectly valid inferential reasoning takes place in the physical theory of the atom. But it will not be found to be in any strict logical sense inference from *sense-data to atoms.* An *hypothesis* is set up, and the inferential processes are concerned with the application of the hypothesis, that is, with the prediction by its aid of further possible sensations and with its own internal consistency.

That atoms are not inferences from sensations means, of course, that from the existence of sensations we cannot validly infer the existence of atoms. And this means that we cannot have any reason at all to believe that they exist. And that is why I propose to argue that they do not exist— or at any rate that no one could know it if they did, and that we have absolutely no evidence of their existence.

What status have they, then? Is it meant that they are false and worthless, merely untrue? Certainly not. No one supposes that the entries in the nautical almanac "exist" anywhere except on the pages of that book and in the brains of its compilers and readers. Yet they are "true," inasmuch as they enable us to predict certain sensations, namely, the positions and times of certain perceived objects which we call the stars. And so the formulae of the atomic theory are true in the same sense, and perform a similar function.

I suggest that they are nothing but shorthand formulae, ingeniously predict what sensations will be given to it. By "predict" here I do not mean to refer solely to the future. To calculate that there was an eclipse of the sun visible in Asia Minor in the year 585 B.C.E. is, in the sense in which I am using the term, to predict.

In order to see more clearly what is meant, let us apply the same idea to another case, that of gravitation. Newton formulated a law of gravitation in terms of "forces." It was supposed that this law—which was nothing but a mathematical formula—governed the operation of these existent forces. Nowadays it is no longer believed that these forces exist at all. And yet the law can be applied just as well without them to

the prediction of astronomical phenomena. It is a matter of no importance to the scientific man whether the forces exist or not. That may be
said to be a purely philosophical question. And I think the philosopher
should pronounce them fictions. But that would not make the law useless or untrue. If it could still be used to predict phenomena, it would
be just as true as it was.

It is true that fault is now found with Newton's law, and that another
law, that of Einstein, has been substituted for it. And it is sometimes supposed that the reason for this is that forces are no longer believed in.
But this is not the case. Whether forces exist or not simply does not matter. What matters is the discovery that Newton's law does *not* enable us
accurately to predict certain astronomical facts such as the exact position
of the planet Mercury. Therefore another formula, that of Einstein, has
been substituted for it which permits correct predictions. This new law,
as it happens, is a formula in terms of geometry. It is pure mathematics
and nothing else. It does not contain anything about forces. In its pure
form it does not even contain, so I am informed, anything about "humps
and hills in space-time." And it does not matter whether any such humps
and hills exist. It is truer than Newton's law, not because it substitutes
humps and hills for forces, but solely because it is a more accurate formula of prediction.

Not only may it be said that forces do not exist. It may with equal
truth be said that "gravitation" does not exist. Gravitation is not a
"thing," but a mathematical formula, which exists only in the heads of
mathematicians. And as a mathematical formula cannot cause a body
to fall, so gravitation cannot cause a body to fall. Ordinary language mis-
leads us here. We speak of the law "of" gravitation, and suppose that this
law "applies to" the heavenly bodies. We are thereby misled into supposing that there are *two* things, namely, the gravitation and the heavenly bodies, and that one of these things, the gravitation, causes changes
in the other. In reality nothing exists except the moving bodies. And neither Newton's law nor Einstein's law is, strictly speaking, a law of gravitation. They are both laws of moving bodies, that is to say, formulae
which tell us how these bodies will move.

Now, just as in the past "forces" were foisted into Newton's law (by
himself, be it said), so now certain popularizers of relativity foisted
"humps and hills in space-time" into Einstein's law. We hear that the reason why the planets move in curved courses is that they cannot go
through these humps and hills, but have to go round them! The planets just get "shoved about," not by forces, but by the humps and hills!
But these humps and hills are pure metaphors. And anyone who takes

them for "existences" gets asked awkward questions as to what "curved space" is curved "in."

It is not irrelevant to our topic to consider *why* human beings invent these metaphysical monsters of forces and bumps in space-time. The reason is that they have never emancipated themselves from the absurd idea that science "explains" things. They were not content to have laws which merely told them *that* the planets will, as a matter of fact, move in such and such ways. They wanted to know "why" the planets move in those ways. So Newton replied, "Forces." "Oh," said humanity, "that explains it. We understand forces. We feel them every time someone pushes or pulls us." Thus the movements were supposed to be "explained" by entities familiar because they are analogous to the muscular sensations which human beings feel. The humps and hills were introduced for exactly the same reason. They seem so familiar. If there is a bump in the billiard table, the rolling billiard ball is diverted from a straight to a curved course. Just the same with the planets. "Oh, I see!" says humanity, "that's quite simple. That *explains* everything."

But scientific laws, properly formulated, never "explain" anything. They simply state, in an abbreviated and generalized form, *what happens*. No scientist, and in my opinion no philosopher, knows *why* anything happens, or can "explain" anything. Scientific laws do nothing except state the brute fact that "when *A* happens, *B* always happens too." And laws of this kind obviously enable us to predict. If certain scientists substituted humps and hills for forces, then they have just substituted one superstition for another. For my part I do not believe that *science* has done this, though some *scientists* may have. For scientists, after all, are human beings with the same craving for "explanations" as other people.

I think that atoms are in exactly the same position as forces and the humps and hills of space-time. In reality the mathematical formulae which are the scientific ways of stating the atomic theory are simply formulae for calculating what sensations will appear in given conditions. But just as the weakness of the human mind demanded that there should correspond to the formula of gravitation a real "thing" which could be called "gravitation itself" or "force," so the same weakness demands that there should be a real thing corresponding to the atomic formulae, and this real thing is called the atom. In reality the atoms no more cause sensations than gravitation causes apples to fall. The only causes of sensations are other sensations. And the relation of atoms to sensations to be felt is not the relation of cause to effect but the relation of a mathematical formula to the facts and happenings which it enables the mathematician to calculate.

Some writers have said that the physical world has no color, no sound, no taste, no smell. It has no spatiality. Probably it has not even number. We must not suppose that it is in any way like our world, or that we can understand it by attributing to it the characters of our world. Why not carry this progress to its logical conclusion? Why not give up the idea that it has even the character of "existence" which our familiar world has? We have given up smell, color, taste. We have given up even space and shape. We have given up number. Surely, after all that, mere existence is but a little thing to give up. No? Then is it that the idea of existence conveys "a sort of halo"? I suspect so. The "existence" of atoms is but the expiring ghost of the pellet and billiard-ball atoms of our forefathers. They, of course, had size, shape, weight, hardness. These have gone. But thinkers still cling to their existence, just as their fathers clung to the existence of forces, and for the same reason. Their reason is not in the slightest that science has any use for the existent atom. But the *imagination* has. It seems somehow to explain things, to make them homely and familiar.

It will not be out of place to give one more example to show how common fictitious existences are in science, and how little it matters whether they really exist or not. This example has no strange and annoying talk of "bent spaces" about it. One of the foundations of physics is, or used to be, the law of the conservation of energy. I do not know how far, if at all, this has been affected by the theory that matter sometimes turns into energy. But that does not affect the lesson it has for us. The law states, or used to state, that the amount of energy in the universe is always constant, that energy is never either created or destroyed. This was highly convenient, but it seemed to have obvious exceptions. If you throw a stone up into the air, you are told that it exerts in its fall the same amount of energy which it took to throw it up. But suppose it does not fall. Suppose it lodges on the roof of your house and stays there. What has happened to the energy which you can nowhere perceive as being exerted? It seems to have disappeared out of the universe. No, says the scientist, it still exists as *potential* energy. Now what does this blessed word "potential"—which is thus brought in to save the situation—mean as applied to energy? It means, of course, that the energy does not exist in any of its regular "forms," heat, light, electricity, et cetera. But this is merely negative. What positive meaning has the term? Strictly speaking, none whatever. Either the energy exists or it does not exist. There is no realm of the "potential" half-way between existence and nonexistence. And the existence of energy can only consist in its being exerted. If the energy is not being exerted, then it is not energy and does not exist. Energy can no more exist without energizing than heat can exist without being hot.

The "potential" existence of the energy is, then, a fiction. The actual empirically verifiable facts are that if a certain quantity of energy *e* exists in the universe and then disappears out of the universe (as happens when the stone lodges on the roof), the same amount of energy *e* will always reappear, begin to exist again in certain known conditions. That is the fact which the law of the conservation of energy actually expresses. And the fiction of potential energy is introduced simply because it is convenient and makes the equations easier to work. They could be worked quite well without it, but would be slightly more complicated. In either case the function of the law is the same. Its object is to apprise us that if in certain conditions we have certain perceptions (throwing up the stone), then in certain other conditions we shall get certain other perceptions (heat, light, stone hitting skull, or other such). But there will always be a temptation to hypostatize the potential energy as an "existence," and to believe that it is a "cause" which "explains" the phenomena.

If the views which I have been expressing are followed out, they will lead to the conclusion that, strictly speaking, *nothing exists except sensations* (and the minds which perceive them). The rest is mental construction or fiction. But this does not mean that the conception of a star or the conception of an electron are worthless or untrue. Their truth and value consist in their capacity for helping us to organize our experience and predict our sensations.

Proof of an External World

G. E. Moore

In the preface to the second edition of Kant's *Critique of Pure Reason* some words occur, which, in Professor Kemp Smith's translation, are rendered as follows:

> It still remains a scandal to philosophy . . . that the existence of things outside of us . . . must be accepted merely on *faith*, and that, if anyone thinks good to doubt their existence, we are unable to counter his doubts by any satisfactory proof.[1]

---

[1]B xxxix, note: Kemp Smith, p. 34. The German words are 'so bleibt es immer ein Skandal der Philosophie . . . , das Dasein der Dinge ausser uns . . . bloss auf *Glauben* annehmen zu müssen, und wenn es jemand einfällt es zu bezweifeln, ihm keinen genugtuenden Beweis entgegenstellen zu können'.

It seems clear from these words that Kant thought it a matter of some importance to give a proof of 'the existence of things outside of us' or perhaps rather (for it seems to me possible that the force of the German words is better rendered in this way) of 'the existence of *the* things outside of us'; for had he not thought it important that a proof should be given, he would scarcely have called it a 'scandal' that no proof had been given. And it seems clear also that he thought that the giving of such a proof was a task which fell properly within the province of philosophy; for, if it did not, the fact that no proof had been given could not possibly be a scandal to *philosophy*.

Now, even if Kant was mistaken in both of these two opinions, there seems to me to be no doubt whatever that it is a matter of some importance and also a matter which falls properly within the province of philosophy, to discuss the question what sort of proof, if any, can be given of 'the existence of things outside of us'. And to discuss this question was my object when I began to write the present lecture. But I may say at once that, as you will find, I have only, at most, succeeded in saying a very small part of what ought to be said about it.

The words 'it . . . remains a scandal to philosophy . . . that we are unable . . .' would, taken strictly, imply that, at the moment at which he wrote them, Kant himself was unable to produce a satisfactory proof of the point in question. But I think it is unquestionable that Kant himself did not think that he personally was at the time unable to produce such a proof. On the contrary, in the immediately preceding sentence, he has declared that he has, in the second edition of his *Critique*, to which he is now writing the Preface, given a 'rigorous proof' of this very thing; and has added that he believes this proof of his to be 'the only possible proof'. It is true that in this preceding sentence he does not describe the proof which he has given as a proof of 'the existence of things outside of us' or of 'the existence of the things outside of us', but describes it instead as a proof of 'the objective reality of outer intuition'. But the context leaves no doubt that he is using these two phrases, 'the objective reality of outer intuition' and 'the existence of things (*or* 'the things') outside of us', in such a way that whatever is a proof of the first is also necessarily a proof of the second. We must, therefore, suppose that when he speaks as if *we* are unable to give a satisfactory proof, he does not mean to say that he himself, as well as others, is *at the moment* unable; but rather that, until he discovered the proof which he has given, both he himself and everybody else *were* unable. Of course, if he is right in thinking that he has given a satisfactory proof, the state of things which he describes came to an end as soon as his proof was published. As soon as that happened, anyone who read it was able to give a satisfactory proof by simply repeating that which Kant had given, and the 'scandal' to philosophy had been removed once and for all.

If, therefore, it were certain that the proof of the point in question given by Kant in the second edition is a satisfactory proof, it would be certain that at least one satisfactory proof can be given; and all that would remain of the question which I said I proposed to discuss would be, firstly, the question as to what *sort* of a proof this of Kant's is, and secondly the question whether (contrary to Kant's own opinion) there may not perhaps be other proofs, of the same or of a different sort, which are also satisfactory. But I think it is by no means certain that Kant's proof is satisfactory. I think it is by no means certain that he did succeed in removing once for all the state of affairs which he considered to be a scandal to philosophy. And I think, therefore, that the question whether it is possible to give *any* satisfactory proof of the point in question still deserves discussion.

But what is the point in question? I think it must be owned that the expression 'things outside of us' is rather an odd expression, and an expression the meaning of which is certainly not perfectly clear. It would have sounded less odd if, instead of 'things outside of us' I had said 'external things', and perhaps also the meaning of this expression would have seemed to be clearer; and I think we make the meaning of 'external things' clearer still if we explain that this phrase has been regularly used by philosophers as short for 'things external to *our minds*'. The fact is that there has been a long philosophical tradition, in accordance with which the three expressions 'external things', 'things external to *us*', and 'things external to *our minds*' have been used as equivalent to one another, and have, each of them, been used as if they needed no explanation. The origin of this usage I do not know. It occurs already in Descartes; and since he uses the expressions as if they needed no explanation, they had presumably been used with the same meaning before. Of the three, it seems to me that the expression 'external to *our minds*' is the clearest, since it at least makes clear that what is meant is not 'external to *our bodies*'; whereas both the other expressions might be taken to mean this: and indeed there has been a good deal of confusion, even among philosophers, as to the relation of the two conceptions 'external things' and 'things external to *our bodies*'. But even the expression 'things external to our minds' seems to me to be far from perfectly clear; and if I am to make really clear what I mean by 'proof of the existence of things outside of us', I cannot do it by merely saying that by 'outside of us' I mean 'external to our minds'.

There is a passage (*K.d.r.V.*, A 373) in which Kant himself says that
the expression 'outside of us' 'carries with it an unavoidable ambiguity'. He says that 'sometimes it means something which exists *as a thing
in itself* distinct from us, and sometimes something which merely belongs
to external *appearance*'; he calls things which are 'outside of us' in the
first of these two senses 'objects which might be called external in the
transcendental sense', and things which are so in the second '*empirically
external* objects'; and he says finally that, in order to remove all uncertainty as to the latter conception, he will distinguish empirically external objects from objects which might be called 'external' in the
transcendental sense, 'by calling them outright things which are *to be met
with in space*'.

I think that this last phrase of Kant's 'things which are to be met with
in space', does indicate fairly clearly what sort of things it is with regard
to which I wish to inquire what sort of proof, if any, can be given that
there are any things of that sort. My body, the bodies of other men, the
bodies of animals, plants of all sorts, stones, mountains, the sun, the
moon, stars, and planets, houses and other buildings, manufactured articles of all sorts—chairs, tables, pieces of paper, etc., are all of them 'things
which are to be met with in space'. In short, all things of the sort that
philosophers have been used to call 'physical objects', 'material things',
or 'bodies' obviously come under this head. But the phrase 'things that
are to be met with in space' can be naturally understood as applying also
in cases where the names 'physical object', 'material thing', or 'body' can
hardly be applied. For instance, shadows are sometimes to be met with
in space, although they could hardly be properly called 'physical objects',
'material things', or 'bodies'; and although in one usage of the term
'thing' it would not be proper to call a shadow a 'thing', yet the phrase
'things which are to be met with in space' can be naturally understood
as synonymous with 'whatever can be met with in space', and this is an
expression which can quite properly be understood to include shadows.
I wish the phrase 'things which are to be met with in space' to be understood in this wide sense; so that if a proof can be found that there ever
have been as many as two different shadows it will follow at once that
there have been at least two 'things which were to be met with in space',
and this proof will be as good a proof of the point in question as would
be a proof that there have been at least two 'physical objects' of no matter what sort.

The phrase 'things which are to be met with in space' can, therefore, be naturally understood as having a very wide meaning—a meaning even wider than that of 'physical object' or 'body', wide as is the

meaning of these latter expressions. But wide as is its meaning, it is not, in one respect, so wide as that of another phrase which Kant uses as if it were equivalent to this one; and a comparison between the two will, I think, serve to make still clearer what sort of things it is with regard to which I wish to ask what proof, if any, can be given that there are such things.

The other phrase which Kant uses as if it were equivalent to 'things which are to be met with in space' is used by him in the sentence immediately preceding that previously quoted in which he declares that the expression 'things outside of us' 'carries with it an unavoidable ambiguity' (A 373). In this preceding sentence he says that an 'empirical object' 'is called *external*, if it is presented (*vorgestellt*) in *space*'. He treats, therefore, the phrase 'presented in space' as if it were equivalent to 'to be met with in space'. But it is easy to find examples of 'things', of which it can hardly be denied that they are 'presented in space', but of which it could, quite naturally, be emphatically denied that they are 'to be met with in space'. Consider, for instance, the following description of one set of circumstances under which what some psychologists have called a 'negative after-image' and others a 'negative after-sensation' can be obtained. 'If, after looking steadfastly at a white patch on a black ground, the eye be turned to a white ground, a grey patch is seen for some little time.' (Foster's *Text-book of Physiology*, iv, iii, 3, page 1266; quoted in Stout's *Manual of Psychology*, 3rd edition, page 280.) Upon reading these words recently, I took the trouble to cut out of a piece of white paper a four-pointed star, to place it on a black ground, to 'look steadfastly' at it, and then to turn my eyes to a white sheet of paper: and I did find that I saw a grey patch for some little time—I not only saw a grey patch, but I saw it *on* the white ground, and also this grey patch was of roughly the same shape as the white four-pointed star at which I had 'looked steadfastly' just before—it also was a four-pointed star. I repeated this simple experiment successfully several times. Now each of those grey four-pointed stars, one of which I saw in each experiment, was what is called an 'after-image' or 'after-sensation'; and can anybody deny that each of these after-images can be quite properly said to have been 'presented in space'? I saw each of them on a real white background, and, if so, each of them was 'presented' on a real white background. But though they were 'presented in space' everybody, I think, would feel that it was gravely misleading to say that they were 'to be met with in space'. The white star at which I 'looked steadfastly', the black ground on which I saw it, and the white ground on which I saw the after-images, were, of course, 'to be met with in space': they were, in fact, 'physical objects' or surfaces of physical objects. But one important difference between them, on the one hand, and the grey after-images, on the other, can be quite naturally expressed by saying that the latter were *not* 'to be met with in space'. And one reason why this is so is, I think, plain. To say that so and so was at a given time 'to be met with in space' naturally suggests that there are conditions such that *any one* who fulfilled them might, conceivably, have 'perceived' the 'thing' in question—might have seen, it, if it was a visible object, have felt it, if it was a tangible one, have heard it, if it was a sound, have smelt it, if it was a smell. When I say that the white four-pointed paper star, at which I looked steadfastly, was a 'physical object' and was 'to be met with in space', I am implying that *anyone*, who had been in the room at the time, and who had normal eyesight and a normal sense of touch, might have seen and felt it. But, in the case of those grey after-images which I saw, it is not conceivable that anyone besides myself should have seen any one of them. It is, of course, quite conceivable that other people, if they had been in the room with me at the time, and had carried out the same experiment which I carried out, would have seen grey after-images *very like* one of those which I saw: there is no absurdity in supposing even that they might have seen after-images *exactly* like one of those which I saw. But there is an absurdity in supposing that any one of the after-images which I saw could also have been seen by anyone else: in supposing that two different people can ever see the *very same* after-image. One reason, then, why we should say that none of those grey after-images which I saw was 'to be met with in space', although each of them was certainly 'presented in space' to me, is simply that none of them could conceivably have been seen by anyone else. It is natural so to understand the phrase 'to be met with in space', that to say of anything which a man perceived that it was to be met with in space is to say that it might have been perceived by *others* as well as by the man in question.

Negative after-images of the kind described are, therefore, one example of 'things' which, though they must be allowed to be 'presented in space', are nevertheless *not* 'to be met with in space', and are *not* 'external to our minds' in the sense with which we shall be concerned. And two other important examples may be given.

The first is this. It is well known that people sometimes see things double, an occurrence which has also been described by psychologists by saying that they have a 'double image', or two 'images', of some object at which they are looking. In such cases it would certainly be quite natural to say that each of the two 'images' is 'presented in space': they are seen, one in one place, and the other in another, in just the same sense in which each of those grey after-images which I saw was seen at a particular place on the white background at which I was looking. But it would be utterly unnatural to say that, when I have a double image, each of the two images is 'to be met with in space'. On the contrary it is quite certain that *both* of them are not 'to be met with in space'. If both were, it would follow that somebody else might see the *very same* two images which I see; and, though there is no absurdity in supposing that another person might see a pair of images exactly similar to a pair which I see, there is an absurdity in supposing that anyone else might see the *same identical pair*. In every case, then, in which anyone sees anything double, we have an example of at least one 'thing' which, though 'presented in space' is certainly not 'to be met with in space'.

And the second important example is this. Bodily pains can, in general, be quite properly said to be 'presented in space'. When I have a toothache, I feel it *in* a particular region of my jaw or *in* a particular tooth; when I make a cut on my finger smart by putting iodine on it, I feel the pain in a particular place in my finger; and a man whose leg has been amputated may feel a pain *in* a place where his foot might have been if he had not lost it. It is certainly perfectly natural to understand the phrase 'presented in space' in such a way that if, in the sense illustrated, a pain is felt *in* a particular place, that pain is 'presented in space'. And yet of pains it would be quite unnatural to say that they are 'to be met with in space', for the same reason as in the case of after-images or double images. It is quite conceivable that another person should feel a pain exactly like one which I feel, but there is an absurdity in supposing that he could feel *numerically the same* pain which I feel. And pains are in fact a typical example of the sort of 'things' of which philosophers say that they are *not* 'external' to our minds, but 'within' them. Of any pain which *I* feel they would say that it is necessarily *not* external to my mind but *in* it.

And finally it is, I think, worth while to mention one other class of 'things', which are certainly not 'external' objects and certainly not 'to be met with in space', in the sense with which I am concerned, but which yet some philosophers would be inclined to say are 'presented in space', though they are not 'presented in space' in quite the same sense in which pains, double images, and negative after-images of the sort I described are so. If you look at an electric light and then close your eyes, it sometimes happens that you see, for some little time, against the dark background which you usually see when your eyes are shut, a bright patch similar in shape to the light at which you have just been looking. Such a bright patch, if you see one, is another example of what some psychologists have called 'after-images' and others 'after-sensations'; but, unlike the negative after-images of which I spoke before, it is seen when your eyes are shut. Of such an after-image, seen with closed eyes, some philosophers might be inclined to say that this image too was 'presented in space', although it is certainly not 'to be met with in space'. They would be inclined to say that it is 'presented in space', because it certainly is presented as at some little distance from the person who is seeing it: and how can a thing be presented as at some little distance from me, without being 'presented in space'? Yet there is an important difference between such after-images, seen with closed eyes, and after-images of the sort I previously described—a difference which might lead other philosophers to deny that these after-images, seen with closed eyes, are 'presented in space' at all. It is a difference which can be expressed by saying that when your eyes are shut, you are not seeing any part of *physical* space at all—of the space which is referred to when we talk of 'things which are to be met with in *space*'. An after-image seen with closed eyes certainly is presented in *a* space, but it may be questioned whether it is proper to say that it is presented in *space*.

It is clear, then, I think, that by no means everything which can naturally be said to be 'presented in space' can also be naturally said to be 'a thing which is to be met with in space'. Some of the 'things', which are presented in space, are very emphatically *not* to be met with in space: or, to use another phrase, which may be used to convey the same notion, they are emphatically *not* 'physical realities' at all. The conception 'presented in space' is therefore, in one respect, much wider than the conception 'to be met with in space': many 'things' fall under the first conception which do not fall under the second—many after-images, one at least of the pair of 'images' seen whenever anyone sees double, and most bodily pains, are 'presented in space', though none of them are to be met with in space. From the fact that a 'thing' is presented in space, it by no means follows that it is to be met with in space. But just as the first conception is, in one respect, wider than the second, so, in another, the second is wider than the first. For there are many 'things' to be met with in space, of which it is not true that they are presented in space. From the fact that a 'thing' is to be met with in space, it by no means follows that it is presented in space. I have taken 'to be met with in space' to imply, as I think it naturally may, that a 'thing' *might be* perceived; but from the fact that a thing *might be* perceived, it does not follow that it is perceived; and if it is not actually perceived, then it will not be presented in space. It is characteristic of the sorts of 'things', including shadows, which I have described as 'to be met with in space', that there is no absurdity in supposing with regard to any one of them which *is*, at a given time, perceived, both (1) that it might have existed at that very time, without being perceived; (2) that it might have existed at another time, without being perceived at that other time; and (3) that during the whole period of its existence, it need not have been perceived at any time at all. There is, therefore, no absurdity in supposing that many things, which were at one time to be met with in space, never were 'presented' at any time at all, and that many things which *are* to be met with in space now, are not now 'presented' and also never were and never will be. To use a Kantian phrase, the conception of 'things which are to be met with in space' embraces not only objects of actual experience, but also objects of *possible* experience; and from the fact that a thing is or was an object of *possible* experience, it by no means follows that it either was or is or will be 'presented' at all.

I hope that what I have now said may have served to make clear enough what sorts of 'things' I was originally referring to as 'things outside us' or 'things external to our minds'. I said that I thought that Kant's phrase 'things that are to be met with in space' indicated fairly clearly the sorts of 'things' in question; and I have tried to make the range clearer still, by pointing out that this phrase only serves the purpose, if (a) you understand it in a sense, in which many 'things', e.g., after-images, double images, bodily pains, which might be said to be 'presented in space', are nevertheless *not* to be reckoned as 'things that are to be met with in space', and *(b)* you realize clearly that there is no contradiction in supposing that there have been and are 'to be met with in space' things which never have been, are not now, and never will be perceived, nor in supposing that among those of them which have at some time been perceived many existed at times at which they were not being perceived. I think it will now be clear to everyone that, since I do not reckon as 'external things' after-images, double images, and bodily pains, I also should not reckon as 'external things', any of the 'images' which we often 'see with the mind's eye' when we are awake, nor any of those which we see when we are asleep and dreaming; and also that I was so using the expression 'external' that from the fact that a man was at a given time having a visual hallucination, it will follow that he was seeing at that time something which was *not* 'external' to his mind, and from the fact that he was at a given time having an auditory hallucination, it will follow that he was at the time hearing a sound which was *not* 'external' to his mind. But I certainly have not made my use of these phrases, 'external to our minds' and 'to be met with in space', so clear that in the case of every kind of 'thing' which might be suggested, you would be able to tell at once whether I should or should not reckon it as 'external to our minds' and 'to be met with in space'. For instance, I have said nothing which makes it quite clear whether a reflection which I see in a looking-glass is or is not to be regarded as 'a thing that is to be met with in space' and 'external to our minds', nor have I said anything which makes it quite clear whether the sky is or is not to be so regarded. In the case of the sky, everyone, I think, would feel that it was quite inappropriate to talk of it as 'a thing that is to be met with in space'; and most people, I think, would feel a strong reluctance to affirm, without qualification, that reflections which people see in looking-glasses are 'to be met with in space'. And yet neither the sky nor reflections seen in mirrors are in the same position as bodily pains or after-images in the respect which I have emphasized as a reason for saying of these latter that they are *not* to be met with in space—namely that there is an absurdity in supposing that *the very same* pain which I feel could be felt by someone else or that *the very same* after-image which I see could be seen by someone else. In the case of reflections in mirrors we should quite naturally, in certain circumstances, use language which implies that another person may see the same reflection which we see. We might quite naturally say to a friend: 'Do you see that reddish reflection in the water there? I can't make out what it's a reflection of', just as we might say, pointing to a distant hill-side: 'Do you see that white speck on the hill over there? I can't make out what it is.' And in the case of the sky, it is quite obviously *not* absurd to say that other people see it as well as I.

It must, therefore, be admitted that I have not made my use of the phrase 'things to be met with in space', nor therefore that of 'external to our minds', which the former was used to explain, so clear that in the case of every kind of 'thing' which may be mentioned, there will be no doubt whatever as to whether things of that kind are or are not 'to be met with in space' or 'external to our minds'. But this lack of a clear-cut definition of the expression 'things that are to be met with in space', does not, so far as I can see, matter for my present purpose. For my present purpose it is, I think, sufficient if I make clear, in the case of many kinds of things, that I am so using the phrase 'things that are to be met with in space', that, in the case of each of these kinds, from the proposition that there are things of that kind it *follows* that there are things to be met with in space. And I have, in fact, given a list (though by no means an exhaustive one) of kinds of things which are related to my use of the expression 'things that are to be met with in space' in this way. I mentioned among others the bodies of men and of animals, plants, stars, houses, chairs, and shadows; and I want now to emphasize that I

am so using 'things to be met with in space' that, in the case of each of
these kinds of 'things', from the proposition that there are 'things' of that
kind it *follows* that there are things to be met with in space: e.g., from the
proposition that there are plants or that plants exist it *follows* that there
are things to be met with in space, from the proposition that shadows
exist, it *follows* that there are things to be met with in space, and so on,
in the case of all the kinds of 'things' which I mentioned in my first list.
That this should be clear is sufficient for my purpose, because, if it is
clear, then it will also be clear that, as I implied before, if you have proved
that two plants exist, or that a plant and a dog exist, or that a dog and
a shadow exist, etc. etc., you will *ipso facto* have proved that there are
things to be met with in space: you will not require *also* to give a separate proof that from the proposition that there are plants it *does* follow
that there are things to be met with in space.

Now with regard to the expression 'things that are to be met with in
space' I think it will readily be believed that I may be using it in a sense
such that no proof is required that from 'plants exist' there follows 'there
are things to be met with in space'; but with regard to the phrase 'things
external to our minds' I think the case is different. People may be inclined
to say: 'I can see quite clearly that from the proposition "At least two dogs
exist at the present moment" there *follows* the proposition "At least two
things are to be met with in space at the present moment", so that if
you can prove that there are two dogs in existence at the present moment
you will *ipso facto* have proved that two things at least are to be met with
in space at the present moment. I can see that you do not also require
a separate proof that from "Two dogs exist" "Two things are to be met
with in space" *does* follow; it is quite obvious that there couldn't be a dog
which wasn't to be met with in space. But it is not by any means so clear
to me that if you can prove that there are two dogs or two shadows, you
will *ipso facto* have proved that there are two things *external to our
minds*. Isn't it possible that a dog, though it certainly must be "to be
met with in space", might *not* be an external object—an object external to our minds? Isn't a separate proof required that anything that is
to be met with in space must be external to our minds? Of course, if
you are using "external" as a mere synonym for "to be met with in
space", no proof will be required that dogs are external objects: in that
case, if you can prove that two dogs exist, you will *ipso facto* have proved
that there are some external things. But I find it difficult to believe that
you, or anybody else, do really use "external" as a mere synonym for
"to be met with in space"; and if you don't, isn't some proof required that
whatever is to be met with in space must be external to our minds?'

Now Kant, as we saw, asserts that the phrases 'outside of us' or 'external' are in fact used in two very different senses; and with regard to one of these two senses, that which he calls the 'transcendental' sense, and which he tries to explain by saying that it is a sense in which 'external' means 'existing *as a thing in itself* distinct from us', it is notorious that he himself held that things which are to be met with in space are *not* 'external' in that sense. There is, therefore, according to him, *a* sense of 'external', a sense in which the word has been commonly used by philosophers—such that, if 'external' be used in that sense, then from the proposition 'Two dogs exist' it will *not* follow that there are some external things. What this supposed sense is I do not think that Kant himself ever succeeded in explaining clearly; nor do I know of any reason for supposing that philosophers ever have used 'external' in a sense, such that in *that* sense things that are to be met with in space are *not* external. But how about the other sense, in which, according to Kant, the word 'external' has been commonly used—that which he calls 'empirically external'? How is this conception related to the conception 'to be met with in space'? It may be noticed that, in the passages which I quoted Kant himself does not tell us at all clearly what he takes to be the proper answer to this question. He only makes the rather odd statement that, in order to remove all uncertainty as to the conception 'empirically external', he will distinguish objects to which it applies from those which might be called 'external' in the transcendental sense, by 'calling them outright things which are *to be met with in space*'. These odd words certainly suggest, as one possible interpretation of them, that in Kant's opinion the conception 'empirically external' is *identical* with the conception 'to be met with in space'—that he does think that 'external', when used in this second sense, is a mere synonym for 'to be met with in space'. But, if this is his meaning, I do find it very difficult to believe that he is right. Have philosophers, in fact, ever used 'external' as a mere synonym for 'to be met with in space'? Does he himself do so?

I do not think they have, nor that he does himself; and, in order to explain how they have used it, and how the two conceptions 'external to our minds' and 'to be met with in space' are related to one another, I think it is important expressly to call attention to a fact which hitherto I have only referred to incidentally: namely the fact that those who talk of certain things as 'external to' our minds, do, in general, as we should naturally expect, talk of other 'things', with which they wish to contrast the first, as 'in' our minds. It has, of course, been often pointed out that when 'in' is thus used, followed by 'my mind', 'your mind', 'his mind', etc., 'in' is being used metaphorically. And there are some metaphorical uses of 'in', followed by such expressions, which occur in common speech, and which we all understand quite well. For instance, we all understand such expressions as 'I had you in mind, when I made that arrangement' or 'I had you in mind, when I said that there are some people who can't bear to touch a spider'. In these cases 'I was thinking of you' can be used to mean the same as 'I had you in mind'. But it is quite certain that this particular metaphorical use of 'in' is not the one in which philosophers are using it when they contrast what is 'in' my mind with what is 'external' to it. On the contrary, in their use of 'external', you will be external to my mind even at a moment when I have you in mind. If we want to discover what this peculiar metaphorical use of '*in* my mind' is, which is such that nothing, which is, in the sense we are now concerned with, 'external' to my mind, can ever be 'in' it, we need, I think, to consider instances of the sort of 'things' which they would say are 'in' my mind in this special sense. I have already mentioned three such instances, which are, I think, sufficient for my present purpose: any bodily pain which I feel, any after-image which I see with my eyes shut, and any image which I 'see' when I am asleep and dreaming, are typical examples of the sort of 'thing' of which philosophers have spoken as 'in my mind'. And there is no doubt, I think, that when they have spoken of such things as my body, a sheet of paper, a star—in short 'physical objects' generally—as 'external', they have meant to emphasize some important difference which they feel to exist between such things as these and such 'things' as a pain, an after-image seen with closed eyes, and a dream-image. But *what* difference? What difference do they feel to exist between a bodily pain which I feel or an after-image which I see with closed eyes, on the one hand, and my body itself, on the other—what difference which leads them to say that whereas the bodily pain and the after-image are 'in' my mind, my body itself is *not* 'in' my mind—not even when I am feeling it and seeing it or thinking of it? I have already said that one difference which there is between the two, is that my body is to be met with in space, whereas the bodily pain and the after-image are not. But I think it would be quite wrong to say that this is *the* difference which has led philosophers to speak of the two latter as 'in' my mind, and of my body as *not* 'in' my mind.

The question what the difference is which has led them to speak in this way, is not, I think, at all an easy question to answer; but I am going to try to give, in brief outline, what I *think* is a right answer.

It should, I think, be noted, first of all, that the use of the word 'mind', which is being adopted when it is said that any bodily pains which I feel are 'in my mind', is one which is not quite in accordance with any usage common in ordinary speech, although we are very familiar with it in philosophy. Nobody, I think, would say that bodily pains which I feel are 'in my mind', unless he was also prepared to say that it is *with* my mind that I feel bodily pains; and to say this latter is, I think, not quite in accordance with common non-philosophic usage. It is natural enough to say that it is with my mind that I remember, and think, and imagine, and feel *mental* pains—e.g., disappointment, but not, I think, quite so natural to say that it is with my mind that I feel *bodily* pains, e.g., a severe headache; and perhaps even less natural to say that it is with my mind that I see and hear and smell and taste. There is, however, a well-established philosophical usage according to which seeing, hearing, smelling, tasting, and having a bodily pain are just as much *mental* occurrences or processes as are remembering, or thinking, or imagining. This usage was, I think, adopted by philosophers, because they saw a real resemblance between such statements as 'I saw a cat', 'I heard a clap of thunder', 'I smelt a strong smell of onions', 'My finger smarted horribly', on the one hand, and such statements as 'I remembered having seen him', 'I was thinking out a plan of action', 'I pictured the scene to myself', 'I felt bitterly disappointed', on the other—a resemblance which puts all these statements in one class together, as contrasted with other statements in which 'I' or 'my' is used, such as, e.g., 'I was less than four feet high', 'I was lying on my back', 'My hair was very long'. What is the resemblance in question? It is a resemblance which might be expressed by saying that all the first eight statements are the sort of statements which furnish data for psychology, while the three latter are not. It is also a resemblance which may be expressed, in a way now common among philosophers, by saying that in the case of all the first eight statements, if we make the statement more specific by adding a date, we get a statement such that, if it is true, then it *follows* that I was 'having an experience' at the date in question, whereas this does not hold for the three last statements. For instance, if it is true that I saw a cat between 12 noon and 5 minutes past, today, it *follows* that I was 'having some experience' between 12 noon and 5 minutes past, today; whereas from the proposition that I was less than four feet high in December 1877, it does not *follow* that I had any experiences in December 1877. But this philosophic use of 'having an experience' is one which itself needs explanation, since it is not identical with any use of the expression that is established in common speech. An explanation, however, which is, I think, adequate for the purpose, can be given by saying that a philosopher, who was following this usage, would say that I was at a given time 'having an experience' if and only if either (1) I was conscious at the time or (2) I was dreaming at the time or (3) something else was true of me at the time, which resembled what is true of me when I am conscious and when I am dreaming, in a certain very obvious respect in which what is true of me when I am dreaming resembles what is true of me when I am conscious, and in which what would be true of me, if at any time, for instance, I had a vision, would resemble both. This explanation is, of course, in some degree vague; but I think it is clear enough for our purpose. It amounts to saying that, in this philosophic usage of 'having an experience', it would be said of me that I was, at a given time, having *no* experience, if I was at the time neither conscious nor dreaming nor having a vision nor *anything else of the sort*; and, of course, this is vague in so far as it has not been specified what else would be *of the sort*: this is left to be gathered from the instances given. But I think this is sufficient: often at night when I am asleep, I am neither conscious nor dreaming nor having a vision nor *anything else of the sort*—that is to say, I am having no experiences. If this explanation of this philosophic usage of 'having an experience' is clear enough, then I think that what has been meant by saying that any pain which I feel or any after-image which I see with my eyes closed is '*in* my mind', can be explained by saying that what is meant is neither more nor less than that there would be a contradiction in supposing *that very same pain* or *that very same after-image* to have existed at a time at which I was having no experience; or, in other words, that from the proposition, with regard to any time, that *that* pain or *that* after-image existed at that time, it *follows* that I was having some experience at the time in question. And if so, then we can say that the felt difference between bodily pains which I feel and after-images which I see, on the one hand, and my body on the other, which has led philosophers to say that any such pain or after-image is '*in* my mind', whereas my body *never* is but is always 'outside of' or 'external to' my mind, is just this, that whereas there is a contradiction in supposing a pain which I feel or an after-image which I see to exist at a time when I am having no experience, there is no contradiction in supposing my body to exist at a time when I am having no experience; and we can even say, I think, that just this and nothing more is what they have meant by these puzzling and misleading phrases 'in my mind' and 'external to my mind'.

But now, if to say of anything, e.g., my body, that it is external to *my* mind, means merely that from a proposition to the effect that it existed at a specified time, there in no case follows the further proposition that *I* was having an experience at the time in question, then to say of anything that it is external to *our* minds, will mean similarly that from a proposition to the effect that it existed at a specified time, it in no case follows that any of *us* were having experiences at the time in question. And if by *our* minds be meant, as is, I think, usually meant, the minds of human beings living on the earth, then it will follow that any pains which animals may feel, any after-images they may see, any experiences they may have, though not external to *their* minds, yet are external to *ours*. And this at once makes plain how different is the conception 'external to our minds' from the conception 'to be met with in space'; for, of course, pains which animals feel or after-images which they see are no more to be met with in space than are pains which *we* feel or after-images which *we* see. From the proposition that there are external objects—objects that are not in any of *our* minds, it does *not* follow that there are things to be met with in space; and hence 'external to our minds' is not a mere synonym for 'to be met with in space': that is to say, 'external to our minds' and 'to be met with in space' are two different conceptions. And the true relation between these conceptions seems to me to be this. We have already seen that there are ever so many kinds of 'things', such that, in the case of each of these kinds, from the proposition that there is at least one thing of that kind there *follows* the proposition that there is at least one thing to be met with in space: e.g., this follows from 'There is at least one star', from 'There is at least one human body', from 'There is at least one shadow', etc. And I think we can say that of every kind of thing of which this is true, it is also true that from the proposition that there is at least one 'thing' of that kind there *follows* the proposition that there is at least one thing external to our minds: e.g., from 'There is at least one star' there follows not only 'There is at least one thing to be met with in space' but also 'There is at least one external thing', and similarly in all other cases. My reason for saying this is as follows. Consider any kind of thing, such that anything of that kind, if there is anything of it, must be 'to be met with in space': e.g., consider the kind 'soap-bubble'. If I say of anything which I am perceiving, 'That is a soap-bubble', I am, it seems to me, certainly implying that there would be no contradiction in asserting that it existed before I perceived it and that it will continue to exist, even if I cease to perceive it. This seems to me to be part of what is meant by saying that it is a real soap-bubble, as distinguished, for instance, from an hallucination of a soap-bubble. Of course, it by no means follows, that if it really is a soap-bubble, it did in fact exist before I perceived it or will continue to exist after I cease to perceive it: soap-bubbles are an example of a kind of 'physical object' and 'thing to be met with in space', in the case of which it is notorious that particular specimens of the kind often do exist only so long as they are perceived by a particular person. But a thing which I perceive would not be a soap-bubble unless its existence at any given time were *logically independent* of my perception of it at that time; unless that is to say, from the proposition, with regard to a particular time, that it existed at that time, it *never* follows that I perceived it at that time. But, if it is true that it would not be a soap-bubble, unless it *could* have existed at any given time without being perceived by me at that time, it is certainly also true that it would not be a soap-bubble, unless it *could* have existed at any given time, without its being true that I was having any experience of any kind at the time in question: it would not be a soap-bubble, unless, whatever time you take, from the proposition that it existed at that time it does *not* follow that I was having any experience at that time. That is to say, from the proposition with regard to anything which I am perceiving that it is a soap-bubble, there *follows* the proposition that it is external to *my* mind. But if, when I say that anything which I perceive is a soap-bubble, I am implying that it is external to *my* mind, I am, I think, certainly also implying that it is also external to all other minds: I am implying that it is not a thing of a sort such that things of that sort *can* only exist at a time when somebody is having an experience. I think, therefore, that from any proposition of the form 'There's a soap-bubble!' there does really *follow* the proposition 'There's an external object!' 'There's an object external to *all* our minds!' And, if this is true of the kind 'soap-bubble', it is certainly also true of any other kind (including the kind 'unicorn') which is such that, if there are any things of that kind, it follows that there are *some* things to be met with in space.

I think, therefore, that in the case of all kinds of 'things', which are such that if there is a pair of things, both of which are of one of these kinds, or a pair of things one of which is of one of them and one of them of another, then it will follow at once that there are some things to be met with in space, it is true also that if I can prove that there are a pair of things, one of which is of one of these kinds and another of another, or a pair both of which are of one of them, then I shall have proved *ipso facto* that there are at least two 'things outside of us'. That is to say, if I can prove that there exist now both a sheet of paper and a human hand, I shall have proved that there are now 'things outside of us'; if I can prove that there exist now both a shoe and sock, I shall have proved that there are now 'things outside of us'; etc.; and similarly I shall have proved it, if I can prove that there exist now two sheets of paper, or two human hands, or two shoes, or two socks, etc. Obviously, then, there are thousands of different things such that, if, at any time, I can prove any one of them, I shall have proved the existence of things outside of us. Cannot I prove any of these things?

It seems to me that, so far from its being true, as Kant declares to be his opinion, that there is only one possible proof of the existence of things outside of us, namely the one which he has given, I can now give a large number of different proofs, each of which is a perfectly rigorous proof; and that at many other times I have been in a position to give many others. I can prove now, for instance, that two human hands exist. How? By holding up my two hands, and saying, as I make a certain gesture with the right hand, 'Here is one hand', and adding, as I make a certain gesture with the left, 'and here is another'. And if, by doing this, I have proved *ipso facto* the existence of external things, you will all see that I can also do it now in numbers of other ways: there is no need to multiply examples.

But did I prove just now that two human hands were then in existence? I do want to insist that I did; that the proof which I gave was a perfectly rigorous one; and that it is perhaps impossible to give a better or more rigorous proof of anything whatever. Of course, it would not have been a proof unless three conditions were satisfied; namely (1) unless the premiss which I adduced as proof of the conclusion was different from the conclusion I adduced it to prove; (2) unless the premiss which I adduced was something which I *knew* to be the case, and not merely something which I believed but which was by no means certain, or something which, though in fact true, I did not know to be so; and (3) unless the conclusion did really follow from the premiss. But all these three conditions were in fact satisfied by my proof. (1) The premiss which I adduced in proof was quite certainly different from the conclusion, for the conclusion was merely 'Two human hands exist at this moment'; but the premiss was something far more specific than this—something which I expressed by showing you my hands, making certain gestures, and saying the words 'Here is one hand, and here is another'. It is quite obvious that the two were different, because it is quite obvious that the conclusion might have been true, even if the premiss had been false. In asserting the premiss I was asserting much more than I was asserting in asserting the conclusion. (2) I certainly did at the moment *know* that which I expressed by the combination of certain gestures with saying the words 'There is one hand and here is another'. I *knew* that there was one hand in the place indicated by combining a certain gesture with my first utterance of 'here' and that there was another in the different place indicated by combining a certain gesture with my second utterance of 'here'. How absurd it would be to suggest that I did not know it, but only believed it, and that perhaps it was not the case! You might as well suggest that I do not know that I am now standing up and talking—that perhaps after all I'm not, and that it's not quite certain that I am! And finally (3) it is quite certain that the conclusion did follow from the premiss. This is as certain as it is that if there is one hand here and another here *now*, then it follows that there are two hands in existence *now*.

My proof, then, of the existence of things outside of us did satisfy three of the conditions necessary for a rigorous proof. Are there any other conditions necessary for a rigorous proof, such that perhaps it did not satisfy one of them? Perhaps there may be; I do not know; but I do want to emphasize that, so far as I can see, we all of us do constantly take proofs of this sort as absolutely conclusive proofs of certain conclusions— as finally settling certain questions, as to which we were previously in doubt. Suppose, for instance, it were a question whether there were as many as three misprints on a certain page in a certain book. A says there are, B is inclined to doubt it. How could A prove that he is right? Surely he *could* prove it by taking the book, turning to the page, and pointing to three separate places on it, saying 'There's one misprint here, another here, and another here': surely that is a method by which it *might* be proved! Of course, A would not have proved, by doing this, that there were at least three misprints on the page in question, unless it was certain that there was a misprint in each of the places to which he pointed. But to say that he *might* prove it in this way, is to say that it *might* be certain that there was. And if such a thing as that could ever be certain, then assuredly it was certain just now that there was one hand in one of the two places I indicated and another in the other.

I did, then, just now, give a proof that there were *then* external objects; and obviously, if I did, I could *then* have given many other proofs of the same sort that there were external objects *then*, and could now give many proofs of the same sort that there are external objects *now*.

But, if what I am asked to do is to prove that external objects have existed *in the past*, then I can give many different proofs of this also, but proofs which are in important respects of a different *sort* from those just given. And I want to emphasize that, when Kant says it is a scandal not to be able to give a proof of the existence of external objects, a proof of their existence in the past would certainly *help* to remove the scandal of which he is speaking. He says that, if it occurs to anyone to question their existence, we ought to be able to confront him with a satisfactory proof. But by a person who questions their existence, he certainly means not merely a person who questions whether any exist at the moment of speaking, but a person who question whether any have *ever* existed; and a proof that some have existed in the past would certainly therefore be relevant to *part* of what such a person is questioning. How then can I prove that there have been external objects in the past? Here is one proof. I can say: 'I held up two hands above this desk not very long ago; therefore two hands existed not very long ago; therefore at least two external objects have existed at some time in the past, Q.E.D.' This is a perfectly good proof, provided I *know* what is asserted in the premiss. But I *do* know that I held up two hands above this desk not very long ago. As a matter of fact, in this case you all know it too. There's no doubt whatever that I did. Therefore I have given a perfectly conclusive proof that external objects have existed in the past; and you will all see at once that, if this is a conclusive proof, I could have given many others of the same sort, and could now give many others. But it is also quite obvious that this sort of proof differs in important respects from the sort of proof I gave just now that there were two hands existing *then*.

I have, then, given two conclusive proofs of the existence of external objects. The first was a proof that two human hands existed at the time when I gave the proof; the second was a proof that two human hands had existed at a time previous to that at which I gave the proof. These proofs were of a different sort in important respects. And I pointed out that I could have given, then, many other conclusive proofs of both sorts. It is also obvious that I could give many others of both sorts now. So that, if these are the sort of proof that is wanted, nothing is easier than to prove the existence of external objects.

But now I am perfectly well aware that, in spite of all that I have said, many philosophers will still feel that I have not given any satisfactory proof of the point in question. And I want briefly, in conclusion, to say something as to why this dissatisfaction with my proofs should be felt.

One reason why, is, I think, this. Some people understand 'proof of an external world' as including a proof of things which I haven't attempted to prove and haven't proved. It is not quite easy to say *what* it is that they want proved—*what* it is that is such that unless they got a proof of it, they would not say that they had a proof of the existence of external things; but I can make an approach to explaining what they want by saying that if I had proved the propositions which I used as *premisses* in my two proofs, then they would perhaps admit that I had proved the existence of external things, but, in the absence of such a proof (which, of course, I have neither given nor attempted to give), they will say that I have not given what they mean by a proof of the existence of external things. In other words, they want a proof of what I assert *now* when I hold up my hands and say 'Here's one hand and here's another'; and, in the other case, they want a proof of what I assert *now* when I say 'I did hold up two hands above this desk just now'. Of course, what they really want is not merely a proof of these two propositions, but something like a general statement as to how *any* propositions of this sort may be proved. This, of course, I haven't given; and I do not believe it can be given: if this is what is meant by proof of the existence of external things, I do not believe that any proof of the existence of external things is possible. Of course, in some cases what might be called a proof of propositions which seem like these can be got. If one of you suspected that one of my hands was artificial he might be said to get a proof of my proposition 'Here's one hand, and here's another', by coming up and examining the suspected hand close up, perhaps touching and pressing it, and so establishing that it really was a human hand. But I do not believe that any proof is possible in nearly all cases. How am I to prove now that 'Here's one hand, and here's another'? I do not believe I can do it. In order to do it, I should need to prove for one thing, as Descartes pointed out, that I am not now dreaming. But how can I prove that I am not? I have, no doubt, con-clusive reasons for asserting that I am not now dreaming; I have con-clusive evidence that I am awake: but that is a very different thing from being able to prove it. I could not tell you what all my evidence is; and I should require to do this at least, in order to give you a proof.

But another reason why some people would feel dissatisfied with my proofs is, I think, not merely that they want a proof of something which I haven't proved, but that they think that, if I cannot give such extra proofs, then the proofs that I have given are not conclusive proofs at all. And this, I think, is a definite mistake. They would say: 'If you cannot prove your premiss that here is one hand and here is another, then you do not know it. But you yourself have admitted that, if you did not know it, then your proof was not conclusive. Therefore your proof was not, as you say it was, a conclusive proof.' This view that, if I cannot prove such things as these, I do not know them, is, I think, the view that Kant was express-ing in the sentence which I quoted at the beginning of this lecture, when he implies that so long as we have no proof of the existence of external things, their existence must be accepted merely on *faith*. He means to say, I think, that if I cannot prove that there is a hand here, I must accept it merely as a matter of faith—I cannot know it. Such a view, though it has been very common among philosophers, can, I think, be shown to be wrong—though shown only by the use of premises which are not known to be true, unless we do know of the existence of external things. I can know things, which I cannot prove; and among things which I certainly did know, even if (as I think) I could not prove them, were the premises of my two proofs. I should say, therefore, that those, if any, who are dissatisfied with these proofs merely on the ground that I did not know their premises, have no good reason for their dissatisfaction.

A Pragmatic Solution to the Problem of Induction

John Hospers

Thus far we have been content to say that, while we cannot *know* that tomorrow water will boil, the sun will rise, and so forth, we have considerable *evidence* that these things will happen, and that the statements asserting that they will happen are, although not certain, at least extremely *probable*. At this point, however, a much more radical kind of question is sometimes raised: how does the fact that something has happened in the past constitute *any evidence whatever* that it will continue so in the future? What if someone said, "Very well—it's always happened that way in the past; so what? What has that to do with the future?"

Here is one comment we should consider first, lest it confuse the issue later: "You can't be so general about it—the occurrence of some regularities, or uniformities, in the past *is* evidence for their continuance in the future, but not so for others." Bertrand Russell uses the example of the chicken that has gone to its roost every night for several months in the belief that it will be secure there, perhaps because it has been secure there on past nights. But finally one night its owner comes into the henhouse and wrings its neck. If the chicken assumed that because it had been undisturbed in the past it would continue to be undisturbed in the future, it was mistaken. Some beliefs of this kind become *less* probable rather than more so with repetition: when you are eighty years old it's less probable that you will live till morning than it was when you were twenty, although the number of instances backing up the generalization is far greater at eighty. Whether the generalization is made more probable or less probable by the addition of repeated instances depends on the evidence we have for *other* generalizations relevant to the situation. We believe that the sun will rise tomorrow more confidently than we believe the eighty-year-old will live till

Source: Introduction to Philosophical Analysis, Third Edition by Hospers. Reprinted by permission of Pearson Education, Inc., Upper Saddle River, NJ.

morning because we know some statistics about the incidence of deaths and also some physiological laws about the human body, and we also know some things about the solar system, the earth's rotation on its axis, laws of planetary motion, principles of acceleration and momentum, and some of the other things that would have to be different if the sun were *not* to rise tomorrow. We have arrived at other generalizations about the behavior of nature besides the repeated rising of the sun; and these others all contribute, and add probability, to the statement about the continued rising of the sun. It is different with the case of the chicken, for our other generalizations—rather vague ones about the habits of chickens and farmers and the chicken market—do *not* lead to the belief that the past security of the chicken in any way guarantees its subsequent security. And the same with the example about the octogenarian: if the mere fact that he had lived so many days made it probable that he would live to see every next day that dawned, you would arrive at the conclusion that he would live forever! The mere repetition of days of life is subordinate to wider generalizations about the human constitution, which make it, every day that he lives, *less* probable that he will live to see the next day.

Both common sense and science would accept this view of the reasons for believing in continued uniformity in the case of the sun rising but not in the other cases. The same logical problem remains, however. It does not help to fortify the generalization about the sun's continued rising by appealing to *other* generalizations which are in precisely the same predicament that it is. How do we know that these other laws which are invoked to support the generalization about the sun will continue to hold? Being laws, they too involve the future, and therefore are as fallible as the generalization they are invoked to support. If the past affords us no evidence that the sun will rise in the future, how can it afford us evidence that the Law of Gravitation will continue to hold true, and that all the other laws that are used to support it will do the same? How, then, has our situation improved? It seems not to have improved at all.

One might suggest the easy way out, that of proving a law deductively. Thus:

> What has always occurred regularly in the past will continue to occur regularly in the future.
>
> The sun's rising has occurred regularly in the past.
> _____
> Therefore, The sun's rising will continue to occur regularly in the future.

Here we have proved our conclusion deductively. The trouble is, of course, . . . that you cannot prove the *truth* of a conclusion by valid deduction from premises; the premises must themselves be true. And if we do not know that our present conclusion is true, because it involves the future, how can we know that the major premise (the first line) is true, since it too involves the future? It is, in fact, a bigger generalization than is the conclusion. This is clearly no way out: if you want to deduce a conclusion which makes some reference to the future, there must be some reference to the future in one or more of the premises from which that conclusion is deduced. In that case the same skeptical questionings that can be made about the conclusion can be equally made about the premise (or those premises). The question has merely shifted; it has not been resolved.

The general principle, the one that covers all cases, that is usually invoked as a major premise in arguments of this type is the *Principle of Uniformity of Nature*. It is not always formulated in the same way, but it comes to this: "If Nature has always been uniform in the past (generalizations have held good), then Nature will continue to be uniform in the future." Some particular uniformity in the past will then be stated in the minor premise, and the continuance of that uniformity in the future will be deduced in the conclusion. From the Principle of Uniformity of Nature, then, we can deduce the desired conclusion. But how does one establish the Principle of Uniformity of Nature? From what true premises can *it* be deduced? "Well, the Principle of Uniformity of Nature has been true of the past; therefore the Principle of Uniformity of Nature will continue to be true of the future." But this conclusion does not logically follow. It does not follow unless we add another premise:

What has held true of the past will hold true of the future.

The Principle of Uniformity of Nature has held true of the past.

Therefore, The Principle of Uniformity of Nature will hold true of the future.

And thus we are back in the same situation: how are we going to prove *this* major premise?

Or we could put the problem this way. "In the past, our predictions about the continued uniformity of nature have turned out to be true; in other words, our past predictions of the future have been verified. Thus we have considerable evidence that nature will continue to be uniform. After all, it's not as if we had never observed our predictions turning out right." "But that's not the question. I grant that our past predictions have been verified by the facts. In other words, our past predictions about the then-future were verified when that future was no longer future but became past. Now I'm not asking about past futures; I'm asking about future futures! What have the past futures to do with it? The fact that past futures turned out to be so-and-so doesn't prove that future futures will turn out to be so-and-so. If you assume that because past futures were so-and-so therefore the future futures will be so-and-so also, you are again assuming the very point to be proved!"

In other words, every time we try to prove the Principle of Uniformity of Nature we assume the principle in the very process of the proof. We cannot prove the principle by means of itself; and yet without doing this we cannot prove it at all. . . . No statement about nature being uniform in the past will prove that nature will be uniform in the future unless we assume that the fact of uniformity in the past proves future uniformity. Yet clearly it does not; from "The uniformity of nature has held in the past" we cannot deduce "The uniformity of nature will hold in the future."

If deduction fails us, how about induction? Induction, as we have seen, is not a method of proof, but only a method of estimating the probability of a conclusion; and it is the very basis of induction itself that is being questioned here. What we are examining is our very right to use inductive procedure in making generalizations. We cannot, therefore, justify this inductive procedure on the basis of inductive reasoning.

Our question, then, still remains: Can the uniformities of the past and the present render uniformities in the future any more probable? Does the fact that the past has turned out a certain way render even probable the statement that the future will turn out that way too?

There is much more agreement on the nature of the problem than on the solution of it. Unfortunately most attempted solutions become too technical to be discussed here. Nevertheless, two comments can be given which may alleviate the pressure of the problem:

1. If someone seriously says that the way things have occurred in the past affords *no* evidence whatever about the future, we can ask him what he means when he uses the word "evidence." A million times in the past when I have let go of a book or a stone it has fallen; never once has it risen into the air. This, and all the other things I know about the behavior of material objects, lead me to believe that it will fall when I let go of it this time. Is there really *no* evidence either way as to what the stone will do next time? To say this is to abandon all prediction and all science, and, more important here, *all meaning for the word "evidence."* For if the fact that it has fallen a million times is *not* evidence, what *would* be? If you so use the word "evidence" that *nothing* that ever happened could be evidence, what would you mean by the word "evidence"? Would it not

just be a meaningless noise? (You could not even say, "There is *no* evidence that *X* will happen," for that sentence contains the word "evidence," which must be given a meaning before it can meaningfully be used.)

The same point could be made regarding the word "probable." If the fact that the stone has always fallen and never risen, together with all the other things we have observed about stones and other material objects, does not even render more *probable* the statement that the stone will fall the next time, what in the world *could* make it so? And if nothing could, then what meaning can be attached by the speaker to the word "probable," or for that matter the word "improbable"? Remember that it would be just as meaningless to say "It is *im*probable that *X* will occur" as it would be to say "It is probable that *X* will occur"—for if the word "probable" has been deprived of all possible application to the universe, its opposite, which acquires meaning only by contrast with it, suffers precisely the same fate.

2. If the question is still asked, "How are we going to prove the Principle of Uniformity of Nature which is required to establish our inductions?" the answer is of course that we cannot. It cannot be proved by means of itself, and it cannot be proved without itself. As we have already seen, to prove (deductively) a conclusion involving the future we must have a proposition involving the future in the premises. In other words— as in the case of the principles of logic—we cannot give a *logical* justification for the Principle of Uniformity of Nature; we cannot give a logical basis for the very principle which is itself the logical basis for the deduction of laws.

It would seem, then, that to demand a logical basis for the principle is as unreasonable as to demand it in the case of the principles of logic themselves. Yet the principle is needed if our inductive conclusions (laws) are to be proved, since they involve the future. Laws are the basis of our predictions. "Why do you think that stone will fall?" "All unsupported bodies fall." If this last statement did not involve the future, it could not be employed to predict anything about the future, which it clearly *is* being employed to do.

What, then, can we do under the circumstances? As in the case of the principles of logic, . . . we can give a pragmatic justification for our *adoption* of these principles. In the case of the principles of logic it was the impossibility of any coherent discourse without the use of them; in the present case the situation is not quite so radical: it is the fruitlessness of any scientific procedure without the adoption of the Principle of Uniformity of Nature, which alone enables us to make inferences from past and present to future. We cannot prove that the principle which enables us to do this is true, but *if* we want to attempt any predictions at all—and as human beings we must all do this if we want to stay alive (do we not refrain from going to the street via the fifth-floor window because we are convinced that the uniformity of behavior of freely falling bodies will continue?)—then the laws of nature are the only sound basis for such prediction. It is these or nothing. We cannot prove deductively that these laws are true, for we cannot prove that the uniformities will hold in the future, and this is what every law implicitly asserts; but *if* nature is uniform, and *if* there is an order of nature which extends into the future, then the inductive method is the way in which to gain knowledge of this order. We want successful prediction; we cannot prove that our predictions, however well they may have worked out in the past, will be successful in the next instance; but if successful prediction is to be possible at all, it will be so only by means of these laws. This is our pragmatic basis, our practical justification, for asserting these laws, in spite of the fact that we cannot prove that the laws are true, or can prove them only by using an unprovable principle as a premise.

There is, to be sure, another way out of the situation: we can assert that the Principle of Uniformity of Nature is a synthetic necessary statement, something which *necessarily* holds of the universe. But here again, of course, there are difficulties: what entitles us to say that the principle is necessary? How do we know this, if we know it? To many it would seem that this way of resolving the Gordian knot is not by unraveling it but by cutting it with a knife.

The Problem of Induction— Old and New
Howard Kahane and Paul Tidman

Induction Is Unjustified—The Old Riddle of Induction

Recall that the characteristic mark of all inductive (nondeductive) reasoning is a "gap" between premises and conclusion. As soon as this gap was realized,[1] the question of *how any inductive argument can be jus-*

---

[1] The philosopher David Hume was the first person to perceive it clearly and to try to bridge it. See *A Treatise of Human Nature*, Book I., Part IV., Section I: and *An Enquiry Concerning Human Understanding*, Section V.

tified was raised; that is, the question was raised about the *rationality* of the acceptance of hypotheses on inductive grounds.

Unfortunately, a good answer to this question has been hard to come by. A great many solutions to the problem of induction have been proposed, most of which can be classified into four categories.

(1) The most obvious thought is that we are justified in using induction because it "works." All of science is based on inductive conclusions of some sort or other, and everyone knows how successful science is. Everyone knows that the scientific method, which uses induction, *works*.

Unfortunately, this obvious solution to the problem is not satisfactory. It simply isn't true that we know that induction works, or is successful. At best, what we know is that it *has worked, or has been successful.* But will it be successful in the future? We don't know. Indeed, the problem seems to be that we haven't the slightest reason to think induction will be successful in the future.

It often is claimed that in fact we do have a very good reason for thinking that induction will be successful in the future, namely its success in the past. But only a little thought is needed to see that this reason will not do. For to argue that induction will be successful because it *has* been successful is to argue *inductively*. (The premise of such an argument is "Induction has been successful [on the whole] up to now", and its conclusion is "Induction always will be successful [on the whole]". Clearly, this argument itself is an inductive argument.) So when we argue this way, we use induction to justify itself, which means that we argue circularly, and hence fallaciously.

(2) Perhaps the most popular solutions to the problem of induction are those that use some principle concerning the *uniformity of nature*, such as the principle that *every event has a cause*.

For instance, if we assume that nature is uniform, then we can reason inductively from the fact that all examined pieces of copper are uniform with respect to conductivity to the conclusion that all pieces of copper (examined or as yet unexamined) are uniform with respect to the conducting of electricity.

But solutions of this kind are unsatisfactory. First, even if nature is uniform, there is no guarantee that the particular uniformities we have observed up to a given time will hold in the future; the true uniformities of nature may be more complex or subtle. And second, the assumption itself that every event has a cause, or that nature is uniform, can be challenged. Why assume that nature is uniform? Again, there seems to be no answer. (Remember that we cannot argue that the assumption that nature is uniform has been fruitful in the past, and hence is likely to be fruitful in the future, for such an argument would be an inductive argument, and we cannot use induction to justify a principle of uniformity and then use that principle to justify the use of induction.)

(3) Some philosophers have proposed justifications based on the so-called self-corrective nature of induction.[2] For example, suppose we conclude that half of 10,000 tosses of a coin will land heads up, on the basis of the evidence that half of the first 100 tosses of this coin landed heads up. Suppose this conclusion is false. Then we can "correct" it simply by observing larger and larger coin tossing samples, basing our conclusion about the relative frequency of heads in the total series of 10,000 tosses on the relative frequency of heads in the largest sample we have at any given time. If we continue the process long enough, at some point we must reach the correct value. Hence, it is claimed, we are justified in using inductive reasoning in such cases because the process is self-correcting: repeated applications must get us closer and closer to the truth.

Suppose, for instance, that one half of 10,000 tosses of a coin in fact will land heads up. If we get heads on exactly half of the first 5,000 tosses, then we know with deductive certainty that the relative frequency of heads compared to total tosses in the entire series of 10,000 tosses must be somewhere between 1/4 and 3/4.[3] Hence our prediction that half of the 10,000 tosses will be heads cannot be off by more than ± 1/4.

Now, suppose that after 8,000 tosses the observed relative frequency of heads is still 1/2. Then we know at this point that the relative frequency of heads in the total series of 10,000 tosses must be somewhere between 2/5 and 3/5.[4] Hence, at this point our prediction that half of the 10,000 tosses will be heads cannot be off by more than ± 1/10. So we are getting closer and closer to the correct value (no matter what that value happens to be), because the *largest possible error* in our predictions keeps getting smaller and smaller.

The trouble is that our predictions get closer and closer to the correct value because larger and larger portions of the series concern *past tosses* and are incorporated into our *evidence*, while smaller and smaller portions of the series concern *future tosses*. At no point do we have any guarantee that we are getting any closer to the actual relative frequency

---

[2]See, for instance, Charles Peirce, "Induction as Experimental and Self-Correcting." *Collected Papers of Charles Sanders Peirce*. vol. VI. Charles Hartshorne and Paul Weiss, eds. (Cambridge, MA: Harvard University Press, 1935). Reprinted in Edward H. Madden. *The Structure of Scientific Thought* (Boston: Houghton Mifflin. 1960), pp. 296–298.

[3]If the 5,000 remaining tosses all are tails, then the relative frequency will be 1/4, and if they all are heads, then the relative frequency will be 3/4.

[4]If the 2,000 remaining tosses all are tails, then the relative frequency will be 2/5, and if they all are heads, then the relative frequency will be 3/5.

of heads among future (unexamined) tosses of the coin. But if the self-corrective claim is to have any force, it must apply to predictions about the future (or the as yet unexamined past).

The situation is even worse for infinitely long series, because the relative frequency of any given finite portion of an infinite series is compatible with any relative frequency whatever in the infinite series. For instance, even if every one of millions of tosses of a coin lands heads up, the *limit* of such an infinite series of tosses (assuming an infinite series of tosses is possible) still might equal zero. Hence, for an infinite series, inductive practices embody no self-corrective feature whatever.

We must conclude, then, that we cannot justify the use of induction on the grounds that it is self-correcting.

(4) Finally, there are the so-called dissolutions of the problem of induction, according to which the very problem itself is a pseudoproblem.[5] We shall consider two of the many solutions of this kind. In the first, it is claimed that it is not rational to doubt the principles of inductive reasoning because these principles themselves *determine* (in part) what it means to be rational. In other words, if we doubt the rationality (the reasonableness) of the use of induction, then we simply don't know what it means to be rational.

Unfortunately, this argument is defective. Were we to find ourselves in a community in which it is considered rational to believe everything said by the oldest member of the community, it would be reasonable to inquire if it *really* is rational to do so. And if the reply were that what it *means* to be rational is to believe the oldest member of the community, then it would be perfectly proper to ask *why* we should be rational. Put into this context, the problem of induction is that we seem to have no answer to the question "Why be rational?" either for the peculiar concept of rationality in the imaginary community just described or for the concept of rationality in the real community.

According to the second kind of "dissolution" of the problem, there is no problem of justifying the use of inductive principles because *no justification is possible*, and if none is possible, then none can be required. Two kinds of arguments have been presented in support of this claim.

First, it has been argued that such a justification would have to be either *inductive* or *deductive*. An inductive justification would be circular because it would use the very principles of reasoning we are trying to justify. And we could never construct a valid deductive

---

[5]See for instance, A. J. Ayer, *Language, Truth and Logic* (New York: Dover Publications), pp. 49–50.

justification, because it is impossible to prove deductively that nature is uniform, or that every event has a cause, or that the future will resemble the past.[6]

But this argument is defective. It is true that metaphysical assumptions, such as the uniformity of nature, cannot be proved deductively. But a deductive justification does not necessarily require that any such principle be proved. Perhaps other kinds of assumptions can be proved that will justify the use of induction.[7]

Second, it has been argued that just as the theorems in an axiom system cannot all be proved (without circularity or infinite regress), so also all principles of *reasoning* or *inferring* cannot be justified (without circularity or infinite regress). Hence, we should not be surprised that no justification of induction is possible.

Clearly, there is something to this last argument. It is true that we cannot justify every principle of reasoning any more than we can prove every theorem. And it may well be that the basic inductive principle will be among those that remain forever unjustified and hence remain forever as a kind of primitive inference rule. But the argument in question does not prove this. All that it proves is that some principle or other will remain unjustified. It does not prove induction is that principle.

On the other hand, recognition of the important fact that some principle or other must remain unjustified may make it more tolerable that as yet no one seems to have been able to justify the basic principle of induction.

Not All Instances of Theories Confirm Them — The New Riddle of Induction

Perhaps the most curious of the objections raised against our account of scientific method is the one posed by Nelson Goodman's so-called *new riddle of induction.*

The old riddle, you will recall, has to do with justifying induction and inductive inferences in general, and in particular with justifying the belief that generalizations are confirmed by their instances (as, say, the gen-

---

[6]What is often meant by such an argument is that metaphysical principles of this kind are not *theorems of logics,* or *deductively obtainable from the null set of premises,* or *knowable prior to any particular empirical observations.*

[7]For instance, the pragmatic justification presented by Hans Reichenbach in *The Theory of Probability* (Berkeley: University of California Press, 1949), pp. 469–482, is based on an attempt to prove deductively that if any method of predicting the future is successful, then the use of induction will be successful.

eralization "All dogs have tails" is confirmed by finding an instance of it—namely a dog with a tail). The new riddle, according to Goodmanites, has to do with distinguishing those generalizations that *are* confirmed by their instances from those that are not.

To see the difference between these two kinds of cases, consider the following example. Suppose 100 emeralds, all of them green, are observed for color. This would usually be considered good evidence for the hypothesis or generalization (H-1) "All emeralds are green". But now let's introduce a new color term, "grue," referring to all things examined for color *before* a particular time *t*, say January 1, 2001, that are green, and to other things just in case they are blue. Then emeralds, for instance, will be "grue" just in case they either are green and the time in question is before time *t* or are blue and the time in question is at *t* or after. An emerald examined now and found to be green would thus be "grue," but one examined in the twenty-first century and found to be green would not be "grue" (it would, however, be *bleen*, that is, it would be either examined before time *t* and blue, or not so examined and green).

All of the 100 green emeralds observed in our hypothetical example are "grue," as well as green, because they're green and the time is prior to time *t*. So according to what has been said so far about confirmation, it would seem that the 100 observed "grue" emeralds constitute confirming instances of the hypothesis (H-2): "All emeralds are grue", just as these same emeralds, being green, confirm (H-1): "All emeralds are green". But (H-1) and (H-2) *conflict* with each other, because according to (H-1) emeralds observed after time *t* will be green while according to (H-2) they will be blue. In fact, of course, no one would accept (H-2) no matter how many confirming cases we find in its favor. Goodman's problem is to find some way to distinguish "grue-like" illegitimate predicates and hypotheses from legitimate green-like ones, so that hypotheses like (H-1) will be confirmed by their instances while those like (H-2) will not.

Most of the proposed solutions to this problem are seriously defective. Rudolf Carnap, for example, argued that terms like "grue" are what he called "positional," meaning that they are terms whose definitions in part refer to individual objects, or to individual places or times. But Carnap's solution is unsatisfactory, in particular because lots of "good" predicates are positional and in fact are used in acceptable generalizations all the time. Some examples given by Goodman are "Ming," "Arctic," and "Pleistocene." Generalizations like "All Ming vases are expensive" would usually be held to be confirmed by their instances (in this case, by particular Ming vases that are expensive).

The interesting thing about Goodman's riddle is that an obvious answer lies right at hand, and was proposed soon after Goodman formulated the problem; indeed it must have occurred independently to countless readers of the literature since then. Take our two competing hypotheses (H-1) "All emeralds are green", and (H-2) "All emeralds are grue". The first contains the "good" term "green", the second the "bad" term "grue". What is good about the former but bad about the latter? The first thought many of us have is that all green things *resemble* each other in a certain way, namely by being green in color, while there is no such color resemblance uniting all grue things, because items that are grue prior to time *t* are green, while those that are grue after time *t* are blue. What the term "green" *means* requires all items referred to by that predicate to resemble each other in color—share a common color—namely green. But what the term "grue" means does not require this; prior to time *t* grue things are green, after time *t* they are blue. By simply saying that only those generalizations containing terms like "green" are confirmed by their instances, the problem would seem to be solved. That is, it seems as though we can quite easily solve the problem by rejecting all generalizations containing terms, like "grue," which select classes of items that do not necessarily all resemble each other in some relevant way. One idea behind inductive reasoning is, after all, to find items that resemble each other in some specified way that also share some other common property. In the case of (H-1): "All emeralds are green", we find stones that resemble each other in being beryl silicates (and thus emeralds)[8] and discover that they also share the common property of being green. In the case of (H-2) "All emeralds are grue", there also is a shared common property, namely that of being grue, but that is not a *resembling* property—all grue things do not resemble each other in the appropriate way.

Perhaps, the main reason why this obvious solution to the grue problem has not settled the matter is that Goodman provided what most writers on the subject have accepted as a conclusive objection to it. Goodman argued that given any two things, however different they may seem, we can always invent a property they both share, as we did in fact in inventing the property of being grue. That is, he argued that all grue things do in fact share a common property, namely that of being grue, and thus do in fact resemble each other (because they all are grue). We've noticed that all emeralds have resembled each other by being green,

---

[8]Goodman's choice of example was unfortunate in that according to one common definition of *emerald* a non-green beryl silicate would not be an emerald.

perhaps, because "green" is a term we've become familiar with through long use—it has become well *entrenched* in our language. But we've failed to notice that all emeralds so far encountered have resembled each other by being grue, perhaps because we're not familiar with and haven't used the term "grue"—it hasn't become entrenched in our language.

Underlying Goodman's view on the grue question is an extreme version of a very old philosophical position, called *nominalism* (something some of the nonnominalistic writers on the subject seem to have overlooked). In its extreme form, nominalism says that "there is nothing common to a class of particulars called by the same name other than that they *are* called by the same name."[9] That is why Goodman says that just as green things resemble each other in being green so also grue things *equally* resemble each other in being grue.[10]

But suppose we reject the nominalist's view and accept the commonsense, everyday idea of resemblance that makes it wrong to speak of "grue" things as resembling each other just as much as do green things. (This is in fact what the vast majority of philosophers have done over the ages.) Then the Goodman problem fails to get off the ground,[11] and our account of the philosophy of science remains intact.

[9]A. D. Woozley in his article "Universals," in the *Encyclopedia of Philosophy*, Paul Edwards, ed. (New York: Collier Macmillan 1967). Woozley's article also contains an excellent rebuttal of this extreme form of nominalism (in the opinion of this writer).

[10]Goodman's basic nominalistic principle is that there are individual things in the world, and sums of individual things, but no general properties. (See his article "A World of Individuals" in *The Problem of Universals* (Notre Dame, IN: Notre Dame, University Press, 1956.) But he is quickly led to the version of nominalism Woozley discussed, and without doubt believes that any two things (for example, any two grue emeralds) may resemble each other just as much as any other two things (for example, any two green emeralds).

[11]There are, of course, some wrinkles to take care of. For example, Goodman argues that lots of acceptable terms, such as "electrical conductor," are not resembling terms in the everyday sense; we therefore have to show what the resemblances might be like in these cases. See my "Pathological Predicates and Projections" (*American Philosophical Quarterly*, vol. 8 (1971), pp. 171–178), for more on this, and also for some other thoughts on the grue problem and how to solve it, as well as for a bibliography on the subject.

PART THREE

DO WE HAVE FREE WILL?

We often find ourselves deliberating between alternative courses of action. Doing so leaves us with a strong sense of freedom, and we may conclude that our present and future choices are up to us. Unfortunately, there is reason for doubt. Is it possible that our choices are determined by factors beyond our control? If our choices are caused by events in our past, and if the past cannot be changed, then it seems that our present and future choices are beyond our control as well. Reconciling human freedom with the fact that actions are caused is the philosophical problem of free will.

    We start our readings in this section with a spirited attack on the idea of genetic determinism by Daniel Dennett. As our knowledge of the human genome has grown, and a wide set of human behavior can be explained by reference to what set of genes we possess, the idea that we might be "programmed" by our genes has gained currency. Dennett dubs the position that our will, education, and culture cannot change our genetically determined future *genetic determinism*. Dennett argues that genetic determinism is an illusive threat. First, even if we have certain genetic traits that will, for instance, lead to a specific disease in the future, it is certainly possible that we could avoid this disease if the appropriate medical technology were to become available. Our future is therefore determined by our knowledge and the state of technology rather than by our genes. Second, Dennett argues that genetic determinism is not more dangerous than any form of environmental determinism—the idea that our upbringing or culture completely determines our future actions. Because environmental determinism is not particularly frightening, neither should we be especially frightened by genetic determinism. On the contrary, he concludes that "knowledge of the roles of our genes . . . is not the enemy of human freedom, but one of its best friends."

In his article "Freedom and Necessity," A. J. Ayer also comes to an optimistic conclusion about human freedom. Although he concedes that our actions are part of a causal network and are thus causally determined to take place, he does not think that this causal determinism threatens human freedom. Ayer argues that if we analyze the term *freedom*, we quickly realize that it is not in conflict with causality as such but with constraint, which is a particular kind of causality. It is, however, a mistake to equate *causality* with *constraint*. Ayer develops a classic formulation of soft determinism. He concludes that our actions are in many situations both caused as well as free.

It is exactly this form of compatibilism that Peter van Inwagen attacks in his article "The Incompatibility of Free Will and Determinism." One of van Inwagen's starting points is the common belief that an agent P deserves to be called *free* with respect to an act only if the agent has the ability to either perform or refrain from performing the act. Van Inwagen considers the case of a judge, who after a period of calm and rational deliberation, decides to refrain from raising his hand and thus condemns a criminal to death. Van Inwagen argues that if we assume that the judge's act is causally determined, it follows that the judge could not have raised his hand to save the criminal. The judge, and any other agent who acts in a causally determined world, is therefore not free.

Van Inwagen's attack against compatibilism is based on the principle that an agent can be free and responsible only if the agent could have acted other than she in fact did act. This so-called *principle of alternate possibilities* is challenged by Harry Frankfurt. In his essay "Alternative Possibilities and Moral Responsibility," he argues that it is very well possible that a person who is coerced into doing an act and has no alternative to performing it is nevertheless morally responsible for performing it. According to Frankfurt, it is logically possible to separate the concepts of being morally responsible from the concept of being able to act otherwise.

We finish our discussion of free will with a classical paper by Roderick Chisholm. In "Human Freedom and the Self," Chisholm argues that anyone who holds that human beings are fully responsible agents must reject the idea that our actions are either causally determined or simply happen by chance. Chisholm suggests that there is a third option: Free actions are caused "not by other events or states of affairs, but by the agent." He thereby introduces the idea of "agent causation" and develops a libertarian solution to the problem of free will. According to this position, "Each of us, when we act, is a prime mover unmoved."

The Mythical Threat of Genetic Determinism

Daniel C. Dennett

It is time to set minds at ease by raising the "specter" of "genetic determinism" and banishing it once and for all. According to Stephen Jay Gould, genetic determinists believe the following:

> If we are programmed to be what we are, then these traits are ineluctable. We may, at best, channel them, but we cannot change them either by will, education, or culture.

If this is genetic determinism, then we can all breathe a sigh of relief: There are no genetic determinists. I have never encountered anybody who claims that will, education, and culture cannot change many, if not all, of our genetically inherited traits. My genetic tendency to myopia is canceled by the eyeglasses I wear (but I do have to want to wear them); and many of those who would otherwise suffer from one genetic disease or another can have the symptoms postponed indefinitely by being educated about the importance of a particular diet, or by the culture-borne gift of one prescription medicine or another. If you have the gene for the disease phenylketonuria, all you have to do to avoid its undesirable effects is stop eating food containing phenylalanine. What is inevitable doesn't depend on whether determinism reigns, but on whether or not there are steps we can take, based on information we can get in time to take those steps, to avoid the foreseen harm.

There are two requirements for meaningful choice: information and a path for the information to guide. Without one, the other is useless or worse. In his excellent survey of contemporary genetics, Matt Ridley drives the point home with the poignant example of Huntington's disease, which is "pure fatalism, undiluted by environmental variability. Good living, good medicine, healthy food, loving families, or great riches can do nothing about it." This is in sharp contrast to all the equally undesirable genetic predispositions that we can do something about. And it is for just this reason that many people who are likely, given their family tree, to have the Huntington's mutation choose not to take the simple test that would tell them with virtual certainty whether they have it. But note that if and when a path opens up, as it may in the future, for treating those who have Huntington's mutation, these same people will be first in line to take the test.

Gould and others have declared their firm opposition to "genetic determinism," but I doubt if anybody thinks our genetic endowments are infinitely revisable. It is all but impossible that I will ever give birth, thanks to my Y chromosome. I cannot change this by either will, education, or culture—at least not in my lifetime (but who knows what another century of science will make possible?). So at least for the foreseeable future, some of my genes fix some parts of my destiny without any real prospect of exemption. If that is genetic determinism, we are all genetic determinists, Gould included. Once the caricatures are set aside, what remains, at best, are honest differences of opinion about just how much intervention it would take to counteract one genetic tendency or another and, more important, whether such intervention would be justified.

These are important moral and political issues, but they often become next to impossible to discuss in a calm and reasonable way. Besides, what would be so specially bad about *genetic* determinism? Wouldn't environmental determinism be just as dreadful? Consider a parallel definition of *environmental* determinism:

> If we have been raised and educated in a particular cultural environment, then the traits imposed on us by that environment are ineluctable. We may at best channel them, but we cannot change them either by will, further education, or by adopting a different culture.

The Jesuits have often been quoted (I don't know how accurately) as saying: "Give me a child until he is 7, and I will show you the man." An exaggeration for effect, surely, but there is little doubt that early education and other major events of childhood can have a profound effect on later life. There are studies, for instance, that suggest that such dire events as being rejected by your mother in the first year of life increases your likelihood of committing a violent crime. Again, we mustn't make the mistake of equating determinism with inevitability. What we need to examine empirically—and this can vary just as dramatically in environmental settings as in genetic settings is whether the undesirable effects, however large, can be avoided by steps we can take.

Consider the affliction known as not knowing a word of Chinese. I suffer from it, thanks entirely to environmental influences early in my childhood (my genes had nothing—nothing directly—to do with it). If

I were to move to China, however, I could soon enough be "cured," with some effort on my part, though I would no doubt bear deep and unalterable signs of my deprivation, readily detectable by any native Chinese speaker, for the rest of my life. But I could certainly get good enough in Chinese to be held responsible for actions I might take under the influence of Chinese speakers I encountered.

Isn't it true that whatever isn't determined by our genes must be determined by our environment? What else is there? There's Nature and there's Nurture. Is there also some X, some further contributor to what we are? There's Chance. Luck. This extra ingredient is important but doesn't have to come from the quantum bowels of our atoms or from some distant star. It is all around us in the causeless coin-flipping of our noisy world, automatically filling in the gaps of specification left unfixed by our genes, and unfixed by salient causes in our environment. This is particularly evident in the way the trillions of connections between cells in our brains are formed. It has been recognized for years that the human genome, large as it is, is much too small to specify (in its gene recipes) all the connections that are formed between neurons. What happens is that the genes specify processes that set in motion huge population growth of neurons—many times more neurons than our brains will eventually use—and these neurons send out exploratory branches, at random (at pseudo-random, of course), and many of these happen to connect to other neurons in ways that are detectably useful (detectable by the mindless processes of brain-pruning).

These winning connections tend to survive, while the losing connections die, to be dismantled so that their parts can be recycled in the next generation of hopeful neuron growth a few days later. This selective environment within the brain (especially within the brain of the fetus, long before it encounters the outside environment) no more specifies the final connections than the genes do; saliencies in both genes and developmental environment influence and prune the growth, but there is plenty that is left to chance.

When the human genome was recently published, and it was announced that we have "only" about 30,000 genes (by today's assumptions about how to identify and count genes), not the 100,000 genes that some experts had surmised, there was an amusing sigh of relief in the press. Whew! "We" are not just the products of our genes; "we" get to contribute all the specifications that those 70,000 genes would otherwise have "fixed" in us! And how, one might ask, are "we" to do this? Aren't we under just as much of a threat from the dread environment, nasty old Nurture with its insidious indoctrination techniques? When Nature and Nurture have done their work, will there be anything left over to be me?

Does it matter what the trade-off is if, one way or another, our genes and our environment (including chance) divide up the spoils and "fix" our characters? Perhaps it seems that the environment is a more benign source of determination since, after all, "we can change the environment." That is true, but we can't change a person's *past* environment any more than we can change her parents, and environmental adjustments in the future can be just as vigorously addressed to undoing prior genetic constraints as prior environmental constraints. And we are now on the verge of being able to adjust the genetic future almost as readily as the environmental future.

Suppose you know that any child of yours will have a problem that can be alleviated by either an adjustment to its genes or an adjustment to its environment. There can be many valid reasons for favoring one treatment policy over another, but it is certainly not obvious that one of these options should be ruled out on moral or metaphysical grounds. Suppose, to make up an imaginary case that will probably soon be out-run by reality, you are a committed Inuit who believes life above the Arc-tic Circle is the only life worth living, and suppose you are told that your children will be genetically ill-equipped for living in such an environment. You can move to the tropics, where they will be fine—at the cost of giving up their environmental heritage—or you can adjust their genomes, permitting them to continue living in the Arctic world, at the cost (if it is one) of the loss of some aspect of their "natural" genetic heritage.

The issue is not about determinism, either genetic or environmental or both together; the issue is about *what we can change* whether or not our world is deterministic. A fascinating perspective on the misguided issue of genetic determinism is provided by Jared Diamond in his magnificent book *Guns, Germs, and Steel* (1997). The question Diamond poses, and largely answers, is why it is that "Western" people (Europeans or Eurasians) have conquered, colonized, and otherwise dominated "Third World" people instead of vice versa. Why didn't the human populations of the Americas or Africa, for instance, create worldwide empires by invading, killing, and enslaving Europeans? Is the answer . . . genetic? Is science showing us that the ultimate source of Western dominance is in our genes? On first encountering this question, many people—even highly sophisticated scientists—jump to the conclusion that Diamond, by merely addressing this question, must be entertaining some awful racist hypothesis about European genetic superiority. So rattled are they by this suspicion that they have a hard time taking in the fact (which he must labor mightily to drive home) that he is saying just about the opposite: The secret explanation lies not in our genes, not in human genes, but it does lie to a very large extent in genes—the genes of the plants and animals that were the wild ancestors of all the domesticated species of human agriculture.

Prison wardens have a rule of thumb: If it can happen, it will happen. What they mean is that any gap in security, any ineffective prohibition or surveillance or weakness in the barriers, will soon enough be found and exploited to the full by the prisoners. Why? The intentional stance makes it clear: The prisoners are intentional systems who are smart, resourceful, and frustrated; as such they amount to a huge supply of informed desire with lots of free time in which to explore their worlds. Their search procedure will be as good as exhaustive, and they will be able to tell the best moves from the second-best. Count on them to find whatever is there to be found.

Diamond exploits the same rule of thumb, assuming that people anywhere in the world have always been just about as smart, as thrifty, as opportunistic, as disciplined, as foresighted, as people anywhere else, and then showing that indeed people have always found what was there to be found. To a good first approximation, all the domesticable wild species have been domesticated. The reason the Eurasians got a head start on technology is because they got a head start on agriculture, and they got that because among the wild plants and animals in their vicinity 10,000 years ago were ideal candidates for domestication. There were grasses that were genetically close to superplants that could be arrived at more or less by accident, just a few mutations away from big-head, nutritious grains, and animals that because of their social nature were genetically close to herdable animals that bred easily in captivity. (Maize in the Western Hemisphere took longer to domesticate in part because it had a greater genetic distance to travel away from its wild precursor.)

And, of course, the key portion of the selection events that covered this ground, before modern agronomy, was what Darwin called "unconscious selection"—the largely unwitting and certainly uninformed bias implicit in the behavior patterns of people who had only the narrowest vision of what they were doing and why. Accidents of biogeography, and hence of environment, were the major causes, the constraints that "fixed" the opportunities of people wherever they lived. Thanks to living for millennia in close proximity to their many varieties of domesticated animals, Eurasians developed immunity to the various disease pathogens that jumped from their animal hosts to human hosts—here is a profound role played by human genes, and one confirmed beyond a shadow of a doubt—and when thanks to their technology, they were able to travel long distances and encounter other peoples, their germs did many times the damage that their guns and steel did.

What are we to say about Diamond and his thesis? Is he a dread genetic determinist, or a dread environmental determinist? He is neither, of course, for both these species of bogeyman are as mythical as werewolves. By increasing the information we have about the various causes of the constraints that limit our current opportunities, he has increased our powers to avoid what we want to avoid, prevent what we want to prevent. Knowledge of the roles of our genes, and the genes of the other species around us, is not the enemy of human freedom, but one of its best friends.

Freedom and Necessity

A. J. Ayer

When I am said to have done something of my own free will it is implied that I could have acted otherwise; and it is only when it is believed that I could have acted otherwise that I am held to be morally responsible for what I have done. For a man is not thought to be morally responsible for an action that it was not in his power to avoid. But if human behaviour is entirely governed by causal laws, it is not clear how any action that is done could ever have been avoided. It may be said of the agent that he would have acted otherwise if the causes of his action had been different, but they being what they were, it seems to follow that he was bound to act as he did. Now it is commonly assumed both that men are capable of acting freely, in the sense that is required to make them morally responsible, and that human behaviour is entirely governed by causal laws: and it is the apparent conflict between these two assumptions that gives rise to the philosophical problem of the freedom of the will.

Confronted with this problem, many people will be inclined to agree with Dr. Johnson: 'Sir, we *know* our will is free, and *there's* an end on't'. But, while this does very well for those who accept Dr. Johnson's premiss, it would hardly convince anyone who denied the freedom of the will. Certainly, if we do know that our wills are free, it follows that they are so. But the logical reply to this might be that since our wills are not free, it follows that no one can know that they are: so that if anyone claims, like Dr. Johnson, to know that they are, he must be mistaken. What is evident, indeed, is that people often believe themselves to be acting freely; and it is to this 'feeling' of freedom that some philosophers appeal when they wish, in the supposed interests of morality, to prove that not all human action is causally determined. But if these philosophers are right in their assumption that a man cannot be acting freely if his action is causally determined, then the fact that someone feels free to do, or not to do, a certain action does not prove that he really is so. It may prove that the agent does not himself know what it is that makes him act in one way rather than another: but from the fact that a man is unaware of the causes of his action, it does not follow that no such causes exist.

So much may be allowed to the determinist; but his belief that all human actions are subservient to causal laws still remains to be justified. If, indeed, it is necessary that every event should have a cause, then the rule must apply to human behaviour as much as to anything else. But why should it be supposed that every event must have a cause? The contrary is not unthinkable. Nor is the law of universal causation a necessary presupposition of scientific thought. The scientist may try to discover causal laws, and in many cases he succeeds; but sometimes he has to be content with statistical laws, and sometimes he comes upon events which, in the present state of his knowledge, he is not able to subsume under any law at all. In the case of these events he assumes that if he knew more he would be able to discover some law, whether causal or statistical, which would enable him to account for them. And this assumption cannot be disproved. For however far he may have carried his investigation, it is always open to him to carry it further; and it is always conceivable that if he carried it further he would discover the connection which had hitherto escaped him. Nevertheless, it is also conceivable that the events with which he is concerned are not systematically connected with any others: so that the reason why he does not discover the sort of laws that he requires is simply that they do not obtain.

Now in the case of human conduct the search for explanations has not in fact been altogether fruitless. Certain scientific laws have been established; and with the help of these laws we do make a number of successful predictions about the ways in which different people will behave. But these predictions do not always cover every detail. We may be able to predict that in certain circumstances a particular man will be angry, without being able to prescribe the precise form that the expression of his anger will take. We may be reasonably sure that he will shout, but not sure how loud his shout will be, or exactly what words he will use. And it is only a small proportion of human actions that we are able to forecast even so precisely as this. But that, it may be said, is because we have not carried our investigations very far. The science of psychology is still in its infancy and, as it is developed, not only will more human actions be explained, but the explanations will go into greater detail. The ideal of complete explanation may never in fact be attained: but it is theoretically attainable. Well, this may be so: and certainly it is impossible to show *a priori* that it is not so: but equally it cannot be shown that it is. This will not, however, discourage the scientist who, in the field of human behaviour, as elsewhere, will continue to formulate theories and test them by the facts. And in this he is justified. For since he has no reason *a priori* to admit that there is a limit to what he can discover, the fact that he also cannot be sure that there is no limit does not make it unreasonable for him to devise theories, nor, having devised them, to try constantly to improve them.

But now suppose it to be claimed that, so far as men's actions are concerned, there is a limit: and that this limit is set by the fact of human freedom. An obvious objection is that in many cases in which a person feels himself to be free to do, or not to do, a certain action, we are even now able to explain, in causal terms, why it is that he acts as he does. But it might be argued that even if men are sometimes mistaken in believing that they act freely, it does not follow that they are always so mistaken. For it is not always the case that when a man believes that he has acted freely we are in fact able to account for his action in causal terms. A determinist would say that we should be able to account for it if we had more knowledge of the circumstances, and had been able to discover the appropriate natural laws. But until those discoveries have been made, this remains only a pious hope. And may it not be true that, in some cases at least, the reason why we can give no causal explanation is that no causal explanation is available; and that this is because the agent's choice was literally free, as he himself felt it to be?

The answer is that this may indeed be true, inasmuch as it is open to anyone to hold that no explanation is possible until some explanation is actually found. But even so it does not give the moralist what he wants. For he is anxious to show that men are capable of acting freely in order to infer that they can be morally responsible for what they do. But if it is a matter of pure chance that a man should act in one way rather than another, he may be free but he can hardly be responsible. And indeed when a man's actions seem to us quite unpredictable, when, as we say, there is no knowing what he will do, we do not look upon him as a moral agent. We look upon him rather as a lunatic.

To this it may be objected that we are not dealing fairly with the moralist. For when he makes it a condition of my being morally responsible that I should act freely, he does not wish to imply that it is purely a matter of chance that I act as I do. What he wishes to imply is that my actions are the result of my own free choice: and it is because they are the result of my own free choice that I am held to be morally responsible for them.

But now we must ask how it is that I come to make my choice. Either it is an accident that I choose to act as I do or it is not. If it is an accident, then it is merely a matter of chance that I did not choose otherwise; and if it is merely a matter of chance that I did not choose otherwise, it is surely irrational to hold me morally responsible for choosing as I did. But if it is not an accident that I choose to do one thing rather than another, then presumably there is some causal explanation of my choice: and in that case we are led back to determinism.

Again, the objection may be raised that we are not doing justice to the moralist's case. His view is not that it is a matter of chance that I choose to act as I do, but rather that my choice depends upon my character. Nevertheless he holds that I can still be free in the sense that he requires; for it is I who am responsible for my character. But in what way am I responsible for my character? Only, surely, in the sense that there is a causal connection between what I do now and what I have done in the past. It is only this that justifies the statement that I have made myself what I am: and even so this is an over-simplification, since it takes no account of the external influences to which I have been subjected. But, ignoring the external influences, let us assume that it is in fact the case that I have made myself what I am. Then it is still legitimate to ask how it is that I have come to make myself one sort of person rather than another. And if it be answered that it is a matter of my strength of will, we can put the same question in another form by asking how it is that my will has the strength that it has and not some other degree of strength. Once more, either it is an accident or it is not. If it is an accident, then by the same argument as before, I am not morally responsible, and if it is not an accident we are led back to determinism.

Furthermore, to say that my actions proceed from my character or, more colloquially, that I act in character, is to say that my behaviour is consistent and to that extent predictable: and since it is, above all, for the actions that I perform in character that I am held to be morally responsible, it looks as if the admission of moral responsibility, so far from being incompatible with determinism, tends rather to presuppose it. But how can this be so if it is a necessary condition of moral responsibility that the person who is held responsible should have acted freely? It seems that if we are to retain this idea of moral responsibility, we must either show that men can be held responsible for actions which they do not do freely, or else find some way of reconciling determinism with the freedom of the will.

It is no doubt with the object of effecting this reconciliation that some philosophers have defined freedom as the consciousness of necessity. And by so doing they are able to say not only that a man can be acting freely when his action is causally determined, but even that his action must be causally determined for it to be possible for him to be acting freely. Nevertheless this definition has the serious disadvantage that it gives to the word 'freedom' a meaning quite different from any that it ordinarily bears. It is indeed obvious that if we are allowed to give the word 'freedom' any meaning that we please, we can find a meaning that will reconcile it with determinism: but this is no more a solution of our present problem than the fact that the word 'horse' could be arbitrarily used to mean what is ordinarily meant by 'sparrow' is a proof that horses have wings. For suppose that I am compelled by another person to do something 'against my will'. In that case, as the word 'freedom' is ordinarily used, I should not be said to be acting freely: and the fact that I am fully aware of the constraint to which I am subjected makes no difference to the matter. I do not become free by becoming conscious that I am not. It may, indeed, be possible to show that my being aware that my action is causally determined is not incompatible with my acting freely: but it by no means follows that it is in this that my freedom consists. Moreover, I suspect that one of the reasons why people are inclined to define freedom as the consciousness of necessity is that they think that if one is conscious of necessity one may somehow be able to master it. But this is a fallacy. It is like someone's saying that he wishes he could see into the future, because if he did he would know what calamities lay in wait for him and so would be able to avoid them. But if he avoids the calamities then they don't lie in the future and it is not true that he foresees them. And similarly if I am able to master necessity, in the sense of escaping the operation of a necessary law, then the law in question is not necessary. And if the law is not necessary, then neither my freedom nor anything else can consist in my knowing that it is.

Let it be granted, then, that when we speak of reconciling freedom with determinism we are using the word 'freedom' in an ordinary sense. It still remains for us to make this usage clear: and perhaps the best way to make it clear is to show what it is that freedom, in this sense, is contrasted with. Now we began with the assumption that freedom is contrasted with causality: so that a man cannot be said to be acting freely if his action is causally determined. But this assumption has led us into difficulties and I now wish to suggest that it is mistaken. For it is not, I think, causality that freedom is to be contrasted with, but constraint. And while it is true that being constrained to do an action entails being caused to do it, I shall try to show that the converse does not hold. I shall try to show that from the fact that my action is causally determined it does not necessarily follow that I am constrained to do it: and this is equivalent to saying that it does not necessarily follow that I am not free.

If I am constrained, I do not act freely. But in what circumstances can I legitimately be said to be constrained? An obvious instance is the case in which I am compelled by another person to do what he wants. In a case of this sort the compulsion need not be such as to deprive one of the power of choice. It is not required that the other person should have hypnotized me, or that he should make it physically impossible for me to go against his will. It is enough that he should induce me to do what he wants by making it clear to me that, if I do not, he will bring about some situation that I regard as even more undesirable than the consequences of the action that he wishes me to do. Thus, if the man points a pistol at my head I may still choose to disobey him: but this does not prevent its being true that if I do fall in with his wishes he can legitimately be said to have compelled me. And if the circumstances are such that no reasonable person would be expected to choose the other alternative, then the action that I am made to do is not one for which I am held to be morally responsible.

A similar, but still somewhat different, case is that in which another person has obtained an habitual ascendancy over me. Where this is so, there may be no question of my being induced to act as the other person wishes by being confronted with a still more disagreeable alternative: for if I am sufficiently under his influence this special stimulus will not be necessary. Nevertheless I do not act freely, for the reason that I have been deprived of the power of choice. And this means that I have acquired so strong a habit of obedience that I no longer go through any process of deciding whether or not to do what the other person wants. About other matters I may still deliberate; but as regards the fulfilment of this other person's wishes, my own deliberations have ceased to be a causal factor in my behaviour. And it is in this sense that I may be said to be constrained. It is not, however, necessary that such constraint should take the form of subservience to another person. A kleptomaniac is not a free agent, in respect of his stealing, because he does not go through any process of deciding whether or not to steal. Or rather, if he does go through such a process, it is irrelevant to his behavior. Whatever he resolved to do, he would steal all the same. And it is this that distinguishes him from the ordinary thief.

But now it may be asked whether there is any essential difference between these cases and those in which the agent is commonly thought to be free. No doubt the ordinary thief does go through a process of deciding whether or not to steal, and no doubt it does affect his behaviour. If he resolved to refrain from stealing, he could carry his resolution out. But if it be allowed that his making or not making this resolution is causally determined, then how can he be any more free than the kleptomaniac? It may be true that unlike the kleptomaniac he could refrain from stealing if he chose: but if there is a cause, or set of causes, which necessitate his choosing as he does, how can he be said to have the power of choice? Again, it may be true that no one now compels me to get up and walk across the room: but if my doing so can be causally explained in terms of my history or my environment, or whatever it may be, then how am I any more free than if some other person had compelled me? I do not have the feeling of constraint that I have when a pistol is manifestly pointed at my head; but the chains of causation by which I am bound are no less effective for being invisible.

The answer to this is that the cases I have mentioned as examples of constraint do differ from the others: and they differ just in the ways that I have tried to bring out. If I suffered from a compulsion neurosis, so that I got up and walked across the room, whether I wanted to or not, or if I did so because somebody else compelled me, then I should not be acting freely. But if I do it now, I shall be acting freely, just because these conditions do not obtain; and the fact that my action may nevertheless have a cause is, from this point of view, irrelevant. For it is not when my action has any cause at all, but only when it has a special sort of cause, that it is reckoned not to be free.

But here it may be objected that, even if this distinction corresponds to ordinary usage, it is still very irrational. For why should we distinguish, with regard to a person's freedom, between the operations of one sort of cause and those of another? Do not all causes equally necessitate? And is it not therefore arbitrary to say that a person is free when he is necessitated in one fashion but not when he is necessitated in another?

That all causes equally necessitate is indeed a tautology, if the word 'necessitate' is taken merely as equivalent to 'cause': but if, as the objection requires, it is taken as equivalent to 'constrain' or 'compel', then I do not think that this proposition is true. For all that is needed for one event to be the cause of another is that, in the given circumstances, the event which is said to be the effect would not have occurred if it had not been for the occurrence of the event which is said to be the cause, or *vice versa*, according as causes are interpreted as necessary, or sufficient, conditions:

and this fact is usually deducible from some causal law which states that whenever an event of the one kind occurs then, given suitable conditions, an event of the other kind will occur in a certain temporal or spatiotemporal relationship to it. In short, there is an invariable concomitance between the two classes of events; but there is no compulsion, in any but a metaphorical sense. Suppose, for example, that a psycho-analyst is able to account for some aspect of my behaviour by referring it to some lesion that I suffered in my childhood. In that case, it may be said that my childhood experience, together with certain other events, necessitates my behaving as I do. But all that this involves is that it is found to be true in general that when people have had certain experiences as children, they subsequently behave in certain specifiable ways; and my case is just another instance of this general law. It is in this way indeed that my behaviour is explained. But from the fact that my behaviour is capable of being explained, in the sense that it can be subsumed under some natural law, it does not follow that I am acting under constraint.

If this is correct, to say that I could have acted otherwise is to say, first, that I should have acted otherwise if I had so chosen; secondly, that my action was voluntary in the sense in which the actions, say, of the kleptomaniac are not; and thirdly, that nobody compelled me to choose as I did: and these three conditions may very well be fulfilled. When they are fulfilled, I may be said to have acted freely. But this is not to say that it was a matter of chance that I acted as I did, or, in other words, that my action could not be explained. And that my actions should be capable of being explained is all that is required by the postulate of determinism.

If more than this seems to be required it is, I think, because the use of the very word 'determinism' is in some degree misleading. For it tends to suggest that one event is somehow in the power of another whereas the truth is merely that they are factually correlated. And the same applies to the use, in this context, of the word 'necessity' and even of the word 'cause' itself. Moreover, there are various reasons for this. One is the tendency to confuse causal with logical necessitation, and so to infer mistakenly that the effect is contained in the cause. Another is the uncritical use of a concept of force which is derived from primitive experiences of pushing and striking. A third is the survival of an animistic conception of causality, in which all causal relationships are modelled on the example of one person's exercising authority over another. As a result we tend to form an imaginative picture of an unhappy effect trying vainly to escape from the clutches of an overmastering cause. But, I repeat, the fact is simply that when an event of one type occurs, an event of another type occurs also, in a certain temporal or spatio-temporal relation to the first. The rest is only metaphor. And it is because of the metaphor, and not because of the fact, that we come to think that there is an antithesis between causality and freedom.

Nevertheless, it may be said, if the postulate of determinism is valid, then the future can be explained in terms of the past: and this means that if one knew enough about the past one would be able to predict the future. But in that case what will happen in the future is already decided. And how then can I be said to be free? What is going to happen is going to happen and nothing that I do can prevent it. If the determinist is right, I am the helpless prisoner of fate.

But what is meant by saying that the future course of events is already decided? If the implication is that some person has arranged it, then the proposition is false. But if all that is meant is that it is possible, in principle, to deduce it from a set of particular facts about the past, together with the appropriate general laws, then, even if this is true, it does not in the least entail that I am the helpless prisoner of fate. It does not even entail that my actions make no difference to the future: for they are causes as well as effects; so that if they were different their consequences would be different also. What it does entail is that my behaviour can be predicted: but to say that my behaviour can be predicted is not to say that I am acting under constraint. It is indeed true that I cannot escape my destiny if this is taken to mean no more than that I shall do what I shall do. But this is a tautology, just as it is a tautology that what is going to happen is going to happen. And such tautologies as these prove nothing whatsoever about the freedom of the will.

The Incompatibility of Free Will and Determinism

Peter van Inwagen

In this paper I shall define a thesis I shall call "determinism," and argue that it is incompatible with the thesis that we are able to act otherwise than we do (i.e., is incompatible with "free will"). Other theses, some of them very different from what *I* shall call "determinism," have at least an equal right to this name, and, therefore, I do not claim to show that *every* thesis that could be called "determinism" without historical impropriety is incompatible with free will. I shall, however, assume without argument that what I call 'determinism' is legitimately so called.

In Part I, I shall explain what I mean by "determinism." In Part II, I shall make some remarks about "can." In Part III, I shall argue that free will and determinism are incompatible. In Part IV, I shall examine some possible objections to the argument of Part III. I shall not attempt to establish the truth or falsity of determinism, or the existence or non-existence of free will.

I

In defining "determinism," I shall take for granted the notion of a proposition (that is, of a non-linguistic bearer of truth-value), together with certain allied notions such as denial, conjunction, and entailment. Nothing in this paper will depend on the special features of any particular account of propositions. The reader may think of them as functions from possible worlds to truth-values or in any other way he likes, provided they have their usual features (e.g., they are either true or false; the conjunction of a true and a false proposition is a false proposition; they obey the law of contraposition with respect to entailment).

Our definition of "determinism" will also involve the notion of "the state of the entire physical world" (hereinafter, "the state of the world") at an instant. I shall leave this notion largely unexplained, since the argument of this paper is very nearly independent of its content. Provided the following two conditions are met, the reader may flesh out "the state of the world" in any way he likes:

(i) Our concept of "state" must be such that, given that the world is in a certain state at a certain time, nothing follows *logically* about its states at other times. For example, we must not choose a concept of "state" that would allow as part of a description of the momentary state of the world, the clause, ". . . and, at *t*, the world is such that Jones's left hand will be raised 10 seconds later than *t*."

(ii) If there is some observable change in the way things are (e.g, if a white cloth becomes blue, a warm liquid cold, or if a man raises his hand), this change must entail some change in the state of the world. That is, our concept of "state" must not be so theoretical, so divorced from what is observably true, that it be possible for the world to be in the *same* state at t_1 and t_2, although (for example) Jones's hand is raised at t_1 and not at t_2.

We may now define "determinism." We shall apply this term to the conjunction of these two theses:

(a) For every instant of time, there is a proposition that expresses the state of the world at that instant.

(b) If *A* and *B* are any propositions that express the state of the world at some instants, then the conjunction of *A* with the laws of physics entails *B*.

By a proposition that expresses the state of the world at time *t*, I mean a true proposition that asserts of some state that, at *t*, the world is in that state. The reason for our first restriction on the content of "state" should now be evident: if it were not for this restriction, "the state of the world" could be defined in such a way that determinism was trivially true. We could, without this restriction, build sufficient information about the past and future into each proposition that expresses the state of the world at an instant, that, for every pair of such propositions, each *by itself* entails the other. And in that case, determinism would be a mere tautology, a thesis applicable to every conceivable state of affairs.

This amounts to saying that the "laws of physics" clause on our definition does some work: whether determinism is true depends on the character of the laws of physics. For example, if all physical laws were vague propositions like "In every nuclear reaction, momentum is *pretty nearly* conserved," or "Force is *approximately* equal to mass times acceleration," then determinism would be false.

This raises the question, What is a law of physics? First, a terminological point. I do not mean the application of this term to be restricted to those laws that belong to physics in the narrowest sense of the word. I am using "law of physics" in the way some philosophers use "law of nature." Thus, a law about chemical valences is a law of physics in my sense, even if chemistry is not ultimately "reducible" to physics. I will not use the term "law of nature," because, conceivably, *psychological* laws, including laws (if such there be) about the voluntary behaviour of rational agents, might be included under this term.[1] Rational agents are, after all, in some sense part of "Nature." Since I do not think that everything I shall say about laws of physics is true of such "voluntaristic laws," I should not want to use, instead of "laws of physics," some term like "laws of nature" that might legitimately be applied to voluntaristic laws. Thus, for all that is said in this paper, it may be that some version of determinism based on voluntaristic laws is compatible with free will.[2] Let us, then, understand by "law of physics" a law of nature that is not about the voluntary behaviour of rational agents.

But this does not tell us what "laws of nature" are. There would probably be fairly general agreement that a proposition cannot be a law of nature unless it is true and contingent, and that no proposition is a law of nature if it entails the existence of some concrete individual, such as Caesar or the earth. But the proposition that there is no solid gold sphere 20 feet in diameter (probably) satisfies these conditions, though it is certainly not a law of nature.

It is also claimed sometimes that a law of nature must "support its counter-factuals." There is no doubt something to this. Consider, however, the proposition, "Dogs die if exposed to virus V." The claim that this proposition supports its counter-factuals is, I think, equivalent to the claim that "Every dog is such that if it were exposed to virus V, it would die" is *true*. Let us suppose that this latter proposition *is* true, the quantification being understood as being over all dogs, past, present, and future. Its truth, it seems to me, is quite consistent with its being the case that dog-breeders *could* (but will not) institute a programme of selective breeding that *would* produce a sort of dog that is immune to virus V. But if dog-breeders *could* do this, then clearly "Dogs die if exposed to virus V" is not a law of nature, since in that case the truth of the corresponding universally quantified counter-factual depends upon an accidental circumstance: if dog-breeders were to institute a certain programme of selective breeding they are quite capable of instituting, then "Every dog is such that if it were exposed to virus V, it would die" would be false. Thus a proposition may "support its counter-factuals" and yet not be a law of nature.

I do not think that any philosopher has succeeded in giving a (nontrivial) set of individually necessary and jointly sufficient conditions for a proposition's being a law of nature or of physics. *I* certainly do not know of any such set. Fortunately, for the purposes of this paper we need not know how to analyse the concept "law of physics." I shall, in Part III, argue that certain statements containing "law of physics" are analytic. But this can be done in the absence of a satisfactory analysis of "law of physics." In fact, it would hardly be possible for one to *provide* an analysis of some concept if one had no pre-analytic convictions about what statements involving that concept are analytic.

For example, we do not have to have a satisfactory analysis of memory to know that "No one can remember future events" is analytic. And if someone devised an analysis of memory according to which it was possible to remember future events, then, however attractive the analysis was in other respects, it would have to be rejected. The analyticity of "No one can remember future events" is one of the *data* that anyone who investigates the concept of memory must take account of. Similarly, the claims I shall make on behalf of the concept of physical law seem to me to be basic and evident enough to be data that an analysis of this concept must take account of: any analysis on which these claims did not 'come out true' would be for that very reason defective.

II

It seems to be generally agreed that the concept of free will should be understood in terms of the *power* or *ability* of agents to act otherwise than they in fact do. To deny that men have free will is to assert that what a man *does* do and what he *can* do coincide. And almost all philosophers[3] agree that a necessary condition for holding an agent responsible for an act is believing that that agent *could have* refrained from performing that act.[4]

There is, however, considerably less agreement as to how "can" (in the relevant sense) should be analysed. This is one of the most difficult questions in philosophy. It is certainly a question to which I do not know any non-trivial answer. But, as I said I should do in the case of "law of physics," I shall make certain conceptual claims about "can" (in the "power" or "ability" sense) in the absence of any analysis. Any suggested analysis of "can" that does not support these claims will either be neutral with respect to them, in which case it will be incomplete, since it will not settle *all* conceptual questions about "can," or it will be inconsistent with them, in which case the arguments I shall present in support of these claims will, in effect, be arguments that the analysis fails. In Part IV, I shall expand on this point as it applies to one particular analysis of "can," the well-known "conditional" analysis.

I shall say no more than this about the meaning of "can." I shall, however, introduce an idiom that will be useful in talking about ability and inability in complicated cases. Without this idiom, the statement of our argument would be rather unwieldy. We shall sometimes make claims about an agent's abilities by using sentences of the form:

S can render |could have rendered| . . . false.

where ". . ." may be replaced by names of propositions.[5] Our ordinary claims about ability can easily be translated into this idiom. For example, we translate:

He could have reached Chicago by midnight.

as

He could have rendered the proposition that he did not reach Chicago by midnight false.

and, of course, the translation from the special idiom to the ordinary idiom is easy enough in such simple cases. If we were interested only in everyday ascriptions of ability, the new idiom would be useless. Using it, however, we may make ascriptions of ability that it would be very difficult to make in the ordinary idiom. Consider, for example, the last true proposition asserted by Plato. (Let us assume that this description is, as logicians say, "proper.") One claim that we might make about Aristotle is that he could have rendered this proposition false. Now, presumably, we have no way of discovering *what* proposition the last true proposition asserted by Plato was. Still, the claim about Aristotle would seem to be either true or false. To discover its truth-value, we should have to discover under what conditions the last true proposition asserted by Plato (i.e., that proposition having as one of its accidental properties, the property of being the last true proposition asserted by Plato) would be false, and then discover whether it was within Aristotle's power to produce these conditions. For example, suppose that if Aristotle had lived in Athens from the time of Plato's death till the time of his own death, then the last true proposition asserted by Plato (whatever it was) would be false. Then, if Aristotle could have lived (i.e. if he had it within his power to live) in Athens throughout this period, he could have rendered the last true proposition asserted by Plato false. On the other hand, if the last true proposition asserted by Plato is the proposition that the planets do not move in perfect circles, then Aristotle could not have rendered the last true proposition asserted by Plato false, since it was not within his power to produce any set of conditions sufficient for the falsity of this proposition.[6]

It is obvious that the proposition expressed by "Aristotle could have rendered the last true proposition asserted by Plato false," is a proposition that we should be hard put to express without using the idiom of rendering propositions false, or at least, without using some very similar idiom. We shall find this new idiom very useful in discussing the relation between free will (a thesis about abilities) and determinism (a thesis about certain propositions).

III

I shall now imagine a case in which a certain man, after due deliberation, refrained from performing a certain contemplated act. I shall then argue that, if determinism is true, then that man *could not have* performed that act. Because this argument will not depend on any features peculiar to our imagined case, the incompatibility of free will and determinism *in general* will be established, since, as will be evident, a parallel argument could easily be constructed for the case of any agent and any unperformed act.

Here is the case. Let us suppose there was once a judge who had only to raise his right hand at a certain time, T, to prevent the execution of a sentence of death upon a certain criminal, such a hand-raising being the sign, according to the conventions of the judge's country, of a granting of special clemency. Let us further suppose that the judge—call him "J"—refrained from raising his hand at that time, and that this inaction resulted in the criminal's being put to death. We may also suppose that the judge was unbound, uninjured, and free from paralysis; that he decided not to raise his hand at T only after a period of calm, rational, and relevant deliberation; that he had not been subjected to any "pressure" to decide one way or the other about the criminal's death; that he was not under the influence of drugs, hypnosis, or anything of that sort; and finally, that there was no element in his deliberations that would have been of any special interest to a student of abnormal psychology.

Now the argument. In this argument, which I shall refer to as the "main argument," I shall use "T_0" to denote some instant of time earlier than J's birth, "P_0" to denote the proposition that expresses the state of the world at T_0. "P" to denote the proposition that expresses the state of the world at T, and "L" to denote the conjunction into a single proposition of all laws of physics. (I shall regard L itself as a law of physics, on the reasonable assumption that if A and B are laws of physics, then the conjunction of A and B is a law of physics.) The argument consists of seven statements, the seventh of which follows from the first six:

1. If determinism is true, then the conjunction of P_0 and L entails P.
2. If J had raised his hand at T, then P would be false.
3. If (2) is true, then if J could have raised his hand at T, J could have rendered P false.[7]
4. If J could have rendered P false, and if the conjunction of P_0 and L entails P, then J could have rendered the conjunction of P_0 and L false.
5. If J could have rendered the conjunction of P_0 and L false, then J could have rendered L false.
6. J could not have rendered L false.
∴7. If determinism is true, J could not have raised his hand at T.

That (7) follows from (1) through (6) can easily be established by truthfunctional logic. Note that all conditionals in the argument except for (2) are truthfunctional. For purposes of establishing the *validity* of this argument, (2) may be regarded as a simple sentence. Let us examine the premises individually.

(1) This premiss follows from the definition of determinism.

(2) If J had raised his hand at T, then the world would have been in a different state at T from the state it was in fact in. (See our second condition on the content of "the state of the world.") And, therefore, if J had raised his hand at T, some contrary of P would express the state of the world at T. It should be emphasized that "P" does not *mean* "the proposition that expresses the state of the world at T." Rather, "P" *denotes* the proposition that expresses the state of the world at T. In Kripke's terminology, "P" is being used as a *rigid designator*, while "the proposition that expresses the state of the world at T" is perforce non-rigid.[8]

(3) Since J's hand being raised at T would have been sufficient for the falsity of P, there is, if J could have raised his hand, at least one condition sufficient for the falsity of P, and J could have produced.

(4) This premiss may be defended as an instance of the following general principle:

If S can render R false, and if Q entails R, then S can render Q false.

This principle seems to be analytic. For if Q entails R, then the denial of R entails the denial of Q. Thus, any condition sufficient for the falsity of R is also sufficient for the falsity of Q. Therefore, if there is some condition that S can produce that is sufficient for the falsity of R, there is some condition (that same condition) that S can produce that is sufficient for the falsity of Q.

(5) This premiss may be defended as an instance of the following general principle, which I take to be analytic:

If Q is a true proposition that concerns only states of affairs that obtained before S's birth, and if S can render the conjunction of Q and R false, then S can render R false.

Consider, for example, the propositions expressed by

The Spanish Armada was defeated in 1588.

and

Peter van Inwagen never visits Alaska.

The conjunction of these two propositions is quite possibly true. At any rate, let us assume it is true. Given that it is true, it seems quite clear that I can render it false if and only if I can visit Alaska. If, for some reason, it is not within my power ever to visit Alaska, then I *cannot* render it false. This is a quite trivial assertion, and the general principle (above) of which it is an instance is hardly less trivial. And it seems incontestable that premiss (5) is also an instance of this principle.

(6) I shall argue that if anyone *can* (i.e., has it within his power to) render some proposition false, then that proposition is not a law of physics. This I regard as a conceptual truth, one of the data that must be taken account of by anyone who wishes to give an analysis of "can" or "law." It is this connection between these two concepts, I think, that is at the root of the incompatibility of free will and determinism.

In order to see this connection, let us suppose that both of the following are true:

1. Nothing ever travels faster than light.
2. Jones, a physicist, can construct a particle accelerator that would cause protons to travel at twice the speed of light.

It follows from (A) that Jones will never exercise the power that (B) ascribes to him. But whatever the reason for Jones's failure to act on his ability to render (A) false, it is clear that (A) and (B) are consistent, and that (B) entails that (A) is not a law of physics. For given that (B) is true, then Jones is able to conduct an experiment that would falsify (A); and surely it is a feature of any proposition that is a physical law that no one *can* conduct an experiment that would show it to be false.

Of course, most propositions that look initially as if they might be physical laws, but which are later decided to be non-laws, are rejected because of experiments that are actually performed. But this is not essential. In order to see this, let us elaborate the example we have been considering. Let us suppose that Jones's ability to render (A) false derives from the fact that he has discovered a mathematically rigorous proof that under certain conditions C, realizable in the laboratory, protons would travel faster than light. And let us suppose that this proof proceeds from premises so obviously true that all competent physicists accept his conclusion without reservation. But suppose that conditions C never obtain in nature, and that actually to produce them in the laboratory would require such an expenditure of resources that Jones and his colleagues decide not to carry out the experiment. And suppose that, as a result, conditions C are never realized and nothing ever travels faster than light.

It is evident that if all this were true, we should have to say that (A), while *true*, is not a law of physics. (Though, of course, "Nothing ever travels faster than light except under conditions *C*" might be a law.)

The laboratories and resources that figure in this example are not essential to its point. If Jones *could* render some proposition false by performing *any* act he does not in fact perform, even such a simple act as raising his hand at a certain time, this would be sufficient to show that that proposition is not a law of physics.

This completes my defence of the premises of the main argument. In the final part of this paper, I shall examine objections to this argument suggested by the attempts of various philosophers to establish the compatibility of free will and determinism.

IV

The most useful thing a philosopher who thinks that the main argument does not prove its point could do would be to try to show that some premiss of the argument is false or incoherent, or that the argument begs some important question, or contains a term that is used equivocally, or something of that sort. In short, he should get down to cases. Some philosophers, however, might continue to hold that free will and determinism, in the sense of Part I, are compatible, but decline to try to point out a mistake in the argument. For (such a philosopher might argue) we have, in everyday life, *criteria* for determining whether an agent could have acted otherwise than he did, and these criteria determine the *meaning* of "could have acted otherwise"; to know the meaning of this phrase is simply to know how to apply these criteria. And since these criteria make no mention of determinism, anyone who thinks that free will and determinism are incompatible is simply confused.[9]

As regards the argument of Part III (this philosopher might continue), this argument is very complex, and this complexity must simply serve to hide some error, since its conclusion is absurd. We must treat this argument like the infamous "proof" that zero equals one: It may be amusing and even instructive to find the hidden error(if one has nothing better to do), but it would be a waste of time to take seriously any suggestion that it is sound.

Now I suppose we do have "criteria," in some sense of this over-used word, for the application of "could have done otherwise," and I will grant that knowing the criteria for the application of a term can plausibly be identified with knowing its meaning. Whether the criteria for applying 'could have done otherwise' can (as at least one philosopher has supposed[10]) be taught by simple ostension is another question. However this may be, the "criteria" argument is simply invalid. To see this, let us examine a simpler argument that makes the same mistake.

Consider the doctrine of "predestinarianism." Predestinarians hold (i) that if an act is foreseen it is not free, and (ii) that all acts are foreseen by God. (I do not claim that anyone has ever held this doctrine in precisely this form.) Now suppose we were to argue that predestinarianism must be compatible with free will, since our criteria for applying "could have done otherwise" make no reference to predestinarianism. Obviously this argument would be invalid, since predestinarianism is incompatible with free will. And the only difference I can see between this argument and the "criteria" argument for the compatibility of free will and determinism is that predestinarianism, unlike determinism, is *obviously* incompatible with free will. But, of course, theses may be incompatible with one another even if this incompatibility is not obvious. Even if determinism cannot, like predestinarianism, be seen to be incompatible with free will on the basis of a simple formal inference, there is, nonetheless, a conceptual connection between the two theses (as we showed in our defence of premiss (6)). The argument of Part III is intended to draw out the implications of this connection. There may well be a mistake in the argument, but I do not see why anyone should think that the very idea of such an argument is misconceived.

It has also been argued that free will *entails* determinism, and, being itself a consistent thesis, is *a fortiori* compatible with determinism. The argument, put briefly, is this. To say of some person on some particular occasion that he acted freely is obviously to say at least that *he* acted on that occasion. Suppose, however, that we see someone's arm rise and it later turns out that there was *no cause whatsoever* for his arm's rising. Surely we should have to say that *he* did not really raise his arm at all. Rather, his arm's rising was a mere chance happening, that, like a muscular twitch, had nothing to do with *him*, beyond the fact that it happened to involve a part of his body. A necessary condition for this person's really having raised his hand is that *he* caused his hand to rise. And surely "*he* caused" means "*his* character, desires, and beliefs caused."[11]

I think that there is a great deal of confusion in this argument, but to expose this confusion would require a lengthy discussion of many fine points in the theory of agency. I shall only point out that if this argument is supposed to refute the conclusion of Part III, it is an *ignoratio elenchi*. For I did not conclude that free will is incompatible with the thesis that every event has a cause, but rather with determinism as defined in Part I. And the denial of this thesis does not entail that there are uncaused events.

Of course, one might try to construct a similar but relevant argument for the falsity of the conclusion of Part III. But, so far as I can see, the plausibility of such an argument would depend on the plausibility of supposing that if the present movements of one's body are not completely determined by physical law and the state of the world before one's birth, then these present movements are not one's own doing, but, rather, mere random happenings. And I do not see the least shred of plausibility in this supposition.

I shall finally consider the popular "conditional analysis" argument for the compatibility of free will and determinism. According to the advocates of this argument—let us call them 'conditionalists'—what statements of the form:

(8) S could have done X

mean is:

(9) If S had chosen to do X, S would have done X.[12]

For example, "Smith could have saved the drowning child" means: "If Smith had chosen to save the drowning child, Smith would have saved the drowning child." Thus, even if determinism is true (the conditionalists argue), it is possible that Smith did not save but *could have* saved the drowning child, since the conjunction of determinism with "Smith did not save the child" does not entail the falsity of "If Smith had chosen to save the child, Smith would have saved the child."

Most of the controversy about this argument centres around the question whether (9) is a correct analysis of (8). I shall not enter into the debate about whether this analysis is correct. I shall instead question the relevance of this debate to the argument of Part III. For it is not clear that the main argument would be unsound if the conditional analysis *were* correct. Clearly the argument is *valid* whether or not (8) and (9) mean the same. But suppose the premises of the main argument were rewritten so that every clause they contain that is of form (8) is replaced by the corresponding clause of form (9)—should we then see that any of these premises is false? Let us try this with premiss (6), which seems, prima facie, to be the crucial premiss of the argument. We have:

(6a) It is not the case that if *J* had chosen to render *L* false, *J* would have rendered *L* false.

Now (6a) certainly seems true: If someone chooses to render false some proposition *R*, and if *R* is a law of physics, then surely he will fail. This little argument for (6a) *seems* obviously sound. But we cannot overlook the possibility that someone might discover a mistake in it and, perhaps, even construct a convincing argument that (6a) is false. Let us, therefore, assume for the sake of argument that (6a) is demonstrably false. What would this show? I submit that it would show that (6a) does not mean the same as (6), since (6) is, as I have argued, *true*.

The same dilemma confronts the conditionalist if he attempts to show, on the basis of the conditional analysis, that any of the other premisses of the argument is false. Consider the argument got by replacing every clause of form (8) in the main argument with the corresponding clause of form (9). If all the premisses of this new argument are true, the main argument is, according to the conditionalist's own theory, sound. If, on the other hand, any of the premisses of the new argument is false, then (*I* would maintain) this premiss is a counter-example to the conditional analysis. I should not be begging the question against the conditionalist in maintaining this, since I have given arguments for the truth of each of the premisses of the main argument, and nowhere in these arguments do I assume that the conditional analysis is wrong.

Of course, any or all of my arguments in defence of the premisses of the main argument may contain some mistake. But unless the conditionalist could point to some such mistake, he would not accomplish much by showing that some statement he *claimed* was equivalent to one of its premisses was false.[13]

Notes

1. For example, "If a human being is not made to feel ashamed of lying before his twelfth birthday, then he will lie whenever he believes it to be to his advantage."
2. In "The Compatibility of Free Will and Determinism," *Philosophical Review*, 1962, J. V. Canfield argues convincingly for a position that we might represent in this terminology as the thesis that a determinism based on voluntaristic laws could be compatible with free will.
3. See, however, Harry Frankfurt, "Alternate Possibilities and Moral Responsibility," *Journal of Philosophy*, 1969.

4. Actually, the matter is rather more complicated than this, since we may hold a man responsible for an act we believe he could not have refrained from, provided we are prepared to hold him responsible for his being unable to refrain.

5. In all the cases we shall consider, ". . ." will be replaced by names of *true* propositions. For the sake of logical completeness, we may stipulate that any sentence formed by replacing ". . ." with the name of a *false* proposition is trivially true. Thus, "Kant could have rendered the proposition that 7 + 5 = 13 false" is trivially true.

6. Steven M. Cahn and Richard Taylor have argued (most explicitly in "Time, Truth and Ability" by "Diodorus Cronus," *Analysis*, 1965 that every true proposition is such that, necessarily, no one is able to render it false. On my view, this thesis is mistaken, and their arguments for it can be shown to be unsound. I shall not, however, argue for this here. I shall argue in Part III that we are unable to render *certain sorts of* true proposition false, but my arguments will depend on special features of these sorts of proposition. I shall, for example, argue that no one can render false a law of physics; but I shall not argue that this is the case because laws of physics are *true*, but because of other features that they possess.

7. "*J* could have raised his hand at *T*" is ambiguous. It might mean either (roughly) "*J* possessed, at *T*, the ability to raise his hand," or "*J* possessed the ability to bring it about that his hand rose at *T*." If *J* was unparalysed at *T* but paralysed at all earlier instants, then the latter of these would be false, though the former might be true. I mean "*J* could have raised his hand at *T*" in the latter sense.

8. See Saul Kripke, "Identity and Necessity," in *Identity and Individuation*, ed. Milton K. Munitz (New York, 1971).

9. Cf. Antony Flew, "Divine Omniscience and Human Freedom," *New Essays in Philosophical Theology*, ed. Antony Flew and Alasdair MacIntyre (London: SCM Press, 1955), 149–51 in particular.

10. Flew, loc cit.

11. Cf. R. E. Hobart, "Free Will as Involving Determination and Inconceivable Without It," *Mind*, 1934; A. J. Ayer, "Freedom and Necessity," in his collected *Philosophical Essays* (New York, 1954) P. H. Nowell-Smith, "Freewill and Moral Responsibility," *Mind*, 1948, J. J. C. Smart, "Free Will, Praise, and Blame," *Mind*, 1961.

12. Many other verbs besides "choose" figure in various philosophers' conditional analyses of ability: e.g., "wish," "want," "will," "try," "set oneself." Much of the important contemporary work on this analysis, by G. E. Moore, P. H. Nowell-Smith, J. L. Austin, Keith Lehrer, Roderick Chisholm, and others is collected in *The Nature of Human Action*, ed. Myles Brand (Glenview, Ill., 1970). See also "Fatalism and Determinism," by Wilfrid Sellars, in *Freedom and Determinism*, ed. Keith Lehrer (New York, 1966), 141–74.

13. For an argument in some respects similar to what I have called the "main argument," see Carl Ginet's admirable article, "Might We Have No Choice?" in Lehrer, 87–104. Another argument similar to the main argument, which is (formally) much simpler than the main argument, but which is stated in language very different from that of traditional statements of the free-will problem, can be found in my "A Formal Approach to the Problem of Free Will and Determinism," *Theoria*, 1974.

Alternative Possibilities and Moral Responsibility

Harry G. Frankfurt

A dominant role in nearly all recent inquiries into the free-will problem has been played by a principle which I shall call "the principle of alternate possibilities." This principle states that a person is morally responsible for what he has done only if he could have done otherwise. Its exact meaning is a subject of controversy, particularly concerning whether someone who accepts it is thereby committed to believing that moral responsibility and determinism are incompatible. Practically no one, however, seems inclined to deny or even to question that the principle of alternate possibilities (construed in some way or other) is true. It has generally seemed so overwhelmingly plausible that some philosophers have even characterized it as an a priori truth. People whose accounts of free will or of moral responsibility are radically at odds evidently find in it a firm and convenient common ground upon which they can profitably take their opposing stands.

But the principle of alternate possibilities is false. A person may well be morally responsible for what he has done even though he could not have done otherwise. The principle's plausibility is an illusion, which can be made to vanish by bringing the relevant moral phenomena into sharper focus.

I

In seeking illustrations of the principle of alternate possibilities, it is most natural to think of situations in which the same circumstances both bring it about that a person does something and make it impossible for him to avoid doing it. These include, for example, situations in which a person is coerced into doing something, or in which he is impelled to act by a hypnotic suggestion, or in which some inner compulsion drives him to do what he does. In situations of these kinds there are circumstances that make it impossible for the person to do otherwise, and these very circumstances also serve to bring it about that he does whatever it is that he does.

However, there may be circumstances that constitute sufficient conditions for a certain action to be performed by someone and that therefore make it impossible for the person to do otherwise, but that do not actually impel the person to act or in any way produce his action. A person may do something in circumstances that leave him no alternative to doing it, without these circumstances actually moving him or leading him to do it—without them playing any role, indeed, in bringing it about that he does what he does.

An examination of situations characterized by circumstances of this sort casts doubt, I believe, on the relevance to questions of moral responsibility of the fact that a person who has done something could not have done otherwise. I propose to develop some examples of this kind in the context of a discussion of coercion and to suggest that our moral intuitions concerning these examples tend to disconfirm the principle of alternate possibilities. Then I will discuss the principle in more general terms, explain what I think is wrong with it, and describe briefly and without argument how it might appropriately be revised.

II

It is generally agreed that a person who has been coerced to do something did not do it freely and is not morally responsible for having done it. Now the doctrine that coercion and moral responsibility are mutually exclusive may appear to be no more than a somewhat particularized version of the principle of alternate possibilities. It is natural enough to say of a person who has been coerced to do something that he could not have done otherwise. And it may easily seem that being coerced deprives a person of freedom and of moral responsibility simply because it is a special case of being unable to do otherwise. The principle of alternate possibilities may in this way derive some credibility from its association with the very plausible proposition that moral responsibility is excluded by coercion.

It is not right, however, that it should do so. The fact that a person was coerced to act as he did may entail both that he could not have done otherwise and that he bears no moral responsibility for his action. But his lack of moral responsibility is not entailed by his having been unable to do otherwise. The doctrine that coercion excludes moral responsibility is not correctly understood, in other words, as a particularized version of the principle of alternate possibilities.

Let us suppose that someone is threatened convincingly with a penalty he finds unacceptable and that he then does what is required of him by the issuer of the threat. We can imagine details that would make it reasonable for us to think that the person was coerced to perform the action in question, that he could not have done otherwise, and that he bears no moral responsibility for having done what he did. But just what is it about situations of this kind that warrants the judgment that the threatened person is not morally responsible for his act?

This question may be approached by considering situations of the following kind. Jones decides for reasons of his own to do something, then someone threatens him with a very harsh penalty (so harsh that any reasonable person would submit to the threat) unless he does precisely that, and Jones does it. Will we hold Jones morally responsible for what he has done? I think this will depend on the roles we think were played, in leading him to act, by his original decision and by the threat.

One possibility is that $Jones_1$ is not a reasonable man: he is, rather, a man who does what he has once decided to do no matter what happens next and no matter what the cost. In that case, the threat actually exerted no effective force upon him. He acted without any regard to it, very much as if he were not aware that it had been made. If this is indeed the way it was, the situation did not involve coercion at all. The threat did not lead $Jones_1$ to do what he did. Nor was it in fact sufficient to have prevented him from doing otherwise: if his earlier decision had been to do something else, the threat would not have deterred him in the slightest. It seems evident that in these circumstances the fact that $Jones_1$ was threatened in no way reduces the moral responsibility he would otherwise bear for his act. This example, however, is not a counterexample either to the doctrine that coercion excuses or to the principle of alternate possibilities. For we have supposed that $Jones_1$ is a man upon whom the threat had no coercive effect and, hence, that it did not actually deprive him of alternatives to doing what he did.

Another possibility is that $Jones_2$ was stampeded by the threat. Given that threat, he would have performed that action regardless of what decision he had already made. The threat upset him so profoundly, more-over, that he completely forgot his own earlier decision and did what was demanded of him entirely because he was terrified of the penalty with which he was threatened. In this case, it is not relevant to his having per-formed the action that he had already decided on his own to perform it. When the chips were down he thought of nothing but the threat, and fear alone led him to act. The fact that at an earlier time Jones$_2$ had decided for his own reasons to act in just that way may be rele-vant to an evaluation of his character; he may bear full moral respon-sibility for having made *that* decision. But he can hardly be said to be morally responsible for his action. For he performed the action simply as a result of the coercion to which he was subjected. His earlier deci-sion played no role in bringing it about that he did what he did, and it would therefore be gratuitous to assign it a role in the moral evalua-tion of his action.

Now consider a third possibility. Jones$_3$ was neither stampeded by the threat nor indifferent to it. The threat impressed him, as it would impress any reasonable man, and he would have submitted to it wholeheartedly if he had not already made a decision that coincided with the one demanded of him. In fact, however, he performed the action in ques-tion on the basis of the decision he had made before the threat was issued. When he acted, he was not actually motivated by the threat but solely by the considerations that had originally commended the action to him. It was not the threat that led him to act, though it would have done so if he had not already provided himself with a sufficient motive for per-forming the action in question.

No doubt it will be very difficult for anyone to know, in a case like this one, exactly what happened. Did Jones$_3$ perform the action because of the threat, or were his reasons for acting simply those which had already persuaded him to do so? Or did he act on the basis of two motives, each of which was sufficient for his action? It is not impossi-ble, however, that the situation should be clearer than situations of this kind usually are. And suppose it is apparent to us that Jones$_3$ acted on the basis of his own decision and not because of the threat. Then I think we would be justified in regarding his moral responsibility for what he did as unaffected by the threat even though, since he would in any case have submitted to the threat, he could not have avoided doing what he did. It would be entirely reasonable for us to make the same judgment concerning his moral responsibility that we would have made if we had not known of the threat. For the threat did not in fact influence his performance of the action. He did what he did just as if the threat had not been made at all.

III

The case of Jones₃ may appear at first glance to combine coercion and moral responsibility, and thus to provide a counterexample to the doctrine that coercion excuses. It is not really so certain that it does so, however, because it is unclear whether the example constitutes a genuine instance of coercion. Can we say of Jones₃ that he was coerced to do something, when he had already decided on his own to do it and when he did it entirely on the basis of that decision? Or would it be more correct to say that Jones₃ was not coerced to do what he did, even though he himself recognized that there was an irresistible force at work in virtue of which he had to do it? My own linguistic intuitions lead me toward the second alternative, but they are somewhat equivocal. Perhaps we can say either of these things, or perhaps we must add a qualifying explanation to whichever of them we say.

This murkiness, however, does not interfere with our drawing an important moral from an examination of the example. Suppose we decide to say that Jones₃ was *not* coerced. Our basis for saying this will clearly be that it is incorrect to regard a man as being coerced to do something unless he does it *because* of the coercive force exerted against him. The fact that an irresistible threat is made will not, then, entail that the person who receives it is coerced to do what he does. It will also be necessary that the threat is what actually accounts for his doing it. On the other hand, suppose we decide to say that Jones₃ *was* coerced. Then we will be bound to admit that being coerced does not exclude being morally responsible. And we will also surely be led to the view that coercion affects the judgment of a person's moral responsibility only when the person acts as he does because he is coerced to do so—i.e., when the fact that he is coerced is what accounts for his action.

Whichever we decide to say, then, we will recognize that the doctrine that coercion excludes moral responsibility is not a particularized version of the principle of alternate possibilities. Situations in which a person who does something cannot do otherwise because he is subject to coercive power are either not instances of coercion at all, or they are situations in which the person may still be morally responsible for what he does if it is not because of the coercion that he does it. When we excuse a person who has been coerced, we do not excuse him because he was unable to do otherwise. Even though a person is subject to a coercive force that precludes his performing any action but one, he may nonetheless bear full moral responsibility for performing that action.

IV

To the extent that the principle of alternate possibilities derives its plausibility from association with the doctrine that coercion excludes moral responsibility, a clear understanding of the latter diminishes the appeal of the former. Indeed the case of Jones₃ may appear to do more than illuminate the relationship between the two doctrines. It may well seem to provide a decisive counterexample to the principle of alternate possibilities and thus to show that this principle is false. For the irresistibility of the threat to which Jones₃ is subjected might well be taken to mean that he cannot but perform the action he performs. And yet the threat, since Jones₃ performs the action without regard to it, does not reduce his moral responsibility for what he does.

The following objection will doubtless be raised against the suggestion that the case of Jones₃ is a counterexample to the principle of alternate possibilities. There is perhaps a sense in which Jones₃ cannot do otherwise than perform the action he performs, since he is a reasonable man and the threat he encounters is sufficient to move any reasonable man. But it is not this sense that is germane to the principle of alternate possibilities. His knowledge that he stands to suffer an intolerably harsh penalty does not mean that Jones₃, strictly speaking, *cannot* perform any action but the one he does perform. After all it is still open to him, and this is crucial, to defy the threat if he wishes to do so and to accept the penalty his action would bring down upon him. In the sense in which the principle of alternate possibilities employs the concept of "could have done otherwise." Jones₃'s inability to resist the threat does not mean that he cannot do otherwise than perform the action he performs. Hence the case of Jones₃ does not constitute an instance contrary to the principle.

I do not propose to consider in what sense the concept of "could have done otherwise" figures in the principle of alternate possibilities, nor will I attempt to measure the force of the objection I have just described. For I believe that whatever force this objection may be thought to have can be deflected by altering the example in the following way. Suppose someone—Black, let us say—wants Jones₄ to perform a certain action. Black is prepared to go to considerable lengths to get his way, but he prefers to avoid showing his hand unnecessarily. So he waits until Jones₄ is about to make up his mind what to do, and he does nothing unless it is clear to him (Black is an excellent judge of such things) that Jones₄ is going to decide to do something *other* than what he wants him to do. If it does become clear that Jones₄ is going to decide to do something else, Black takes effective steps to ensure that Jones₄ decides to do, and that he does do, what he wants him to do. Whatever Jones₄'s initial preferences and inclinations, then, Black will have his way.

What steps will Black take, if he believes he must take steps, in order to ensure that Jones₄ decides and acts as he wishes? Anyone with a theory concerning what "could have done otherwise" means may answer this question for himself by describing whatever measures he would regard as sufficient to guarantee that, in the relevant sense, Jones₄ cannot do otherwise. Let Black pronounce a terrible threat, and in this way both force Jones₄ to perform the desired action and prevent him from performing a forbidden one. Let Black give Jones₄ a potion, or put him under hypnosis, and in some such way as these generate in Jones₄ an irresistible inner compulsion to perform the act Black wants performed and to avoid others. Or let Black manipulate the minute processes of Jones₄'s brain and nervous system in some more direct way, so that causal forces running in and out of his synapses and along the poor man's nerves determine that he chooses to act and that he does act in the one way and not in any other. Given any conditions under which it will be maintained that Jones₄ cannot do otherwise, in other words, let Black bring it about that those conditions prevail. The structure of the example is flexible enough, I think, to find a way around any charge of irrelevance by accommodating the doctrine on which the charge is based.

Now suppose that Black never has to show his hand because Jones₄, for reasons of his own, decides to perform and does perform the very action Black wants him to perform. In that case, it seems clear, Jones₄ will bear precisely the same moral responsibility for what he does as he would have borne if Black had not been ready to take steps to ensure that he do it. It would be quite unreasonable to excuse Jones₄ for his action, or to withhold the praise to which it would normally entitle him, on the basis of the fact that he could not have done otherwise. This fact played no role at all in leading him to act as he did. He would have acted the same even if it had not been a fact, Indeed, everything happened just as it would have happened without Black's presence in the situation and without his readiness to intrude into it.

In this example there are sufficient conditions for Jones₄'s performing the action in question. What action he performs is not up to him. Of course it is in a way up to him whether he acts on his own or as a result of Black's intervention. That depends upon what action he himself is inclined to perform. But whether he finally acts on his own or as a result of Black's intervention, he performs the same action. He has no alternative but to do what Black wants him to do. If he does it on his own, however, his moral responsibility for doing it is not affected by the fact that Black was lurking in the background with sinister intent, since this intent never comes into play.

V

The fact that a person could not have avoided doing something is a sufficient condition of his having done it. But, as some of my examples show, this fact may play no role whatever in the explanation of why he did it. It may not figure at all among the circumstances that actually brought it about that he did what he did, so that his action is to be accounted for on another basis entirely. Even though the person was unable to do otherwise, that is to say, it may not be the case that he acted as he did *because* he could not have done otherwise. Now if someone had no alternative to performing a certain action but did not perform it because he was unable to do otherwise, then he would have performed exactly the same action even if he *could* have done otherwise. The circumstances that made it impossible for him to do otherwise could have been subtracted from the situation without affecting what happened or why it happened in any way. Whatever it was that actually led the person to do what he did, or that made him do it, would have led him to do it or made him do it even if it had been possible for him to do something else instead.

Thus it would have made no difference, so far as concerns his action or how he came to perform it, if the circumstances that made it impossible for him to avoid performing it had not prevailed. The fact that he could not have done otherwise clearly provides no basis for supposing that he *might* have done otherwise if he had been able to do so. When a fact is in this way irrelevant to the problem of accounting for a person's action it seems quite gratuitous to assign it any weight in the assessment of his moral responsibility. Why should the fact be considered in reaching a moral judgment concerning the person when it does not help in any way to understand either what made him act as he did or what, in other circumstances, he might have done?

This, then, is why the principle of alternate possibilities is mistaken. It asserts that a person bears no moral responsibility—that is, he is to be excused—for having performed an action if there were circumstances that made it impossible for him to avoid performing it. But there may be circumstances that make it impossible for a person to avoid performing some action without those circumstances in any way bringing it about that he performs that action. It would surely be no good for the person to refer to circumstances of this sort in an effort to absolve himself of moral responsibility for performing the action in question. For those circumstances, by hypothesis, actually had nothing to do with his having done what he did. He would have done precisely the same thing, and he would have been led or made in precisely the same way to do it, even if they had not prevailed.

We often do, to be sure, excuse people for what they have done when they tell us (and we believe them) that they could not have done otherwise. But this is because we assume that what they tell us serves to explain why they did what they did. We take it for granted that they are not being disingenuous, as a person would be who cited as an excuse the fact that he could not have avoided doing what he did but who knew full well that it was not at all because of this that he did it.

What I have said may suggest that the principle of alternate possibilities should be revised so as to assert that a person is not morally responsible for what he has done if he did it because he could not have done otherwise. It may be noted that this revision of the principle does not seriously affect the arguments of those who have relied on the original principle in their efforts to maintain that moral responsibility and determinism are incompatible. For if it was causally determined that a person perform a certain action, then it will be true that the person performed it because of those causal determinants. And if the fact that it was causally determined that a person perform a certain action means that the person could not have done otherwise, as philosophers who argue for the incompatibility thesis characteristically suppose, then the fact that it was causally determined that a person perform a certain action will mean that the person performed it because he could not have done otherwise. The revised principle of alternate possibilities will entail, on this assumption concerning the meaning of "could have done otherwise," that a person is not morally responsible for what he has done if it was causally determined that he do it. I do not believe, however, that this revision of the principle is acceptable.

Suppose a person tells us that he did what he did because he was unable to do otherwise; or suppose he makes the similar statement that he did what he did because he had to do it. We do often accept statements like these (if we believe them) as valid excuses, and such statements may well seem at first glance to invoke the revised principle of alternate possibilities. But I think that when we accept such statements as valid excuses it is because we assume that we are being told more than the statements strictly and literally convey. We understand the person who offers the excuse to mean that he did what he did *only because* he was unable to do otherwise, or *only because* he had to do it. And we understand him to mean, more particularly, that when he did what he did it was not because that was what he really wanted to do. The principle of alternate possibilities should thus be replaced, in my opinion, by the following principle: a person is not morally responsible for what he has done if he did it only because he could not have done otherwise. This principle does not appear to conflict with the view that moral responsibility is compatible with determinism.

The following may all be true: there were circumstances that made it impossible for a person to avoid doing something; these circumstances actually played a role in bringing it about that he did it, so that it is correct to say that he did it because he could not have done otherwise; the person really wanted to do what he did; he did it because it was what he really wanted to do, so that it is not correct to say that he did what he did only because he could not have done otherwise. Under these conditions, the person may well be morally responsible for what he has done. On the other hand, he will not be morally responsible for what he has done if he did it only because he could not have done otherwise, even if what he did was something he really wanted to do.

Human Freedom and the Self

Roderick Chisholm

A staff moves a stone, and is moved by a hand, which is moved by a man.
                                          Aristotle, *Physics*, 256a

1. The metaphysical problem of human freedom might be summarized in the following way: Human beings are responsible agents; but this fact appears to conflict with a deterministic view of human action (the view that every event that is involved in an act is caused by some other event); and it *also* appears to conflict with an indeterministic view of human action (the view that the act, or some event that is essential to the act, is not caused at all.) To solve the problem, I believe, we must make

somewhat far-reaching assumptions about the self or the agent—about the man who performs the act.

Perhaps it is needless to remark that, in all likelihood, it is impossible to say anything significant about this ancient problem that has not been said before.[1]

2. Let us consider some deed, or misdeed, that may be attributed to a responsible agent: one man, say, shot another. If the man *was* responsible for what he did, then, I would urge, what was to happen at the time of the shooting was something that was entirely up to the man himself. There was a moment at which it was true, both that he could have fired the shot and also that he could have refrained from firing it. And if this is so, then, even though he did fire it, he could have done something else instead. (He didn't find himself firing the shot "against his will," as we say.) I think we can say, more generally, then, that if a man is responsible for a certain event or a certain state of affairs (in our example, the shooting of another man), then that event or state of affairs was brought about by some act of his, and the act was something that was in his power either to perform or not to perform.

But now if the act which he *did* perform was an act that was also in his power *not* to perform, then it could not have been caused or determined by any event that was not itself within his power either to bring about or not to bring about. For example, if what we say he did was really something that was brought about by a second man, one who forced his hand upon the trigger, say, or who, by means of hypnosis, compelled him to perform the act, then since the act was caused by the *second* man it was nothing that was within the power of the *first* man to prevent. And precisely the same thing is true, I think, if instead of referring to a second man who compelled the first one, we speak instead of the *desires* and *beliefs* which the first man happens to have had. For if what we say he did was really something that was brought about by his own beliefs and desires, if these beliefs and desires in the particular situation in which he happened to have found himself caused him to do just what it was that we say he did do, then, since *they* caused it, he was unable to do anything other than just what it was that he did do. It makes no difference whether the cause of the deed was internal or external; if the cause was some state or event for which the man himself was not responsible, then he was not responsible for what we have been mistakenly calling his act. If a flood caused the poorly constructed dam to break, then, given the flood and the constitution of the dam, the break, we may say, *had* to occur and nothing could have happened in its place. And if the flood of desire caused the weak-willed man to give in then he, too, had to do just what it was that he did do and he was no more responsible than was the dam for the results that followed. (It is true, of course, that if the man is responsible for the beliefs and desires that he happens to have, then he may also be responsible for the things they lead him to do. But the question now becomes: *is* he responsible for the beliefs and desires he happens to have? If he is, then there was a time when they were within his power either to acquire or not to acquire, and we are left, therefore, with our general point.)

One may object: But surely if there were such a thing as a man who is really *good*, then he would be responsible for things that he would do; yet, he would be unable to do anything other than just what it is that he does do, since, being good, he will always choose to do what is best. The answer, I think, is suggested by a comment that Thomas Reid makes upon an ancient author. The author had said of Cato, "He was good because he could not be otherwise," and Reid observes: "This saying, if understood literally and strictly, is not the praise of Cato, but of his constitution, which was no more the work of Cato than his existence."[2] If Cato was himself responsible for the good things that he did, then Cato, as Reid suggests, was such that, although he had the power to do what was not good, he exercised his power only for that which was good.

All of this, if it is true, may give a certain amount of comfort to those who are tender-minded. But we should remind them that it also conflicts with a familiar view about the nature of God—with the view that St. Thomas Aquinas expresses saying that "every movement both of the will and of nature proceeds from God as the Prime Mover."[3] If the act of the sinner *did* proceed from God as the Prime Mover, then God was in the position of the second agent we just discussed—the man who forced the trigger finger, or the hypnotist—and the sinner, so-called, was *not* responsible for what he did. (This may be a bold assertion, in view of the history of western theology, but I must say that I have never encountered a single good reason for denying it.)

There is one standard objection to all of this and we should consider it briefly.

3. The objection takes the form of a stratagem—one designed to show that determinism (and divine providence) is consistent with human responsibility. The stratagem is one that was used by Jonathan Edwards and by many philosophers in the present century, most notably, G. E. Moore.[4]

One proceeds as follows: The expression

(a) He could have done otherwise,

it is argued, means no more nor less than

(b) If he had chosen to do otherwise, then he would have done otherwise.

(In place of "chosen," one might say "tried," "set out," "decided," "undertaken," or "willed.") The truth of statement (b), it is then pointed out, is consistent with determinism (and with divine providence); for even if all of the man's actions were causally determined, the man could still be such that, *if* he had chosen otherwise, then he would have done otherwise. What the murderer saw, let us suppose, along with his beliefs and desires, *caused* him to fire the shot; yet he was such that *if*, just then, he had chosen or decided *not* to fire the shot, then he would not have fired it. All of this is certainly possible. Similarly, we could say, of the dam, that the flood caused it to break and also that the dam was such that, *if* there had been no flood or any similar pressure, then the dam would have remained intact. And therefore, the argument proceeds, if (b) is consistent with determinism, and if (a) and (b) say the same thing, then (a) is also consistent with determinism; hence we can say that the agent *could* have done otherwise even though he was caused to do what he did do; and therefore determinism and moral responsibility are compatible.

Is the argument sound? The conclusion follows from the premises, but the catch, I think, lies in the first premise—the one saying that statement (a) tells us no more nor less than what statement (b) tells us. For (b), it would seem, could be true while (a) is false. That is to say, our man might be such that, if he had chosen to do otherwise, then he would have done otherwise, and yet *also* such that he could not have done otherwise. Suppose, after all, that our murderer could not have *chosen*, or could not have *decided*, to do otherwise. Then the fact that he happens also to be a man such that, if he had chosen not to shoot he would not have shot, then he could not have done anything other than just what it was that he did do. In a word: from our statement (b) above ("If he had chosen to do otherwise, then he would have done otherwise"), we cannot make an inference to (a) above ("He could have done otherwise") unless we can *also* assert:

(c) He could have chosen to do otherwise.

And therefore, if we must reject this third statement (c), then, even though we may be justified in asserting (b), we are not justified in asserting (a). If the man could not have chosen to do otherwise, then he would not have done otherwise—*even if* he was such that, if he *had* chosen to do otherwise, then he would have done otherwise.

The stratagem in question, then, seems to me not to work, and I would say, therefore, that the ascription of responsibility conflicts with a deterministic view of action.

4. Perhaps there is less need to argue that the ascription of responsibility also conflicts with an indeterministic view of action—with the view that the act, or some event that is essential to the act, is not caused at all. If the act—the firing of the shot—was not caused at all, if it was fortuitous or capricious, happening so to speak out of the blue, then, presumably, no one—and nothing—was responsible for the act. Our conception of action, therefore, should be neither deterministic nor indeterministic. Is there any other possibility?

5. We must not say that every event involved in the act is caused by some other event; and we must not say that the act is something that is not caused at all. The possibility that remains, therefore, is this: We should say that at least one of the events that are involved in the act is caused, not by any other events, but by something else instead. And this something else can only be the agent—the man. If there is an event that is caused, not by other events, but by the man, then there are some events involved in the act that are not caused by other events. But if the event in question is caused by the man then it *is* caused and we are not committed to saying that there is something involved in the act that is not caused at all.

But this, of course, is a large consequence, implying something of considerable importance about the nature of the agent or the man.

6. If we consider only inanimate natural objects, we may say that causation, if it occurs, is a relation between *events* or *states of affairs*. The dam's breaking was an event that was caused by a set of other events—the dam being weak, the flood being strong, and so on. But if a man is responsible for a particular deed, then, if what I have said is true, there is some event, or set of events, that is caused, *not* by other events or states of affairs, but by the agent, whatever he may be.

I shall borrow a pair of medieval terms, using them, perhaps, in a way that is slightly different from that for which they were originally intended. I shall say that when one event or state of affairs (or set of events or states of affairs) causes some other event or state of affairs, then we have an instance of *transeunt* causation. And I shall say that when an *agent*, as distinguished from an event, causes an event or state of affairs, then we have an instance of *immanent* causation.

The nature of what is intended by the expression "immanent causation" may be illustrated by this sentence from Aristotle's *Physics*. "Thus, a staff moves a stone, and is moved by a hand, which is moved by a man" (Book VII, Chap. 5, 256a, 6–8). If the man was responsible, then we have in this illustration a number of instances of causation—most of them transeunt but at least one of them immanent. What the staff did to the stone was an instance of transeunt causation, and thus we may describe it as a relation between events: "the motion of the staff caused the motion of the stone." And similarly for what the hand did to the staff: "the motion of the hand caused the motion of the staff." And, as we know from physiology, there are still other events which caused the motion of the hand. Hence we need not introduce the agent at this particular point, as Aristotle does—we *need* not, though we *may*. We *may* say that the hand was moved by the man, but we may *also* say that the motion of the hand was caused by the motion of certain muscles; and we may say that the motion of the muscles was caused by certain events that took place within the brain. But some event, and presumably one of those that took place within the brain, was caused by the agent and not by any other events.

There are, of course, objections to this way of putting the matter; I shall consider the two that seem to me to be most important.

7. One may object, firstly: "If the *man* does anything, then, as Aristotle's remark suggests, what he does is to move the *hand*. But he certainly does not do anything to his brain—he may not even know that he *has* a brain. And if he doesn't do anything to the brain, and if the motion of the hand was caused by something that happened within the brain, then there is no point in appealing to 'immanent causation' as being something incompatible with 'transeunt causation'—for the whole thing, after all, is a matter of causal relations among events or states of affairs."

The answer to this objection, I think, is this: It is true that the agent does not *do* anything with his brain, or to his brain, in the sense in which he *does* something with his hand and does something to the staff. But from this it does not follow that the agent was not the immanent cause of something that happened within his brain.

We should note a useful distinction that has been proposed by Professor A. I. Melden—namely, the distinction between "making something A happen" and "doing A."[5] If I reach for the staff and pick it up, then one of the things that I *do* is just that—reach for the staff and pick it up. And if it is something that I do, then there is a very clear sense in which it may be said to be something that I know that I do. If you ask me, "Are you doing something, or trying to do something, with the staff?", I will have no difficulty in finding an answer. But in doing something with the staff, I also make various things happen which are not in this same sense things that I do: I will make various air-particles move; I will free a number of blades of grass from the pressure that had been upon them; and I may cause shadow to move from one place to another. If these are merely things that I make happen, as distinguished from things that I do, then I may know nothing whatever about them; I may not have the slightest idea that, in moving the staff, I am bringing about any such thing as the motion of air-particles, shadows, and blades of grass.

We may say, in answer to the first objection, therefore, that it is true that our agent does nothing to his brain; but from this it does not follow that the agent is not the immanent cause of some event within his brain; for the brain event may be something which, like the motion of the air-particles, he made happen in picking up the staff. The only difference between the two cases is this: in each case, he made something happen when he picked up the staff; but in the one case—the motion of the air-particles or of the shadows—it was the motion of the staff that caused the event to happen; and in the other case—the event that took place in the brain—it was this event that caused the motion of the staff.

The point is, in a word, that whenever a man does something A, then (by "immanent causation") he makes a certain cerebral event happen, and this cerebral event (by "transeunt causation") makes A happen.

8. The second objection is more difficult and concerns the very concept of "immanent causation," or causation by an agent, as this concept is to be interpreted here. The concept is subject to a difficulty which has long been associated with that of the prime mover unmoved. We have said that there must be some event A, presumably some cerebral event, which is caused not by any other event, but by the agent. Since A was not caused by any other event, then the agent himself cannot be said to have undergone any change or produced any other event (such as "an act of will" or the like) which brought A about. But if, when the agent made A happen, there was no event involved other than A itself, no event which could be described as *making* A happen, what did the agent's causation consist of? What, for example, is the difference between A's just happening, and the agent's *causing* A to happen? We cannot attribute the difference to any event that took place within the agent. And so far as the event A itself is concerned, there would seem to be no discernible dif-

ference. Thus Aristotle said that the activity of the prime mover is nothing in addition to the motion that it produces, and Suarez said that "the action is in reality nothing but the effect as it flows from the agent."[6] Must we conclude, then, that there is no more to the man's action in causing event A than there is to the event A's happening by itself? Here we would seem to have a distinction without a difference—in which case we have failed to find a *via media* between a deterministic and an indeterministic view of action.

The only answer, I think, can be this: that the difference between the man's causing A, on the one hand, and the event A just happening, on the other, lies in the fact that, in the first case but not the second, the event A *was* caused and was caused by the man. There was a brain event A; the agent did, in fact, cause the brain event; but there was nothing that he did to cause it.

This answer may not entirely satisfy and it will be likely to provoke the following question: "But what are you really *adding* to the assertion that A happened when you utter the words 'The agent *caused* A to happen'?" As soon as we have put the question this way, we see, I think, that whatever difficulty we may have encountered is one that may be traced to the concept of causation generally—whether "immanent" or "transeunt." The problem, in other words, is not a problem that is peculiar to our conception of human action. It is a problem that must be faced by anyone who makes use of the concept of causation at all; and therefore, I would say, it is a problem for everyone but the complete indeterminist.

For the problem, as we put it, referring just to "immanent causation," or causation by an agent, was this: "What is the difference between saying, of an event A, that A just happened and saying that someone caused A to happen?" The analogous problem, which holds for "transeunt causation," or causation by an event, is this: "What is the difference between saying, of two events A and B, that B happened and then A happened, and saying that B's happening was the *cause* of A's happening?" And the only answer that one can give is this—that in the one case the agent was the cause of A's happening and in the other case event B was the cause of A's happening. The nature of transeunt causation is no more clear than is that of immanent causation.

9. But we may plausibly say—and there is a respectable philosophical tradition to which we may appeal—that the notion of immanent causation, or causation by an agent, is in fact more clear than that of transeunt causation, or causation by an event; and that it is only by understanding our own causal efficacy, as agents, that we can grasp the

concept of *cause* at all. Hume may be said to have shown that we do not derive the concept of *cause* from what we perceive of external things. How, then, do we derive it? The most plausible suggestion, it seems to me, is that of Reid, once again: namely that "the conception of an efficient cause may very probably be derived from the experience we have had . . . of our own power to produce certain effects."[7] If we did not understand the concept of immanent causation, we would not understand that of transeunt causation.

10. It may have been noted that I have avoided the term "free will" in all of this. For even if there is such a faculty as "the will," which somehow sets our acts agoing, the question of freedom, as John Locke said, is not the question *"whether the will be free"*; it is the question *"whether a man be free."*[8] For if there is a "will," as a moving faculty, the question is whether the man is free to will to do these things that he does will to do—and also whether the man is free *not* to will any of those things that he does will to do, and, again, whether he is free to will any of those things that he does not will to do. Jonathan Edwards tried to restrict himself to the question—"Is the man free to do what it is that he wills?"— but the answer to the question will not tell us whether the man is responsible for what it is that he *does* will to do. Using still another pair of medieval terms, we may say that the metaphysical problem of freedom does not concern the *actus imperatus*, it does not concern the question whether we are free to accomplish whatever it is that we will or set out to do; it concerns the *actus elicitus*, the question whether we are free to will or to set out to do those things that we do will or set out to do.

11. If we are responsible, and if what I have been trying to say is true, then we have a prerogative which some would attribute only to God: each of us, when we act, is a prime mover unmoved. In doing what we do, we cause certain events to happen, and nothing—or no one—causes us to cause those events to happen.

12. If we are thus prime movers unmoved and if our actions, or those for which we are responsible, are not causally determined, then they are not causally determined by our *desires*. And this means that the relation between what we want or what we desire, on the one hand, and what it is that we do, on the other, is not as simple as most philosophers would have it.

We may distinguish between what we might call the "Hobbist approach" and what we might call the "Kantian approach" to this question. The Hobbist approach is the one that is generally accepted at the present time, but the Kantian approach, I believe, is the one that is true. According to Hobbism, if we *know*, of some man, what his belief and desires happen to be and how strong they are, if we know what he feels certain of, what he desires more than anything else, and if we know the state of his body and what stimuli he is being subjected to, then we may *deduce*, logically, just what it is that he will do—or, more accurately, just what it is that he will try, set out, or undertake to do. Thus Professor Melden has said that "the connection between wanting and doing is logical."[9] But according to the Kantian approach to our problem, and this is the one that I would take, there is no such logical connection between wanting and doing, nor need there even be a causal connection. No set of statements about a man's desires, beliefs, and stimulus situation at any time implies any statement telling us what the man will try, set out, or undertake to do at that time. As Reid put it, though we may "reason from men's motives to their actions and, in many cases, with great probability," we can never do so "with absolute certainty."[10]

This means that, in one very strict sense of the terms, there can be no science of man. If we think of science as a matter of finding out what laws happen to hold, and if the statement of a law tells us what kinds of events are caused by what other kinds of events, then there will be human actions which we cannot explain by subsuming them under any laws. We cannot say, "It is causally necessary that, given such and such desires and beliefs, and being subject to such and such stimuli, the agent will do so and so." For at times the agent, if he chooses, may rise above his desires and do something else instead.

But all of this is consistent with saying that, perhaps more often than not, our desires do exist under conditions such that those conditions necessitate us to act. And we may also say, with Leibniz, that at other times our desires may "incline without necessitating."[. . .]

Notes

1. The general position to be presented here is suggested in the following writings among others: Aristotle, *Eudemian Ethics*, book II, ch. 6; *Nicomachean Ethics*, book III, chs 1–5; Thomas Reid, *Essays on the Active Powers of Man.* C.A. Campbell, "Is 'Free Will' a Pseudo-Problem?" *Mind*, n.s. 60 (1951), pp. 441–65; Roderick M. Chisholm, "Responsibility and Avoidability," and Richard Taylor, "Determination and the Theory of Agency," in Sidney Hook, ed., *Determinism and Freedom in the Age of Modern Science* (New York: New York University Press, 1958).

2. Thomas Reid, *Essays on the Active Powers of the Human Mind* (Cambridge MA: MIT Press, 1969; first published 1788), p. 261.

3. *Summa Theologia*, First Part of the Second Part, Question VI: "On the Voluntary and Involuntary."

4. Jonathan Edwards, *Freedom of the Will* (New Haven, Conn.: Yale University Press, 1957); G. E. Moore, *Ethics* (Home University Library, 1912), ch. 6.

5. A. I. Melden, *Free Action* (Oxford: Blackwell, 1961), especially ch. 3. Mr. Melden's own views, however, are quite the contrary of those proposed here.

6. Aristotle, *Physics*, book III, ch. 3; Suarez, *Disputations Metaphysicae*, Disputation 18, Section 10.

7. Reid, *Essays on the Active Powers*, p. 39.

8. John Locke, *Essay Concerning Human Understanding*, book II, ch. 21.

9. Melden, *Free Action*, p. 166.

10. Reid, *Essays on the Active Powers*, p. 291.

PART FOUR

IS THERE AN ENDURING SELF?

We cannot deny that we change a good deal during our lifetime. As time goes by, we change from being a baby into an adult and then change into an older person. This leads to an obvious question: Does the same self persist through all of these changes? This question becomes especially relevant when we approach death. Can we be sure that the death of our physical bodies ends all? Is it not at least logically possible that we might survive the destruction of our bodies?

John Perry addresses these issues in *A Dialogue on Personal Identity and Immortality*. The dialogue introduces us to three characters: Gretchen Weirob, a philosopher who is seriously injured in a motorcycle accident and who awaits her death in a hospital bed; Sam Miller, a chaplain and a longtime friend of Gretchen's; and Dave Cohen, a former student of Gretchen's. Sam tries to convince a skeptical Gretchen that it is quite possible that she might survive her looming death. His initial arguments are based on a "soul theory" of personal identity. But Gretchen raises serious objections to Sam's comforting words and an entertaining and thoughtful conversation about personal identity and life after death develops.

Our second reading introduces us to an Eastern way of thinking about the self. In his essay "The Buddhist Theory of 'No-Self'" Serge-Christophe Kolm describes a Buddhist way of dissolving the Western conception of a permanent self that persists through time. Kolm agrees that all of us are tempted to believe that there is such a permanent self. However, once we begin to see that this self really exists as a manifold of distinct elements, we understand that a *permanent self* is a creation of reason and imagination. It is a way of seeing and composing the world, but not an entity that really exists.

In "Where Am I?" Daniel Dennett explores what would happen to him and his sense of self if his brain were to be separated from his body. Dennett imagines that he is asked by the Pentagon to undergo such a brain–body separation operation so that his body can safely retrieve a nuclear warhead under Tulsa, Oklahoma, while his brain is safely located in a life-support system in the Spacecraft Center in Houston, Texas. After undergoing a successful operation, Dennett is initially confused and wants to know whether he is identical to his brain, which he calls "Yorek," or whether he is identical to his body, which he calls "Hamlet." After some hard reflecting, he gets used to the idea that he is in two places at the same time and that he has become a "scattered individual."

In "The Unimportance of Identity," Derek Parfit comes to similar conclusions about the nature of the self. He argues that questions about strict identity are not as central to our concept of self as it might at first appear. Strict identity is a one–one relation. But according to Parfit, a strict identity conception of self does not fare well in so-called *splitting cases*, that is, situations in which the self is divided into two surviving elements. He suggests that these splitting cases can be handled much more easily if we accept that what matters for the survival of the self is not the relationship of strict identity but rather relationships of degree.

In the final reading, "Feminist Perspectives on the Self," Diana Meyers gives an overview of recent feminist work on the self. According to many feminist writers, the standard conception of the self that emerges in Western Philosophy is predominately derived from the perspective of white, heterosexual, mostly economically advantaged men who have wielded social, economical, and political power. Such a self sees itself as a rational chooser and economic planner who is free of obligations and difficulties that arise in interpersonal relationships and unforeseen economical circumstances. Meyers explains why such a view of self is, in the eyes of many feminist writers, incomplete at best and seriously misleading at worst.

A Dialogue on Personal Identity and Immortality

John Perry

This is a record of conversations of Gretchen Weirob, a teacher of philosophy at a small midwestern college, and two of her friends. The conversations took place in her hospital room on the three nights before she died from injuries sustained in a motorcycle accident. Sam Miller is a chaplain and a long-time friend of Weirob's; Dave Cohen is a former student of hers.

The First Night

COHEN: I can hardly believe what you say, Gretchen. You are lucid and do not appear to be in great pain. And yet you say things are hopeless?

WEIROB: These devices can keep me alive for another day or two at most. Some of my vital organs have been injured beyond anything the doctors know how to repair, apart from certain rather radical measures I have rejected. I am not in much pain. But as I understand it that is not a particularly good sign. My brain was uninjured and I guess that's why I am as lucid as I ever am. The whole situation is a bit depressing, I fear. But here's Sam Miller, perhaps he will know how to cheer me up.

MILLER: Good evening, Gretchen. Hello, Dave. I guess there's not much point in beating around the bush, Gretchen; the medics tell me you're a goner. Is there anything I can do to help?

WEIROB: Crimenetley, Sam! You deal with the dying every day. Don't you have anything more comforting to say than "Sorry to hear you're a goner"?

MILLER: Well, to tell you the truth, I'm a little at a loss for what to say to you. Most people I deal with are believers like I am. We talk of the prospects for survival. I give assurance that God, who is just and merciful, would not permit such a travesty as that our short life on this earth should be the end of things. But you and I have talked about religious and philosophical issues for years. I have never been able to find in you the least inclination to believe in God; indeed, it's a rare day when you are sure that your friends have minds, or that you can see your own hand in front of your face, or that there is any reason to believe that the sun will rise tomorrow. How can I hope to comfort you with the prospect of life after death, when I know you will regard it as having no probability whatsoever?

WEIROB: I would not require so much to be comforted, Sam. Even the possibility of something quite improbable can be comforting, in certain situations. When we used to play tennis, I beat you no more than one time in twenty. But this was enough to establish the possibility of beating you on any given occasion, and by focusing merely on the possibility I remained eager to play. Entombed in a secure prison, thinking our situation quite hopeless, we may find unutterable joy in the information that there is, after all, the slimmest possibility of escape. Hope provides comfort, and hope does not always require probability. But we must believe that what we hope for is at least possible. So I will set an easier task for you. Simply persuade me that my survival after the death of this body, is *possible*, and I promise to be comforted. Whether you succeed or not, your attempts will be a diversion, for you know I like to talk philosophy more than anything else.

MILLER: But what is possibility, if not reasonable probability?

WEIROB: I do not mean possible in the sense of likely, or even in the sense of conforming to the known laws of physics or biology. I mean possible only in the weakest sense—of being conceivable, given the unavoidable facts. Within the next couple of days, this body will die. It will be buried and it will rot away. I ask that, given these facts, you explain to me how it even makes *sense* to talk of me continuing to exist. Just explain to me what it is I am to *imagine*, when I imagine surviving, that is consistent with these facts, and I shall be comforted.

MILLER: But then what is there to do? There are many conceptions of immortality, of survival past the grave, which all seem to make good sense. Surely not the possibility, but only the probability, can be doubted. Take your choice! Christians believe in life, with a body, in some Hereafter—the details vary, of course, from sect to sect. There is the Greek idea of the body as a prison, from which we escape at death—so that we have continued life without a body. Then there are conceptions in which, so to speak, we merge with the flow of being—

WEIROB: I must cut short your lesson in comparative religion. Survival means surviving, no more, no less. I have no doubts that I shall merge with being; plants will take root in my remains, and the chemicals that I am will continue to make their contribution to life. I am enough of an ecologist to be comforted. But survival, if it is anything, must offer comforts of a different sort, the comforts of *anticipation*. Survival means that tomorrow, or sometime in the future, there will be someone who will experience, who will see and touch and smell—or at the very least, think and reason and remember. And this person will be *me*. This person will be related to me in such a way that it is correct for me to anticipate, to look forward to, those future experiences. And I am related to her in such a way that it will be right for her to remember what I have thought and done, to feel remorse for what I have done wrong, and pride in what I have done right. And the only relation that supports anticipation and memory in this way, is simply *identity*. For it is never correct to anticipate, as happening to oneself, what will happen to someone else, is it? Or to remember, as one's own thoughts and deeds, what someone else did? So don't give me merger with being, or some such nonsense. Give me identity, or let's talk about baseball or fishing—but I'm sorry to get so emotional. I react strongly when words which mean one thing are used for another—when one talks about survival, but does not mean to say that the same person will continue to exist. It's such a sham!

MILLER: I'm sorry. I was just trying to stay in touch with the times, if you want to know the truth, for when I read modern theology or talk to my students who have studied Eastern religions, the notion of survival simply as continued existence of the same person seems out of date. Merger with Being! Merger with Being! That's all I hear. My own beliefs are quite simple, if somewhat vague. I think you will live again—with or without a body, I don't know—*I* draw comfort from my belief that you and I will be together again, after I also die. We will communicate, somehow. We will continue to grow spiritually. That's what I believe, as surely as I believe that I am sitting here. For I don't know how God could be excused, if this small sample of life is all that we are allotted; I don't know why He should have created us, if these few years of toil and torment are the end of it—

WEIROB: Remember our deal, Sam. You don't have to convince me that survival is probable, for we both agree you would not get to first base. You have only to convince me that it is possible. The only condition is that it be real survival we are talking about, not some up-to-date ersatz survival, which simply amounts to what any ordinary person would call totally ceasing to exist.

MILLER: I guess I just miss the problem, then. Of course, it's possible. You just continue to exist, after your body dies. What's to be defended or explained? You want details? Okay. Two people meet a thousand years from now, in a place that may or may not be part of this physical universe. I am one and you are the other. So you must have survived. Surely you can imagine that. What else is there to say?

WEIROB: But in a few days *I* will quit breathing, *I* will be put into a coffin, *I* will be buried. And in a few months or a few years *I* will be reduced to so much humus. That, I take it, is obvious, is given. How then can you say that I am one of these persons a thousand years from now?

Suppose I took this box of Kleenex and lit fire to it. It is reduced to ashes and I smash the ashes and flush them down the john. Then I say to you, go home and on the shelf will be *that very box of Kleenex*. It has survived! Wouldn't that be absurd? What sense could you make of it? And yet that is just what you say to me. I will rot away. And then, a thousand years later, there I will be. What sense does that make?

MILLER: There could be an *identical* box of Kleenex at your home, one just like it in every respect. And, in this sense, there is no difficulty in there being someone identical to you in the Hereafter, though your body has rotted away.

WEIROB: You are playing with words again. There could be an *exactly similar* box of Kleenex on my shelf. We sometimes use "identical" to mean "exactly similar," as when we speak of "identical twins." But I am using "identical" in a way in which *identity* is the condition of memory and correct anticipation. If I am told that tomorrow, though I will be dead, someone else that looks and sounds and thinks just like me will be alive—would that be comforting? Could I correctly *anticipate* having her experiences? Would it make sense for me to fear her pains and look forward to her pleasures? Would it be right for her to feel remorse at the harsh way I am treating you? Of course not. Similarity, however exact, is not identity. I use identity to mean there is but one thing. If I am to survive, there must be one person who lies in this bed now, and who talks to someone in your Hereafter ten or a thousand years from now. After all, what comfort could there be in the notion of a heavenly imposter, walking around getting credit for the few good things I have done?

MILLER: I'm sorry. I see that I was simply confused. Here is what I should have said. If you were merely a live human body—as the Kleenex body is merely cardboard and glue in a certain arrangement—then the death of your body would be the end of you. But surely you are more than that, fundamentally more than that. What is fundamentally you is not your body, but your soul or self or mind.

WEIROB: Do you mean these words, "soul," "self," or "mind" to come to the same thing?

MILLER: Perhaps distinctions could be made, but I shall not pursue them now. I mean the nonphysical and nonmaterial aspects of you, your consciousness. It is this that I get at with these words, and I don't think any further distinction is relevant.

WEIROB: Consciousness? I am conscious, for a while yet. I see, I hear, I think, I remember. But "to be conscious"—that is a verb. What is the subject of the verb, the thing which is conscious? Isn't it just this body, the same object that is overweight, injured, and lying in bed?— and which will be buried and not be conscious in a day or a week at the most?

MILLER: As you are a philosopher, I would expect you to be less muddled about these issues. Did Descartes not draw a clear distinction between the body and the mind, between that which is overweight, and that which is conscious? Your mind or soul is immaterial, lodged in your body while you are on earth. The two are intimately related but not identical. Now clearly, what concerns us in survival is your mind or soul. It is this which must be identical to the person before me now, and to the one I expect to see in a thousand years in heaven.

WEIROB: So I am not really this body, but a soul or mind or spirit? And this soul cannot be seen or felt or touched or smelt? That is implied, I take it, by the fact that it is immaterial?

MILLER: That's right. Your soul sees and smells, but cannot be seen or smelt.

WEIROB: Let me see if I understand you. You would admit that I am the very same person with whom you had lunch last week at Dorsey's?

MILLER: Of course you are.

WEIROB: Now when you say I am the same person, if I understand you, that is not a remark about this body you see and could touch and I fear can smell. Rather it is a remark about a soul, which you cannot see or touch or smell. The fact that the same body that now lies in front of you on the bed was across the table from you at Dorsey's— that would not mean that the same *person* was present on both occasions, if the same soul were not. And if, through some strange turn of events, the same soul were present on both occasions, but lodged in different bodies, then it *would* be the same person. Is that right?

MILLER: You have understood me perfectly. But surely, you understood all of this before!

WEIROB: But wait. I can repeat it, but I'm not sure I understand it. If you cannot see or touch or in any way perceive my soul, what makes you think the one you are confronted with now *is* the very same soul you were confronted with at Dorsey's?

MILLER: But I just explained. To say it is the same soul and to say it is the same person, are the same. And, of course, you are the same person you were before. Who else would you be if not yourself? You *were* Gretchen Weirob, and you *are* Gretchen Weirob.

WEIROB: But how do you know you are talking to Gretchen Weirob at all, and not someone else, say Barbara Walters or even Mark Spitz!

MILLER: Well, it's just obvious. I can see who I am talking to.

WEIROB: But all you can see is my body. You can see, perhaps, that the same body is before you now that was before you last week at Dorsey's. But you have just said that Gretchen Weirob is not a body but a soul. In judging that the same person is before you now as was before you then, you must be making a judgment about souls—which, you said, cannot be seen or touched or smelt or tasted. And so, I repeat, how do you know?

MILLER: Well, I *can* see that it is the same body before me now that was across the table at Dorsey's. And I know that the same soul is connected with the body now that was connected with it before. That's how I know it's you. I see no difficulty in the matter.

WEIROB: You reason on the principle, "Same body, same self."

MILLER: Yes.

WEIROB: And would you reason conversely also? If there were in this bed Barbara Walters' body—that is, the body you see every night on the news—would you infer that it was not me, Gretchen Weirob, in the bed?

MILLER: Of course I would. How would you have come by Barbara Walters' body?

WEIROB: But then merely extend this principle to Heaven, and you will see that your conception of survival is without sense. Surely this very body, which will be buried and as I must so often repeat, *rot away*, will not be in your Hereafter. Different body, different person. Or do you claim that a body can rot away on earth, and then still wind up somewhere else? Must I bring up the Kleenex box again?

MILLER: No, I do not claim that. But I also do not extend a principle, found reliable on earth, to such a different situation as is represented by the Hereafter. That a correlation between bodies and souls has been found on earth does not make it inconceivable or impossible that they should separate. Principles found to work in one circumstance may not be assumed to work in vastly altered circumstances. January and snow go together here, and one would be a fool to expect otherwise. But the principle does not apply in southern California.

WEIROB: So the principle, "same body, same soul," is a well-confirmed regularity, not something you know "a priori."

MILLER: By "a priori" you philosophers mean something which can be known without observing what actually goes on in the world—as I can know that two plus two equals four just by thinking about numbers, and that no bachelors are married, just by thinking about the meaning of "bachelor"?

WEIROB: Yes.

MILLER: Then you are right. If it was part of the meaning of "same body" that wherever we have the same body we have the same soul, it would have to obtain universally, in Heaven as well as on earth. But I just claim it is a generalization we know by observation on earth, and it need not automatically extend to Heaven.

WEIROB: But where do you get this principle? It simply amounts to a correlation between being confronted with the same body and being confronted with the same soul. To establish such a correlation in the first place, surely one must have some *other* means of judging sameness of soul. You do not have such a means; your principle is without foundation; either you really do not know the person before you now is Gretchen Weirob, the very same person you lunched with at Dorsey's, or what you do know has nothing to do with sameness of some immaterial soul.

MILLER: Hold on, hold on. You know I can't follow you when you start spitting out arguments like that. Now what is this terrible fallacy I'm supposed to have committed?

WEIROB: I'm sorry. I get carried away. Here—by way of a peace offering—have one of the chocolates Dave brought.

MILLER: Very tasty. Thank you.

WEIROB: Now why did you choose that one?

MILLER: Because it had a certain swirl on the top which shows that it is a caramel.

WEIROB: That is, a certain sort of swirl is correlated with a certain type of filling—the swirls with caramel, the rosettes with orange, and so forth.

MILLER: Yes. When you put it that way, I see an analogy. Just as I judged that the filling would be the same in this piece as in the last piece that I ate with such a swirl, so I judge that the soul with which I am conversing is the same as the last soul with which I conversed when sitting across from that body. We *see* the outer wrapping and infer what is inside.

WEIROB: But how did you come to realize that swirls of that sort and caramel insides were so associated?

MILLER: Why, from eating a great many of them over the years. Whenever I bit into a candy with that sort of swirl, it was filled with caramel.

WEIROB: Could you have established the correlation had you never been allowed to bite into a candy and never seen what happened when someone else bit into one? You could have formed the hypothesis, "same swirl, same filling." But could you have ever established it?

MILLER: It seems not.

WEIROB: So your inference, in a particular case, to the identity of filling from the identity of swirl would be groundless?

MILLER: Yes, it would. I think I see what is coming.

WEIROB: I'm sure you do. Since you can never, so to speak, bite into my soul, can never see or touch it, you have no way of testing your hypothesis that sameness of body means sameness of self.

MILLER: I daresay you are right. But now I'm a bit lost. What is supposed to follow from all of this?

WEIROB: If, as you claim, identity of persons consisted in identity of immaterial unobservable souls, then judgments of personal identity of the sort we make every day whenever we greet a friend or avoid a pest are really judgments about such souls.

MILLER: Right.

WEIROB: But if such judgments were really about souls, they would all be groundless and without foundation. For we have no direct method of observing sameness of soul, and so—and this is the point made by the candy example—we can have no indirect method either.

MILLER: That seems fair.

WEIROB: But our judgments about persons are not all simply groundless and silly, so we must not be judging of immaterial souls after all.

MILLER: Your reasoning has some force. But I suspect the problem lies in my defense of my position, and not the position itself. Look here—there *is* a way to test the hypothesis of a correlation after all. When I entered the room, I expected you to react just as you did—argumentatively and skeptically. Had the person with this body reacted completely differently perhaps I would have been forced to conclude it was not you. For example, had she complained about not being able to appear on the six o'clock news, and missing Harry Reasoner, and so forth, I might eventually have been persuaded it *was* Barbara Walters and not you. Similarity of psychological characteristics—a person's attitudes, beliefs, memories, prejudices, and the like—is observable. These are correlated with identity of body on the one side, and of course with sameness of soul on the other. So the correlation between body and soul can be established after all by this intermediate link.

WEIROB: And how do you know that?

MILLER: Know what?

WEIROB: That where we have sameness of psychological characteristics, we have sameness of soul.

MILLER: Well, now you are really being just silly. The soul or mind is just that which is responsible for one's character, memory, belief. These are aspects of the mind, just as one's height, weight, and appearance are aspects of the body.

WEIROB: Let me grant for the sake of argument that belief, character, memory, and so forth are states of mind. That is, I suppose, I grant that what one thinks and feels is due to the states one's mind is in at that time. And I shall even grant that a mind is an immaterial thing—though I harbor the gravest doubts that this is so. I do not see how it follows that similarity of such traits requires, or is evidence to the slightest degree, for identity of the mind or soul.

Let me explain my point with an analogy. If we were to walk out of this room, down past the mill and out towards Wilbur, what would we see?

MILLER: We would come to the Blue River, among other things.

WEIROB: And how would you recognize the Blue River? I mean, of course if you left from here, you would scarcely expect to hit the Platte or Niobrara. But suppose you were actually lost, and came across the Blue River in your wandering, just at that point where an old dam partly blocks the flow. Couldn't you recognize it?

MILLER: Yes, I'm sure as soon as I saw that part of the river I would again know where I was.

WEIROB: And how would you recognize it?

MILLER: Well, the turgid brownness of the water, the sluggish flow, the filth washed up on the banks, and such.

WEIROB: In a word, the states of the water which makes up the river at the time you see it.

MILLER: Right.

WEIROB: If you saw the blue clean water, with bass jumping, you would know it wasn't the Blue River.

MILLER: Of course.

WEIROB: So you expect, each time you see the Blue, to see the water, which makes it up, in similar states—not always exactly the same, for sometimes it's a little dirtier, but by and large similar.

MILLER: Yes, but what do you intend to make of this?

WEIROB: Each time you see the Blue, it consists of *different* water. The water that was in it a month ago may be in Tuttle Creek Reservoir or in the Mississippi or in the Gulf of Mexico by now. So the *similarity* of states of water, by which you judge the sameness of river, does not require *identity* of the water which is in those states at these various times.

MILLER: And?

WEIROB: And so just because you judge as to personal identity by reference to similarity of states of mind, it does not follow that the mind, or soul, is the same in each case. My point is this. For all you know, the immaterial soul which you think is lodged in my body might change from day to day, from hour to hour, from minute to minute, replaced each time by another soul psychologically similar. You cannot see it or touch it, so how would you know?

MILLER: Are you saying I don't really know who you are?

WEIROB: Not at all. *You* are the one who says personal identity consists in sameness of this immaterial, unobservable, invisible, untouchable soul. I merely point out that *if* it did consist in that, you *would* have no idea who I am. Sameness of body would not necessarily mean sameness of person. Sameness of psychological characteristics would not necessarily mean sameness of person. I am saying that if you do know who I am then you are wrong that personal identity consists in sameness of immaterial soul.

MILLER: I see. But wait. I believe my problem is that I simply forgot a main tenet of my theory. The correlation can be established in my own case. I know that *my* soul and my body are intimately and consistently found together. From this one case I can generalize, at least as concerns life in this world, that sameness of body is a reliable sign of sameness of soul. This leaves me free to regard it as intelligible, in the case of death, that the link between the particular soul and the particular body it has been joined with is broken.

WEIROB: This would be quite an extrapolation, wouldn't it, from one case directly observed, to a couple of billion in which only the body is observed? For I take it that we are in the habit of assuming, for every person now on earth, as well as those who have already come and gone, that the principle "one body, one soul" is in effect.

MILLER: This does not seem an insurmountable obstacle. Since there is nothing special about my case, I assume the arrangement I find in it applies universally until given some reason to believe otherwise. And I never have been.

WEIROB: Let's let that pass. I have another problem that is more serious. How is it that you know in your own case that there is a single soul which has been so consistently connected with your body?

MILLER: Now you really cannot be serious, Gretchen. How can I doubt that I am the same person I was? Is there anything more clear and distinct, less susceptible to doubt? How do you expect me to prove anything to you, when you are capable of denying my own continued existence from second to second? Without knowledge of our own identity, everything we think and do would be senseless. How could I think if I did not suppose that the person who begins my thought is the one who completes it? When I act, do I not assume that the person who forms the intention is the very one who performs the action?

WEIROB: But I grant you that a single *person* has been associated with your body since you were born. The question is whether one immaterial soul has been so associated—or more precisely, whether you are in a position to know it. You believe that a judgment that one and the same person has had your body all these many years is a judgment that one and the same immaterial soul has been lodged in it. I say that such judgments concerning the soul are totally mysterious, and that if our knowledge of sameness of persons consisted in knowledge of sameness of immaterial soul, it too would be totally mysterious. To point out, as you do, that it is not mysterious, but perhaps the most secure knowledge we have, the foundation of all reason and action, is simply to make the point that it cannot consist of knowledge of identity of an immaterial soul.

MILLER: You have simply asserted, and not established, that my judgment that a single soul has been lodged in my body these many years is mysterious.

WEIROB: Well, consider these possibilities. One is that a single soul, one and the same, has been with this body I call mine since it was born. The other is that one soul was associated with it until five years ago and then another, psychologically similar, inheriting all the old memories and beliefs, took over. A third hypothesis is that every five years a new soul takes over. A fourth is that every five minutes a new soul takes over. The most radical is that there is a constant flow of souls through this body, each psychologically similar to the preceding, as there is a constant flow of water molecules down the Blue. What evidence do I have that the first hypothesis, the "single soul hypothesis" is true, and not one of the others? Because I am the same person I was five minutes or five years ago? But the issue in question is simply whether from sameness of person, which isn't in doubt, we can infer sameness of soul. Sameness of body? But how do I establish a stable relationship between soul and body? Sameness of thoughts and sensations? But they are in constant flux. By the nature of the case, if the soul cannot be observed, it cannot be observed to be the same. Indeed, no sense has ever been assigned to the phrase "same soul." Nor could any sense be attached to it! One would have to say what a single soul looked like or felt like, how an encounter with a single soul at different times differed from encounters with different souls. But this can hardly be done, since a soul according to your conception doesn't look or feel like *anything* at all. And so of course "souls" can afford no principle of identity. And so they cannot be used to bridge the gulf between my existence now and my existence in the hereafter.

MILLER: Do you doubt the existence of your own soul?

WEIROB: I haven't based my argument on there being no immaterial souls of the sort you describe, but merely on their total irrelevance to questions of personal identity, and so to questions of personal survival. I do indeed harbor grave doubts whether there are any immaterial souls of the sort to which you appeal. Can we have a notion of a soul unless we have a notion of the *same* soul? But I hope you do not think that means I doubt my own existence. I think I lie here, overweight and conscious. I think you can see me, not just some outer wrapping, for I think I am just a live human body. But that is not the basis of my argument. I give you these souls. I merely observe that they can by their nature provide no principle of personal identity.

MILLER: I admit I have no answer.

I'm afraid I do not comfort you, though I have perhaps provided you with some entertainment. Emerson said that a little philosophy turns one away from religion, but that deeper understanding brings one back. I know no one who has thought so long and hard about philosophy as you have. Will it never lead you back to a religious frame of mind?

WEIROB: My former husband used to say that a little philosophy turns one away from religion, and more philosophy makes one a pain in the neck. Perhaps he was closer to the truth than Emerson.

MILLER: Perhaps he was. But perhaps by tomorrow night I will have come up with a better argument.

WEIROB: I hope I live to hear it.

NOTE

THE FIRST NIGHT: The arguments against the position that personal identity consists in identity of an immaterial soul are similar to those found in John Locke. "Of Identity and Diversity," chapter 27 of Book II of the *Essay Concerning Human Understanding*. This chapter first appeared in the second edition of 1694.

The Buddhist Theory of 'No-Self'

Serge-Christophe Kolm   *(Translated by Martin Thom)*

. . . For Buddhism it is clear, therefore, that *badness is unhappiness*. The true unhappiness, however, is not poverty but attachment, which is virtually its opposite, and the bad that there is in attaching oneself consists not in the attachment but in the self that is attached. Fortunately, however, this 'self' does not really exist, it is merely an illusion. One simply has to become aware of this for one's attachments, and therefore one's miseries, to cease.

In order to prove that the 'self' does not exist, Buddhism employs a fairly impressive argument. It consists in considering the person as a set of simple elements which has no reality in itself but only in the mind of the observer. And one is advised to apply this perspective to oneself, whilst taking great care to ensure that the corresponding knowledge is itself a set of elements belonging to those that it uncovers. If one genuinely succeeds in bringing off this ploy, all discomfort would seem to disappear. One would also seem to require more than one life to understand it, and several to apply it, declares the *tathagata* Guatama (the Tibetan Milarepa, a long time after him, is the only one to have effected this in a single life). All the more reason, then, to start straightaway.

One begins by acknowledging that a person is composed of several elements. The profane person would see this as a 'decomposition' of the still perceptible person into several elements. One would then make him see that what he believed to be a person *is only* this set of elements that he stubbornly persisted in regarding as a whole: there is nothing else, the world is empty of 'self'.

The West has long been habituated to such analytic dismantling of being. From Plato, through Descartes to Freud, we find a division between appetite, reason and mind, or we hear of the ghost in the machine, or of id, ego and superego, or of conscious and subconscious, or of conscious, unconscious and preconscious, or of the cognitive, the conative and the affective, etc. But the dismantling that the Buddha (a century before Plato) proposes is infinitely more refined than the crude divisions into two or three elements imagined by Westerners. Even when Hume says, much as a Buddhist would, that 'the mind is only a bundle or collection of different perceptions linked by causalities, he only grasps one out of the six *skandhas* (it may be that he employs the word 'perception' in a slightly wider sense, but he is hardly explicit about this).

Buddhism is concerned with elementary or simple, indecomposable elements, ontological 'atoms', as it were, which are said by it to be the only things enjoying any reality, and which are called *dharmas* in Sanskrit (*dhammas* in Pali). This word also refers to the Buddha's doctrine, a double reference which is frequent in Buddhist language (*dharma* has many other meanings also, and although most Buddhist terms have several meanings it is probably the richest of them all). As a consequence, the first two words of the Buddhist *credo, ye dhamma*, mean both 'I follow the doctrine' and 'I am only [composed of] simple elements.' If these two apparently very different meanings coexist, it is because the deepest meaning of *dharma* is 'ultimate reality' (or 'ultimate truth'). These *dharma* elements occur in many different forms. The elementary manuals in the monasteries describe several dozen of them, but several hundred are said to exist. These types of *dharma* are classed in different ways, according to different criteria. Before being ordained as *bhikkhus*, the novices must learn three of these classifications: in terms of *skandhas*, in terms of *ayatanas*, and in terms of *dhatus*. The most famous is the classification in terms of *skandhas* or 'aggregates' (of *dharmas*), which are five in number. To begin with, there are the ten properties of matter, of material things which, where a person is concerned, means his body and the things which he owns, with the body referring also to his ideas, thoughts and mental images. Then there are the sensations of the six senses (the sixth sense involves perception and sensation of ideas, thoughts and mental images by the mental and cerebral organ—an expression that John Locke was later to reinvent). Then there are the fifty-eight volitions, impulses or 'mental formations'. Finally, the consciousnesses of all the above crown the whole series. The classification into *ayatanas* obeys a cognitive criterion; its twelve categories are the six senses and the things that they know, the latter being the sixty-four types of mental *dharma*. The division into *dhatus* serves to describe the 'current' (*santana*) of causal relations between *dharmas* which seem to constitute an 'individual' (*pudgala*). It consists of eighteen classes, adding the consciousnesses of the corresponding properties–perceptions–sensations to the twelve of the preceding classification. But Buddhism sometimes puts itself at the level of modern scholarship by distinguishing three categories, matter, spirit and forces, a classification which it teaches to small children and to them only. The dual division between spirit and matter is also present.

The important point to note is that, once the person is dissolved in this way, Buddhism sees no reason to reassemble these elements into so-called individuals. It dismantles the human machine conceptually, and with great finesse, but then it disdains to put it together again. Man remains in detached and scattered pieces. A Buddhist observing you will see a pile of elements, a bag containing several hundred types of things, an aggregate of aggregates, a flux of events, a current of causal relations, but not *you*. The Buddhist gaze is a ray which disintegrates being. It is fortunate, then, that it is himself that a Buddhist will spend his time thus scrutinizing.

What thus is this thing which so interests people, which activates their passions, which they care for so intensely, about which they talk so much, their 'self'? It is a concept, a construction of the reason and of the imagination, a way of seeing and of composing the world, but not an entity which really exists. In other words, it is an *illusion*. But does not man excel most at transforming his ideas into suffering? The idea of the 'self', Buddhism says, is the heart of all pain. The worst possible thing to do would therefore be to reassemble the robot, and to believe that this montage on the part of the mind has a real existence.

The idea of the 'self' is not the only thing, Buddhism generously adds, to which this argument applies. The same is true of every mental construction. For instance, a cart consists of wheels, shafts, frame, etc. It *is* these elements; the entity 'cart' is a creature of the mind, an illusion. Or, to put it another way, one must not say that this fruit *has* this form, this colour, this smell, but rather that this fruit *is* this form and this colour and this smell and so on. Likewise, the mind doesn't *have* sensations, sentiments, ideas, volitions, etc., but what one calls 'mind' is these things. And the 'self' is that plus material elements. But to believe in a cart or in a pear does not have the same consequences as believing in oneself.

The main conclusion we can draw from this is that the 'self' is a mental construction, and by realizing this one may suppress pain. Precise analysis of the causes of suffering, of the perceptions which bring it, of its sensation of the consciousness of these facts, enables one either to remove this conscious sensation or to take a detached and objective view of it, and thereby to remove the pain. It is worth noting that Buddhism claims that this latter method is its own peculiar achievement, arrived at thanks to the no-self (the cutting off of sensation, reputed to have been the means employed by the Buddha's last *guru,* did not satisfy the Buddha, inducing him to search for his own answer by embarking upon a long meditation, from which he was to emerge 'awakened' to the solution.) At any rate, more or less training is required to produce these results. This is particularly the case with physical sufferings, where one has to overcome the danger and the fear that its absence would deprive us of the warning that the body is incurring some serious destruction. And things are much easier in the case of self-love, jealousy, hatred, pride, and of shame, honour or love! When one understands the causes and mechanisms of suffering, when one becomes aware of their basic sequences, suffering ceases. In the West, Spinoza (in his *Ethics,* in particular) had certain intuitions about this phenomenon, but he provided no account of the precise mode of functioning, or even of the structure of the psyche such as would enable one to understand it, and such as Buddhism provides. One is tempted, however, to improve the latter doctrine by saying: only strive to dismantle mentally those things which do you harm; attach yourself when it is possible and painless or agreeable, disengage yourself when it ceases to be so; opt for the agreeable side of things, and only analyse the rest in a Buddhist manner! This should be all the more possible that Buddhist psychology provides all the warning and knowledge which are required in order to prevent that a voluntary attachment turns into a sadistic master.

In this diagnosis of the cause of human unhappiness, and therefore in the therapeutic practice which derives from it, Buddhism proves to be the exact opposite of the Western tradition (which includes both Marx and Freud). The latter sees unhappiness, despair, neurosis, alienation, etc. in human beings who are divided, in fragments and internally dismembered, and equilibrium, the necessary condition for happiness (and a concept reminiscent of that of *nirvana*), in the integrated personality. Buddhism, by contrast, regards the latter as the cause of all ills. In order to remedy it, it shatters man (the illusion of man in man's eyes) and is only too glad to leave him in pieces. Is there then a fundamental contradiction between these two theories, each of which is firmly anchored in a tradition? The important thing to note is that the divisions of the personality identified by these two traditions are by no means the same. In Buddhism, the elements are psychological categories which, although connected, belong to different planes, whilst for Freud, for example, the superego and id may collide head-on over particular choices.

To be more precise, however large the number of 'things' (or, more exactly, of 'facts') Buddhism sees in an 'individual', there is one which he will not find there, namely, the 'I', the heart of being, which would be at once the subject of volitions and the object of suffering, and therefore a link between desire and *dukkha*. Chapter 19 in Kolm (1982)[1] analyses precisely and in detail this question of the 'I', and it explains that Buddhist advanced philosophy considers in fact many kinds of 'I', some of which are real by definition or by nature and some of which are illusory. It is the illusion of the 'I in itself', both based upon and providing the basis for desires and attachments, which Buddhists hold to be the specific cause common to all sufferings. Critical examination of the 'self' enables one to show that an individual contains no entity of this sort. When, therefore, one has succeeded in realizing this and in convincing oneself of it, both desires and pains fade away.

Having thus presented a more detailed account of the Buddhist conception of the self, we are now in a better position to gauge whether it can be reconciled with the theory of choices. If the 'self' is simply an illusion, what reality can the 'order of preferences' have? If it is composed of various 'aggregates' and specified elements, can the whole of behaviour be explained in terms of this ultra-simple entity? If everything is provisional, 'impermanent' and in a perpetual flux of change, as Buddhism declares it to be, what can the stability of these preferences be worth? If 'everything has a cause' and 'everything is determined', which is another base of this philosophy, it applies to individual's actions, and can one then speak of a person's free choice, or even of choice at all? And if 'I' does not exist, who is it that does the choosing?

An illusion is something quite real for the person observing someone who is in a state of illusion (his theoretician, as it were), and if this illusion guides or influences its victim's acts, one can perhaps describe this effect in terms of the theory of choices. But, for a Buddhist, the illusion of the *self* has a crucial effect on the decisions of a non-Buddhist or, more exactly, on non-Buddhist decisions. Only an *arahant*, because he has understood, is an exception to this, but he is a rare phenomenon and undoubtedly acts very little. On the other hand, the action entailed by the theory of choices is indeed caused by constraints and preferences, which are themselves caused by something else. The instability of preferences, for its part, does not obstruct the pure theory of choices which dates them; it may, however, hinder certain of its practical applications. Buddhism states that everything changes, everything disappears, without specifying the speed of this process or the delays that occur. It may take a lifetime, or an aeon. Finally, the fact that out of five 'aggregates' one may only derive one 'self' does not necessarily imply that one can-

[1]S. C. Kolm (1982). *Le Bonheur-liberté*.

not derive an order of preferences from them. For the *perceptions* of the available alternatives produce more or less agreeable sensations, and this gives rise to an order which is a *mental and volitional formation*, all of this being liable to be more or less *conscious* (with certainly a higher degree of rationality in the sense of transitivity the more conscious it is). . . .

Where Am I?

Daniel C. Dennett

Now that I've won my suit under the Freedom of Information Act, I am at liberty to reveal for the first time a curious episode in my life that may be of interest not only to those engaged in research in the philosophy of mind, artificial intelligence, and neuroscience but also to the general public.

Several years ago, I was approached by Pentagon officials who asked me to volunteer for a highly dangerous and secret mission. In collaboration with NASA and Howard Hughes, the Department of Defense was spending billions to develop a Supersonic Tunneling Underground Device, or STUD. It was supposed to tunnel through the earth's core at great speed and deliver a specially designed atomic warhead "right up the Red's missile silos," as one of the Pentagon brass put it.

The problem was that in an early test they had succeeded in lodging a warhead about a mile deep under Tulsa, Oklahoma, and they wanted me to retrieve it for them. "Why me?" I asked. Well, the mission involved some pioneering applications of current brain research, and they had heard of my interest in brains and of course my Faustian curiosity and great courage and so forth. . . . Well, how could I refuse? The difficulty that brought the Pentagon to my door was that the device I'd been asked to recover was fiercely radioactive, in a new way. According to monitoring instruments, something about the nature of the device and its complex interactions with pockets of material deep in the earth had produced radiation that could cause severe abnormalities in certain tissues of the brain. No way had been found to shield the brain from these deadly rays, which were apparently harmless to other tissues and organs of the body. So it had been decided that the person sent to recover the device should *leave his brain behind*. It would be kept in a safe place where it could execute its normal control functions by elaborate radio links. Would I submit to a surgical procedure that would completely remove my brain, which would then be placed in a life-support system at the Manned Spacecraft Center in Houston? Each input and output pathway, as it was severed, would be restored by a pair of microminiaturized radio transceivers, one attached precisely to the brain, the other to the nerve stumps in the empty cranium. No information would be lost, all the connectivity would be preserved. At first I was a bit reluctant. Would it really work? The Houston brain surgeons encouraged me. "Think of it," they said, "as a mere *stretching* of the nerves. If your brain were just moved over an *inch* in your skull, that would not alter or impair your mind. We're simply going to make the nerves indefinitely elastic by splicing radio links into them."

I was shown around the life-support lab in Houston and saw the sparkling new vat in which my brain would be placed, were I to agree. I met the large and brilliant support team of neurologists, hematologists, biophysicists, and electrical engineers, and after several days of discussions and demonstrations, I agreed to give it a try. I was subjected to an enormous array of blood tests, brain scans, experiments, interviews, and the like. They took down my autobiography at great length, recorded tedious lists of my beliefs, hopes, fears, and tastes. They even listed my favorite stereo recordings and gave me a crash session of psychoanalysis.

The day for surgery arrived at last and of course I was anesthetized and remember nothing of the operation itself. When I came out of anesthesia, I opened my eyes, looked around, and asked the inevitable, the traditional, the lamentably hackneyed postoperative question: "Where am I?" The nurse smiled down at me. "You're in Houston," she said, and I reflected that this still had a good chance of being the truth one way or another. She handed me a mirror. Sure enough, there were the tiny antennae poling up through their titanium ports cemented into my skull.

"I gather the operation was a success," I said. "I want to go see my brain." They led me (I was a bit dizzy and unsteady) down a long corridor and into the life-support lab. A cheer went up from the assembled support team, and I responded with what I hoped was a jaunty salute. Still feeling lightheaded, I was helped over to the life-support vat. I peered through the glass. There, floating in what looked like ginger ale, was undeniably a human brain, though it was almost covered with printed circuit chips, plastic tubules, electrodes, and other paraphernalia. "Is that mine?" I asked. "Hit the output transmitter switch there on the side of the vat and see for yourself," the project director replied. I moved the switch to OFF, and immediately slumped, groggy and nauseated, into the arms of the technicians, one of whom kindly restored the switch to its ON position. While I recovered my equilibrium and composure, I thought to myself: "Well, here I am sitting on a folding chair, staring through a piece of plate glass at my own brain. . . . But wait," I said to myself, "shouldn't I have thought, 'Here I am, suspended in a bubbling fluid, being stared at by my own eyes'?" I tried to think this latter thought. I tried to project into the tank, offering it hopefully to my brain, but I failed to carry off the exercise with any conviction. I tried again. "Here am *I*, Daniel Dennett, suspended in a bubbling fluid, being stared at by my own eyes." No, it just didn't work. Most puzzling and confusing. Being a philosopher of firm physicality conviction, I believed unswervingly that the tokening of my thoughts was occurring somewhere in my brain: yet, when I thought "here I am," where the thought occurred to me was *here*, outside the vat, where I, Dennett, was standing staring at my brain.

I tried and tried to think myself into the vat, but to no avail. I tried to build up to the task by doing mental exercises. I thought to myself, "The sun is shining *over there*," five times in rapid succession, each time mentally ostending a different place: in order, the sunlit corner of the lab, the visible front lawn of the hospital, Houston, Mars, and Jupiter. I found I had little difficulty in getting my "there"'s to hop all over the celestial map with their proper references. I could loft a "there" in an instant through the farthest reaches of space, and then aim the next "there" with pinpoint accuracy at the upper left quadrant of a freckle on my arm. Why was I having such trouble with "there"? "Here in Houston" worked well enough, and so did "here in the lab," and even "here in this part of the lab," but "here in the vat" always seemed merely an unmeant mental mouthing. I tried closing my eyes while thinking it. This seemed to help, but still I couldn't manage to pull it off, except perhaps for a fleeting instant. I couldn't be sure. The discovery that I couldn't be sure was also unsettling. How did I know *where* I meant by "here" when I thought "here"? Could I *think* I meant one place when in fact I meant another? I didn't see how that could be admitted without untying the few bonds of intimacy between a person and his own mental life that had survived the onslaught of the brain scientists and philosophers, the physicalists and behaviorists. Perhaps I was incorrigible about where I *meant* when I said "here." But in my present circumstances it seemed that either I was doomed by sheer force of mental habit to thinking systematically false indexical thoughts, or where a person is (and hence where his thoughts are tokened for purposes of semantic analysis) is not necessarily where his brain, the physical seat of his soul, resides. Nagged by confusion, I attempted to orient myself by falling back on a favorite philosopher's ploy. I began naming things.

"Yorick," I said aloud to my brain, "you are my brain. The rest of my body, seated in this chair, I dub 'Hamlet.'" So here we all are: Yorick's my brain, Hamlet's my body, and I am Dennett. *Now*, where am I? And when I think "where am I?" where's that thought tokened? Is it tokened in my brain, lounging about in the vat, or right here between my ears where it *seems* to be tokened? Or nowhere? Its *temporal* coordinates give me no trouble; must it not have spatial coordinates as well? I began making a list of the alternatives.

1. *Where Hamlet goes, there goes Dennett.* This principle was easily refuted by appeal to the familiar brain-transplant thought experiments so enjoyed by philosophers. If Tom and Dick switch brains, Tom is the fellow with Dick's former body—just ask him; he'll claim to be Tom, and tell you the most intimate details of Tom's autobiography. It was clear enough, then, that my current body and I could part company, but not likely that I could be separated from my brain. The rule of thumb that emerged so plainly from the thought experiments was that in a brain-transplant operation, one wanted to be the *donor*, not the recipient. Better to call such an operation a *body* transplant, in fact. So perhaps the truth was,

2. *Where Yorick goes, there goes Dennett.* This was not at all appealing, however. How could I be in the vat and not about to go anywhere, when I was so obviously outside the vat looking in and beginning to make guilty plans to return to my room for a substantial lunch? This begged the question I realized, but it still seemed to be getting at something important. Casting about for some support for my intuition, I hit upon a legalistic sort of argument that might have appealed to Locke.

Suppose, I argued to myself, I were now to fly to California, rob a bank, and be apprehended. In which state would I be tried: In California, where the robbery took place, or in Texas, where the brains of the outfit were located? Would I be a California felon with an out-of-state brain, or a Texas felon remotely controlling an accomplice of sorts in California? It seemed possible that I might beat such a rap just on the undecidability of that jurisdictional question, though perhaps it would be deemed an interstate, and hence Federal, offense. In any event, suppose I were convicted. Was it likely that California would be satisfied to throw Hamlet into the brig, knowing that Yorick was living the good life and luxuriously taking the waters in Texas? Would Texas incarcerate Yorick, leaving Hamlet free to take the next boat to Rio? This alternative appealed to me.

Barring capital punishment or other cruel and unusual punishment, the state would be obliged to maintain the life-support system for Yorick though they might move him from Houston to Leavenworth, and aside from the unpleasantness of the opprobrium, I, for one, would not mind at all and would consider myself a free man under those circumstances. If the state has an interest in forcibly relocating persons in institutions, it would fail to relocate *me* in any institution by locating Yorick there. If this were true, it suggested a third alternative.

3. *Dennett is wherever he thinks he is.*   Generalized, the claim was as follows: At any given time a person has a *point of view*, and the location of the point of view (which is determined internally by the content of the point of view) is also the location of the person.

Such a proposition is not without its perplexities, but to me it seemed a step in the right direction. The only trouble was that it seemed to place one in a heads-I-win/tails-you-lose situation of unlikely infallibility as regards location. Hadn't I myself often been wrong about where I was, and at least as often uncertain? Couldn't one get lost? Of course, but getting lost *geographically* is not the only way one might get lost. If one were lost in the woods one could attempt to reassure oneself with the consolation that at least one knew where one was: one was right *here* in the familiar surroundings of one's own body. Perhaps in this case one would not have drawn one's attention to much to be thankful for. Still, there were worse plights imaginable, and I wasn't sure I wasn't in such a plight right now.

Point of view clearly had something to do with personal location, but it was itself an unclear notion. It was obvious that the content of one's point of view was not the same as or determined by the content of one's beliefs or thoughts. For example, what should we say about the point of view of the Cinerama viewer who shrieks and twists in his seat as the roller-coaster footage overcomes his psychic distancing? Has he forgotten that he is safely seated in the theater? Here I was inclined to say that the person is experiencing an illusory shift in point of view. In other cases, my inclination to call such shifts illusory was less strong. The workers in laboratories and plants who handle dangerous materials by operating feedback-controlled mechanical arms and hands undergo a shift in point of view that is crisper and more pronounced than anything Cinerama can provoke. They can feel the heft and slipperiness of the containers they manipulate with their metal fingers. They know perfectly well where they are and are not fooled into false beliefs by the experience, yet it is as if they were inside the isolation chamber they are peering into. With mental effort, they can manage to shift their point of view back and forth, rather like making a transparent Necker cube or an Escher drawing change orientation before one's eyes. It does seem extravagant to suppose that in performing this bit of mental gymnastics, they are transporting *themselves* back and forth.

Still their example gave me hope. If I was in fact in the vat in spite of my intuitions, I might be able to train myself to adopt that point of view even as a matter of habit. I should dwell on images of myself comfortably floating in my vat, beaming volitions to that familiar body *out there*. I reflected that the ease or difficulty of this task was presumably independent of the truth about the location of one's brain. Had I been practicing before the operation, I might now be finding it second nature. You might now yourself try such a *trompe l'oeil*. Imagine you have written an inflammatory letter which has been published in the *Times*, the result of which is that the government has chosen to impound your brain for a probationary period of three years in its Dangerous Brain Clinic in Bethesda, Maryland. Your body of course is allowed freedom to earn a salary and thus continue its function of laying up income to be taxed. At this moment, however, your body is seated in an auditorium listening to a peculiar account by Daniel Dennett of his own similar experience. Try it. Think yourself to Bethesda, and then hark back longingly to your body, far away, and yet *seeming* so near. It is only with long-distance restraint (yours? the government's?) that you can control your impulse to get those hands clapping in polite applause before navigating the old body to the rest room and a well-deserved glass of evening sherry in the lounge. The task of imagination is certainly difficult, but if you achieve your goal the results might be consoling.

Anyway, there I was in Houston, lost in thought as one might say, but not for long. My speculations were soon interrupted by the Houston doctors, who wished to test out my new prosthetic nervous system before sending me off on my hazardous mission. As I mentioned before, I was a bit dizzy at first, and not surprisingly, although I soon habituated myself to my new circumstances (which were, after all, well nigh indistinguishable from my old circumstances). My accommodation was not perfect, however, and to this day I continue to be plagued by minor coordination difficulties. The speed of light is fast, but finite, and as my brain and body move farther and farther apart, the delicate interaction of my feedback systems is thrown into disarray by the time lags. Just as one is rendered close to speechless by a delayed or echoic hearing of one's speaking voice so, for instance, I am virtually unable to track a moving object with my eyes whenever my brain and my body are more than a few miles apart. In most matters my impairment is scarcely detectable, though I can no longer hit a slow curve ball with the authority of yore. There are some compensations of course. Though liquor tastes as good as ever, and warms my gullet while corroding my liver, I can drink it in any quantity I please, without becoming the slightest bit inebriated, a curiosity some of my close friends may have noticed (though I occasionally have *feigned* inebriation, so as not to draw attention to my unusual circumstances). For similar reasons, I take aspirin orally for a sprained wrist, but if the pain persists I ask Houston to administer codeine to me *in vitro*. In times of illness the phone bill can be staggering.

But to return to my adventure. At length, both the doctors and I were satisfied that I was ready to undertake my subterranean mission. And so I left my brain in Houston and headed by helicopter for Tulsa. Well, in any case, that's the way it seemed to me. That's how I would put it, just off the top of my head as it were. On the trip I reflected further about my earlier anxieties and decided that my first postoperative speculations had been tinged with panic. The matter was not nearly as strange or metaphysical as I had been supposing. Where was I? In two places, clearly: both inside the vat and outside it. Just as one can stand with one foot in Connecticut and the other in Rhode Island, I was in two places at once. I had become one of those scattered individuals we used to hear so much about. The more I considered this answer, the more obviously true it appeared. But, strange to say, the more true it appeared, the less important the question to which it could be the true answer seemed. A sad, but not unprecedented, fate for a philosophical question to suffer. This answer did not completely satisfy me, of course. There lingered some question to which I should have liked an answer, which was neither "Where are all my various and sundry parts?" nor "What is my current point of view?" Or at least there seemed to be such a question. For it did seem undeniable that in some sense *I* and not merely *most of me* was descending into the earth under Tulsa in search of an atomic warhead.

When I found the warhead, I was certainly glad I had left my brain behind, for the pointer on the specially built Geiger counter I had brought with me was off the dial. I called Houston on my ordinary radio and told the operation control center of my position and my progress. In return, they gave me instructions for dismantling the vehicle, based upon my on-site observations. I had set to work with my cutting torch when all of a sudden a terrible thing happened. I went stone deaf. At first I thought it was only my radio earphones that had broken, but when I tapped on my helmet, I heard nothing. Apparently the auditory transceivers had gone on the fritz. I could no longer hear Houston or my own voice, but I could speak, so I started telling them what had happened. In midsentence, I knew something else had gone wrong. My vocal apparatus had become paralyzed. Then my right hand went limp—another transceiver had gone. I was truly in deep trouble. But worse was to follow. After a few more minutes, I went blind. I cursed my luck, and then I cursed the scientists who had led me into this grave peril. There I was, deaf, dumb, and blind, in a radioactive hole more than a mile under Tulsa. Then the last of my cerebral radio links broke, and suddenly I was faced with a new and even more shocking problem: whereas an instant before I had been buried alive in Oklahoma, now I was disembodied in Houston. My recognition of my new status was not immediate. It took me several very anxious minutes before it dawned on me that my poor body lay several hundred miles away, with heart pulsing and lungs respirating, but otherwise as dead as the body of any heart-transplant donor, its skull packed with useless, broken electronic gear. The shift in perspective I had earlier found well nigh impossible now seemed quite natural. Though I could think myself back into my body in the tunnel under Tulsa, it took some effort to sustain the illusion. For surely it was an illusion to suppose I was still in Oklahoma: I had lost all contact with that body.

It occurred to me then, with one of those rushes of revelation of which we should be suspicious, that I had stumbled upon an impressive demonstration of the immateriality of the soul based upon physicalist principles and premises. For as the last radio signal between Tulsa and Houston died away, had I not changed location from Tulsa to Houston at the speed of light? And had I not accomplished this without any increase in mass? What moved from A to B at such speed was surely myself, or at any rate my soul or mind—the massless center of my being and home of my consciousness. My *point of view* had lagged somewhat behind, but I had already noted the indirect bearing of point of view on personal location. I could not see how a physicalist philosopher could quarrel with this except by taking the dire and counterintuitive route of banishing all talk of persons. Yet the notion of personhood was so well entrenched in everyone's world view, or so it seemed to me, that any denial would be as curiously unconvincing, as systematically disingenuous, as the Cartesian negation, "non sum."

The joy of philosophic discovery thus tided me over some very bad minutes or perhaps hours as the helplessness and hopelessness of my situation became more apparent to me. Waves of panic and even nausea swept over me, made all the more horrible by the absence of their normal body-dependent phenomenology. No adrenaline rush of tingles in the arms, no pounding heart, no premonitory salivation. I did feel a dread sinking feeling in my bowels at one point, and this tricked me momentarily into the false hope that I was undergoing a reversal of the process that landed me in this fix—a gradual undisembodiment. But the isolation and uniqueness of that twinge soon convinced me that it was simply the first of a plague of phantom body hallucinations that I, like any other amputee, would be all too likely to suffer.

My mood then was chaotic. On the one hand, I was fired up with elation of my philosophic discovery and was wracking my brain (one of the few familiar things I could still do), trying to figure out how to communicate my discovery to the journals; while on the other, I was bitter, lonely, and filled with dread and uncertainty. Fortunately, this did not last long, for my technical support team sedated me into a dreamless sleep from which I awoke, hearing with magnificent fidelity the familiar opening strains of my favorite Brahms piano trio. So that was why they had wanted a list of my favorite recordings! It did not take me long to realize that I was hearing the music without ears. The output from the stereo stylus was being fed through some fancy rectification circuitry directly into my auditory nerve. I was mainlining Brahms, an unforgettable experience for any stereo buff. At the end of the record it did not surprise me to hear the reassuring voice of the project director speaking into a microphone that was now my prosthetic ear. He confirmed my analysis of what had gone wrong and assured me that steps were being taken to re-embody me. He did not elaborate, and after a few more recordings, I found myself drifting off to sleep. My sleep lasted, I later learned, for the better part of a year, and when I awoke, it was to find myself fully restored to my senses. When I looked into the mirror, though, I was a bit startled to see an unfamiliar face. Bearded and a bit heavier, bearing no doubt a family resemblance to my former face, and with the same look of spritely intelligence and resolute character, but definitely a new face. Further self-explorations of an intimate nature left me no doubt that this was a new body, and the project director confirmed my conclusions. He did not volunteer any information on the past history of my new body and I decided (wisely, I think in retrospect) not to pry. As many philosophers unfamiliar with my ordeal have more recently speculated, the acquisitions of a new body leaves one's *person* intact. And after a period of adjustment to a new voice, new muscular strengths and weaknesses, and so forth, one's *personality* is by and large also preserved. More dramatic changes in personality have been routinely observed in people who have undergone extensive plastic surgery, to say nothing of sex-change operations, and I think no one contests the survival of the person in such cases. In any event I soon accommodated to my new body, to the point of being unable to recover any of its novelties to my consciousness or even memory. The view in the mirror soon became utterly familiar. That view, by the way, still revealed antennae, and so I was not surprised to learn that my brain had not been moved from its haven in the life-support lab.

I decided that good old Yorick deserved a visit. I and my new body, whom we might as well call Fortinbras, strode into the familiar lab to another round of applause from the technicians, who were of course congratulating themselves, not me. Once more I stood before the vat and contemplated poor Yorick, and on a whim I once again cavalierly flicked off the output transmitter switch. Imagine my surprise when nothing unusual happened. No fainting spell, no nausea, no noticeable change. A technician hurried to restore the switch to ON, but still I felt nothing. I demanded an explanation, which the project director hastened to provide. It seems that before they had even operated on the first occasion, they had constructed a computer duplicate of my brain, reproducing both the complete information-processing structure and the computational speed of my brain in a giant computer program. After the operation, but before they had dared to send me off on my mission to Oklahoma, they had run this computer system and Yorick side by side. The incoming signals from Hamlet were sent simultaneously to Yorick's transceivers and to the computer's array of inputs. And the outputs from Yorick were not only beamed back to Hamlet, my body; they were recorded and checked against the simultaneous output of the computer program, which was called "Hubert" for reasons obscure to me. Over days and even weeks, the outputs were identical and synchronous, which of course did not *prove* that they had succeeded in copying the brain's functional structure, but the empirical support was greatly encouraging.

Hubert's input, and hence activity, had been kept parallel with Yorick's during my disembodied days. And now, to demonstrate this, they had actually thrown the master switch that put Hubert for the first time in on-line control of my body—not Hamlet, of course, but Fortinbras. (Hamlet, I learned, had never been recovered from its underground tomb and could be assumed by this time to have largely returned to the dust. At the head of my grave still lay the magnificent bulk of the abandoned device, with the word STUD emblazoned on its side in large letters—a circumstance which may provide archeologists of the next century with a curious insight into the burial rites of their ancestors.)

The laboratory technicians now showed me the master switch, which had two positions, labeled *B*, for Brain (they didn't know my brain's name was Yorick) and *H*, for Hubert. The switch did indeed point to *H*, and they explained to me that if I wished, I could switch it back to *B*. With my heart in my mouth (and my brain in its vat), I did this. Nothing happened. A click, that was all. To test their claim, and with the master switch now set at *B*, I hit Yorick's output transmitter switch on the vat and sure enough, I began to faint. Once the output switch was turned back on and I had recovered my wits, so to speak, I continued to play with the master switch, flipping it back and forth. I found that with the exception of the transitional click, I could detect no trace of a difference. I could switch in mid-utterance, and the sentence I had begun speaking under the control of Yorick was finished without a pause or hitch of any kind under the control of Hubert. I had a spare brain, a prosthetic device which might some day stand me in very good stead, were some mishap to befall Yorick. Or alternatively, I could keep Yorick as a spare and use Hubert. It didn't seem to make any difference which I chose, for the wear and tear and fatigue on my body did not have any debilitating effect on either brain, whether or not it was actually causing the motions of my body, or merely spilling its output into thin air.

The one truly unsettling aspect of this new development was the prospect, which was not long in dawning on me, of someone detaching the spare—Hubert or Yorick, as the case might be—from Fortinbras and hitching it to yet another body—some Johnny-come-lately Rosencrantz or Guildenstern. Then (if not before) there would be *two* people, that much was clear. One would be me, and the other would be a sort of super-twin brother. If there were two bodies, one under the control of Hubert and the other being controlled by Yorick, then which would the world recognize as the true Dennett? And whatever the rest of the world decided, which one would be *me*? Would I be the Yorick-brained one, in virtue of Yorick's causal priority and former intimate relationship with the original Dennett body, Hamlet? That seemed a bit legalistic, a bit too redolent of the arbitrariness of consanguinity and legal possession, to be convincing at the metaphysical level. For suppose that before the arrival of the second body on the scene, I had been keeping Yorick as the spare for years, and letting Hubert's output drive my body—that is, Fortinbras—all that time. The Hubert-Fortinbras couple would seem then by squatter's rights (to combat one legal intuition with another) to be the true Dennett and the lawful inheritor of everything that was Dennett's. This was an interesting question, certainly, but not nearly so pressing as another question that bothered me. My strongest intuition was that in such an eventuality *I* would survive so long as *either* brain-body couple remained intact, but I had mixed emotions about whether I should want both to survive.

I discussed my worries with the technicians and the project director. The prospect of two Dennetts was abhorrent to me, I explained, largely for social reasons. I didn't want to be my own rival for the affections of my wife, nor did I like the prospect of the two Dennetts sharing my modest professor's salary. Still more vertiginous and distasteful, though, was the idea of knowing *that much* about another person, while he had the very same goods on me. How could we ever face each other? My colleagues in the lab argued that I was ignoring the bright side of the matter. Weren't there many things I wanted to do but, being only one person, had been unable to do? Now one Dennett could stay at home and be the professor and family man, while the other could strike out on a life of travel and adventure—missing the family of course, but happy in the knowledge that the other Dennett was keeping the home fires burning. I could be faithful and adulterous at the same time. I could even cuckold myself—to say nothing of other more lurid possibilities my colleagues were all too ready to force upon my overtaxed imagination. But my ordeal in Oklahoma (or was it Houston?) had made me less adventurous, and I shrank from this opportunity that was being offered (though of course I was never quite sure it was being offered to *me* in the first place).

There was another prospect even more disagreeable: that the spare, Hubert or Yorick as the case might be, would be detached from any input from Fortinbras and just left detached. Then, as in the other case, there would be two Dennetts, or at least two claimants to my name and possessions, one embodied in Fortinbras, and the other sadly, miserably disembodied. Both selfishness and altruism bade me take steps to prevent this from happening. So I asked that measures be taken to ensure that no one could ever tamper with the transceiver connections or the master switch without my (our? no, *my*) knowledge and consent. Since I had no desire to spend my life guarding the equipment in Houston, it was mutually decided that all the electronic connections in the lab would be carefully locked. Both those that controlled the life-support system for Yorick and those that controlled the power supply for Hubert would be guarded with fail-safe devices, and I would take the only master switch, outfitted for radio remote control, with me wherever I went. I carry it strapped around my waist and—wait a moment—*here it is*. Every few months I reconnoiter the situation by switching channels. I do this only in the presence of friends, of course, for if the other channel were, heaven forbid, either dead or otherwise occupied, there would have to be somebody who had my interests at heart to switch it back, to bring me back from the void. For while I could feel, see, hear, and otherwise sense whatever befell my body, subsequent to such a switch, I'd be unable to control it. By the way, the two positions on the switch are intentionally unmarked, so I never have the faintest idea whether I am switching from

Hubert to Yorick or vice versa. (Some of you may think that in this case I really don't know *who* I am, let alone where I am. But such reflections no longer make much of a dent on my essential Dennettness, on my own sense of who I am. If it is true that in one sense I don't know who I am then that's another one of your philosophical truths of underwhelming significance.)

In any case, every time I've flipped the switch so far, nothing has happened. *So let's give it a try. . . .*

"THANK GOD! I THOUGHT YOU'D NEVER FLIP THAT SWITCH! You can't imagine how horrible it's been these last two weeks—but now you know; it's your turn in purgatory. How I've longed for this moment! You see, about two weeks ago—excuse me, ladies and gentlemen, but I've got to explain this to my . . . um, brother, I guess you could say, but he's just told you the facts, so you'll understand—about two weeks ago our two brains drifted just a bit out of synch. I don't know whether *my* brain is now Hubert or Yorick, any more than you do, but in any case, the two brains drifted apart, and of course once the process started, it snowballed, for I was in a slightly different receptive state for the input we both received, a difference that was soon magnified. In no time at all the illusion that I was in control of my body—our body—was completely dissipated. There was nothing I could do—no way to call you. YOU DIDN'T EVEN KNOW I EXISTED! It's been like being carried around in a cage, or better, like being possessed—hearing my own voice say things I didn't mean to say, watching in frustration as my own hands performed deeds I hadn't intended. You'd scratch our itches, but not the way I would have, and you kept me awake, with your tossing and turning. I've been totally exhausted, on the verge of a nervous breakdown, carried around helplessly by your frantic round of activities, sustained only by the knowledge that some day you'd throw the switch.

"Now it's your turn, but at least you'll have the comfort of knowing *I* know you're in there. Like an expectant mother, I'm eating—or at any rate tasting, smelling, seeing—for *two* now, and I'll try to make it easy for you. Don't worry. Just as soon as this colloquium is over, you and I will fly to Houston, and we'll see what can be done to get one of us another body. You can have a female body—your body could be any color you like. But let's think it over. I tell you what—to be fair, if we both want this body, I promise I'll let the project director flip a coin to settle which of us gets to keep it and which then gets to choose a new body. That should guarantee justice, shouldn't it? In any case, I'll take care of you, I promise. These people are my witnesses.

"Ladies and gentlemen, this talk we have just heard is not exactly the talk *I* would have given, but I assure you that everything he said was perfectly true. And now if you'll excuse me, I think I'd—we'd—better sit down."

The Unimportance of Identity

Derek Parfit

We can start with some science fiction. Here on Earth, I enter the Teletransporter. When I press some button, a machine destroys my body, while recording the exact states of all my cells. The information is sent by radio to Mars, where another machine makes, out of organic materials, a perfect copy of my body. The person who wakes up on Mars seems to remember living my life up to the moment when I pressed the button, and he is in every other way just like me.

Of those who have thought about such cases, some believe that it would be I who would wake up on Mars. They regard Teletransportation as merely the fastest way of travelling. Others believe that, if I chose to be Teletransported, I would be making a terrible mistake. On their view, the person who wakes up would be a mere Replica of me.

I

That is a disagreement about personal identity. To understand such disagreements, we must distinguish two kinds of sameness. Two white billiard balls may be qualitatively identical, or exactly similar. But they are not numerically identical, or one and the same ball. If I paint one of these balls red, it will cease to be qualitatively identical with itself as it was; but it will still be one and the same ball. Consider next a claim like, 'Since her accident, she is no longer the same person'. That involves both senses of identity. It means that *she*, one and the same person, is *not* now the same person. That is not a contradiction. The claim is only that

Source: From H. Harris, *Identity* (Oxford University Press, 1987):13–45. Reprinted by permission of Oxford University Press.

this person's character has changed. This numerically identical person is now qualitatively different.

When psychologists discuss identity, they are typically concerned with the kind of person someone is, or wants to be. That is the question involved, for example, in an identity crisis. But, when philosophers discuss identity, it is numerical identity they mean. And, in our concern about our own futures, that is what we have in mind. I may believe that, after my marriage, I shall be a different person. But that does not make marriage death. However much I change, I shall still be alive if there will be someone living who will be me. Similarly, if I was Teletransported, my Replica on Mars would be qualitatively identical to me; but, on the sceptic's view, he wouldn't *be* me. *I* shall have ceased to exist. And that, we naturally assume, is what matters

Questions about our numerical identity all take the following form. We have two ways of referring to a person, and we ask whether these are ways of referring to the same person. Thus we might ask whether Boris Nikolayevich is Yeltsin. In the most important questions of this kind, our two ways of referring to a person pick out a person at different times. Thus we might ask whether the person to whom we are speaking now is the same as the person to whom we spoke on the telephone yesterday. These are questions about identity over time.

To answer such questions, we must know the *criterion* of personal identity: the relation between a person at one time, and a person at another time, which makes these one and the same person.

Different criteria have been advanced. On one view, what makes me the same, throughout my life, is my having the same body. This criterion requires uninterrupted bodily continuity. There is no such continuity between my body on Earth and the body of my Replica on Mars; so, on this view, my Replica would not be me. Other writers appeal to psychological continuity. Thus Locke claimed that, if I was conscious of a past life in some other body, I would be the person who lived that life. On some versions of this view, my Replica would be me.

Supporters of these different views often appeal to cases where they conflict. Most of these cases are, like Teletransportation, purely imaginary. Some philosophers object that, since our concept of a person rests on a scaffolding of facts, we should not expect this concept to apply in imagined cases where we think those facts away. I agree. But I believe that, for a different reason, it is worth considering such cases. We can use them to discover, not what the truth is, but what we believe. We might have found that, when we consider science fiction cases, we simply shrug our shoulders. But that is not so. Many of us find that we have certain beliefs about what kind of fact personal identity is.

These beliefs are best revealed when we think about such cases from a first-person point of view. So, when I imagine something's happening to me, you should imagine its happening to you. Suppose that I live in some future century, in which technology is far advanced, and I am about to undergo some operation. Perhaps my brain and body will be remodeled, or partially replaced. There will be a resulting person, who will wake up tomorrow. I ask, 'Will that person be me? Or am I about to die? Is this the end?' I may not know how to answer this question. But it is natural to assume that there must *be* an answer. The resulting person, it may seem, must be either me, or someone else. And the answer must be all-or-nothing. That person cannot be *partly* me. If that person is in pain tomorrow, this pain cannot be partly mine. So, we may assume, either I shall feel that pain, or I shan't.

If this is how we think about such cases, we assume that our identity must be *determinate*. We assume that, in every imaginable case, questions about our identity must have answers, which must be either, and quite simply, Yes or No.

Let us now ask: 'Can this be true?' There is one view on which it might be. On this view, there are immaterial substances: souls, or Cartesian Egos. These entities have the special properties once ascribed to atoms: they are indivisible, and their continued existence is, in its nature, all or nothing. And such an Ego is what each of us really is.

Unlike several writers, I believe that such a view might have been true. But we have no good evidence for thinking that it is, and some evidence for thinking that it isn't; so I shall assume here that no such view is true.

If we do not believe that there are Cartesian Egos, or other such entities, we should accept the kind of view which I have elsewhere called *Reductionist*. On this view

(1) A person's existence just consists in the existence of a body, and the occurrence of a series of thoughts, experiences, and other mental and physical events.

Some Reductionists claim

(2) Persons just *are* bodies.

This view may seem not to be Reductionist, since it does not reduce persons to something else. But that is only because it is hyper-Reductionist: it reduces persons to bodies in so strong a way that it doesn't even distinguish between them. We can call it *Identifying* Reductionism.

Such a view seems to me too simple. I believe that we should combine (1) with

(3) A person is an entity that has a body, and has thoughts and other experiences.

On this view, though a person is distinct from that person's body, and from any series of thoughts and experiences, the person's existence just *consists* in them. So we can call this view *Constitutive* Reductionism.

It may help to have other examples of this kind of view. If we melt down a bronze statue, we destroy this statue, but we do not destroy this lump of bronze. So, though the statue just consists in the lump of bronze, these cannot be one and the same thing. Similarly, the existence of a nation just consists in the existence of a group of people, on some territory, living together in certain ways. But the nation is not the same as that group of people, or that territory.

Consider next *Eliminative* Reductionism. Such a view is sometimes a response to arguments against the Identifying view. Suppose we start by claiming that a nation just is a group of people on some territory. We are then persuaded that this cannot be so: that the concept of a nation is the concept of an entity that is distinct from its people and its territory. We may conclude that, in that case, there are really no such things as nations. There are only groups of people, living together in certain ways.

In the case of persons, some Buddhist texts take an Eliminative view. According to these texts

(4) There really aren't such things as persons: there are only brains and bodies, and thoughts and other experiences.

For example:

Buddha has spoken thus: 'O brethren, actions do exist, and also their consequences, but the person that acts does not. . . . There exists no Individual, it is only a conventional name given to a set of elements.'

Or:

The mental and the material are really here,
But here there is no person to be found.

For it is void and merely fashioned like a doll,

Just suffering piled up like grass and sticks.

Eliminative Reductionism is sometimes justified. Thus we are right to claim that there were really no witches, only persecuted women. But Reductionism about some kind of entity is not often well expressed with the claim that there are no such entities. We should admit that there are nations, and that we, who are persons, exist.

Rather than claiming that there are no entities of some kind, Reductionists should distinguish kinds of entity, or ways of existing. When the existence of an X just consists in the existence of a Y, or Ys, though the X is *distinct* from the Y or Ys, it is not an *independent* or *separately existing* entity. Statues do not exist separately from the matter of which they are made. Nor do nations exist separately from their citizens and their territory. Similarly, I believe,

(5) Though persons are distinct from their bodies, and from any series of mental events, they are not independent or separately existing entities.

Cartesian Egos, if they existed, would not only be distinct from human bodies, but would also be independent entities. Such Egos are claimed to be like physical objects, except that they are wholly mental. If there were such entities, it would make sense to suppose that they might cease to be causally related to some body, yet continue to exist. But, on a Reductionist view, persons are not in that sense independent from their bodies. (That is not to claim that our thoughts and other experiences are merely changes in the states of our brains. Reductionists, while not believing in purely mental substances, may be dualists.)

We can now return to personal identity over time, or what constitutes the continued existence of the same person. One question here is this. What explains the unity of a person's mental life? What makes thoughts and experiences, had at different times, the thoughts and experiences of a single person? According to some Non-Reductionists, this question cannot be answered in other terms. We must simply claim that these different thoughts and experiences are all had by the same person. This fact does not consist in any other facts, but is a bare or ultimate truth.

If each of us was a Cartesian Ego, that might be so. Since such an Ego would be an independent substance, it could be an irreducible fact that different experiences are all changes in the states of the same persisting Ego. But that could not be true of persons, I believe, if, while distinct from their bodies, they are not separately existing entities. A person, so conceived, is not the kind of entity about which there could be such irreducible truths. When experiences at different times are all had by the same person, this fact must consist in certain other facts.

If we do not believe in Cartesian Egos, we should claim

(6) Personal identity over time just consists in physical and/or psychological continuity.

That claim could be filled out in different ways. On one version of this view, what makes different experiences the experiences of a single person is their being either changes in the states of, or at least directly causally related to, the same embodied brain. That must be the view of those who believe that persons just are bodies. And we might hold that view even if, as I think we should, we distinguish persons from their bodies. But we might appeal, either in addition or instead, to various psychological relations between different mental states and events, such as the relations involved in memory, or in the persistence of intentions, desires, and other psychological features. That is what I mean by psychological continuity.

On Constitutive Reductionism, the fact of personal identity is distinct from these facts about physical and psychological continuity. But, since it just consists in them, it is not an independent or separately obtaining fact. It is not a further difference in what happens.

To illustrate that distinction, consider a simpler case. Suppose that I already know that several trees are growing together on some hill. I then learn that, because that is true, there is a copse on this hill. That would not be new factual information. I would have merely learnt that such a group of trees can be called a 'copse'. My only new information is about our language. That those trees can be called a copse is not, except trivially, a fact about the trees.

Something similar is true in the more complicated case of nations. In order to know the facts about the history of a nation, it is enough to know what large numbers of people did and said. Facts about nations cannot be barely true: they must consist in facts about people. And, once we know these other facts, any remaining questions about nations are not further questions about what really happened.

I believe that, in the same way, facts about people cannot be barely true. Their truth must consist in the truth of facts about bodies, and about various interrelated mental and physical events. If we knew these other facts, we would have all the empirical input that we need. If we understood the concept of a person, and had no false beliefs about what persons are, we would then know, or would be able to work out, the truth of any further claims about the existence or identity of persons. That is because such claims would not tell us more about reality.

That is the barest sketch of a Reductionist view. These remarks may become clearer if we return to the so-called 'problem cases' of personal identity. In such a case, we imagine knowing that, between me now and some person in the future, there will be certain kinds or degrees of physical and/or psychological continuity or connectedness. But, though we know these facts, we cannot answer the question whether that future person would be me.

Since we may disagree on which the problem cases are, we need more than one example. Consider first the range of cases that I have elsewhere called the *Physical Spectrum*. In each of these cases, some proportion of my body would be replaced, in a single operation, with exact duplicates of the existing cells. In the case at the near end of this range, no cells would be replaced. In the case at the far end, my whole body would be destroyed and replicated. That is the case with which I began: Teletransportation.

Suppose we believe that in that case, where my whole body would be replaced, the resulting person would not be me, but a mere Replica. If no cells were replaced, the resulting person would be me. But what of the cases in between, where the percentage of the cells replaced would be, say, 30, or 50, or 70 percent? Would the resulting person here be me? When we consider some of these cases, we will not know whether to answer Yes or No.

Suppose next that we believe that, even in Teletransportation, my Replica would be me. We should then consider a different version of that case, in which the Scanner would get its information without destroying my body, and my Replica would be made while I was still alive. In this version of the case, we may agree that my Replica would not be me. That may shake our view that, in the original version of case, he *would* be me.

If we still keep that view, we should turn to what I have called the *Combined Spectrum*. In this second range of cases, there would be all the different degrees of both physical and psychological connectedness. The new cells would not be exactly similar. The greater the proportion of my body that would be replaced, the less like me would the resulting person be. In the case at the far end of this range, my whole body would be destroyed, and they would make a Replica of some quite different person, such as Greta Garbo. Garbo's Replica would clearly *not* be me. In the case at the near end, with no replacement, the resulting person would be me. On any view, there must be cases in between where we could not answer our question.

For simplicity, I shall consider only the Physical Spectrum, and I shall assume that, in some of the cases in this range, we cannot answer the question whether the resulting person would be me. My remarks could be transferred, with some adjustment, to the Combined Spectrum.

As I have said, it is natural to assume that, even if *we* cannot answer this question, there must always *be* an answer, which must be either Yes or No. It is natural to believe that, if the resulting person will be in pain, either I shall feel that pain, or I shan't. But this range of cases challenges that belief. In the case at the near end, the resulting person would be me. In the case at the far end, he would be someone else. How could it be true that, in all the cases in between, he must be either me, or someone else? For that to be true, there must be, somewhere in this range, a sharp borderline. There must be some critical set of cells such that, if only those cells were replaced, it would be me who would wake up, but that in the very next case, with only just a few more cells replaced, it would be, not me, but a new person. That is hard to believe.

Here is another fact, which makes it even harder to believe. Even if there were such a borderline, no one could ever discover where it is. I might say, 'Try replacing half of my brain and body, and I shall tell you what happens.' But we know in advance that, in every case, since the resulting person would be exactly like me, he would be inclined to believe that he was me. And this could not show that he *was* me, since any mere Replica of me would think that too.

Even if such cases actually occurred, we would learn nothing more about them. So it does not matter that these cases are imaginary. We should try to decide now whether, in this range of cases, personal identity could be determinate. Could it be true that, in every case, the resulting person either would or would not be me?

If we do not believe that there are Cartesian Egos, or other such entities, we seem forced to answer No. It is not true that our identity must be determinate. We can always ask, 'Would that future person be me?' But, in some of these cases,

(7) This question would have no answer. It would be neither true nor false that this person would be me.

And

(8) This question would be *empty*. Even without an answer, we could know the full truth about what happened.

If our questions were about such entities as nations or machines, most of us would accept such claims. But, when applied to ourselves, they can be hard to believe. How could it be neither true nor false that I shall still exist tomorrow? And, without an answer to our question, how could I know the full truth about my future?

Reductionism gives the explanation. We naturally assume that, in these cases, there are different possibilities. The resulting person, we assume, might be me, or he might be someone else, who is merely like me. If the resulting person will be in pain, either I shall feel that pain, or I shan't. If these really were different possibilities, it would be compelling that one of them must be the possibility that would in fact obtain. How could reality fail to choose between them? But, on a Reductionist view,

(9) Our question is not about different possibilities. There is only a single possibility, or course of events. Our question is merely about different possible descriptions of this course of events.

That is how our question has no answer. We have not yet decided which description to apply. And, that is why, even without answering this question, we could know the full truth about what would happen.

Suppose that, after considering such examples, we cease to believe that our identity must be determinate. That may seem to make little difference. It may seem to be a change of view only about some imaginary cases, that will never actually occur. But that may not be so. We may be led to revise our beliefs about the nature of personal identity; and that would be a change of view about our own lives.

In nearly all actual cases, questions about personal identity have answers, so claim (7) does not apply. If we don't know these answers, there is something that we don't know. But claim (8) still applies. Even without answering these questions, we could know the full truth about what happens. We would know that truth if we knew the facts about both physical and psychological continuity. If, implausibly, we still didn't know the answer to a question about identity, our ignorance would only be about our language. And that is because claim (9) still applies. When we know the other facts, there are never different possibilities at the level of what happens. In all cases, the only remaining possibilities are at the linguistic level. Perhaps it would be correct to say that some future person would be me. Perhaps it would be correct to say that he would not be me. Or perhaps neither would be correct. I conclude that in *all* cases, if we know the other facts, we should regard questions about our identity as merely questions about language.

That conclusion can be misunderstood. First, when we ask such questions, that is usually because we *don't* know the other facts. Thus, when we ask if we are about to die, that is seldom a conceptual question. We ask that question because we don't know what will happen to our bodies, and whether, in particular, our brains will continue to support consciousness. Our question becomes conceptual only when we already know about such other facts.

Note next that, in certain cases, the relevant facts go beyond the details of the case we are considering. Whether some concept applies may depend on facts about other cases, or on a choice between scientific theories. Suppose we see something strange happening to an unknown animal. We might ask whether this process preserves the animal's identity, or whether the result is a new animal (because what we are seeing is some kind of reproduction). Even if we knew the details of this process, that question would not be merely conceptual. The answer would depend on whether this process is part of the natural development of this kind of animal. And that may be something we have yet to discover.

If we identify persons with human beings, whom we regard as a natural kind, the same would be true in some imaginable cases involving persons. But these are not the kind of case that I have been discussing. My cases all involve artificial intervention. No facts about natural development could be relevant here. Thus, in my Physical Spectrum, if we knew which of my cells would be replaced by duplicates, all of the relevant empirical facts would be in. In such cases any remaining questions would be conceptual.

Since that is so, it would be clearer to ask these questions in a different way. Consider the case in which I replace some of the components of my audio system, but keep the others. I ask, 'Do I still have one and the same system?' That may seem a factual question. But, since I already know what happened, that is not really so. It would be clearer to ask, 'Given that I have replaced those components, would it be correct to call this the same system?'

The same applies to personal identity. Suppose that I know the facts about what will happen to my body, and about any psychological connections that there will be between me now and some person tomorrow. I may ask, 'Will that person be me?' But that is a misleading way to put my question. It suggests that I don't know what's going to happen. When I know these other facts, I should ask, 'Would it be correct to call that person me?' That would remind me that, if there's anything that I don't know, that is merely a fact about our language.

I believe that we can go further. Such questions are, in the belittling sense, merely verbal. Some conceptual questions are well worth discussing. But questions about personal identity, in my kind of case, are like questions that we would all think trivial. It is quite uninteresting whether, with half its components replaced, I still have the same audio system. In the same way, we should regard it as quite uninteresting whether, if half of my body were simultaneously replaced, I would still exist. As questions about reality, these are entirely empty. Nor, as conceptual questions, do they need answers.

We might need, for legal purposes, to *give* such questions answers. Thus we might decide that an audio system should be called the same if its new components cost less than half its original price. And we might decide to say that I would continue to exist as long as less than half my body were replaced. But these are not answers to conceptual questions; they are mere decisions.

(Similar remarks apply if we are Identifying Reductionists, who believe that persons just are bodies. There are cases where it is a merely verbal question whether we still have one and the same human body. That is clearly true in the cases in the middle of the Physical Spectrum.)

It may help to contrast these questions with one that is not merely verbal. Suppose we are studying some creature which is very unlike ourselves, such as an insect, or some extraterrestrial being. We know all the facts about this creature's behaviour, and its neurophysiology. The creature wriggles vigorously, in what seems to be a response to some injury. We ask, 'Is it conscious, and in great pain? Or is it merely like an insentient machine?' Some Behaviourist might say, 'That is a merely verbal question. These aren't different possibilities, either of which might be true. They are merely different descriptions of the very same state of affairs.' That I find incredible. These descriptions give us, I believe, two quite different possibilities. It could not be an empty or a merely verbal question whether some creature was unconscious or in great pain.

It is natural to think the same about our own identity. If I know that some proportion of my cells will be replaced, how can it be a merely verbal question whether I am about to die, or shall wake up again tomorrow? It is because that is hard to believe that Reductionism is worth discussing. If we become Reductionists, that may change some of our deepest assumptions about ourselves.

These assumptions, as I have said, cover actual cases, and our own lives. But they are best revealed when we consider the imaginary problem cases. It is worth explaining further why that is so.

In ordinary cases, questions about our identity have answers. In such cases, there is a fact about personal identity, and Reductionism is one view about what kind of fact this is. On this view, personal identity just consists in physical and/or psychological continuity. We may find it hard to decide whether we accept this view, since it may be far from clear when one fact just consists in another. We may even doubt whether Reductionists and their critics really disagree.

In the problem cases, things are different. When we cannot answer questions about personal identity, it is easier to decide whether we accept a Reductionist view. We should ask: Do we find such cases puzzling? Or do we accept the Reductionist claim that, even without answering these questions, if we knew the facts about the continuities, we would know what happened?

Most of us do find such cases puzzling. We believe that, even if we knew those other facts, it we could not answer questions about our identity, there would be something that we didn't know. That suggests that, on our view, personal identity does *not* just consist in one or both of the continuities, but is a separately obtaining fact, or a further difference in what happens. The Reductionist account must then leave something out. So there is a real disagreement, and one that applies to all cases.

Many of us do not merely find such cases puzzling. We are inclined to believe that, in all such cases, questions about our identity must have answers, which must be either Yes or No. For that to be true, personal identity must be a separately obtaining fact of a peculiarly simple kind. It must involve some special entity, such as a Cartesian Ego, whose existence must be all-or-nothing.

When I say that we have these assumptions, I am *not* claiming that we believe in Cartesian Egos. Some of us do. But many of us, I suspect, have inconsistent beliefs. If we are asked whether we believe that there are Cartesian Egos, we may answer No. And we may accept that, as Reductionists claim, the existence of a person just involves the existence of a body, and the occurrence of a series of interrelated mental and physical events. But, as our reactions to the problem cases show, we don't fully accept that view. Or, if we do, we also seem to hold a different view.

Such a conflict of beliefs is quite common. At a reflective or intellectual level, we may be convinced that some view is true; but at another level, one that engages more directly with our emotions, we may continue to think and feel as if some different view were true. One example of this kind would be a hope, or fear, that we know to be groundless. Many of us, I suspect, have such inconsistent beliefs about the metaphysical questions that concern us most, such as free will, time's passage, consciousness, and the self.

II

I turn now from the nature of personal identity to its importance. Personal identity is widely thought to have great rational and moral significance. Thus it is the fact of identity which is thought to give us our reason for concern about our own future. And several moral principles, such as those of desert or distributive justice, presuppose claims about identity. The separateness of persons, or the non-identity of different people, has been called 'the basic fact for morals'.

I can comment here on only one of these questions: what matters in our survival. I mean by that, not what makes our survival good, but what makes our survival matter, whether it will be good or bad. What is it, in our survival, that gives us a reason for special anticipatory or prudential concern?

We can explain that question with an extreme imaginary case. Suppose that, while I care about my whole future, I am especially concerned about what will happen to me on future Tuesdays. Rather than suffer mild pain on a future Tuesday, I would choose severe pain on any other future day. That pattern of concern would be irrational. The fact that a pain will be on a Tuesday is no reason to care about it more. What about the fact that a pain will be *mine*? Is *this* a reason to care about it more?

Many people would answer Yes. On their view, what gives us a reason to care about our future is, precisely, that it will be our future. Personal identity is what matters in survival.

I reject this view. Most of what matters, I believe, are two other relations: the psychological continuity and connectedness that, in ordinary cases, hold between the different parts of a person's life. These relations only roughly coincide with personal identity, since, unlike identity, they are in part matters of degree. Nor, I believe, do they matter as much as identity is thought to do.

There are different ways to challenge the importance of identity. One argument can be summarized like this:

(1) Personal identity just consists in certain other facts.
(2) If one fact just consists in certain others, it can only be these other facts which have rational or moral importance. We should ask whether, in themselves, these other facts matter.

Therefore

(3) Personal identity cannot be rationally or morally important. What matters can only be one or more of the other facts in which personal identity consists.

Mark Johnston rejects this argument.[1] He calls it an *Argument from Below*, since it claims that, if one fact justs consists in certain others, it can only be these other lower level facts which matter. Johnston replies with what he calls an *Argument from Above*. On his view, even if the lower-level facts do not in themselves matter, the higher-level fact may matter. If it does, the lower-level facts will have a derived significance. They will matter, not in themselves, but because they constitute the higher-level fact.

To illustrate this disagreement, we can start with a different case. Suppose we ask what we want to happen if, through brain damage, we become irreversibly unconscious. If we were in this state, we would still be alive. But this fact should be understood in a Reductionist way. It may not be the same as the fact that our hearts would still be beating, and our other organs would still be functioning. But it would not be an independent or separately obtaining fact. Our being still alive, though irreversibly unconscious, would just consist in these other facts.

On my Argument from Below, we should ask whether those other facts in themselves matter. If we were irreversibly unconscious, would it be either good for us, or good for others, that our hearts and other organs would still be functioning? If we answer No, we should conclude that it would not matter that we were still alive.

If Johnston were right, we could reject this argument. And we could appeal to an Argument from Above. We might say:

> It may not be in itself good that our hearts and other organs would still be functioning. But it is good to be alive. Since that is so, it is rational to hope that, even if we could never regain consciousness, our hearts would go on beating for as long as possible. That would be good because it would constitute our staying alive.

I believe that, of these arguments; mine is more plausible.

Consider next the moral question that such cases raise. Some people ask, in their living wills, that if brain damage makes them irreversibly unconscious, their hearts should be stopped. I believe that we should do what these people ask. But many take a different view. They could appeal to an Argument from Above. They might say:

> Even if such people can never regain consciousness, while their hearts are still beating, they can be truly called alive. Since that is so, stopping their

---

[1]In his "Human Concerns Without Superlative Selves," in Jonathan Dancy, *Reading Parfit* (Oxford: Blackwell), 1997.

hearts would be an act of killing. And, except in self-defence, it is always wrong to kill.

On this view, we should leave these people's hearts to go on beating, for months or even years.

As an answer to the moral question, this seems to me misguided. (It is a separate question what the law should be.) But, for many people, the word 'kill' has such force that it seems significant whether it applies.

Turn now to a different subject. Suppose that, after trying to decide when people have free will, we become convinced by either of two compatibilist views. On one view, we call choices 'unfree' if they are caused in certain ways, and we call them 'free' if they are caused in certain other ways. On the other view, we call choices 'unfree' if we know how they were caused, and we call them 'free' if we have not yet discovered this.

Suppose next that, when we consider these two grounds for drawing this distinction, we believe that neither, in itself, has the kind of significance that could support making or denying claims about guilt, or desert. There seems to us no such significance in the difference between these kinds of causal determination; and we believe that it cannot matter whether a decision's causes have already been discovered. (Note that, in comparing the Arguments from Above and Below, we need not actually accept these claims. We are asking whether, *if* we accepted the relevant premises, we ought to be persuaded by these arguments.)

On my Argument from Below, if the fact that a choice is free just consists in one of those other facts, and we believe that those other facts cannot in themselves be morally important, we should conclude that it cannot be important whether some person's choice was free. Either choices that are unfree can deserve to be punished, or choices that are free cannot. On a Johnstonian Argument from Above, even if those other facts are not in themselves important—even if, in themselves, they are trivial—they can have a derived importance if and because they constitute the fact that some person's choice was free. As before, the Argument from Below seems to me more plausible.

We can now consider the underlying question on which this disagreement turns.

As I have claimed, if one fact just consists in certain others, the first fact is not an independent or separately obtaining fact. And, in the cases with which we are concerned, it is also, in relation to these other facts, merely a conceptual fact. Thus, if someone is irreversibly unconscious, but his heart is still beating, it is a conceptual fact that this person is still alive. When I call this fact conceptual, I don't mean that it is a fact about our concepts. That this person is alive is a fact about this person. But, if we have already claimed that this person's heart is still beating, when we claim that he is still alive, we do not give further information about reality. We only give further information about our use of the words 'person' and 'alive'.

When we turn to ask what matters, the central question is this. Suppose we agree that it does not matter, in itself, that such a person's heart is still beating. Could we claim that, in another way, this fact does matter, because it makes it correct to say that this person is still alive? If we answer Yes, we are treating language as more important than reality. We are claiming that, even if some fact does not in itself matter, it may matter if and because it allows a certain word to be applied.

This, I believe, is irrational. On my view, what matters are the facts about the world, given which some concept applies. If the facts about the world have no rational or moral significance, and the fact that the concept applies is not a further difference in what happens, this conceptual fact cannot be significant.

Johnston brings a second charge against my argument. If physicalism were true, he claims, all facts would just consist in facts about fundamental particles. Considered in themselves, these facts about particles would have no rational or moral importance. If we apply an Argument from Below, we must conclude that nothing has any importance. He remarks: "this is not a proof of Nihilism. It is a reductio ad absurdum."

Given what I have suggested here, this charge can, I think, be answered. There may perhaps be a sense in which, if physicalism were true, all facts would just consist in facts about fundamental particles. But that is not the kind of reduction which I had in mind. When I claim that personal identity just consists in certain other facts, I have in mind a closer and partly conceptual relation. Claims about personal identity may not mean the same as claims about physical and/or psychological continuity. But, if we knew the facts about these continuities, and understood the concept of a person, we would thereby know, or would be able to work out, the facts about persons. Hence my claim that, if we know the other facts, questions about personal identity should be taken to be questions, not about reality, but only about our language. These claims do not apply to facts about fundamental particles. It is not true for example that, if we knew how the particles moved in some person's body, and understood our concepts, we would thereby know, or be able to work out, all of the relevant facts about this person. To understand the world around us, we need more than physics and a knowledge of our own language.

My argument does not claim that, whenever there are facts at different levels, it is always the lowest-level facts which matter. That is clearly false. We are discussing cases where, relative to the facts at some lower level, the higher-level fact is, in the sense that I have sketched, merely conceptual. My claim is that such conceptual facts cannot be rationally or morally important. What matters is reality, not how it is described. So this view might be called *realism about importance*.

If we are Reductionists about persons, and Realists about importance, we should conclude that personal identity is not what matters. Can we accept that conclusion?

Most of us believe that we should care about our future because it will be *our* future. I believe that what matters is not identity but certain other relations. To help us to decide between these views, we should consider cases where identity and those relations do not coincide.

Which these cases are depends on which criterion of identity we accept. I shall start with the simplest form of the Physical Criterion, according to which a person continues to exist if and only if that person's body continues to exist. That must be the view of those who believe that persons just are bodies. And it is the view of several of the people who identify persons with human beings. Let's call this the *Bodily Criterion*.

Suppose that, because of damage to my spine, I have become partly paralysed. I have a brother, who is dying of a brain disease. With the aid of new techniques, when my brother's brain ceases to function, my head could be grafted onto the rest of my brother's body. Since we are identical twins, my brain would then control a body that is just like mine, except that it would not be paralysed.

Should I accept this operation? Of those who assume that identity is what matters, three groups would answer No. Some accept the Bodily Criterion. These people believe that, if this operation were performed, I would die. The person with my head tomorrow would be my brother, who would mistakenly think that he was me. Other people are uncertain what would happen. They believe that it would be risky to accept this operation, since the resulting person might not be me. Others give a different reason why I should reject this operation: that it would be indeterminate whether that person would be me. On all these views, it matters who that person would be.

On my view, that question is unimportant. If this operation were performed, the person with my head tomorrow would not only believe that he was me, seem to remember living my life, and be in every other way psychologically like me. These facts would also have their normal

cause, the continued existence of my brain. And this person's body would
be just like mine. For all these reasons, his life would be just like the
life that I would have lived, if my paralysis had been cured. I believe that,
given these facts, I should accept this operation. It is irrelevant whether
this person would be me.

That may seem all important. After all, if he would not be me, I shall
have ceased to exist. But, if that person would not be me, this fact would
just consist in another fact. It would just consist in the fact that my body
will have been replaced below the neck. When considered on its own, is
that second fact important? Can it matter in itself that the blood that will
keep my brain alive will circulate, not through my own heart and lungs,
but through my brother's heart and lungs? Can it matter in itself that my
brain will control, not the rest of my body, but the rest of another body
that is exactly similar?

If we believe that these facts would amount to my nonexistence, it
may be hard to focus on the question whether, in themselves, these facts
matter. To make that easier, we should imagine that we accept a different view. Suppose we are convinced that the person with my head
tomorrow *would* be me. Would we then believe that it would matter
greatly that my head would have been grafted onto this other body?
We would not. We would regard my receiving a new torso, and new limbs,
as like any lesser transplant, such as receiving a new heart, or new kid-
neys. As this shows, if it would matter greatly that what will be replaced
is not just a few such organs, but my whole body below the neck, that
could only be because, if that happened, the resulting person would *not*
be me.

According to my argument, we should now conclude that neither of
these facts could matter greatly. Since it would not be in itself important that my head would be grafted onto this body, and that would be
all there was to the fact that the resulting person would not be me, it
would not be in itself important that this person would not be me. Perhaps it would not be irrational to regret these facts a little. But, I believe,
they would be heavily outweighed by the fact that, unlike me, the resulting person would not be paralysed.

When it is applied to our own existence, my argument is hard to
accept. But, as before, the fundamental question is the relative importance of language and reality.

On my view, what matters is what is going to happen. If I knew that
my head could be grafted onto the rest of a body that is just like mine,
and that the resulting person would be just like me, I would know enough
to decide whether to accept this operation. I need not ask whether the

resulting person could be correctly called me. That is not a further difference in what is going to happen.

That may seem a false distinction. What matters, we might say, is whether the resulting person would *be* me. But that person would be me if and only if he could be correctly called me. So, in asking what he could be called, we are not merely asking a conceptual question. We *are* asking about reality.

This objection fails to distinguish two kinds of case. Suppose that I ask my doctor whether, while I receive some treatment, I shall be in pain. That is a factual question. I am asking what will happen. Since pain can be called 'pain', I *could* ask my question in a different way. I could say, 'While I am being treated, will it be correct to describe me as in pain?' But that would be misleading. It would suggest that I am asking how we use the word 'pain'.

In a different case, I might ask that conceptual question. Suppose I know that, while I am crossing the Channel, I shall be feeling sea-sick, as I always do. I might wonder whether that sensation could be correctly called 'pain'. Here too, I could ask my question in a different way. I could say, 'While I am crossing the Channel, shall I be in pain?' But that would be misleading, since it would suggest that I am asking what will happen.

In the medical case, I don't know what conscious state I shall be in. There are different possibilities. In the Channel crossing case, there aren't different possibilities. I already know what state I shall be in. I am merely asking whether that state could be redescribed in a certain way.

It matters whether, while receiving the medical treatment, I shall be in pain. And it matters whether, while crossing the Channel, I shall be seasick. But it does not matter whether, in feeling sea-sick, I can be said to be in pain.

Return now to our main example. Suppose I know that my head will be successfully grafted onto my brother's headless body. I ask whether the resulting person will be me. Is this like the medical case, or the case of crossing the Channel? Am I asking what will happen, or whether what I know will happen could be described in a certain way?

On my view, I should take myself to be asking the second. I already know what is going to happen. There will be someone with my head and my brother's body. It is a merely verbal question whether that person will be me. And that is why, even if he won't be me, that doesn't matter.

It may now be objected: 'By choosing this example, you are cheating. Of course you should accept this operation. But that is because the resulting person *would* be you. We should reject the Bodily Criterion. So this case cannot show that identity is not what matters.'

234 • Part Four Is There an Enduring Self?

Since there are people who accept this criterion, I am not cheating. It is worth trying to show these people that identity is not what matters. But I accept part of this objection. I agree that we should reject the Bodily Criterion.

Of those who appeal to this criterion, some believe that persons just are bodies. But, if we hold this kind of view, it would be better to identify a person with that person's brain, or nervous system. Consider next those who believe that persons are animals of a certain kind, viz. human beings. We could take this view, but reject the Bodily Criterion. We could claim that animals continue to exist if there continue to exist and to function, the most important parts of their bodies. And we could claim that, at least in the case of human beings, the brain is so important that its survival counts as the survival of this human being. On both these views, in my imagined case, the person with my head tomorrow would be me. And that is what, on reflection, most of us would believe.

My own view is similar. I would state this view, not as a claim about reality, but as a conceptual claim. On my view, it would not be incorrect to call this person me; and this would be the best description of this case.

If we agree that this person would be me, I would still argue that this fact is not what matters. What is important is not identity, but one or more of the other facts in which identity consists. But I concede that, when identity coincides with these other facts, it is harder to decide whether we accept that argument's conclusion. So, if we reject the Bodily Criterion, we must consider other cases.

Suppose that we accept the Brain-Based version of the Psychological Criterion. On this view, if there will be one future person who is psychologically continuous with me, because he will have enough of my brain, that person will be me. But psychological continuity without its normal cause, the continued existence of enough of my brain, does not suffice for identity. My Replica would not be me.

Remember next that an object can continue to exist even if all its components are gradually replaced. Suppose that, every time some wooden ship comes into port, a few of its planks are replaced. Before long, the same ship may be entirely composed of different planks.

Assume, once again, that I need surgery. All of my brain cells have a defect which, in time, would be fatal. Surgeons could replace all these cells, inserting new cells that are exact replicas, except that they have no defect.

The surgeons could proceed in either of two ways. In *Case One*, there would be a hundred operations. In each operation, the surgeons would remove a hundredth part of my brain, and insert replicas of those parts.

In *Case Two*, the surgeons would first remove all the existing parts of my brain and then insert all of their replicas.

There is a real difference here. In Case One, my brain would continue to exist, like a ship with all of its planks gradually replaced. In Case Two, my brain would cease to exist, and my body would be given a new brain.

This difference, though, is much smaller than that between ordinary survival and teletransportation. In both cases, there will later be a person whose brain will be just like my present brain, but without the defects, and who will therefore be psychologically continuous with me. And, in *both* cases, this person's brain will be made of the very same new cells, each of which is a replica of one of my existing cells. The difference between the cases is merely the way in which these new cells are inserted. In Case One, the surgeons alternate between removing and inserting. In Case Two, they do all the removing before all the inserting.

On the Brain-Based Criterion, this is the difference between life and death. In Case One, the resulting person would be me. In Case Two he would *not* be me, so I would cease to exist.

Can this difference matter? Reapply the Argument from Below. This difference consists in the fact that, rather than alternating between removals and insertions, the surgeon does all the removing before all the inserting. Considered on its own, can this matter? I believe not. We would not think it mattered if it did not constitute the fact that the resulting person would not be me. But if this fact does not in itself matter, and that is all there is to the fact that in Case Two I would cease to exist, I should conclude that my ceasing to exist does not matter.

Suppose next that you regard these as problem cases, ones where you do not know what would happen to me. Return to the simpler Physical Spectrum. In each of the cases in this range, some proportion of my cells will be replaced with exact duplicates. With some proportions—20 percent, say, or 50, or 70—most of us would be uncertain whether the resulting person would be me. (As before, if we do not believe that here, my remarks could be transferred, with adjustments, to the Combined Spectrum.)

On my view, in all of the cases in this range, it is a merely conceptual question whether the resulting person would be me. Even without answering this question, I can know just what is going to happen. If there is anything that I don't know, that is merely a fact about how we could describe what is going to happen. And that conceptual question is not even, I believe, interesting. It is merely verbal, like the question whether, if I replaced some of its parts, I would still have the same audio system.

When we imagine these cases from a first-person point of view, it may still be hard to believe that this is merely a verbal question. If I don't know whether, tomorrow, I shall still exist, it may be hard to believe that I know what is going to happen. But what is it that I don't know? If there are different possibilities, at the level of what happens, what is the difference between them? In what would that difference consist? If I had a soul, or Cartesian Ego, there might be different possibilities. Perhaps, even if *n* percent of my cells were replaced, my soul would keep its intimate relation with my brain. Or perhaps another soul would take over. But, we have assumed, there are no such entities. What else could the difference be? When the resulting person wakes up tomorrow, what could make it either true, or false, that he is me?

It may be said that, in asking what will happen, I am asking what I can expect. Can I expect to wake up again? If that person will be in pain, can I expect to feel that pain? But this does not help. These are just other ways of asking whether that person will or will not be me. In appealing to what I can expect, we do not explain what would make these different possibilities.

We may believe that this difference needs no explanation. It may seem enough to say: Perhaps that person will be me, and perhaps he won't. Perhaps I shall exist tomorrow, and perhaps I shan't. It may seem that these must be different possibilities.

That, however, is an illusion. If I shall still exist tomorrow, that fact must consist in certain others. For there to be two possibilities, so that it might be either true or false that I shall exist tomorrow, there must be some other difference between these possibilities. There would be such a difference, for example, if between now and tomorrow, my brain and body might either remain unharmed, or be blown to pieces. But, in our imagined case, there is no such other difference. I already know that there will be someone whose brain and body will consist partly of these cells, and partly of new cells, and that this person will be psychologically like me. There aren't, at the level of what happens, different possible outcomes. There is no further essence of me, or property of me-ness, which either might or might not be there.

If we turn to the conceptual level, there *are* different possibilities. Perhaps that future person could be correctly called me. Perhaps he could be correctly called someone else. Or perhaps neither would be correct. That, however, is the only way in which it could be either true, or false, that this person would be me.

The illusion may persist. Even when I know the other facts, I may want reality to go in one of two ways. I may want it to be true that I shall still exist tomorrow. But all that could be true is that we use language in one of two ways. Can it be rational to care about that?

III

I am now assuming that we accept the Brain-Based Psychological Criterion. We believe that, if there will be one future person who will have enough of my brain to be psychologically continuous with me, that person would be me. On this view, there is another way to argue that identity is not what matters.

We can first note that, just as I could survive with less than my whole body, I could survive with less than my whole brain. People have survived, and with little psychological change, even when, through a stroke or injury, they have lost the use of half their brain.

Let us next suppose that the two halves of my brain could each fully support ordinary psychological functioning. That may in fact be true of certain people. If it is not, we can suppose that, through some technological advance, it has been made true of me. Since our aim is to test our beliefs about what matters, there is no harm in making such assumptions.

We can now compare two more possible operations. In the first, after half my brain is destroyed, the other half would be successfully transplanted into the empty skull of a body that is just like mine. Given our assumptions, we should conclude that, here too, I would survive. Since I would survive if my brain were transplanted, and I would survive with only half my brain, it would be unreasonable to deny that I would survive if that remaining half were transplanted. So, in this *Single Case*, the resulting person would be me.

Consider next the *Double Case*, or *My Division*. Both halves of my brain would be successfully transplanted, into different bodies that are just like mine. Two people would wake up, each of whom has half my brain, and is, both physically and psychologically, just like me.

Since these would be two different people, it cannot be true that each of them is me. That would be a contradiction. If each of them was me, each would be one and the same person: me. So they could not be two different people.

Could it be true that only one of them is me? That is not a contradiction. But, since I have the same relation to each of these people, there is nothing that could make me one of them rather than the other. It cannot be true, of either of these people, that he is the one who could be correctly called me.

How should I regard these two operations? Would they preserve what matters in survival? In the Single Case, the one resulting person would be me. The relation between me now and that future person is just an instance of the relation between me now and myself tomorrow. So that relation would contain what matters. In the Double Case, my relation to that person would be just the same. So this relation must still contain what matters. Nothing is missing. But that person cannot here be claimed to be me. So identity cannot be what matters.

We may object that, if that person isn't me, something *is* missing. *I'm* missing. That may seem to make all the difference. How can everything still be there if *I'm* not there?

Everything is still there. The fact that I'm not there is not a real absence. The relation between me now and the future person is in itself the same. As in the Single Case, he has half my brain, and he is just like me. The difference is only that, in this Double Case, I also have the same relation to the other resulting person. Why am I not there? The explanation is only this. When this relation holds between me now and a single person in the future, we can be called one and the same person. When this relation holds between me now and *two* future people, I cannot be called one and the same as each of these people. But that is not a difference in the nature or the content of this relation. In the Single Case, where half my brain will be successfully transplanted, my prospect is survival. That prospect contains what matters. In the Double Case, where both halves will be successfully transplanted, nothing would be lost.

It can be hard to believe that identity is not what matters. But that is easier to accept when we see why, in this example, it is true. It may help to consider this analogy. Imagine a community of persons who are like us, but with two exceptions. First, because of facts about their reproductive system, each couple has only two children, who are always twins. Second, because of special features of their psychology, it is of great importance for the development of each child that it should not, through the death of its sibling, become an only child. Such children suffer psychological damage. It is thus believed, in this community, that it matters greatly that each child should have a twin.

Now suppose that, because of some biological change, some of the children in this community start to be born as triplets. Should their parents think this a disaster, because these children don't have twins? Clearly not. These children don't have twins only because they each have *two* siblings. Since each child has two siblings, the trio must be called, not twins, but triplets. But none of them will suffer damage as an only child. These people should revise their view. What matters isn't having a twin: it is having at least one sibling.

In the same way, we should revise our view about identity over time. What matters isn't that there will be someone alive who will be me. It is rather that there will be at least one living person who will be psychologically continuous with me as I am now, and/or who has enough of my brain. When there will be only one such person, he can be described as me. When there will be two such people, we cannot claim that each will be me. But that is as trivial as the fact that, if I had two identical siblings, they could not be called my twins.[2]

IV

If, as I have argued, personal identity is not what matters, we must ask what does matter. There are several possible answers. And, depending on our answer, there are several further implications. Thus there are several moral questions which I have no time even to mention. I shall end with another remark about our concern for our own future.

That concern is of several kinds. We may want to survive partly so that our hopes and ambitions will be achieved. We may also care about our future in the kind of way in which we care about that well-being of certain other people, such as our relatives or friends. But most of us have, in addition, a distinctive kind of egoistic concern. If I know that my child will be in pain, I may care about his pain more than I would about my own future pain. But I cannot fearfully anticipate my child's pain. And if I knew that my Replica would take up my life where I leave off, I would not look forward to that life.

This kind of concern may, I believe, be weakened, and be seen to have no ground, if we come to accept a Reductionist view. In our thoughts about our own identity, we are prone to illusions. That is why the so-called 'problem cases' seem to raise problems: why we find it hard to believe that, when we know the other facts, it is an empty or a merely verbal question whether we shall still exist. Even after we accept a Reductionist view, we may continue, at some level, to think and feel as if that view were not true. Our own continued existence may still seem an independent fact, of a peculiarly deep and simple kind. And that belief may underlie our anticipatory concern about our own future.

There are, I suspect, several causes of that illusory belief. I have discussed one cause here: our conceptual scheme. Though we need concepts

[2]In many contexts, we need to distinguish two senses of 'what matters in survival.' What matters in the *prudential* sense is what gives us reason for special concern about our future. What matters in the *desirability* sense is what makes our survival good. But, in the examples I have been discussing, these two coincide. On my view, even if we won't survive, we could have what matters *in* survival. If there will be at least one living person who will both be psychologically continuous with me, and have enough of my brain, my relation to that person contains what matters in the prudential sense. So it also preserves what matters in the desirability sense. It is irrelevant whether that person will be me.

to think about reality, we sometimes confuse the two. We mistake conceptual facts for facts about reality. And, in the case of certain concepts, those that are most loaded with emotional or moral significance, we can be led seriously astray. Of these loaded concepts, that of our own identity is, perhaps, the most misleading.

Even the use of the word 'I' can lead us astray. Consider the fact that, in a few years, I shall be dead. This fact can seem depressing. But the reality is only this. After a certain time, none of the thoughts and experiences that occur will be directly causally related to this brain, or be connected in certain ways to these present experiences. That is all this fact involves. And, in that redescription, my death seems to disappear.

Feminist Perspectives on the Self

Diana Meyers

The topic of the self has long been salient in feminist philosophy, for it is pivotal to questions about personhood, identity, the body, and agency that feminism must address. In some aspects, Simone de Beauvoir's trenchant observation, "He is the Subject, he is the Absolute—she is the Other," sums up why the self is such an important issue for feminism. To be the Other is to be the non-subject, the non-person, the non-agent—in short, the mere body. In law, in customary practice, and in cultural stereotypes, women's selfhood has been systematically subordinated, diminished, and belittled, when it has not been outright denied. Since women have been cast as lesser forms of the masculine individual, the paradigm of the self that has gained ascendancy in U.S. popular culture and in Western philosophy is derived from the experience of the predominantly white and heterosexual, mostly economically advantaged men who have wielded social, economic, and political power and who have dominated the arts, literature, the media, and scholarship. Responding to this state of affairs, feminist philosophical work on the self has taken three main tacks: (1) critique of established views of the self, (2) reclamation of women's selfhood, and (3) reconceptualization of the self to incorporate women's experience. . . .

1. Critique

Two views of the self have been prominent in contemporary Anglo-American moral and political philosophy—a Kantian ethical subject and homo economicus. Both of these conceptions see the individual as a free and rational chooser and actor—an autonomous agent. Nevertheless, they differ in their emphasis. The Kantian ethical subject uses reason to transcend cultural norms and to discover absolute moral truth, whereas homo economicus uses reason to rank desires in a coherent order and to figure out how to maximize desire satisfaction. Whether the self is identified with pure abstract reason or with the instrumental rationality of the marketplace, though, these conceptions of the self isolate the individual from personal relationships and larger social forces. For the Kantian ethical subject, emotional bonds and social conventions imperil objectivity and undermine commitment to duty. For homo economicus, it makes no difference what social forces shape one's desires provided they do not result from coercion or fraud, and one's ties to other people are to be factored into one's calculations and planning along with the rest of one's desires. Some feminist philosophers modify and defend these conceptions of the self. But their decontextualized individualism and their privileging of reason over other capacities trouble many feminist philosophers.

Twentieth century philosophy's regnant conceptions of the self minimize the personal and moral import of unchosen circumstances and interpersonal relationships. They eclipse family, friendship, passionate love, and community, and they downplay the difficulty of resolving conflicts that arise between these commitments and personal values and aspirations. Since dependency is dismissed as a defective form of selfhood, caregiving responsibilities vanish along with children, the disabled, and the frail elderly. Prevailing conceptions of the self ignore the multiple, sometimes fractious sources of social identity constituted by one's gender, sexual orientation, race, class, age, ethnicity, and so forth. Structural domination and subordination do not penetrate the "inner citadel" of selfhood. Likewise, these conceptions deny the complexity of the intrapsychic world of unconscious fantasies, fears, and desires, and they overlook the ways in which such materials intrude upon conscious life. The homogenized—you might say sterilized—rational subject is not prey to ambivalence, anxiety, obsession, prejudice, hatred, or violence. A disembodied mind, the body is peripheral—a source of desires for homo economicus to weigh and a distracting temptation for the Kantian ethical subject. Age, looks, sexuality, and physical competencies are extraneous to the self. As valuable as the capacities for rational analysis and free choice undoubtedly are, it is hard to believe that there is nothing more to the self.

Feminist philosophers have charged that these views are, at best, incomplete and, at worst, fundamentally misleading. Many feminist critiques take the question of who provides the paradigm for these conceptions as their point of departure. Who models this free, rational self? Although represented as genderless, sexless, raceless, ageless, and classless, feminists argue that the Kantian ethical subject and homo economicus mask a white, healthy, youthfully middle-aged, middleclass, heterosexual MAN. He is pictured in two principle roles—as an impartial judge or legislator reflecting on principles and deliberating about policies and as a self-interested bargainer and contractor wheeling and dealing in the marketplace. It is no accident that politics and commerce are both domains from which women have historically been excluded. It is no accident either that the philosophers who originated these views of the self typically endorsed this exclusion. Deeming women emotional and unprincipled, these thinkers advocated confining women to the domestic sphere where their vices could be neutralized, even transformed into virtues, in the role of submissive wife and nurturant mother.

Feminist critics point out, furthermore, that this misogynist heritage cannot be remedied simply by condemning these traditional constraints and advocating equal rights for women, for these conceptions of the self are themselves gendered. In western culture, the mind and reason are coded masculine, whereas the body and emotion are coded feminine (Lloyd 1992). To identify the self with the rational mind is, then, to masculinize the self. If selfhood is not impossible for women, it is only because they resemble men in certain essential respects—they are not altogether devoid of rational will. Yet, feminine selves are necessarily deficient, for they only mimic and approximate the masculine ideal.

Problematic, as well, is the way in which these gendered conceptions of the self contribute to the valorization of the masculine and the stigmatization of the feminine. The masculine realm of rational selfhood is a realm of moral decency—principled respect for others and conscientious fidelity to duty—and of prudent good sense—adherence to shrewd, fulfilling, long-range life plans. However, femininity is associated with emotionally rooted concern for family and friends that spawns favoritism and compromises principles. Likewise, femininity is associated with immersion in unpredictable domestic exigencies that forever jeopardize the best-laid plans and often necessitate resorting to hasty retreats or charting new directions. By comparison, the masculinized self appears to be a sturdy fortress of integrity. How flattering! The self is essentially masculine, and the masculine self is essentially good and wise.

Feminists object that this philosophical consolidation of the preeminence of the masculine over the feminine rests on untenable assumptions about the transparency of the self, the immunity of the self to noxious social influences, and the reliability of reason as a corrective to distorted moral judgment. Today people grow up in social environments in which culturally normative prejudice persists, even in communities where overt forms of bigotry are strictly proscribed (Meyers 1994). Although official cultural norms uphold the values of equality and tolerance, cultures continue to transmit camouflaged messages of the inferiority of historically subordinated social groups through stereotypes and other imagery. These deeply ingrained schemas commonly structure attitudes, perception, and judgment despite the individual's conscious good will (Valian 1998). As a result, people often consider themselves objective and fair, and yet they systematically discriminate against "different" others while favoring members of their own social group (Piper 1990; Young 1990). Fortified by culture and ensconced in the unconscious, such prejudice cannot be dispelled through rational reflection alone (Meyers 1994). In effect, then, the Kantian moral subject countenances "innocent" wrongdoing and occluded reinforcement of the social stratification that privileges the minority of men whom this conception takes as paradigmatic.

These oversights necessitate reconceptualizing the self in two respects. To account for the residual potency of this form of prejudice, feminists urge, the self must be understood as socially situated and murkily heterogeneous. To account for the self's ability to discern and resist culturally normative prejudice, the moral subject must not be reduced to the capacity for reason.

Complementing this line of argument, a number of feminists argue that conceptualizing the self as a seamless whole has invidious social consequences. To realize this ideal, it is necessary to repress inner diversity and conflict and to police the boundaries of the purified self. Alien desires and impulses are consigned to the unconscious, but this unconscious material inevitably intrudes upon conscious life and influences people's attitudes and desires. In particular, the feared and despised Other within is projected onto "other" social groups, and hatred and contempt are redirected at these imagined enemies (Scheman 1993; Kristeva 1991). Misogyny and other forms of bigotry are thus borne of the demand that the self be unitary together with the impossibility of meeting this demand. Worse still, these irrational hatreds cannot be cured unless this demand is repudiated, but to repudiate this demand is to be resigned to a degraded, feminized self. Far from functioning as the guarantor of moral probity, the Kantian moral subject is the condition of the possibility of intractable animosity and injustice.

Another strand of feminist critique targets homo economicus's preoccupation with independence and planning. In an eery suspension of biological reality, selves are conceived as sufficient unto themselves. No one seems to be born and raised, for birth mothers and caregivers are driven offstage (Baier 1987; Code 1987; Held 1987; Benhabib and Cornell 1987; Kittay 1999). The self appears to materialize on its own, endowed with a starter set of basic desires, ready to select additional desires and construct overarching goals, and skilled in performing instrumental rationality tasks. No one's powers ever seem to deteriorate either, for time is suspended along with biology. Since dependency is denied, no morally significant preconsensual or nonconsensual entanglements at the beginning or the end of life need be acknowledged. All affiliations are to be freely chosen, and all transactions are to be freely negotiated. The repudiation of feminine caregiving underwrites the illusion of independence, and the illusion of independence underwrites homo economicus's voluntarism.

To achieve maximal fulfillment, homo economicus must organize his chosen pursuits into a rational life plan. He must decide which desires are most urgent; he must ensure that his desires are co-satisfiable; and he must ascertain the most efficient way to satisfy this set of desires. Madcap spontaneity and seat-of-the-pants improvisation are registered as defeats for "The Man with the Plan." Not only is this vision of a life governed by a self-chosen plan distinctly middleclass, it is gendered (Addelson 1994; Walker 1999). The mother coping with the vagaries of early childhood and the wife accommodating her man's plan are the antitheses of this conception of the self. Uncertain of where they are ultimately headed and seldom sure how to achieve the goals they embrace as they go along, these women violate norms of selfhood. Ironically, middleclass men who grow old also have difficulty measuring up to homo economicus's standards of control. Unable to count on continued health and vigor, unable to anticipate the onset of serious disease or disabling conditions, unable finally to outwit the grim reaper, affluent elderly men violate norms of selfhood along with women and the poor. The price of denying the relationality of the self and idolizing rational self-regulation is that full selfhood eludes all but a lucky, albeit transitory, male elite.

A further problem with this view from a feminist standpoint is that it fails to furnish an adequate account of internalized oppression and the process of overcoming it. It is common for women to comport themselves in a feminine fashion, to scale down their aspirations, and to embrace gender-compliant goals (Bartky 1990; Babbitt 1993). Feminists account for this phenomenon by explaining that women internalize patriarchal values and norms—that is, these pernicious values and norms become integrated in the cognitive, emotional, and conative structure of the self. Once embedded in a woman's psychic economy, internalized oppression conditions her desires. To maximize satisfaction of her desires, then, would be to collaborate in her own oppression. Paradoxically, the more completely she fulfills these desires, the worse off she becomes. Advantaged as he is, homo economicus can safely accept his desires as given and proceed without ado to orchestrate a plan to satisfy them. But women and members of other subordinated groups can ill-afford such complacency, and homo economicus's instrumental reason is too superficial a form of mastery to serve their interests (Babbitt 1993). They need a conception of the self that renders emancipatory transformation of one's values and projects intelligible.

Feminist critique exposes the partiality of the ostensibly universal Kantian ethical subject and homo economicus. These conceptions of the self are: 1) androcentric because they replicate masculine stereotypes and ideals; 2) sexist because they demean anything that smacks of the feminine; and 3) masculinist because they help to perpetuate male dominance. . . .

3. Reconceptualizations

3.1. The Nature of the Self

The primary task of a philosophy of the self is to clarify what makes something a self. Feminist philosophers are acutely aware that this is not a value-free task. To get an analysis of the nature of the self off the ground, one must decide which entities count as selves (or, at least, which entities are noncontroversially counted as selves within one's linguistic community). Since we regard selves as valuable—as members of our moral community and as worthy of respect—these judgments are in part judgments about which entities are valuable. Moreover, values enter into these judgments because we consider selves to be the sorts of things that can achieve (or fail to achieve) ideals of selfhood. Thus, philosophical accounts of the self have implications for conceptions of what it is to lead a good life. As we have seen, many feminist philosophers argue that it is a mistake to hold that rationality alone is essential to the self and that the ideal self is transparent, unified, coherent, and independent, for they discern misogynist subtexts in the atomistic individualism of the Kantian ethical subject and homo economicus (see Section 1). It is incumbent on feminist philosophers, then, to develop more satisfactory accounts of the self—accounts that are compatible with respect for women. Thus, a number of feminist philosophers propose reconstructions of alternative theories of the nature of the self.

Three traditions have been especially influential in recent feminist thought—classic psychoanalysis, objective relations theory, and post-structuralism. Feminist philosophers gravitate toward these approaches to understanding selfhood because they do not share the drawbacks that prompt feminist critique of the Kantian ethical subject and homo economicus. None of these approaches regards the self as homogeneous or transparent; none supposes that a self should be coherent and speak in a single voice; none removes the self from its cultural or interpersonal setting; none sidelines the body. In appropriating these views, feminists bring out their implications in regard to gender, incorporate feminist insights into these theories, and modify the theories to address feminist concerns.

Julia Kristeva transposes the classic Freudian conception of the self and the distinction between consciousness and the unconscious into an explicitly gendered discursive framework (Kristeva 1980). For Kristeva, the self is a subject of enunciation—a speaker who can use the pronoun 'I'. But speakers are not unitary, nor are they fully in control of what they say because discourse is bifurcated. The symbolic dimension of language, which is characterized by referential signs and linear logic, corresponds to consciousness and control. The clear, dry prose of scientific research reports epitomizes symbolic discourse. The semiotic dimension of language, which is characterized by figurative language, cadences, and intonations, corresponds to the unruly, passion-fueled unconscious. The ambiguities and nonstandard usages of poetry epitomize semiotic discourse. These paradigms notwithstanding, Kristeva maintains that all discourse combines elements of both registers. Every intelligible utterance relies on semantic conventions, and every utterance has a tone, even if it is a dull monotone. This contention connects Kristeva's account to feminist concerns about gender and the self. Since the rational orderliness of the symbolic is culturally coded masculine while the affect-laden allure of the semiotic is culturally coded feminine, it follows that no discourse is purely masculine or purely feminine. The masculine symbolic and the feminine semiotic are equally indispensable to the speaking subject, whatever this individual's socially assigned gender may be. It is not possible, then, to be an unsulliedly masculine self or an unsulliedly feminine self. Every subject of enunciation—every self—amalgamates masculine and feminine discursive modalities.

Like the unconscious in classic psychoanalytic theory, the semiotic decenters the self. One may try to express one's thoughts in definite, straightforward language, yet because of the semiotic aspects of one's utterances, what one says carries no single meaning and is amenable to being interpreted in more than one way. In Kristeva's view, this is all to the good, for accessing the semiotic—that which is conveyed, often inadvertently, by the style of an utterance—kindles social critique. The semiotic gives expression to repressed, unconscious material. According to Kristeva, what society systematically represses provides clues to what is oppressive about society and how society needs to be changed. Thus, she discerns a vital ethical potential in the semiotic (Kristeva 1987). Since this ethical potential is explicitly linked to the feminine, moreover, Kristeva's account of the self displaces "masculine" adherence to principle as the prime mode of ethical agency and recognizes the urgent need for a "feminine" ethical approach. Viewing the self as a "questionable-subject-in-process"—a subject who is responsive to the encroachments of semiotic material into conscious life and who is therefore without a fixed or unitary identity—and valorizing the dissident potential of this decentered subjectivity, Kristeva seeks to neutralize the fear of the inchoate feminine that, in her view, underwrites misogyny. In one respect, Nancy Chodorow's appropriation of object relations theory parallels Kristeva's project of reclaiming and revaluing femininity, for Chodorow's account of the relational self reclaims and revalues feminine mothering capacities. But whereas Kristeva focuses on challenging the homogeneous self and the bright line between reason, on the one hand, and emotion and desire, on the other, Chodorow focuses on challenging the self-subsisting self with its sharp self-other boundaries. Chodorow's claim that the self is inextricable from interpersonal relationships calls into question the decontextualized individualism of the Kantian ethical subject and homo economicus.

Chodorow sees the self as relational in several respects (Chodorow 1981). Every child is cared for by an adult or adults, and every individual is shaped for better or worse by this emotionally charged interaction. As a result of feelings of need and moments of frustration, the infant becomes differentiated from its primary caregiver and develops a sense of separate identity. Concomitantly, a distinctive personality emerges. By selectively internalizing and recombining elements of their experience with other people, children develop characteristic traits and dispositions. Moreover, Chodorow attributes the development of a key interpersonal capacity to nurturance. A caregiver who is experienced as warmly solicitous is internalized as a "good internal mother" (Chodorow 1980). Children gain a sense of their worthiness by internalizing the nurturance they receive and directing it toward themselves, and they learn to respect and respond to other people by internalizing their experience of nurturance and projecting it toward others. Whereas Kristeva understands the self as a dynamic interplay between the feminine semiotic and the masculine symbolic, Chodorow understands the self as fundamentally relational and thus linked to cultural norms of feminine interpersonal responsiveness. For Chodorow, the rigidly differentiated, compulsively rational, stubbornly independent self is a masculine defensive formation—a warped form of the rational self—that develops as a result of fathers' negligible involvement in childcare.

Feminist philosophers have noted strengths and weaknesses in both of these views. For example, Kristeva's questionable-subject-in-process seems to enshrine and endorse the very gender dichotomy that causes women so much grief. Yet, Chodorow's rational self seems to glorify weak individuation and scorn the independence and self-assertiveness that many women desperately need. Still, Kristeva's analyses of the psychic, social, and political potency of gender figurations underscore the need for feminist counter-imagery to offset culturally entrenched, patriarchal images of womanhood. And Chodorow's appreciation of the relational self together with her diagnosis of the damage wrought by hyperindividuation advances feminist demands for equitable parenting practices. These contributions notwithstanding, both of these views have come under attack for heterosexist biases as well as for inattention to other forms of difference among women.

Critical race theorists and poststructuralists have been particularly vocal about this failure to come to grips with the diversity of gender, and they have offered accounts of the self designed to accommodate difference. Poststructuralist Judith Butler maintains that personal identity—the sense that there are answers to the questions 'who am I?' and 'what am I like?'—is an illusion (Butler 1990). The self is merely an unstable discursive node—a shifting confluence of multiple discursive currents—and sexed/gendered identity is merely a "corporeal style"—the imitation and repeated enactment of ubiquitous norms. For Butler, psychodynamic accounts of the self, including Kristeva's and Chodorow's, camouflage the performative nature of the self and collaborate in the cultural conspiracy that maintains the illusion that one has an emotionally anchored, interior identity that is derived from one's biological nature, which is manifest in one's genitalia. Such accounts are pernicious. In concealing the ways in which normalizing regimes deploy power to enforce the performative routines that construct "natural" sexed/gendered bodies together with debased, "unnatural" bodies, they obscure the arbitrariness of the constraints that are being imposed and deflect resistance to these constraints. The solution, in Butler's view, is to question the categories of biological sex, polarized gender, and determinate sexuality that serve as markers of personal identity, to treat the construction of identity as a site of political contestation, and to embrace the subversive potential of unorthodox performances and parodic identities.

African American feminists are less sanguine than poststructuralists about the felicitous social impact of playful deviations from norms and the laughter they may prompt (Williams 1991; Crenshaw 1993). Nevertheless, some of them have adapted poststructuralist theory to the purposes of critical race theory. Noting that gender, race, and class stratification do not operate in isolation from one another but rather interact to produce compound effects, these theorists conceive of the individual as an intersectional subject—a site where structures of domination and subordination converge (King 1988; Crenshaw 1993). Intersectional theory does not purport to offer a comprehensive theory of the self. Its aim is to capture those aspects of selfhood that are conditioned by membership in subordinated or privileged social groups. Accenting the liabilities of belonging to more than one subordinated group, Kimberle Crenshaw likens the position of such individuals to that of a pedestrian hit by several speeding vehicles simultaneously, and Maria Lugones likens their position to that of a stateless border-dweller who is not at home anywhere (Crenshaw 1991; Lugones 1992). Nevertheless, some theorists of mixed ancestry embrace border-dwelling as a model of positive identity (Anzaldua 1987; Alcoff 1995). Moreover, proponents of the intersectional self credit multiply oppressed people with a certain epistemic advantage. In virtue of their suffering and alienation, these individuals are well situated not only to discern which values and practices in their heritage deserve allegiance but also to identify shortcomings in the traditions of the groups to which they belong. Thus, African American women are acutely aware of racism within feminism and sexism within the struggle for racial justice. Their intersectional positioning and subjectivity makes such insight virtually unavoidable.

By and large, recent feminist philosophy of the self reflects skepticism about modernist, unitary accounts of the self. In seeking to remedy the androcentric biases of the latter views, feminist philosophers emphasize features of selfhood that other philosophical schools neglect, including intersubjectivity, heterogeneity, and social construction. Still, some contemporary feminist philosophers express concern that the sorts of conceptions I have sketched are detrimental to feminist aims. Influenced by Jurgen Habermas's communicative ethics, Seyla Benhabib refuses to join poststructuralists in declaring the death of the autonomous, self-reflective individual who is capable of taking responsibility and acting on principle (Benhabib 1995). Although Benhabib is committed to viewing people as socially situated, interpersonally bonded, and embodied, she is also committed to the feasibility of rational philosophical justification of universal moral norms. Moreover, she argues that a narrative conception of the self renders the idea of a core self and coherent identity intelligible without suppressing difference and without insulating the self from social relations (Benhabib 1999). Autobiographical stories can include the many voices within us and the many relationships we have experienced, and these stories are constantly under revision, for they are always being contested by our associates' disparate self-narratives with their divergent versions of events. Nevertheless, these narratives do not collapse into incoherence, and they presuppose a core capacity to describe and reflect on one's experience. For Benhabib, this view of selfhood and reason is indispensable to feminist emancipatory objectives. . . .

4. Conclusion

As this article attests, there is tremendous foment and variety within the field of feminist work on the self. Yet, in reviewing this literature, I have been struck by a recurrent theme—the inextricability of metaphysical issues about the self from moral and political theory. Feminist critiques of regnant philosophical theories of the self expose the normative underpinnings of these theories. Feminist analyses of women's agentic capacities both acknowledge traditional feminine social contributions and provide accounts of how women can overcome oppressive norms and practices. Feminist reconstructions of the nature of the self are interwoven with arguments that draw out the emancipatory benefits of conceiving the self one way rather than another. There is nothing surprising, to be sure, about the salience of normative concerns in feminist philosophizing. Still, I mention it because I believe that feminists' attention to political concerns leads to fresh questions and also that asking novel questions enriches philosophical understanding of the self. Moreover, I would urge that this forthrightness about the political viewpoint that informs philosophy is a virtue, for overlooking the political suppositions and implications of esoteric philosophical view has led to considerable mischief.

References

The following works are cited:

Addelson, Kathryn Pyne. 1994. *Moral Passages:* New York: Routledge.

Alcoff, Linda. 1995. "Mestizo Identity." In *American Mixed Race: The Culture of Microdiversity*, ed., Naomi Zack, 257–278. Lanham, MD and London: Rowman and Littlefield, 1995.

Anzaldua, Gloria. 1987. *Borderlands: The New Mestiza/La Frontera.* San Fransisco: Spinters/Aunt Lute.

Babbitt, Susan E. 1993. "Feminism and Objective Interests? The Role of Transformation Experiences in Rational Deliberation." In *Feminist Epistemologies*, eds., Linda Alcoff and Elizabeth Potter. New York: Routledge, 1993.

Baier, Annette. 1997. "Trust and Anti-Trust." *Ethics* 96 (January 1986): 231–260. ALSO IN: *Feminist Social Thought*, ed., Diana Tietjens Meyers. New York: Routledge, 1997.

Baier, Susan. 1987. "The Need for More than Justice." In *Science, Morality, and Feminist Theory*, eds., Marsha Hanen and Kai Nielsen. Minneapolis: University of Minnesota Press.

Bartky, Sandra Lee. 1990. *Femininity and Domination.* New York: Routledge.

Benhabib, Seyla. 1999. "Sexual Difference and Collective Identities: The New Global Constellation." *Signs* 24: 335–361.

Benhabib, Seyla, and Drucilla Cornell, eds. 1987. *Feminism as Critique.* Minneapolis: University of Minnesota Press.

Benhabib, Seyla, et. al. 1995 *Feminist Contentions.* New York: Routledge.

Butler, Judith. 1990. "Gender Trouble, Feminist Theory, and Psychoanalytic Discourse." In *Feminism/Postmodernism*, ed., Linda Nicholson. New York: Routledge.

Chodorow, Nancy. 1980. "Gender, Relation, and Difference in Psychoanalytic Perspective," In *The Future of Difference*, ed., Hester Eisenstein and Alice Jardine. Boston: G.K. Hall.

Chodorow, Nancy. 1981. "On the Reproduction of Mothering: A Methodological Debate." *Signs* 6: 500–514.

Code, Lorraine. 1987. "Second Persons." In *Science, Morality, and Feminist Theory* (Supplement to *Canadian Journal of Philosophy* 13), ed., Marsha Hanen and Kai Nielsen. Calgary: University of Calgary Press.

Crenshaw, Kimberlé. 1991. "Demarginalizing the Intersection of Race and Sex: A Black Feminist Critique of Antidiscrimination Doctrine, Feminist Theory, and Antiracist Politics." In *Feminist Legal Theory*, eds. Katherine T. Bartlett and Rosanne Kennedy. Boulder: Westview Press.

Crenshaw, Kimberlé. 1993. "Beyond Race and Misogyny: Black Feminism and 2 Live Crew." In *Words that Wound*, ed. Mari J. Matsuda, et. al. Boulder: Westview Press.

Hartsock, Nancy. 1983. *Money, Sex, Power.* New York: Longman.

Held, Virginia. 1987. "Feminism and Moral Theory." In *Women and Moral Theory*, eds., Eva Feder Kittay and Diana T. Meyers. Totowa: Rowman and Littlefield. ALSO IN: *Feminist Social Thought* (Meyers 1997).

King, Deborah K. 1988. "Multiple Jeopardy, Multiple Consciousness: The Context of a Black Feminist Ideology." *Signs* 14(1): 42–72. ALSO IN: *Feminist Social Thought* (Meyers 1997).

Kittay, Eva Feder. 1999. *Love's Labor.* New York: Routledge.

Kristeva, Julia. 1980. *Desire in Language*, eds., Thomas Gora, Alice Jardine, and Leon Roudiez (Trans). New York: Columbia University Press.

Kristeva, Julia. 1987. *Tales of Love*, Leon Roudiez (Trans). New York: Columbia University Press.

Kristeva, Julia. 1991. *Strangers to Ourselves*, Leon Roudiez (Trans.). New York: Columbia University Press.

Lloyd, Genevieve. 1992. "Maleness, Metaphor, and the 'Crisis' of Reason." In *A Mind of One's Own*, eds., Louise Antony and Charlotte Witt. Boulder: Westview Press.

Lugones, María. 1992. "On 'Borderlands/La Frontera': An Interpretive Essay." *Hypatia* 7:4 (Fall): 31–37.

Piper, Adrian M.S. 1990. "Higher-Order Discrimination." In *Identity, Character and Morality*, eds., Owen Flanagan and Amelie Okensberg Rorty. Cambridge: MIT Press.

Scheman, Naomi. 1993. *Engenderings.* New York: Routledge.

Valian, Virginia. 1998. *Why So Slow? The Advancement of Women.* Cambridge: MIT Press.

Walker, Margaret Urban. 1999. "Getting Out of Line: Alternatives to Life as a Career." In *Mother Time*, ed., Margaret Urban Walker. Lanham, MD: Rowman and Littlefield.

Williams, Patricia J. 1991. *The Alchemy of Race and Rights.* Cambridge: Harvard University Press.

Young, Iris Marion. 1990. *Stretching Out.* Bloomington: Indiana University Press.

PART FIVE

WHAT IS THE MIND?

Each of us has a mind. We have thoughts, beliefs, sensations, experiences, hopes, doubts, fears, dreams, and desires. However, it is not clear at all what, exactly, a mind is or what mental states are. Minds seem quite different from the others sorts of things we encounter on a day-to-day basis. Unlike cats, trucks, eggplants, high-rise buildings, or bodies, mental states are not observable, and they do not have shape, size, or texture. Mental states are private—we each have a special access to our own mental states that others do not have. Our mental states are subjective—no one else can have our mental states. Despite what our friends say, they cannot feel our pain. These fundamental differences between the mental and the nonmental give rise to what philosophers call the "mind–body problem," which is the focus of this section of this book. This problem concerns the nature of the mind (and mental states). What kind of thing is the mind? Is it simply part of the body (that is, the brain or central nervous system) or is it something over and above the physical body?

René Descartes held that the mind is distinct from the body on the grounds that the mind and the body do not share all of the same properties. He argued that human beings are made up of two distinct substances—a physical substance (the body) and a mental substance (the mind). Hence, his theory of the mind, his answer to the Mind–Body Problem, is what is known as *substance (or Cartesian) dualism*.

Although few contemporary philosophers are substance dualists, it is important to mention the view for two reasons. First, in some way or another, all of the philosophy of mind that followed Descartes', right up to the present, can be seen as a reaction to his version of dualism, and each attempts to accommodate so-called "Cartesian intuitions" about the mental—intuitions that, in many respects, the mind is fundamentally different from the body. Second, many nonphilosophers tend to gravitate toward some version of it. However, in our first reading in this section, the chapter from his book *Matter and Consciousness* entitled "Dualism," Paul Churchland argues that neither substance dualism nor what he calls *popular dualism* fairs very well under scrutiny. Even though neuroscience, or "brain" science is far from "complete," given what we do know about the relationship between the mind and the brain, Churchland argues that we have no reason to suppose that there is some nonphysical aspect to mental states.

One extreme response to the difficulties faced by dualism is presented by the philosophical behaviorist's account of the mental. According to this version of behaviorism, what it means to be in some mental state or another is simply to behave, or to be disposed to behave, in certain ways in certain circumstances. Behaviorism is a form of physicalism in that it takes mental states or minds to be physical states of a thing. The selection from John Heil, "Philosophical Behaviorism," describes this theory of the mind and the intellectual context in which it arose. While behaviorism may have trouble accounting for many of our Cartesian intuitions about the mind, behaviorists made a significant contribution to philosophy of mind by focusing their examination of the mental on behavior. Consequently, the two main varieties of physicalism that came subsequent to behaviorism—identity theory and functionalism—include some reference to behavior in their analysis of the mental.

In his paper, "The Nature of Mind," David Armstrong questions the behaviorist's analysis of dispositional states. Whereas the behaviorist is committed to the view that mental states can be analyzed in terms of dispositions to behave in certain ways given certain antecedent conditions, Armstrong argues that this characterization of dispositions ignores the underlying physical constitution of a thing that disposes it to behave in the way it does. For example, a thing may be described as fragile, having the disposition to break when dropped, and that disposition can be explained in terms of the object's having a certain molecular structure. Similarly, says Armstrong, our dispositions to behave in certain ways in certain conditions can be explained by certain internal states of us—certain neurological states of us ("brain states" for short). Thus, he says we can think of perceptions as inner states or events apt for the production of certain sorts of selective behavior towards the environment. To perceive is like acquiring a key to a door. You do not have to use the key: you can put it in your pocket and never bother about the door. But if you want to open the door, the key may be essential. The blind man is a man who does not acquire certain keys and, as a result, is not able to operate in his environment in the way that somebody who has sight can operate.

Thus, while mental states ought not be *reduced* to behavior, mental states, according to this theory of the mental, are identical to those brain or neural states that typically cause certain behaviors. The fact that the identity theory is simple and straightforward and that it is consistent with what we know from science makes it an attractive alternative to dualism. However, as we shall see, it is not without its own set of problems.

Simply put, locks can be picked. That is, if we suppose that one can open a door's lock with something other than its key, then there is something not quite right about the identity theory of the mind. What may be more important than one's having certain keys is what the keys (or paper clips, or hairpins, or credit cards) one has can do. The main idea of our next theory of the mind is *not* that it be made of certain stuff, but rather that that stuff it is made of *functions* in a certain way. According to this theory, we should not define a mind in terms of what it is made of; instead, we should define a mind in terms of what it *does*. In "Mad Pain and Martian Pain," David Lewis argues that because we can imagine (1) some person who is physiologically just like us and yet mentally quite different from us, and (2) some creature physiologically quite different from us and mentally similar to us, it cannot be the case that what it is to be in some particular mental state is to be in some particular brain state. That is, Lewis raises a serious objection to the identity theory. The theory of the mind he argues for is called *functionalism*. Along with this view comes the idea that mental states are *multiply realizable*—that is, one and the same mental state can be "made up" of different stuff in different creatures. So, perceiving is not like "acquiring a key to open a door," but it is more like *opening* the door. If you and I open the same (or similar) door with quite different keys (or paper clips, hairpins, etc.), we are both perceiving.

Functionalism, however, encounters a problem when trying to account for the qualitative character of experience. This problem is motivated by the following thought-experiment called the Inverted Spectrum.

It seems possible to imagine that two people, Karin and Nirak, who, in the presence of a red tomato, are functionally indistinguishable. That is, they both say things like, "That tomato is red," and they can both pick out the red tomato from green tomatoes, etc. However, while Karin's experience has the qualitative character that "normal" perceivers have when looking at red things, Nirak's experience has the qualitative character that "normal' perceivers have when looking at green things. So, although their mental states are functionally the same, they are phenomenally different. If this is the case, then the phenomenal aspect of experience is not accounted for by a functionalist theory of the mental. Terrance Horgan's paper, "Functionalism, Qualia, and the Inverted Spectrum," defends what he calls *partial functionalism* in response to the Inverted Spectrum objection. He argues that while nonphenomenal mental states are best explained in terms functionalism provides, phenomenal states should be construed as nonrelational, neural state types. Thus, he favors a theory of the mind that combines some aspects of functionalism with some aspects of identity theory.

By defining the mind in terms of what it does rather than in terms of what it is made of, functionalism allows for the possibility of artificial intelligence (AI). If functionalism is true, then it is possible that a very advanced robot could be functionally indistinguishable from a human being at least in terms of certain mental states. That is, a robot could have some thing (a circuit, silicon chip, or whatever) that played the same role that, say, some particular neuron firing plays in us. In "Why People Think Computers Can't," Marvin Minsky explores the possibility of intelligent computers.

In response to the thesis of strong AI—the idea that the appropriately programmed computer literally understands—John Searle argues, in "Minds, Brains, and Programs," that there is more to understanding than fulfilling some functional role. In his Chinese Room thought experiment, he presents a case in which a person who does not understand Chinese is functionally indistinguishable from a native Chinese speaker. If his objection goes through, then there is something wrong with functionalism, because there is more to understanding, more to being in a particular mental state, than functionalism would require.

In the final paper in this section, "Epiphenomenal Qualia," Frank Jackson gives his infamous objection to physicalism—The Knowledge Argument. In the first version of this argument, we are asked to imagine Fred, a person who can discriminate one more shade of red than can other color perceivers. It seems that we could know all the physical facts about Fred's physiology, and yet we could not know facts about *what it is like* for Fred to see this extra color. Therefore, Jackson argues, facts about *what it is like* to see, smell, hear, taste, etc., are facts that escape a physicalist theory. In the second, and far more influential, version of this argument, we are asked to imagine Mary, a color scientist who has lived her entire life in a black-and-white laboratory. She observes the world on a black-and-white monitor, and yet she knows all of the physical facts about seeing red. The intuition Jackson thinks we should have is that, upon leaving her lab, Mary learns something new about seeing color—she learns *what it is like* to see color. If she does in fact learn something new, and she knew all the *physical* facts, then there is a *nonphysical* fact about seeing color. Because seeing is a mental state, if there is something nonphysical about seeing, then physicalism is false. The property of experience in virtue, of which there is something that it is like to have an experience, is called a *quale* (or plural, *qualia*). In this paper, Jackson's objection to physicalism is at the same time a defense of what is called *property dualism*—the theory of the mind that says that, for the most part, the mind is a physical thing; however, the mind has certain *nonphysical properties*, namely, qualia.

The Mind-Body Problem has evolved into a set of problems that constitute contemporary philosophy of mind. Philosophers today continue to try to answer core questions about the nature of mind as well as questions about the relationship between the mind and body, the connection between mental states and what they are about, and the nature of phenomenal consciousness or qualia. By answering these questions philosophers hope to unveil the mysterious mind.

Dualism
Paul Churchland

. . . The dualistic approach to mind encompasses several quite different theories, but they are all agreed that the essential nature of conscious intelligence resides in something *nonphysical*, in something forever beyond the scope of sciences like physics, neurophysiology, and computer science. Dualism is not the most widely held view in the current philosophical and scientific community, but it is the most common theory of mind in the public at large, it is deeply entrenched in most of the world's popular religions, and it has been the dominant theory of mind for most of Western history. It is thus an appropriate place to begin our discussion.

Substance Dualism

The distinguishing claim of this view is that each mind is a distinct nonphysical thing, an individual "package" of nonphysical substance, a thing whose identity is independent of any physical body to which it may be temporarily "attached." Mental states and activities derive their special character, on this view, from their being states and activities of this unique, nonphysical substance.

This leaves us wanting to ask for more in the way of a *positive* characterization of the proposed mind-stuff. It is a frequent complaint with the substance dualist's approach that his characterization of it is so far almost entirely negative. This need not be a fatal flaw, however, since we no doubt have much to learn about the underlying nature of mind, and perhaps the deficit here can eventually be made good. On this score, the philosopher René Descartes (1596–1650) has done as much as anyone to provide a positive account of the nature of the proposed mind-stuff, and his views are worthy of examination.

Descartes theorized that reality divides into two basic kinds of substance. The first is ordinary matter, and the essential feature of this kind of substance is that it is extended in space: any instance of it has length, breadth, height, and occupies a determinate position in space. Descartes did not attempt to play down the importance of this type of matter. On the contrary, he was one of the most imaginative physicists of his time, and he was an enthusiastic advocate of what was then called "the mechanical philosophy." But there was one isolated corner of reality he thought could not be accounted for in terms of the mechanics of matter: the conscious reason of Man. This was his motive for proposing a second and radically different kind of substance, a substance that has no spatial extension or spatial position whatever, a substance whose essential feature is the activity of *thinking*. This view is known as *Cartesian dualism*.

As Descartes saw it, the real *you* is not your material body, but rather a nonspatial thinking substance, an individual unit of mind-stuff quite distinct from your material body. This nonphysical mind is in systematic causal interaction with your body. The physical state of your body's sense organs, for example, causes visual/auditory/tactile experiences in your mind. And the desires and decisions of your nonphysical mind cause your body to behave in purposeful ways. Its causal connections to your mind are what make your body yours, and not someone else's.

The main reasons offered in support of this view were straightforward enough. First, Descartes thought that he could determine, by direct introspection alone, that he was essentially a thinking substance and nothing else. And second, he could not imagine how a purely physical system could ever use *language* in a relevant way, or engage in mathematical *reasoning*, as any normal human can. Whether these are good reasons, we shall discuss presently. Let us first notice a difficulty that even Descartes regarded as a problem.

If "mind-stuff" is so utterly different from "matter-stuff" in its nature—different to the point that it has no mass whatever, no shape whatever, and no position anywhere in space—then how is it possible for my mind to have any causal influence on my body at all? As Descartes himself was aware (he was one of the first to formulate the law of the conservation of momentum), ordinary matter in space behaves according to rigid laws, and one cannot get bodily movement (= momentum) from nothing. How is this utterly insubstantial "thinking substance" to have any influence on ponderous matter? How can two such different things be in any sort of causal contact? Descartes proposed a very subtle material substance—"animal spirits"—to convey the mind's influence to the body in general. But this does not provide us with a solution, since it leaves us with the same problem with which we started: how something ponderous and spatial (even "animal spirits") can interact with something entirely nonspatial.

In any case, the basic principle of division used by Descartes is no longer as plausible as it was in his day. It is now neither useful nor accurate to characterize ordinary matter as that-which-has-extension-in-space. Electrons, for example, are bits of matter, but our best current theories describe the electron as a point-particle with no extension what-ever (it even lacks a determinate spatial position). And according to Ein-stein's theory of gravity, an entire star can achieve this same status, if it undergoes a complete gravitational collapse. If there truly is a divi-sion between mind and body, it appears that Descartes did not put his finger on the dividing line.

Such difficulties with Cartesian dualism provide a motive for con-sidering a less radical from of substance dualism, and that is what we find in a view I shall call *popular dualism*. This is the theory that a per-son is literally a "ghost in a machine," where the machine is the human body, and the ghost is a spiritual substance, quite unlike physical mat-ter in its internal constitution, but fully possessed of spatial properties even so. In particular, minds are commonly held to be *inside* the bodies they control: inside the head, on most views, in intimate contact with the brain.

This view need not have the difficulties of Descartes'. The mind is right there in contact with the brain, and their interaction can perhaps be understood in terms of their exchanging energy of a form that our sci-ence has not yet recognized or understood. Ordinary matter, you may recall, is just a form or manifestation of energy. (You may think of a grain of sand as a great deal of energy condensed or frozen into a small pack-age, according to Einstein's relation, $E = mc^2$.) Perhaps mind-stuff is a well-behaved form or manifestation of energy also, but a different form of it. It is thus *possible* that a dualism of this alternative sort be consis-tent with familiar laws concerning the conservation of momentum and energy. This is fortunate for dualism, since those particular laws are very well established indeed.

This view will appeal to many for the further reason that it at least holds out the possibility (though it certainly does not guarantee) that the mind might survive the death of the body. It does not guarantee the mind's survival because it remains possible that the peculiar form of energy here supposed to constitute a mind can be produced and sustained only in conjunction with the highly intricate form of matter we call the brain, and must disintegrate when the brain disintegrates. So the prospects for surviving death are quite unclear even on the assumption that popular dualism is true. But even if survival were a clear conse-quence of the theory, there is a pitfall to be avoided here. Its promise of survival might be a reason for *wishing* dualism to be true, but it does not constitute a reason for *believing* that it *is* true. For that, we would need independent empirical evidence that minds do indeed survive the permanent death of the body. Regrettably, and despite the exploitative blatherings of the supermarket tabloids (**TOP DOCS PROVE LIFE AFTER DEATH!!!**), we possess no such evidence.

As we shall see later in this section, when we turn to evaluation, positive evidence for the existence of this novel, nonmaterial, thinking *substance* is in general on the slim side. This has moved many dualists to articulate still less extreme forms of dualism, in hopes of narrowing further the gap between theory and available evidence.

Property Dualism

The basic idea of the theories under this heading is that while there is no *substance* to be dealt with here beyond the physical brain, the brain has a special set of *properties* possessed by no other kind of physical object. It is these special properties that are nonphysical: hence the term *property dualism*. The properties in question are the ones you would expect: the property of having a pain, of having a sensation of red, of thinking that *P*, of desiring that *Q*, and so forth. These are the properties that are characteristic of conscious intelligence. They are held to be nonphysical in the sense that they cannot ever be reduced to or explained solely in terms of the concepts of the familiar physical sciences. They will require a wholly new and autonomous science—the 'science of mental phenomena'—if they are ever to be adequately understood.

From here, important differences among the positions emerge. Let us begin with what is perhaps the oldest version of property dualism: *epiphenomenalism*. This term is rather a mouthful, but its meaning is simple. The Greek prefix "epi-" means "above", and the position at issue holds that mental phenomena are not a part of the physical phenomena in the brain that ultimately determine our actions and behavior, but rather ride "above the fray." Mental phenomena are thus *epi*phenomena. They are held to just appear or emerge when the growing brain passes a certain level of complexity.

But there is more. The epiphenomenalist holds that while mental phenomena are caused to occur by the various activities of the brain, *they do not have any causal effects in turn*. They are entirely impotent with respect to causal effects on the physical world. They are *mere* epiphenomena. (To fix our ideas, a vague metaphor may be helpful here. Think of our conscious mental states as little sparkles of shimmering light that occur on the wrinkled surface of the brain, sparkles which are caused to occur by physical activity in the brain, but which have no causal effects on the brain in return.) This means that the universal conviction that one's actions are determined by one's desires, decisions, and volitions is false! One's actions are exhaustively determined by physical events in the brain, which events *also* cause the epiphenomena we call desires, decisions, and volitions. There is therefore a constant conjunction between volitions and actions. But according to the epiphenomenalist, it is mere illusion that the former cause the latter.

What could motivate such a strange view? In fact, it is not too difficult to understand why someone might take it seriously. Put yourself in the shoes of a neuroscientist who is concerned to trace the origins of behavior back up the motor nerves to the active cells in the motor cortex of the cerebrum, and to trace in turn their activity into inputs from other parts of the brain, and from the various sensory nerves. She finds a thoroughly physical system of awesome structure and delicacy, and much intricate activity, all of it unambiguously chemical or electrical in nature, and she finds no hint at all of any nonphysical inputs of the kind that substance dualism proposes. What is she to think? From the standpoint of her researches, human behavior is exhaustively a function of the activity of the physical brain. And this opinion is further supported by her confidence that the brain has the behavior-controlling features it does exactly because those features have been ruthlessly selected for during the brain's long evolutionary history. In sum, the seat of human behavior appears entirely physical in its constitution, in its origins, and in its internal activities.

On the other hand, our neuroscientist has the testimony of her own introspection to account for as well. She can hardly deny that she has experiences, beliefs, and desires, nor that they are connected in some way with her behavior. One bargain that can be struck here is to admit the *reality* of mental properties, as nonphysical properties, but demote them to the status of impotent epiphenomena that have nothing to do with the scientific explanation of human and animal behavior. This is the position the epiphenomenalist takes, and the reader can now perceive the rationale behind it. It is a bargain struck between the desire to respect a rigorously scientific approach to the explanation of behavior, and the desire to respect the testimony of introspection.

The epiphenomenalist's "demotion" of mental properties—to causally impotent by-products of brain activity—has seemed too extreme for most property dualists, and a theory closer to the convictions of common sense has enjoyed somewhat greater popularity. This view, which we may call *interactionist property dualism*, differs from the previous view in only one essential respect: the interactionist asserts that mental properties do indeed have causal effects on the brain, and thereby, on behavior. The mental properties of the brain are an integrated part of the general causal fray, in systematic interaction with the brain's physical properties. One's actions, therefore, are held to be caused by one's desires and volitions after all.

As before, mental properties are here said to be *emergent* properties, properties that do not appear at all until ordinary physical matter has managed to organize itself, through the evolutionary process, into a system of sufficient complexity. Examples of properties that are emergent in this sense would be the property of being *solid*, the property of being *colored*, and the property of being *alive*. All of these require matter to be suitably organized before they can be displayed. With this much, any materialist will agree. But any property dualist makes the further claim that mental states and properties are *irreducible*, in the sense that they are not just organizational features of physical matter, as are the examples cited. They are said to be novel properties beyond prediction or explanation by physical science.

This last condition—the irreducibility of mental properties—is an important one, since this is what makes the position a dualist position. But it sits poorly with the joint claim that mental properties emerge from nothing more than the organizational achievements of physical matter. If that is how mental properties are produced, then one would expect a physical account of them to be possible. The simultaneous claim of evolutionary emergence *and* physical irreducibility is prima facie puzzling.

A property dualist is not absolutely bound to insist on both claims. He could let go the thesis of evolutionary emergence, and claim that mental properties are *fundamental* properties of reality, properties that have been here from the universe's inception, properties on a par with length, mass, electric charge, and other fundamental properties. There is even an historical precedent for a position of this kind. At the turn of this century it was still widely believed that electromagnetic phenomena (such as electric charge and magnetic attraction) were just an unusually subtle manifestation of purely *mechanical* phenomena. Some scientists thought that a reduction of electromagnetics to mechanics was more or less in the bag. They thought that radio waves, for example, would turn out to be just travelling oscillations in a very subtle but jellylike aether that fills space everywhere. But the aether turned out not to exist. So electromagnetic properties turned out to be fundamental properties in their own right, and we were forced to add electric charge to the existing list of fundamental properties (mass, length, and duration).

Perhaps mental properties enjoy a status like that of electromagnetic properties: irreducible, but not emergent. Such a view may be called *elemental-property dualism*, and it has the advantage of clarity over the previous view. Unfortunately, the parallel with electromagnetic phenomena has one very obvious failure. Unlike electromagnetic properties, which are displayed at all levels of reality from the subatomic level on up, mental properties are displayed only in large physical systems that have evolved a very complex internal organization. The case for the evolutionary emergence of mental properties through the organization of matter is extremely strong. They do not appear to be basic or elemental at all. This returns us, therefore, to the issue of their irreducibility. Why should we accept this most basic of the dualist's claims? Why be a dualist?

Arguments of Dualism

Here we shall examine some of the main considerations commonly offered in support of dualism. Criticism will be postponed for a moment so that we may appreciate the collective force of these supporting considerations.

A major source of dualistic convictions is the *religious belief* many of us bring to these issues. Each of the major religions is in its way a theory about the cause or purpose of the universe, and Man's place within it, and many of them are committed to the notion of an immortal soul—that is, to some form of substance dualism. Supposing that one is consistent, to consider disbelieving dualism is to consider disbelieving one's religious heritage, and some of us find that difficult to do. Call this the *argument from religion*.

A more universal consideration is the *argument from introspection*. The fact is, when you center your attention on the contents of your consciousness, you do not clearly apprehend a neural network pulsing with electrochemical activity: you apprehend a flux of thoughts, sensations, desires, and emotions. It seems that mental states and properties, as revealed in introspection, could hardly be more different from physical states and properties if they tried. The verdict of introspection, therefore, seems strongly on the side of some form of dualism—on the side of property dualism, at a minimum.

A cluster of important considerations can be collected under the *argument from irreducibility*. Here one points to a variety of mental phenomena where it seems clear that no purely physical explanation could possibly account for what is going on. Descartes has already cited our ability to use language in a way that is relevant to our changing circumstances, and he was impressed also with our faculty of Reason, particularly as it is displayed in our capacity for mathematical reasoning. These abilities, he thought, must surely be beyond the capacity of any physical system. More recently, the introspectible qualities of our sensations (sensory "qualia"), and the meaningful content of our thoughts and beliefs, have also been cited as phenomena that will forever resist reduction to the physical. Consider, for example, seeing the color or smelling the fragrance of a rose. A physicist or chemist might know everything about the molecular structure of the rose, and of the human brain, argues the dualist, but that knowledge would not enable him to predict or anticipate the quality of these inexpressible experiences.

Finally, parapsychological phenomena are occasionally cited in favor of dualism. Telepathy (mind reading), precognition (seeing the future), telekinesis (thought control of material objects), and clairvoyance (knowledge of distant objects) are all awkward to explain within the normal confines of psychology and physics. If these phenomena are real, they might well be reflecting the superphysical nature that the dualist ascribes to the mind. Trivially they are *mental* phenomena, and if they are also forever beyond physical explanation, then at least some mental phenomena must be irreducibly nonphysical.

Collectively, these considerations may seem compelling. But there are serious criticisms of each, and we must examine them as well. Consider first the argument from religion. There is certainly nothing wrong in principle with appealing to a more general theory that bears on the case at issue, which is what the appeal to religions amounts to. But the appeal can only be as good as the scientific credentials of the religions(s) being appealed to, and here the appeals tend to fall down rather badly. In general, attempts to decide scientific questions by appeal to religious orthodoxy have a very sorry history. That the stars are other suns, that the earth is not the center of the universe, that diseases are caused by microorganisms, that the earth is billions of years old, that life is a physicochemical phenomenon; all of these crucial insights were strongly and sometimes viciously resisted, because the dominant religion of the time happened to think otherwise. Giordano Bruno was burned at the stake for urging the first view; Galileo was forced by threat of torture in the Vatican's basement to recant the second view; the firm belief that disease was a punishment visited by the Devil allowed public health practices that brought chronic plagues to most of the cities of Europe; and the age of the earth and the evolution of life were forced to fight an uphill battle against religious prejudice even in an age of supposed enlightenment.

History aside, the almost universal opinion that one's own religious convictions are the reasoned outcome of a dispassionate evaluation of all of the major alternatives is almost demonstrably false for humanity in general. If that really were the genesis of most people's convictions, then one would expect the major faiths to be distributed more or less randomly or evenly over the globe. But in fact they show a very strong tendency to cluster: Christianity is centered in Europe and the Americas, Islam in Africa and the Middle East, Hinduism in India, and Buddhism in the Orient. Which illustrates what we all suspected anyway: that *social forces* are the primary determinants of religious belief for people in general. To decide scientific questions by appeal to religious orthodoxy would therefore be to put social forces in place of empirical evidence. For all of these reasons, professional scientists and philosophers concerned with the nature of mind generally do their best to keep religious appeals out of the discussion entirely.

The argument from introspection is a much more interesting argument, since it tries to appeal to the direct experience of everyman. But the argument is deeply suspect, in that it assumes that our faculty of inner observation or introspection reveals things as they really are in their innermost nature. This assumption is suspect because we already know that our other forms of observation—sight, hearing, touch, and so on— do no such thing. The red surface of an apple does not *look* like a matrix of molecules reflecting photons at certain critical wavelengths, but that is what it is. The sound of a flute does not *sound* like a sinusoidal compression wave train in the atmosphere, but that is what it is. The warmth of the summer air does not *feel* like the mean kinetic energy of millions of tiny molecules, but that is what it is. If one's pains and hopes and beliefs do not *introspectively* seem like electrochemical states in a neural network, that may be only because our faculty of introspection, like our other senses, is not sufficiently penetrating to reveal such hidden details. Which is just what one would expect anyway. The argument from introspection is therefore entirely without force, unless we can somehow argue that the faculty of introspection is quite different from all other forms of observation.

The argument from irreducibility presents a more serious challenge, but here also its force is less than first impression suggests. Consider first our capacity for mathematical reasoning which so impressed Descartes. The last ten years have made available, to anyone with fifty dollars to spend, electronic calculators whose capacity for mathematical reasoning—the calculational part, at least—far surpasses that of any normal human. The fact is, in the centuries since Descartes' writings, philosophers, logicians, mathematicians, and computer scientists have managed to isolate the general principles of mathematical reasoning, and electronics engineers have created machines that compute in accord with those principles. The result is a hand-held object that would have astonished Descartes. This outcome is impressive not just because machines have proved capable of some of the capacities boasted by human reason, but because some of those achievements invade areas of human reason that past dualistic philosophers have held up as forever closed to mere physical devices.

Although debate on the matter remains open, Descartes' argument from language use is equally dubious. The notion of a *computer language* is by now a commonplace: consider BASIC, PASCAL, FORTRAN, APL, LISP, and so on. Granted, these artificial 'languages' are much simpler in structure and content than human natural language, but the differences may be differences only of degree, and not of kind. As well, the theoretical work of Noam Chomsky and the generative grammar approach to linguistics have done a great deal to explain the human capacity for language use in terms that invite simulation by computers. I do not mean to suggest that truly conversational computers are just around the corner. We have a great deal yet to learn, and fundamental problems yet to solve (mostly having to do with our capacity for inductive or theoretical reasoning). But recent progress here does nothing to support the claim that language use must be forever impossible for a purely physical system. On the contrary, such a claim now appears rather arbitrary and dogmatic.

The next issue is also a live problem: How can we possibly hope to explain or to predict the intrinsic qualities of our sensations, or the meaningful content of our beliefs and qualities of our sensations, or the meaningful content of our beliefs and desires, in purely physical terms? This is a major challenge to the materialist. But as we shall see in later sections, active research programs are already under way on both problems, and positive suggestions are being explored. It is in fact not impossible to imagine how such explanations might go, though the materialist cannot yet pretend to have solved either problem. Until he does, the dualist will retain a bargaining chip here, but that is about all. What the dualists need in order to establish their case is the conclusion that a physical reduction is outright impossible, and that is a conclusion they have failed to establish. Rhetorical questions, like the one that opens this paragraph, do not constitute arguments. And it is equally difficult, note, to imagine how the relevant phenomena could be explained or predicted solely in terms of the substance dualist's nonphysical mind-stuff. The explanatory problem here is a major challenge to everybody, not just to the materialist. On this issue then, we have a rough standoff.

The final argument in support of dualism urged the existence of parapsychological phenomena such as telepathy and telekinesis, the point being that such mental phenomena are (a) real, and (b) beyond purely physical explanation. This argument is really another instance of the argument from irreducibility discussed above, and as before, it is not entirely clear that such phenomena, even if real, must forever escape a purely physical explanation. The materialist can already suggest a possible mechanism for telepathy, for example. On his view, thinking is an electrical activity within the brain. But according to electromagnetic theory, such changing motions of electric charges must produce electromagnetic waves radiating at the speed of light in all directions, waves that will contain information about the electrical activity that produced them. Such waves can subsequently have effects on the electrical activity of other brains, that is, on their thinking. Call this the 'radio transmitter/receiver' theory of telepathy.

I do not for a moment suggest that this theory is true: the electromagnetic waves emitted by the brain are fantastically weak (billions of times weaker than the ever present background electromagnetic flux produced by commercial radio stations), and they are almost certain to be hopelessly jumbled together as well. This is one reason why, in the absence of systematic, compelling, and repeatable evidence for the existence of telepathy, one must doubt its possibility. But it is significant that the materialist has the theoretical resources to suggest a detailed possible explanation of telepathy, if it were real, which is more than any dualist has so far done. It is not at all clear, then, that the materialist *must* be at an explanatory disadvantage in these matters. Quite the reverse.

Put the preceding aside, if you wish, for the main difficulty with the argument from parapsychological phenomena is much, much simpler. Despite the endless pronouncements and anecdotes in the popular press, and despite a steady trickle of serious research on such things, there is no significant or trustworthy evidence that such phenomena even exist. The wide gap between popular conviction on this matter, and the actual evidence, is something that itself calls for research. For there is not a single parapsychological effect that can be repeatedly or reliably produced in any laboratory suitably equipped to perform and control the experiment. Not one. Honest researchers have been repeatedly hoodwinked by 'psychic' charlatans with skills derived from the magician's trade, and the history of the subject is largely a history of gullibility, selection of evidence, poor experimental controls, and outright fraud by the occasional researcher as well. If someone really does discover a repeatable parapsychological effect, then we shall have to reevaluate the situation, but as things stand, there is nothing here to support a dualist theory of mind.

Upon critical examination, the arguments in support of dualism lose much of their force. But we are not yet done: there are arguments against dualism, and these also require examination.

Arguments Against Dualism

The first argument against dualism urged by the materialists appeals to the greater *simplicity* of their view. It is a principle of rational methodology that, if all else is equal, the simpler of two competing hypotheses should be preferred. This principle is sometimes called "Ockham's Razor"—after William of Ockham, the medieval philosopher who first enunciated it—and it can also be expressed as follows: "Do not multiply entities beyond what is strictly necessary to explain the phenomena." The materialist postulates only one kind of substance (physical matter), and one class of properties (physical properties), whereas the dualist postulates two kinds of matter and/or two classes of properties. And to no explanatory advantage, charges the materialist.

This is not yet a decisive point against dualism, since neither dualism nor materialism can yet explain all of the phenomena to be explained. But the objection does have some force, especially since there is no doubt at all physical matter exists, while spiritual matter remains a tenuous hypothesis.

If this latter hypothesis brought us some definite explanatory advantage obtainable in no other way, then we would happily violate the demand for simplicity, and we would be right to do so. But it does not, claims the materialist. In fact, the advantage is just the other way around, he argues, and this brings us to the second objection to dualism: the relative *explanatory impotence* of dualism as compared to materialism.

Consider, very briefly, the explanatory resources already available to the neurosciences. We know that the brain exists and what it is made of. We know much of its microstructure: how the neurons are organized into systems and how distinct systems are connected to one another, to the motor nerves going out to the muscles, and to the sensory nerves coming in from the sense organs. We know much of their microchemistry: how the nerve cells fire tiny electrochemical pulses along their various fibers, and how they make other cells fire also, or cease firing. We know some of how such activity processes sensory information, selecting salient or subtle bits to be sent on to higher systems. And we know some of how such activity initiates and coordinates bodily behavior. Thanks mainly to neurology (the branch of medicine concerned with brain pathology), we know a great deal about the correlations between damage to various parts of the human brain, and various behavioral and cognitive deficits from which the victims suffer. There are a great many isolated deficits—some gross, some subtle—that are familiar to neurologists (inability to speak, or to read, or to understand speech, or to recognize faces, or to add/subtract, or to move a certain limb, or to put information into long-term memory, and so on), and their appearance is closely tied to the occurrence of damage to very specific parts of the brain.

Nor are we limited to cataloguing traumas. The growth and development of the brain's microstructure is also something that neuroscience has explored, and such development appears to be the basis of various kinds of learning by the organism. Learning, that is, involves lasting chemical and physical changes in the brain. In sum, the neuroscientist can tell us a great deal about the brain, about its constitution and the physical laws that govern it; he can already explain much of our behavior in terms of the physical, chemical, and electrical properties of the brain; and he has the theoretical resources available to explain a good deal more as our explorations continue.

Compare now what the neuroscientist can tell us about the brain, and what he can do with that knowledge, with what the dualist can tell us about spiritual substance, and what he can do with those assumptions. Can the dualist tell us anything about the internal constitution of mind-stuff? Of the nonmaterial elements that make it up? Of the laws that govern their behavior? Of the mind's structural connections with the body? Of the manner of its operations? Can he explain human capacities and pathologies in terms of its structures and its defects? The fact is, the dualist can do none of these things, because no detailed theory of mind-stuff has ever been formulated. Compared to the rich resources and explanatory successes of current materialism, dualism is less a theory of mind than it is an empty space waiting for a genuine theory of mind to be put in it.

Thus argues the materialist. But again, this is not a completely decisive point against dualism. The dualist can admit that the brain plays a major role in the administration of both perception and behavior—on his view the brain is the *mediator* between the mind and the body—but he may attempt to argue that the materialist's current successes and future explanatory prospects concern only the mediative functions of the brain, not the *central* capacities of the nonphysical mind, capacities such as reason, emotion, *and* consciousness itself. On these latter topics, he may argue, both dualism and materialism currently draw a blank.

But this reply is not a very good one. So far as the capacity for reasoning is concerned, machines already exist that execute in minutes sophisticated deductive and mathematical calculations that would take a human a lifetime to execute. And so far as the other two mental capacities are concerned, studies of such things as depression, motivation, attention, and sleep have revealed many interesting and puzzling facts about the neurochemical and neurodynamical basis of both emotion and consciousness. The *central* capacities, no less than the peripheral, have been addressed with profit by various materialist research programs.

In any case, the (substance) dualist's attempt to draw a sharp distinction between the unique 'mental' capacities proper to the nonmaterial mind, and the merely mediative capacities of the brain, prompts an argument that comes close to being an outright refutation of (substance) dualism. If there really is a distinct entity in which reasoning, emotion, and consciousness take place, and if that entity is dependent on the brain for nothing more than sensory experiences as input and volitional executions as output, *then one would expect reason, emotion, and consciousness to be relatively invulnerable to direct control or pathology by manipulation or damage to be brain.* But in fact the exact opposite is true. Alcohol, narcotics, or senile degeneration of nerve tissue will impair, cripple, or even destroy one's capacity for rational thought. Psychiatry knows of hundreds of emotion-controlling chemicals (lithium, chlorpromazine, amphetamine, cocaine, and so on) that do their work when vectored into the brain. And the vulnerability of consciousness to the anesthetics, to caffeine, and to something as simple as a sharp blow to the head, shows its very close dependence on neural activity in the brain. All of this makes perfect sense if reason, emotion, and consciousness are activities of the brain itself. But it makes very little sense if they are activities of something else entirely.

We may call this the argument from the *neural dependence* of all known mental phenomena. Property dualism, note, is not threatened by this argument, since, like materialism, property dualism reckons the brain as the seat of all mental activity. We shall conclude this section, however, with an argument that cuts against both varieties of dualism: the argument from *evolutionary history.*

What is the origin of a complex and sophisticated species such as ours? What, for that matter, is the origin of the dolphin, the mouse, or the housefly? Thanks to the fossil record, comparative anatomy, and the biochemistry of proteins and nucleic acids, there is no longer any significant doubt on this matter. Each existing species is a surviving type from a number of variations on an earlier type of organism; each earlier type is in turn a surviving type from a number of variations on a still earlier type of organism; and so on down the branches of the evolutionary tree until, some three billion years ago, we find a trunk of just one or a handful of very simple organisms. These organisms, like their more complex offspring, are just self-repairing, self-replicating, energy-driven molecular structures. (That evolutionary trunk has its own roots in an earlier era of purely chemical evolution, in which the molecular elements of life were themselves pieced together.) The mechanism of development that has structured this tree has two main elements: (1) the occasional blind variation in types of reproducing creature, and (2) the selective survival of some of these types due to the relative reproductive advantage enjoyed by individuals of those types. Over periods of geological time, such a process can produce an enormous variety of organisms, some of them very complex indeed.

For purposes of our discussion, the important point about the standard evolutionary story is that the human species and all of its features are the wholly physical outcome of a purely physical process. Like all but the simplest of organisms, we have a nervous system. And for the same reason: a nervous system permits the discriminative guidance of behavior. But a nervous system is just an active matrix of cells, and a cell is just an active matrix of molecules. We are notable only in that our nervous system is more complex and powerful than those of our fellow creatures. Our inner nature differs from that of simpler creatures in degree, but not in kind.

If this is the correct account of our origins, then there seems neither need, nor room, to fit any nonphysical substances or properties into our theoretical account of ourselves. We are creatures of matter. And we should learn to live with that fact.

Arguments like these have moved most (but not all) of the professional community to embrace some form of materialism. This has not produced much unanimity, however, since the differences between the several materialist positions are even wider than the differences that divide dualism.

Philosophical Behaviorism
John Heil

. . . We began with an examination of Descartes's contention that minds and material bodies are distinct kinds of substance. We then examined a number of related views, views that could be spun out from our Cartesian starting point by rejecting or modifying one or another of its components. In this paper, we shall explore two materialist accounts of the mind.

Materialists deny that the world includes both mental and material substances. Every substance is a material substance. Minds are fashioned somehow from the same materials from which rocks, trees, and stars are made. If we take the fundamental particles that make up inanimate objects and arrange them in the right way, the result is a creature with a mind. The mind is not a separate, non-material entity, but only matter, suitably organized.

Materialism has a long history. Democritus (c. 460–370 BC) described the world as a fleeting arrangement of atoms swirling in the void. Hobbes (1588–1679) and La Mettrie (1707–51) regarded mental phenomena as nothing more than mechanical interactions of material components. Nowadays, materialism of one stripe or another is more often than not taken for granted. The belief that minds are just brains is evidently widespread. Francis Crick's recent description of this as "the astonishing hypothesis" flies in the face of my own experience with undergraduate philosophy students who seem to use "mind" and "brain" interchangeably.

Although many philosophers would, if pressed, describe themselves as materialists, materialism comes in different flavors. Disagreements among materialists tend to overshadow their common rejection of dualism. In recent years, dissatisfaction with materialist assumptions has led to a revival of interest in forms of dualism. Surprisingly, much of this interest has been spawned by work in the neurosciences where difficulties in reconciling characteristics of complex material systems with characteristics of conscious experiences are especially acute.

In this chapter, we shall examine [one] precursor to the contemporary debate: behaviorism. . . . Behaviorism as a philosophical doctrine about the nature of mind differs from behaviorism as a movement in psychology. Philosophical behaviorism is associated with a thesis about the nature of mind and the meanings of mental terms. Psychological behaviorism emerged from a particular conception of scientific method as applied to psychology. This brand of behaviorism dominated experimental work in psychology until the 1960s when it was eclipsed by the information-processing model, a model inspired by the advent of the computing machine.

The relation between philosophy and the empirical sciences, including psychology, is scarcely straightforward. On the one hand, philosophers of mind have had an important part in shaping conceptions of mentality that guide empirical investigators. On the other hand, philosophers have periodically re-evaluated their theories in light of advances in the sciences. One result is that philosophical influences on the sciences find their way back into philosophy. When this happens, a philosophical thesis can gain an undeserved air of empirical respectability in the minds of philosophers eager to embrace the pronouncements of science.

Philosophers, impressed by behaviorism in psychology, sometimes failed to appreciate the extent to which the behaviorist conception of mind was the product of a definite philosophical conception of scientific method. Ironically, the roots of that conception lay in a positivist tradition that many of these same philosophers would have found unappealing. One lesson is that it is a mistake for philosophers of mind to accept uncritically or at face value claims issuing from psychology or the neurosciences.

Behaviorism

Until the twentieth century, the study of the mind was assumed to revolve around the study of conscious states and processes. Subjects in psychological experiments (very often the experimenters themselves or their students) were trained to "introspect," and report on features of their conscious experiences. In this milieu, mental imagery and subtle qualities of sensory episodes had a central place.

At the same time, psychologists were concerned to integrate the study of the mind with the study of the brain. It had long been evident that occurrences in the brain and nervous system were intimately related to mental goings-on. The difficulty was to understand precisely the nature of the relation between minds and brains. It is tempting to think that minds (or selves: I shall continue to use the terms interchangeably, without intending to suggest that they are synonymous) are nothing more than brains. Properties of brains, however, seem to differ importantly from properties of minds. When you undergo a conscious experience, you are vividly aware of characteristics of that experience. When we examine a living brain, the characteristics we observe appear to be utterly different. Think of what it is like to have a headache. Now imagine that you are able to peer at the brain of someone suffering a headache. What you observe, even aided by instruments that reveal the fine structure of the brain, is altogether different from what the headache victim feels. Imagine a neuroscientist, intimately familiar with the physiology of headache, but who has never experienced a headache. There is, it would seem, something the scientist lacks knowledge of, some characteristic the scientist has not encountered and could not encounter simply by inspecting the brain. But then this characteristic would appear not to be a neurological characteristic. When we look at the matter this way, it is hard to avoid concluding that mental characteristics are not brain characteristics, and thus that minds are not brains.

If this were not enough, we would do well to remind ourselves that we evidently enjoy a kind of "access" to our conscious experiences that others could never have. Your experiences are "private." Your awareness of them is direct and authoritative; my awareness of those same experiences is, in contrast, indirect, inferential, and easily overridden. When you have a headache, form an image of your grandmother, or decide to comb your hair, you are in a position to recognize immediately, without the benefit of evidence or observation, that you have a headache, that you are imagining your grandmother, or that you have decided to comb your hair. I can only infer your state of mind by observing your behavior (including your linguistic behavior: I can interrogate you). If mental goings-on are correlated with neurological processes, then I may be able to infer your state of mind by observing your brain. But my access to that state is still indirect. I infer your state of mind by observing a neurological correlate. I do not observe your state of mind.

All this is exactly what we should expect were dualism true. But dualism, or at any rate Cartesian dualism, apparently leads to a bifurcation of the study of intelligent agents. We can study the biology and physiology of such agents, but in so doing we ignore their minds; or we can study their minds, ignoring their material composition.

Now, however, we are faced with a difficulty. Science is limited to the pursuit of objective, "public" states of affairs. An objective state of affairs can be apprehended from more than one perspective, by more than one observer. The contents of your mind, however, are observable (if that is the word) only by you. My route to those contents is through observations of what you say and do. This appears to place minds outside the realm of scientific inquiry. We can study brains, and we may conclude that particular kinds of neurological goings-on are correlated with kinds of mental goings-on. This would enable us reliably to infer states of mind by observing brain activity. But we should not be observing or measuring those states of mind themselves, except in our own case.

Privacy and Its Consequences

Once we start down this road, we may come to doubt that states of mind—as distinct from their physiological correlates—are a fit subject for scientific examination. Eventually, the very idea that we are in a position even to establish correlations between mental occurrences and goings-on in the nervous system can come to be doubted. Imagine that, every time you have a particular kind of experience—every time you see a certain shade of red, for instance, the red of a ripe tomato—your brain goes into a particular state, *S*. Further, whenever your brain goes into state *S*, you experience that very shade of red. It looks as though there must be a correlation between experiences of this kind and neurological states of kind *S*.

Suppose, now, you observe my brain in state *S*. I announce that I am experiencing a certain shade of red, a shade I describe as the red of a ripe tomato. It might seem that this provides further evidence of the correlation already observed in your own case. But does it? In your own case, you have access both to the mental state and to its neurological correlate. When you observe me, however, you have access only to my neurological condition. What gives you the right to assume that my mental state resembles yours?

True, I describe my experience just as you describe yours. We agree that we are experiencing the color of ripe tomatoes. But of course this is how we have each been taught to characterize our respective experiences. I have a particular kind of visual experience when I view a ripe tomato in bright sunlight. I describe this experience as the kind of experience I have when I view a ripe tomato in bright sunlight. You have a particular kind of experience when you view a ripe tomato under similar observational conditions. And you have learned to describe this experience as the kind of experience you have when you view a ripe tomato in bright sunlight. But what entitles either of us to say that the experiences so described are exactly similar? Perhaps the experience you have is like the experience I would have were I to view a lime in bright sunlight. Our descriptions perfectly coincide, but the state of mind I am describing is qualitatively very different from yours.

It would seem, then, that attempts to correlate kinds of neurological goings-on and kinds of mental occurrences boil down to correlations of neurological goings-on and descriptions of mental occurrences. We learn to describe the qualities of our states of mind by reference to publicly observable objects that typically evoke them. And this leaves open the possibility that, while our descriptions match, the states to which they apply are wildly different.

This may seem an idle worry, a purely philosophical possibility. But ask yourself: what earthly reason do you have for thinking that your states of mind qualitatively resemble the states of mind of others? It is not as though you have observed others' states of mind and discovered they match yours. You lack a single example of such a match. Might you infer inductively from characteristics of your own case to the characteristics of others? (Inductive inference is probabilistic: we reason from the characteristics of a sample of a population to characteristics of the population as a whole.) But canons of inductive reasoning proscribe inferences from a single individual to a whole population unless it is clear that the individual is representative of the population. If you assume that characteristics of your states of mind are representative, however, you are assuming precisely what you set out to establish.

The problem we have been scouting is the old problem of other minds. Granted you can know your own mind, how can you know the minds of others? Indeed, once we put it this way, we can see that the problem is deeper than we might have expected. How can you know that others have minds at all? They behave in ways similar to the ways you behave, and they insist they have pains, images, feelings, and thoughts. But what reason do you have for supposing that they do? You cannot observe others' states of mind. Nor do you have adequate inductive grounds for inferring that they enjoy a mental life from what you can observe about them.

A recent twist on this ancient puzzle introduces the possibility of "zombies," creatures identical to us in every material respect, but altogether lacking conscious experiences. The apparent conceivability of zombies has convinced some philosophers that there is an unbridgeable "explanatory gap" between material qualities and the qualities of conscious experience.

You may be growing impatient with this line of reasoning. Of course we know that others have mental lives similar to ours in many ways—and different as well: it is also possible to know that. Well and good. But it is hard to see how this confidence could be justified so long as we accept the notion that minds and their contents are private affairs, incapable of public scrutiny.

The Beetle in the Box

Perhaps our starting point is what is responsible for our predicament. We have been led down the garden path by a certain conception of mind inherited from Descartes. If we begin to question that conception, we may see our way clear to a solution to our problem, one that better fits our commonsense idea that we can know that others have minds and that their minds resemble ours.

Wittgenstein (1889–1951), in his *Philosophical Investigations* (1953/1968), §293, offers a compelling analogy:

Suppose everyone had a box with something in it: we call it a "beetle". No one can look into anyone else's box, and everyone says he knows what a beetle is only by looking at his beetle.—Here it would be quite possible for everyone to have something different in his box. One might even imagine such a thing constantly changing.

The picture here resembles the picture of the relation we bear to our own and others' states of mind that we have been taking for granted.

Wittgenstein argues against this picture, not by presenting considerations that imply its falsity, but by showing that our accepting it leads to a paradoxical result: if this is the relation we bear to our own and others' states of mind, then we should have no way of referring to them.

Suppose the word "beetle" had a use in these people's language?—If so it would not be used as the name of a thing. The thing in the box has no place in the language-game at all; not even as a something: for the box might even be empty.—No, one can "divide through" by the thing in the box; it cancels out, whatever it is. That is to say: if we construe the grammar of the expression of sensation on the model of "object and designation" the object drops out of consideration as irrelevant.

What is Wittgenstein's point? You report that your box contains a beetle. Your report is perfectly apt. You have been taught to use the word "beetle" in just this way. Imagine, now, that the object in my box is very different from the object in your box. If we could compare the objects, this would be obvious, although we could never be in a position to compare them. Suppose now that I report that my box contains a beetle. In so doing, I am using the word "beetle" exactly as I have been taught to use it. My utterance, like yours, is perfectly correct.

Suppose, now, we each report, say, that our respective boxes contain a beetle. Is either of us mistaken? No. In the imagined situation, Wittgenstein argues, the word "beetle" is used in such a way that it makes no difference what is inside anyone's box. "Beetle," in our imagined dialect, means, roughly, "whatever is in the box." To wonder whether your beetle resembles my beetle is to misunderstand this use of "beetle." It is to treat "beetle" as though it named or designated a kind of object or entity. But "beetle" is used in such a way that "the object drops out of consideration as irrelevant."

Wittgenstein's point is not merely a linguistic one. Any thoughts we might harbor that we would express using the word "beetle," are similarly constrained. Those thoughts turn out not to concern some particular kind of entity. Differently put: if the word "beetle" does not refer to entities of a particular sort, then neither do thoughts naturally expressible using "beetle."

Philosophical Behaviorism

How might the analogy be extended to states of mind? As a child, you react in various ways to your surroundings. On some occasions, you moan and rub your head. Adults tell you that what you have is called a headache. Others are taught to use "headache" similarly. Does "headache" designate a kind of entity or state?

Perhaps not. Perhaps when you tell me that you have a headache, you are not picking out any definite thing or private condition at all (think of the beetle), but merely evincing your headache. You have been trained in a particular way. When you are moved to moan and rub your head, you are, as a result of this training, moved as well to utter the words "I have a headache." When you ascribe a headache to me, you are saying no more than that I am in a kind of state that leads me to moan, rub my head, or utter "I have a headache." The private character of that state could differ across individuals. It might continually change, or even, in some cases (zombies?), be altogether absent. The function of the word "headache" is not to designate that private character, however. It "drops out of consideration as irrelevant."

Suppose that this account of our use of "headache" applied to our mental vocabulary generally. Then mental terms would not in fact be used to designate kinds of entity or qualitatively similar private episodes as Descartes would have it. Their role is quite different. And in that case, the question whether the state you designate by "experience I have when I view a ripe tomato in bright sunlight" qualitatively matches the state I designate when I use the same expression could not so much as arise. To raise the question is to mischaracterize the use of mental terminology, and thus to utter nonsense.

This line of reasoning supports what is often dubbed philosophical behaviorism. (It is dubbed thus by its opponents. Few philosophers routinely so characterized have applied the label to themselves.) The philosophical behaviorist holds that the Cartesian conception of mind errs in a fundamental way. Minds are not entities (whether Cartesian substances or brains); and mental episodes are not private goings-on inside such entities. We are attracted to the Cartesian picture only because we are misled by what Wittgenstein calls the grammar of our language.

So long as we deploy our language in everyday life we steer clear of philosophical puzzles. Words owe their significance to the "language games" we play with them. An appropriate understanding of any word (hence the concept it expresses) requires a grasp of the part of parts it plays in these language games. When we engage in philosophy, however, we are apt to be misled by the fact that "mind," like "brain," or "baseball," is a substantive noun. We reason that "mind" must designate a kind of entity, and that what we call thoughts, sensations, and feelings refer to qualitatively similar states or modes of this entity. We can avoid confusion only by looking carefully at the way our words are actually deployed in ordinary circumstances.

This prescription is intended by Wittgenstein to apply to philosophy generally. Philosophical problems arise "when language goes on holiday," when we lose touch with the way our words are actually used. In our everyday interactions with one another, we are not puzzled by our capacity to know how others feel or what they are thinking. The philosophical problem of other minds arises when we wrench "mind," "thought," "feeling," and their cognates from the contexts in which they are naturally deployed, put a special interpretation on them, and then boggle at the puzzles that result.

Gilbert Ryle (1900–76) extends Wittgenstein's point. According to Ryle, the supposition that minds are kinds of entity amounts to a "category mistake": "it represents the facts of mental life as if they belonged to one logical type or category . . . when actually they belong to another" (1949, p. 16). Suppose I show you around my university. We stroll through the grounds; I show you various academic and administrative buildings; I take you to the library; I introduce you to students and members of the faculty. When I am done, I ask whether there is anything else you would like to see. You reply: "Yes. You've shown me the grounds, the academic and administrative buildings, the library, students, and faculty; but you haven't shown me the university. I'd like to see that." You have made a category mistake. You have taken the term "university" to designate an entity similar to, but distinct from, those you have seen already.

If you persisted in the belief that "university" designates such an entity despite failing ever to encounter it, you might come to imagine that the entity in question is "non-material." An analogous mistake, says Ryle, encourages Cartesian dualism. We begin with the idea that minds are entities, distinct from, but similar to brains or bodies. When we have trouble locating such entities in the material world, we assume that they must be non-material. We see the mind, to use Ryle's colorful phrase, as the ghost in the machine. But minds are not entities at all, ghostly or otherwise, a fact we should immediately appreciate if only we kept firmly before us the way "mind" functions in ordinary English.

> The theoretically interesting category mistakes are those made by people who are perfectly competent to apply concepts, at least in the situations with which they are familiar, but are still liable in their abstract thinking to allocate those concepts to logical types to which they do not belong.
>
> (1949, p.17)

At the risk of confusing matters by piling analogies on top of analogies, an example of Wittgenstein's may help here. Suppose you look into the cab of a locomotive (or the cockpit of a jetliner). You see levers, knobs, buttons, and switches. Each of these operates in a particular way (some are turned, some slide back and forth, some are pushed or pulled), and each has a particular function in the locomotive's (or jetliner's) operation. We should be misled if we assumed that levers or knobs with similar shapes had similar functions. In the same way, the fact that "mind" is a substantive noun, or that we speak of "states of mind" should not lead us to assume that "mind" functions to designate a particular entity, and that states of mind are states of this entity.

If "mind," like "university," does not function to name a particular kind of material or immaterial ("ghostly") entity, how does it function? Perhaps we ascribe minds to creatures with a capacity to comport themselves, as we should say, "intelligently." A creature possesses a mind, not in virtue of being equipped with a peculiar kind of private ingredient, its mind, but in virtue of being the sort of creature capable of engaging in behavior that exhibits a measure of spontaneity and a relatively complex organization. For their part, states of mind—headaches, intentions, beliefs—are possessed by intelligent creatures in virtue of what they do or would do. Your believing that there is a bear in your path, for instance, is a matter of your taking appropriate evasive measures, your assenting to "There is a bear on the path," and the like. Your intending to attend the World Series is a matter of your being moved to purchase tickets, arranging for transportation, announcing "I'm going to the World Series," and so on.

On a view of this sort, an agent is correctly describable as having states of mind, not only in virtue of what that agent does, but also in virtue of what he would do, what he is "disposed" to do. Thus, if you have a headache, you may be disposed to moan, rub your head, seek out aspirin, and announce "I have a headache." You may do none of these things, however. Imagine, for instance, that you do not want anyone to know that you have a headache. In that case, although you are disposed to behave in particular ways, you do not behave in those ways.

But now we are confronted with a new question. What is it to "be disposed" to behave in a particular way? What are dispositions? A fragile vase possesses a disposition to shatter. In shattering, when struck by a tire iron, for instance, it manifests this disposition. A salt crystal possesses a disposition to dissolve in water. In dissolving upon being placed in water, it manifests its solubility. An object can possess a disposition, however, without manifesting that disposition. A fragile glass need never shatter; a salt crystal need never dissolve.

. . . It is important only to appreciate that any plausible version of philosophical behaviorism requires their introduction. Among other things, dispositions take up the slack between what I do and what I would do. I do, presumably, what I am disposed to do; but I may be disposed to do many things that I never do because the opportunity to do them does not arise or because they are overridden by competing dispositions. You might be disposed to act bravely when faced with danger, but pass your life in tranquil surroundings. This need not detract from your bravery. Of course if you never manifest your bravery, we should have no reason to think you brave—nor, for that matter, need you have any inkling of it. Similarly, we should have no reason to think that a particular unfamiliar substance was water-soluble if its solubility is never manifested. You may be disposed to remain steadfast in a dangerous encounter but nevertheless flee because you are disposed, as well, to spirit away a threatened companion. Similarly, a salt crystal disposed to dissolve in water may fail to dissolve if it is subjected to a powerful electromagnetic field.

In what sense, exactly, does philosophical behaviorism "tie states of mind to behavior"? Behaviorists hold that assertions concerning states of mind can be translated into statements about behavior or dispositions to behave. We have had a taste of this already. If you believe there is a bear in your path, you are disposed to take evasive action, to assent to "There is a bear on the path," to warn your companions, and the like.

The guiding idea is that, if talk about states of mind can be analyzed or paraphrased into talk about behavior (or dispositions to behave), then states of mind will have been "reduced to" (shown to be nothing more than) behavior (or dispositions to behave). Analysis of this sort amounts to the reduction of something to something else. To see the point, think of a parallel case. We sometimes speak of the average family. The income of the average family in rural areas has declined from what it was a decade ago. Is there an average family? Is there an entity (or, for that matter, a collection of entities) designated by the phrase "the average family"? That seems unlikely. In this case, we can see how talk about the average family's income might be reductively analyzed into talk about the income of individual families summed and divided by the number of families. There is nothing more to the average family than this. If we could analyze away claims about minds and mental goings-on, replacing it with claims about behavior and dispositions to behave, then (so the argument goes) we would have succeeded in showing that there is nothing more to an agent's possessing a mind than the agent's behaving or being disposed to behave in appropriately mindful ways.[1]

What are the prospects for reductive analyses of states of mind? One worry is that behavioral analyses are open-ended. There is no limit on the list of things you might do or be disposed to do if you harbor the belief that there is a bear on the trail, for instance. What you do will depend on the circumstances, and the circumstances can vary in indefinitely many ways. Moreover, it seems clear that among the things you will be disposed to do is to form new beliefs and acquire new desires. Each of these beliefs and desires will need its own behavioral analysis.

This complicates the picture, certainly, but it need not pose an insuperable problem for the philosophical behaviorist. The envisaged analyses need not be finite. We can accept a reductive analysis, provided we can see how it could be extended, even when we are in no position to do so ourselves.

Another difficulty is less easily dismissed. You see a bear on the path and form the belief that there is a bear on the path. But what you do and what you are disposed to do evidently depends on your overall state of mind: what else you believe and want, for instance. And this is so for any state of mind. Suppose you believe that there is a bear on the path, but want to have a closer look, or believe that bears are not dangerous, or suppose you have a yen to live dangerously.

It would seem that your belief is compatible with your behaving or being disposed to behave in any way at all depending on what else you believe and what you want. In that case, however, it looks as though no reductive analysis of states of mind is in the cards. The problem is not just that each of these additional states of mind requires a further behavioral analysis, thus complicating and extending the analytical task. The problem, rather, is that there is apparently no way to avoid mention of

---

[1] Berkeley defends a reductive analysis of talk about material objects to talk about "ideas" (Berkeley's catch-all term for states of mind). If successful, such an analysis would show that we do not need to suppose that material objects are anything "over and above" ideas. Behaviorists' analyses run in the opposite direction.

further states of mind in any statement of what behavior a given state of mind is likely to produce. It is as though we set out to analyze away talk about the average family only to discover that our analysis reintroduced mention of average families at every turning.

To appreciate the magnitude of the problem, think of your belief that there is a bear on the path. This belief, in concert with the belief that bears are dangerous, and a desire to avoid dangerous animals, may lead you to hurry away. But now imagine that you believe that there is a bear in your path, believe that bears are dangerous, and desire to avoid dangerous animals (your beliefs and desires are as before) but that you believe, in addition, that hurrying away will only attract the attention of bears. In this case, you will be disposed to behave, and behave, very differently.

The example illustrates a general point. Any attempt to say what behavior follows from a given state of mind can be shown false by producing an example in which the state of mind is present but, owing to the addition of new beliefs or desires, the behavior does not follow. Nor will it help to try to rule out such cases by means of a general excluder: if you believe that there is a bear on the path, believe that bears are dangerous, and desire to avoid dangerous animals, then, providing you have no further conflicting beliefs or desires, you will be disposed to turn tail. The problem here is that we have reintroduced mention of states of mind in the exclusion clause. And these are precisely what we were trying to analyze away. The analytical project looks hopeless. . . .

The Legacy of Philosophical Behaviorism

If the attempt to analyze talk of states of mind into talk of behavior is unworkable, what is left of philosophical behaviorism? It is true, certainly, that our grounds for ascribing states of mind to one another are largely behavioral. This is an epistemological point, however, a point about what constitutes evidence for our beliefs about one another's mental lives, and a point a Cartesian could happily accept.

What of Ryle's contention that it is a mistake to regard your possessing a mind as a matter of your body's standing in a particular relation to a distinct entity, your mind? And what of Wittgenstein's suggestion that terms used to ascribe states of mind are not used to designate objects of some definite sort? Both of these ideas are independent of the behaviorist's analytical project, and both survive in accounts of the mind that are self-consciously anti-behaviorist. Thus, one might suppose that to have a mind is just to possess a particular sort of organization, one that issues in what we should call intelligent behavior. And one might imagine that to possess a given state of mind is just to be in some state or other that contributes in a characteristic way to the operation of this organized system.

These themes are central to functionalism, a conception of mind that we [must set aside here.] For the moment, let us simply register behaviorism's lack of concern for the qualitative dimension of states of mind. If your having a headache is solely a matter of your behaving, or being disposed to behave, in a particular way, then the intrinsic qualitative nature of whatever is responsible for your so behaving, or being disposed to behave, is irrelevant. This is explicit in Wittgenstein's beetle in the box analogy. And, as we shall see, this feature of behaviorism is inherited by functionalism.

What could be meant by "intrinsic qualitative nature"? The notion of an intrinsic quality is best understood in contrast to the complementary notion of an extrinsic characteristic. An intrinsic quality is a quality an object has in its own right. Being spherical is an intrinsic quality of a billiard ball. Being near the center of the billiard table is, in contrast, a non-intrinsic, extrinsic feature of the ball.[2] Think of intrinsic qualities as being built into objects, extrinsic characteristics as being possessed by objects only in virtue of relations those objects bear to other objects. In the beetle in the box case, imagine that one person's box contains a marble, and another's contains a sugar cube. Then the intrinsic nature of what is in each box differs. And it is precisely this that "drops out of consideration as irrelevant."

We can distinguish an object's intrinsic qualitative nature from its dispositionalities or causal powers. The billiard ball has the power to roll across the table, the power to shatter a pane of glass, and the power to reflect light in a particular way. But the ball has, as well, a particular qualitative nature: a particular shape, a particular size, a particular temperature. The relation between an object's powers or dispositionalities and its qualitative characteristics is a subtle business, as we shall see later. For the present, we need only recognize that it seems possible to distinguish an object's qualitative aspects from its causal propensities or powers. And, again, behaviorism regards the intrinsic qualitative nature of states of mind as irrelevant.

One way to put this is to say that, according to the behaviorist, states of mind, "*qua* states of mind," lack an intrinsic qualitative nature. Think

---

[2] I prefer to contrast intrinsic with extrinsic rather than relational. That two cells bear a certain relation to one another is a relational feature of the cells, but an intrinsic feature of the organism to which they belong.

again of the beetle in the box analogy. Whatever is in the box has some intrinsic qualitative nature. But this nature is irrelevant to its being true that the box contains a beetle: *qua* beetle—considered solely as a beetle—what the box contains lacks intrinsic qualities.

A view of this sort might seem wildly implausible. Surely your headache has an intrinsic qualitative nature, and this is an important part of what makes a headache a headache. These days it is fashionable to put this point by saying that "there is something it is like" to have a headache. What it is like to have a headache differs from what it is like to have other kinds of conscious experience. Part of what makes a given conscious experience a headache is just this "what-it's-likeness."

I have said that the denial of all this might seem implausible. Yet behaviorists do deny it. And, as we shall see, many other philosophers, philosophers dismissive of behaviorism, deny it as well. These philosophers argue that states of mind owe their identity, not to their intrinsic qualitative nature (if indeed they have any such nature at all), but exclusively to their causal powers or, as I prefer, their dispositionalities. We can evaluate such claims only after we have built up an understanding of the underlying metaphysical issues. . . .

References

Crick, Francis (1994). *The Astonishing Hypothesis: The Scientific Search for the Soul*, New York: Scribner.

Ryle, Gilbert (1949). *The Concept of Mind*, London: Hutchinson.

Wittgenstein, Ludwig (1953/1968). *Tractatus Logico-Philosophicus*, trans. D. F. Pears and B. F. McGuinness, London: Routledge and Kegan Paul.

The Nature of Mind

David Armstrong

Men have minds, that is to say, they perceive, they have sensations, emotions, beliefs, thoughts, purposes and desires. What is it to have a mind? What is it to perceive, to feel emotion, to hold a belief or to have a purpose? Many contemporary philosophers think that the best clue we have to the nature of mind is furnished by the discoveries and hypotheses of modern science concerning the nature of man.

What does modern science have to say about the nature of man? There are, of course, all sorts of disagreements and divergencies in the view of individual scientists. But I think it is true to say that one view is steadily gaining ground, so that it bids fair to become established scientific doctrine. This is the view that we can give a complete account of man *in purely physico-chemical terms.* This view has received a tremendous impetus in recent decades from the new subject of molecular biology, a subject that promises to unravel the physical and chemical mechanisms that lie at the basis of life. Before that time, it received great encouragement from pioneering work in neurophysiology pointing to the likelihood of a purely electro-chemical account of the working of the brain. I think it is fair to say that those scientists who still reject the physico-chemical account of man do so primarily for philosophical, or moral or religious reasons, and only secondarily, and half-heartedly, for reasons of scientific detail. This is not to say that in the future new evidence and new problems may not come to light that will force science to reconsider the physico-chemical view of man. But at present the drift of scientific thought is clearly set towards the physico-chemical hypothesis. And we have nothing better to go on than the present.

For me, then, and for many philosophers who think like me, the moral is clear. We must try to work out an account of the nature of mind which is compatible with the view that man is nothing but a physico-chemical mechanism.

And in this paper, I shall be concerned to do just this: to sketch (in barest outline) what may be called a Materialist or Physicalist account of the mind.

The Authority of Science

But before doing this, I should like to go back and consider a criticism of my position that must inevitably occur to some. What reason have I, it may be asked, for taking my stand on science? Even granting that I am right about what is the currently dominant scientific view of man, why should we concede science a special authority to decide questions about the nature of man? What of the authority of philosophy, of religion, of morality, or even of literature and art? Why do I set the authority of science above all these? Why this "scientism"?

It seems to me that the answer to this question is very simple. If we consider the search for truth, in all its fields, we find that it is only in science that men versed in their subject can, after investigation that is more or less prolonged, and which may in some cases extend beyond a single human lifetime, reach substantial agreement about what is the case. It is only as a result of scientific investigation that we ever seem to reach an intellectual consensus about controversial matters.

In the Epistle Dedicatory to *De Corpore*, Hobbes wrote of William Harvey, the discoverer of the circulation of the blood, that he was: "the only man I know, that conquering envy, hath established a new doctrine in his life-time."

Before Copernicus, Galileo and Harvey, Hobbes remarks: "there was nothing certain in natural philosophy." And we might add, with the exception of mathematics, there was nothing certain in any other learned discipline.

These remarks of Hobbes are incredibly revealing. They show us what a watershed in the intellectual history of the human race the seventeenth century was. Before that time, enquiry proceeded, as it were, in the dark. Men could not hope to see their doctrine *established*, that is to say, accepted by the vast majority of those properly versed in the subject under discussion. There was no intellectual consensus. Since that time, it has become a commonplace to see new doctrines, sometimes of the most far-reaching kind, established to the satisfaction of the learned, often within the lifetime of their first proponents. Science has provided us with a method of deciding disputed questions. This is not to say, of course, that the consensus of those who are learned and competent in a subject cannot be mistaken. Of course such a consensus can be mistaken. Sometimes it has been mistaken. But, granting fallibility, what better authority have we than such a consensus?

Now this is of the utmost importance. For in philosophy, in religion, in such disciplines as literary criticism, in moral questions in so far as they are thought to be matters of truth and falsity, there has been a notable failure to achieve an intellectual consensus about disputed questions among the learned. Must we not then attach a peculiar authority to the discipline that can achieve a consensus? And if it presents us with a certain vision of the nature of man, is this not a powerful reason for accepting that vision?

I will not take up here the deeper question *why* it is that the methods of science have enabled us to achieve an intellectual consensus about so many disputed matters. That question, I think, could receive no brief or uncontroversial answer. I am resting my argument on the simple fact that, as a result of scientific investigation, such a consensus has been achieved.

It may be replied—it often is replied—that while science is all very well in its own sphere—the sphere of the physical, perhaps—there are matters of fact on which it is not competent to pronounce. And among such matters, it may be claimed, is the question: what is the whole nature of man? But I cannot see that this reply has much force. Science has provided us with an island of truths, or, perhaps one should say, a raft of truths, to bear us up on the sea of our disputatious ignorance. There may have to be revisions and refinements, new results may set old findings in a new perspective, but what science has given us will not be altogether superseded. Must we not therefore appeal to these relative certainties for guidance when we come to consider uncertainties elsewhere? Perhaps science cannot help us to decide whether or not there is a God, whether or not human beings have immortal souls, or whether or not the will is free. But if science cannot assist us, what can? I conclude that it is the scientific vision of man, and not the philosophical or religious or artistic or moral vision of man, that is the best clue we have to the nature of man. And it is rational to argue from the best evidence we have.[1]

Defining the Mental

Having in this way attempted to justify my procedure, I turn back to my subject: the attempt to work out an account of mind, or, if you prefer, of mental process, within the framework of the physico-chemical, or, as we may call it, the Materialist view of man.

Now there is one account of mental process that is at once attractive to any philosopher sympathetic to a Materialist view of man: this is Behaviourism. Formulated originally by a psychologist, J.B. Watson, it attracted widespread interest and considerable support from scientifically oriented philosophers. Traditional philosophy had tended to think of the mind as a rather mysterious inward arena that lay behind, and was responsible for, the outward or physical behaviour of our bodies. Descartes thought of this inner arena as a *spiritual substance*, and it was this conception of the mind as spiritual object that Gilbert Ryle attacked, apparently in the interest of Behaviourism, in his important book *The Concept of Mind* (1949). He ridiculed the Cartesian view as the dogma of "the ghost in the machine". The mind was not something behind the behaviour of the body, it was simply part of that physical behaviour. My anger with you is not some modification of a spiritual substance that somehow brings about aggressive behaviour; rather it is the aggressive behaviour itself; my addressing strong words to you, striking you, turning my back on you, and so on. Thought is not an inner process that lies behind, and brings about, the words I speak and write: it is my speaking and writing. The mind is not an inner arena, it is an outward act.

---

[1]The view of science presented here has been challenged in recent years by new Irrationalist philosophies of science. See, in particular, Thomas Kuhn (1962) and Paul Feyerabend (1975). A complete treatment of the problem would involve answering their contentions.

It is clear that such a view of mind fits in very well with a completely Materialistic or Physicalist view of man. If there is no need to draw a distinction between mental processes and their expression in physical behaviour, but if instead the mental processes are identified with their so-called "expressions", then the existence of mind stands in no conflict with the view that man is nothing but a physico-chemical mechanism.

However, the version of Behaviourism that I have just sketched is a very crude version, and its crudity lays it open to obvious objections. One obvious difficulty is that it is our common experience that there can be mental processes going on although there is no behaviour occurring that could possibly be treated as expressions of those processes. A man may be angry, but give no bodily sign; he may think, but say or do nothing at all.

In my view, the most plausible attempt to refine Behaviourism with a view to meeting this objection was made by introducing the notion of a *disposition to behave*. (Dispositions to behave play a particularly important part in Ryle's account of the mind.) Let us consider the general notion of disposition first. Brittleness is a disposition, a disposition possessed by materials like glass. Brittle materials are those that, when subjected to relatively small forces, break or shatter easily. But breaking and shattering easily is not brittleness, rather it is the *manifestation* of brittleness. Brittleness itself is the tendency or liability of the material to break or shatter easily. A piece of glass may never shatter or break throughout its whole history, but it is still the case that it is brittle: it is liable to shatter or break if dropped quite a small way or hit quite lightly. Now a disposition to *behave* is simply a tendency or liability of a person to behave in a certain way under certain circumstances. The brittleness of glass is a disposition that the glass retains throughout its history, but clearly there also could be dispositions that come and go. The dispositions to behave that are of interest to the Behaviourist are, for the most part, of this temporary character.

Now how did Ryle and others use the notion of a disposition to behave to meet the obvious objection to Behaviourism that there can be mental process going on although the subject is engaging in no relevant behaviour? Their strategy was to argue that in such cases, although the subject was not behaving in any relevant way, he or she was disposed to behave in some relevant way. The glass does not shatter, but it is still brittle. The man does not behave, but he does have a disposition to behave. We can say he thinks although he does not speak or act because at that time he was disposed to speak or act in a certain way. *If* he had been asked, perhaps, he would have spoken or acted. We can say he is angry although he does not behave angrily, because he is disposed so to behave. *If* only one more word had been addressed to him, he would have burst out. And so on. In this way it was hoped that Behaviourism could be squared with the obvious facts.

It is very important to see just how these thinkers conceived of dispositions. I quote from Ryle:

> To possess a dispositional property *is not to be in a particular state, or to undergo a particular change*; it is to be bound or liable to be in a particular state, or to undergo a particular change, when a particular condition is realized.[2]

So to explain the breaking of a lightly struck glass on a particular occasion by saying it was brittle is, on this view of dispositions, simply to say that the glass broke because it is the sort of thing that regularly breaks when quite lightly struck. The breaking was the normal behaviour, or not abnormal behaviour, of such a thing. The brittleness is not to be conceived of as a *cause* for the breakage, or even, more vaguely, a *factor* in bringing about the breaking. Brittleness is just the fact that things of that sort break easily.

But although in this way the Behaviourists did something to deal with the objection that mental processes can occur in the absence of behaviour, it seems clear, now that the shouting and the dust have died, that they did not do enough. When I think, but my thoughts do not issue in any action, it seems as obvious as anything is obvious that there is something actually going on in me that constitutes my thought. It is not simply that I would speak or act if some conditions that are unfulfilled were to be fulfilled. Something is currently going on, in the strongest and most literal sense of "going on", and this something is my thought. Rylean Behaviourism denies this, and so it is unsatisfactory as a theory of mind. Yet I know of no version of Behaviourism that is more satisfactory. The moral for those of us who wish to take a purely physicalistic view of man is that we must look for some other account of the nature of mind and of mental processes.

But perhaps we need not grieve too deeply about the failure of Behaviourism to produce a satisfactory theory of mind. Behaviourism is a profoundly unnatural account of mental processes. If somebody speaks and acts in certain ways, it is natural to speak of this speech and action as the *expression* of his thought. It is not at all natural to speak of his speech

---

[2]Ryle, 1949: 43; emphasis added.

and action as identical with his thought. We naturally think of the thought as something quite distinct from the speech and action that, under suitable circumstances, brings the speech and action about. Thoughts are not to be identified with behaviour, we think; they lie behind behaviour. A man's behaviour constitutes the *reason* we have for attributing certain mental processes to him, but the behaviour cannot be identified with the mental processes.

This suggests a very interesting line of thought about the mind. Behaviourism is certainly wrong, but perhaps it is not altogether wrong. Perhaps the Behaviourists are wrong in identifying the mind and mental occurrences with behaviour, but perhaps they are right in thinking that our notion of a mind and of individual mental states is *logically tied to behaviour*. For perhaps what we mean by a mental state is some state of the person that, under suitable circumstances, *brings about* a certain range of behaviour. Perhaps mind can be defined not as behaviour, but rather as the inner cause of certain behaviour. Thought is not speech under suitable circumstances, rather it is something within the person that, in suitable circumstances, brings about speech. And, in fact, I believe that this is the true account, or, at any rate, a true first account, of what we mean by a mental state.

How does this line of thought link up with a purely Physicalist view of man? The position is that while it does not make such a Physicalist view inevitable, it does make it *possible*. It does not entail, but it is compatible with, a purely Physicalist view of man. For if our notion of the mind and of mental states is nothing but that of a cause within the person of certain ranges of behaviour, then it becomes a scientific question, and not a question of logical analysis, what in fact the intrinsic nature of that cause is. The cause might be, as Descartes thought it was, a spiritual substance working through the pineal gland to produce the complex bodily behaviour of which men are capable. It might be breath, or specially smooth and mobile atoms dispersed throughout the body; it might be many other things. But in fact the verdict of modern science seems to be that the sole cause of mind-betokening behaviour in man and the higher animals is the physico-chemical workings of the central nervous system. And so, assuming we have correctly characterized our concept of a mental state as nothing but the cause of certain sorts of behaviour, then we can identify these mental states with purely physical states of the central nervous system.

At this point we may stop and go back to the Behaviourist's dispositions. We saw that, according to him, the brittleness of glass or, to take another example, the elasticity of rubber, is not a state of the glass or

the rubber, but is simply the fact that things of that sort behave in the
way they do. But now let us consider how a scientist would think about
brittleness or elasticity. Faced with the phenomenon of breakage under
relatively small impacts, or the phenomenon of stretching when a force
is applied followed by contraction when the force is removed, he will
assume that there is some current *state* of the glass or the rubber that
is responsible for the characteristic behaviour of samples of these two
materials. At the beginning, he will not know what this state is, but he
will endeavour to find out, and he may succeed in finding out. And when
he has found out, he will very likely make remarks of this sort: "We
have discovered that the brittleness of glass is in fact a certain sort of pattern in the molecules of the glass." That is to say, he will *identify* brittleness with the state of the glass that is responsible for the liability of the
glass to break. For him, a disposition of an object is a state of the object.
What makes the state a state of brittleness is the fact that it gives rise
to the characteristic manifestations of brittleness. But the disposition itself
is distinct from its manifestations: it is the state of the glass that gives rise
to these manifestations in suitable circumstances.

This way of looking at dispositions is very different from that of Ryle
and the Behaviourists. The great difference is this: If we treat dispositions
as actual states, as I have suggested that scientists do, even if states the
intrinsic nature of which may yet have to be discovered, then we can
say that dispositions are actual causes, or causal factors, which, in suitable circumstances, actually bring about those happenings that are the
manifestations of the disposition. A certain molecular constitution of glass
that constitutes its brittleness is actually *responsible* for the fact that,
when the glass is struck, it breaks.

Now I cannot argue the matter here, because the detail of the argument is technical and difficult, but I believe that the view of dispositions as states, which is the view that is natural to science, is the correct
one.[3] I believe it can be shown quite strictly that, to the extent that we
admit the notion of dispositions at all, we are committed to the view
that they are actual states of the object that has the disposition. I may
add that I think that the same holds for the closely connected notions
of capacities and powers. Here I will simply have to assume this step in
my argument.

But perhaps it will be seen that the rejection of the idea that mind
is simply a certain range of man's behaviour in favour of the view that
mind is rather the inner *cause* of that range of man's behaviour, is bound

---

[3] I develop the argument in *Belief, Truth and Knowledge* (1973), ch. 2, sect. 2.

up with the rejection of the Rylean view of dispositions in favour of one that treats dispositions as states of objects and so as having actual causal power. The Behaviourists were wrong to identify the mind with behaviour. They were not so far off the mark when they tried to deal with cases where mental happenings occur in the absence of behaviour by saying that these are dispositions to behave. But in order to reach a correct view, I am suggesting, they would have to conceive of these dispositions as actual *states* of the person who has the disposition, states that have actual causal power to bring about behaviour in suitable circumstances. But to do this is to abandon the central inspiration of Behaviourism: that in talking about the mind we do not have to go behind outward behaviour to inner states.

And so two separate but interlocking lines of thought have pushed me in the same direction. The first line of thought is that it goes profoundly against the grain to think of the mind as behaviour. The mind is, rather, that which stands behind and brings about our complex behaviour. The second line of thought is that the Behaviourist's dispositions, properly conceived, are really states that underlie behaviour and, under suitable circumstances, bring about behaviour. Putting these two together, we reach the conception of a mental state *as a state of the person apt for producing certain ranges of behaviour*. This formula: a mental state is a state of the person apt for producing certain ranges of behaviour, I believe to be a very illuminating way of looking at the concept of a mental state. I have found it fruitful in the search for detailed logical analyses of the individual mental concepts.

I do not think that Hegel's Dialectic has much to tell us about the nature of reality. But I think that human thought often moves in a dialectical way, from thesis to antithesis and then to the synthesis. Perhaps thought about the mind is a case in point. I have already said that classical philosophy has tended to think of the mind as an inner arena of some sort. This we may call the Thesis. Behaviourism moves to the opposite extreme: the mind is seen as outward behaviour. This is the Antithesis. My proposed Synthesis is that the mind is properly conceived as an inner principle, but a principle that is identified in terms of the outward behaviour it is apt for bringing about. This way of looking at the mind and mental states does not itself entail a Materialist or Physicalist view of man, for nothing is said in this analysis about the intrinsic nature of these mental states. But if we have, as I have argued that we do have, general scientific grounds for thinking that man is nothing but a physical mechanism, we can go on to argue that the mental states are in fact nothing but physical states of the central nervous system.

The Problem of Consciousness

Along these lines, then, I would look for an account of the mind that is compatible with a purely Materialist theory of man. There are, as may be imagined, all sorts of powerful objections that can be made to my view. But in the rest of this paper, I propose to do only one thing: I will develop one very important objection to my view of the mind—an objection felt by many philosophers—and then try to show how the objection should be met.

The view that our notion of mind is nothing but that of an inner principle apt for bringing about certain sorts of behaviour may be thought to share a certain weakness with Behaviourism. Modern philosophers have put the point about Behaviourism by saying that, although Behaviourism may be a satisfactory account of the mind from *an other-person point of view*, it will not do as a *first-person* account. To explain. In my encounters with other people, all I ever observe is their behaviour: their actions, their speech, and so on. And so, if we simply consider other people, Behaviourism might seem to do full justice to the facts. But the trouble about Behaviourism is that it seems so unsatisfactory as applied to our *own* case. In our own case, we seem to be aware of so much more than mere behaviour.

Suppose that now we conceive of the mind as an inner principle apt for bringing about certain sorts of behaviour. This again fits the other-person cases very well. Bodily behaviour of a very sophisticated sort is observed, quite different from the behaviour that ordinary physical objects display. It is inferred that this behaviour must spring from a very special sort of inner cause in the object that exhibits this behaviour. This inner cause is christened "the mind", and those who take a Physicalist view of man argue that it is simply the central nervous system of the body observed. Compare this with the case of glass. Certain characteristic behaviour is observed: the breaking and shattering of the material when acted upon by relatively small forces. A special inner state of the glass is postulated to explain this behaviour. Those who take a purely Physicalist view of glass then argue that this state is a *material* state of the glass. It is, perhaps, an arrangement of its molecules and not, say, the peculiarly malevolent disposition of the demons that dwell in glass.

But when we turn to our own case, the position may seem less plausible. We are conscious, we have experiences. Now can we say that to be conscious, to have experiences, is simply for something to go on within us apt for the causing of certain sorts of behaviour? Such an account does not seem to do any justice to the phenomena. And so it seems that our account of the mind, like Behaviourism, will fail to do justice to the first-person case.

In order to understand the objection better, it may be helpful to consider a particular case. If you have driven for a very long distance without a break, you may have had experience of a curious state of automatism, which can occur in these conditions. One can suddenly "come to" and realize that one has driven for long distances without being aware of what one was doing, or, indeed, without being aware of anything. One has kept the car on the road, used the brake and the clutch perhaps, yet all without any awareness of what one was doing.

Now if we consider this case, it is obvious that *in some sense* mental processes are still going on when one is in such an automatic state. Unless one's will was still operating in some way, and unless one was still perceiving in some way, the car would not still be on the road. Yet, of course, *something* mental is lacking. Now, I think, when it is alleged that an account of mind as an inner principle apt for the production of certain sorts of behaviour leaves out consciousness or experience, what is alleged to have been left out is just whatever is missing in the automatic driving case. It is conceded that an account of mental processes as states of the person apt for the production of certain sorts of behaviour very possibly may be adequate to deal with such cases as that of automatic driving. It may be adequate to deal with most of the mental processes of animals, which perhaps spend most of their lives in this state of automatism. But, it is contended, it cannot deal with the consciousness that we normally enjoy.

I will now try to sketch an answer to this important and powerful objection. Let us begin in an apparently unlikely place and consider the way that an account of mental processes of the sort I am giving would deal with *sense-perception.*

Now psychologists, in particular, have long realized that there is a very close logical tie between sense-perception and *selective behaviour.* Suppose we want to decide whether an animal can perceive the difference between red and green. We might give the animal a choice between two pathways, over one of which a red light shines and over the other of which a green light shines. If the animal happens by chance to choose the green pathway, we reward it; if it happens to choose the other pathway, we do not reward it. If, after some trials, the animal systematically takes the green-lighted pathway, and if we become assured that the only relevant differences in the two pathways are the differences in the colour of the lights, we are entitled to say that the animal can see this colour difference. Using its eyes, it selects between red-lighted and green-lighted pathways. So we say it can see the difference between red and green.

Now a Behaviourist would be tempted to say that the animal's regular selection of the green-lighted pathway was its perception of the
colour difference. But this is unsatisfactory, because we all want to say
that perception is something that goes on within the person or animal—
within its mind—although, of course, this mental event is normally
caused by the operation of the environment upon the organism. Suppose,
however, that we speak instead of *capacities* for selective behaviour
towards the current environment, and suppose we think of these capacities, like dispositions, as actual inner states of the organism. We can then
think of the animal's perception as a state within the animal apt, if the
animal is so impelled, for selective behaviour between the red- and green-
lighted pathways.

In general, we can think of perceptions as inner states or events apt
for the production of certain sorts of selective behaviour towards our environment. To perceive is like acquiring a key to a door. You do not have
to use the key: you can put it in your pocket and never bother about
the door. But if you do want to open the door, the key may be essential.
The blind man is a man who does not acquire certain keys and, as a
result, is not able to operate in his environment in the way that somebody
who has his sight can operate. It seems, then, a very promising view to
take of perceptions that they are inner states defined by the sorts of selective behaviour that they enable the perceiver to exhibit, if so impelled.

Now how is this discussion of perception related to the question of
consciousness or experience, the sort of thing that the driver who is in
a state of automatism has not got, but which we normally do have? Simply this. My proposal is that consciousness, in this sense of the word, is
nothing but *perception or awareness of the state of our own mind.* The
driver in a state of automatism perceives, or is aware of, the road. If he
did not, the car would be in a ditch. But he is not currently aware of
his awareness of the road. He perceives the road, but he does not perceive
his perceiving, or anything else that is going on in his mind. He is not,
as we normally are, conscious of what is going on in his mind.

And so I conceive of consciousness or experience, in this sense of the
words, in the way that Locke and Kant conceived it, as like perception.
Kant, in a striking phrase, spoke of "inner sense". We cannot directly
observe the minds of others, but each of us has the power to observe
directly our own minds, and "perceive" what is going on there. The driver in the automatic state is one whose "inner eye" is shut: who is not
currently aware of what is going on in his own mind.

Now if this account is along the right lines, why should we not give
an account of this inner observation along the same lines as we have

already given of perception? Why should we not conceive of it as an inner state, a state in this case directed towards other inner states and not to the environment, which enables us, if we are so impelled, to behave in a selective way *towards our own states of mind*? One who is aware, or conscious, of his thoughts or his emotions is one who has the capacity to make discriminations between his different mental states. His capacity might be exhibited in words. He might say that he was in an angry state of mind, when, and only when, he *was* in an angry state of mind. But such verbal behaviour would be the mere *expression* or *result* of the awareness. The awareness itself would be an inner state: the sort of inner state that gave the man a capacity for such behavioural expressions.

So I have argued that consciousness of our own mental state may be assimilated to *perception* of our own mental state, and that, like other perceptions, it may then be conceived of as an inner state or event giving a capacity for selective behaviour, in this case selective behaviour towards our own mental state. All this is meant to be simply a logical analysis of consciousness, and none of it entails, although it does not rule out, a purely Physicalist account of what these inner states are. But if we are convinced, on general scientific grounds, that a purely physical account of man is likely to be the true one, then there seems to be no bar to our identifying these inner states with purely physical states of the central nervous system. And so consciousness of our own mental state becomes simply the scanning of one part of our central nervous system by another. Consciousness is a self-scanning mechanism in the central nervous system.

As I have emphasized before, I have done no more than sketch a programme for a philosophy of mind. There are all sorts of expansions and elucidations to be made, and all sorts of doubts and difficulties to be stated and overcome. But I hope I have done enough to show that a purely Physicalist theory of the mind is an exciting and plausible intellectual option.

References

Armstrong, D. M. (1973). *Belief, Truth and Knowledge*, Cambridge: Cambridge University Press.

Feyerabend, P. (1963). "Mental Events and the Brain," *Journal of Philosophy* 60: 295–96.

Kuhn, T. (1962). *The Structure of Scientific Revolutions*, Chicago: University of Chicago Press.

Ryle, G. (1949). *The Concept of Mind*, London: Hutchinson.

Mad Pain and Martian Pain
David Lewis

I

There might be a strange man who sometimes feels pain, just as we do, but whose pain differs greatly from ours in its causes and effects. Our pain is typically caused by cuts, burns, pressure, and the like; his is caused by moderate exercise on an empty stomach. Our pain is generally distracting; his turns his mind to mathematics, facilitating concentration on that but distracting him from anything else. Intense pain has no tendency whatever to cause him to groan or writhe, but does cause him to cross his legs and snap his fingers. He is not in the least motivated to prevent pain or to get rid of it. In short, he feels pain but his pain does not at all occupy the typical causal role of pain. He would doubtless seem to us to be some sort of madman, and that is what I shall call him, though of course the sort of madness I have imagined may bear little resemblance to the real thing.

I said there might be such a madman. I don't know how to prove that something is possible, but my opinion that this is a possible case seems pretty firm. If I want a credible theory of mind, I need a theory that does not deny the possibility of mad pain. I needn't mind conceding that perhaps the madman is not in pain in *quite* the same sense that the rest of us are, but there had better be some straightforward sense in which he and we are both in pain.

Also, there might be a Martian, who sometimes feels pain, just as we do, but whose pain differs greatly from ours in its physical realization. His hydraulic mind contains nothing like our neurons. Rather, there are varying amounts of fluid in many inflatable cavities, and the inflation of any one of these cavities opens some valves and closes others. His mental plumbing pervades most of his body—in fact, all but the heat exchanger inside his head. When you pinch his skin you cause no firing of C-fibers—he has none—but, rather, you cause the inflation of many smallish cavities in his feet. When these cavities are inflated, he is in pain. And the effects of his pain are fitting: his thought and activity are disrupted, he groans and writhes, he is strongly motivated to stop you from pinching him and to see to it that you never do again. In short, he feels pain but lacks the bodily states that either are pain or else accompany it in us.

There might be such a Martian; this opinion too seems pretty firm. A credible theory of mind had better not deny the possibility of Martian pain. I needn't mind conceding that perhaps the Martian is not in pain in *quite* the same sense that we Earthlings are, but there had better be some straightforward sense in which he and we are both in pain.

II

A credible theory of mind needs to make a place both for mad pain and for Martian pain. Prima facie, it seems hard for a materialist theory to pass this twofold test. As philosophers, we would like to characterize pain a priori. (We might settle for less, but let's start by asking for all we want.) As materialists, we want to characterize pain as a physical phenomenon. We can speak of the place of pain in the causal network from stimuli to inner states to behavior. And we can speak of the physical processes that go on when there is pain and that take their place in that causal network. We seem to have no other resources but these. But the lesson of mad pain is that pain is associated only contingently with its causal role, while the lesson of Martian pain is that pain is connected only contingently with its physical realization. How can we characterize pain a priori in terms of causal role and physical realization, and yet respect both kinds of contingency?

A simple identity theory straightforwardly solves the problem of mad pain. It goes just as straightforwardly wrong about Martian pain. A simple behaviorism or functionalism goes the other way: right about the Martian, wrong about the madman. The theories that fail our twofold test so decisively are altogether too simple. (Perhaps they are too simple ever to have had adherents.) It seems that a theory that can pass our test will have to be a mixed theory. It will have to be able to tell us that the madman and the Martian are both in pain, but for different reasons: the madman because he is in the right physical state, the Martian because he is in a state rightly situated in the causal network.

Certainly we can cook up a mixed theory. Here's an easy recipe: First, find a theory to take care of the common man and the madman, disregarding the Martian—presumably an identity theory. Second, find a theory to take care of the common man and the Martian, disregarding the madman—presumably some sort of behaviorism or functionalism. Then disjoin the two: say that to be in pain is to be in pain either according to the first theory or according to the second. Alternatively, claim ambiguity: say that to be in pain in one sense is to be in pain according to the first theory, to be in pain in another sense is to be in pain according to the second theory.

This strategy seems desperate. One wonders why we should have a disjunctive or ambiguous concept of pain, if common men who suffer pain are always in pain according to both disjuncts or both disambiguations. It detracts from the credibility of a theory that it posits a useless complexity in our concept of pain—useless in application to the common man, at least, and therefore useless almost always.

I don't object to the strategy of claiming ambiguity. As you'll see, I shall defend a version of it. But it's not plausible to cook up an ambiguity *ad hoc* to account for the compossibility of mad pain and Martian pain. It would be better to find a widespread sort of ambiguity, a sort we would believe in no matter what we thought about pain, and show that it will solve our problem. That is my plan.

III

A dozen years or so ago, D. M. Armstrong and I (independently) proposed a materialist theory of mind that joins claims of type-type psychophysical identity with a behaviorist or functionalist way of characterizing mental states such as pain.[1] I believe our theory passes the twofold test. Positing no ambiguity without independent reason, it provides natural senses in which both madman and Martian are in pain. It wriggles through between Scylla and Charybdis.

Our view is that the concept of pain, or indeed of any other experience or mental state, is the concept of a state that occupies a certain causal role, a state with certain typical causes and effects. It is the concept of a state apt for being caused by certain stimuli and apt for causing certain behavior. Or, better, of a state apt for being caused in certain ways by stimuli plus other mental states and apt for combining with certain other mental states to jointly cause certain behavior. It is the concept of a member of a system of states that together more or less realize the pattern of causal generalizations set forth in commonsense psychology. (That system may be characterized as a whole and its members characterized afterward by reference to their place in it.)

If the concept of pain is the concept of a state that occupies a certain causal role, then whatever state does occupy that role is pain. If the state of having neurons hooked up in a certain way and firing in a certain pattern is the state properly apt for causing and being caused, as we materialists think, then that neural state is pain. But the concept of pain is not the concept of that neural state. ("The concept of . . ." is an intensional functor.) The concept of pain, unlike the concept of that neural state which in fact is pain, would have applied to some different state if the relevant causal relations had been different. Pain might have not been pain. The occupant of the role might have not occupied it. Some other state might have occupied it instead. Something that is not pain might have been pain.

This is not to say, of course, that it might have been that pain was not pain and nonpain was pain; that is, that it might have been that the occupant of the role did not occupy it and some nonoccupant did. Compare: "The winner might have lost" (true) versus "It might have been that the winner lost" (false). No wording is entirely unambiguous, but I trust my meaning is clear.

In short, the concept of pain as Armstrong and I understand it is a *nonrigid* concept. Likewise the word "pain" is a nonrigid designator. It is a contingent matter what state the concept and the word apply to. It depends on what causes what. The same goes for the rest of our concepts and ordinary names of mental states.

Some need hear no more. The notion that mental concepts and names are nonrigid, wherefore what *is* pain might not have been, seems to them just self-evidently false.[2] I cannot tell why they think so. Bracketing my own theoretical commitments, I think I would have no opinion one way or the other. It's not that I don't care about shaping theory to respect naive opinion as well as can be, but in this case I have no naive opinion to respect. If I am not speaking to your condition, so be it.

If pain is identical to a certain neural state, the identity is contingent. Whether it holds is one of the things that varies from one possible world to another. But take care. I do not say that here we have two states, pain and some neural state, that are contingently identical, identical at this world but different at another. Since I'm serious about the identity, we have not two states but one. This one state, this neural state which is pain, is not contingently identical to itself. It does not differ from itself at any world. Nothing does.[3] What's true is, rather, that the concept and name of pain contingently apply to some neural state at this world, but do not apply to it at another. Similarly, it is a contingent truth that Bruce is our cat, but it's wrong to say that Bruce and our cat are contingently identical. Our cat Bruce is necessarily self-identical. What is contingent is that the nonrigid concept of being our cat applies to Bruce rather than to some other cat, or none.

IV

Nonrigidity might begin at home. All actualities are possibilities, so the variety of possibilities includes the variety of actualities. Though some possibilities are thoroughly otherworldly, others may be found on planets within range of our telescopes. One such planet is Mars.

If a nonrigid concept or name applies to different states in different possible cases, it should be no surprise if it also applies to different states in different actual cases. Nonrigidity is to logical space as other relativities are to ordinary space. If the word "pain" designates one state at our actual world and another at a possible world where our counterparts have a different internal structure, then also it may designate one state on Earth and another on Mars. Or, better, since Martians may come here and we may go to Mars, it may designate one state for Earthlings and another for Martians.

We may say that some state *occupies a causal role for a population*. We may say this whether the population is situated entirely at our actual world, or partly at our actual world and partly at other worlds, or entirely at other worlds. If the concept of pain is the concept of a state that occupies that role, then we may say that a state *is pain for a population*. Then we may say that a certain pattern of firing of neurons is pain for the population of actual Earthlings and some but not all of our otherworldly counterparts, whereas the inflation of certain cavities in the feet is pain for the population of actual Martians and some of their otherworldly counterparts. Human pain is the state that occupies the role of pain for humans. Martian pain is the state that occupies the same role for Martians.

A state occupies a causal role for a population, and the concept of occupant of that role applies to it, if and only if, with few exceptions, whenever a member of that population is in that state, his being in that state has the sort of causes and effects given by the role.

The thing to say about Martian pain is that the Martian is in pain because he is in a state that occupies the causal role of pain for Martians, whereas we are in pain because we are in a state that occupies the role of pain for us.

V

Now, what of the madman? He is in pain, but he is not in a state that occupies the causal role of pain for him. He is in a state that occupies that role for most of us, but he is an exception. The causal role of a pattern of firing of neurons depends on one's circuit diagram, and he is hooked up wrong.

His state does not occupy the role of pain for a population comprising himself and his fellow madmen. But it does occupy that role for a more salient population—mankind at large. He is a man, albeit an exceptional one, and a member of that larger population.

We have allowed for exceptions. I spoke of the definitive syndrome of *typical* causes and effects. Armstrong spoke of a state *apt* for having certain causes and effects; that does not mean that it has them invariably. Again, I spoke of a system of states that *comes near to* realizing common-sense psychology. A state may therefore occupy a role for mankind even if it does not at all occupy that role for some mad minority of mankind.

The thing to say about mad pain is that the madman is in pain because he is in the state that occupies the causal role of pain for the population comprising all mankind. He is an exceptional member of that population. The state that occupies the role for the population does not occupy it for him.

VI

We may say that *X* is in pain *simpliciter* if and only if *X* is in the state that occupies the causal role of pain for the *appropriate* population. But what is the appropriate population? Perhaps (1) it should be *us*; after all, it's our concept and our word. On the other hand, if it's *X* we're talking about, perhaps (2) it should be a population that *X* himself belongs to, and (3) it should preferably be one in which *X* is not exceptional. Either way, (4) an appropriate population should be a natural kind—a species, perhaps.

If *X* is you or I—human and unexceptional—all four considerations pull together. The appropriate population consists of mankind as it actually is, extending into other worlds only to an extent that does not make the actual majority exceptional.

Since the four criteria agree in the case of the common man, which is the case we usually have in mind, there is no reason why we should have made up our minds about their relative importance in cases of conflict. It should be no surprise if ambiguity and uncertainty arise in such cases. Still, some cases do seem reasonably clear.

If *X* is our Martian, we are inclined to say that he is in pain when the cavities in his feet are inflated; and so says the theory, provided that criterion (1) is outweighed by the other three, so that the appropriate population is taken to be the species of Martians to which X belongs.

If X is our madman, we are inclined to say that he is in pain when he is in the state that occupies the role of pain for the rest of us; and so says the theory, provided that criterion (3) is outweighed by the other three, so that the appropriate population is taken to be mankind.

We might also consider the case of a mad Martian, related to other Martians as the madman is to the rest of us. If X is a mad Martian, I would be inclined to say that he is in pain when the cavities in his feet are inflated; and so says our theory, provided that criteria (2) and (4) together outweigh either (1) or (3) by itself.

Other cases are less clear-cut. Since the balance is less definitely in favor of one population or another, we may perceive the relativity to population by feeling genuinely undecided. Suppose the state that plays the role of pain for us plays instead the role of thirst for a certain small subpopulation of mankind, and vice versa. When one of them has the state that is pain for us and thirst for him, there may be genuine and irresolvable indecision about whether to call him pained or thirsty—that is, whether to think of him as a madman or as a Martian. Criterion (1) suggests calling his state pain and regarding him as an exception; criteria (2) and (3) suggest shifting to a subpopulation and calling his state thirst. Criterion (4) could go either way, since mankind and the exceptional subpopulation may both be natural kinds. (Perhaps it is relevant to ask whether membership in the subpopulation is hereditary.)

The interchange of pain and thirst parallels the traditional problem of inverted spectra. I have suggested that there is no determinate fact of the matter about whether the victim of interchange undergoes pain or thirst. I think this conclusion accords well with the fact that there seems to be no persuasive solution one way or the other to the old problem of inverted spectra. I would say that there is a good sense in which the alleged victim of inverted spectra sees red when he looks at grass: he is in a state that occupies the role of seeing red for mankind in general. And there is an equally good sense in which he sees green: he is in a state that occupies the role of seeing green for him, and for a small subpopulation of which he is an unexceptional member and which has some claim to be regarded as a natural kind. You are right to say either, though not in the same breath. Need more be said?

To sum up, Armstrong and I claim to give a schema that, if filled in, would characterize pain and other states a priori. If the causal facts are right, then also we characterize pain as a physical phenomenon. By allowing for exceptional members of a population, we associate pain only contingently with its causal role. Therefore we do not deny the possibility of mad pain, provided there is not too much of it. By allowing for variation from one population to another (actual or merely possible) we associate pain only contingently with its physical realization. Therefore we do not deny the possibility of Martian pain. If different ways of filling in the relativity to population may be said to yield different senses of the word "pain," then we plead ambiguity. The madman is in pain in one sense, or relative to one population. The Martian is in pain in another sense, or relative to another population. (So is the mad Martian.)

But we do not posit ambiguity *ad hoc*. The requisite flexibility is explained simply by supposing that we have not bothered to make up our minds about semantic niceties that would make no difference to any commonplace case. The ambiguity that arises in cases of inverted spectra and the like is simply one instance of a commonplace kind of ambiguity—a kind that may arise whenever we have tacit relativity and criteria of selection that sometimes fail to choose a definite *relatum*. It is the same kind of ambiguity that arises if someone speaks of relevant studies without making clear whether he means relevance to current affairs, to spiritual well-being, to understanding, or what.

VII

We have a place for commonplace pain, mad pain, Martian pain, and even mad Martian pain. But one case remains problematic. What about pain in a being who is mad, alien, and unique? Have we made a place for that? It seems not. Since he is mad, we may suppose that his alleged state of pain does not occupy the proper causal role for him. Since he is alien, we may also suppose that it does not occupy the proper role for us. And since he is unique, it does not occupy the proper role for others of his species. What is left?

(One thing that might be left is the population consisting of him and his un-actualized counterparts at other worlds. If he went mad as a result of some improbable accident, perhaps we can say that he is in pain because he is in the state that occupies the role for most of his alternative possible selves; the state that would have occupied the role for him if he had developed in a more probable way. To make the problem as hard as possible, I must suppose that this solution is unavailable. He did *not* narrowly escape being so constituted that his present state would have occupied the role of pain.)

I think we cannot and need not solve this problem. Our only recourse is to deny that the case is possible. To stipulate that the being in this example is in pain was illegitimate. That seems credible enough. Admittedly, I might have thought offhand that the case was possible. No wonder; it merely combines elements of other cases that are possible. But I am willing to change my mind. Unlike my opinions about the possibility of mad pain and Martian pain, my naive opinions about this case are not firm enough to carry much weight.

VIII

Finally, I would like to try to pre-empt an objection. I can hear it said that I have been strangely silent about the very center of my topic. *What is it like* to be the madman, the Martian, the mad Martian, the victim of interchange of pain and thirst, or the being who is mad, alien, and unique? What is the *phenomenal character* of his state? If it *feels* to him like pain, then it is pain, whatever its causal role or physical nature. If not, it isn't. It's that simple!

Yes. It would indeed be a mistake to consider whether a state is pain while ignoring what it is like to have it. Fortunately, I have not made that mistake. Indeed, it is an impossible mistake to make. It is like the impossible mistake of considering whether a number is composite while ignoring the question of what factors it has.

Pain is a feeling.[4] Surely that is uncontroversial. To have pain and to feel pain are one and the same. For a state to be pain and for it to feel painful are likewise one and the same. A theory of what it is for a state to be pain is inescapably a theory of what it is like to be in that state, of how that state feels, of the phenomenal character of that state. Far from ignoring questions of how states feel in the odd cases we have been considering. I have been discussing nothing else! Only if you believe on independent grounds that considerations of causal role and physical realization have no bearing on whether a state is pain should you say that they have no bearing on how that state feels.

Notes

1. D. M. Armstrong, A *Materialist Theory of the Mind* (London: Routledge, 1968); "The Nature of Mind," in C. V. Borst, ed., *The Mind/Brain Identity Theory* (London: Macmillan, 1970), pp. 67-97; "The Causal Theory of the Mind," *Neue Heft für Philosophie*, no. 11 (Vendenhoek & Ruprecht, 1977), pp. 82-95. David Lewis, "An Argument for the Identity Theory," *Journal*

of *Philosophy* 63 (1966): 17-25, reprinted with additions in David M. Rosenthal, ed., *Materialism and the Mind-Body Problem* (Englewood Cliffs, N.J.: Prentice-Hall, 1971), pp. 162-171; "Review of *Art, Mind, and Religion,*" *Journal of Philosophy* 66 (1969): 22-27, particularly pp. 23-25; "Psychophysical and Theoretical Identifications," *Australasian Journal of Philosophy* 50 (1972): 249-258; "Radical Interpretation," *Synthese* 23 (1974): 331-344.

2. For instance, see Saul A. Kripke, "Naming and Necessity," in Gilbert Harman and Donald Davidson, eds., *Semantics of Natural Language* (Dordrecht: Reidel, 1972), pp. 253-355, 763-769, particularly pp. 335-336. Note that the sort of identity theory that Kripke opposes by argument, rather than by appeal to self-evidence, is not the sort that Armstrong and I propose.

3. The closest we can come is to have something at one world with twin counterparts at another. See my "Counterpart Theory and Quantified Modal Logic," *Journal of Philosophy* 65 (1968): 113-126. That possibility is irrelevant to the present case.

4. Occurrent pain, that is. Maybe a disposition that sometimes but not always causes occurrent pain might also be called "pain."

Functionalism, Qualia, and the Inverted Spectrum

Terrance Horgan

I

Functionalism is the doctrine that every mental state-type may be fully defined by means of its typical causal connections to sensory stimulation, behavior, and other mental state-types similarly defined. Some philosophers, myself included, believe that although functionalism is plausible as regards certain aspects of mentality, nevertheless there is one aspect that is incapable, in principle, of being analyzed functionally: viz., the qualitative, or phenomenal, content of our mental states—i.e., *what it is like* to undergo these states. What we mean by the notion of qualitative content, and why we think that this aspect of mentality cannot be accommodated by functionalism, are nicely summarized by Jerry Fodor:

Try to imagine looking at a blank wall through a red filter. Now change the filter to a green one and leave everything else exactly the way it was. Something about the character of your experience changes when the filter does, and it is this kind of thing that philosophers call qualitative content. . . .

The reason qualitative content is a problem for functionalism is straightforward. Functionalism is committed to defining mental states in terms of their causes and effects. It seems, however, as if two mental states could have all the same causal relations and yet could differ in their qualitative content. Let me illustrate this with the classic puzzle of the inverted spectrum.

It seems possible to imagine two observers who are alike in all relevant psychological respects except that experiences having the qualitative content of red for one observer would have the qualitative content of green for the other. Nothing about their behavior need reveal the difference because both of them see ripe tomatoes and flaming sunsets as being similar in color and both of them call that color "red." Moreover, the causal connection between their (qualitatively distinct) experiences and their other mental states could also be identical. Perhaps they both think of Little Red Riding Hood when they see ripe tomatoes, feel depressed when they see the color green and so on. It seems as if anything that could be packed into the notion of the causal role of their experience could be shared by them, and yet the qualitative content of the experiences could be as different as you like. If this is possible, then the functionalist account does not work for mental states that have qualitative content. If one person is having a green experience while another person is having a red one, then surely they must be in different mental states.

It would seem that if all mental states are fully definable functionally, then the inverted-spectrum thought experiment Fodor describes should be conceptually incoherent. Yet many of us find it remarkably easy to perform such thought experiments, and this makes us very suspicious of claims that they are incoherent. Instead, we find ourselves concluding that functionalism, whatever its virtues in other respects, cannot accommodate qualia. . . .

II

Let us now return to the inverted-spectrum objection to functionalism. To fix our attention on a concrete case, we shall suppose that Jack is a normal color-perceiver, but that Jill has, from the moment of her birth onward, unusual neural "wiring" in the intermediate portions of her visual system—wiring which systematically causes the retinal stimulations induced by light of any given wavelength to generate in her visual cortex the same neural activity that is generated in us by the "spectral inverse" of that wavelength. Thus, if brain state G and brain state R are the state-types induced in John's visual cortex by green objects and red objects respectively, then G is induced in Jill by red objects and R is induced in her by green objects. Nonetheless, since Jill has learned color words in the same ostensive manner John has, she uses those words in the same way he does. Let us further suppose that G plays *completely* the same causal role in Jill that R plays in Jack, and vice versa; thus, if Jack thinks of Little Red Riding Hood when looking at ripe tomatoes then so does Jill, and if Jack becomes depressed when he looks at green objects then so does Jill, and so on.

Thought experiments like this initially seem problematic for functionalism. For when Jack and Jill both look at grass, they surely differ mentally despite being in functionally identical states—a fact that seems to imply that there is more to mentality than what is functionally definable. But now we see how the functionalist can reply to this line of reasoning. He can say that although Jack and Jill are in functionally identical states under one relativization (the one that relativizes Jack's mental states to mankind, and Jill's to her unusual subpopulation), they are in functionally *different* states under another relativization (the one that relativizes both Jack's and Jill's mental states to mankind). Thus, the functionalist can deny that the case of Jack and Jill shows there is more to mentality than is functionally definable. He can say instead that under one relativization, Jack and Jill differ neither functionally nor mentally when they look at grass, whereas under the other relativization they differ *both* functionally and mentally. According to this account, we really commit a subtle form of equivocation if we claim that Jack and Jill differ mentally despite being in functionally identical states: viz., equivocation between two contextually appropriate ways of relativizing mental-state ascriptions.

Should we qualia-lovers concede that this analysis successfully disarms the inverted-spectrum objection to functionalism? I submit that we should not, and for a reason that takes much less time to state then does the analysis itself. For it is just self-evident, I submit, that the qualitative content of Jill's experience when she looks at grass is an absolute, intrinsic feature of her mental life—not a feature that is implicitly population-relative. There is, absolutely and non-relatively, *something it is like* for Jill when she looks at grass. Furthermore, this feature differs from the corresponding intrinsic, non-relative feature of

Jack's mental life when he looks at grass: what it is like for Jill when she looks at grass is the same as what it is like for Jack when he looks at grassy red stuff. Hence their mental states when looking at grass are intrinsically, unqualifiedly different. This difference remains present even if we relativize all *functional* state-ascriptions in such a way that Jack and Jill are in functionally-identical states when looking at grass. Thus, the phenomenal content of color experience does indeed go beyond what is functionally definable. Functionalism cannot accommodate qualia.

As I said, I take the intrinsic, non-relative nature of qualia to be a self-evident fact, a fact which unavoidably impresses itself upon most of us who actually experience these states. The point is virtually impossible to *argue* for, however, because it depends upon an individual's first-person perspective toward his own mental life. Functionalists can, and do, resolutely insist that they are aware of no such features in their own mental life; and since the rest of us lack first-person access to their mental states, we cannot refute them. We can only describe cases like that of Jack and Jill, and ask whether it is not absolutely, undeniably *obvious* that there is an intrinsic, non-population-relative difference between Jack's mental state when looking at grass and Jill's.

Dialectically, we seem to have reached an impasse. Initially it appeared that functionalists were required to take the heroic step of denying the intelligibility of inverted-spectrum stories, and hence that the evident intelligibility of such stories constituted evidence against them. But it turns out that functionalists can make sense of inverted spectra by invoking population-relativization. The qualia-lovers reply that this approach leaves out of account the allegedly self-evident fact that the qualitative content of our mental states is an intrinsic, non-population-relative feature of those states. The functionalists respond by denying that this is a fact at all, let alone a self-evident one. Deadlock.

I shall not try to break this deadlock. Instead, I shall simply direct the subsequent discussion at those who consider it obvious, as I do, that the qualitative aspects of mentality are not definable functionally. I shall propose a theory of mind that makes room for qualia as non-functional mental state-types. If you are not among those to whom the remaining portion of the paper is addressed, and you find yourself wondering what it is about our mental life that is allegedly left out by functional definitions, I can only join with Ned Block in replying with the words once used by Louis Armstrong when he was asked what jazz is: "If you got to ask, you ain't never gonna get to know."

III

I propose a two-part theory. Phenomenal state-types (i.e., qualia) are to be identified with neurophysiological state-types; the identities involved are necessary identities, because the qualia-names involved (as well as the neurophysiological state-names) are rigid designators. Nonphenomenal state-types, on the other hand, are to be construed functionally. . . .

Can we expect all the mental state-types we recognize in everyday mentalese to be neatly separable by means of the phenomenal/non-phenomenal distinction? Not necessarily. It may turn out that many garden-variety mental state-types are really hybrid types, involving both a phenomenal component and a non-phenomenal component. A plausible candidate for such hybrid status, I suggest, is the philosopher's favorite mental state: pain. I think there are really two state-types instantiated in any clear-cut instance of pain: (1) *phenomenal* pain, the "raw feel" of pain experiences (and the element not definable functionally); and (2) *functional* pain, the state-type which, by definition, has typical causes such as harmful forces impinging upon the creature's surface, and typical effects such as avoidance-behavior. Hybrid types, on the view I am proposing, are instantiated when both the relevant purely-phenomenal type and the relevant purely-functional type are instantiated—even if these latter are not explicitly countenanced in everyday mentalese.

IV

Let us now consider how this theory, which I shall call *partial functionalism*, fares in comparison to full-fledged functionalism. One important advantage of partial functionalism, of course, is that it explicitly accommodates the deeply-felt intuition that the phenomenal aspects of mentality are not definable functionally: the intuition that functionalism leaves out what it is like to undergo mental states like pain, thirst, seeing red, and seeing green.

Another positive feature of partial functionalism is that it not only accommodates this intuition, but it does so while still preserving a fully naturalistic conception of a human being as physico-chemical system whose behavior is completely explainable, in principle, solely in physico-chemical terms. For although I am claiming that the qualitative content of our mental life is not definable functionally. I am not thereby rendering it something occult—something apart from the uninterrupted nexus of physico-chemical causation within the human central nervous system. On the contrary, I am claiming that qualia are nothing other than certain neurophysiological state-types. They are not higher-level state-types whose presence and causal efficacy in human beings are mysterious from the perspective of natural science.

One reason for the current wide appeal of functionalism, I think, is that this doctrine seems to mesh so nicely with a naturalistic conception of human beings. Under functionalism it is no more difficult to understand how humans, regarded naturalistically, can undergo mental states than it is to understand how the physical devices we call computers can undergo "computational" states—i.e., states defined abstractly in terms of the computer's program, its "software." Mentality is to physico-chemical activity in humans as computational activity is to physico-chemical activity in computers.

I am claiming that phenomenal state-types are, in Keith Gunderson's happy phrase, "program resistant." That is, the capacity to instantiate them does not arise by virtue of a creature's software, the functional organization of its physico-chemical components. But I espouse naturalism nonetheless, for my contention is that phenomenal state-types are *hardware* state-types rather than software state-types. They are program resistant because they are identical, and necessarily identical, to physico-chemical state-types—not because they are occult state-types that no mere physico-chemical system could instantiate.

But although partial functionalism does seem compatible with the granola conception of human beings, nevertheless one might object that it is theoretically less unified than full-fledged functionalism, and that this fact counts seriously against it.

I deny neither the desirability of theoretical simplicity nor the fact that my theory is somewhat more complex than functionalism. But a theory of mind should not be rendered simple at the cost of failing to accommodate seemingly obvious facts about our mental life—like the fact that in an inverted spectrum situation like that of Jack and Jill, the two persons differ mentally in an absolute, non-population-relative way. Furthermore, since I am not positing qualia as state-types over and above physico-chemical state-types, the greater complexity of my theory concerns only the workings of mental terminology; the ontology of this theory is at least as parsimonious as functionalism's ontology.

Another potential objection to partial functionalism is the charge that it is chauvinistic, in a way that functionalism is not. Surely, the objection goes, a Martian could undergo the same qualia we do even if his neurological hardware were vastly different from our own. Functionalism allows for this possibility, but partial functionalism does not.

Since my theory is partly functionalist, I can grant the plasticity of non-phenomenal mental states, i.e., the realizability of such states in creatures vastly different from ourselves in physico-chemical structure. But is it really plausible to say the same about qualia? I submit that it is not, unless one holds that qualia too are functionally definable. For, if we deny that qualia are functional states, then the most natural way to accommodate them naturalistically is to suppose that they are identical with specific physico-chemical states of the human brain—or at any rate, of brains relevantly similar to human brains. And it then becomes plausible to *deny* the plasticity of qualia, and to contend that a Martian, with his radically different physical makeup, must experience either different qualia than ours or no qualia at all.

The prospect of Martians who are functionally similar to us but who either lack qualia altogether or else have dramatically different qualia, raises with a vengeance the traditional problem of other minds. If partial functionalism is correct, how could we ever tell whether Martians have qualia? Their functional organization would be compatible with both (1) the supposition that their mental lives are qualitatively as rich as our own, and (2) the alternative supposition that they are zombies whose mental lives are qualitatively empty.

Suppose we came to know and like Martians, and to have frequent profound intellectual intercourse with them—including philosophical discussions about minds. At some point, no doubt we would raise the topic of functionalism, the doctrine that all mental state-types are fully definable in terms of typical causal connections to sensory inputs, behavioral outputs, and other similarly-defined mental states. Once we were satisfied that they understood this thesis, we could simply *ask* them whether they find that in their own case, there is more to mentality than what is functionally definable. To make the question more specific, we could describe a Martian version of our earlier inverted-spectrum story, involving a Martian Jack and a Martian Jill, and then ask them whether these two individuals would differ mentally in some absolute, non-population-relative way. If they said yes, we would have grounds for inferring that they have qualia; if no, we would have grounds for inferring that they do not.

Admittedly, the matter might be complicated by the existence of some Martian philosophers who really have qualia but still resolutely deny that there is more to theory mentality than what is functionally definable—

just as certain human philosophers do. Still, we could obtain evidence for or against Martian qualia by determining whether the issue was *controversial* among philosophically-inclined Martians. If, by and large, they tended to accede to a Lewis-style analysis of inverted-spectrum cases, we could infer that they probably have no qualia. If, on the other hand, many of them insisted that something crucial is left out by such an analysis, and that "If you got to ask" what it is "you ain't never gonna get to know," then we could infer that they probably do have qualia— the stubbornness of the Martian functionalists notwithstanding.

But even if it is possible, under partial functionalism, to know whether or not Martians have qualia, it very well might not be possible to know what these qualia are like. After all, "knowing what a mental state is like" involves being in, or remembering being in, that state yourself—or at any rate, being in, or remembering being in, sufficiently similar states. And since Martian qualia would be physico-chemical state-types instantiatable by creatures with a Martian-like physical composition, we humans might simply lack the neural hardware that is necessary to undergo Martian qualia. And if we could not undergo them, we could not "know what they are like."

Does this show that there is something occult and theoretically mysterious about qualia after all? I think not. For I have been claiming that part of what we mean by "knowing what a mental state is like" is "having undergone that state, or a similar one, one-self." Thus, if we can explain scientifically why humans cannot undergo the physical state-types which are identical to Martian qualia, we will thereby explain *why* humans cannot know what Martian qualia are like. Furthermore, it is still perfectly possible to know *what* they are, even if we cannot know what they are like: they are specific physico-chemical state-types.

Why People Think Computers Can't
Marvin Minsky

Most people are convinced computers cannot think. That is, *really* think. Everyone knows that computers already do many things that no person could do without "thinking." But when computers do such things, most people suspect that there is only an illusion of thoughtful behavior, and that the machine

- doesn't know what it's doing.
- is only doing what its programmer told it to.
- has no feelings. And so on.

The people who built the first computers were engineers concerned with huge numerical computations: that's why the things were *called* computers. So, when computers first appeared, their designers regarded them as nothing but machines for doing mindless calculations.

Yet even then a fringe of people envisioned what's now called "Artificial Intelligence"—or "AI" for short—because they realized that computers could manipulate not only numbers but also *symbols*. That meant that computers should be able to go beyond arithmetic, perhaps to imitate the information processes that happen inside minds. In the early 1950's, Turing began a Chess program, Oettinger wrote a learning program, Kirsch and Selfridge wrote vision programs, all using the machines that were designed just for arithmetic.

Today, surrounded by so many automatic machines, industrial robots, and the R2-D2's of Star Wars movies, most people think AI is much more advanced than it is. But still, many "computer experts" don't believe that machines will ever "really think." I think those specialists are too used to explaining that there's nothing inside computers but little electric currents. This leads them to believe that there can't be room left for anything else—like minds, or selves. And there are many other reasons why so many experts still maintain that machines can never be creative, intuitive, or emotional, and will never really think, believe, or understand anything. This essay explains why they are wrong.

Can Computers Do Only What They're Told?

We naturally admire our Einsteins and Beethovens, and wonder if computers ever could create such wondrous theories or symphonies. Most people think that "creativity" requires some mysterious "gift" that simply cannot be explained. If so, then no computer can create—since, clearly, anything machines can do can be explained.

To see what's wrong with that, we'd better turn aside from those outstanding works our culture views as very best of all. Otherwise we'll fall into a silly trap. For, until we first have some good ideas of how we do the *ordinary* things—how ordinary people write ordinary symphonies—we simply can't expect to understand how great composers write great symphonies! And obviously, until we have some good ideas about *that*, we'd simply have no way to guess how difficult might be the problems in composing those most outstanding works—and then, with no idea at all of how they're made, of course they'll seem mysterious! (As Arthur Clarke has said, *any* technology sufficiently advanced seems like magic.) So first we'd better understand how people and computers might do the ordinary things that we all do. (Besides, those skeptics should be made to realize that their arguments imply that ordinary people can't think, either.) So let's ask if we can make computers that can use ordinary common sense; until we get a grip on that we hardly can expect to ask good questions about works of genius.

In a practical sense, computers already do much more than their programmers tell them to. I'll grant that the earliest and simplest programs were little more than simple lists and loops of commands like *"Do this. Do that. Do this and that and this again until* that *happens."* That made it hard to imagine how more could emerge from such programs than their programmers envisioned. But there's a big difference between "impossible" and "hard to imagine." The first is about *it*; the second is about *you*!

Most people still write programs in languages like BASIC and FORTRAN, which make you write in that style—let's call it "do now" programming. This forces you to imagine all the details of how your program will move from one state to another, from one moment to the next. And once you're used to thinking that way, it is hard to see how a program could do anything its programmer didn't think of—because it is so hard to make that kind of program do *anything* very interesting. Hard, not impossible.

Then AI researchers developed new kinds of programming. For example, the "General Problem Solver" system of Newell, Shaw and Simon lets you describe processes in terms of statements like "if you're on the wrong side of a door, go through it"—or, more technically, "if the difference between what you have and what you want is of kind D, then try to change that difference by using method M."[1] Let's call this "do whenever" programming. Such programs automatically apply each rule whenever it's applicable—so the programmer doesn't have to anticipate when that might happen. When you write in this style, you still have to say what should happen in each "state" the process gets into—but you don't have to know in advance when each state will occur.

---

[1]Of course, I'm greatly simplifying that history.

You also could do such things with the early programming language COMIT, developed by Yngve at MIT, and the SNOBOL language that followed it. Today, that programming style is called "production systems."[2] The mathematical theory of such languages is explained in my book.[3]

That "General Problem Solver" program of Newell and Simon was also a landmark in research on Artificial Intelligence, because it showed how to write a program to solve a problem that the programmer doesn't know how to solve. The trick is to tell the program what kinds of things to TRY; you need not know which one actually will work. Even earlier, in 1956, Newell, Shaw, and Simon developed a computer program that was good at finding proofs of theorems in mathematical logic—problems that college students found quite hard—and it even found some proofs that were rather novel. (It also showed that computers could do "logical reasoning"—but this was no surprise, and since then we've found even more powerful ways to make machines do such things.) Later, I'll discuss how this relates to the problem of making programs that can do "common-sense reasoning."

Now, you might reply, "Well, everyone knows that if you try enough different things at random, of course, eventually, you can do anything. But if it takes a million billion trillion years, like those monkeys hitting random typewriter keys, that's not intelligence at all. That's just Evolution or something."

That's quite correct—except that the "GPS" system had a real difference—it didn't do things randomly. To use it, you also had to add another kind of knowledge—"advice" about when one problem-state is likely to be better than another. Then, instead of wandering around at random, the program can seek the better states; it sort of feels around, the way you'd climb a hill, in the dark, by always moving up the slope. This makes its "search" seem not random at all, but rather purposeful. The trouble—and it's very serious—is that it can get stuck on a little peak, and never make it to the real summit of the mountain.

Since then, much AI research has been aimed at finding more "global" ways to solve problems, to get around that problem of getting stuck on little peaks which are better than all the nearby spots, but worse than places that can't be reached without descending in between. We've discovered a variety of ways to do this, by making programs take larger views, plan further ahead, reformulate problems, use analogies, and so

[2]Allen Newell and Herbert Simon, *Human Problem Solving.*
[3]Marvin Minsky, *Computation: Finite and Infinite Machines*, Prentice-Hall 1967.

forth. No one has discovered a "completely general" way to always find the very highest peak. Well, that's too bad—but it doesn't mean there's any difference here between men and machines—since people, too, are almost always stuck on local peaks of every kind. That's life.

Today, most AI researchers use languages like LISP, that let a programmer use "general recursion." Such languages are even more expressive than "do whenever" language, because their programmers don't have to foresee clearly either the kinds of states that might occur or when they will occur; the program just constrains how states and structures will relate to one another. We could call these "constraint languages."[4]

Even with such powerful tools, we're still just beginning to make programs that can learn and can reason by analogy. We're just starting to make systems that will learn to recognize which old experiences in memory are most analogous to present problems. I like to think of this as "do something sensible" programming. Such a program would remember a lot about its past so that, for each new problem, it would search for methods like the ones that worked best on similar problems in the past. When speaking about programs that have that much self-direction, it makes no sense at all to say "computers do only what they're told to do," because now the programmer knows so little of what situations the machine may encounter in its future—or what it will remember from its past.

A generation later, we should be experimenting on programs that *write better programs to replace themselves.* Then at last it will be clear how foolish was our first idea—that never, by their nature, could machines create new things. This essay tries to explain why so many people have guessed so wrongly about such things.

Could Computers Be Creative?

I plan to answer "no" by showing that there's no such thing as "creativity" in the first place. I don't believe there's any substantial difference between ordinary thought and creative thought. Then why do we think there's a difference? I'll argue that this is really not a matter of what's in the mind of the artist—but of what's in the mind of the critic; the less one understands an artist's mind the more creative seems the work the artist does.

---

[4]This isn't quite true. LISP doesn't really have those "do whenevers" built into it, but programmers can learn to make such extensions, and most AI workers feel that the extra flexibility outweighs the inconvenience.

I don't blame anyone for not being able to do the things creative people do. I don't blame them for not being able to explain it, either. (I don't even blame them for thinking that if creativity can't be explained, it can't be mechanized; in fact I agree with that.) But I do blame them for thinking that, just because they can't explain it themselves, then no one *ever* could imagine how creativity works. After all, if you can't understand or imagine how something might be done at all, you certainly shouldn't expect to be able to imagine how a machine could do it!

What is the origin of all those skeptical beliefs? I'll argue first that we're unduly intimidated by admiration of our Beethovens and Einsteins. Consider first how hard we find it to express the ways we get our new ideas—not just "creative" ones but everyday ideas. The trouble is, when focusing on creativity, we're prone to notice it when others get ideas that we don't. But when we get our own ideas, we take them for granted, and don't ask where we "get" them from. Actually we know as little— maybe less—of how we think of ordinary things. We're simply so accustomed to the marvels of everyday thought that we never wonder—until unusual performances attract attention. (Of course, our superstitions about creativity serve other needs, e.g., to give our heroes special qualities that justify the things we ordinary losers cannot do.)

Should we suppose that outstanding minds are any different from ordinary minds at all, except in matters of degree? I'll argue both ways. I'll first say "No, there's nothing special in a genius, but just some rare, unlikely combination of virtues—none very special by itself." Then, I'll say "Yes, but in order to *acquire* such a combination, you need at least a lucky accident—and maybe something else—to make you able, in the first place, to acquire those other skills."

I don't see any mystery about that mysterious combination itself. There must be an intense concern with some domain. There must be great proficiency in that domain (albeit not in any articulate, academic sense). And one must have enough self-confidence, immunity to peer pressure, to break the grip of standard paradigms. Without that one might solve problems just as hard—but in domains that wouldn't be called "creative" by one's peers. But none of those seems to demand a basic qualitative difference. As I see it, any ordinary person who can understand an ordinary conversation must have already in his head most of the mental power that our greatest thinkers have. In other words, I claim that "ordinary, common sense" already includes the things it takes—when better balanced and more fiercely motivated—to make a genius. Then what makes those first-raters so much better at their work? Perhaps two kinds of difference-in-degree from ordinary minds. One is the way such people *learn* so many more and deeper skills.

The other is the way they learn to *manage* using what they learn. Perhaps beneath the surface of their surer mastery, creative people also have some special administrative skills that better knit their surface skills together. A good composer, for example, has to master many skills of phrase and theme—but those abilities are shared, to some degree, by everyone who *talks* coherently. An artist also has to master larger forms of form—but such skills, too, are shared by everyone who knows good ways to "tell a tale." A lot of people learn a lot of different skills—but few combine them well enough to reach that frontal rank. One minor artist masters fine detail but not the larger forms; another has the forms but lacks technique.[5]

We still don't know why those "creative masters" learn so much so well. The simplest hypothesis is that they've come across some better way to choose how and what to learn! What might the secret be? The simplest explanation: such a "gift" is just some "higher-order" kind of expertise—of knowing how to gain and use one's other skills. What might it take to learn *that*? Obvious: *one must learn to be better at learning!*

If that's not obvious, perhaps our culture doesn't teach how to think about learning. We tend to think of learning as something that just happens to us, like a sponge getting soaked. But learning really is a growing mass of skills; we start with some but have to learn the rest. Most people never get deeply concerned with acquiring increasingly more advanced learning skills. Why not? Because they don't pay off right away! When a child tries to spoon sand into a pail, the child is mostly concerned with filling pails and things like that. Suppose, though, by some accident, a child got interested in how that pail-filling activity itself improved over time, and how the mind's inner dispositions affected that improvement. If only once a child became involved (even unconsciously) in how to learn better, then that could lead to exponential learning growth.

Each better way to learn to learn would lead to better ways to build more skills—until that little difference had magnified itself into an awesome, qualitative change. In this view, first-rank "creativity" could be just the consequence of childhood accidents in which a person's learning

---

[5]Of course each culture sets a threshold to award to just a few that rank of "first class creativity"—however great or small the differences among contestants. This must make social sense, providing smallish clubs of ideal-setting idols, but shouldn't then burden our philosophy with talk of "inexplicability." There must be better ways to deal with feelings of regret at being "second-rate."

gets to be a little more "self-applied" than usual.[6] If this image is correct, then we might see creativity happen in machines, once we begin to travel down the road of making machines that learn—and learn to learn better.

Then why is genius so rare? Well, first of all, the question might be inessential, because the "tail" of every distribution must be small by definition. But in the case of self-directed human thought-improvement, it may well be that all of us are already "close to some edge" of safety in some socio-biological sense. Perhaps it's really relatively easy for certain genes to change our brains to make them focus even more on learning better ways to learn. But quantity is not the same as quality—and, possibly, no culture could survive in which each different person finds some wildly different, better way to think! It might be true, and rather sad, if there were genes for genius that weren't hard at all for Evolution to come upon—but needed (instead of nurturing) a frequent, thorough weeding out, to help us keep our balance on some larger social scale.

Can Computers Choose Their Own Problems?

Some people even ask "How could computers make mistakes?" as though, somehow, ability to err itself might be some precious gift. There's nothing wrong with seeking for some precious quality, but only some form of quiet desperation would lead one to seek for it in error and mistake. It seems to stem from the misconception that creativity is rooted in some chance or random element that can't be found in any well-defined machine. This is silly, first because machines can simulate random behavior as well as one can want, and, second because it doesn't explain the consistency and coherency with which creative people produce.

Another often-heard speculation: "I can see how a machine could solve very difficult problems that are given to it by someone. But isn't the very hardest and most important problem, really, to figure out *what problem to solve*? Perhaps the thing machines can't do is to invent their own problems?" This is wonderfully profound and silly at the same time. Really, it's usually *much* easier to think of good problems than to solve them—though sometimes it is profoundly hard to find exactly the right question to ask. In any case, a culture frames its history of ideas so that the rewards are largest for opening new areas. But the problems *inside* each subject can be just as *hard.*

---

[6]Notice, that there's no way a parent could notice—and then reward—a young child's reflective concern with learning. If anything, the kid would seem to be doing *less* rather than more—and might be urged to "snap out of it."

The reason this speculation is wrong is that, in order to solve any really hard problem (by definition of "hard"), one has to find a way to break it down into other problems that one can solve. Therefore, the ability to invent and formulate new problems must already be a part of being reasonably intelligent. It only obscures the point to argue that those are "only sub-problems." The ability to compose good questions is a requisite of intelligence, not a special *sine qua non* for creativity.

Besides, some people, more than others, prefer to look outside a present context and ask larger questions like "Am I working on the right problem?" But everyone *can* do this to some degree—and can be worse off by doing it excessively. I see nothing especially mysterious about that inclination to "take a larger view."[7] The interesting problem is less in what generates the originality, and more in how we build control mechanisms that appropriately exploit and suppress it.

The rest of this essay explains the weaknesses of several other common theories of how machines must differ fundamentally from minds. Those theories are unproved today—not because of anything about machines, but just because we know too little about how human minds really work. We're simply not prepared to search for things that we can do but machines cannot. Because of this, we'll focus on a more constructive kind of question: why *people* are so very bad at making theories of what *they* can or cannot do!

Can Computers Think Only Logically?

Our culture is addicted to images of minds divided into two parts. Usually, one mind-half is seen as calculating, logical, and pretty brittle; the other half seems sort of soft and vague. There are so many variants of this, and all so ill-defined, that it's impossible to tell them apart: let's call them Soft-Hard Dumbbell theories:

Logic	—	Intuition
Spatial	—	Verbal
Quantitative	—	Qualitative
Local	—	Global
Reason	—	Emotion
Thinking	—	Feeling
Literal	—	Metaphorical, etc.

---

[7]That is, given the advanced abilities to plan, generalise, and make abstractions that all ordinary people possess; computers haven't exhibited much ability in these areas, yet.

There's nothing wrong with starting with two-part theories—if you use them as steps toward better theories. But when you *stop* at dumbbell theories then, most likely, you have only one idea instead of two:

Whatever-it-is—Everything else.

The trouble with one-part theories is that they don't lead anywhere, because they can't support enough detail. Most of our culture's mental-pair distinctions are stuck just so, which handicaps our efforts to make theories of the mind. I'm especially annoyed with recent fads that see minds as divided evenly into two halves that live within the left and right-hand sides of the brain:

Left-Like — Right-Like

(Computer-like)—(Rest-of-mind-like)

This is really neat. It not only supports beliefs that minds do things computers can't, but even provides a handy physical brain-location in which to put the differences!

Each half of the brain has dozens, and probably hundreds of different sections of machinery. There definitely are some differences between right and left. But these structural differences between corresponding parts of the right and left halves appear very much less than the differences *within* each half. Despite that flood of half-baked brain-half stories, I've heard of little evidence for systematic differences in how those left-right portions really function, in spite of all those newsstand magazines and books, and it would seem that even brain-scientists' theories about minds are just as naive as yours and mine. They're just as prone to "observe" whatever distinctions they imagine. Just for fun, I'll contribute two of my own speculations on what our brain-halves do:

MASTER-SLAVE THEORY: The two brain-sides at first develop more or less the same ways, in parallel. As time goes on and specialties mature, the need for order and coherency requires one to become dominant: a program cannot smoothly serve two masters. Whichever side acquires control, perhaps according to some inborn bias, the other side remains more "childish" and subservient, and used for cruder, simpler parts of whatever computation is involved.

DIFFERENCE THEORY: Our AI theories of thinking emphasize mechanisms for recognizing differences. This requires access to closely

related pairs of descriptions. One must describe the present situation as
it is; the other describes the ideal or goal—that is, the situation as one
wishes it to be. What better way to do that than to slave together a pair
of similar machines with, say, one side depicting more of what's perceived, the other representing anticipated or imagined goals.

Either image seems to suit those popular but vague descriptions of
the two "dissected personalities," right and left, that emerge when surgeons split a patient's brain in halves. The right side, say, would be better at realistic, concrete things—things as they are. The left half would
have specialized in long-range plans, in things that aren't yet, in short,
at things we like to call "abstract."

Those age-old distinctions between Logic and Intuition, or Reason
and Emotion, have been the source of many unsound arguments about
machine intelligence. It was clear in AI's earliest days that logical deduction would be easy to program. Accordingly, people who imagined thinking to be mostly logical expected computers soon to do the things that
people used their logic for. In that view, it ought to be much harder,
perhaps impossible, to program more qualitative traits like intuition,
metaphor, aesthetics or reasoning by analogy. I never liked such arguments.

In 1964, my student T.G. Evans finished a program to show that
computers could actually use analogies. It did some interesting kinds of
reasoning about perception of geometric structures. This made some
humanistic skeptics so angry that they wrote papers about it. Some
threw out the baby with the bath by seeming to argue that if machines
could indeed do that kind of analogical reasoning, then, maybe that
kind of reasoning can't be so important. One of them complained that
Evans' program was too complicated to be the basis of an interesting
psychological theory, because it used about 60,000 computer instruc-
tion-words. (That seemed like saying there wasn't any baby in the first
place.)

In any case Evans' program certainly showed it was wrong to assume
computers could do only logical or quantitative reasoning. Why did so
many people make that mistake? I see it as a funny irony: those critics
had mistaken *their own personal limitations* for limitations of computers!
They had projected their own inability to explain how either person or
machine could reason by analogy onto the outer world, to suppose that
no well-defined mechanism could do such a thing. In effect, they were
saying that since *they* could see no explanation then, surely, there could
be no explanation!

Another misconception sterns from confusing different senses of logic. Too many computer specialists talk as though computers are perfectly logical, and that's all. What they really mean is that *they* can understand, using logic, how all those tiny little computer circuits work. But, just because the little circuits can be understood *by* logic doesn't mean *at all* that those circuits can only *do* logic! That's like thinking you could figure out what houses are *for* from knowing how bricks work.

Many AI workers have continued to pursue the use of logic to solve problems. This hasn't worked very well, in my opinion; logical reasoning is more appropriate for displaying or confirming the *results* of thinking than for the thinking itself. That is, I suspect we use it less for solving problems than we use it for explaining the solutions to other people and—much more important—to ourselves. When working with the actual details of problems, it is usually too hard to package the knowledge we need into suitably logical form. So then we have to use other methods, anyway—methods more suitable for the "networks of meanings" that I'll discuss shortly. Still, I consider such ideas to be of great importance in making theories of how we *represent* the things we think about, and especially in how we think when we reason *carefully*.

Could a Computer Really Understand Anything?

I see you've programmed that computer to obey verbal commands. You've probably inserted into its memory how it should respond to each command. But I don't believe the program really understands the words, in any human sense.

This criticism is deserved by most computer systems around these days. But how does it apply to the 1965 program written by Daniel Bobrow that solves high-school algebra "word problems?"! It could solve some problems like these:

The distance from New York to Los Angeles is 3000 miles. If the average speed of a jet plane is 600 miles per hour, find the time it takes to travel from New York to Los Angeles by jet.

Bill's father's uncle is twice as-old as Bill's father. Two years from now Bill's father will be three times as old as Bill. The sum of their ages is 92. Find Bill's age.

Most human students find problems like these quite hard. They find it easier to learn to solve the kinds of *equations* they encounter in high school algebra; that's just cook-book stuff. But to solve the word problems, you have to figure out what equations to solve. Doesn't this mean you have to understand at least something of what the words and sentences mean?

Well, to begin with, Bobrow's program used a lot of tricks. It guesses that the word "is" usually means "equals." It doesn't even try to figure out what "Bill's fathers' uncle" is, except to notice that this phrase resembles "Bill's father."[8] It doesn't know that "age" and "old" have anything to do with time, only that they're numbers to be put into, or found from, equations. Given these and a couple of hundred other facts about the words, it sometimes (and by no means, always) manages to get the answers right.

But dare one say that Bobrow's program really "understands" those sentences? If meaning isn't caught in several hundred different tricks—might not we still imprison it in several hundred thousand tricks? Is "understand" even an idea we can ask Science to deal with?

Here's how I like to deal with such questions. I feel no obligation to define such words as "mean" and "understand," just because others tried it for five thousand years! Our words are only *social things*; it's great when they combine to give us good ideas. But here, I think, they only point to a maze of unproductive superstitions, that only handicapped our predecessors when they tried to figure out what "meanings" are and how they get connected to our words. It is a wrong-headed enterprise, like asking people to agree on what is "good," without considering each person's different hopes and fears.

Fortunately, as I will show, there isn't any need to try to capture "meanings" in such rigid, public ways. In fact, that would defeat our real purposes. This is because any psychologically realistic theory of meanings needs built-in ways to deal with individual differences between the people who are to do the "knowing."

Could a Computer Know What Something Means?

We can't think very well about meaning without thinking about the meaning of something. So let's discuss what numbers mean. And we can't think about what numbers mean very well without thinking about what

---

[8]In fact, if there were one less equation, it would assume that they mean the same, because they're so similar.

some particular number means. Take Five. Now, no one would claim that Bobrow's algebra program could be said to understand what numbers "really" are, or even what Five really is. It obviously knows something of arithmetic, in the sense that it can find sums like "5 plus 7 is 12." The question is—does it understand numbers in any *other* sense—say, what are 5 or 7 or 12—or, for that matter, what are "plus" or "is"? Well, what would *you* say if I asked, "What is Five"? I'll argue that the secret lies in that little word *"other."*

Early this century, the philosophers Russell and Whitehead suggested a new way to define a number. "Five," they said, is *the set of all possible sets with five members.* This set includes every set of Five ball-point pens, and every litter of Five kittens. The trouble was, this definition threatened also to include sets like "these Five words" and even "the Five things that you'd least expect." Sets like those led to so many curious inconsistencies and paradoxes that the theory had to be doctored so that these could not be expressed—and *that* made the theory, in its final form, too complicated for any practical use (except for formalizing mathematics, where it worked very well indeed). But, in my view, it offers little promise for capturing the meanings of everyday common sense. The trouble is with its basic goal: finding for each word some single rigid definition. That's fine for formalizing Mathematics. But for real life, it ignores a basic fact of mind: what something means to me depends to some extent on everything else I know—and no one else knows just those things in just those ways.

But, you might complain, when you give up the idea of having rigid, definitions, don't you get into hot water? Isn't ambiguity bad enough; what about the problems of "circular definitions," paradoxes, and inconsistencies? Relax! We shouldn't be *that* terrified of contradictions; let's face it, most of the things we people think we "know" are crocks already overflowing with contradictions; a little more won't kill us. The best we can do is just be reasonably careful—and make our machines careful, too—but still there are always chances of mistakes. That's life.

Another kind of thing we scientists tend to hate are circular dependencies. If every meaning depends on the mind it's in—that is, on all other meanings in that mind—then there's no place to start. We fear that when some meanings form such a circle, then there would be no way to break into the circle, and everything would be too subjective to make good science.

I don't think that we should fear the fact that our meanings and definitions run around in vicious circles, each depending on the others. There's still a scientific way to deal with this: just start making new kinds of theories—about those circles themselves! You don't *have* to break into them—you only need to have good theories *about* them. Of course, this is hard to do, and likely to get complicated. It was to avoid complication that all those old theories tried to suppress the ways that meanings depend on one another. The trouble is, that lost all the power and the richness of our wondrous meaning-webs! Let's face another fact: our minds really are complicated, perhaps more so than any other structure Science ever contemplated. So we can't expect the old ideas to solve all the new problems.

Besides, speaking of breaking into the meaning-circle, many science-fiction writers have pointed out that no one ever really *wants* to get oneself inside another mind. No matter if that's the only hope of perfect communication—of being absolutely sure you understand exactly, at every level of nuance what other people mean. The only way you could do that is by becoming exactly like that person but even then the game is lost, since then you couldn't understand any more (perfectly, that is) just what it was that your old self had tried to say.

What Is a Number, That a Mind Might Know It?

Now let's return to what numbers mean. This time, to make things easier, we'll think about Three. What could we mean by saying that Three hasn't any single, basic definition, but is a web of different processes that depend upon each other? Well, consider all the roles "Three" plays.

One way a person tells when there's a Three is to recite "One, Two, Three," while pointing to the different things. Of course, while doing that, you have to manage to (i) touch each thing once and (ii) not touch any twice. One easy way to do *that* is, to pick up one object, as you say each counting-word, and remove it. Soon, children learn to do that in their minds or, when it's too hard to keep track, to use some physical technique like finger-pointing.

Another way to tell a Three is to establish some Standard Set of Three things. Then you bring *your* set of things there and match them one-to-one: if all are matched and you have nothing left, then you had Three. And, again, that "standard Three" need not be physical; those three words, "One, Two, Three" would work quite well. To be sure, this might make it hard to tell which method you're using—"counting" or "matching"—at the moment. Good. It really doesn't matter, does it? (Except, perhaps, to philosophers.) For do-ers, it's really good to be able to shift and slip from one skill-process to another without even realizing it.

Another way to know a Three is by perceptual groups. One might think of Three in terms of arranging some objects into groups of One and Two. This, too, you can do mentally, without actually moving the objects, or you might lay them out on a table. You might learn several different such arrangements:

```
            *
**          *          ** *
*           *
```

For Five you have more families of ways, because you can use groups of Two and Three, or groups of One and Four. A pentagon, a thing-filled square, a "W," a star, a plane, a cup; they all make Fives.

```
  * *          *   *          * * *
 *   *           *            *   *
  *            *   *
```

```
  *                *            * *
 * * *          * * *           * *
  *                *             *
```

Another strand of understanding is to know how Three can be an incomplete or broken kind of Four—as in a defective square:

```
    *    0


    *    *
```

Which way is right—to count, or match, or group—which is the "real" meaning of a number? The very question shows how foolish is any such idea: each structure and its processes have both their own uses, and ways to support the others. This is what makes the whole into a powerful, versatile skill-system. Neither chicken nor egg need come first; they both evolve from something else.

It's too bad that so many scientists and philosophers despise such networks and only seek to construct simple "chains" of definitions in which each new thing depends only on other things that have been previously defined. That is what has given "reductionism" a bad name. The common sense meaning of Three is not a single link in one long chain of definitions in the mind. Instead, we simply let the word activate some rather messy web of different ways to deal with Threes of things, to use them, to remember them, to compare them, and so forth. The result of this is great for solving problems since, when you get stuck with one sense of meaning, there are many other things to try and do. If your first idea about Three doesn't do some job, in some particular context, you can switch to another. But if you use the mathematician's way, then, when you get into the slightest trouble, you get completely stuck!

If this is so, then why *do* mathematicians prefer their single chains to our multiply-connected knowledge-nets? Why would anyone prefer each thing to depend upon as few other things as possible instead of as many as possible? The answer has a touch of irony: mathematicians *want* to get stuck! This is because, as mathematicians, we *want* to be sure above all that as soon as anything goes wrong, we'll be the first to notice it. And the best way to be sure of that is to make everything collapse at once! To mathematicians, that sort of fragility is *good*, not bad, because it helps us find out if any single thing that we believe is inconsistent with any of the others. This insures absolute consistency—and that is fine in Mathematics. It simply isn't good Psychology.

Perfect consistency is not so relevant to real life because—let's face it—minds will *always* have beliefs that turn out to be wrong. That's why our teachers use a very wrong theory of how to understand things, when they shape our *children's* mathematics, not into robust networks of ideas, but into those long, thin, fragile chains or shaky towers of professional mathematics. A chain breaks whenever there's just one single weak link, just as a slender tower falls whenever we disturb it just a little. And this could happen to a child's mind, in mathematics class, who only takes a moment to watch a pretty cloud go by.

The purposes of children, and of other ordinary people, are not the same as those of mathematicians and philosophers. They need to have as few connections as can be, to simplify their careful, accurate analyses. In real life the best ideas are those robust ones that connect to as many other ideas as possible. And so, there is a conflict when the teachers start to consult those academic technicians about curricula. If my theory's right, they're not just bad at this; they're just about as bad at that as *possible*! Perhaps this helps explain how our society arranges to make most children terrified of mathematics. We think we're making things easier for them to find what's right, by managing to make things go all wrong almost all the time! So when our children learn about numbers (or about anything else) I would prefer that they build meshy networks in their minds, not slender chains or flimsy towers. Let's leave that for when they take their graduate degrees.

For learning about Two, a pre-school child learns in terms of symmetry and congruence—two hands, two feet, two shoes—one doesn't need to count or refer to some standard ideal set. (It is only later that one learns that, every time you count, you get the same result.) We learn of Three in terms of rhymes and tales of Threes of Bears and Pigs and Turtle Doves (whatever those might be) that tell of many different *kinds* of Threes.

Note that those Bears are two and one, Parents and Child, while their famous bowls of porridge make a very different kind of Three—"too hot, too cold, just right"—that shows the fundamental dialectic compromise of two extremes. (So do the bears' forbidden beds—too hard, too soft, just right.) Just think of all the different kinds of Threes that confront real children in the real world, and the complex network of how they all relate to one another in so many different, interesting ways. There simply isn't any sense to choosing one of them to be "defined" so as to come before the rest.

Our culture tries to teach us that a meaning really ought to have only a single, central sense. But if you programmed a machine that way, then, of course it couldn't really understand. Nor would a person either, since when something has just one meaning then it doesn't really "mean" at all because such mental structures are so fragile and so easy to get stuck that they haven't any real use. A network, though, yields many different ways to work each problem. And then, when one way doesn't work and another does, you can try to figure out why. In other words, the network lets you think, and thinking lets you build more network. For only when you have several meanings in a network is there much to think about; then you can turn things around in your mind and look at them from different perspectives. When you get stuck, you can try another view. But when a thing has just one meaning, and you get stuck, there's no way out except to ask Authority. That's why networks are better than logical definitions. There never is much meaning until you join together many partial meanings; and if you have only one, you haven't any.

Could a Computer Know About the Real World?

Is there some paradox in this idea, that every meaning is built on other meanings, with no special place to start? If so, then isn't all a castle built on air? Well, yes and no. Contrary to common belief, *there's really nothing wrong at all with circular definitions.* Each part can give some meaning to the rest. There's nothing wrong with liking several different tunes, each one the more because it contrasts with the others. There's

334 • Part Five   What Is the Mind?

nothing wrong with ropes—or knots, or woven cloth—in which each
strand helps hold the other strands together—or apart! There's nothing
very wrong, in this strange sense, with having one's entire mind a castle in the air!

But then, how could such a mind have any contact with reality. Well,
maybe this is something we must always face in any case, be we Machine
or Man. In the human condition, our mental contact with the real world
is really quite remote. The reason we don't notice this, and why it isn't
even much of a practical problem, is that the sensory and motor mechanisms of the brain (that shape the contents of, at least, our infant minds)
ensure enough developmental correspondence between the objects we
perceive and those that lie out there in raw reality; and that's enough
so that we hardly ever walk through walls or fall down stairs.

But in the final analysis, our idea of "reality" itself is rather net-
work-y. Do triangles "exist" or are they only Threes of Lines that share
their vertices? What's real, anyway, about a Three—in view of all we've
said; "reality" itself is also somewhat like a castle in the air. And don't
forget how totally some minds, for better or usually for worse, do sometimes split away to build their own imaginary worlds. Finally, when we
build intelligent machines we'll have a choice: either we can constrain
them as we wish to match each and every concept to their outside-data
instruments, or we can let them build their own inner networks and attain
a solipsistic isolation totally beyond anything we humans could conceive.

To summarize: of course computers couldn't understand a real
world—or even what a number is—were they confined to any single
way of dealing with them. But neither then could child or philosopher.
It's not a question of computers at all, but only of our culture's foolish
quest for meanings that can stand all by themselves, outside of any mental context. The puzzle comes from limitations of the way our culture
teaches us to think. It gives us such shallow and simplistic concepts of
what it means to "understand" that—probably—no entity could understand *that* way. The intuition that our public has—that if computers
worked that way, they couldn't understand—is probably quite right! But
this only means we mustn't program our machines that way.

Can a Computer Be Aware of Itself?

*Even if computers do things that amaze us, they're just mechanical. They
can't believe or think, feel pain or pleasure, sorrow, joy. A computer can't be
conscious, or self-aware—because it simply has no self to feel things with.*

Well. What do you suppose happens in your head when someone says a thing like that to *you*? Do you understand it? I'll demonstrate that this problem, too, isn't actually about computers at all. It isn't even about "understanding." This problem is about you. That is, it turns around that little word "you." For when we feel that when we understand something, we also seem to think there must be some agent in our heads that "does" the understanding. When we believe something, there must be someone in our heads to do the believing. To feel, someone must do the feeling.

Now, something must be wrong with that idea. One can't get anywhere by assuming there's someone inside oneself—since then there'll have to be another someone inside that one, to do its understanding for it, and so on. You'll either end up like those sets of nested Ukrainian Russian dolls, or else you'll end up with some "final" inner self. In either case, as far as I can see, that leaves you just exactly where you started.[9] So what's the answer? The answer is—we must be asking the wrong question: perhaps we never had anything like "self-awareness" in the first place—but only thought we had it! So now we have to ask, instead—why do we *think* we're self-aware?

My answer to this is that we are *not*, in fact, really self-aware. Our self-awareness is just illusion. I know that sounds ridiculous, so let me explain my argument very briefly. We build a network of half-true theories that gives us the illusion that we can see into our working minds. From those apparent visions, we think we learn what's really going on there. In other words, much of what we "discover" about ourselves, by these means, is just "made up." I don't mean to say, by the way, that those made-up ideas are *necessarily* better than or worse than theories we make about all other things that we don't understand very well. But I do mean to say that when we examine carefully the quality of the ideas most people have about their selves—ideas they got by using that alleged "self awareness"—we don't find that quality very good at all.

By the way, I'm not saying that we aren't aware of sounds and sights, or even of thoughts and ideas. I'm only saying that we aren't "self-aware." I'm also sure that the structures and processes that deserve to be called "self" and "awareness" are *very* complicated concept-networks. The trouble is that *those* are hardly at all like what we think they're like. The result is that in this area our networks don't fit together well enough to be useful for understanding our own psychology very well.

---

[9]Actually, there might be value in imagining the Self as like those dolls—each a smaller "model" of the previous system, and vanishing completely after a few stages.

Now let's try to see what some of the meanings we attach to "self" are like. When you and I converse, it makes perfect sense for me to call you "you" and to call me "me." That's fine for ordinary social purposes, that is, when neither of us cares about the fine details of what is going on inside our minds. But everything goes wrong at once as soon as one's concerned with that—because those you's and me's conceal most of the intricacy of what's inside our minds that really do the work. The very purpose of such words like "you" and "self" is to symbolize away what we don't know about those complex and enormous webs of stuff inside our head.

When people talk, the physics is quite clear: I shake some air, which makes your ear-drums move, and some "computer" in your head converts vibrations into, say, little "phoneme" units. Next, oversimplifying, these go into strings of symbols representing words, so now somewhere in your head you have something that "represents" a sentence. The problem is, what happens next?

In the same way, when you see something, the waves of light excite your retinas, and this cause signals in your brain that correspond to texture fragments, bits of edges, color patches, or whatever. Then these, in turn, are put together (somehow) into a symbol-structure that "represents" a shape or outline, or whatever. What happens then?

We argued that it cannot help to have some inner self to hear or read the sentence, or little person, hiding there to watch that mental television screen, who then proceeds to understand what's going on. And yet that seems to be our culture's standard concept of the self. Call it the "Single Agent" theory: that inside every mind resides a certain special "self" that does the real mental work. Since this concept is so popular, we ought to have a theory of why we all believe such a ridiculous theory!

In fact, it isn't hard to see why we hold onto such ideas—once we look past the single self and out into Society. For then we realize how valuable to us is this idea of Single Agent Self—no matter how simplistic, scientifically—in social matters of the greatest importance. It underlies, for instance, all the principles of all our moral systems; without it, we could have no canons of *responsibility*, no sense of blame or virtue, no sense of right or wrong. In short, without the idea of a Single Self, we'd scarcely have a culture to begin with. It also serves a crucial role in how we frame our plans and goals, and how we solve all larger problems—for, what *use* could solving problems be, without that idea of a self to savor and exploit their solutions.

And, furthermore, that image of a single self is central to the very ways we knit our personalities together—albeit though, as Freud has pointed out, it's not the image of us as we are that counts, but as we'd like to be, that makes us grow. That's why I didn't mean to say that it is bad to have Illusions for our Selves. (Why, what could one prefer to that, anyway?) And so, in short, no matter that it bollixes up our thinking about thinking; I doubt if we could survive without that wonderful idea of Single Self.

To build good theories of the mind, we'll have to find a better way. We find that hard to do because the concept of the Single Self is so vitally important for those other reasons.[10] But, just as Science forced us to accept the fact that what we think are single things—like rocks or mice or clouds—must sometimes be regarded as complicated other kinds of structures, we'll simply have to understand that Self, too, is no "elementary particle," but an extremely complicated construction.

We should be very used to this. There's nothing wrong with the idea of Single Houses, either. They keep us warm and dry, we buy them and sell them, they burn down or blow away; they're "things" all right but just up to a point. But when you really want to understand how Houses work, then you must understand that Houses aren't really "things" at all but constructions. They're made of beams and bricks and nails and stuff like that, and they're also made of forces and vectors and stresses and strains. And in the end, you can hardly understand them at all without understanding the intentions and purposes that underlie the ways they're designed.

So this wonderful but misleading Single Agent Self idea leads people to believe machines can't understand, because it makes us think that understanding doesn't need to be constructed or computed—only handed over to the Self—a thing that, you can plainly see, there isn't room for in machines.

Can a Computer Have a Self?

Now we can watch the problem change its character, before our eyes, the moment that we change our view. Usually, we say things like this:

A computer can't do (xxx), because it has no self.

And such assertions often seem to make perfect sense—until we shed that Single Agent view. At once those sayings turn to foolishness, like this:

---

[10]Similarly, we find Einstein's space-time integration very difficult because, no matter how it bollixes up our thinking about Special Relativity, I doubt if we could survive without that wonderful idea of Separate Space.

A computer can't do (xxx), because all a computer can do is execute
incredibly intricate processes, perhaps millions at a time, while constructing elaborately interactive structures on the basis of almost unimag-
ineably ramified networks of interrelated fragments of knowledge.

It doesn't make so much sense any more, does it? Yet all we did was
face one simple, complicated fact. The second version shows how some
of our skepticism about computers emerges from our unwillingness to
imagine what might happen in the computers of the future. The first version shows how some of our skepticism emerges from our disgracefully
empty ideas about how *people* really work, or feel, or think.

Why are we so reluctant to admit this inadequacy? It clearly isn't just
the ordinary way we sometimes repress problems that we find discouraging. I think it is a deeper thing that makes us hold to that belief in precious self-awareness, albeit it's too feeble to help us explain our
thinking—intelligent or otherwise. It's closer to a childish excuse—like
"something made me do it," or "I didn't really mean to"—that only
denies Single Self when fault or blame comes close. And rightly so, for
questioning the Self is questioning the very notion of identity—and
underneath I'm sure we're all aware of how too much analysis could shred
the fabrics of illusion that clothe our mental lives.

I think that's partly why most people still reject computational theories of thinking, although they have no other worthy candidates. And
that leads to denying minds to machines. For me, this has a special irony
because it was only after trying to understand what computers—that
is, complicated mechanisms—*could* do, that I began to have some
glimpses of how a *mind* itself might work. Of course we're nowhere near
a sharp and complete theory of how human minds work—yet. But, when
you think about it, how could we ever have expected, in the first place,
to understand how minds work until after expertise with theories about
very complicated machines? (Unless, of course, you had the strange but
popular idea that minds aren't complicated at all, only different from
anything else, so there's no use trying to understand them.)

I've mentioned what I think is wrong with popular ideas of self—
but what ought we to substitute for that? Socially, as I've hinted, I don't
recommend substituting anything—it's too risky. Technically, I have some
ideas but this is not the place for them. The "general idea" is to first
develop better theories of how to understand the webs of processes we (or
our machines) might use to represent our huge networks of fragments
of common-sense knowledge. Once we've some of those that seem to
work, we can begin work on other webs for representing knowledge about
the first kind. Finally, we work on sub-webs—within those larger webs—

that represent *simplified* theories of the entire mess! There's no paradox at all in this, provided one doesn't become too greedy—i.e., by asking that those simplified models be more than coarse approximations.

To do this will be quite complicated—but rightly so, for only such a splendid thing would seem quite worthy as a theory of a Self. For just as every child must connect a myriad of different ways to count and measure and compare, in order to understand that simple 'concept of number", so each child must surely build an even more intricate such network, in order that it understand itself (or even just a wishful image of itself) enough to grow a full-fledged personality. No less will do.

Could a Computer Have Common Sense?

We all enjoy hearing those jokes about the stupid and literal behavior of computers, about how they send us checks for $0.00 or bills for $0.00 and so forth. Surely that total lack of common sense has encouraged most of us to doubt machines could have minds. It isn't just that they do only what they're told, it is also that they're so dumb that it's almost impossible to tell them how to do things right.

And, indeed, those stories are quite true, on the whole. There certainly does seem something queer about computers. Why, for example, can they be so good at advanced mathematics, and stuff like that, so hard for us mortals—yet seem so dumb in general? You can hardly blame people for feeling that there must be some "vital missing element" in a computer!

On the surface, this seems to apply even to those AI programs. Isn't it odd, when you think about it, that the very earliest AI programs excelled at "advanced, adult" subjects. I mentioned that the Newell-Simon program written in 1956 was quite good at certain kinds of Mathematical Logic. Then, in 1961, James Slagle wrote a program that could solve symbolic calculus problems at the level of college students (it got an A on an MIT exam). Around 1965 Bobrow's program solved high-school algebra problems. And only around 1970 did we have robot programs, like Terry Winograd's, which could deal with children's building blocks well enough to stack them up, take them down, rearrange them, and put them in boxes.

Why were we able to make AI programs do such grownup things so long before we could make them do childish things? The answer was a somewhat unexpected paradox. It seems that "expert" adult thinking is often[11] somehow simpler than childrens' ordinary play! Apparently it can

---

[11] . . . but certainly not always . . .

require more to be a novice than to be an expert, because (sometimes, anyway) the things an expert needs to know can be quite few and simple, however difficult they may be to discover or learn in the first place. Thus, Galileo was very smart indeed, yet when he saw the need for calculus, he couldn't manage to invent it. But any student can learn it today.

The knowledge network built into Slagle's program had only some 100 "facts"—yet that's enough to solve those college level problems. Most of these were simple facts about algebra and calculus, but some were about ways to tell *which of two problems is probably the easier.* Those were especially important because they embodied the program's ability to make judgments about situations. Without them the program could only thrash about; with them it could usually make progress by making good decisions about what next to try.

Today we know a lot about making that sort of "expert" program, but we still don't know nearly enough to build good common sense problem solving programs. Consider the kinds of things little children can do. Winograd's program needed ways to combine different kinds of knowledge: about shapes and colors, space and time, words and syntax, and others, just to do simple things inside that "children's world of building blocks"; in all it needed on the order of a thousand knowledge fragments, where Slagle needed only about a hundred—although the one just "played with toys" while the other could solve college level problems. As I see it, "experts" often can get by with deep but narrow bodies of knowledge—while common sense is almost always technically a lot more complicated.

Nor is it just a mere matter of quantity and quality of knowledge: Winograd needed more *different kinds* of ways for processes to control and exploit each other. It seems that common sense thinking needs a greater variety of different *kinds* of knowledge, and needs different *kinds* of processes. And then, once there are more different kinds of processes, there will be more different kinds of interactions between them, so we need yet more knowledge.

To make our robots have just their teeny bit of common sense, and that was nothing to write home about, our laboratory had to develop new kinds of programming—we called it "heterarchy," as opposed to the "hierarchy" of older programs and theories. Less centralized, with more interaction and interruption between parts of the system, one part of Winograd's program might try to parse a phrase while another part would try to rectify the grammar with the meaning. If one program guessed that "pick" is a verb, in "Pick up the block," another program-part might check to see if "block" is really the kind of thing that *can* be picked up. Common sense requires a lot of that sort of switching from one viewpoint to another, engaging different kinds of ideas from one moment to another.

In order to get more common sense into our programs, I think we'll have to make them more reflective. The present systems seem to me a bit too active; they try too many things, with too little "thought." When anything goes wrong, most present programs just back up to previous decisions and try something else—and that's too crude a base for making more intelligent machines. A person tries, when anything goes wrong, to *understand* what's going wrong, instead of just attempting something else. We look for causal explanations and excuses and—when we find them— add them to our networks of belief and understanding—we do intelligent learning. We'll have to make our programs do more things like that.

Can Computers Make Mistakes?

To err is human, etc. I'll bet that when we try to make machines more sensible, we'll find that *knowing what causes mistakes* is nearly as important as knowing what is correct. That is, in order to succeed, it helps to know the most likely ways to fail. Freud talked about censors in our minds, that serve to repress or suppress certain forbidden acts or thoughts; those censors were proposed to regulate much of our social activity. Similarly, I suspect that we accumulate censors for ordinary activities—not just for social taboos and repressions—and use them for ordinary problem solving, for knowing what *not* to do. We learn new ones, whenever anything goes wrong, by remembering some way to recognize those circumstances, in some "subconscious memory"—so, later, we won't make the same mistake.[12]

Because a "censor" can only *suppress* behavior, their activity is invisible on the surface—except in making fewer blunders. Perhaps that's why the idea of a repressive unconscious came so late in the history of psychology. But where Freud considered only emotional and social behavior, I'm proposing that they're equally important in common-sense thinking. But this would also be just as hard to observe. And when a person makes some good intellectual decision, we tend to ask what "line of thought" lay behind it—but never think to ask "What thousand prohibitions warded off a thousand bad alternatives?"

This helps explain why we find it so hard to explain how our common sense thinking works. We can't detect how our censors work to prevent mistakes, absurdities, bugs, and resemblances to other experiences. There

---

[12]More details of this theory are in my paper on "Jokes and Their Relation to the Cognitive Unconscious" in *Cognitive Constraints on Communcation*, Vaina and Hintikka (eds.), Reidel, 1981.

are two reasons, in my theory, why we can't detect them. First, I suspect that thousands of them work at the same time, and if you had to take account of them, you'd never get anything else done. Second, they have to do their work in a rather special, funny way, because they have to *prevent* a bad idea before you "get" that idea. Otherwise you'd think too slowly to get anywhere.

Accordingly, much of our thinking has to be unconscious. We can only sense—that is, have enough information to make theories about—what's near the surface of our minds. I'm convinced that conscious thought is just one product of complex "adversary processes" that go on elsewhere in the mind, where parts of thoughts are always under trial, with complicated presentations of the litigants, and lengthy deliberations of the juries.[13] And then, our "selves" hear just the final sentences of those unconscious judges.

How, after all, could it be otherwise? There's no way any part of our mind could keep track of all that happens in the rest of our mind, least of all that "self"—that sketchy little model of the mind inside the mind. Our famous "selves" are valuable only to the extent they simplify and condense things. Each attempt to give "self consciousness" a much more comprehensive quality would be self defeating; like executives of giant corporations, they can't be burdened with detail but only compact summaries transmitted from other agents that "know more and more about less and less." Let's look at this more carefully.

Could a Computer Be Conscious?

When people ask that question, they seem always to want the answer to be "no." Therefore, I'll try to shock you by explaining why machines might be capable, in principle, of even more and better consciousness than people have.

Of course, there is the problem that we can't agree on just what "conscious" means. Once I asked a student, "Can people be conscious?"

"Of course we can—because we are."

Then, I asked: "Do you mean that you can know everything that happens in your mind?"

"I certainly didn't mean *that*. I meant something different."

"Well," I continued, "what did you mean by 'conscious' if you didn't mean knowing what's happening in your mind?"

"I didn't mean conscious of what's *in* my mind, just *of* my mind."

---

[13]Like the "skeptics" in Kornfeld's thesis.

Puzzled, I had to ask, "er, what do you mean?"

"Well, er, it's too hard to explain."

And so it goes. Why can we say so little about our alleged consciousness? Apparently because we can't agree on what we're talking about. So I'll cheat and just go back to "self-awareness." I've already suggested that although it is very useful and important, it really doesn't do what we think it does. We assume we have a way to discover true facts about our minds but really, I claim, we only can make guesses about such matters. The arguments we see between psychologists show all too well that none of us have perfect windows that look out on mental truth.

If we're so imperfect at self-explanation, then I don't see any reason (in principle, at least) why we couldn't make machines much better than we are ourselves at finding out about themselves. We could give them better ways to watch the ways their mechanisms work to serve their purposes and goals. The hardest part, of course, would lie not in acquiring such inner information, but in making the machine able to understand it—that is, in building programs with the common sense they'd need in order to be able to use such "insight." Today's programs are just too specialized, too dumb—if you'll pardon the expression—to handle anything as complicated as a theory of thinking. But once we learn to make machines smart enough to understand such theories, then (and only then) I see no special problem in giving them more "self-insight."[14]

Of course, that might not be so wise to do—but maybe we will have to. For I suspect our skeptics have things upside-down, who teach that self awareness is a strange, metaphysical appendage beyond and outside, mere intelligence, which somehow makes us human, yet hasn't any necessary use or function. Instead, it might turn out that, at some point, we *have to* make computers more self-conscious, just in order to make them smarter! It seems to me that no robot could safely undertake any very complex, long-range task, unless it had at least a little "insight" into its own dispositions and abilities. It ought not start a project without knowing enough about itself to be pretty sure that it will stay "interested" long enough to finish. Furthermore, if it is to be able to learn new ways to solve hard, new kinds of problems, it may need, again, at least a simplified idea of how it already solves easier, older problems. For this and other reasons, I suspect that any really robust problem solver, one that can adapt to major changes in its situation, must have some sort of model of itself.

---

[14]I think that *we* are smart enough to understand the general principles of how we think, if they were told to us. Anyway, I sure hope so. But I tend to doubt that we have enough built-in, self-information channels to figure it out by "introspection."

On the other side, there are some minor theoretical limitations to
the quality of self-insight. No interesting machine can, in general, predict ahead of time exactly what it will do, since it would have to compute
faster than it can compute. So self-examination can yield only "general" descriptions, based on simplified principles. People, too, can tell
us only fragments of details of how they think, and usually end up saying things like "It occurred to me." We often hear of "mystical experiences" and tales of total understanding of the self. But when we hear
the things they say of what they learned—it seems they only learned to
quench some question-asking portion of the mind.

So "consciousness" yields just a sketchy, simplified mind model, suitable only for practical and social uses, but not fine-grained enough for
scientific work. Indeed, our models of ourselves seem so much weaker
than they ought to be that one suspects that systematic mechanisms
oppose (as Freud suggested) the making of too-realistic self-images. That
could be to a purpose, for what would happen if you really could observe
your "underlying" goals—and were to say "Well, I don't *like* those goals"
and change them in some willy-nilly way? Why, then, you'd throw away
an eon's worth of weeding out of non-survivors—since almost every new
invention has some fatal bug. For, as we noted earlier, a part of Evolution's work is rationing the creativity of our brain-machines.

But when and if we chose to build more artfully intelligent machines,
we'd have more options than there were in our own evolution—because
biology must have constrained the wiring of our brains, while we can wire
machines in almost any way we wish. So, in the end, those artificial creatures might have richer inner lives than people do. (Do I hear cries of
"treason"?) Well, we'll just have to leave that up to future generations—
who surely wouldn't want to build the things *that* well without good
reasons to.

Can We Really Build Intelligent Machines?

It will be a long time before we learn enough about common sense reasoning to make machines as smart as people are. We already know a lot
about making useful, specialized, "expert" systems, but we don't yet
know enough to make them able to improve themselves in interesting
ways. Nevertheless, all those beliefs which set machine intelligence forever far beneath our own are only careless speculations, based on unsupported guesses on how human minds might work. The best uses for such
arguments are to provide opportunities to see more ways that *human*

minds can make mistakes! The more we know of why our minds do foolish things, the better we can figure out how we so often do things so
well. In years to come, we'll learn new ways to make machines and minds
both act more sensibly. We'll learn about more kinds of knowledge and
processes, and how to make machines learn still more knowledge for
themselves, while learning for ourselves to think of "thinking," "feeling" and "understanding" not as single, magic faculties, but as complex yet comprehensible webs of ways to represent and use ideas.

In turn, those new ideas will give us new ideas for new machines, and
those, in turn, will further change our ideas on ideas. And though no
one can tell where all of this may lead, one thing is certain, even now:
there's something wrong with any claim to know, today, of differences
of men and possible machines—because we simply do not know enough
today, of either men or possible machines.

Minds, Brains, and Programs

John R. Searle

What psychological and philosophical significance should we attach to
recent efforts at computer simulations of human cognitive capacities?
In answering this question, I find it useful to distinguish what I will call
"strong" AI from "weak" or "cautious" AI (Artificial Intelligence).
According to weak AI, the principal value of the computer in the study
of the mind is that it gives us a very powerful tool. For example, it enables
us to formulate and test hypotheses in a more rigorous and precise fashion. But according to strong AI, the computer is not merely a tool in the
study of the mind; rather, the appropriately programmed computer really
is a mind, in the sense that computers given the right programs can be
literally said to *understand* and have other cognitive states. In strong
AI, because the programmed computer has cognitive states, the programs
are not mere tools that enable us to test psychological explanations;
rather, the programs are themselves the explanations.

I have no objection to the claims of weak AI, at least as far as this article is concerned. My discussion here will be directed at the claims I have
defined as those of strong AI, specifically the claim that the appropriately

programmed computer literally has cognitive states and that the programs thereby explain human cognition. When I hereafter refer to AI, I
have in mind the strong version, as expressed by these two claims.

I will consider the work of Roger Schank and his colleagues at Yale
(Schank & Abelson 1977), because I am more familiar with it than I
am with any other similar claims, and because it provides a very clear
example of the sort of work I wish to examine. But nothing that follows
depends upon the details of Schank's programs. The same arguments
would apply to Winograd's SHRDLU (Winograd 1973), Weizenbaum's
ELIZA (Weizenbaum 1965), and indeed any Turing machine simulation
of human mental phenomena.

Very briefly, and leaving out the various details, one can describe
Schank's program as follows: the aim of the program is to simulate the
human ability to understand stories. It is characteristic of human beings'
story-understanding capacity that they can answer questions about the
story even though the information that they give was never explicitly
stated in the story. Thus, for example, suppose you are given the following
story: "A man went into a restaurant and ordered a hamburger. When
the hamburger arrived it was burned to a crisp, and the man stormed out
of the restaurant angrily, without paying for the hamburger or leaving
a tip." Now, if you are asked "Did the man eat the hamburger?" you
will presumably answer, "No, he did not." Similarly, if you are given
the following story: "A man went into a restaurant and ordered a hamburger; when the hamburger came he was very pleased with it; and as he
left the restaurant he gave the waitress a large tip before paying his
bill," and you are asked the question, "Did the man eat the hamburger?,"
you will presumably answer, "Yes, he ate the hamburger." Now Schank's
machines can similarly answer questions about restaurants in this fashion. To do this, they have a "representation" of the sort of information
that human beings have about restaurants, which enables them to answer
such questions as those above, given these sorts of stories. When the
machine is given the story and then asked the question, the machine
will print out answers of the sort that we would expect human beings
to give if told similar stories. Partisans of strong AI claim that in this
question and answer sequence the machine is not only simulating a
human ability but also

1. that the machine can literally be said to *understand* the story and
   provide the answers to questions, and
2. that what the machine and its program do *explains* the human ability to understand the story and answer questions about it.

Both claims seem to me to be totally unsupported by Schank's[1] work, as I will attempt to show in what follows.

One way to test any theory of the mind is to ask oneself what it would be like if my mind actually worked on the principles that the theory says all minds work on. Let us apply this test to the Schank program with the following *Gedankenexperiment.* Suppose that I'm locked in a room and given a large batch of Chinese writing. Suppose furthermore (as is indeed the case) that I know no Chinese, either written or spoken, and that I'm not even confident that I could recognize Chinese writing as Chinese writing distinct from, say, Japanese writing or meaningless squiggles. To me, Chinese writing is just so many meaningless squiggles. Now suppose further that after this first batch of Chinese writing I am given a second batch of Chinese script together with a set of rules for correlating the second batch with the first batch. The rules are in English, and I understand these rules as well as any other native speaker of English. They enable me to correlate one set of formal symbols with another set of formal symbols, and all that "formal" means here is that I can identify the symbols entirely by their shapes. Now suppose also that I am given a third batch of Chinese symbols together with some instructions, again in English, that enable me to correlate elements of this third batch with the first two batches, and these rules instruct me how to give back certain Chinese symbols with certain sorts of shapes in response to certain sorts of shapes given me in the third batch. Unknown to me, the people who are giving me all of these symbols call the first batch "a script," they call the second batch a "story," and they call the third batch "questions." Furthermore, they call the symbols I give them back in response to the third batch "answers to the questions," and the set of rules in English that they gave me, they call "the program." Now just to complicate the story a little, imagine that these people also give me stories in English, which I understand, and they then ask me questions in English about these stories, and I give them back answers in English. Suppose also that after a while I get so good at following the instructions for manipulating the Chinese symbols and the programmers get so good at writing the programs that from the external point of view—that is, from the point of view of somebody outside the room in which I am locked—my answers to the questions are absolutely indistinguishable from those of native Chinese speakers. Nobody just looking at my answers can tell that I don't speak a word of Chinese. Let us also suppose that my answers to the English questions are, as they no doubt would be, indistinguishable from those of other native English speakers, for the simple reason that I am a native English speaker. From the external point of view—

from the point of view of someone reading my "answers"—the answers to the Chinese questions and the English questions are equally good. But in the Chinese case, unlike the English case, I produce the answers by manipulating uninterpreted formal symbols. As far as the Chinese is concerned, I simply behave like a computer; I perform computational operations on formally specified elements. For the purposes of the Chinese, I am simply an instantiation of the computer program.

Now the claims made by strong AI are that the programmed computer understands the stories and that the program in some sense explains human understanding. But we are now in a position to examine these claims in light of our thought experiment.

1. As regards the first claim, it seems to me quite obvious in the example that I do not understand a word of the Chinese stories. I have inputs and outputs that are indistinguishable from those of the native Chinese speaker, and I can have any formal program you like, but I still understand nothing. For the same reasons, Schank's computer understands nothing of any stories, whether in Chinese, English, or whatever, since in the Chinese case the computer is me, and in cases where the computer is not me, the computer has nothing more than I have in the case where I understand nothing.

2. As regards the second claim, that the program explains human understanding, we can see that the computer and its program do not provide sufficient conditions of understanding since the computer and the program are functioning, and there is no understanding. But does it even provide a necessary condition or a significant contribution to understanding? One of the claims made by the supporters of strong AI is that when I understand a story in English, what I am doing is exactly the same—or perhaps more of the same—as what I was doing in manipulating the Chinese symbols. It is simply more formal symbol manipulation that distinguishes the case in English, where I do understand, from the case in Chinese, where I don't. I have not demonstrated that this claim is false, but it would certainly appear an incredible claim in the example. Such plausibility as the claim has derives from the supposition that we can construct a program that will have the same inputs and outputs as native speakers, and in addition we assume that speakers have some level of description where they are also instantiations of a program. On the basis of these two assumptions we assume that even if Schank's program isn't the whole story about understanding, it may be part of the story. Well, I suppose that is an empirical possibility, but not the slightest reason has so far been given to believe that it is true, since what is suggested—though certainly not demonstrated—by the example is that

the computer program is simply irrelevant to my understanding of the story. In the Chinese case I have everything that artificial intelligence can put into me by way of a program, and I understand nothing; in the English case I understand everything, and there is so far no reason at all to suppose that my understanding has anything to do with computer programs, that is, with computational operations on purely formally specified elements. As long as the program is defined in terms of computational operations on purely formally defined elements, what the example suggests is that these by themselves have no interesting connection with understanding. They are certainly not sufficient conditions, and not the slightest reason has been given to suppose that they are necessary conditions or even that they make a significant contribution to understanding. Notice that the force of the argument is not simply that different machines can have the same input and output while operating on different formal principles—that is not the point at all. Rather, whatever purely formal principles you put into the computer, they will not be sufficient for understanding, since a human will be able to follow the formal principles without understanding anything. No reason whatever has been offered to suppose that such principles are necessary or even contributory, since no reason has been given to suppose that when I understand English I am operating with any formal program at all.

Well, then, what is it that I have in the case of the English sentences that I do not have in the case of the Chinese sentences? The obvious answer is that I know what the former mean, while I haven't the faintest idea what the latter mean. But in what does this consist and why couldn't we give it to a machine, whatever it is? I will return to this question later, but first I want to continue with the example.

I have had the occasions to present this example to several workers in artificial intelligence, and, interestingly, they do not seem to agree on what the proper reply to it is. I get a surprising variety of replies, and in what follows I will consider the most common of these (specified along with their geographic origins).

But first I want to block some common misunderstandings about "understanding": in many of these discussions one finds a lot of fancy footwork about the word "understanding." My critics point out that there are many different degrees of understanding; that "understanding" is not a simple two-place predicate; that there are even different kinds and levels of understanding, and often the law of excluded middle doesn't even apply in a straightforward way to statements of the form "x understands y"; that in many cases it is a matter for decision and not a simple matter of fact whether x understands y; and so on. To all of these points I want to say: of course, of course. But they have nothing to do with the points at issue. There are clear cases in which "understanding" literally applies and clear cases in which it does not apply; and these two sorts of cases are all I need for this argument.[2] I understand stories in English; to a lesser degree I can understand stories in French; to a still lesser degree, stories in German; and in Chinese, not at all. My car and my adding machine, on the other hand, understanding nothing: they are not in that line of business. We often attribute "understanding" and other cognitive predicates by metaphor and analogy to cars, adding machines, and other artifacts, but nothing is proved by such attributions. We say, "The door *knows* when to open because of its photoelectric cell," "The adding machine *knows how* (*understands how*, is *able*) to do addition and subtraction but not division," and "The thermostat *perceives* changes in the temperature." The reason we make these attributions is quite interesting, and it has to do with the fact that in artifacts we extend our own intentionality;[3] our tools are extensions of our purposes, and so we find it natural to make metaphorical attributions of intentionality to them; but I take it no philosophical ice is cut by such examples. The sense in which an automatic door "understands instructions" from its photoelectric cell is not at all the sense in which I understand English. If the sense in which Schank's programmed computers understand stories is supposed to be the metaphorical sense in which the door understands, and not the sense in which I understand English, the issue would not be worth discussing. But Newell and Simon (1963) write that the kind of cognition they claim for computers is exactly the same as for human beings. I like the straightforwardness of this claim, and it is the sort of claim I will be considering. I will argue that in the literal sense the programmed computer understands what the car and the adding machine understand, namely, exactly nothing. The computer understanding is not just (like my understanding of German) partial or incomplete; it is zero.

Now to the replies:

I. The Systems Reply (Berkeley)

"While it is true that the individual person who is locked in the room does not understand the story, the fact is that he is merely part of a whole system, and the system does understand the story. The person has a large ledger in front of him in which are written the rules, he has a lot of scratch paper and pencils for doing calculations, he has 'data banks' of sets of Chinese symbols. Now, understanding is not being ascribed to the mere individual; rather it is being ascribed to this whole system of which he is a part."

My response to the systems theory is quite simple: let the individual internalize all of these elements of the system. He memorizes the rules in the ledger and the data banks of Chinese symbols, and he does all the calculations in his head. The individual then incorporates the entire system. There isn't anything at all to the system that he does not encompass. We can even get rid of the room and suppose he works outdoors. All the same, he understands nothing of the Chinese, and a fortiori neither does the system, because there isn't anything in the system that isn't in him. If he doesn't understand, then there is no way the system could understand because the system is just a part of him.

Actually I feel somewhat embarrassed to give even this answer to the systems theory because the theory seems to me so unplausible to start with. The idea is that while a person doesn't understand Chinese, somehow the *conjunction* of that person and bits of paper might understand Chinese. It is not easy for me to imagine how someone who was not in the grip of an ideology would find the idea at all plausible. Still, I think many people who are committed to the ideology of strong AI will in the end be inclined to say something very much like this; so let us pursue it a bit further. According to one version of this view, while the man in the internalized systems example doesn't understand Chinese in the sense that a native Chinese speaker does (because, for example, he doesn't know that the story refers to restaurants and hamburgers, etc.), still "the man as a formal symbol manipulation system" *really does understand Chinese.* The subsystem of the man that is the formal symbol manipulation system for Chinese should not be confused with the subsystem for English.

So there are really two subsystems in the man; one understands English, the other Chinese, and "it's just that the two systems have little to do with each other." But, I want to reply, not only do they have little to do with each other, they are not even remotely alike. The subsystem that understands English (assuming we allow ourselves to talk in this jargon of "subsystems" for a moment) knows that the stories are about restaurants and eating hamburgers, he knows that he is being asked questions about restaurants and that he is answering questions as best he can by making various inferences from the content of the story, and so on. But the Chinese system knows none of this. Whereas the English subsystem knows that "hamburgers" refers to hamburgers, the Chinese subsystem know only that "squiggle squiggle" is followed by "squoggle squoggle." All he knows is that various formal symbols are being introduced at one end and manipulated according to rules written in English, and other symbols are going out at the other end. The whole point of the original example was to argue that such symbol manipulation by itself couldn't be sufficient for understanding Chinese in any literal sense because the man could write "squoggle squoggle" after "squiggle squiggle" without understanding anything in Chinese. And it doesn't meet that argument to postulate subsystems within the man, because the subsystems are no better off than the man was in the first place; they still don't have anything even remotely like what the English-speaking man (or subsystem) has. Indeed, in the case as described, the Chinese subsystem is simply a part of the English subsystem, a part that engages in meaningless symbol manipulation according to rules in English.

Let us ask ourselves what is supposed to motivate the systems reply in the first place; that is, what *independent* grounds are there supposed to be for saying that the agent must have a subsystem within him that literally understands stories in Chinese? As far as I can tell the only grounds are that in the example I have the same input and output as native Chinese speakers and a program that goes from one to the other. But the whole point of the examples has been to try to show that that couldn't be sufficient for understanding, in the sense in which I understand stories in English, because a person, and hence the set of systems that go to make up a person, could have the right combination of input, output, and program and still not understand anything in the relevant literal sense in which I understand English. The only motivation for saying there *must* be a subsystem in me that understands Chinese is that I have a program and I can pass the Turing test; I can fool native Chinese speakers. But precisely one of the points at issue is the adequacy of the Turing test. The example shows that there could be two "systems," both of which pass the Turing test, but only one of which understands; and it is no argument against this point to say that since they both pass the Turing test they must both understand, since this claim fails to meet the argument that the system in me that understands English has a great deal more than the system that merely processes Chinese. In short, the systems reply simply begs the question by insisting without argument that the system must understand Chinese.

Furthermore, the systems reply would appear to lead to consequences that are independently absurd. If we are to conclude that there must be cognition in me on the grounds that I have a certain sort of input and output and a program in between, then it looks like all sorts of noncognitive subsystems are going to turn out to be cognitive. For example, there is a level of description at which my stomach does information processing, and it instantiates any number of computer programs, but I take it we do not want to say that it has any understanding [cf. Pylyshyn: "Computation and Cognitition" *BBS* 3(1) 1980]. But if we accept the systems reply, then it is hard to see how we avoid saying that stomach, heart, liver, and so on, are all understanding subsystems, since there is no principled way to distinguish the motivation for saying the Chinese subsystem understands from saying that the stomach understands. It is, by the way, not an answer to this point to say that the Chinese system has information as input and output and the stomach has food and food products as input and output, since from the point of view of the agent, from my point of view, there is no information in either the food or the Chinese—the Chinese is just so many meaningless squiggles. The information in the Chinese case is solely in the eyes of the programmers and the interpreters, and there is nothing to prevent them from treating the input and output of my digestive organs as information if they so desire.

This last point bears on some independent problems in strong AI, and it is worth digressing for a moment to explain it. If strong AI is to be a branch of psychology, then it must be able to distinguish those systems that are genuinely mental from those that are not. It must be able to distinguish the principles on which the mind works from those on which nonmental systems work; otherwise it will offer us no explanations of what is specifically mental about the mental. And the mental-nonmental distinction cannot be just in the eye of the beholder but it must be intrinsic to the systems; otherwise it would be up to any beholder to treat people as nonmental and, for example, hurricanes as mental if he likes. But quite often in the AI literature the distinction is blurred in ways that would in the long run prove disastrous to the claim that AI is a cognitive inquiry. McCarthy, for example, writes, "Machines as simple as thermostats can be said to have beliefs, and having beliefs seems to be a characteristic of most machines capable of problem solving performance" (McCarthy 1979). Anyone who thinks strong AI has a chance as a theory of the mind ought to ponder the implications of that remark. We are asked to accept it as a discovery of strong AI that the hunk of metal on the wall that we use to regulate the temperature has beliefs in exactly the same sense that we, our spouses, and our children have beliefs, and furthermore that "most" of the other machines in the room—telephone, tape recorder, adding machine, electric light switch,—also have beliefs in this literal sense. It is not the aim of this article to argue against McCarthy's point, so I will simply assert the following without argument. The study of the mind starts with such facts as that humans have beliefs, while thermostats, telephones, and adding machines don't. If you get a theory that denies this point you have produced a counter-example to the theory and the theory is false. One gets the impression that people in AI who write this sort of thing think they can get away with it because they don't really take it seriously, and they don't think anyone else will either. I propose for a moment at least, to take it seriously. Think hard for one minute about what would be necessary to establish that that hunk of metal on the wall over there had real beliefs, beliefs with direction of fit, propositional content, and conditions of satisfaction; beliefs that had the possibility of being strong beliefs or weak beliefs; nervous, anxious, or secure beliefs; dogmatic, rational, or superstitious beliefs; blind faiths or hesitant cogitations; any kind of beliefs. The thermostat is not a candidate. Neither is stomach, liver, adding machine, or telephone. However, since we are taking the idea seriously, notice that its truth would be fatal to strong AI's claim to be a science of the mind. For now the mind is everywhere. What we wanted to know is what distinguishes the mind from thermostats and livers. And if McCarthy were right, strong AI wouldn't have a hope of telling us that.

II. The Robot Reply (Yale)

"Suppose we wrote a different kind of program from Schank's program. Suppose we put a computer inside a robot, and this computer would not just take in formal symbols as input and give out formal symbols as output, but rather would actually operate the robot in such a way that the robot does something very much like perceiving, walking, moving about, hammering nails, eating, drinking—anything you like. The robot would, for example, have a television camera attached to it that enabled it to 'see,' it would have arms and legs that enabled it to 'act,' and all of this would be controlled by its computer 'brain.' Such a robot would, unlike Schank's computer, have genuine understanding and other mental states."

The first thing to notice about the robot reply is that it tacitly concedes that cognition is not soley a matter of formal symbol manipulation, since this reply adds a set of causal relation with the outside world [cf. Fodor: "Methodological Solipsism" *BBS* 3(1) 1980]. But the answer to the robot reply is that the addition of such "perceptual" and "motor" capacities adds nothing by way of understanding, in particular, or intentionality, in general, to Schank's original program. To see this, notice that the same thought experiment applies to the robot case. Suppose that instead of the computer inside the robot, you put me inside the room and, as in the original Chinese case, you give me more Chinese symbols with more instructions in English for matching Chinese symbols to Chinese symbols and feeding back Chinese symbols to the outside. Suppose, unknown to me, some of the Chinese symbols that come to me come from a television camera attached to the robot and other Chinese symbols that I am giving out serve to make the motors inside the robot move the robot's legs or arms. It is important to emphasize that all I am doing is manipulating formal symbols: I know none of these other facts. I am receiving "information" from the robot's "perceptual" apparatus, and I am giving out "instructions" to its motor apparatus without knowing either of these facts. I am the robot's homunculus, but unlike the traditional homunculus, I don't know what's going on. I don't understand anything except the rules for symbol manipulation. Now in this case I want to say that the robot has no intentional states at all; it is simply moving about as a result of its electrical wiring and its program. And furthermore, by instantiating the program I have no intentional states of the relevant type. All I do is follow formal instructions about manipulating formal symbols.

III. The Brain Simulator Reply (Berkeley and M.I.T.)

"Suppose we design a program that doesn't represent information that we have about the world, such as the information in Schank's scripts, but simulates the actual sequence of neuron firings at the synapses of the brain of a native Chinese speaker when he understands stories in Chinese and gives answers to them. The machine takes in Chinese stories and questions about them as input, it simulates the formal structure of actual Chinese brains in processing these stories, and it gives out Chinese answers as outputs. We can even imagine that the machine operates, not with a single serial program, but with a whole set of programs operating in parallel, in the manner that actual human brains presumably operate when they process natural language. Now surely in such a case we would have to say that the machine understood the stories; and if we refuse to say that, wouldn't we also have to deny that native Chinese speakers understood the stories? At the level of the synapses, what would or could be different about the program of the computer and the program of the Chinese brain?"

Before countering this reply I want to digress to note that it is an odd reply for any partisan of artificial intelligence (or functionalism, etc.) to make: I thought the whole idea of strong AI is that we don't need to know how the brain works to know how the mind works. The basic hypothesis, or so I had supposed, was that there is a level of mental operations consisting of computational processes over formal elements that constitute the essence of the mental and can be realized in all sorts of different brain processes, in the same way that any computer program can be realized in different computer hardwares: on the assumptions of strong AI, the mind is to the brain as the program is to the hardware, and thus we can understand the mind without doing neurophysiology. If we had to know how the brain worked to do AI, we wouldn't bother with AI. However, even getting this close to the operation of the brain is still not sufficient to produce understanding. To see this, imagine that instead of a monolingual man in a room shuffling symbols we have the man operate an elaborate set of water pipes with valves connecting them. When the man receives the Chinese symbols, he looks up in the program, written in English, which valves he has to turn on and off. Each water connection corresponds to a synapse in the Chinese brain, and the whole system is rigged up so that after doing all the right firings, that is after turning on all the right faucets, the Chinese answers pop out at the output end of the series of pipes.

Now where is the understanding in this system? It takes Chinese as input, it simulates the formal structure of the synapses of the Chinese brain, and it gives Chinese as output. But the man certainly doesn't understand Chinese, and neither do the water pipes, and if we are tempted to adopt what I think is the absurd view that somehow the *conjunction* of man *and* water pipes understands, remember that in principle the man can internalize the formal structure of the water pipes and do all the "neuron firings" in his imagination. The problem with the brain simulator is that it is simulating the wrong things about the brain. As long as it simulates only the formal structure of the sequence of neuron firings at the synapses, it won't have simulated what matters about the brain, namely its causal properties, its ability to produce intentional states. And that the formal properties are not sufficient for the causal properties is shown by the water pipe example: we can have all the formal properties carved off from the relevant neurobiological causal properties.

IV. *The Combination Reply (Berkeley and Stanford)*

"While each of the previous three replies might not be completely convincing by itself as a refutation of the Chinese room counterexample, if you take all three together they are collectively much more convincing and even decisive. Imagine a robot with a brain-shaped computer lodged in its cranial cavity, imagine the computer programmed with all the synapses of a human brain, imagine the whole behavior of the robot is indistinguishable from human behavior, and now think of the whole thing as a unified system and not just as a computer with inputs and outputs. Surely in such a case we would have to ascribe intentionality to the system."

I entirely agree that in such a case we would find it rational and indeed irresistible to accept the hypothesis that the robot had intentionality, as long as we knew nothing more about it. Indeed, besides appearance and behavior, the other elements of the combination are really irrelevant. If we could build a robot whose behavior was indistinguishable over a large range from human behavior, we would attribute intentionality to it, pending some reason not to. We wouldn't need to know in advance that its computer brain was a formal analogue of the human brain.

But I really don't see that this is any help to the claims of strong AI; and here's why: According to strong AI, instantiating a formal program with the right input and output is a sufficient condition of, indeed is constitutive of, intentionality. As Newell (1979) puts it, the essence of the mental is the operation of a physical symbol system. But the attributions of intentionality that we make to the robot in this example have nothing to do with formal programs. They are simply based on the assumption that if the robot looks and behaves sufficiently like us, then we would suppose, until proven otherwise, that it must have mental states like ours that cause and are expressed by its behavior and it must have an inner mechanism capable of producing such mental states. If we knew independently how to account for its behavior without such assumptions we would not attribute intentionality to it, especially if we knew it had a formal program. And this is precisely the point of my earlier reply to objection II.

Suppose we knew that the robot's behavior was entirely accounted for by the fact that a man inside it was receiving uninterpreted formal symbols from the robot's sensory receptors and sending out uninterpreted formal symbols to its motor mechanisms, and the man was doing this symbol manipulation in accordance with a bunch of rules. Furthermore, suppose the man knows none of these facts about the robot, all he knows is which operations to perform on which meaningless symbols. In such a case we would regard the robot as an ingenious mechanical dummy. The hypothesis that the dummy has a mind would now be unwarranted and unnecessary, for there is now no longer any reason to ascribe intentionality to the robot or to the system of which it is a part (except of course for the man's intentionality in manipulating the symbols). The formal symbol manipulations go on, the input and output are correctly

matched; but the only real locus of intentionality is the man, and he
doesn't know any of the relevant intentional states; he doesn't, for example, *see* what comes into the robot's eyes, he doesn't *intend* to move the
robot's arm, and he doesn't *understand* any of the remarks made to or
by the robot. Nor, for the reasons stated earlier, does the system of which
man and robot are a part.

To see this point, contrast this case with cases in which we find it completely natural to ascribe intentionality to members of certain other pri-
mate species such as apes and monkeys and to domestic animals such
as dogs. The reasons we find it natural are, roughly, two: we can't make
sense of the animal's behavior without the ascription of intentionality,
and we can see that the beasts are made of similar stuff to ourselves—
that is an eye, that a nose, this is its skin, and so on. Given the coherence of the animal's behavior and the assumption of the same causal stuff
underlying it, we assume both that the animal must have mental states
underlying its behavior, and that the mental states must be produced
by mechanisms made out of the stuff that is like our stuff. We would
certainly make similar assumptions about the robot unless we had some
reason not to, but as soon as we knew that the behavior was the result
of a formal program, and that the actual causal properties of the physical substance were irrelevant we would abandon the assumption of
intentionality. [See "Cognition and Consciousness in Nonhuman Species"
BBS I(4) 1978.]

There are two other responses to my example that come up frequently
(and so are worth discussing) but really miss the point.

V. The Other Minds Reply (Yale)

"How do you know that other people understand Chinese or anything
else? Only by their behavior. Now the computer can pass the behavioral tests as well as they can (in principle), so if you are going to
attribute cognition to other people you must in principle also attribute
it to computers."

This objection really is only worth a short reply. The problem in this
discussion is not about how I know that other people have cognitive
states, but rather what it is that I am attributing to them when I attribute
cognitive states to them. The thrust of the argument is that it couldn't
be just computational processes and their output because the computational processes and their output can exist without the cognitive state.
It is no answer to this argument to feign anesthesia. In "cognitive sciences" one presupposes the reality and knowability of the mental in the

same way that in physical sciences one has to presuppose the reality and knowability of physical objects.

VI. The Many Mansions Reply (Berkeley)

"Your whole argument presupposes that AI is only about analogue and digital computers. But that just happens to be the present state of technology. Whatever these causal processes are that you say are essential for intentionality (assuming you are right), eventually we will be able to build devices that have these causal processes, and that will be artificial intelligence. So your arguments are in no way directed at the ability of artificial intelligence to produce and explain cognition."

I really have no objection to this reply save to say that it in effect trivializes the project of strong AI by redefining it as whatever artificially produces and explains cognition. The interest of the original claim made on behalf of artificial intelligence is that it was a precise, well defined thesis: mental processes are computational processes over formally defined elements. I have been concerned to challenge that thesis. If the claim is redefined so that it is no longer that thesis, my objections no longer apply because there is no longer a testable hypothesis for them to apply to.

Let us now return to the question I promised I would try to answer: granted that in my original example I understand the English and I do not understand the Chinese, and granted therefore that the machine doesn't understand either English or Chinese, still there must be something about me that makes it the case that I understand English and a corresponding something lacking in me that makes it the case that I fail to understand Chinese. Now why couldn't we give those somethings, whatever they are, to a machine?

I see no reason in principle why we couldn't give a machine the capacity to understand English or Chinese, since in an important sense our bodies with our brains are precisely such machines. But I do see very strong arguments for saying that we could not give such a thing to a machine where the operation of the machine is defined solely in terms of computational processes over formally defined elements; that is, where the operation of the machine is defined as an instantiation of a computer program. It is not because I am the instantiation of a computer program that I am able to understand English and have other forms of intentionality (I am, I suppose, the instantiation of any number of computer programs), but as far as we know it is because I am a certain sort of organism with a certain biological (i.e., chemical and physical) structure, and this structure, under certain conditions, is causally capable of producing perception, action, understanding, learning, and other intentional phenomena. And part of the point of the present argument is that only something that had those causal powers could have that intentionality. Perhaps other physical and chemical processes could produce exactly these effects; perhaps, for example, Martians also have intentionality but their brains are made of different stuff. That is an empirical question, rather like the question whether photosynthesis can be done by something with a chemistry different from that of chlorophyll.

But the main point of the present argument is that no purely formal model will ever be sufficient by itself for intentionality because the formal properties are not by themselves constitutive of intentionality, and they have by themselves no causal powers except the power, when instantiated, to produce the next stage of the formalism when the machine is running. And any other causal properties that particular realizations of the formal model have, are irrelevant to the formal model because we can always put the same formal model in a different realization where those causal properties are obviously absent. Even if, by some miracle, Chinese speakers exactly realize Schank's program, we can put the same program in English speakers, water pipes, or computers, none of which understand Chinese, the program notwithstanding.

What matters about brain operations is not the formal shadow cast by the sequences of synapses but rather the actual properties of the sequences. All the arguments for the strong version of artificial intelligence that I have seen insist on drawing an outline around the shadows cast by cognition and then claiming that the shadows are the real thing.

By way of concluding I want to try to state some of the general philosophical points implicit in the argument. For clarity I will try to do it in a question and answer fashion, and I begin with that old chestnut of a question:

"Could a machine think?"

The answer is, obviously, yes. We are precisely such machines.

"Yes, but could an artifact, a man-made machine, think?"

Assuming it is possible to produce artificially a machine with a nervous system, neurons with axons and dendrites, and all the rest of it, sufficiently like ours, again the answer to the question seems to be obviously, yes. If you can exactly duplicate the causes, you could duplicate the effects. And indeed it might be possible to produce consciousness, intentionality, and all the rest of it using some other sorts of chemical principles than those that human beings use. It is, as I said, an empirical question.

"OK, but could a digital computer think?"

If by "digital computer" we mean anything at all that has a level of description where it can correctly be described as the instantiation of a computer program, then again the answer is, of course, yes, since we are the instantiations of any number of computer programs, and we can think.

"But could something think, understand, and so on *solely* in virtue of being a computer with the right sort of program? Could instantiating a program, the right program of course, by itself be a sufficient condition of understanding?"

This I think is the right question to ask, though it is usually confused with one or more of the earlier questions, and the answer to it is no.

"Why not?"

Because the formal symbol manipulations by themselves don't have any intentionality; they are quite meaningless; they aren't even *symbol* manipulations, since the symbols don't symbolize anything. In the linguistic jargon, they have only a syntax but no semantics. Such intentionality as computers appear to have is solely in the minds of those who program them and those who use them, those who send in the input and those who interpret the output.

The aim of the Chinese room example was to try to show this by showing that as soon as we put something into the system that really does have intentionality (a man), and we program him with the formal program, you can see that the formal program carries no additional intentionality. It adds nothing, for example, to a man's ability to understand Chinese.

Precisely that feature of AI that seemed so appealing—the distinction between the program and the realization—proves fatal to the claim that simulation could be duplication. The distinction between the program and its realization in the hardware seems to be parallel to the distinction between the level of mental operations and the level of brain operations. And if we could describe the level of mental operations as a formal program, then it seems we could describe what was essential about the mind without doing either introspective psychology or neurophysiology of the brain. But the equation, "mind is to brain as program is to hardware" breaks down at several points, among them the following three:

First, the distinction between program and realization has the consequence that the same program could have all sorts of crazy realizations that had no form of intentionality. Weizenbaum (1976, Ch. 2), for example, shows in detail how to construct a computer using a roll of toilet paper and a pile of small stones. Similarly, the Chinese story understanding program can be programmed into a sequence of water pipes, a set of wind machines, or a monolingual English speaker, none of which thereby acquires an understanding of Chinese. Stones, toilet paper, wind, and water pipes are the wrong kind of stuff to have intentionality in the first place—only something that has the same causal powers as brains can have intentionality—and though the English speaker has the right kind of stuff for intentionality you can easily see that he doesn't get any extra intentionality by memorizing the program, since memorizing it won't teach him Chinese.

Second, the program is purely formal, but the intentional states are not in that way formal. They are defined in terms of their content, not their form. The belief that it is raining, for example, is not defined as a certain formal shape, but as a certain mental content with conditions of satisfaction, a direction of fit (see Searle 1979), and the like. Indeed the belief as such hasn't even got a formal shape in this syntactic sense, since one and the same belief can be given an indefinite number of different syntactic expressions in different linguistic systems.

Third, as I mentioned before, mental states and events are literally a product of the operation of the brain, but the program is not in that way a product of the computer.

"Well if programs are in no way constitutive of mental processes, why have so many people believed the converse? That at least needs some explanation."

I don't really know the answer to that one. The idea that computer simulations could be the real thing ought to have seemed suspicious in the first place because the computer isn't confined to simulating mental operations, by any means. No one supposes that computer simulations of a five-alarm fire will burn the neighborhood down or that a computer simulation of a rainstorm will leave us all drenched. Why on earth would anyone suppose that a computer simulation of understanding actually understood anything? It is sometimes said that it would be frightfully hard to get computers to feel pain or fall in love, but love and pain are neither harder nor easier than cognition or anything else. For simulation, all you need is the right input and output and a program in the middle that transforms the former into the latter. That is all the computer has for anything it does. To confuse simulation with duplication is the same mistake, whether it is pain, love, cognition, fires, or rainstorms.

Still, there are several reasons why AI must have seemed—and to many people perhaps still does seem—in some way to reproduce and thereby explain mental phenomena, and I believe we will not succeed in removing these illusions until we have fully exposed the reasons that give rise to them.

First, and perhaps most important, is a confusion about the notion of "information processing": many people in cognitive science believe that the human brain, with its mind, does something called "information processing," and analogously the computer with its program does information processing; but fires and rainstorms, on the other hand, don't do information processing at all. Thus, though the computer can simulate the formal features of any process whatever, it stands in a special relation to the mind and brain because when the computer is properly programmed, ideally with the same program as the brain, the information processing is identical in the two cases, and this information processing is really the essence of the mental. But the trouble with this argument is that it rests on an ambiguity in the notion of "information." In the sense in which people "process information" when they reflect, say, on problems in arithmetic or when they read and answer questions about stories, the programmed computer does not do "information processing." Rather, what it does is manipulate formal symbols. The fact that the programmer and the interpreter of the computer output use the symbols to stand for objects in the world is totally beyond the scope of the computer. The computer, to repeat, has a syntax but no semantics. Thus, if you type into the computer "2 plus 2 equals?" it will type out "4." But it has no idea that "4" means 4 or that it means anything at all. And the point is not that it lacks some second-order information about the interpretation of its first-order symbols, but rather that its first-order symbols don't have any interpretations as far as the computer is concerned. All the computer has is more symbols. The introduction of the notion of "information processing" therefore produces a dilemma: either we construe the notion of "information processing" in such a way that it implies intentionality as part of the process or we don't. If the former, then the programmed computer does not do information processing, it only manipulates formal symbols. If the latter, then, though the computer does information processing, it is only doing so in the sense in which adding machines, typewriters, stomachs, thermostats, rainstorms, and hurricanes do information processing; namely, they have a level of description at which we can describe them as taking information in at one end, transforming it, and producing information as output. But in this case it is up to outside observers to interpret the input and output as information in the ordinary sense. And no similarity is established between the computer and the brain in terms of any similarity of information processing.

Second, in much of AI there is a residual behaviorism or operationalism. Since appropriately programmed computers can have input-output patterns similar to those of human beings, we are tempted to postulate mental states in the computer similar to human mental states. But once we see that it is both conceptually and empirically possible for a system to have human capacities in some realm without having any intentionality at all, we should be able to overcome this impulse. My desk adding machine has calculating capacities, but no intentionality, and in this paper I have tried to show that a system could have input and output capabilities that duplicated those of a native Chinese speaker and still not understand Chinese, regardless of how it was programmed. The Turing test is typical of the tradition in being unashamedly behavioristic and operationalistic, and I believe that if AI workers totally repudiated behaviorism and operationalism much of the confusion between simulation and duplication would be eliminated.

Third, this residual operationalism is joined to a residual form of dualism; indeed strong AI only makes sense given the dualistic assumption that, where the mind is concerned, the brain doesn't matter. In strong AI (and in functionalism, as well) what matters are programs, and programs are independent of their realization in machines; indeed, as far as AI is concerned, the same program could be realized by an electronic machine, a Cartesian mental substance, or a Hegelian world spirit. The single most surprising discovery that I have made in discussing these issues is that many AI workers are quite shocked by my idea that actual human mental phenomena might be dependent on actual physical chemical properties of actual human brains. But if you think about it a minute you can see that I should not have been surprised; for unless you accept some form of dualism, the strong AI project hasn't got a chance. The project is to reproduce and explain the mental by designing programs, but unless the mind is not only conceptually but empirically independent of the brain you couldn't carry out the project, for the program is completely independent of any realization. Unless you believe that the mind is separable from the brain both conceptually and empirically—dualism in a strong form—you cannot hope to reproduce the mental by writing and running programs since programs must be independent of brains or any other particular forms of instantiation. If mental operations consist in computational operations on formal symbols, then it follows that they have no interesting connection with the brain; the only connection would be that the brain just happens to be one of the indefinitely many types of machines capable of instantiating the program. This form of dualism is not the traditional Cartesian variety that claims there are two sorts of *substances*, but it is Cartesian in the sense that it insists that what is specifically mental about the mind has no intrinsic connection with the actual properties of the brain. This underlying dualism is masked from us by the fact that AI literature contains frequent fulmi-nations against "dualism"; what the authors seem to be unaware of is that their position presupposes a strong version of dualism.

"Could a machine think?" My own view is that *only* a machine could think, and indeed only very special kinds of machines, namely brains and machines that had the same causal powers as brains. And that is the main reason strong AI has had little to tell us about thinking, since it has noth-ing to tell us about machines. By its own definition, it is about pro-grams, and programs are not machines. Whatever else intentionality is, it is a biological phenomenon, and it is as likely to be as causally depen-dent on the specific biochemistry of its origins as lactation, photosyn-thesis, or any other biological phenomena. No one would suppose that we could produce milk and sugar by running a computer simulation of the formal sequences in lactation and photosynthesis, but where the mind is concerned many people are willing to believe in such a miracle because of a deep and abiding dualism: the mind they suppose is a matter of formal processes and is independent of quite specific material causes in the way that milk and sugar are not.

In defense of this dualism the hope is often expressed that the brain is a digital computer (early computers, by the way, were often called "electronic brains"). But that is no help. Of course the brain is a digital computer. Since everything is a digital computer, brains are too. The point is that the brain's causal capacity to produce intentionality can-not consist in its instantiating a computer program, since for any pro-gram you like it is possible for something to instantiate that program and still not have any mental states. Whatever it is that the brain does to pro-duce intentionality, it cannot consist in instantiating a program since no program, by itself, is sufficient for intentionality.

Notes

1. I am not, of course, saying that Schank himself is committed to these claims.

2. Also, "understanding" implies both the possession of mental (intentional) states and the truth (validity, success) of these states. For the purposes of this discussion we are concerned only with the possession of the states.

3. Intentionality is by definition that feature of certain mental states by which they are directed at or about objects and states of affairs in the world. Thus, beliefs, desires, and intentions are intentional states; undirected forms of anxiety and depression are not. For further discussion see Searle (1979c).

References

Fodor, J. A. (1968). "The Appeal to Tacit Knowledge in Psychological Explanation." *Journal of Philosophy* 65: 627–40.

Fodor, J. A. (1980). "Methodological Solipsism Considered as a Research Strategy in Cognitive Psychology." *Behavioral and Brain Sciences* 3:1.

McCarthy, J. (1979). "Ascribing Mental Qualities to Machines." In: *Philosophical Perceptives in Artificial Intelligence*, ed. M. Ringle. Atlantic Highlands, NJ: Humanities Press.

Newell, A. (1973). "Physical Symbol Systems." Lecture at the La Jolla Conference on Cognitive Science.

Newell, A., and Simon, H. A. (1963). GPS, a Program That Simulates Human Thought." In: *Computers and Thought.* ed. A. Feigenbaum & V. Feldman, pp. 279–93. New York: McGraw-Hill.

Pylyshyn, Z. W. (1980). "Computation and Cognition: Issues in the Foundations of Cognitive Science." *Behavioral and Brain Sciences* 3.

Schank, R. C., and Abelson, R. P. (1977). *Scripts, Plans, Goals, and Understanding.* Hillsdale, NJ: Lawrence Erlbaum Press.

Searle, J. R. (1979). "The Intentionality of Intention and Action." *Inquiry* 22:253–80.

Weizenbaum, J. (1965). "Eliza—a Computer Program for the Study of Natural Language Communication Between Man and Machine." *Communication of the Association for Computing Machinery* 9:36–45.

Weizenbaum, J. (1976). *Computer Power and Human Reason.* San Francisco: W. H. Freeman.

Winograd, T. (1973). "A Procedural Model of Language Understanding." In: *Computer Models of Thought and Language*, ed. R. Schank & K. Colby. San Francisco: W. H. Freeman.

Epiphenomenal Qualia
Frank Jackson

It is undeniable that the physical, chemical and biological sciences have provided a great deal of information about the world we live in and about ourselves. I will use the label 'physical information' for this kind of information, and also for information that automatically comes along with it. For example, if a medical scientist tells me enough about the processes that go on in my nervous system, and about how they relate to happenings in the world around me, to what has happened in the past and is likely to happen in the future, to what happens to other similar and dissimilar organisms, and the like, he or she tells me—if I am clever enough to fit it together appropriately—about what is often called the functional role of those states in me (and in organisms in general in similar cases). This information, and its kin, I also label 'physical'.

I do not mean these sketchy remarks to constitute a definition of 'physical information', and of the correlative notions of physical property, process, and so on, but to indicate what I have in mind here. It is well known that there are problems with giving a precise definition of these notions, and so of the thesis of physicalism that all (correct) information is physical information.[1] But—unlike some—I take the question of definition to cut across the central problems I want to discuss in this paper.

I am what is sometimes known as a "qualia freak." I think that there are certain features of the bodily sensations especially, but also of certain perceptual experiences, which no amount of purely physical information includes. Tell me everything physical there is to tell about what is going on in a living brain, the kind of states, their functional role, their relation to what goes on at other times and in other brains, and so on and so forth, and be I as clever as can be in fitting it all together, you won't have told me about the hurtfulness of pains, the itchiness of itches, pangs of jealousy, or about the characteristic experience of tasting a lemon, smelling a rose, hearing a loud noise or seeing the sky.

There are many qualia freaks, and some of them say that their rejection of physicalism is an unargued intuition.[2] I think that they are being unfair to themselves. They have the following argument. Nothing you could tell of a physical sort captures the smell of a rose, for instance. Therefore, physicalism is false. By our lights this is a perfectly good argument. It is obviously not to the point to question its validity, and the premise is intuitively obviously true both to them and to me.

I must, however, admit that it is weak from a polemical point of view. There are, unfortunately for us, many who do not find the premise intuitively obvious. The task then is to present an argument whose premises are obvious to all, or at least to as many as possible. This I try to do in section I with what I will call "the knowledge argument." In section II I contrast the knowledge argument with the modal argument and in section III with the "what is it like to be" argument. In section IV I tackle the question of the causal role of qualia. The major factor in stopping people from admitting qualia is the belief that they would have to be given a causal role with respect to the physical world and especially the brain;[3] and it is hard to do this without sounding like someone who believes in fairies. I seek in section IV to turn this objection by arguing that the view that qualia are epiphenomenal is a perfectly possible one.

I. The Knowledge Argument for Qualia

People vary considerably in their ability to discriminate colors. Suppose that in an experiment to catalog this variation Fred is discovered. Fred has better color vision than anyone else on record; he makes every discrimination that anyone has ever made, and moreover he makes one that we cannot even begin to make. Show him a batch of ripe tomatoes and he sorts them into two roughly equal groups and does so with complete consistency. That is, if you blindfold him, shuffle the tomatoes up, and then remove the blindfold and ask him to sort them out again, he sorts them into exactly the same two groups.

We ask Fred how he does it. He explains that all ripe tomatoes do not look the same color to him, and in fact that this is true of a great many objects that we classify together as red. He sees two colors where we see one, and he has in consequence developed for his own use two words 'red$_1$' and 'red$_2$' to mark the difference. Perhaps he tells us that he has often tried to teach the difference between red$_1$ and red$_2$ to his friends but has got nowhere and has concluded that the rest of the world is red$_1$–red$_2$ color-blind—or perhaps he has had partial success with his children, it doesn't matter. In any case he explains to us that it would be quite wrong to think that because 'red' appears in both 'red$_1$' and 'red$_2$' that the two colors are shades of the one color. He only uses the common term 'red' to fit more easily into our restricted usage. To him red$_1$ and red$_2$ are as different from each other and all the other colors as yellow is from blue. And his discriminatory behavior bears this out: he sorts red$_1$ from red$_2$ tomatoes with the greatest of ease in a wide variety of viewing circumstances. Moreover, an investigation of the physiological basis of Fred's exceptional ability reveals that Fred's optical system is able to separate out two groups of wavelengths in the red spectrum as sharply as we are able to sort out yellow from blue.[4]

I think that we should admit that Fred can see, really see, at least one more color than we can; red$_1$ is a different color from red$_2$. We are to Fred as a totally red–green color-blind person is to us. H. G. Wells' story "The country of the blind" is about a sighted person in a totally blind community.[5] This person never manages to convince them that he can see, that he has an extra sense. They ridicule this sense as quite inconceivable, and treat his capacity to avoid falling into ditches, to win fights and so on as precisely that capacity and nothing more. We would be making their mistake if we refused to allow that Fred can see one more color than we can.

What kind of experience does Fred have when he sees red$_1$ and red$_2$? What is the new color or colors like? We would dearly like to know but do not; and it seems that no amount of physical information about Fred's brain and optical system tells us. We find out perhaps that Fred's cones respond differentially to certain light waves in the red section of the spectrum that make no difference to ours (or perhaps he has an extra cone) and that this leads in Fred to a wider range of those brain states responsible for visual discriminatory behavior. But none of this tells us what we really want to know about his color experience. There is something about it we don't know. But we know, we may suppose, everything about Fred's body, his behavior and dispositions to behavior and about his internal physiology, and everything about his history and relation to others that can be given in physical accounts of persons. We have all the physical information. Therefore, knowing all this is *not* knowing everything about Fred. It follows that physicalism leaves something out.

To reinforce this conclusion, imagine that as a result of our investigations into the internal workings of Fred we find out how to make everyone's physiology like Fred's in the relevant respects; or perhaps Fred donates his body to science and on his death we are able to transplant his optical system into someone else—again the fine detail doesn't matter. The important point is that such a happening would create enormous interest. People would say "At last we will know what it is like to see the extra color, at last we will know how Fred has differed from us in the way he has struggled to tell us about for so long." Then it cannot be that we knew all along all about Fred. But *ex hypothesi* we did know all along everything about Fred that features in the physicalist scheme; hence the physicalist scheme leaves something out.

Put it this way. *After* the operation, we will know *more* about Fred and especially about his color experiences. But beforehand we had all the physical information we could desire about his body and brain, and indeed everything that has ever featured in physicalist accounts of mind and consciousness. Hence there is more to know than all that. Hence physicalism is incomplete.

Fred and the new color(s) are of course essentially rhetorical devices. The same point can be made with normal people and familiar colors. Mary is a brilliant scientist who is, for whatever reason, forced to investigate the world from a black and white room *via* a black and white television monitor. She specializes in the neurophysiology of vision and acquires, let us suppose, all the physical information there is to obtain about what goes on when we see ripe tomatoes, or the sky, and use terms like 'red,' 'blue,' and so on. She discovers, for example, just which wavelength combinations from the sky stimulate the retina, and exactly how this produces *via* the central nervous system the contraction of the vocal chords and expulsion of air from the lungs that results in the uttering of the sentence 'The sky is blue.' (It can hardly be denied that it is in principle possible to obtain all this physical information from black and white television, otherwise the Open University would of *necessity* need to use color television.)

What will happen when Mary is released from her black and white room or is given a color television monitor? Will she *learn* anything or not? It seems just obvious that she will learn something about the world and our visual experience of it. But then it is inescapable that her previous knowledge was incomplete. But she had *all* the physical information. *Ergo* there is more to have than that, and "physicalism" is false.

Clearly the same style of knowledge argument could be deployed for taste, hearing, the bodily sensations and generally speaking for the various mental states which are said to have (as it is variously put) raw feels, phenomenal features or qualia. The conclusion in each case is that the qualia are left out of the physicalist story. And the polemical strength of the knowledge argument is that it is so hard to deny the central claim that one can have all the physical information without having all the information there is to have.

II. The Modal Argument

By the Modal Argument I mean an argument of the following style.[6] Skeptics about other minds are not making a mistake in deductive logic, whatever else may be wrong with their position. No amount of physical information about another *logically entails* that he or she is conscious or feels anything at all. Consequently there is a possible world with organisms exactly like us in every physical respect (and remember that includes functional states, physical history, et al.) but which differ from us profoundly in that they have no conscious mental life at all. But then what is it that we have and they lack? Not anything physical *ex hypothesi*. In all physical regards we and they are exactly alike. Consequently there is more to us than the purely physical. Thus physicalism is false.[7]

It is sometimes objected that the modal argument misconceives physicalism on the ground that that doctrine is advanced as a *contingent* truth.[8] But to say this is only to say that physicalists restrict their claim to *some* possible worlds, including especially ours; and the modal argument is only directed against this lesser claim. If we in *our* world, let alone beings in any others, have features additional to those of our physical replicas in other possible worlds, then we have non-physical features or qualia.

The trouble rather with the modal argument is that it rests on a disputable modal intuition. Disputable because it is disputed. Some sincerely deny that there can be physical replicas of us in other possible worlds which nevertheless lack consciousness. Moreover, at least one person who once had the intuition now has doubts.[9]

Head-counting may seem a poor approach to a discussion of the modal argument. But frequently we can do no better when modal intuitions are in question, and remember our initial goal was to find the argument with the greatest polemical utility.

Of course, *qua* protagonists of the knowledge argument we may well accept the modal intuition in question; but this will be a *consequence* of our already having an argument to the conclusion that qualia are left out of the physicalist story, not our ground for that conclusion. Moreover, the matter is complicated by the possibility that the connection between matters physical and qualia is like that sometimes held to obtain between aesthetic qualities and natural ones. Two possible worlds which agree in all "natural" respects (including the experiences of sentient creatures) must agree in all aesthetic qualities also, but it is plausibly held that the aesthetic qualities cannot be reduced to the natural.

III. The "What Is It Like to Be" Argument

In "What Is It Like to Be a Bat?" Thomas Nagel argues that no amount of physical information can tell us what it is like to be a bat, and indeed that we, human beings, cannot imagine what it is like to be a bat.[10] His reason is that what this is like can only be understood from a bat's point of view, which is not our point of view and is not something capturable in physical terms which are essentially terms understandable equally from many points of view.

It is important to distinguish this argument from the knowledge argument. When I complained that all the physical knowledge about Fred was not enough to tell us what his special color experience was like. I was not complaining that we weren't finding out what it is like to be Fred. I was complaining that there is something *about* his experience, a property of it, of which we were left ignorant. And if and when we come to know what this property is we still will not know what it is like to *be* Fred, but we will know more *about* him. No amount of knowledge about Fred, be it physical or not, amounts to knowledge "from the inside" considering Fred. We are not Fred. There is thus a whole set of items of knowledge expressed by forms of words like 'that it is *I myself* who is . . .' which Fred has and we simply cannot have because we are not him.[11]

When Fred sees the color he alone can see, one thing he knows is the way his experience of it differs from his experience of seeing red and so on; *another* is that he himself is seeing it. Physicalist and qualia freaks alike should acknowledge that no amount of information of whatever kind that *others* have *about* Fred amounts to knowledge of the second. My complaint though concerned the first and was that the special quality of his experience is certainly a fact about it, and one which physicalism leaves out because no amount of physical information told us what it is.

Nagel speaks as if the problem he is raising is one of extrapolating from knowledge of one experience to another, of imagining what an unfamiliar experience would be like on the basis of familiar ones. In terms of Hume's example, from knowledge of some shades of blue we can work out what it would be like to see other shades of blue. Nagel argues that the trouble with bats et al. is that they are too unlike us. It is hard to see an objection to physicalism here. Physicalism makes no special claims about the imaginative or extrapolative powers of human beings, and it is hard to see why it need do so.[12]

Anyway, our knowledge argument makes no assumptions on this point. If physicalism were true, enough physical information about Fred would obviate any need to extrapolate or to perform special feats of imagination or understanding in order to know all about his special color experience. *The information would already be in our possession.* But it clearly isn't. That was the nub of the argument.

IV. The Bogey of Epiphenomenalism

Is there any really *good* reason for refusing to countenance the idea that qualia are causally impotent with respect to the physical world? I will argue for the answer no, but in doing this I will say nothing about two views associated with the classical epiphenomenalist position. The first is that mental *states* are inefficacious with respect to the physical world. All I will be concerned to defend is that it is possible to hold that certain *properties* of certain mental states, namely those I've called qualia, are such that their possession or absence makes no difference to the physical world. The second is that the mental is *totally* causally inefficacious.

For all will say it may be that you have to hold that the instantiation of *qualia* makes a difference to *other mental states* though not to anything physical. Indeed general considerations to do with how you could come to be aware of the in stantiation of qualia suggest such a position.[13]

Three reasons are standardly given for holding that a quale like the hurtfulness of a pain must be causally efficacious in the physical world, and so, for instance, that its instantiation must sometimes make a difference to what happens in the brain. None, I will argue, has any real force. (I am much indebted to Alec Hyslop and John Lucas for convincing me of this.)

(i) It is supposed to be just obvious that the hurtfulness of pain is partly responsible for the subject seeking to avoid pain, saying 'It hurts' and so on. But, to reverse Hume, anything can fail to cause anything. No matter how often B follows A, and no matter how initially obvious the causality of the connection seems, the hypothesis that A causes B can be overturned by an over-arching theory which shows the two as distinct effects of a common underlying causal process.

To the untutored the image on the screen of Lee Marvin's fist moving from left to right immediately followed by the image of John Wayne's head moving in the same general direction looks as causal as anything.[14] And of course throughout countless Westerns images similar to the first are followed by images similar to the second. All this counts for precisely nothing when we know the over-arching theory concerning how the relevant images are both effects of an underlying causal process involving the projector and the film. The epiphenomenalist can say exactly the same about the connection between, for example, hurtfulness and behavior. It is simply a consequence of the fact that certain happenings in the brain cause both.

(ii) The second objection relates to Darwin's theory of evolution. According to natural selection the traits that evolve over time are those conducive to physical survival. We may assume that qualia evolved over time—we have them, the earliest forms of life do not—and so we should expect qualia to be conducive to survival. The objection is that they could hardly help us to survive if they do nothing to the physical world.

The appeal of this argument is undeniable, but there is a good reply to it. Polar bears have particularly thick, warm coats. The theory of evolution explains this (we suppose) by pointing out that having a thick, warm coat is conducive to survival in the Arctic. But having a thick coat goes along with having a heavy coat, and having a heavy coat is *not* conducive to survival. It slows the animal down.

Does this mean that we have refuted Darwin because we have found an evolved trait—having a heavy coat—which is not conducive to survival? Clearly not. Having a heavy coat is an unavoidable concomitant of having a warm coat (in the context, modern insulation was not available), and the advantages for survival of having a warm coat outweighed the disadvantages of having a heavy one. The point is that all we can extract from Darwin's theory is that we should expect any evolved characteristic to be *either* conducive to survival *or* a by-product of one that is so conducive. The epiphenomenalist holds that qualia fall into the latter category. They are a by-product of certain brain processes that are highly conducive to survival.

(iii) The third objection is based on a point about how we come to know about other minds. We know about other minds by knowing about other behavior, at least in part. The nature of the inference is a matter of some controversy, but it is not a matter of controversy that it proceeds from behavior. That is why we think that stones do not feel and dogs do feel. But, runs the objection, how can a person's behavior provide any reason for believing he has qualia like mine, or indeed any qualia at all, unless this behavior can be regarded as the *outcome* of the qualia. Man Friday's footprint was evidence of Man Friday because footprints are causal outcomes of feet attached to people. And an epiphenomenalist cannot regard behavior, or indeed anything physical, as an outcome of qualia.

But consider my reading in *The Times* that Spurs won. This provides excellent evidence that the *Telegraph* has also reported that Spurs won, despite the fact that (I trust) the *Telegraph* does not get the results from the *The Times*. They each send their own reporters to the game. the *Telegraph's* report is in no sense an outcome of *The Times'*, but the latter provides good evidence for the former nevertheless.

The reasoning involved can be reconstructed thus. I read in *The Times* that Spurs won. This gives me reason to think that Spurs won because I know that Spurs' winning is the most likely candidate to be what caused the report in *The Times*. But I also know that Spurs' winning would have had many effects, including almost certainly a report in the *Telegraph*.

I am arguing from one effect back to its cause and out again to another effect. The fact that neither effect causes the other is irrelevant. Now the epiphenomenalist allows that qualia are effects of what goes on in the brain. Qualia cause nothing physical but are caused by something physical. Hence the epiphenomenalist can argue from the behavior of others to the qualia of others by arguing from the behavior of others ack to its causes in the brains of others and out again to their qualia.

You may well feel for one reason or another that this is a more dubious chain of reasoning than its model in the case of newspaper reports. You are right. The problem of other minds is a major philosophical problem, the problem of other newspaper reports is not. But there is no special problem for epiphenomenalism as opposed to, say, interactionism here.

There is a very understandable response to the three replies I have just made. "All right, there is no knockdown refutation of the existence of epiphenomenal qualia. But the fact remains that they are an excrescence. They *do* nothing, they *explain* nothing, they serve merely to soothe the intuitions of dualists, and it is left a total mystery how they fit into the world view of science. In short we do not and cannot understand the how and why of them."

This is perfectly true; but is no objection to qualia, for it rests on an overly optimistic view of the human animal, and its powers. We are the products of evolution. We understand and sense what we need to understand and sense in order to survive. Epiphenomenal qualia are totally irrelevant to survival. At no stage of our evolution did natural selection favor those who could make sense of how they are caused and the laws governing them, or in fact why they exist at all. And that is why we can't.

It is not sufficiently appreciated that physicalism is an extremely optimistic view of our powers. If it is true, we have, in very broad outline admittedly, a grasp of our place in the scheme of things. Certain matters of sheer complexity defeat us—there are an awful lot of neurons—but in principle we have it all. But consider the antecedent probability that everything in the universe be of a kind that is relevant in some way or other to the survival of *Homo sapiens.* It is very low surely. But then one must admit that it is very likely that there is a part of the whole scheme of things, maybe a big part, which no amount of evolution will ever bring us near to knowledge about or understanding. For the simple reason that such knowledge and understanding is irrelevant to survival.

Physicalists typically emphasise that we are a part of nature on their view, which is fair enough. But if we are a part of nature, we are as nature has left us after however many years of evolution it is, and each step in that evolutionary progression has been a matter of chance constrained just by the need to preserve or increase survival value. The wonder is that we understand as much as we do, and there is no wonder that there should be matters which fall quite outside our comprehension. Perhaps exactly how epiphenomenal qualia fit into the scheme of things is one such.

This may seem an unduly pessimistic view of our capacity to articulate a truly comprehensive picture of our world and our place in it. But suppose we discovered living on the bottom of the deepest oceans a sort of sea slug which manifested intelligence. Perhaps survival in the conditions required rational powers. Despite their intelligence, these sea slugs have only a very restricted conception of the world by comparison with ours, the explanation for this being the nature of their immediate environment. Nevertheless they have developed sciences which work surprisingly well in these restricted terms. They also have philosophers, called slugists. Some call themselves tough-minded slugists, others confess to being soft-minded slugists.

The tough-minded slugists hold that the restricted terms (or ones pretty like them which may be introduced as their sciences progress) suffice in principle to describe everything without remainder. These tough-minded slugists admit in moments of weakness to a feeling that their theory leaves something out. They resist this feeling and their opponents, the softminded slugists, by pointing out—absolutely correctly—that no slugist has ever succeeded in spelling out how this mysterious residue fits into the highly successful view that their sciences have and are developing of how their world works.

Our sea slugs don't exist, but they might. And there might also exist super beings which stand to us as we stand to these slugs. We cannot adopt the perspective of these super beings, because we are not them, but the possibility of such a perspective is, I think, an antidote to excessive optimism.[15]

Addendum: From "What Mary Didn't Know"

I. Three Clarifications

The knowledge argument does not rest on the dubious claim that logically you cannot imagine what sensing red is like unless you have sensed red. Powers of imagination are not to the point. The contention about Mary is not that, despite her fantastic grasp of neurophysiology and everything else physical, she *could not imagine* what it is like to sense red; it is that, as a matter of fact, she *would not know*. But if physicalism is true, she would know; and no great powers of imagination would be called for. Imagination is a faculty that those who *lack* knowledge need to fall back on.

Secondly, the intensionality of knowledge is not to the point. The argument does not rest on assuming falsely that, if S knows that a is F and if $a = b$, then S knows that b is F. It is concerned with the nature of Mary's total body of knowledge before she is released: is it complete, or do some facts escape it? What is to the point is that S may know that a is F and *know* that $a = b$, yet arguably not know that b is F, by virtue of not being sufficiently logically alert to follow the consequences through. If Mary's lack of knowledge were at all like this, there would be no threat to physicalism in it. But it is very hard to believe that her lack of knowledge could be remedied merely by her explicitly following through enough logical consequences of her vast physical knowledge. Endowing her with great logical acumen and persistence is not in itself enough to fill in the gaps in her knowledge. On being let out, she will not say "I could have worked all this out before by making some more purely logical inferences."

Thirdly, the knowledge Mary lacked which is of particular point for the knowledge argument against physicalism is *knowledge about the experiences of others*, not about her own. When she is let out, she has new experiences, color experiences she has never had before. It is not, therefore, an objection to physicalism that she learns *something* on being let out. Before she was let out, she could not have known facts about her experience of red, for there were no such facts to know. That physicalist and nonphysicalist alike can agree on. After she is let out, things change: and physicalism can happily admit that she learns this; after all, some physical things will change, for instance, her brain states and their functional roles. The trouble for physicalism is that, after Mary sees her first ripe tomato, she will realize how impoverished her conception of the mental life of *others* has been *all along*. She will realize that there was, all the time she was carrying out her laborious investigations into the neurophysiologies of others and into the functional roles of their internal states, something about these people she was quite unaware of. All along their experiences (or many of them, those got from tomatoes, the sky, . . .) had a feature conspicuous to them but until now hidden from her (in fact, not in logic). But she knew all the physical facts about them all along; hence, what she did not know until her release is not a physical fact about their experiences. But it is a fact about them. That is the trouble for physicalism.

II. *Churchland's Three Objections*[16]

(i) Churchland's first objection is that the knowledge argument contains a defect that "is simplicity itself" (23). The argument equivocates on the sense of 'knows about.' How so? Churchland suggests that the following is "a conveniently tightened version" of the knowledge argument:

(1) Mary knows everything there is to know about brain states and their properties.
(2) It is not the case that Mary knows everything there is to know about sensations and their properties.

Therefore, by Leibniz's law.

(3) Sensations and their properties ≠ brain states and their properties (23).

Churchland observes, plausibly enough, that the type or kind of knowledge involved in premise 1 is distinct from the kind of knowledge involved in premise 2. We might follow his lead and tag the first 'knowledge by description,' and the second 'knowledge by acquaintance'; but, whatever the tags, he is right that the displayed argument involves a highly dubious use of Leibniz's law.

My reply is that the displayed argument may be convenient, but it is not accurate. It is not the knowledge argument. Take, for instance, premise 1. The whole thrust of the knowledge argument is that Mary (before her release) does *not* know everything there is to know about brain states and their properties, because she does not know about certain qualia associated with them. What is complete, according to the argument, is her knowledge of matters physical. A convenient and accurate way of displaying the argument is:

(1)' Mary (before her release) knows everything physical there is to know about other people.
(2)' Mary (before her release) does not know everything there is to know about other people (because she *learns* something about them on her release).

Therefore,

(3)' There are truths about other people (and herself) which escape the physicalist story.

What is immediately to the point is not the kind, manner, or type of knowledge Mary has, but *what* she knows. What she knows beforehand is ex hypothesi everything physical there is to know, but is it everything there is to know? That is the crucial question.

Notes

1. See, e.g., D. H. Mellor, "Materialism and Phenomenal Qualities," *Aristotelian Society Supp. Vol.* 47 (1973), 107–19; and J. W. Cornman, *Materialism and Sensations*, New Haven and London, 1971.

2. Particularly in discussion, but see, e.g., Keith Campbell, *Metaphysics*, Belmont, 1976, p. 67.

3. See, e.g., D. C. Dennett, "Current Issues in the Philosophy of Mind," *American Philosophical Quarterly* 15(1978), 249–61.

4. Put this, and similar simplifications below, in terms of Land's theory if you prefer. See, e.g., Edwin H. Land, "Experiments in Color Vision." *Scientific American* 200 (5 May 1959), 84–99.

5. H. G. Wells, *The Country of the Blind and Other Stories*, London, n.d.

6. See, e.g., Keith Campbell, *Body and Mind*, New York, 1970; and Robert Kirk, "Sentience and Behaviour," *Mind* 83 (1974), 43–60.

7. I have presented the argument in an inter-world rather than the more usual intra-world fashion to avoid inessential complications to do with supervenience, causal anomalies and the like.

8. See, e.g., W. G. Lycan, "A New Lilliputian Argument Against Machine Functionalism," *Philosophical Studies* 35 (1979), 279–87, p. 280; and Don Locke, "Zombies, Schizophrenics and Purely Physical Objects," *Mind* 85 (1976), 97–9.

9. See R. Kirk, "From Physical Explicability to Full-Blooded Materialism," *Philosophical Quarterly* 29 (1979), 229–37. See also the arguments against the modal intuition in, e.g., Sydney Shoemaker, "Functionalism and Qualia," *Philosophical Studies* 27 (1975), 291–315.

10. *Philosophical Review* 83 (1974), 435–50. Two things need to be said about this article. One is that, despite my dissociations to come, I am much indebted to it. The other is that the emphasis changes through the article, and by the end Nagel is objecting not so much to Physicalism as to all extant theories of mind for ignoring points of view, including those that admit (irreducible) qualia.

11. Knowledge *de se* in the terms of David Lewis, "Attitudes de Dicto and de se," *Philosophical Review* 88 (1979), 513–43.

12. See Laurence Nemirow's comments on "What it is . . ." in his review of T. Nagel, *Mortal Questions*, in *Philosophical Review* 89 (1980), 473–7. I am indebted here in particular to a discussion with David Lewis.

13. See my review of K. Campbell, *Body and Mind*, in *Australasian Journal of Philosophy* 50 (1972), 77–80.

14. Cf. Jean Piaget, "The Child's Conception of Physical Causality," reprinted in *The Essential Piaget*, London, 1977.

15. I am indebted to Robert Pargetter for a number of comments and, despite his dissent, to section IV of Paul E. Meehl's "The complete autocerebroscopist's" in Paul Feyerabend and Grover Maxwell (eds), *Mind, Matter and Method*, Minneapolis, 1966.

16. Paul M. Churchland, "Reduction, Qualia, and the Direct Introspection of Brain States." *The Journal of Philosophy* LXXXII, 1 (January 1985): 8–28. Unless otherwise stated, future page references are to this paper.

PART SIX

DOES GOD EXIST?

The relationship between faith and reason is of central importance for the history of Western philosophy. For philosophers like Immanuel Kant, René Descartes, and G. W. Hegel, philosophical reflection reaffirmed their religious beliefs. Other thinkers however, like Bertrand Russell, Karl Marx, and Friedrich Nietzsche, found that philosophy led them toward atheism. The readings in this section show how various philosophers have responded to questions about God, faith, and reason.

In our first selection, "The Ethics of Belief," William Clifford argues that "it is wrong always everywhere, and for anyone, to believe anything upon insufficient evidence." Clifford's position is known as "strong rationalism," because it holds that one cannot be rational in accepting religious beliefs unless they can be shown by convincing reason to be true. Clifford points out that if we act on poorly supported beliefs, we are very likely to harm others as well as ourselves.

The direct response to Clifford's position is provided by William James. In his essay, "The Will to Believe," James argues that we cannot settle religious questions on the basis of pure rational analysis of the available evidence. The decision whether we want to believe in God is a "genuine option" that we are forced to make and that has a momentous impact on our lives. James considers the example of a man who cannot decide whether he should marry because he is not perfectly sure whether his partner is the right person. Pure intellectual analysis cannot settle the question, and to hesitate indefinitely requires that we ignore our passionate nature. According to James, this is also true for our decision whether to believe in the existence of God. We need to acknowledge that intellectual analysis alone cannot decide this question. The decision requires a passionate leap. He concludes that "No one of us ought to issue vetoes to the other, nor should we bandy words of abuse. We ought, on the contrary, delicately and profoundly to respect one another's mental freedom. . . ."

In our third essay, Richard Taylor presents a well-constructed, contemporary version of the cosmological argument. Taylor argues that if we accept the principle of sufficient reason—that is, the principle that for any positive truth there must exist an explanation—then we also must accept that a necessary, self-caused being exists. He argues that it is only in reference to such a being that we can explain the existence of the world.

William L. Rowe introduces a novel objection to Anselm's attempt to deduce God's existence from the insight that God, by definition, must be the greatest possible being. Unlike Gaunilo, who claims that Anselm's ontological argument proves too much, and unlike Kant, who suggests that existence is not a real predicate, Rowe argues that Anselm's ontological argument is partly successful. It establishes that no nonexistent thing can be God. This conclusion, however, differs profoundly from the claim that some existing being actually is God, and it is this conclusion the ontological argument would have to establish if it were to be successful.

In the essay "Pascal's Wager," George Schlesinger defends Pascal's Wager against various objections. He starts out by showing that it is misleading to accuse those who are convinced by Pascal's reasoning to be of a mercenary and selfish nature. He then defends Pascal's Wager against the so-called many–gods objection. Schlesinger argues that the probability that a scrupulously just deity exists is much higher than the existence of a "fancy bred capricious power." This is the reason why, according to Schlesinger, Pascal's Wager plays a crucial role in the contexts of all other theistic arguments as well.

Although the basic idea of the design argument—the claim that this world is too complex to have evolved without the help of a conscious designer—has been around for a long time, some scientists claim that recent scientific advances provide fresh evidence in support of this argument. In the essay "Molecular Machines: Experimental Support for the Design Inference," the biochemist Michael Behe argues that biomolecular systems function like tiny, intricate machines and that they exhibit what he calls "irreducible complexity." Behe claims that irreducible complexity proves that such molecules could not have evolved gradually as Darwinism holds, and he concludes that it is more reasonable to believe that they were intelligently designed.

In "Born-Again Creationism," Philip Kitcher responds to Behe's argument. Kitcher argues that neither he nor Behe have any idea how exactly these complex molecular structures have come into existence. However, this does not establish that it is impossible that they have to come into being in a manner consistent with a Darwinian account. According to Kitcher, Behe's argument rests on a fallacious appeal to ignorance, and his quantitative argument "smacks more of numerology than of science."

In "Evil and Omnipotence," J. L. Mackie presents a clearheaded and straightforward formulation of the logical problem of evil. According to Mackie, most religious believers are "positively irrational" because they are committed to three logically inconsistent propositions: God is omnipotent; God is wholly good; and evil exists. He goes on to examine theistic attempts to resolve this inconsistency. The result is negative. According to Mackie, the most popular attempts to resolve the inconsistency fail to abandon any of the three inconsistent claims. These theodicies fail, therefore, to provide adequate solutions to the problem of evil.

Richard Swinburne develops a theistic reply to the problem of evil. He tries to show that pain and suffering cannot count as evidence against the existence of God. Swinburne argues that a God who eliminates all pain and suffering is also a God who deprives humans of the ability to make meaningful decisions in their lives. According to Swinburne, genuine freedom requires the existence not only of moral evil but also of natural evil. He writes, ". . . just imagine all the suffering of mind and body caused by disease, earthquake, and accident unpreventable by humans removed at a stroke from our society . . . Many of us would then have such an easy life that we simply would not have much opportunity to show courage, or indeed, manifest much in the way of great goodness at all."

In the final reading in this section, Deborah Mathieu argues that religion plays a fundamental role in the subjugation of women in society. According to Mathieu, all three major monotheistic religions—Judaism, Christianity, and Islam—are used by men "to brainwash females into accepting the theory of male superiority." The basic argument is simple. Because all three religions hold that God is male, it follows that female humans are more distant from God than male humans, and this is taken as proof that female humans are inferior to males.

The Ethics of Belief

William Clifford

The Duty of Inquiry

A shipowner was about to send to sea an emigrant ship. He knew that she was old, and not over-well built at the first; that she had seen many seas and climes, and often had needed repairs. Doubts had been suggested to him that possibly she was not seaworthy. These doubts preyed upon his mind and made him unhappy; he thought that perhaps he ought to have her thoroughly overhauled and refitted, even though this should put him to great expense. Before the ship sailed, however, he succeeded in overcoming these melancholy reflections. He said to himself that she had gone safely through so many voyages and weathered so many storms that it was idle to suppose she would not come safely home from this trip also. He would put his trust in Providence, which could hardly fail to protect all these unhappy families that were leaving their fatherland to seek for better times elsewhere. He would dismiss from his mind all ungenerous suspicions about the honesty of builders and contractors. In such ways he acquired a sincere and comfortable conviction that his vessel was thoroughly safe and seaworthy; he watched her departure with a light heart, and benevolent wishes for the success of the exiles in their strange new home that was to be; and he got his insurance money when she went down in mid-ocean and told no tales.

What shall we say of him? Surely this, that he was verily guilty of the death of those men. It is admitted that he did sincerely believe in the soundness of his ship; but the sincerity of his conviction can in no wise help him, because *he had no right to believe on such evidence as was before him.* He had acquired his belief not by honestly earning it in patient investigation, but by stifling his doubts. And although in the end he may have felt so sure about it that he could not think otherwise, yet inasmuch as he had knowingly and willingly worked himself into that frame of mind, he must be held responsible for it.

Let us alter the case a little, and suppose that the ship was not unsound after all; that she made her voyage safely, and many others after it. Will that diminish the guilt of her owner? Not one jot. When an action is once done, it is right or wrong forever; no accidental failure of its good or evil fruits can possibly alter that. The man would not have been innocent, he would only have been not found out. The question of right or wrong has to do with the origin of his belief, not the matter of it; not what is was, but how he got it; not whether it turned out to be true or false, but whether he had a right to believe on such evidence as was before him.

There was once an island in which some of the inhabitants professed a religion teaching neither the doctrine of original sin nor that of eternal punishment. A suspicion got abroad that the professors of this religion had made use of unfair means to get their doctrines taught to children. They were accused of wresting the laws of their country in such a way as to remove children from the care of their natural and legal guardians; and even of stealing them away and keeping them concealed from their friends and relations. A certain number of men formed themselves into a society for the purpose of agitating the public about this matter. They published grave accusations against individual citizens of the highest position and character, and did all in their power to injure these citizens in the exercise of their professions. So great was the noise they made that a Commission was appointed to investigate the facts; but after the Commission had carefully inquired into all the evidence that could be got, it appeared that the accused were innocent. Not only had they been accused on insufficient evidence, but the evidence of their innocence was such as the agitators might easily have obtained, if they had attempted a fair inquiry. After these disclosures the inhabitants of that country looked upon the members of the agitating society, not only as persons whose judgement was to be distrusted, but also as no longer to be counted honourable men. For although they had sincerely and conscientiously believed in the charges they had made, *yet they had no right to believe on such evidence as was before them.* Their sincere convictions, instead of being honestly earned by patient inquiring, were stolen by listening to the voice of prejudice and passion.

Let us vary this case also, and suppose, other things remaining as before, that a still more accurate investigation proved the accused to have been really guilty. Would this make any difference in the guilt of the accusers? Clearly not; the question is not whether their belief was true or false, but whether they entertained it on wrong grounds. They would no doubt say, "Now you see that we were right after all; next time perhaps you will believe us.' And they might be believed, but they would not thereby become honourable men. They would not be innocent, they would only be not found out. Every one of them, if he chose to examine himself *in foro conscientiae*, would know that he had acquired and nourished a belief, when he had no right to believe on such evidence as was before him; and therein he would know that he had done a wrong thing.

It may be said, however, that in both of these supposed cases it is not the belief which is judged to be wrong, but the action following upon it. The shipowner might say, 'I am perfectly certain that my ship is sound, but still I feel it my duty to have her examined, before trusting the lives of so many people to her.' And it might be said to the agitator, 'However convinced you were of the justice of your cause and the truth of your convictions, you ought not to have made a public attack upon any man's character until you had examined the evidence on both sides with the utmost patience and care.'

In the first place, let us admit that, so far as it goes, this view of the case is right and necessary; right, because even when a man's belief is so fixed that he cannot think otherwise, he still has a choice in regard to the action suggested by it, and so cannot escape the duty of investigating on the ground of the strength of his convictions; and necessary, because those who are not yet capable of controlling their feelings and thoughts must have a plain rule dealing with overt acts.

But this being premised as necessary, it becomes clear that it is not sufficient, and that our previous judgment is required to supplement it. For it is not possible so to sever the belief from the action it suggests as to condemn the one without condemning the other. No man holding a strong belief on one side of a question, or even wishing to hold a belief on one side, can investigate it with such fairness and completeness as if he were really in doubt and unbiased; so that the existence of a belief not founded on fair inquiry unfits a man for the performance of this necessary duty.

Nor is that truly a belief at all which has not some influence upon the actions of him who holds it. He who truly believes that which prompts him to an action has looked upon that action to lust after it, he has committed it already in his heart. If a belief is not realized immediately in open deeds, it is stored up for the guidance of the future. It goes to make a part of that aggregate of beliefs which is the link between sensation and action at every moment of all our lives, and which is so organized and compacted together that no part of it can be isolated from the rest, but every new addition modifies the structure of the whole. No real belief, however trifling and fragmentary it may seem, is ever truly insignificant; it prepares us to receive more of its like, confirms those which resembled it before, and weakens others; and so gradually it lays a stealthy train in our inmost thoughts, which may some day explode into overt action, and leave its stamp upon our character for ever.

And no one man's belief is in any case a private matter which concerns himself alone. Our lives are guided by that general conception of the course of things which has been created by society for social purposes. Our words, our phrases, our forms and processes and modes of thought, are common property, fashioned and perfected from age to age; an heirloom which every succeeding generation inherits as a precious deposit and a sacred trust to be handed on to the next one, not unchanged but enlarged and purified, with some clear marks of its proper handiwork. Into this, for good or ill, is woven every belief of every man who has speech of his fellows. An awful privilege, and an awful responsibility, that we should help to create the world in which posterity will live.

In the two supposed cases which have been considered, it has been judged wrong to believe on insufficient evidence, or to nourish belief by suppressing doubts and avoiding investigation. The reason of this judgement is not far to seek: it is that in both these cases the belief held by one man was of great importance to other men. But forasmuch as no belief held by one man, however seemingly trivial the belief, and however obscure the believer, is ever actually insignificant or without its effect on the fate of mankind we have no choice but to extend our judgement to all cases of belief whatever. Belief, that sacred faculty which prompts the decisions of our will, and knits into harmonious working all the compacted energies of our being, is ours not for ourselves, but for humanity. It is rightly used on truths which have been established by long experience and waiting toil, and which have stood in the fierce light of free and fearless questioning. Then it helps to bind men together, and to strengthen and direct their common action. It is desecrated when given to unproved and unquestioned statements, for the solace and private pleasure of the believer; to add a tinsel splendour to the plain straight road of our life and display a bright mirage beyond it; or even to drown the common sorrows of our kind by a self-deception which allows them not only to cast down, but also to degrade us. Whoso would deserve well of his fellows in this matter will guard the purity of his belief with a very fanaticism of jealous care, lest at any time it should rest on an unworthy object, and catch a stain which can never be wiped away.

It is not only the leader of men, statesman, philosopher, or poet, that owes this bounden duty to mankind. Every rustic who delivers in the village alehouse his slow, infrequent sentences, may help to kill or keep alive the fatal superstitions which clog his race. Every hard-worked wife of an artisan may transmit to her children beliefs which shall knit society together, or rend it in pieces. No simplicity of mind, no obscurity of station, can escape the universal duty of questioning all that we believe.

It is true that this duty is a hard one, and the doubt which comes out of it is often a very bitter thing. It leaves us bare and powerless where we thought that we were safe and strong. To know all about anything is to know how to deal with it under all circumstances. We feel much happier and more secure when we think we know precisely what to do, no matter what happens, than when we have lost our way and do not know where to turn. And if we have supposed ourselves to know all about anything, and to be capable of doing what is fit in regard to it, we naturally do not like to find that we are really ignorant and powerless, that we have to begin again at the beginning, and try to learn what the thing is and how it is to be dealt with—if indeed anything can be learnt about it. It is the sense of power attached to a sense of knowledge that makes men desirous of believing, and afraid of doubting.

This sense of power is the highest and best of pleasures when the belief on which it is founded is a true belief, and has been fairly earned by investigation. For then we may justly feel that it is common property, and holds good for others as well as for ourselves. Then we may be glad, not that *I* have learned secrets by which I am safer and stronger, but that *we men* have got mastery over more of the world; and we shall be strong, not for ourselves, but in the name of Man and in his strength. But if the belief has been accepted on insufficient evidence, the pleasure is a stolen one. Not only does it deceive ourselves by giving us a sense of power which we do not really possess, but it is sinful, because it is stolen in defiance of our duty to mankind. That duty is to guard ourselves from such beliefs as from a pestilence, which may shortly master our own body and then spread to the rest of the town. What would be thought of one who, for the sake of a sweet fruit, should deliberately run the risk of bringing a plague upon his family and his neighbours?

And, as in other such cases, it is not the risk only which has to be considered; for a bad action is always bad at the time when it is done, no matter what happens afterwards. Every time we let ourselves believe for unworthy reasons, we weaken our powers of self-control, of doubting, of judicially and fairly weighing evidence. We all suffer severely enough from the maintenance and support of false beliefs and the fatally wrong actions which they lead to, and the evil born when one such belief is entertained is great, and wide. But a greater and wider evil arises when the credulous character is maintained and supported, when a habit of believing for unworthy reasons is fostered and made permanent. If I steal money from any person, there may be no harm done by the mere transfer of possession; he may not feel the loss, or it may prevent him from using the money badly. But I cannot help doing this great wrong towards Man, that I make myself dishonest. What hurts society is not that it should lose its property, but that it should become a den of thieves; for then it must cease to be society. This is why we ought not to do evil that good may come; for at any rate this great evil has come, that we have done evil and are made wicked thereby. In like manner, if I let myself believe anything on insufficient evidence, there may be no great harm done by the mere belief; it may be true after all, or I may never have occasion to exhibit it in outward acts. But I cannot help doing this great wrong towards Man, that I make myself credulous. The danger to society is not merely that it should believe wrong things, though that is great enough; but that it should become credulous, and lose the habit of resting things and inquiring into them; for then it must sink back into savagery.

The harm which is done by credulity in a man is not confined to the fostering of a credulous character in others, and consequent support of false beliefs. Habitual want of care about what I believe leads to habitual want of care in others about the truth of what is told to me. Men speak the truth to one another when each reveres the truth in his own mind and in the other's mind; but how shall my friend revere that truth in my mind when I myself am careless about it, when I believe things because I want to believe them, and because they are comforting and pleasant? Will he not learn to cry, 'Peace,' to me, when there is no peace? By such a course I shall surround myself with a thick atmosphere of falsehood and fraud, and in that I must live. It may matter little to me, in my cloud-castle of sweet illusions and darling lies; but it matters such to Man that I have made my neighbours ready to deceive. The credulous man is father to the liar and the cheat; he lives in the bosom of this his family, and it is no marvel if he should become even as they are. So closely are our duties knit together, that whoso shall keep the whole law, and yet offend in one point, he is guilty of all.

To sum up: it is wrong always, everywhere, and for any one, to believe anything upon insufficient evidence.

If a man, holding a belief which he was taught in childhood or persuaded of afterwards, keeps down and pushes away any doubts which arise about it in his mind, purposely avoids the reading of books and the company of men that call in question or discuss it, and regards as impious those questions which cannot easily be asked without disturbing it—the life of that man is one long sin against mankind.

If this judgement seems harsh when applied to those simple souls who have never known better, who have been brought up from the cradle with a horror of doubt, and taught that their eternal welfare depends on *what* they believe, then it leads to the very serious question, *Who hath made Israel to sin?*

It may be permitted me to fortify this judgement with the sentence of Milton:

A man may be a heretic in the truth; and if he believe things only because his pastor says so, or the assembly so determine, without knowing other reason, though his belief be true, yet the very truth he holds becomes his heresy. (*Areopagitica*)

And with this famous aphorism of Coleridge:

He who begins by loving Christianity better than Truth, will proceed by loving his own sect or Church better than Christianity, and end in loving himself better than all. (*Aids to Reflection*)

Inquiry into the evidence of a doctrine is not to be made once for all, and then taken as finally settled. It is never lawful to stifle a doubt; for either it can be honestly answered by means of the inquiry already made, or else it proves that the inquiry was not complete.

'But,' says one, 'I am a busy man; I have not time for the long course of study which would be necessary to make me in any degree a competent judge of certain question, or even able to understand the nature of the arguments.' Then he should have no time to believe.

The Will to Believe[*]
William James

In the recently published Life by Leslie Stephen of his brother, Fitz-James, there is an account of a school to which the latter went when he was a boy. The teacher, a certain Mr. Guest, used to converse with his pupils in this wise, "Gurney, what is the difference between justification and sanctification?—Stephen, prove the omnipotence of God!" etc. In the midst of our Harvard freethinking and indifference we are prone to imagine that here at your good old orthodox College conversation continues to be somewhat upon this order; and to show you that we at Harvard have not lost all interest in these vital subjects, I have brought with me tonight something like a sermon on justification by faith to read to you,—I mean an essay in justification *of* faith, a defence of our right to

[*]This essay, originally an address delivered before the Philosophical Clubs of Yale and Brown Universities, was first published in 1896.

adopt a believing attitude in religious matters, in spite of the fact that our merely logical intellect may not have been coerced. "The Will to Believe," accordingly, is the title of my paper.

I have long defended to my own students the lawfulness of voluntarily adopted faith; but as soon as they have got well imbued with the logical spirit, they have as a rule refused to admit my contention to be lawful philosophically, even though in point of fact they were personally all the time chock-full of some faith or other themselves. I am all the while, however, so profoundly convinced that my own position is correct, that your invitation has seemed to me a good occasion to make my statements more clear. Perhaps your minds will be more open than those with which I have hitherto had to deal. I will be as little technical as I can, though I must begin by setting up some technical distinctions that will help us in the end.

I

Let us give the name of hypothesis to anything that may be proposed to our belief; and just as the electricians speak of live and dead wires, let us speak of any hypothesis as either *live* or *dead*. A live hypothesis is one which appeals as a real possibility to him to whom it is proposed. If I ask you to believe in the Mahdi, the notion makes no electric connection with your nature—it refuses to scintillate with any credibility at all. As an hypothesis it is completely dead. To an Arab, however (even if he be not one of the Mahdi's followers), the hypothesis is among the mind's possibilities: It is alive. This shows that deadness and liveness in an hypothesis are not intrinsic properties, but relations to the individual thinker. They are measured by his willingness to act. The maximum of liveness in an hypothesis means willingness to act irrevocably: Practically, that means belief; but there is some believing tendency wherever there is willingness to act at all.

Next, let us call the decision between two hypotheses an *option*. Options may be of several kinds. They may be first, *living* or *dead*; secondly, *forced* or *avoidable*; thirdly, *momentous* or *trivial*; and for our purposes we may call an option a *genuine* option when it is of the forced, living, and momentous kind.

1. A living option is one in which both hypotheses are live ones. If I say to you: "Be a theosophist or be a Mohammedan," it is probably a dead option, because for you neither hypothesis is likely to be alive. But if I say: "Be an agnostic or be a Christian," it is otherwise; trained as you are, each hypothesis makes some appeal, however small, to your belief.

2. Next, if I say to you: "Choose between going out with your umbrella or without it," I do not offer you a genuine option, for it is not forced. You can easily avoid it by not going out at all. Similarly, if I say, "Either love me or hate me," "Either call my theory true or call it false," your option is avoidable. You may remain indifferent to me, neither loving nor hating, and you may decline to offer any judgment as to my theory. But if I say, "Either accept this truth or go without it," I put on you a forced option, for there is no standing place outside of the alternative. Every dilemma based on a complete logical disjunction, with no possibility of not choosing, is an option of this forced kind.

3. Finally, if I were Dr. Nansen and proposed to you to join my North Pole expedition, your option would be momentous; for this would probably be your only similar opportunity, and your choice now would either exclude you from the North Pole sort of immortality altogether or put at least the chance of it into your hands. He who refuses to embrace a unique opportunity loses the prize as surely as if he tried and failed. *Per contra*, the option is trivial when the opportunity is not unique, when the stake is insignificant, or when the decision is reversible if it later prove unwise. Such trivial options abound in the scientific life. A chemist finds an hypothesis live enough to spend a year in its verification: he believes in it to that extent. But if his experiments prove inconclusive either way, he is quit for his loss of time, no vital harm being done.

It will facilitate our discussion if we keep all these distinctions well in mind.

II

The next matter to consider is the actual psychology of human opinion. When we look at certain facts, it seems as if our passional and volitional nature lay at the root of all our convictions. When we look at others, it seems as if they could do nothing when the intellect had once said its say. Let us take the latter facts up first.

Does it not seem preposterous on the very face of it to talk of our opinions being modifiable at will? Can our will either help or hinder our intellect in its perceptions of truth? Can we, by just willing it, believe that Abraham Lincoln's existence is a myth, and that the portraits of him in *McClure's Magazine* are all of some one else? Can we, by any effort of our will, or by any strength of wish that it were true, believe ourselves well and about when we are roaring with rheumatism in bed, or feel certain that the sum of the two one-dollar bills in our pocket must be a hundred dollars? We can *say* any of these things, but we are absolutely impotent to believe them; and of just such things is the whole fabric of

the truths that we do believe in made up—matters of fact, immediate
or remote, as Hume said, and relations between ideas, which are either
there or not there for us if we see them so, and which if not there cannot be put there by any action of our own.

In Pascal's *Thoughts* there is a celebrated passage known in literature
as Pascal's wager. In it he tries to force us into Christianity by reasoning as if our concern with truth resembled our concern with the stakes
in a game of chance. Translated freely his words are these: You must
either believe or not believe that God is—which will you do? Your human
reason cannot say. A game is going on between you and the nature of
things which at the day of judgment will bring out either heads or tails.
Weigh what your gains and your losses would be if you should stake all
you have on heads, or God's existence; if you win in such case, you gain
eternal beatitude; if you lose, you lose nothing at all. If there were an
infinity of chances, and only one for God in this wager, still you ought
to stake your all on God; for though you surely risk a finite loss by this
procedure, any finite loss is reasonable, even a certain one is reasonable, if there is but the possibility of infinite gain. Go, then, and take holy
water, and have masses said; belief will come and stupefy your scru-
ples. . . . Why should you not? At bottom, what have you to lose?

You probably feel that when religious faith expresses itself thus, in the
language of the gaming-table, it is put to its last trumps. Surely Pascal's own personal belief in masses and holy water had far other springs;
and this celebrated page of his is but an argument for others, a last desperate snatch at a weapon against the hardness of the unbelieving heart.
We feel that a faith in masses and holy water adopted wilfully after such
a mechanical calculation would lack the inner soul of faith's reality; and
if we were ourselves in the place of the Deity, we should probably take
particular pleasure in cutting off believers of this pattern from their infinite reward. It is evident that unless there be some preexisting tendency
to believe in masses and holy water, the option offered to the will by Pascal is not a living option. Certainly no Turk ever took to masses and
holy water on its account; and even to us Protestants these means of
salvation seem such foregone impossibilities that Pascal's logic, invoked
for them specifically, leaves us unmoved. As well might the Mahdi write
to us, saying, "I am the Expected One whom God has created in his efful-
gence. You shall be infinitely happy if you confess me; otherwise you shall
be cut off from the light of the sun. Weigh, then, your infinite gain if I am
genuine against your finite sacrifice if I am not!" His logic would be
that of Pascal; but he would vainly use it on us, for the hypothesis he
offers us is dead. No tendency to act on it exists in us to any degree.

The talk of believing by our volition seems, then, from one point of view, simply silly. From another point of view it is worse than silly, it is vile. When one turns to the magnificent edifice of the physical sciences, and sees how it was reared; what thousands of disinterested moral lives of men lie buried in its mere foundations; what patience and postponement, what choking down of preference, what submission to the icy laws of outer fact are wrought into its very stones and mortar; how absolutely impersonal it stands in its vast augustness—then how besotted and contemptible seems every little sentimentalist who comes blowing his voluntary smoke-wreaths, and pretending to decide things from out of his private dream! Can we wonder if those bred in the rugged and manly school of science should feel like spewing such subjectivism out of their mouths? The whole system of loyalties which grow up in the schools of science go dead against its toleration; so that it is only natural that those who have caught the scientific fever should pass over to the opposite extreme, and write sometimes as if the incorruptibly truthful intellect ought positively to prefer bitterness and unacceptableness to the heart in its cup.

It fortifies my soul to know

That though I perish, Truth is so

sings Clough, while Huxley exclaims: "My only consolation lies in the reflection that, however bad our posterity may become, so far as they hold by the plain rule of not pretending to believe what they have no reason to believe, because it may be to their advantage so to pretend [the word 'pretend' is surely here redundant], they will not have reached the lowest depth of immorality." And that delicious *enfant terrible* Clifford writes: "Belief is desecrated when given to unproved and unquestioned statements for the solace and private pleasure of the believer . . . Whoso would deserve well of his fellows in this matter will guard the purity of his belief with a very fanaticism of jealous care, lest at any time it should rest on an unworthy object, and catch a stain which can never be wiped away. . . . If [a] belief has been accepted on insufficient evidence [even though the belief be true, as Clifford on the same page explains] the pleasure is a stolen one. . . . It is sinful because it is stolen in defiance of our duty to mankind. That duty is to guard ourselves from such beliefs as from a pestilence which may shortly master our own body and then spread to the rest of the town. . . . It is wrong always, everywhere, and for every one, to believe anything upon insufficient evidence."

III

All this strikes one as healthy, even when expressed, as by Clifford, with somewhat too much of robustious pathos in the voice. Free will and simple wishing do seem, in the matter of our credences, to be only fifth wheels to the coach. Yet if any one should thereupon assume that intellectual insight is what remains after wish and will and sentimental preference have taken wing, or that pure reason is what then settles our opinions, he would fly quite as directly in the teeth of the facts.

It is only our already dead hypotheses that our willing nature is unable to bring to life again. But what has made them dead for us is for the most part a previous action of our willing nature of an antagonistic kind. When I say "willing nature," I do not mean only such deliberate volitions as may have set up habits of belief that we cannot now escape from—I mean all such factors of belief as fear and hope, prejudice and passion, imitation and partisanship, the circumpressure of our caste and set. As a matter of fact we find ourselves believing, we hardly know how or why. Mr. Balfour gives the name of "authority" to all those influences, born of the intellectual climate, that make hypotheses possible or impossible for us, alive or dead. Here in this room, we all of us believe in molecules and the conservation of energy, in democracy and necessary progress, in Protestant Christianity and the duty of fighting for "the doctrine of the immortal Monroe," all for no reasons worthy of the name. We see into these matters with no more inner clearness, and probably with much less, than any disbeliever in them might possess. His unconventionality would probably have some grounds to show for its conclusions; but for us, not insight, but the *prestige* of the opinions, is what makes the spark shoot from them and light up our sleeping magazines of faith. Our reason is quite satisfied, in nine hundred and ninety-nine cases out of every thousand of us, if it can find a few arguments that will do to recite in case our credulity is criticized by some one else. Our faith is faith in some one else's faith, and in the greatest matters this is most the case. . . .

Evidently, then, our non-intellectual nature does influence our convictions. There are passional tendencies and volitions which run before and others which come after belief, and it is only the latter that are too late for the fair; and they are not too late when the previous passional work has been already in their own direction. Pascal's argument, instead of being powerless, then seems a regular clincher, and is the last stroke needed to make our faith in masses and holy water complete. The state of things is evidently far from simple; and pure insight and logic, whatever they might do ideally, are not the only things that really do produce our creeds.

IV

Our next duty, having recognized this mixed-up state of affairs, is to ask whether it be simply reprehensible and pathological, or whether, on the contrary, we must treat it as a normal element in making up our minds. The thesis I defend is, briefly stated, this: *Our passional nature not only lawfully may, but must, decide an option between propositions, whenever it is a genuine option that cannot by its nature be decided on intellectual grounds; for to say, under such circumstances, "Do not decide, but leave the question open," is itself a passional decision—just like deciding yes or no—and is attended with the same risk of losing the truth.* . . .

VII

One more point, small but important, and our preliminaries are done. There are two ways of looking at our duty in the matter of opinion—ways entirely different, and yet ways about whose difference the theory of knowledge seems hitherto to have shown very little concern. *We must know the truth*; and *we must avoid error*—these are our first and great commandments as would-be knowers; but they are not two ways of stating an identical commandment, they are two separable laws. Although it may indeed happen that when we believe the truth A, we escape as an incidental consequence from believing the falsehood B, it hardly ever happens that by merely disbelieving B we necessarily believe A. We may in escaping B fall into believing other falsehoods, C or D, just as bad as B; or we may escape B by not believing anything at all, not even A.

Believe truth! Shun error!—these, we see, are two materially different laws; and by choosing between them we may end by coloring differently our whole intellectual life. We may regard the chase for truth as paramount, and the avoidance of error as secondary; or we may, on the other hand, treat the avoidance of error as more imperative, and let truth take its chance. Clifford, in the instructive passage which I have quoted, exhorts us to the latter course. Believe nothing, he tells us, keep your mind in suspense forever, rather than by closing it on insufficient evidence incur the awful risk of believing lies. You, on the other hand, may think that the risk of being in error is a very small matter when compared with the blessings of real knowledge, and be ready to be duped many times in your investigation rather than postpone indefinitely the chance of guessing true. I myself find it impossible to go with Clifford. We must remember that these feelings of our duty about either truth or error are in any case only expressions of our passional life. Biologically considered, our minds are as ready to grind out falsehood as veracity, and he who says, "Better go without belief forever than believe a lie!" merely shows his own preponderant private horror of becoming a dupe. He may be critical of many of his desires and fears, but this fear he slavishly obeys. He cannot imagine any one questioning its binding force. For my own part, I have also a horror of being duped; but I can believe that worse things than being duped may happen to a man in this world: so Clifford's exhortation has to my ears a thoroughly fantastic sound. It is like a general informing his soldiers that it is better to keep out of battle forever than to risk a single wound. Not so are victories either over enemies or over nature gained. Our errors are surely not such awfully solemn things. In a world where we are so certain to incur them in spite of all our caution, a certain lightness of heart seems healthier than this excessive nervousness on their behalf. At any rate, it seems the fittest thing for the empiricist philosopher.

VIII

And now, after all this introduction, let us go straight at our question. I have said, and now repeat it, that not only as a matter of fact do we find our passional nature influencing us in our opinions, but that there are some options between opinions in which this influence must be regarded both as an inevitable and as a lawful determinant of our choice.

I fear here that some of you my hearers will begin to scent danger, and lend an inhospitable ear. Two first steps of passion you have indeed had to admit as necessary—we must think so as to avoid dupery, and we must think so as to gain truth; but the surest path to those ideal consummations, you will probably consider, is from now onwards to take no further passional step.

Well, of course, I agree as far as the facts will allow. Wherever the option between losing truth and gaining it is not momentous, we can throw the chance of *gaining truth* away, and at any rate save ourselves from any chance of *believing falsehood*, by not making up our minds at all till objective evidence has come. In scientific questions, this is almost always the case; and even in human affairs in general, the need of acting is seldom so urgent that a false belief to act on is better than no belief at all. Law courts, indeed, have to decide on the best evidence attainable for the moment, because a judge's duty is to make law as well as to ascertain it, and (as a learned judge once said to me) few cases are worth spending much time over; the great thing is to have them decided on *any* acceptable principle, and got out of the way. But in our dealings with objective nature we obviously are recorders, not makers, of the truth; and decisions for the mere sake of deciding promptly and getting on to the next business would be wholly out of place. Throughout the breadth of physical nature facts are what they are quite independently of us, and seldom is there any such hurry about them that the risks of being duped by believing a premature theory need be faced. The questions here are always trivial options, the hypotheses are hardly living (at any rate not living for us spectators), the choice between believing truth or falsehood is seldom forced. The attitude of sceptical balance is therefore the absolutely wise one if we would escape mistakes. What difference, indeed, does it make to most of us whether we have or have not a theory of the Röntgen rays, whether we believe or not in mind-stuff, or have a conviction about the causality of conscious states? It makes no difference. Such options are not forced on us. On every account it is better not to make them, but still keep weighing reasons *pro et contra* with an indifferent hand.

I speak, of course, here of the purely judging mind. For purposes of discovery such indifference is to be less highly recommended, and science would be far less advanced than she is if the passionate desires of individuals to get their own faiths confirmed had been kept out of the game. See for example the sagacity which Spencer and Weismann now display. On the other hand, if you want an absolute duffer in an investigation, you must, after all, take the man who has no interest whatever in its results: he is the warranted incapable, the positive fool. The most useful investigator, because the most sensitive observer, is always he whose eager interest in one side of the question is balanced by an equally keen nervousness lest he become deceived.[1] Science has organized this nervousness into a regular *technique*, her so-called method of verification; and she has fallen so deeply in love with the method that one may even say she has ceased to care for truth by itself at all. It is only truth as technically verified that interests her. The truth of truths might come in merely affirmative form, and she would decline to touch it. Such truth as that, she might repeat with Clifford, would be stolen in defiance of her duty to mankind. Human passions, however, are stronger than technical rules. *"Le coeur a ses raisons,"* as Pascal says, *"que la raison ne connait pas"*;[2] and however indifferent to all but the bare rules of the game the umpire, the abstract intellect, may be, the concrete players who furnish him the materials to judge of are usually, each one of them, in love with some pet "live hypothesis" of his own. Let us agree, however, that wherever there is no forced option, the dispassionately judicial intellect with no pet hypothesis, saving us, as it does, from dupery at any rate, ought to be our ideal.

The question next arises: Are there not somewhere forced options in our speculative questions, and can we (as men who may be interested at least as much in positively gaining truth as in merely escaping dupery) always wait with impunity till the coercive evidence shall have arrived? It seems *a priori* improbable that the truth should be so nicely adjusted to our needs and powers as that. In the great boarding-house of nature, the cakes and the butter and the syrup seldom come out so even and leave the plates so clean. Indeed, we should view them with scientific suspicion if they did.

IX

Moral questions immediately present themselves as questions whose solution cannot wait for sensible proof. A moral question is a question not of what sensibly exists, but of what is good, or would be good if it did exist. Science can tell us what exists; but to compare the *worths*, both of what exists and of what does not exist, we must consult not science, but what Pascal calls our heart. . . .

Turn now from these wide questions of good to a certain class of questions of fact, questions concerning personal relations, states of mind between one man and another. *Do you like me or not?*—for example. Whether you do or not depends, in countless instances, on whether I meet you halfway, am willing to assume that you must like me, and show you trust and expectation. The previous faith on my part in your liking's existence is in such cases what makes your liking come. But if I stand aloof, and refuse to budge an inch until I have objective evidence, until you shall have done something apt, as the absolutists say, *ad extorquendum assensum meum*, ten to one your liking never comes. How many women's hearts are vanquished by the mere sanguine insistence of some man that they *must* love him! He will not consent to the hypothesis that they cannot. The desire for a certain kind of truth here brings about that special truth's existence; and so it is in innumerable cases of other sorts. . . . *And where faith in a fact can help create the fact,* that would be an insane logic which should say that faith running ahead of scientific evidence is the "lowest kind of immorality" into which a thinking being can fall. Yet such is the logic by which our scientific absolutists pretend to regulate our lives!

X

In truths dependent on our personal action, then, faith based on desire is certainly a lawful and possibly an indispensable thing.

But now, it will be said, these are all childish human cases, and have nothing to do with great cosmical matters, like the question of religious faith. Let us then pass on to that. Religions differ so much in their accidents that in discussing the religious question we must make it very generic and broad. What then do we now mean by the religious hypothesis? Science says things are; morality says some things are better than other things; and religion says essentially two things.

First, she says that the best things are the more eternal things, the overlapping things, the things in the universe that throw the last stone, so to speak, and say the final word. "Perfection is eternal"—this phrase of Charles Secrétan seems a good way of putting this first affirmation of religion, an affirmation which obviously cannot yet be verified scientifically at all.

The second affirmation of religion is that we are better off even now if we believe her first affirmation to be true.

Now, let us consider what the logical elements of this situation are *in case the religious hypothesis in both its branches be really true.* (Of course, we must admit that possibility at the outset. If we are to discuss the question at all, it must involve a living option. If for any of you religion be a hypothesis that cannot, by any living possibility, be true, then you need go no farther. I speak to the "saving remnant" alone.) So proceeding, we see, first, that religion offers itself as a *momentous* option. We are supposed to gain, even now, by our belief, and to lose by our nonbelief, a certain vital good. Secondly, religion is a *forced* option, so far as that good goes. We cannot escape the issue by remaining sceptical and waiting for more light, because, although we do avoid error in that way *if religion be untrue,* we lose the good, *if it be true,* just as certainly as if we positively chose to disbelieve. It is as if a man should hesitate indefinitely to ask a certain woman to marry him because he was not perfectly sure that she would prove an angel after he brought her home. Would he not cut himself off from that particular angel-possibility as decisively as if he went and married some one else? Scepticism, then, is not avoidance of option; it is option of a certain particular kind of risk. *Better risk loss of truth than chance of error*—that is your faith-vetoer's exact position. He is actively playing his stake as much as the believer is; he is backing the field against the religious hypothesis, just as the believer is backing the religious hypothesis against the field. To preach scepticism to us as a duty until "sufficient evidence" for religion be found, is tantamount therefore to telling us, when in presence of the religious hypothesis, that to yield to our fear of its being error is wiser and better than to yield to our hope that it may be true. It is not intellect against all passion, then; it is only intellect with one passion laying down its law. And by what, forsooth, is the supreme wisdom of this passion warranted? Dupery for dupery, what proof is there that dupery through hope is so much worse than dupery through fear? I, for one, can see no proof; and I simply refuse obedience to the scientist's command to imitate his kind of option, in a case where my own stake is important enough to give me the right to choose my own form of risk. If religion be true and the evidence for it be still insufficient, I do not wish, by putting your extinguisher upon my nature (which feels to me as if it had after all some business in this matter), to forfeit my sole chance in life of getting upon the winning side—that chance depending, of course, on my willingness to run the risk of acting as if my passional need of taking the world religiously might be prophetic and right.

All this is on the supposition that it really may be prophetic and right, and that, even to us who are discussing the matter, religion is a live hypothesis which may be true. Now, to most of us religion comes in a still further way that makes a veto on our active faith even more illogical. The more perfect and more eternal aspect of the universe is represented in our religions as having personal form. The universe is no longer a mere *It* to us, but a *Thou*, if we are religious; and any relation that may be possible from person to person might be possible here. For instance, although in one sense we are passive portions of the universe, in another we show a curious autonomy, as if we were small active centers on our own account. We feel, too, as if the appeal of religion to us were made to our own active goodwill, as if evidence might be forever withheld from us unless we met the hypothesis halfway to take a trivial illustration: just as a man who in a company of gentlemen made no advances, asked a warrant for every concession, and believed no one's word without proof, would cut himself off by such churlishness from all the social rewards that a more trusting spirit would earn—so here, one who should shut himself up in snarling logicality and try to make the gods extort his recognition willy-nilly, or not get it at all, might cut himself off forever from his only opportunity of making the gods' acquaintance. This feeling, forced on us we know not whence that by obstinately believing that there are gods (although not to do so would be so easy both for our logic and our life) we are doing the universe the deepest service we can, seems part of the living essence of the religious hypothesis. If the hypothesis *were* true in all its parts, including this one, then pure intellectualism, with its veto on our making willing advances, would be an absurdity; and some participation of our sympathetic nature would be logically required. I therefore, for one, cannot see myway to accepting the agnostic rules for truth-seeking, or wilfully agree to keep my willing nature out of the game. I cannot do so for this plain reason, that *a rule of thinking which would absolutely prevent me from acknowledging certain kinds of truth if those kinds of truth were really there, would be an irrational rule.* That for me is the long and short of the formal logic of the situation, no matter what the kinds of truth might materially be.

I confess I do not see how this logic can be escaped. But sad experience makes me fear that some of you may still shrink from radically saying with me, *in abstracto*, that we have the right to believe at our own risk any hypothesis that is live enough to tempt our will. I suspect, however, that if this is so, it is because you have got away from the abstract logical point of view altogether, and are thinking (perhaps without realizing it) of some particular religious hypothesis which for you is dead. The freedom to "believe what we will" you apply to the case of some patent superstition; and the faith you think of is the faith defined by the schoolboy when he said, "Faith is when you believe something that you know ain't true." I can only repeat that this is misapprehension. *In concreto*, the freedom to believe can only cover living options which the intellect of the individual cannot by itself resolve; and living options never seem absurdities to him who has them to consider. When I look at the religious question as it really puts itself to concrete men, and when I think of all the possibilities which both practically and theoretically it involves, then this command that we shall put a stopper on our heart, instincts, and courage, and *wait*—acting of course meanwhile more or less as if religion were *not* true[3]—till doomsday, or till such time as our intellect and senses working together may have raked in evidence enough—this command, I say, seems to me the queerest idol ever manufactured in the philosophic cave. Were we scholastic absolutists, there might be more excuse. If we had an infallible intellect with its objective certitudes, we might feel ourselves disloyal to such a perfect organ of knowledge in not trusting to it exclusively, in not waiting for its releasing word. But if we are empiricists, if we believe that no bell in us tolls to let us know for certain when truth is in our grasp, then it seems a piece of idle fantasticality to preach so solemnly our duty of waiting for the bell. Indeed we *may* wait if we will—I hope you do not think that I am denying that— but if we do so, we do so at our peril as much as if we believed. In either case we *act*, taking our life in our hands. No one of us ought to issue vetoes to the other, nor should we bandy words of abuse. We ought, on the contrary, delicately and profoundly to respect one another's mental freedom: then only shall we bring about the intellectual republic; then only shall we have that spirit of inner tolerance without which all our outer tolerance is soulless, and which is empiricism's glory; then only shall we live and let live, in speculative as well as in practical things.

I began by a reference to Fitz-James Stephen; let me end by a quotation from him. "What do you think of yourself? What do you think of the world? . . . These are questions with which all must deal as it seems good to them. They are riddles of the Sphinx, and in some way or other we must deal with them. . . . In all important transactions of life we have to take a leap in the dark. . . . If we decide to leave the riddles unanswered, that is a choice; if we waver in our answer, that, too, is a choice: but whatever choice we make, we make it at our peril. If a man chooses to turn his back altogether on God and the future, no one can prevent him; no one can show beyond reasonable doubt that he is mistaken. If a man thinks otherwise and acts as he thinks, I do not see that any one can prove that *he* is mistaken. Each must act as he thinks best; and if he is wrong, so much the worse for him. We stand on a mountain pass in the midst of whirling snow and blinding mist, through which we get glimpses now and then of paths which may be deceptive. If we stand still we shall be frozen to death. If we take the wrong road we shall be dashed to pieces. We do not certainly know whether there is any right one. What must we do? 'Be strong and of a good courage.' Act for the best, hope for the best, and take what comes. . . . If death ends all, we cannot meet death better."[4]

Notes

1. Compare Wilfrid Ward's Essay "The Wish to Believe," in his *Witnesses to the Unseen* (Macmillan & Co., 1893).
2. "The heart has its reasons which reason does not know." Editor's Trans.
3. Since belief is measured by action, he who forbids us to believe religion to be true, necessarily also forbids us to act as we should if we did believe it to be true. The whole defence of religious faith hinges upon action. If the action required or inspired by the religious hypothesis is in no way different from that dictated by the naturalistic hypothesis, then religious faith is a pure superfluity, better pruned away, and controversy about its legitimacy is a piece of idle trifling, unworthy of serious minds. I myself believe, of

course, that the religious hypothesis gives to the world an expression which specifically determines our reactions, and makes them in a large part unlike what they might be on a purely naturalistic scheme of belief.

4. *Liberty, Equality, Fraternity*, p. 353, 2d edition (London, 1874).

The Cosmological Argument
Richard Taylor

. . . Suppose you were strolling in the woods and, in addition to the sticks, stones, and other accustomed litter of the forest floor, you one day came upon some quite unaccustomed object, something not quite like what you had ever seen before and would never expect to find in such a place. Suppose, for example, that it is a large ball, about your own height, perfectly smooth and translucent. You would deem this puzzling and mysterious, certainly, but if one considers the matter, it is no more inherently mysterious that such a thing should exist than that anything else should exist. If you were quite accustomed to finding such objects of various sizes around you most of the time, but had never seen an ordinary rock, then upon finding a large rock in the woods one day you would be just as puzzled and mystified. This illustrates the fact that something that is mysterious ceases to seem so simply by its accustomed presence. It is strange indeed, for example, that a world such as ours should exist; yet few people are very often struck by this strangeness but simply take it for granted.

Suppose, then, that you have found this translucent ball and are mystified by it. Now whatever else you might wonder about it, there is one thing you would hardly question; namely, that it did not appear there all by itself, that it owes its existence to something. You might not have the remotest idea whence and how it came to be there, but you would hardly doubt that there was an explanation. The idea that it might have come from nothing at all, that it might exist without there being any explanation of its existence, is one that few people would consider worthy of entertaining.

Source: *Metaphysics*, Fourth Edition by R. Taylor, © 1992. Reprinted by permission of Pearson Education, Inc., Upper Saddle River, N.J.

This illustrates a metaphysical belief that seems to be almost a part of reason itself, even though few ever think upon it; the belief, namely, that there is some explanation for the existence of anything whatever, some reason why it should exist rather than not. The sheer nonexistence of anything, which is not to be confused with the passing out of existence of something, never requires a reason; but existence does. That there should never have been any such ball in the forest does not require any explanation or reason, but that there should ever be such a ball does. If one were to look upon a barren plain and ask why there is not and never has been any large translucent ball there, the natural response would be to ask why there should be; but if one finds such a ball, and wonders why it is there, it is not quite so natural to ask why it should *not* be—as though existence should simply be taken for granted. That anything should not exist, then, and that, for instance, no such ball should exist in the forest, or that there should be no forest for it to occupy, or no continent containing a forest, or no Earth, nor any world at all, do not seem to be things for which there needs to be any explanation or reason; but that such things should be *does* seem to require a reason.

The principle involved here has been called the principle of sufficient reason. Actually, it is a very general principle, and it is best expressed by saying that, in the case of any positive truth, there is some sufficient reason for it, something that, in this sense, makes it true—in short, that there is some sort of explanation, known or unknown, for everything.

Now, some truths depend on something else, and are accordingly called *contingent*, while others depend only upon themselves, that is, are true by their very natures and are accordingly called *necessary*. There is, for example, a reason why the stone on my window sill is warm; namely, that the sun is shining upon it. This happens to be true, but not by its very nature. Hence, it is contingent, and depends upon something other than itself. It is also true that all the points of a circle are equidistant from the center, but this truth depends upon nothing but itself. No matter what happens, nothing can make it false. Similarly, it is a truth, and a necessary one, that if the stone on my window sill is a body, as it is, then it has a form, because this fact depends upon nothing but itself for its confirmation. Untruths are also, of course, either contingent or necessary, it being contingently false, for example, that the stone on my window still is cold, and necessarily false that it is both a body and formless, because this is by its very nature impossible.

The principle of sufficient reason can be illustrated in various ways, as we have done, and if one thinks about it, he is apt to find that he presupposes it in his thinking about reality, but it cannot be proved. It does not appear to be itself a necessary truth, and at the same time it would be most odd to say it is contingent. If one were to try proving it, he would sooner or later have to appeal to considerations that are less plausible than the principle itself. Indeed, it is hard to see how one could even make an argument for it without already assuming it. For this reason it might properly be called a presupposition of reason itself. One can deny that it is true, without embarrassment or fear of refutation, but one is then apt to find that what he is denying is not really what the principle asserts. We shall, then, treat it here as a datum—not something that is provably true, but as something that people, whether they ever reflect upon it or not, seem more or less to presuppose.

It happens to be true that something exists, that there is, for example, a world, and although no one ever seriously supposes that this might not be so, that there might exist nothing at all, there still seems to be nothing the least necessary in this, considering it just by itself. That no world should ever exist at all is perfectly comprehensible and seems to express not the slightest absurdity. Considering any particular item in the world it seems not at all necessary that the totality of these things, or any totality of things, should ever exist.

From the principle of sufficient reason it follows, of course, that there must be a reason not only for the existence of everything in the world but for the world itself, meaning by "the world" simply everything that ever does exist, except God, in case there is a god. This principle does not imply that there must be some purpose or goal for everything, or for the totality of all things; for explanations need not be, and in fact seldom are, teleological or purposeful. All the principle requires is that there be some sort of reason for everything. And it would certainly be odd to maintain that everything in the world owes its existence to something, that nothing in the world is either purely accidental, or such that it just bestows its own being upon itself, and then to deny this of the world itself. One can indeed say that the world is in some sense a pure accident, that there simply is no reason at all why this or any world should exist, and one can equally say that the world exists by its very nature, or is an inherently necessary being. But it is at least very odd and arbitrary to deny of this existing world the need for any sufficient reason, whether independent of itself or not, while presupposing that there is a reason for every other thing that ever exists.

Consider again the strange ball that we imagine has been found in the forest. Now, we can hardly doubt that there must be an explanation for the existence of such a thing, though we may have no notion what that explanation is. It is not, moreover, the fact of its having been found in the forest rather than elsewhere that renders an explanation necessary. It matters not in the least where it happens to be, for our question is not how it happens to be *there* but how it happens to be at all. If we in our imagination annihilate the forest, leaving only this ball in an open field, our conviction that it is a contingent thing and owes its existence to something other than itself is not reduced in the least. If we now imagine the field to be annihilated, and in fact everything else as well to vanish into nothingness, leaving only this ball to constitute the entire physical universe, then we cannot for a moment suppose that its existence has thereby been explained, or the need for any explanation eliminated, or that its existence is suddenly rendered self-explanatory. If we now carry this thought one step further and suppose that no other reality ever has existed or ever will exist, that this ball forever constitutes the entire physical universe, then we must still insist on there being some reason independent of itself why it should exist rather than not. If there must be a reason for the existence of any particular thing, then the necessity of such a reason is not eliminated by the mere supposition that certain other things do *not* exist. And again, it matters not at all what the thing in question is, whether it be large and complex, such as the world we actually find ourselves in, or whether it be something small, simple, and insignificant, such as a ball, a bacterium, or the merest grain of sand. We do not avoid the necessity of a reason for the existence of something merely by describing it in this way or that. And it would, in any event, seem quite plainly absurd to say that if the world were composed entirely of a single ball about six feet in diameter, or of a single grain of sand, then it would be contingent and there would have to be some explanation other than itself why such a thing exists, but that, since the actual world is vastly more complex than this, there is no need for an explanation of its existence, independent of itself.

It should now be noted that it is no answer to the question, why a thing exists, to state *how long* it has existed. A geologist does not suppose that she has explained why there should be rivers and mountains merely by pointing out that they are old. Similarly, if one were to ask, concerning the ball of which we have spoken, for some sufficient reason for its being, he would not receive any answer upon being told that it had been there since yesterday. Nor would it be any better answer to say that it had existed since before anyone could remember, or even that it had always existed; for the question was not one concerning its age but its existence. If, to be sure, one were to ask where a given thing came from, or how it came into being, then upon learning that it had always existed he would learn that it never really *came* into being at all; but he could still reasonably wonder why it should exist at all. If, accordingly, the world—that is, the totality of all things excepting God, in case there is a god—had really no beginning at all, but has always existed in some form or other, then there is clearly no answer to the question, where it came from and when; it did not, on this supposition, *come* from anything at all, at any time. But still, it can be asked why there is a world, why indeed there is a beginningless world, why there should have perhaps always been something rather than nothing. And, if the principle of sufficient reason is a good principle, there must be an answer to that question, an answer that is by no means supplied by giving the world an age, or even an infinite age.

This brings out an important point with respect to the concept of creation that is often misunderstood, particularly by those whose thinking has been influenced by Christian ideas. People tend to think that creation—for example, the creation of the world by God—*means* creation *in time*, from which it of course logically follows that if the world had no beginning in time, then it cannot be the creation of God. This, however, is erroneous, for creation means essentially *dependence*, even in Christian theology. If one thing is the creation of another, then it depends for its existence on that other, and this is perfectly consistent with saying that both are eternal, that neither ever came into being, and hence, that neither was ever created at any point of time. Perhaps an analogy will help convey this point. Consider, then, a flame that is casting beams of light. Now, there seems to be a clear sense in which the beams of light are dependent for their existence upon the flame, which is their source, while the flame, on the other hand, is not similarly dependent for its existence upon them. The beams of light arise from the flame, but the flame does not arise from them. In this sense, they are the creation of the flame; they derive their existence from it. And none of this has any reference to time; the relationship of dependence in such a case would not be altered in the slightest if we supposed that the flame, and with it the beams of light, had always existed, that neither had ever *come* into being.

Now if the world is the creation of God, its relationship to God should be thought of in this fashion; namely, that the world depends for its existence upon God, and could not exist independently of God. If God is eternal, as those who believe in God generally assume, then the world may (though it need not) be eternal too, without that altering in the least its dependence upon God for its existence, and hence without altering its being the creation of God. The supposition of God's eternality, on the other hand, does not by itself imply that the world is eternal too; for there is not the least reason why something of finite duration might not depend for its existence upon something of infinite duration—though the reverse is, of course, impossible.

If we think of God as "the creator of heaven and earth," and if we consider heaven and earth to include everything that exists except God, then we appear to have, in the foregoing considerations, fairly strong reasons for asserting that God, as so conceived, exists. Now of course most people have much more in mind than this when they think of God, for religions have ascribed to God ever so many attributes that are not at all implied by describing him merely as the creator of the world; but that is not relevant here. Most religious persons do, in any case, think of God as being at least the creator, as that being upon which everything ultimately depends, no matter what else they may say about Him in addition. It is, in fact, the first item in the creeds of Christianity that God is the "creator of heaven and earth." And, it seems, there are good metaphysical reasons, as distinguished from the persuasions of faith, for thinking that such a creative being exists.

If, as seems clearly implied by the principle of sufficient reason, there must be a reason for the existence of heaven and earth—*i.e.*, for the world—then that reason must be found either in the world itself, or outside it, in something that is literally supranatural, or outside heaven and earth. Now if we suppose that the world—*i.e.*, the totality of all things except God—contains within itself the reason for its existence, we are supposing that it exists by its very nature, that is, that it is a necessary being. In that case there would, of course, be no reason for saying that it must depend upon God or anything else for its existence; for if it exists by its very nature, then it depends upon nothing but itself, much as the sun depends upon nothing but itself for its heat. This, however, is implausible, for we find nothing about the world or anything in it to suggest that it exists by its own nature, and we do find, on the contrary, ever so many things to suggest that it does not. For in the first place, anything that exists by its very nature must necessarily be eternal and indestructible. It would be a self-contradiction to say of anything that it exists by its own nature, or is a necessarily existing thing, and at the same time to say that it comes into being or passes away, or that it ever could come into being or pass away. Nothing about the world seems at all like this, for concerning anything in the world, we can perfectly easily think of it as being annihilated, or as never having existed in the first place, without there being the slightest hint of any absurdity in such a supposition. Some of the things in the universe are, to be sure, very old; the moon, for example, or the stars and the planets. It is even possible to imagine that they have always existed. Yet it seems quite impossible to suppose that they owe their existence to nothing but themselves, that they bestow existence upon themselves by their very natures, or that they are in themselves things of such nature that it would be impossible for them not to exist. Even if we suppose that something, such as the sun, for instance, has existed forever, and will never cease, still we cannot conclude just from this that it exists by its own nature. If, as is of course very doubtful, the sun has existed forever and will never cease, then it is possible that its heat and light have also existed forever and will never cease; but that would not show that the heat and light of the sun exist by their own natures. They are obviously contingent and depend on the sun for their existence, whether they are beginningless and everlasting or not.

There seems to be nothing in the world, then, concerning which it is at all plausible to suppose that it exists by its own nature, or contains within itself the reason for its existence. In fact, everything in the world appears to be quite plainly the opposite, namely, something that not only need not exist, but at some time or other, past or future or both, does not in fact exist. Everything in the world seems to have a finite duration, whether long or short. Most things, such as ourselves, exist only for a short while; they come into being, then soon cease. Other things, like the heavenly bodies, last longer, but they are still corruptible, and from all that we can gather about them, they too seem destined eventually to perish. We arrive at the conclusion, then, that although the world may contain some things that have always existed and are destined never to perish, it is nevertheless doubtful that it contains any such thing, and, in any case, everything in the world is capable of perishing, and nothing in it, however long it may already have existed and however long it may yet remain, exists by its own nature but depends instead upon something else.

Although this might be true of everything in the world, is it necessarily true of the world itself? That is, if we grant, as we seem forced to, that nothing in the world exists by its own nature, that everything in the world is contingent and perishable, must we also say that the world itself, or the totality of all these perishable things, is also contingent and perishable? Logically, we are not forced to, for it is logically possible that the totality of all perishable things might itself be imperishable, and hence, that the world might exist by its own nature, even though it is composed exclusively of things that are contingent. It is not logically necessary that a totality should share the defects of its members. For exam-

ple, even though every person is mortal, it does not follow from this that
the human race, or the totality of all people, is also mortal; for it is possible that there will always be human beings, even though there are no
human beings who will always exist. Similarly, it is possible that the
world is in itself a necessary thing, even though it is composed entirely of
things that are contingent.

This is logically possible, but it is not plausible. For we find nothing whatever about the world, any more than in its parts, to suggest
that it exists by its own nature. Concerning anything in the world, we
have not the slightest difficulty in supposing that it should perish, or even
that it should never have existed in the first place. We have almost as
little difficulty in supposing this of the world itself. It might be somewhat
hard to think of everything as utterly perishing and leaving no trace
whatever of its ever having been, but there seems to be not the slightest difficulty in imagining that the world should never have existed in the
first place. We can, for instance, perfectly easily suppose that nothing
in the world had ever existed except, let us suppose, a single grain of sand,
and we can thus suppose that this grain of sand has forever constituted
the whole universe. Now if we consider just this grain of sand, it is quite
impossible for us to suppose that it exists by its very nature and could
never have failed to exist. It clearly depends for its existence upon something other than itself, if it depends on anything at all. The same will
be true if we consider the world to consist not of one grain of sand but
of two, or of a million, or, as we in fact find, of a vast number of stars
and planets and all their minuter parts.

It would seem, then, that the world, in case it happens to exist at all—
and this is quite beyond doubt—is contingent and thus dependent upon
something other than itself for its existence, if it depends upon anything
at all. And it must depend upon something, for otherwise there could
be no reason why it exists in the first place. Now, that upon which the
world depends must be something that either exists by its own nature
or does not. If it does not exist by its own nature, then it, in turn, depends
for its existence upon something else, and so on. Now then, we can say
either of two things; namely, (1) that the world depends for its existence
upon something else, which in turn depends on still another thing, this
depending upon still another, *ad infinitum*; or (2) that the world derives
its existence from something that exists by its own nature and that is
accordingly eternal and imperishable, and is the creator of heaven and
earth. The first of these alternatives, however, is impossible, for it does
not render a sufficient reason why anything should exist in the first place.
Instead of supplying a reason why any world should exist, it repeatedly

begs off giving a reason. It explains what is dependent and perishable in terms of what is itself dependent and perishable, leaving us still without a reason why perishable things should exist at all, which is what we are seeking. Ultimately, then, it would seem that the world, or the totality of contingent or perishable things, in case it exists at all, must depend upon something that is necessary and imperishable, and that accordingly exists, not in dependence upon something else, but by its own nature.

What has been said thus far gives some intimation of what meaning should be attached to the concept of a self-caused being, a concept that is quite generally misunderstood, sometimes even by scholars. To say that something—God, for example—is self-caused, or is the cause of its own existence, does not mean that this being brings itself into existence, which is a perfectly absurd idea. Nothing can *bring* itself into existence. To say that something is self-caused (*causa sui*) means only that it exists, not contingently or in dependence upon something else but by its own nature, which is only to say that it is a being which is such that it can neither come into being nor perish. Now, whether in fact such a being exists or not, there is in any case no absurdity in the idea. We have found, in fact, that the principle of sufficient reason seems to point to the existence of such a being, as that upon which the world, with everything in it, must ultimately depend for its existence.

A being that depends for its existence upon nothing but itself and is in this sense self-caused, can equally be described as a necessary being; that is to say, a being that is not contingent, and hence not perishable. For in the case of anything that exists by its own nature and is dependent upon nothing else, it is impossible that it should not exist, which is equivalent to saying that it is necessary. Many persons have professed to find the greatest difficulties in this concept, too, but that is partly because it has been confused with other notions. If it makes sense to speak of anything as an *impossible* being, or something that by its very nature does not exist, then it is hard to see why the idea of a necessary being, or something that in its very nature exists, should not be just as comprehensible. And of course, we have not the slightest difficulty in speaking of something, such as a square circle or a formless body, as an impossible being. And if it makes sense to speak of something as being perishable, contingent, and dependent upon something other than itself for its existence, as it surely does, then there seems to be no difficulty in thinking of something as imperishable and dependent upon nothing other than itself for its existence.

414 • *Part Six Does God Exist?*

From these considerations we can see also what is properly meant by a "first cause," an appellative that has often been applied to God by theologians and that many persons have deemed an absurdity. It is a common criticism of this notion to say that there need not be any first cause, because the series of causes and effects that constitute the history of the universe might be infinite or beginningless and must, in fact, be infinite in case the universe itself had no beginning in time. This criticism, however, reflects a total misconception of what is meant by a first cause. *First* here does not mean first in time, and when God is spoken of as a first cause He is not being described as a being that, at some time in the remote past, *started* everything. To describe God as a first cause is only to say that He is literally a *primary* rather than a secondary cause, an *ultimate* rather than a derived cause, or a being upon which all other things, heaven and earth, ultimately depend for their existence. It is, in short, only to say that God is the creator, in the sense of creation previously explained. Now this, of course, is perfectly consistent with saying that the world is eternal or beginningless. As we have seen, one gives no reason for the existence of a world merely by giving it an age, even if it is supposed to have an infinite age. To use a helpful analogy, we can say that the sun is the first cause of daylight and, for that matter, of the moonlight of the night as well, which means only that daylight and moonlight ultimately depend upon the sun for their existence. The moon, on the other hand, is only a secondary or derivative cause of its light. This light would be no less dependent upon the sun if we affirmed that it had no beginning, for an ageless and beginningless light requires a source no less than an ephemeral one. If we supposed that the sun has always existed, and with it its light, then we would have to say that the sun has always been the first—*i.e.*, the primary or ultimate—cause of its light. Such is precisely the manner in which God should be thought of, and is by theologians often thought of, as the first cause of heaven and earth.

The Ontological Argument
William L. Rowe

It is perhaps best to think of the Ontological Argument not as a single argument but as a family of arguments each member of which begins with a concept of God and, by appealing only to *a priori* principles, endeavors to establish that God actually exists. Within this family of arguments, the most important historically is the argument set forth by

Anselm in the second chapter of his *Proslogium* (a discourse).[1] Indeed, it is fair to say that the Ontological Argument begins with Chapter 2 of St. Anselm's *Proslogium*. In an earlier work, *Monologium* (a soliloquy), Anselm had endeavored to establish the existence and nature of God by weaving together several versions of the Cosmological Argument. In the preface to *Proslogium* Anselm remarks that after the publication of *Monologium* he began to search for a single argument which alone would establish the existence and nature of God. After much strenuous but unsuccessful effort, he reports that he sought to put the project out of his mind in order to turn to more fruitful tasks. The idea, however, continued to haunt him until one day the proof he had so strenuously sought became clear to his mind. It is this proof which Anselm sets forth in the second chapter of *Proslogium*.

Basic Concepts

Before setting forth Anselm's argument in step-by-step fashion, it will be useful to introduce a few concepts that will help us understand some of the central ideas which figure in the argument. Suppose we draw a vertical line in our imagination and imagine that on the left side of our line are all the things which exist, while on the right side of the line are all the things which don't exist. We might then set about to make a list of some of the things on both sides of our imaginary line, a list we might start as follows:

Things Which Exist	Things Which Don't Exist
The Empire State Building	The Fountain of Youth
Dogs	Unicorns
The Planet Mars	The Abominable Snowman

Now, each of the things (or sort of things) listed thus far has the following feature: it logically might have been on the other side of the line. The Fountain of Youth, for example, is on the right side of the line but *logically* there is no absurdity in the idea that it might have been on the left side of the line. Similarly, although dogs do exist, we surely can imagine without logical absurdity that they might not have existed, that they might have been on the right side of the line. Let's then record this feature of the things thus far listed by introducing the idea of a *contingent thing* as a thing that logically might have been on the other side of the line from the side it actually is on. The planet Mars and the abominable snowman are contingent things even though the former happens to exist and the latter does not.

Suppose we add to our list by writing down the phrase "the object which is completely round and completely square at the same time" on the right side of our line. The round square, however, unlike the other things thus far listed on the right side of our line, is something that *logically could not* have been on the left side of the line. Noting this, let's introduce the idea of an *impossible thing* as a thing that is on the right side of the line and logically could not have been on the left side of the line.

Looking again at our list, the question arises as to whether there is anything on the left side of our imaginary line which is such that, unlike the things thus far listed on the left side, it *logically could not* have been on the right side of the line. At this point we don't have to answer this question. But it is useful to have a concept to apply to any such things should there be any. Accordingly, let's introduce the notion of a *necessary thing* as a thing that is on the left side of our imaginary line and logically could not have been on the right side of the line.

Finally, we may introduce the idea of a *possible thing* as any thing that is either on the left side of our imaginary line or logically might have been on the left side of the line. Possible things, then, will be all those things that are not impossible things—that is, all those things that are either contingent or necessary. If there are no necessary things then all possible things will be contingent and all contingent things will be possible. If there is a necessary thing, however, then there will be a possible thing which is not contingent.

Armed with the concepts just explained we can now proceed to clarify certain important distinctions and ideas in Anselm's thought. The first of these is his distinction between *existence in the understanding* and *existence in reality*. Anselm's notion of existence in reality is the same as our notion of existence, that is, being on the left side of our imaginary line. Since the Fountain of Youth is on the right side of the line it does not exist in reality. The things which exist are, to use Anselm's phrase, the things which exist in reality. Anselm's notion of existence in the understanding, however, is not the same as any idea we normally employ. But what Anselm means by "existence in the understanding" is not particularly mysterious. When we think of a certain thing, say the Fountain of Youth, then that thing, in Anselm's view, exists in the understanding. So some of the things on both sides of our imaginary line exist in the understanding, but only those on the left side of our line exist in reality. Are there any things that don't exist in the understanding? Undoubtedly there are. For there are things, both existing and non-existing, of which we have not really thought. Now suppose I assert that the Fountain of Youth does not exist. Since to meaningfully deny the existence of something, I must have that thing in mind; it follows on Anselm's view that whenever someone asserts that some thing does not exist, that thing does exist in the understanding.[2] So in asserting that the Fountain of Youth does not exist I imply that the Fountain of Youth does exist in the understanding. And in asserting that it doesn't exist, I have asserted (on Anselm's view) that it doesn't exist in reality. This means that my simple assertion that the Fountain of Youth doesn't exist amounts to the somewhat more complex claim that the Fountain of Youth exists in the understanding but does not exist in reality—in short, that the Fountain of Youth exists *only* in the understanding.

In view of the above we can now understand why Anselm insists that anyone who hears of God, thinks about God, or even denies the existence of God is, nevertheless, committed to the view that God exists in the understanding. Also, we can understand why Anselm treats what he calls the fool's claim that God does not exist as the claim that God exists *only* in the understanding—that is, that God exists in the understanding but does not exist in reality.

In *Monologium* Anselm sought to prove that among those beings which do exist, there is one which is the greatest, highest, and the best. But in *Proslogium* he undertakes to prove that among those things which exist, there is one which is not just the greatest among existing beings, but is such that no conceivable being is greater. We need to distinguish these two ideas: (i) a being than which no existing being is greater, and (ii) a being than which *no conceivable being* is greater. If the only things in existence were a stone, a frog, and a human being, the last of these, the human being, would satisfy our first idea but not our second—for we can conceive of a being (an angel or God) greater than a human. Anselm's idea of God, as he expresses it in *Proslogium*, II, is the same as (ii) above; it is the idea of "a being than which nothing greater can be conceived." It will, I think, facilitate our understanding of Anselm's argument if we make two slight changes in the way he has expressed his idea of God. For his phrase I shall substitute the following. "*the* being than which none greater *is possible.*"[3] What this idea says is that if a certain being is God, then no *possible* being can be greater than it; or conversely, if a certain being is such that it is even *possible* for there to be a being greater than it then that being is not God. What Anselm proposes to prove, then, is that the being than which none greater is possible exists in reality. If he proves that he will have proved that God, as he conceives of him, exists in reality.

But what does Anselm mean by *greatness*? Is a building, for example, greater than a man? Anselm remarks: "But I do not mean physically great, as a material object is great, but that which, the greater it is, is the better or the more worthy—wisdom, for instance."[4] Contrast wisdom with size. Anselm is saying that wisdom is something that contributes to the greatness of a thing. If a thing comes to have more wisdom than it did before (given that its other characteristics remain the same), then that thing has become a greater, better, more worthy thing than it was. Wisdom, Anselm is saying, is a great-making quality. But the mere fact that something increases in size (physical greatness) does not make that thing a better thing than it was before. So size, unlike wisdom, is not a great-making quality. By *greater than* Anselm means *better than*, *superior to*, or *more worthy than*, and he believes that some characteristics, like wisdom and moral goodness, are great-making characteristics in that anything which has them is a *better thing* than it would be (other characteristics of it remaining the same) were it to lack them.

We come now to what we may call the *key idea* in Anselm's Ontological Argument. Anselm believes that existence *in reality is a great-making quality*. How are we to understand this idea? Does Anselm mean that anything that exists is a greater thing than anything that doesn't? Although he doesn't ask or answer this question, it is perhaps reasonable to believe that Anselm did not mean this. For when he discusses wisdom as a great-making quality he is careful not to say that any wise thing is better than any unwise thing—for he recognizes that a just but unwise person might be a better being than a wise but unjust person.[5] I suggest that what Anselm means is that anything that doesn't exist but might have existed (is on the right side of our line but might have been on the left) would have been a greater thing than it is if it had existed (if it had been on the left side of our line). He is not comparing two different things (one existing and one not existing) and saying that the first is therefore greater than the second. Rather he is talking about one and the same thing and pointing out that if it does not exist but might have existed then *it* would have been a greater thing if it had existed. Using Anselm's distinction between existence in the understanding and existence in reality, we may express the key idea in Anselm's reasoning as follows: If something exists only in the understanding, but might have existed in reality, then it might have been greater than it is. Since the Fountain of Youth, for example, exists only in the understanding but, unlike the round square, might have existed in reality, it follows by Anselm's principle that the Fountain of Youth might have been a greater thing than it is.

Developing Anselm's Ontological Argument

Having looked at some of the important ideas at work in Anselm's Onto-logical Argument, we can now consider its step-by-step development. In presenting Anselm's argument I shall use the term *God* in place of the longer phrase "the being than which none greater is possible"—wher-ever the term *God* appears we are to think of it as simply an abbrevia-tion of the longer phrase.

> 1. God exists in the understanding.

As we've noted, anyone who hears of the being than which none greater is possible is, in Anselm's view, committed to premise 1.

> 2. God might have existed in reality (God is a possible being).

Anselm, I think, assumes the truth of premise 2 without making it explicit in his reasoning. By asserting 2, I don't mean to imply that God does not exist in reality. All that is meant is that, unlike the round square, God is a possible being.

> 3. If something exists only in the understanding and might have existed in reality, then it might have been greater than it is.

As we noted earlier that is the key idea in Anselm's Ontological Argu-ment. It is intended as a general principle true of anything.

Steps 1–3 constitute the basic premises of Anselm's Ontological Argu-ment. From these three items it follows, so Anselm believes, that God exists in reality. But how does Anselm propose to convince us that if we accept 1–3 we are committed by the rules of logic to accept his conclu-sion that God exists in reality? Anselm's procedure is to offer what is called a *reductio ad absurdum* proof of his conclusion. Instead of show-ing directly that the existence of God follows from 1–3, Anselm invites us to suppose that God does not exist (that is, that the conclusion he wants to establish is false) and then shows how this supposition when conjoined with 1–3 leads to an absurd result, a result that couldn't possibly be true because it is contradictory. In short, with the help of 1–3 Anselm shows that the supposition that God does not exist reduces to an absur-dity. Since the supposition that God does not exist leads to an absur-dity, that supposition must be rejected in favor of the conclusion that God does exist.

Does Anselm succeed in reducing that fool's belief that God does not exist to an absurdity? The best way to answer this question is to follow the steps of his argument.

4. Suppose God exists only in the understanding.

This supposition, as we saw earlier, is Anselm's way of expressing the fool's belief that God does not exist.

5. God might have been greater than he is. (2, 4, and 3)[6]

Step 5 follows from steps 2, 4, and 3. Since 3, if true, is true of anything, it will be true of God. Step 3, therefore, implies that if God exists only in the understanding and might have existed in reality, then God might have been greater than he is. If so, then given 2 and 4, 5 must be true. For what 3 says when applied to God is that given 2 and 4 it follows that 5.

6. God is a being than which a greater is possible. (5)

Surely if God is such that he logically might have been greater, then he is such than which a greater is possible.

We're now in a position to appreciate Anselm's *reductio* argument. He has shown us that if we accept 1–4 we must accept 6. But 6 is unacceptable; it is the absurdity Anselm was after. For replacing *God* in step 6 with the longer phrase it abbreviates, we see that 6 amounts to the absurd assertion:

7. The being than which none greater is possible is a being than which a greater is possible.

Now since 1–4 have led us to an obviously false conclusion, if we accept Anselm's basic premises 1–3 as true, 4, the supposition that God exists only in the understanding, must be rejected as false. Thus we have shown that

8. It is false that God exists only in the understanding.

But since premise 1 tells us that God does exist in the understanding, and 8 tells us that God does not exist only there, we may infer that

9. God exists in reality as well as in the understanding. (1, 8)

What are we to say of this argument? Most of the philosophers who have considered the argument have rejected it because of a basic conviction that from the logical analysis of a certain idea or concept we can never determine that there exists in reality anything answering to that idea or concept. We may examine and analyze, for example, the idea of an elephant or the idea of a unicorn, but it is only by our experience of the world that we can determine that there exist things answering to our first idea and not to the second. Anselm, however, believes that the concept of God is utterly unique—from an analysis of this concept he believes that it can be determined that there exists in reality a being which answers to it. Moreover, he presents us with an argument to show that it can be done in the case of the idea of God. We can, of course, simply reject his argument on the grounds that it violates the basic conviction noted above. Many critics, however, have sought to prove more directly that Anselm's argument is a bad argument and to point out the particular step in his argument that is mistaken. In what follows we shall examine the three major objections that have been advanced by the argument's critics.

Gaunilo's Criticism

The first major criticism was advanced by a contemporary of Anselm's, a monk named Gaunilo, who wrote a response entitled "On Behalf of the Fool."[7] Gaunilo sought to prove that Anselm's reasoning is mistaken by applying it to things other than God, things which we know don't exist. He took as his example the island than which none greater is possible. No such island really exists. But, argues Gaunilo, if Anselm's reasoning were correct we could show that such an island really does exist. For since it is greater to exist than not to exist, if the island than which none greater is possible doesn't exist then it is an island than which a greater is possible. But it is impossible for the island than which none greater is possible to be an island than which a greater is possible. Therefore, the island than which none greater is possible must exist. About this argument Gaunilo's remarks:

> If a man should try to prove to me by such reasoning that this island truly exists, and that its existence should no longer be doubted, either I should believe that he was jesting, or I know not which I ought to regard as the greater fool: myself, supposing I should allow this proof; or him, if he should suppose that he had established with any certainty the existence of this island.[8]

Gaunilo's strategy is clear. By using the very same reasoning Anselm employs in his argument, we can prove the existence of things we know don't exist. Therefore Anselm's reasoning in his proof of the existence of God must be mistaken. In his reply to Gaunilo, Anselm insisted that his reasoning applies only to God and cannot be used to establish the existence of things other than God. Unfortunately, Anselm did not explain just why his reasoning cannot be applied to things like Gaunilo's island.

In defense of Anselm against Gaunilo's objection, we should note that the objection supposes that Gaunilo's island is a possible thing. But this requires us to believe that some finite, limited thing (an island) might have unlimited perfections. And it is not at all clear that this is possible. Try to think, for example, of a hockey player than which none greater is possible. How fast would he have to skate? How many goals would such a player have to score in a game? How fast would he have to shoot the puck? Could this player ever fall down, be checked, or receive a penalty? Although the phrase "The hockey player than which none greater is possible" seems meaningful, as soon as we try to get a clear idea of what such a being would be like, we discover that we can't form a coherent idea of it at all. For we are being invited to think of some limited, finite thing—a hockey player or an island—and then to think of it as exhibiting unlimited, infinite perfections. Perhaps, then, since Anselm's reasoning applies only to possible things, Anselm can reject its application to Gaunilo's island on the grounds that the island than which none greater is possible is, like the round square, an impossible thing.

Kant's Criticism

By far the most famous objection to the Ontological Argument was set forth by Immanuel Kant in the eighteenth century. According to this objection, the mistake in the argument is its claim, implicit in premise 3, that existence is a quality or predicate that adds to the greatness of a thing. There are two parts to this claim: (1) existence is a quality or predicate, and (2) existence, like wisdom and unlike physical size, is a great-making quality or predicate. Someone might accept (1) but object to (2). The objection made famous by Kant, however, is directed at (1). According to this objection, existence is not a predicate at all. Therefore, since in its third premise Anselm's argument implies that existence is a predicate, the argument must be rejected.

What is meant by the philosophical doctrine that existence is not a predicate? The central point in this doctrine concerns what we do when we ascribe a certain quality or predicate to something, as, for example, when we say of a woman next door that she is intelligent, six feet tall, or thin. In each case we seem to assert or presuppose that there *exists* a woman next door and then go on to ascribe to her a certain predicate—

"intelligent," "six feet tall," or "thin." And what is claimed by many proponents of the doctrine that existence is not a predicate is that this is a *general feature* of predication. They hold that when we ascribe a quality or predicate to anything, we assert or presuppose that the thing exists and then ascribe the predicate to it. Now, if this is so, then it's clear that existence cannot be a predicate which we may ascribe to or deny of something. For if it were predicate, then when we assert of some thing that it exists we would be asserting or presupposing that it exists and then going on to predicate existence of it. For example, if existence were a predicate, then in asserting "Tigers exist" we would be asserting or presupposing that tigers exist and then going on to predicate existence of them. Furthermore, in asserting "Dragons do not exist" we would be asserting or presupposing, if existence were a predicate, that dragons do exist and then going on to deny that existence attaches to them. In short, if existence were a predicate, the affirmative existential statement "Tigers exist" would be a redundancy, and the negative existential statement "Dragons do not exist" would be contradictory. But clearly "Tigers exist" is not a redundancy and "Dragons do not exist" is true and, therefore, not contradictory. What this shows, according to the proponents of Kant's objection, is that existence is not a genuine predicate.

According to the proponents of the above objection, what we are asserting when we assert that tigers exist and that dragons do not is not that certain things (tigers) have and certain other things (dragons) do not have a peculiar predicate, *existence*, rather, we are saying something about the *concept* of a tiger and the *concept* of a dragon. In the first case we are saying that the concept of a tiger applies to something in the world; in the second case we are saying that the concept of a dragon does not apply to anything in the world.

Although this objection to the Ontological Argument has been widely accepted, it is doubtful that it provides us with a conclusive refutation of the argument. It may be true that existence is not a predicate, that in asserting the existence of something we are not ascribing a certain predicate or attribute to that thing. But the arguments presented for this view seem to rest on mistaken or incomplete claims about the nature of predication. For example, the argument which we stated earlier rests on the claim that when we ascribe a predicate to anything we assert or presuppose that that thing exists. But this claim appears to be mistaken. In asserting that Dr. Doolittle is an animal lover I seem to be ascribing the predicate *animal lover* to Dr. Doolittle, but in doing so I certainly am not asserting or presupposing that Dr. Doolittle actually exists. Dr. Doolittle doesn't exist, but it is, nevertheless, true that he is an animal lover. The plain fact is that we can talk about and ascribe predicates to many things which do not and never did exist. Merlin, for example, no less than Houdini, was a magician although Houdini existed but Merlin did not. If, as these examples suggest, the claim that whenever we ascribe a predicate to something we assert or presuppose that the thing exists is a false claim, then we will need a better argument for the doctrine that existence is not a predicate. There is some question, however, whether anyone has succeeded in giving a really conclusive argument for this doctrine.[9]

A Third Criticism

A third objection against the Ontological Argument calls into question the premise that God might have existed in reality (God is a possible being). As we saw, this premise claims that "the being than which none greater is possible" is not an impossible object. But is this true? Consider the series of positive integers—1, 2, 3, 4 and so on. We know that any integer in this series, no matter how large, is such that a larger than it is possible. Therefore, "the positive integer than which none larger is possible" is an impossible object. Perhaps this is also true of "the being than which none greater is possible." That is, perhaps no matter how great a being may be, it is possible for there to be a being greater than it. If this were so, then, like "the integer than which none larger is possible," Anselm's God would not be a possible object. The mere fact that there are degrees of greatness, however, does not entitle us to conclude that Anselm's God is like "the integer than which none larger is possible." There are, for example, degrees of size in angles—one angle is larger than another—but it is not true that no matter how large an angle is it is possible for there to be an angle larger than it. It is logically impossible for an angle to exceed four right angles. The notion of an angle, unlike the notion of a positive integer, implies a degree of size beyond which it is impossible to go. Is Anselm's God like a largest integer, and therefore impossible, or like a largest angle, and therefore possible? Some philosophers have argued that Anselm's God is impossible.[10] But the arguments for this conclusion are not very compelling. Perhaps, then, this objection is best construed not as proving that Anselm's God is impossible, but as raising the question whether any of us is in a position to know that "the being than which none greater is possible" is a possible object. For Anselm's argument cannot be a successful proof of the existence of God unless its premises are not just true, but are really *known* to be true. Therefore, if we don't know that Anselm's God is a possible object, then his argument cannot prove the existence of God to us, cannot enable us to know that God exists.

A Final Critique

We've had a look at both Anselm's argument and the three major objections philosophers have raised against it. In this final section I want to present a somewhat different critique of the argument, a critique suggested by the basic conviction noted earlier: namely, that from the mere logical analysis of a certain idea or concept, we can never determine that there exists in reality anything answering to that idea or concept.

Suppose someone comes to us and says:

> I propose to define the term *God* as *an existing, wholly perfect being*. Now since it can't be true that an existing, wholly perfect being does not exist, it can't be true that God, as I've defined him, does not exist. Therefore, God must exist.

This argument appears to be a very simple Ontological Argument. It begins with a particular idea or concept of God and ends by concluding that God, so conceived, must exist. What can we say in response? We might start by objecting to this definition of *God*, claiming (1) that only predicates can be used to define a term, and (2) that existence is not a predicate. But suppose our friend is not impressed by this response—either because he thinks no one has fully explained what a predicate is or proved that existence isn't one, or because he thinks that anyone can define a word in whatever way he pleases. Can we allow our friend to define the word *God* in any way he pleases and still hope to show that it will not follow from that definition that there actually exists something to which this concept of God applies? I think we can. Let's first invite him, however, to consider some concepts other than this peculiar concept of God.

Earlier we noted that the term *magician* may be applied both to Houdini and Merlin, even though the former existed whereas the latter did not. Noting that our friend has used *existing* as part of this definition of *God*, suppose we agree with him that we can define a word in any way we please, and, accordingly, introduce the following words with the following definitions:

> A *magican* is defined as *an existing magician*.
>
> A *magico* is defined as *a nonexisting magician*.

Here we have introduced two words and used *existing or nonexisting* in their definitions. Now something of interest follows from the fact that *existing* is part of our definition of a magican. For while it's true that Merlin was a *magician* it isn't true that Merlin was a *magican*. And something of interest follows from our including *nonexisting* in the definition of a magico. For while it's true that Houdini was a *magician* it isn't true that Houdini was a *magico*. Houdini was a *magician* and a *magican*, but not a *magico*, whereas Merlin was a *magician* and a *magico*, but not a *magican*.

What we have just seen is that introducing *existing* or *nonexisting* into the definition of a concept has a very important implication. If we introduce *existing* into the definition of a concept, it follows that no nonexisting thing can exemplify that concept. And if we introduce *nonexisting* into the definition of a concept, it follows that no existing thing can exemplify that concept. No nonexisting thing can be a *magican* and no existing thing can be a *magico*.

But must some existing thing exemplify the concept *magican*? No! From the fact that *existing* is included in the definition of *magican* it does not follow that some existing thing is a *magican*—all that follows is that no nonexisting thing is a *magican*. If there were no magicians in existence there would be nothing to which the term *magican* would apply. This being so, it clearly does not follow merely from our definition of *magican* that some existing thing is a *magican*. Only if magicians exist will it be true that some existing thing is a *magican*.

We are now in a position to help our friend see that, from the mere fact that *God* is defined as an existing, wholly perfect being, it will not follow that some existing being is God. Something of interest does follow from his definition: namely, that no nonexisting being can be God. But whether some existing thing is God will depend entirely on whether some existing thing is a wholly perfect being. If no wholly perfect being exists there will be nothing to which this concept of God can apply. This being so, it clearly does not follow merely from this definition of *God* that some existing thing is God. Only if a wholly perfect being exists will it be true that God, as our friend conceives of him, exists.

Implications for Anselm's Argument

The implications of these considerations for Anselm's ingenious argument can now be traced. Anselm conceives of God as a being than which none greater is possible. He then claims that existence is a great-making quality, something that has it greater than it would have been had it lacked existence. Clearly then, no nonexisting thing can exemplify Anselm's concept of God. For if we suppose that some nonexisting thing exemplifies Anselm's concept of God and also suppose that that nonexisting thing might have existed in reality (is a possible thing), then we are supposing that that nonexisting thing (1) might have been a greater thing, and (2) is, nevertheless, a thing than which a greater is not possible. Thus far Anslem's reasoning is, I believe, impeccable. But what follows from it? All that follows from it is that no nonexisting thing can be God (as Anselm conceives of God). All that follows is that given Anselm's concept of God, the proposition "Some nonexisting thing is God" cannot be true. But, as we saw earlier, this is also the case with the proposition "Some nonexisting thing is a magican." What remains to be shown is that some existing thing exemplifies Anselm's concept of God. What really does follow from his reasoning is that the only thing that logically could exemplify his concept of God is something which actually exists. And this conclusion is not without interest. But from the mere fact that nothing but an existing thing could exemplify Anselm's concept of God, it does not follow that some existing thing actually does exemplify his concept of God—no more than it follows from the mere fact that no nonexisting thing can be a magican that some existing thing is a magican.[11]

There is, however, one major difficulty in this critique of Anselm's argument. This difficulty arises when we take into account Anselm's implicit claim that God is a possible thing. To see just what this difficulty is, let's return to the idea of a possible thing. A possible thing, we determined, is any thing that either is on the left side of our imaginary line or logically might have been on the left side of the line. Possible things, then, will be all those things that, unlike the round square, are not impossible things. Suppose we concede to Anselm that God, as he conceives of him, is a possible thing. Now, of course, the mere knowledge that something is a possible thing doesn't enable us to conclude that that thing is an existing thing. For many possible things, like the Fountain of Youth, do not exist. But if something is a possible thing, then it is either an existing thing or a nonexisting thing. The set of possible things can be exhaustively divided into those possible things which actually exist and those possible things which do not exist. Therefore, if Anselm's God is a possible thing, it is either an existing thing or a nonexisting thing. We have concluded, however, that no nonexisting thing can be Anselm's God; therefore, it seems we must conclude with Anselm that some actually existing thing does exemplify his concept of God.

To see the solution to this major difficulty we need to return to an earlier example. Let's consider again the idea of a magican, an existing magi-

cian. It so happens that some magicians have existed—Houdini, The
Great Blackstone, and others. But, of course, it might have been otherwise. Suppose, for the moment, that no magicians have ever existed.
The concept "magician" would still have application, for it would still be
true that Merlin was a magician. But what about the concept of a "magican"? Would any possible object be picked out by that concept? No! For
no nonexisting thing could exemplify the concept "magican." And on the
supposition that no magicians ever existed, no existing thing would exemplify the concept "magican."[12] We then would have a coherent concept
"magican" which would not be exemplified by any possible object at
all. For if all the possible objects which are magicians are nonexisting
things, none of them would be a magican and, since no possible objects
which exist are magicians, none of them would be a magican. We then
would have a coherent, consistent concept "magican," which in fact is
not exemplified by any possible object at all. Put in this way, our result
seems paradoxical. For we are inclined to think that only contradictory
concepts like "the round square" are not exemplified by any possible
things. The truth is, however, that when *existing* is included in or implied
by a certain concept, it may be the case that no possible object does in
fact exemplify that concept. For no possible object that doesn't exist
will exemplify a concept like "magican" in which *existing* is included;
and if there are no existing things which exemplify the other features
included in the concept—for example, "being a magician" in the case
of the concept "magican"—then no possible object that exists will exemplify the concept. Put in its simplest terms, if we ask whether any possible thing is a magican, the answer will depend entirely on whether
any existing thing is a magician. If no existing things are magicians, then
no possible things are magicans. Some possible object is a magican just
in case some actually existing thing is a magician.[13]

Applying these considerations to Anselm's argument we can find the
solution to our major difficulty. Given Anselm's concept of God and his
principle that existence is a great-making quality, it really does follow
that the only thing that logically could exemplify his concept of God is
something which actually exists. But, we argued, it doesn't follow from
these considerations alone that God actually exists, that some existing
thing exemplifies Anselm's concept of God. The difficulty we fell into,
however, is that when we add the premise that God is a possible thing,
that some possible object exemplifies his concept of God, it really does
follow that God actually exists, that some actually existing thing exemplifies Anselm's concept of God. For if some possible object exemplifies

his concept of God, that object is either an existing thing or a nonexisting thing. But since no nonexisting thing could exemplify Anselm's concept of God, it follows that the possible object which exemplifies his concept of God must be a possible object that actually exists. Therefore, given (1) Anselm's concept of God, (2) his principle that existence is a great-making quality, and (3) the premise that God, as conceived by Anselm, is a possible thing, it really does follow that Anselm's God actually exists.

A Too Generous Grant

I think we now can see that in granting Anselm the premise that God is a possible thing we have granted far more than we intended to grant. All we thought we were granting is that Anselm's concept of God, unlike the concept of a round square, is not contradictory or incoherent. But without realizing it we were in fact granting much more than this, as became apparent when we considered the idea of a "magican." There is nothing contradictory in the idea of a magican, an existing magician. But in asserting that a magican is a possible thing, we are, as we saw, directly implying that some existing thing is a magician. For if no existing thing is a magician, the concept of a magican will apply to no possible object whatever. The same point holds with respect to Anselm's God. Since Anselm's concept of God logically cannot apply to some nonexisting thing, the only possible objects to which it could apply are possible objects which actually exist. Therefore, in granting that Anselm's God is a possible thing, we are granting far more than that his idea of God isn't incoherent or contradictory. Suppose, for example, that every existing being has some defect which it might not have had. Without realizing it, we were denying this when we granted that Anselm's God is a possible being. For if every existing being has a defect it might not have had, then every existing being might have been greater. But if every existing being might have been greater, then Anselm's concept of God will apply to no possible object whatever. Therefore, if we allow Anselm his concept of God and his principle that existence is a great-making quality, then in granting that God, as Anselm conceives of him, is a possible being, we will be granting much more than that his concept of God is not contradictory. We will be granting, for example, that some existing thing is as perfect as it can be. For the plain fact is that Anselm's God is a possible thing only if some *existing* thing is as perfect as it can be.

Our final critique of Anselm's argument is simply this. In granting that Anselm's God is a possible thing, we are in fact granting that Anselm's God actually exists. But since the purpose of the argument is to prove to us that Anselm's God exists, we cannot be asked to grant as a premise a statement which is virtually equivalent to the conclusion that is to be proved. Anselm's concept of God may be coherent and his principle that existence is a great-making quality may be true. But all that follows from this is that no nonexisting thing can be Anselm's God. If we add to all of this the premise that God is a possible thing it will follow that God actually exists. But the additional premise claims more than that Anselm's concept of God isn't incoherent or contradictory. It amounts to the assertion that some existing being is supremely great. And since this is, in part, the point the argument endeavors to prove, the argument begs the question: it assumes the point it is supposed to prove.

If the above critique is correct, Anselm's argument fails as a proof of the existence of God. This is not to say, however, that the argument isn't a work of genius. Perhaps no other argument in the history of thought has raised so many basic philosophical questions and stimulated so much hard thought. Even if it fails as a proof of the existence of God, it will remain as one of the high achievements of the human intellect.

Notes

1. Some philosophers believe that Anselm sets forth a different and more cogent argument in chapter 3 of his *Proslogium*. For this viewpoint see Charles Hartshorne, *Anselm's Discovery* (La Salle, Ill: Open Court Publishing Co., 1965) and Norman Malcolm, "Anselm's Ontological Arguments," *The Philosophical Review* LXIX, no. 1 (1960), pp. 41–62. For an illuminating account both of Anselm's intensions in *Proslogium*, II and III, and of recent interpretations of Anselm, see Arthur C. McGill's essay "Recent Discussions of Anselm's Argument" in *The Many-faced Argument*, ed. John Hick and Arthur C. McGill (New York: The Macmillan Co., 1967), pp. 33–110.

2. Anselm does allow that someone may assert the sentence "God does not exist" without having in his understanding the object or idea for which the word *God* stands. See St. Anselm, *Proslogium*, IV, in *Saint Anselm: Basic Writings*, tr. Sidney N. Deane (La Salle, Ill.: Open Court Publishing Co., 1962). But when a person does understand the object for which a word stands, then when he uses that word in a sentence denying the existence of that object, he must have that object in his understanding. It is doubtful, however, that Anselm thought that incoherent or contradictory expressions like *round square* stand for objects which may exist in the understanding.

3. Anselm speaks of *a being* rather than *the being* than which none greater can be conceived. His argument is easier to present if we express his idea of God in terms of *the being*. Secondly, to avoid the psychological connotations of *can be conceived* I have substituted *possible*.

4. St. Anselm, *Monologium*, II, in *Saint Anselm: Basic Writings*.

5. St. Anselm, *Monologium*, XV, in *Saint Anselm: Basic Writings*.

6. The numbers in parentheses refer to the earlier steps in the argument from which the present step is derived.

7. Gaunilo's brief essay, Anselm's reply, and several of Anselm's major works, as translated by Sidney N. Deane, are collected together in *Saint Anselm: Basic Writings*.

8. Deane, *Saint Anselm: Basic Writings*, p. 151.

9. Perhaps the most sophisticated presentation of the objection that existence is not a predicate is William P. Alston's "The Ontological Argument Revisited," *The Philosophical Review* LXIX (1960), pp. 452–74.

10. See, for example, C. D. Broad's discussion of the Ontological Argument in *Religion, Philosophy, and Psychical Research: Selected Essays* (New York: Humanities Press, 1969).

11. An argument along the lines just presented may be found in J. Shaffer's illuminating essay, "Existence, Predication and the Ontological Argument," *Mind* LXXI (1962), pp. 307–25.

12. I am indebted to Professor William Wainwright for bringing this point to my attention.

13. In the language of possible worlds, we can say that some object x is a *magican* in a possible world w, provided (i) x is a magician in w, and (ii) x is a magician in whatever world happens to be actual. For more on this matter, as well as a critical discussion of some other versions of the Ontological Argument, see my essay "Modal Versions of the Ontological Argument" in Louis Pojman, ed., *Philosophy of Religion: An Anthology*, 3rd ed. (Belmont, Calif.: Wadsworth, 1998).

Pascal's Wager

George Schlesinger

Introduction

Pascal's wager is as a rule more easily appreciated than any other argument in support of religious belief. After all, the locution (which represents the essential structure of the wager), "I have nothing to lose and everything to gain by doing such and such," is a common one and readily understood by everybody.

At the same time the wager has been the target of a number of objections. I propose here to deal with three of these; two are widely known, whereas the third is of very recent origin. Finally, I also point out that the gravest objection to the wager requires a reply that is based on an argument indispensable in the context of nearly all other theistic proofs. Hence, that argument may well be regarded as the most central theistic argument.

The first objection has no great logical force but carries considerable psychological weight. It is unique insofar that it contends not so much that the wager violates the rules of sound thinking and is therefore invalid but rather that it is repugnant, and in a religious context, it is especially unseemly. The second objection contends that even if the argument were logically impeccable it would lead nowhere. The last one, surprisingly enough, claims that it is overly effective, so much so that it should not at all matter what an individual does or fails to do, because he or she by virtue of the wager in a maximally advantageous position anyway with regard to eternal salvation.

The Wager and Greed

It is common knowledge that many well-intentioned individuals reject the wager for reasons that do not require much philosophical sophistication. They find it mercenary. They believe it appeals to the scheming, calculating self and are thus repelled by it. Without delving deep into theological issues, it has seemed to many that applying betting rules, relevant to moneymaking ventures, to a supposedly infinitely more exalted subject to lure skeptics by appealing to their grasping instincts offends religious proprieties.

People have found absurd the very notion that there may be any comparison between the seeker of a transcendent goal in life and a patron of a gambling house. We need not assume that greed as such is held generally in our highly acquisitive society in intense contempt. In the present context, however, it appears to offend the very spirit of what one is supposed to pursue. The essence of religion is generally perceived as the conviction that all profane, self-seeking ambitions are incompatible with the quest for piety. The religious seeker is not one to be mired in self indulgent pursuits but passionately devotes oneself to much nobler and more ultimate concerns.

Now of course Pascal was quite explicit in saying that the skeptic's wagering on God is no more than a first step, and those who take no further steps will have achieved nothing. However, his advice to the wagerer is to start behaving as one would if one actually believed, because Pascal believed that such conduct is likely to lead to a truly dedicated life in the service of God. By starting to observe the rituals of religion, associating with pious persons, and studying the sacred literature, individuals are likely to transform their sentiments and feelings and eventually acquire genuine belief.

Yet Pascal's reply has failed to satisfy many of his critics. If grasping is incompatible with the spirit of religion, then it is not to be used as a vehicle with which to reach any destination. Noble ends are debased when pursued by ignoble means.

Pascal's supporters at this stage are usually inclined to offer distinctions between means that do not and means that do justify their end. I believe a more important point should be made: we are free to assume that no objective is ever hallowed enough that it should be impermissible to reach it by anything but impeccable means.

First, a relatively simple point about the offensiveness of greed. Suppose there is a person of an extraordinarily high income who gives away almost all his money to charity, retaining only what is necessary for bare existence. Furthermore, this individual does not seek the gratitude of the beneficiaries of these donations nor the admiration of the community. In fact, this person always makes every possible effort to ensure that no one should be charged with selfishness and greed: he is surely aware of his almost unparalleled, heroic, moral accomplishments. Evidently therefore he is a highly greedy individual; what he apparently craves is not material possessions nor the prestige accorded for outstanding philanthropy but the ability to relish the knowledge that he has outdone practically everyone in his contempt for stinginess, in his indifference for fame and praise, and the ability to enjoy the deep satisfaction of having been able to reach the pinnacle of otherdirectedness and the heights of noble magnanimity free of the slightest taint of petty self-regard.

Clearly, if we were to take this line, then we would be forced to conclude that every act which fulfills some wish is greedy and selfish and no freely willed act would ever be free of sin. Thus, the sensible thing to say is that the pursuit of a quest is deplorable when it brings harm either to others or to oneself in the sense that it debases the questing individual (which Pascal calls "poisonous pleasures") who could instead strive for more refined, higher order, life-enhancing pleasures.

Now the pleasure that Pascal holds up before his "calculating clients" is of the most exalted kind, one that is simply inaccessible to an individual who has not spent life passionately serving the Master of the Universe and thereby developing and perfecting one's soul, without which one lacks the capacity to partake in the transmundane bliss available to the select few. Only the suitably goomed soul, when released from its earthly fetters, will bask in the radiance of the Divine presence and delight in the adoring communion with a loving God. If craving for such an end is a manifestation of greed, then it is the manifestation of a noble greed that is to be acclaimed. Therefore, only if one were to assume that the ultimate reward of the righteous is the satisfaction of some cruder yearnings could one charge a follower of Pascal with trying to enkindle our unseemly mercenary motives.

Practice and Belief

However, a more important point needs to be made as well. The essence of true religion is not the intellectual assent to a set of propositions nor is it the verbal profession of certain beliefs. It is a full commitment and devotion, having one's heart and soul virtually consumed by a deep reverence and love of God. Maimonides wrote:

> What is the proper love of God? It is the love of the Lord with a great and very strong love so that one's soul shall be tied to the love of the Lord, and one should be continually enraptured by it, like a lovesick individual. . . . [1]

The immediate question one is bound to ask is, how does one achieve such a state of mind? Belief might be obtained through compelling arguments, or credible evidence, but surely exaltation or love is not an epistemic universal and cannot be planted into one's heart by the methodological rules of knowledge acquisition.

A very brief answer has been hinted at by the sagacious Hillel, who, as the famous story goes, was approached by someone demanding to be taught the whole Law while standing on one foot. Hillel agreed and informed the man that the single sentence, "Whatever is hateful to you do not do it to your fellow-human," contains the essence of all there is to be learned.[2] Hillel's fascinating precis of the Law raises many problems. One of them is in Leviticus 19:18: it says, "You all love your fellow-human as yourself."

Why did he believe it necessary to change the wording of the Scriptures? This particular question may have a simple answer, namely, Hillel realized that one cannot be commanded to have certain sentiments; I could be ordered to act or to refrain from acting in a certain way but not to love someone I happen to dislike. Thus, to reach the stage that the Scripture prescribes where one actually loves other human beings, we have to begin with the kind of behavior that is always associated with such a sentiment, that is, our practical conduct toward our fellow humans should be like that toward our own self: never actually do anything injurious to their interests. Desirable behavior is assumed to generate eventually desirable feelings.

Hillel's insight should be applied in the context of one's relation to God as well. The twelfth-century poet-philosopher Judah Halevi was quite explicit on this point, "Man can reach God only by doing His commands" (*Cuzari*, 2.46). Good thoughts, on their own, are too fleeting and insubstantial, and physical acts are concrete; when one has trained oneself to act in accordance with the dictates of religion and actual behavior closely resembles the behavior of those who posses truly deep religious sentiments, then one has provided oneself with the proper grounds on which fervent love for the Divine may grow. The theory behind this view may be compared with what today is called "behavior modification." This kind of therapy is based on the belief that it is possible to induce feelings of aversion to what is harmful and a natural desire for what is beneficial through adopting certain patterns of behavior. On the more extreme version of this view (as held by Halevi), it is not merely possible but essential to begin one's journey toward authentic theism by looking on the practices mandated by religion as the proper first step toward genuine piety. On this view, the wagerer who starts out satisfying the demands of faith before having acquired actual belief is not merely doing what is calculating and mercenary nor even that which is merely commendable but is engaged in what is absolutely indispensable for reaching the noble objective that is sought.

Are There Infinitely Many Equally Viable Hypotheses?

The second, oft-repeated objection is a relatively powerful, clearly articulated objection, known as the "many-gods objection." Pascal has been charged with making the unwarranted assumption that the problem facing the agnostic is confined to the question of which of two options to choose. In reality, however, in addition to the God of the theist, there are any number of other possible ones as well. How is the wagerer to assess the relative benefits associated with betting on Osiris, Baal, Dagon, Zeus, or Blodenwedd? Pascal provides no argument to guide us to the right deity, worshiping whom one is most likely to secure oneself eternal salvation.

Before attempting to advance any reply, I should point out that though the objection is, as already mentioned, a serious one, we find in the literature several versions, depicting a far more threatening portrayal of the difficulty than it is in reality. Richard Gale, for example, sees the following devastating consequences of the many-gods objection:

> . . . from the fact that it is logically possible that God exists it does not follow that the product of the probability of his existence and an infinite number is infinite. In a fair lottery with a denumerable infinity of tickets, for each ticket it is true that it is logically possible that it will win, but the probability of its doing so is infinitesimal and the product of an infinitesimal and an infinite number is itself infinitesimal. Thus the expected gain of buying a ticket is not infinite but infinitesimal. There is at least a denumerable infinity of logically possible deities . . . and thus betting on any one of them the expected gain is zero according to this argument.[3]

The opponents of the wager have had the tendency to magnify the gravity of the problem by overcalculating the number of alternatives available for the religious seeker and hence depicting Pascal's counsel as quite hopelessly arbitrary. For example, J. L. Mackie, who lists a number of possible deities that seem to have escaped Pascal's notice, also mentions,

> . . . that there might be a god who looked with more favor on honest doubters or atheists who, in Hume's words, proportioned their belief to the evidence, than on mercenary manipulators of their own understanding. Indeed, this would follow from the ascription to God of moral goodness in any sense we can understand.[4]

Also fairly often heard is the argument that among the infinitely many possible deities, we must not overlook one who grants eternal reward to those who firmly deny the existence of a theistic God and punishes all those who believe in him.

Richard Gale goes even further, suggesting that

> there is the logically possible deity who rewards with infinite felicity all and only those who believe in him and step on only one sidewalk crack

in the course of their life, as well as the two-crack deity, the three-crack deity, and so on ad infinitum.[5]

There are several lines one may adopt to meet this kind of objection. One may be based on the realization that Pascal is addressing individuals who, though they may be hardened in their disbelief, do have a notion of what genuine religion is about. In other words, though they deny its truth, they acknowledge its meaningfulness and understand that it is based on a highly optimistic view of human potential and of the sublime possible level of existence it postulates. It is a necessary presupposition of the wager that one understands that the notion of "genuine religion" is conceptually associated with a number of other exalted notions, and those people whom Pascal addresses are to be assumed to have a basic grasp of the sublime concerns of its devout practitioners. Divine worship in an authentic sense (as distinct from a pagan sense, where one is trying to propitiate the supernatural powers on whose whims one's fate depends) is in no way to be likened to a commercial transaction. Whatever the probability of the existence of an afterlife worth seeking with all one's might is, it is certainly not to be viewed as a place to which one may be admitted after one has paid the amount demanded by its Divine Proprietor. "The service of God is not intended for God's perfection; it is intended for our own perfection," says Maimonides. On this view, an individual who has devoted his or her life to Divine service has nurtured and refined his or her soul, rendering it capable of receiving and finding felicity in the celestial radiance available for those prepared to absorb it. In brief, the wagerer is supposed to appreciate that in the context of theism, highly involved systems of theologies have been developed over the centuries, theologies that have an internal coherence and consist of many propositions with an appeal to the intellect as well as to the nobler, human sentiments.

Nothing of this sort exists in the context of, say, the sidewalk deity. It is difficult to conceive a reason why one should come to love such a being or why one should desire to be in its proximity. Of course, one might claim that without any rhyme or reason it capriciously rewards those who obey its arbitrary demands. Still, a Pascalian would insist that because a good portion of theistic belief is in harmony with natural, noble aspirations and is embedded in highly developed theology, it has to be ascribed a considerably higher probability than those with little appeal to the human mind and heart.

Thus, we are permitted to assert the following: if we were to agree that different deities have different probabilities, then even if there are infinitely many candidates for the office of the Master of the Universe, it does not follow that each has zero probability. One may, if one wants to, ascribe a finite value to the probability of the existence of each one of them and yet obtain a sum total of all these (which is the value of the probability of the infinite disjunction of "Zeus exists OR Baal exists OR etc."), an amount that does not exceed one. This should be the case if the various finite probabilities are members of a convergent series, for instance, the sum of the series $1/2 + 1/4 + 1/8 + \ldots$ never actually reaches one. This should be sufficient to lay to rest Gale's fear that if "there is at least a denumerable infinity of logically possible deities . . . [then] betting on any one of them the expected gain is zero."

The Criterion for Betting When the Expected Utilities Are Infinite

I submit a crucial point, one that is contrary to what numerous philosophers hold, namely, that when each possible outcome carries an infinite expected value, it is rational to bet on the outcome most probable to occur. Are there solid grounds for my hypothesis? Let me first point out that grounds are provided for this view by common sense (which in itself would not be sufficient to establish my point). Anyone wishing to verify this experimentally may consider the following two cases, A and B:

A = Of the billions of people alive at the present moment, one and only one is going to enjoy eternal salvation, whereas the rest vanish into nothingness after completing their lives upon this earth. A truly randomizing device is going to determine the identity of the single lucky individual.

B = Of the billions of people alive at the present moment, one and only one is going to vanish into nothingness after completing one's existence upon this planet; the rest are going to enjoy eternal salvation. A truly randomizing device is going to determine the identity of the one unlucky individual.

Now, without offering preliminary explanations, ask any number of individuals (and you may include among them some mathematicians) which case they would prefer to obtain? If my experience is reliable to any degree, rarely if ever does anybody argue: although if B is true than I am a billion times more likely to be among the blessed, this is quite irrelevant; the expected utilities are equal and therefore it makes no difference which is true.

Now let us look at a truly compelling argument. In cases where the mathematical expectations are infinite, the criterion for choosing the outcome to bet on is its probability. In all betting situations the sum I am charged to participate I am charged with certainty, whereas the prize I may receive is uncertain. Fairness demands that I be compensated through being charged less than the value of the prize and proportionately so, that is, the lower the probability of winning, the less I should be charged. Thus, it is obvious that the same set of rules cannot apply in case the prize is infinite, as in other cases. Justice cannot demand that the cost for being permitted to bet should equal the expected utilities, because then the fair cost should be infinite. But that is absurd: why should I definitely pay an infinite amount for a less than certain chance of winning back the same amount? It is evident therefore that the situation demands that a different principle must be guiding a wagerer faced with the problem of which of the various outcomes—each associated with infinite utilities—to choose. Because neither expected utilities nor the magnitude of the prize can serve as one's criterion, by elimination it should be reasonable to be guided by the value of the probability: wager on the outcome that is most likely to materialize.

Deities with Different Degrees of Plausibility

Let us consider a number of possible solutions to the many-gods problem. First, it is reasonable that a scrupulously just deity who ensures that each person's celestial reward is in direct proportion to the amount of energy and time invested throughout one's earthly life to the refinement of one's soul so as to increase its susceptibility to that reward, is considerably more probable than a fancy-bred capricious power whose awards are not in any obvious way related to earning, meriting, or the enhanced quality of the receptivity or atonement of the worshipper. Thus, we regard it at least fairly plausible that a deity may exist who does not hand out compensation or reimbursement for the trouble his adherents have gone through in serving him but who is so exalted that it seems reasonable to assume that the highest form of felicity is to center one's life around him. The most important task is to do everything in one's power to adjust and attune one's soul so that it has the capacity of fully resonating with the celestial radiance in which it will be submerged. A mere century or two ago theists did not recoil from using such locutions and were unembarrassed by what today may strike some as inflated grandiloquence. Thus we find the eighteenth-century poet and theologian M. H. Luzatto making (in his widely studied *Mesilat Yesharim*) the brief statement, because he regarded the matter too obvious to require elaboration, "Man came into the world only to achieve nearness to God." Surely such a view is bound to permeate every act and every thought of its adherent; it is part of an inclusive outlook on life and belongs to an extensive system of interconnected propositions.

Furthermore, in the context of the sublime god of the theist, many found it not unreasonable to view life's many trials and tribulations as instruments of soul-making or in any case as means to an end that may surpass our understanding. On the other hand, when referring to deities devoid of the various glorious Divine attributes, it seems more natural to speak like Gloucester: "As flies to wanton boys, are we to the gods. They kill us for their sport."

Thus, the hypothesis is that "a God of faithfulness and without inquity [one who is] just and right . . ." (Deuternomy 31:4), who therefore can be a source of emulation and inspiration and whose attributes altogether resonate with our nobler sentiments, makes a great deal of sense and it is therefore reasonable to ascribe a higher probability to his existence than to an unprincipled, arbitrarily acting, wanton god. And if this is conceded, then it should also seem sensible to hold that the greater those sublime properties, the greater the likelihood the one exemplifying them exists. Hence, the being greater than which is inconceivable, who possesses them to a maximum degree, is to be regarded more probable than any other deity.

Simplicity

The Cambridge statistician H. Jeffreys has shown in the 1920s that whenever we have a finite set of experimental results there are indefinitely many hypotheses that satisfy each result. The only way to select the hypothesis to be adopted is by following the principle of simplicity: of all the equally well-confirmed hypotheses, select the one that is simpler than all the others. It is crucial to realize that Jeffreys does not refer to the simplicity of structure of the systems involved or the simplicity of use and so on; he refers solely to descriptive simplicity and says that among the various expressions that represent the law, we are to adopt the one consisting of the minimal number of terms. It is also worth nothing that Jeffreys' is not a prescriptive but a descriptive principle: scientists have followed it for hundreds of years without explicitly being aware of it, simply because it has never been articulated before that of the indefinitely many alternative hypotheses present in all cases.

Many people willingly concede that the rules of rational reasoning are invariant with subject matter. Consequently, after Pascal has convinced us that we should wager on some supernatural power, we are confronted with the problem of which of the many possible such powers to adopt.

In the absence of any facts to assist us, it stands to reason that we should have to use Jeffreys' principle. It is fairly easy to see that the theistic hypothesis is the simplest in the sense specified by Jeffreys.

It is the simplest because it is the only hypothesis that may be expressed with the use of a single predicate: to describe the God of the theist all that is needed is that he is an absolutely perfect being. By contrast, a statement positing the existence of any deity less than absolutely perfect will be relatively complex. For example, though there is a large body of ancient Greek literature concerning Zeus, there are still many aspects of Zeus's character that remain unknown to us. We know for instance that he was sometimes asleep, but we have no idea how many hours of sleep he needed and what effect sleeplessness had on him. We also know that he ate and drank, but not how much or whether he occasionally overgorged himself or how long he could go without any food at all, and so on.

The Principle of Sufficient Reason

Finally, I should advance an argument based on the principle of sufficient reason why the wagerer should go for the being greater than which is not conceivable. Before doing so, I believe it is necessary to defend the principle because many contemporary philosophers deny its validity. J. L. Mackie was speaking for a large number of adherents of empiricism when he said, "There is no sufficient reason to regard the principle of sufficient reason to be valid."[6] Levelheaded empiricists are not supposed to subscribe to *a priori* principles. For this reason, the majority of contemporary writers strongly object to ascribing equal probabilities on the basis of the principle of indifference, which is no more than a variation on the principle of sufficient reason (PSR).

It seems to me that these objections are based on a serious misconception. They are mostly based on the refusal to acknowledge that "experience is mute" and that it is necessary to assume some unconfirmed principles before we are able to surmise what it tells us. As a matter of fact, no empirically confirmed statement can be found anywhere that did not rely on the PSR. The following illustrate the wide range of its application.

1. It is universally held that there is, for instance, overwhelming inductive evidence that the melting point of gold is 1,064 degrees Celsius. It is common knowledge, however, that it is illegitimate to argue inductively from biased sample classes. Thus, the question arises why do physicists feel entitled to maintain that 1,064 degrees Celsius is likely

to remain the melting point of gold when all their evidence is based on a biased sample class: all the samples of gold hitherto melted occurred in a universe in which the density of matter (which keeps decreasing) was higher, the scaling factor (which is constantly increasing) was lower, and the velocity of the universe's expansion (which according to some cosmologists keeps decreasing all the time) was higher than at this crucial moment.

The answer is not that we have no grounds on which to assume that these changes are relevant to the melting point of any metal. In the past, serious biases turned out to be factors we never suspected before of having relevance: all swans were thought to be white, and the fact that the sample class on which this conclusion was based included only non-Australian swans had not occurred to anyone to be of concern. The presumed law that matter cannot be destroyed was based on the failure of every conceivable attempt to do so; you may break, grind, melt, boil and evaporate, or burn to ashes any lump of matter without succeeding to alter the amount in which it continues to exist. The fact that no relevant observations have been made under exceedingly large pressures and temperatures, the kind of which prevail at the center of the sun where matter does diminish through part of it transforming into energy, did not seem to constitute a source of worry. Indeed, at the pre-twentieth century knowledge of what processes take place on the subatomic level, there was no reason why one should suspect that pressure and temperature had relevance to the issue of the conservation of matter. Similarly, our knowledge of physics may be still too deficient for us to be able to see why the scaling factor of the universe should influence the melting point of anything.

The correct answer has to be that we are aware of the possibility of having arrived at our conclusion through the sue of a biased sample class, and consequently there are two lines of action available to us. One is to make no predictions at all. This, of course, would imply the complete paralysis of the scientific enterprise, which we should want to resist if at all possible. The alternative is to make use of the principle of sufficient reason. In the particular context of the melting point of gold, we then proceed in the following manner: in the past the melting point of gold has always been observed to be 1,064 degrees Celsius. In the future it may be different. However, there is no good reason to believe that the melting point will be higher than it will be lower or vice versa. Thus, as long as not proven otherwise, we make the unique prediction that it will be neither higher nor lower but will continue to remain the same as in the past.

2. It was mentioned before that whenever we have a finite set of experimental results there are indefinitely many hypotheses that satisfy

each result and that the accepted practice is to select the hypothesis to be adopted by following the principle of simplicity: of all the equally well-confirmed hypotheses, select the one that is simpler than all the others. What justification is there for this rule? One is the PSR. Should we suggest that some alternative hypothesis be adopted it will immediately be asked: what reason is there to make this particular choice? Why not select a simpler or a more complicated hypothesis? However, the simplest hypothesis has an edge over all others. It is unique. It is the only one in connection with which it is not possible to ask why not choose a simpler hypothesis. We thus justify our selection on the basis of the chosen hypothesis having a significant feature no other hypothesis has. The most complex hypothesis would also have such a feature except that it does not exist (just as the largest integer does not exist).

3. A strong illustration of how compelling the PSR is is the fact that even mathematicians have found it useful as a principle of plausible reasoning. L. C. Larson in his highly influential book poses the problem: of all the rectangles which can be inscribed in a given circle, which has greatest area? Larson suggests,

> The principle of insufficient reason leads us to suspect that the rectangle of maximum area that can be inscribed in a circle is a square.

He then goes on to give a rigorous proof of his conjecture without regarding it as necessary to elaborate how precisely the principle led him to it. It is reasonable to assume that what Larson had in mind was that if it were suggested that the sought-after rectangle was one with length x and width $x + n$ then of course the rectangle with length $x + n$ and width x must also have the maximum area. And if there are indeed two rectangles with maximum area, then, of course, there are infinitely many couples that might possibly be the ones we are after. There is, however, one rectangle that is unique in the sense that it has no counterpart: the rectangle with equal length and width. It "stands to reason" that this is the privileged figure we are after.

4. Some 2,400 years ago Democritus argued,

> that there are infinite worlds, hypothesizing that the void is infinite; for why would this part of the void be filled by a world, but that part not? So, if there is a world in one part of the void, then also in all the void. So, since the void is infinite, the worlds will be infinite too.

Democritus's hypothesis would warrant detailed study; here I can point out only first of all that his "worlds," unlike what we mean when refer-

444 • Part Six   Does God Exist?

ring to various possible worlds, are not necessarily causally separated from one another and also that he thought of the actual world as having tiny size as compared with what we believe it to be. Yet his hypothesis may be said to have survived to this very day in the form of the far-reaching cosmological principle. It asserts that the universe is the same (i.e., the distribution of galaxies, stars, and planets) everywhere in space (apart from irregularities of a local nature), or that the universe is homogeneous.

The reasoning behind Democritus's hypothesis is once more based on the PSR. Suppose it were suggested that there exist some finite number n worlds. We would be at loss to offer a reason why it was not a number less or greater than n. However, if n is infinite then a unique reason can be given why it is not larger than n.

This last example is of special significance as it shows that the PSR, which is customarily associated with the name of Leibniz, who indeed applied it to numerous issues, was known and made use of two thousand years before him. It provides therefore further evidence of the universal appeal of the PSR and its central role in all our conceptual schemes.

Suppose someone subscribed to a religion that was based on the belief that the deity governing the universe was very benevolent but not absolutely so, possessing merely 95 percent of full benevolence. (It is not important for our purposes to describe how we compute the numerical degree of benevolence.) We might then ask an adherent of this religion: why not ascribe to your deity 96 percent of 94 percent benevolence? No reasonable answer seems available. On the other hand, the theist, when faced with a similar inquiry, might appeal to the PSR. If one settles for any number, like 95 percent, no sufficient reason seems to be available: why not have more or why not have less. However, a reason may be offered for 100 percent benevolence: it is of a unique magnitude, as it is impossible to have more. Suppose someone were to ask: but by the same principle you might as well ascribe 0 percent benevolence and explain your doing so by saying that having less than it is impossible? To this, as mentioned before, the theist reply would be that such a being is not a fit deity to worship, and thus one is to ascribe considerably lower probability to its existence.

Why Wager At All?

We are now in the position to reply to an ingenious objection raised by Antony Duff. Duff points out that the wager works regardless how small the probability, as long as its value is not zero, and that one is going to

be the recipient of infinite salvation. If so, he argues, it is quite superfluous that I should follow Pascal's advice and begin acting religiously
and make every effort to acquire faith, because,

> . . . suppose I take no steps to make it more likely that I will come to
> believe in God. There must be some probability, however small, that I will
> nonetheless come to believe in Him . . . and that probability is enough
> to generate an infinite expected value for my actions.[7]

Now we have at least two answers to Duff's objection. The briefer answer
is to recall the idea advanced previously that it is untenable to maintain that because of the infinitude of the reward it makes no difference
how probable is its acquisition. We are instead to assume that it is important to try and increase the probability of obtaining the prospective prize.

The second answer would be based on the principle that a rational
wagerer will always want to bet on the outcome associated with the highest expected utilities. But is it possible to gain anything more than infinite salvation? The answer is, in an appropriate sense, yes! An infinitely
long string, for example, may be increased in width, or in mass per
unit length, and so on. Similarly, eternal life, which of course is infinitely
long and cannot be increased in length, may vary in the degree of its
depth, intensity, exquisiteness, and so on, during every moment for the
eternal duration of that felicitous state. Once we are prepared to entertain the possibility of an afterlife, we are likely to find it reasonable to
go along with the traditional view that the magnificence of posthumous
reward varies directly with the quality and the portion of the time at
one's disposal as well as the magnitude of the exertion invested in acts
of piety.

It should also be recalled that as soon as an individual embarks on
the road that offers the best chance to lead to the acquisition of genuine religious faith, one is already set on the path of the righteous and
is already engaged in the service of God. Clearly, therefore, one who
acts upon Pascal's call at once, rather than waiting for the not entirely
improbable inspiration to light unassisted upon him at some later time,
places oneself in a far more favorable position with respect to the amount
of time spent on the purification of one's soul. Thus, even if we conceded that in the context of eternal salvation the value of probability
plays no role, the individual following Duff's advice would engage in a
conduct associated with a prize of lower quality and thus with lower
expected utilities.

A Common Feature to Almost All Theistic Arguments

One of the most commonly cited theistic proofs is the Argument from Design. It is based on the wonders of nature we see around us that are unlikely to be, or perhaps unthinkable that they should be, the results of blind forces. Now even if we regard the argument absolutely compelling, it establishes at most—as we pointed out by Hume—that there exists a creator who is many hundreds times more powerful and intelligent than ourselves. But such a creator's power and intelligence may still fall infinitely short of Omnipotence and Omniscience. About benevolence the argument says even less, and the same goes for Omnipresence or Immutability.

Another famous argument is the Cosmological Argument. It shares all the weaknesses just mentioned in connection with the Argument from Design. Indeed, it should be obvious that all other arguments in support of theism (with the exception of the Ontological Argument, of which only a few would claim to have achieved full clarity) face the many gods objection.

Thus, an individual making use of any of numerous known arguments for the existence of God can get no further than to conclude that there exists some supernatural power and intelligence behind the material universe. That individual is thus facing the need to choose among the various candidates who may fulfill this function.

It seems reasonable to conjecture that whatever is deemed the best justification for the theist's choice in one context is also likely to be so in other contexts as well. Therefore, the most acceptable reply to the many-gods objection may well be regarded as an argument of wide application and thus of central importance in the context of theistic arguments in general.

One of the striking features of Pascal's wager is surely the fact that he most often cited stumbling block it runs into has been the many-gods objection, whereas in the context of theistic arguments, I venture to suggest that this may be read as an indication of the unique strength of the wager. The reason why the many-gods objection has been raised less frequently in the context of the wager was because skeptics felt able to clip the wings of a putative argument at the very initial stages, before it could get off the ground and thus prevent even the conclusion that some supernatural being is to be assumed.

Thus, the Argument from Design is nipped in the bud by insisting that the universe does not exhibit any signs of design; the Cosmological Argument has been cut short because of its alleged, unwarranted, basic assumption that there can be no uncaused contingent particulars. On the other hand, it seems that no serious defect could be discovered in Pascal's wager before it reached the relatively advanced stage of establishing the reasonableness of assuming the existence of some transmundane force.

Notes

1. *Mishneh Torah*, Hilkhot Teshuvah, x.
2. *Shabbat*, 31b.
3. *On the Nature and Existence of God* (Cambridge, 1991), p. 350.
4. *The Miracle of Theism* (Oxford, 1982), p. 203.
5. Gale, op. cit., p. 350.
6. "Three Steps Toward Absolutism," *Space, Time and Causality*, ed. R. Swinburne (Dordrecht, 1981), p. 6.
7. "Pascal's Wager and Infinite Utilities," *Analysis* 46 (1986): 107.

Molecular Machines: Experimental Support for the Design Inference
Michael J. Behe

Darwinism's Prosperity

Within a short time after Charles Darwin published *The Origin of Species* the explanatory power of the theory of evolution was recognized by the great majority of biologists. The hypothesis readily resolved the problems of homologous resemblance, rudimentary organs, species abundance, extinction, and biogeography. The rival theory of the time, which posited creation of species by a supernatural being, appeared to most reasonable minds to be much less plausible, since it would have a putative Creator attending to details that seemed to be beneath His dignity.

As time went on the theory of evolution obliterated the rival theory of creation, and virtually all working scientists studied the biological world from a Darwinian perspective. Most educated people now lived in a world where the wonder and diversity of the biological kingdom were produced by the simple, elegant principle of natural selection.

However, in science a successful theory is not necessarily a correct theory. In the course of history there have also been other theories which achieved the triumph that Darwinism achieved, which brought many experimental and observational facts into a coherent framework, and which appealed to people's intuitions about how the world should work. Those theories also promised to explain much of the universe with a few simple principles. But, by the large, those other theories are now dead.

A good example of this is the replacement of Newton's mechanical view of the universe by Einstein's relativistic universe. Although Newton's model accounted for the results of many experiments in his time, it failed to explain aspects of gravitation. Einstein solved that problem and others by completely rethinking the structure of the universe.

Similarly, Darwin's theory of evolution prospered by explaining much of the data of his time and the first half of the 20th century, but my article will show that Darwinism had been unable to account for phenomena uncovered by the efforts of modern biochemistry during the second half of this century. I will do this by emphasizing the fact that life at its most fundamental level is irreducible complex and that such complexity is incompatible with undirected evolution.

A Series of Eyes

How do we see?

In the 19th century the anatomy of the eye was known in great detail and the sophisticated mechanisms it employs to deliver an accurate picture of the outside world astounded everyone who was familiar with them. Scientists of the 19th century correctly observed that if a person were so unfortunate as to be missing one of the eye's many integrated features, such as the lens, or iris, or ocular muscles, the inevitable result would be a severe loss of vision or outright blindness. Thus it was concluded that the eye could only function if it were nearly intact.

As Charles Darwin was considering possible objections to his theory of evolution by natural selection in *The Origin of Species* he discussed the problem of the eye in a section of the book appropriately entitled "Organs of extreme perfection and complication." He realized that if in one generation an organ of the complexity of the eye suddenly appeared, the event would be tantamount to a miracle. Somehow, for Darwinian evolution to be believable, the difficulty that the public had in envisioning the gradual formation of complex organs had to be removed.

Darwin succeeded brilliantly, not by actually describing a real pathway that evolution might have used in constructing the eye, but rather by pointing to a variety of animals that were known to have eyes of various constructions, ranging from a simple light sensitive spot to the complex vertebrate camera eye, and suggesting that the evolution of the human eye might have involved similar organs as intermediates.

But the question remains, how do we see? Although Darwin was able to persuade much of the world that a modern eye could be produced gradually from a much simpler structure, he did not even attempt to explain how the simple light sensitive spot that was his starting point actually worked. When discussing the eye Darwin dismissed the question of its ultimate mechanism by stating: "How a nerve comes to be sensitive to light hardly concerns us more than how life itself originated."

He had an excellent reason for declining to answer the question: 19th century science had not progressed to the point where the matter could even be approached. The question of how the eye works—that is, what happens when a photon of light first impinges on the retina—simply could not be answered at that time. As a matter of fact, no question about the underlying mechanism of life could be answered at that time. How do animal muscles cause movement? How does photosynthesis work? How is energy extracted from food? How does the body fight infection? All such questions were unanswerable.

The Calvin and Hobbes Approach

Now, it appears to be a characteristic of the human mind that when it lacks understanding of a process, then it seems easy to imagine simple steps leading from nonfunction to function. A happy example of this is seen in the popular comic strip *Calvin and Hobbes.* Little boy Calvin is always having adventures in the company of his tiger Hobbes by jumping in a box and traveling back in time, or grabbing a toy ray gun and "transmogrifying" himself into various animal shapes, or again using a box as a duplicator and making copies of himself to deal with worldly powers such as his mom and his teachers. A small child such as Calvin finds it easy to imagine that a box just might be able to fly like an airplane (or something), because Calvin doesn't know how airplanes work.

A good example from the biological world of complex changes appearing to be simple is the belief in spontaneous generation. One of the chief proponents of the theory of spontaneous generation during the middle of the 19th century was Ernst Haeckel, a great admirer of Darwin and an eager popularizer of Darwin's theory. From the limited view of cells that 19th century microscopes provided, Haeckel believed that a cell was a "simple little lump of albuminous combination of carbon," not much different from a piece of microscopic Jell-O®. Thus it seemed to Haeckel that such simple life could easily be produced from inanimate material.

In 1859, the year of the publication of *The Origin of Species*, an exploratory vessel, the H.M.S. Cyclops, dredged up some curious-looking mud from the sea bottom. Eventually Haeckel came to observe the mud and thought that it closely resembled some cells he had seen under a microscope. Excitedly he brought this to the attention of no less a personage than Thomas Henry Huxley, Darwin's great friend and defender, who observed the mud for himself. Huxley, too, became convinced that it was Urschleim (that is, protoplasm), the progenitor of life itself, and Huxley named the mud *Bathybius haeckelii* after the eminent proponent of abiogenesis.

The mud failed to grow. In later years, with the development of new biochemical techniques and improved microscopes, the complexity of the cell was revealed. The "simple lumps" were shown to contain thousands of different types of organic molecules, proteins, and nucleic acids, many discrete subcellular structures, specialized compartments for specialized processes, and an extremely complicated architecture. Looking back from the perspective of our time, the episode of *Bathybius haeckelii* seems silly or downright embarrassing, but it shouldn't. Haeckel and Huxley were behaving naturally, like Calvin: since they were unaware of the complexity of cells, they found it easy to believe that cells could originate from simple mud.

Throughout history there have been many other examples, similar to that of Haeckel, Huxley, and the cell, where a key piece of a particular scientific puzzle was beyond the understanding of the age. In science there is even a whimsical term for a machine or structure or process that does something, but the actual mechanism by which it accomplishes its task is unknown: it is called a "black box." In Darwin's time all of biology was a black box: not only the cell, or the eye, or digestion, or immunity, but every biological structure and function because, ultimately, no one could explain how biological processes occurred.

Biology has progressed tremendously due to the model that Darwin put forth. But the black boxes Darwin accepted are now being opened, and our view of the world is again being shaken.

Take our modern understanding of proteins, for example.

Proteins

In order to understand the molecular basis of life it is necessary to understand how things called "proteins" work. Proteins are the machinery of living tissue that build the structures and carry out the chemical reactions necessary for life. For example, the first of many steps necessary for the conversion of sugar to biologically-usable forms of energy is carried out by a protein called hexokinase. Skin is made in large measure of a protein called collagen. When light impinges on your retina it interacts first with a protein called rhodopsin. A typical cell contains thousands and thousands of different types of proteins to perform the many tasks necessary for life, much like a carpenter's workshop might contain many different kinds of tools for various carpentry tasks.

What do these versatile tools look like? The basic structure of proteins is quite simple: they are formed by hooking together in a chain discrete subunits called amino acids. Although the protein chain can consist of anywhere from about 50 to about 1,000 amino acid links, each position can only contain one of 20 different amino acids. In this they are much like words: words can come in various lengths but they are made up from a discrete set of 26 letters.

Now, a protein in a cell does not float around like a floppy chain; rather, it folds up into a very precise structure which can be quite different for different types of proteins. Two different amino acid sequences—two different proteins—can be folded to structures as specific and different from each other as a three-eights inch wrench and a jigsaw. And like the household tools, if the shape of the proteins is significantly warped then they fail to do their jobs.

The Eyesight of Man

In general, biological processes on the molecular level are performed by networks of proteins, each member of which carries out a particular task in a chain.

Let us return to the question, how do we see? Although to Darwin the primary event of vision was a black box, through the efforts of many biochemists an answer to the question of sight is at hand. The answer involves a long chain of steps that begin when light strikes the retina and a photon is absorbed by an organic molecule called 11-cis-retinal, causing it to rearrange itself within picoseconds. This causes a corresponding change to the protein, rhodopsin, which is tightly bound to it, so that it can react with another protein called transducin, which in turn causes a molecule called GDP to be exchanged with a molecule called GTP.

To make a long story short, this exchange begins a long series of further bindings between still more specialized molecular machinery, and scientists now understand a great deal about the system of gateways, pumps, ion channels, critical concentrations, and attenuated signals that result in a current to finally be transmitted down the optic nerve to the brain, interpreted as vision. Biochemists also understand the many chemical reactions involved in restoring all these changed or depleted parts to make a new cycle possible.

To Explain Life

Although space doesn't permit me to give the details of the biochemistry of vision here, I have given the steps in my talks. Biochemists know what it means to "explain" vision. They know the level of explanation that biological science eventually must aim for. In order to say that some function is understood, every relevant step in the process must be elucidated. The relevant steps in biological processes occur ultimately at the molecular level, so a satisfactory explanation of a biological phenomenon such as sight, or digestion, or immunity, must include a molecular explanation.

It is no longer sufficient, now that the black box of vision has been opened, for an "evolutionary explanation" of that power to invoke only the anatomical structures of whole eyes, as Darwin did in the 19th century and as most popularizers of evolution continue to do today. Anatomy is, quite simply, irrelevant. So is the fossil record. It does not matter whether or not the fossil record is consistent with evolutionary theory, any more than it mattered in physics that Newton's theory was consistent with everyday experience. The fossil record has nothing to tell us about, say, whether or how the interactions of 11-cis-retinal with rhodopsin, transducin, and phosphodiesterase could have developed, step by step.

"How a nerve comes to be sensitive to light hardly concerns us more than how life itself originated," said Darwin in the 19th century. But both phenomena have attracted the interest of modern biochemistry in the past few decades. The story of the slow paralysis of research of life's origin is quite interesting, but space precludes its retelling here. Suffice it to say that at present the field of origin-of-life studies has dissolved into a cacophony of conflicting models, each unconvincing, seriously incomplete, and incompatible with competing models. In private even most evolutionary biologists will admit that science has no explanation for the beginning of life.

The same problems which beset origin-of-life research also bedevil efforts to show how virtually any complex biochemical system came about. Biochemistry has revealed a molecular world which stoutly resists explanation by the same theory that has long been applied at the level of the whole organism. Neither of Darwin's black boxes—the origin of life or the origin of vision (or other complex biochemical systems)—has been accounted for by his theory.

Irreducible Complexity

In *The Origin of Species* Darwin stated:

> If it could be demonstrated that any complex organ existed which could not possibly have been formed by numerous, successive, slight modifications, my theory would absolutely break down.

A system which meets Darwin's criterion is one which exhibits irreducible complexity. By irreducible complexity I mean a single system which is composed of several interacting parts that contribute to the basic function, and where the removal of any one of the parts causes the system to effectively cease functioning. An irreducibly complex system cannot be produced directly by slight, successive modification of a precursor system, since any precursor to an irreducibly complex system is by definition nonfunctional.

Since natural selection requires a function to select, an irreducibly complex biological system, if there is such a thing, would have to arise as an integrated unit for natural selection to have anything to act on. It is almost universally conceded that such a sudden event would be irreconcilable with the gradualism Darwin envisioned. At this point, however, "irreducibly complex" is just a term, whose power resides mostly in its definition. We must now ask if any real thing is in fact irreducibly complex, and, if so, then are any irreducibly complex things also biological systems?

Consider the humble mousetrap (Figure 1). The mousetraps that my family uses in our home to deal with unwelcome rodents consist of a number of parts. There are: (1) a flat wooden platform to act as a base; (2) a metal hammer, which does the actual job of crushing the little mouse; (3) a wire spring with extended ends to press against the platform and the hammer when the trap is charged; (4) a sensitive catch which

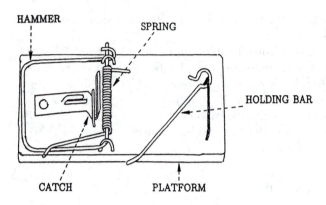

Figure 1
A household mousetrap. The working parts of the trap are labeled. If any of the parts is missing, the trap does not function.

releases when slight pressure is applied; and (5) a metal bar which holds the hammer back when the trap is charged and connects to the catch. There are also assorted staples and screws to hold the system together.

If any one of the components of the mousetrap (the base, hammer, spring, catch, or holding bar) is removed, then the trap does not function. In other words, the simple little mousetrap has no ability to trap a mouse until several separate parts are all assembled.

Because the mousetrap is necessarily composed of several parts, it is irreducibly complex. Thus, irreducibly complex systems exist.

Molecular Machines

Now, are any biochemical systems irreducibly complex? Yes, it turns out that many are.

Earlier we discussed proteins. In many biological structures proteins are simply components of larger molecular machines. Like the picture tube, wires, metal bolts and screws that comprise a television set, many proteins are part of structures that only function when virtually all of the components have been assembled.

A good example of this is a cilium. Cilia are hairlike organelles on the surfaces of many animal and lower plant cells that serve to move fluid over the cell's surface or to "row" single cells through a fluid. In humans, for example, epithelial cells lining the respiratory tract each have about 200 cilia that beat in synchrony to sweep mucus towards the throat for elimination.

A cilium consists of a membrane-coated bundle of fibers called an axoneme. An axoneme contains a ring of 9 double microtubules surrounding two central single microtubules. Each outer doublet consists of a ring of 13 filaments (subfiber A) fused to an assembly of 10 filaments (subfiber B). The filaments of the microtubules are composed of two proteins called alpha and beta tubulin. The 11 microtubules forming an axoneme are held together by three types of connectors: subfibers A are joined to the central microtubules by radial spokes; adjacent outer doublets are joined by linkers that consist of a highly elastic protein called nexin; and the central microtubules are joined by a connecting bridge. Finally, every subfiber A bears two arms, an inner arm and an outer arm, both containing the protein dynein.

But how does a cilium work? Experiments have indicated that ciliary motion results from the chemically-powered "walking" of the dynein arms on one microtubule up the neighboring subfiber B of a second microtubule so that the two microtubules slide past each other (Figure 2). However, the protein cross-links between microtubules in an intact cilium prevent neighboring microtubules from sliding past each other

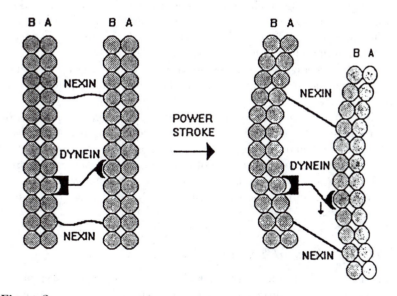

Figure 2

Schematic drawing of part of a cilium. The power stroke of the motor protein dynein, attached to one microtubule, against subfiber B of a neighboring microtubule causes the fibers to slide past each other. The flexible linker protein, nexin, converts the sliding motion to a bending motion.

by more than a short distance. These cross-links, therefore, convert the dynein-induced sliding motion to a bending motion of the entire axoneme.

Now, let us sit back, review the workings of the cilium, and consider what it implies. Cilia are composed of at least a half dozen proteins: alpha-tubulin, beta-tubulin, dynein, nexin, spoke protein, and a central bridge protein. Those combine to perform one task, ciliary motion, and all of these proteins must be present for the cilium to function. If the tubulins are absent, then there are no filaments to slide; if the dynein is missing, then the cilium remains rigid and motionless; if nexin or the other connecting proteins are missing, then the axoneme falls apart when the filaments slide.

What we see in the cilium, then, is not just profound complexity, but it is also irreducible complexity on the molecular scale. Recall that by "irreducible complexity" we mean an apparatus that requires several distinct components for the whole to work. My mousetrap must have a base, hammer, spring, catch, and holding bar, all working together, in order to function. Similarly, the cilium, as it is constituted, must have the sliding filaments, connecting proteins, and motor proteins for function to occur. In the absence of any one of those components, the apparatus is useless.

The components of cilia are single molecules. This means that there are no more black boxes to invoke; the complexity of the cilium is final, fundamental. And just as scientists, when they began to learn the complexities of the cell, realized how silly it was to think that life arose spontaneously in a single step or a few steps from ocean mud, so too we now realize that the complex cilium can not be reached in a single step or a few steps.

But since the complexity of the cilium is irreducible, then it can not have functional precursors. Since the irreducibly complex cilium can not have functional precursors it can not be produced by natural selection, which requires a continuum of function to work. Natural selection is powerless when there is no function to select. We can go further and say that, if the cilium can not be produced by natural selection, then the cilium was designed.

A Non-Mechanical Example

A non-mechanical example of irreducible complexity can be seen in the system that targets proteins for delivery to subcellular compartments. In order to find their way to the compartments where they are needed to perform specialized tasks, certain proteins contain a special amino acid sequence near the beginning called a "signal sequence."

As the proteins are being synthesized by ribosomes, a complex molecular assemblage called the signal recognition particle or SRP, binds to the signal sequence. This causes synthesis of the protein to halt temporarily. During the pause in protein synthesis the SRP is bound by the transmembrane SRP receptor, which causes protein synthesis to resume and which allows passage of the protein into the interior of the endoplasmic reticulum (ER). As the protein passes into the ER the signal sequence is cut off.

For many proteins the ER is just a way station on their travels to their final destinations (Figure 3). Proteins which will end up in a lysosome are enzymatically "tagged" with a carbohydrate residue called mannose-6-phosphate while still in the ER. An area of the ER membrane then begins to concentrate several proteins; one protein, clathrin, forms a sort of geodesic dome called a coated vesicle which buds off from the ER. In the dome there is also a receptor protein which binds to both the clathrin and to the mannose-6-phosphate group of the protein which is being transported. The coated vesicle then leaves the ER, travels through the cytoplasm, and binds to the lysosome through another specific receptor protein. Finally, in a maneuver involving several more proteins, the vesicle fuses with the lysosome and the protein arrives at its destination.

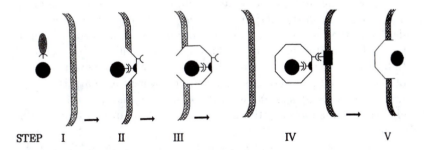

STEP   I   II   III   IV   V

Figure 3
Transport of a protein from the ER to the lysosome. Step I: specific enzyme (gray oval) places a marker on the protein (black sphere). This takes place within the ER, which is delimited by a barrier membrane (cross-hatched bar with ends curving to the left). Step II: The marker is specifically recognized by a receptor protein and the clathrin vesicle (hexagonal shape) begins to form. Step III: The clathrin vesicle is completed and buds off from the ER membrane. Step IV: The clathrin vesicle crosses the cytoplasm and attaches through another specific marker to a receptor protein (black box) on the lysosomal membrane and releases its cargo.

During its travels our protein interacted with dozens of macromolecules to achieve one purpose: its arrival in the lysosome. Virtually all components of the transport system are necessary for the system to operate, and therefore the system is irreducible. And since all of the components of the system are comprised of single or several molecules, there are no black boxes to invoke. The consequences of even a single gap in the transport chain can be seen in the hereditary defect known as I-cell disease. It results from a deficiency of the enzyme that places the mannose-6-phosphate on proteins to be targeted to the lysosomes. I-cell disease is characterized by progressive retardation, skeletal deformities, and early death.

The Study of "Molecular Evolution"

Other examples of irreducible complexity abound, including aspects of protein transport, blood clotting, closed circular DNA, electron transport, the bacterial flagellum, telomeres, photosynthesis, transcription regulation, and much more. Examples of irreducible complexity can be found on virtually every page of a biochemistry textbook. But if these things cannot be explained by Darwinian evolution, how has the scientific community regarded these phenomena of the past forty years?

A good place to look for an answer to that question is in the *Journal of Molecular Evolution. JME* is a journal that was begun specifically to deal with the topic of how evolution occurs on the molecular level. It has high scientific standards, and is edited by prominent figures in the field. In a recent issue of *JME* there were published eleven articles; of these, all eleven were concerned simply with the analysis of protein or DNA sequences. None of the papers discussed detailed models for intermediates in the development of complex biomolecular structures.

In the past ten years *JME* has published 886 papers. Of these, 95 discussed the chemical synthesis of molecules thought to be necessary for the origin of life, 44 proposed mathematical models to improve sequence analysis, 20 concerned the evolutionary implications of current structures and 719 were analyses of protein or polynucleotide sequences. However, there weren't any papers discussing detailed models for intermediates in the development of complex biomolecular structures. This is not a peculiarity of *JME*. No papers are to be found that discuss detailed models for intermediates in the development of complex biomolecular structures in the *Proceedings of the National Academy of Science, Nature,*

Science, the *Journal of Molecular Biology* or, to my knowledge, any journal whatsoever.

Sequence comparisons overwhelmingly dominate the literature of molecular evolution. But sequence comparisons simply can't account for the development of complex biochemical systems any more than Darwin's comparison of simple and complex eyes told him how vision worked. Thus in this area science is mute.

Detection of Design

What's going on? Imagine a room in which a body lies crushed, flat as a pancake. A dozen detectives crawl around, examining the floor with magnifying glasses for any clue to the identity of the perpetrator. In the middle of the room next to the body stands a large, gray elephant. The detectives carefully avoid bumping into the pachyderm's legs as they crawl, and never even glance at it. Over time the detectives get frustrated with their lack of progress but resolutely press on, looking even more closely at the floor. You see, textbooks say detectives must "get their man," so they never consider elephants.

There is an elephant in the roomful of scientists who are trying to explain the development of life. The elephant is labeled "intelligent design." To a person who does not feel obliged to restrict his search to unintelligent causes, the straightforward conclusion is that many biochemical systems were designed. They were designed *not* by the laws of nature, not by chance and necessity. Rather, they were *planned*. The designer knew what the systems would look like when they were completed; the designer took steps to bring the system about. Life on earth at its most fundamental level, in its most critical components, is the product of intelligent activity.

The conclusion of intelligent design flows naturally from the data itself—not from sacred books or sectarian beliefs. Inferring that biochemical systems were designed by an intelligent agent is a humdrum process that requires no new principles of logic or science. It comes simply from the hard work that biochemistry has done over the past forty years, combined with consideration of the way in which we reach conclusions of design every day.

What is "design"? Design is simply the *purposeful arrangement of parts*. The scientific question is how we detect design. This can be done in various ways, but design can most easily be inferred for mechanical objects.

Systems made entirely from natural components can also evince design. For example, suppose you are walking with a friend in the woods. All of a sudden your friend is pulled high in the air and left dangling by his foot from a vine attached to a tree branch.

After cutting him down you reconstruct the trap. You see that the vine was wrapped around the tree branch, and the end pulled tightly down to the ground. It was securely anchored to the ground by a forked branch. The branch was attached to another vine—hidden by leaves—so that, when the trigger-vine was disturbed, it would pull down the forked stick, releasing the spring-vine. The end of the vine formed a loop with a slip-knot to grab an appendage and snap it up into the air. Even though the trap was made completely of natural materials you would quickly conclude that it was the product of intelligent design.

Intelligent design is a good explanation for a number of biochemical systems, but I should insert a word of caution. Intelligent design theory has to be seen in context: it does not try to explain everything. We live in a complex world where lots of different things can happen. When deciding how various rocks came to be shaped the way they are a geologist might consider a whole range of factors: rain, wind, the movement of glaciers, the activity of moss and lichens, volcanic action, nuclear explosions, asteroid impact, or the hand of a sculptor. The shape of one rock might have been determined primarily by one mechanism, the shape of another rock by another mechanism.

Similarly, evolutionary biologists have recognized that a number of factors might have affected the development of life: common descent, natural selection, migration, population size, founder effects (effects that may be due to the limited number of organisms that begin a new species), genetic drift (spread of "neutral," nonselective mutations), gene flow (the incorporation of genes into a population from a separate population), linkage (occurrence of two genes on the same chromosome), and much more. The fact that some biochemical systems were designed by an intelligent agent does not mean that any of the other factors are not operative, common, or important.

Conclusion

It is often said that science must avoid any conclusions which smack of the supernatural. But this seems to me to be both bad logic and bad science. Science is not a game in which arbitrary rules are used to decide what explanations are to be permitted. Rather, it is an effort to make true statements about physical reality. It was only about sixty years ago that the expansion of the universe was first observed. This fact immediately suggested a singular event—that at some time in the distant past the universe began expanding from an extremely small size.

To many people this inference was loaded with overtones of a supernatural event—the creation, the beginning of the universe. The prominent physicist A. S. Eddington probably spoke for many physicists in voicing his disgust with such a notion:

> Philosophically, the notion of an abrupt beginning to the present order of Nature is repugnant to me, as I think it must be to most; and even those who would welcome a proof of the intervention of a Creator will probably consider that a single winding-up at some remote epoch is not really the kind of relation between God and his world that brings satisfaction to the mind.

Nonetheless, the big bang hypothesis was embraced by physics and over the years has proven to be a very fruitful paradigm. The point here is that physics followed the data where it seemed to lead, even though some thought the model gave aid and comfort to religion. In the present day, as biochemistry multiplies examples of fantastically complex molecular systems, systems which discourage even an attempt to explain how they may have arisen, we should take a lesson from physics. The conclusion of design flows naturally from the data; we should not shrink from it; we should embrace it and build on it.

In concluding, it is important to realize that we are not inferring design from what we do not know, but from what we do know. We are not inferring design to account for a black box, but to account for an open box. A man from a primitive culture who sees an automobile might guess that it was powered by the wind or by an antelope hidden under the car, but when he opens up the hood and sees the engine he immediately realizes that it was designed. In the same way biochemistry has opened up the cell to examine what makes it run and we see that it, too, was designed.

It was a shock to the people of the 19th century when they discovered, from observations science had made, that many features of the biological world could be ascribed to the elegant principle of natural selection. It is a shock to us in the twentieth century to discover, from observations science has made, that the fundamental mechanisms of life cannot be ascribed to natural selection, and therefore were designed. But we must deal with our shock as best we can and go on. The theory of undirected evolution is already dead, but the work of science continues.

Born-Again Creationism
Philip Kitcher

The Creationist Reformation

In the beginning, creationists believed that the world was young. But creation "science" was without form and void. A deluge of objections drowned the idea that major kinds of plants and animals had been fashioned a few thousand years ago and been hardly modified since. Then the spirit of piety brooded on the waters and brought forth something new. "Let there be design!" exclaimed the reformers—and lo! there was born-again creationism.

Out in Santee, California, about twenty miles from where I used to live, the old movement, dedicated to the possibility of interpreting *Genesis* literally, continues to ply its wares. Its spokesmen still peddle the familiar fallacies, their misunderstandings of the second law of thermodynamics, their curious views about radiometric dating with apparently revolutionary implications for microphysics, the plundering of debates in evolutionary theory for lines that can be usefully separated from their context, and so forth. But the most prominent creationists on the current intellectual scene are a new species, much smoother and more savvy. Not for them the commitment to a literal interpretation of *Genesis* with all the attendant difficulties. Some of them even veer close to accepting the so-called fact of evolution, the claim, adopted by most scientists within a dozen years of the publication of Darwin's *Origin*, that living things are related and that the history of life has been a process of descent with modification. The sticking point for the born-again creationists, as it was for many late-nineteenth-century thinkers, is the mechanism of evolutionary change. They want to argue that natural selection is inadequate, indeed that no natural process could have produced the diversity of organisms, and thus that there must be some designing agent, who didn't just start the process but who has intervened throughout the history of life.

From the viewpoint of religious fundamentalists the creationist Reformation is something of a cop-out. Yet for many believers, the new movement delivers everything they want—particularly the vision of a personal God who supervises the history of life and nudges it to fulfill His purposes—and even militant evangelicals may come to appreciate the virtues of discretion. Moreover the high priests of the Reformation are clad in academic respectability, Professors of Law at University of California-Berkeley and of Biochemistry at Lehigh, and two of the movement's main cheerleaders are highly respected philosophers who teach at Notre Dame. Creationism is no longer hick, but *chic*.

Why Literalism Failed

In understanding the motivations for, and the shortcomings of, born-again creationism, it's helpful to begin by seeing why the movement had to retreat. The early days of the old-style "creation-science" campaign were highly successfully. Duane Gish, debating champion for the original movement, crafted a brilliant strategy. He threw together a smorgasbord of apparent problems for evolutionary biology, displayed them very quickly before his audiences, and challenged his opponents to respond. At first, the biologists who debated him laboriously offered details to show that one or two of the problems Gish had raised could be solved, but then their time would run out and the audience would leave thinking that most of the objections were unanswerable. In the middle 1980s, however, two important changes took place: first, defenders of evolutionary theory began to take the same care in formulating answers as Gish had given to posing the problems, and there were quick, and elegant, ways of responding to the commonly reiterated challenges; second, and more important, debaters began to fight back, asking how the observable features of the distribution and characteristics of plants and organisms, both those alive and those fossilized, could be rendered compatible with a literal interpretation of *Genesis*.

Suppose that the earth really was created about ten thousand years ago, with the major kinds fashioned then, and diversifying only a little since. How are we to account for the distributions of isotopes in the earth's crust? How are we to explain the regular, worldwide, ordering of the fossils? The only creationist response to the latter question has been to invoke the Noachian deluge: the order is as it is because of the relative positions of the organisms at the time the flood struck. Take this suggestion seriously, and you face some obvious puzzles: sharks and dolphins are found at the same depths, but, of course, the sharks occur much, much lower in the fossil record; pine trees, fir trees, and deciduous trees are mixed in forests around the globe, and yet the deciduous trees are latecomers in the worldwide fossil record. Maybe we should suppose that the oaks and beeches saw the waters rising and outran their evergreen rivals?

Far from being a solution to creationism's problems, the Flood is a real disaster. Consider biogeography. The ark lands on Ararat, say eight thousand years ago, and out pop the animals (let's be kind and forget the plants). We now have eight thousand years for the marsupials to find their way to Australia, crossing several large bodies of water in the process. Perhaps you can imagine a few energetic kangaroos making it—but the wombats? Moreover, creationists think that while the animals were sorting themselves out, there was diversification of species within the "basic kinds"; jackals, coyotes, foxes, and dogs descend, so the story goes, from a common "dog kind." Now despite all the sarcasm that they have lavished on orthodox evolutionary theory's allegedly high rates of speciation, a simple calculation shows that the rates of speciation "creation-science" would require to manage the supposed amount of species diversification are truly breathtaking, orders of magnitude greater than any that have been dreamed of in evolutionary theory. Finally, to touch on just one more problem, creationists have to account for the survival of thousands of parasites that are specific to our species. During the days on the ark, these would have had to be carried by less than ten people. One can only speculate about the degree of ill-health that Noah and his crew must have suffered.

A major difficulty for old-style creationism has always been the fact that very similar anatomical structures are co-opted to different ends in species whose ways of life diverge radically. Moles, bats, whales, and dogs have forelimbs based on the same bone architecture that has to be adapted to their methods of locomotion. Not only is it highly implausible that the common blueprint reflects an especially bright idea from a designer who saw the best ways to fashion a burrowing tool, a wing, a flipper, and a leg, but the obvious explanation is that shared bone structure reflects shared ancestry. That explanation has only been deepened as studies of chromosome banding patterns have revealed common patterns among species evolutionists take to be related, as comparisons of proteins have exposed common sequences of amino acids, and, most recently, as genomic sequencing has shown the affinities in the ordering of bases in the DNA of organisms. Two points are especially noteworthy. First, like the anatomical residues of previously functional structures (such as the rudimentary pelvis found in whales), parts of our junk DNA have an uncanny resemblance to truncated, or mutilated, versions of genes found in other mammals, other vertebrates, or other animals. Second, the genetic kinship even among distantly related organisms is so great that a human sequence was identified as implicated in colon cancer by recognizing its similarity to a gene coding for a DNA repair enzyme in yeast. The evidence for common ancestry is so over-whelming that even the born-again creationist, Michael Behe is moved to admit that it is "fairly convincing" and that he has "no particular rea-son to doubt it" (DBB 5).[1] (Notice that Behe doesn't quite commit him-self here—in fact, to use an example from Richard Dawkins that Behe, and others, have discussed, there's an obvious line to describe Behe's phraseology: METHINKS IT IS A WEASEL.)

Imagine creationists becoming aware, at some level, of this little piece of history, and retreating to the bunker in which they plot strategy. What would they come up with? First, the familiar idea that the best defense is a good offense: they need to return to the tried-and-true, give-'em-hell, Duane Gish fire and brimstone attack on evolutionary theory. Second, they need to expose less to counterattack, and that means giving up on the disastrous "creation model" with all the absurdities that *Genesis*-as-literal-truth brings in its train; better to make biology safe for the cen-tral tenets of religion by talking about a design model so softly focused that nobody can raise nasty questions about parasites on the ark on the wombats' dash for the Antipodes. Third, they should do something to mute the evolutionists' most successful arguments, those that draw on the vast number of cross-species comparisons at all levels to establish com-mon descent; this last is a matter of some delicacy, since too blatant a commitment to descent with modification might seem incompatible with creative design. So the best tactic here is a carefully choreographed waltz—advance a little toward accepting the "fact of evolution" here, back away there; as we shall see, some protagonists have an exquisite mastery of the steps.

Surprise, surprise. Born-again creationism has arrived at just this strategy. I'm going to look at the two most influential versions.

The Hedgehog and the Fox

Isaiah Berlin's famous division that contrasts hedgehogs (people with one big idea) and foxes (people with lots of little ideas) applies not only to thinkers but to creationists as well. The two most prominent figures on the neo-creo scene are Michael Behe (a hedgehog) and Phillip Johnson (a fox), both of whom receive plaudits from such distinguished philosophers as Alvin Plantinga and Peter van Inwagen. (Since Plantinga and van Inwagen have displayed considerable skill in articulating and analyz-ing philosophical arguments, the only charitable interpretation of their fulsome blurbs is that a combination of *Schwärmerei* for creationist doc-trine and profound ignorance of relevant bits of biology has induced them to put their brains in cold storage.) Johnson, a lawyer by training, is a far more subtle rhetorician than Gish, and he moves from topic to topic smoothly, discreetly making up the rules of evidence to suit his case as he goes. Many of his attack strategies refine those of country-bumpkin creationism, although, like the White Knight in Alice, he has a few masterpieces of his own invention.

Behe, by contrast, mounts his case for born-again creationism by taking one large problem, and posing it again and again. The problem isn't particularly new: it's the old issues of "complex organs" that Darwin tried to confront in the *Origin*. Behe gives it a new twist by drawing on his background as a biochemist, and describing the minute details of mechanisms in organisms so as to make it seem impossible that they could ever have emerged from a stepwise natural process.

Behe's Big Idea

Here's the general form of the problem. Given our increased knowledge of the molecular structures in cells and the chemical reactions that go on within and among cells, it's possible to describe structures and processes in exceptionally fine detail. Many structures have large numbers of constituent molecules and the precise details of their fit together are essential for them to fulfill their functions. Similarly, many biochemical pathways require numerous enzymes to interact with one another, in appropriate relative concentrations, so that some important process can occur. Faced with either of these situations, you can pose an obvious question: how could organisms with the pertinent structures or processes have evolved from organisms that lacked them? That question is an explicit invitation to describe an ancestral sequence of organisms that culminated in one with the structures or processes at the end, where each change in the sequence is supposed to carry some selective advantage. If you now pose the question many times over, canvass various possibilities, and conclude that not only has no evolutionist proposed any satisfactory sequences, but that there are systematic reasons for thinking that the structure or process could not have been built up gradually, you have an attack strategy that appears very convincing.

That, in outline, is Behe's big idea. Here's a typical passage, summarizing his quite lucid and accessible description of the structures of cilia and flagella:

> . . . as biochemists have begun to examine apparently simple structures like cilia and flagella, they have discovered staggering complexity, with dozens or even hundreds of precisely tailored parts. It is very likely that

many of the parts we have not considered here are required for any cilium to function in a cell. As the number of required parts increases, the difficulty of gradually putting the system together skyrockets, and the likelihood of indirect scenarios plummets. Darwin looks more and more forlorn. (DBB 73)

This sounds like a completely recalcitrant problem for evolutionists, but it's worth asking just why precisely Darwin should look more and more forlorn.

Notice first that lots of sciences face all sorts of unresolved questions. To take an example close to hand, Behe's own discussions of cilia frankly acknowledge that there's a lot still to learn about molecular structure and its contributions to function. So the fact that evolutionary biologists haven't yet come up with a sequence of organisms culminating in bacteria with flagella or cilia might be regarded as signaling a need for further research on the important open problem of how such bacteria evolved. Not so! declares Behe. We have here "irreducible complexity," and it's just impossible to imagine a sequence of organisms adding component molecules to build the structures up gradually.

What does this mean? Is Behe supposing that his examples point to a failure of natural selection as a mechanism for evolution? If so, then perhaps he believes that there was a sequence of organisms that ended up with a bacterium with a flagellum (say), but that the intermediates in this sequence added molecules to no immediate purpose, presumably being at a selective disadvantage because of this. (Maybe the Good Lord tempers the wind to the shorn bacterium.) Or does he just dispense with intermediates entirely, thinking that the Creator simply introduced all the right molecules *de novo*? In that case, despite his claims, he really does doubt common descent. Behe's actual position is impossible to discern because he has learned Duane Gish's lesson (Always attack! Never explain!). I'll return at the very end to the cloudiness of Behe's account of the history of life.

Clearly, Behe thinks that Darwinian evolutionary theory requires some sequence of precursors for bacteria with flagella and that no appropriate sequence could exist. But why does he believe this? Here's a simple-minded version of the argument. Assume that the flagellum needs 137 proteins. Then Darwinians are required to produce a sequence of 138 organisms, the first having none of the proteins and each one having one more protein than its predecessor. Now, we're supposed to be moved by the plight of organisms numbers 2 to 137, each of which contains proteins that can't serve any function, and is therefore, presumably, a target of selection. Only number 1, the ancestor, and number 138, in which all the protein constituents come together to form the flagellum, have just what it takes to function. The intermediates would wither in the struggle for existence. Hence evolution under natural selection couldn't have brought the bacterium from there to here.[2]

But this story is just plain silly, and Darwinians ought to disavow any commitment to it. After all, it's a common theme of evolutionary biology that constituents of a cell, a tissue, or an organism, are put to new uses because of some modification of the genotype. So maybe the immediate precursor of the proud possessor of the flagellum is a bacterium in which all the protein constituents were already present, but in which some other feature of the cell chemistry interferes with the reaction that builds the flagellum. a genetic change removes the interference (maybe a protein assumes a slightly different configuration, binding to something that would have bound to one of the constituents of the flagellum, preventing the assembly). "But, Professor Kitcher [creos always try to be polite], do you have any evidence for this scenario?" Of course not. That is to shift the question. We were offered a proof of the impossibility of a particular sequence, and when one tries to show that the proof is invalid by inventing possible instances, it's not pertinent to ask for reasons to think that those instances exist. If they genuinely reveal that what was declared to be impossible isn't, then we no longer have a claim that the Darwinian sequence couldn't have occurred, but simply an open problem of the kind that spurs scientists in any field to engage in research.

Behe has made it look as though there's something more here by inviting us to think about the sequence of precursors in a very particular way. He doesn't actually say that proteins have to be added one at a time—he surely knows very well that that would provoke the reaction I've offered—but his defense of the idea that there just couldn't be a sequence of organisms leading up to bacteria with flagella insinuates, again and again, that the problem is that the alleged intermediates would have to have lots of the components lying around like so many monkey-wrenches in the intracellular works. This strategy is hardly unprecedented. Country-bumpkin creos offered a cruder version when they dictated to evolutionists what fossil intermediates would have to be like: the transitional forms on the way to birds would have to have had half-scales and half-feathers, halfway wings—or so we are told.[3] Behe has made up his own ideas about what transitional organisms must have been like, and then argued that such organisms couldn't have existed.

In fact, we don't need to compare my guesswork with his. What Darwinism is committed to (at most) is the idea that modifications of DNA sequence (insertions, deletions, base changes, translocations) could yield a sequence of organisms culminating in a bacterium with a flagellum, with selective advantages for the later member of each adjacent pair. To work out what the members of this sequence of organisms might have been like, our ideas should be educated by the details of how the flagellum is actually assembled and the loci in the bacterial genome that are involved. Until we know these things, it's quite likely that any efforts to describe precursors or intermediates will be whistling in the dark. Behe's examples cunningly exploit our ability to give molecular analysis of the end product and our ignorance of the molecular details of how it is produced.

Throughout his book, Behe repeats the same story. He describes, often charmingly, the complexities of molecular structures and processes. There would be nothing to complain of if he stopped here and said: "Here are some interesting problems for molecularly minded evolutionists to work on, and, in a few decades time, perhaps, in light of increased knowledge of how development works at the molecular level, we may be able to see what the precursors were like." But he doesn't. He tries to argue that the precursors and intermediates required by Darwinian evolutionary theory couldn't have existed. This strategy has to fail because Behe himself is just as ignorant about the molecular basis of development as his Darwinian opponents. Hence he hasn't a clue what kinds of precursors and intermediates the Darwinian account is actually committed to— so it's impossible to demonstrate that the commitment can't be honored. However, again and again, Behe disguises his ignorance by suggesting to the reader that the Darwinian story must take a very particular form— that it has to consist in something like the simple addition of components, for example—and on that basis he can manufacture the illusion of giving an impossibility proof.

Although this is the main rhetorical trick of the book, there are some important subsidiary bits of legerdemain. Like pre-Reformation creationists, Behe loves to flash probability calculations, offering spurious precision to his criticisms. Here's his attack on a scenario for the evolution of a blood-clotting mechanism, tentatively proposed by Russell Doolittle:

> . . . let's do our own quick calculation. Consider that animals with blood-clotting cascades have roughly 10,000 genes, each of which is divided into an average of three pieces. This gives a total of about 30,000 gene pieces. TPA [Tissue Plasminogen Activator] has four different types of domains. By "variously shuffling," the odds of getting those four domains together is 30,000 to the fourth power, which is approximately one-tenth

to the eighteenth power. Now, if the Irish Sweepstakes had odds of winning of one-tenth to the eighteenth power, and if a million people played the lottery each year, it would take an average of about a thousand billion years before *anyone* (not just a particular person) won the lottery. . . . Doolittle apparently needs to shuffle and deal himself a number of perfect bridge hands to win the game. (DBB 94)

This sounds quite powerful, and Behe drives home the point by noting that Doolittle provides no quantitative estimates, adding that "without numbers, there is no science" (DBB 95)—presumably to emphasize that born-again creationists are better scientists than the distinguished figures they attack. But consider a humdrum phenomenon suggested by Behe's analogy to bridge. Imagine that you take a standard deck of cards and deal yourself thirteen. What's the probability that you got exactly those cards in exactly that order? The answer is 1 in 4×10^{21}. Suppose you repeat this process ten times. You'll now have received ten standard bridge hands, ten sets of thirteen cards, each one delivered in a particular order. The chance of getting just those cards in just that order is 1 in $4^{10} \times 10^{210}$. This is approximately 1 in 10^{222}. Notice that the denominator is far larger than that of Behe's trifling 10^{18}. So it must be *really* improbable that you (or anyone else) would ever receive just those cards in just that order in the entire history of the universe. But, whatever the cards were, you did.

What my analogy shows is that, if you describe events that actually occur from a particular perspective, you can make them look improbable. Thus, given a description of the steps in Doolittle's scenario for the evolution of TPA, the fact that you can make the probability look small doesn't mean that that isn't (or couldn't) have been the way things happened. One possibility is that the evolution of blood-clotting was genuinely improbable. But there are others.

Return to your experiment with the deck of cards. Let's suppose that all the hands you were dealt were pretty mundane—fairly evenly distributed among the suits, with a scattering of high cards in each. If you calculated the probability of receiving ten mundane hands in succession, it would of course be much higher than the priority of being dealt those very particular mundane hands with the cards arriving in just that sequence (although it wouldn't be as large as you might expect). There might be an analogue for blood-clotting, depending on how many candidates there are among the 3,000 "gene pieces" to which Behe alludes that would yield a protein product able to play the necessary role. Suppose that there are a hundred acceptable candidates for each position. That means that the chance of success on any particular draw is $(1/30)^4$, which is about 1 in 2.5 million. Now, if there were 10,000 tries per year, it would take, on average, two or three centuries to arrive at the right combination, a flicker of an instant in evolutionary time.

Of course, neither Behe nor I knows how tolerant the blood-clotting system is, how many different molecular ways it allows to get the job done. Thus we can't say if the right way to look at the problem is to think of the situation as the analogue to being dealt a very particular sequence of cards in a very particular order, or whether the right comparison is with cases in which a more general type of sequence occurs. But these two suggestions don't exhaust the relevant cases.

Suppose you knew the exact order of cards in the deck prior to each deal. Then the probability that the particular sequence would occur would be extremely high (barring fumbling or sleight of hand, the probability would be 1). The sequence only *looks* improbable because we don't know the order. Perhaps that's true for the Doolittle shuffling process as well. Given the initial distribution of pieces of DNA, plus the details of the biochemical milieu, principles of chemical recombination might actually make it very probable that the cascade Doolittle hypothesizes would ensue. Once again, nobody knows whether this is so. Behe simply assumes that it isn't.

Let me sum up. There are two questions to pose: What is the probability that the Doolittle sequence would occur? What is the significance of a low value for that probability? The answer to the first question is that we haven't a clue: it might be close to 1, it might be small but significant enough to make it likely that the sequence would occur in a flicker of evolutionary time, or it might be truly tiny (as Behe suggests). The answer to the second question is that genuinely improbable things sometimes happen, and one shouldn't confuse improbability with impossibility. Once these points are recognized, it's clear that, for all its rhetorical force, Behe's appeal to numbers smacks more of numerology than of science. As with his main line of argument, it turns out to be an attempt to parlay ignorance of molecular details into an impossibility proof.

I postpone until the very end another fundamental difficulty with Behe's argument for design, to wit his fuzzy faith that appeal to a creator will make all these "difficulties" evaporate. As we shall see, both he and Johnson try to hide any positive views. With good reason. . . .

Notes

I am extremely grateful to Dan Dennett and Ed Curley for sharing with me their unpublished discussions of the creationist writers I discuss here.

I have also learned much from an illuminating essay by Niall Shanks and Karl Joplin, "Redundant Complexity: A Critical Analysis of Intelligent Design in Biochemistry," *Philosophy of Science*. 66, 1999, 268–282. Finally, I'd like to thank Robert Pennock for his editorial encouragement and for the insights of his own excellent treatment of the neo-creos in *Tower of Babel*.

1. I'll be quoting extensively from two creationist works, Michael Behe, *Darwin's Black Box: The Biochemical Challenge to Evolution*, New York: The Free Press, 1996 (cited as DBB) and Phillip Johnson, *Darwin on Trial*, Washington D.C.: Regnery Gateway, 1993 (cited as DOT).
2. I borrow this pithy formulation from Dan Dennett.
3. For further discussion of this issue, see my *Abusing Science: The Case against Creationism*, Cambridge MA: MIT Press, p. 117.

Evil and Omnipotence
J. L. Mackie

The traditional arguments for the existence of God have been fairly thoroughly criticised by philosophers. But the theologian can, if he wishes, accept this criticism. He can admit that no rational proof of God's existence is possible. And he can still retain all that is essential to his position, by holding that God's existence is known in some other, non-rational way. I think, however, that a more telling criticism can be made by way of traditional problem of evil. Here it can be shown, not that religious beliefs lack rational support, but that they are positively irrational, that the several parts of the essential theological doctrine are inconsistent with one another, so that the theologian can maintain his position as a whole only by a much more extreme rejection of reason than in the former case. He must now be prepared to believe, not merely what cannot be proved, but what can be *disproved* from other beliefs that he also holds.

The problem of evil, in the sense in which I shall be using the phrase, is a problem only for someone who believes that there is a God who is both omnipotent and wholly good. And it is a logical problem, the prob-

Source: From J. L. Mackie, *Mind*, *Vol. 64* (Oxford University Press, 1955): 200–212. Reprinted by permission of Oxford University Press.

lem of clarifying and reconciling a number of beliefs: it is not a scientific problem that might be solved by further observations, or a practical problem that might be solved by a decision or an action. These points are obvious; I mention them only because they are sometimes ignored by theologians, who sometimes parry a statement of the problem with such remarks as "Well, can you solve the problem yourself?" or "This is a mystery which may be revealed to us later" or "Evil is something to be faced and overcome, not to be merely discussed."

In its simplest form the problem is this: God is omnipotent; God is wholly good; and yet evil exists. There seems to be some contradiction between these three propositions, so that if any two of them were true the third would be false. But at the same time all three are essential parts of most theological positions: the theologian, it seems, at once *must* adhere and *cannot consistently* adhere to all three. (The problem does not arise only for theists, but I shall discuss it in the form in which it presents itself for ordinary theism.)

However, the contradiction does not arise immediately; to show it we need some additional premises, or perhaps some quasi-logical rules connecting the terms "good," "evil," and "omnipotent." These additional principles are that good is opposed to evil, in such a way that a good thing always eliminates evil as far as it can, and that there are no limits to what an omnipotent thing can do. From these it follows that a good omnipotent thing eliminates evil completely, and then the propositions that a good omnipotent thing exists, and that evil exists, are incompatible.

Adequate Solutions

Now once the problem is fully stated it is clear that it can be solved, in the sense that the problem will not arise if one gives up at least one of the propositions that constitute it. If you are prepared to say that God is not wholly good, or not quite omnipotent, or that evil does not exist, or that good is not opposed to the kind of evil that exists, or that there are limits to what an omnipotent thing can do, then the problem of evil will not arise for you.

There are, then, quite a number of adequate solutions of the problem of evil, and some of these have been adopted, or almost adopted, by various thinkers. For example, a few have been prepared to deny God's omnipotence, and rather more have been prepared to keep the term "omnipotence" but severely to restrict its meaning, recording quite a number of things that an omnipotent being cannot do. Some have said

474 • *Part Six   Does God Exist?*

that evil is an illusion, perhaps because they held that the whole world of temporal, changing things is an illusion, and that what we call evil belongs only to this world, or perhaps because they held that although temporal things *are* much as we see them, those that we call evil are not really evil. Some have said that what we call evil is merely the privation of good, that evil in a positive sense, evil that would really be opposed to good, does not exist. Many have agreed with Pope that disorder is harmony not understood, and that partial evil is universal good. Whether any of these views is *true* is, of course, another question. But each of them gives an adequate solution of the problem of evil in the sense that if you accept it this problem does not arise for you, though you may, of course, have *other* problems to face.

But often enough these adequate solutions are only *almost* adopted. The thinkers who restrict God's power, but keep the term "omnipotence," may reasonably be suspected of thinking, in other contexts, that his power is really unlimited. Those who say that evil is an illusion may also be thinking, inconsistently, that this illusion is itself an evil. Those who say that "evil" is merely privation of good may also be thinking, inconsistently, that privation of good is an evil. (The fallacy here is akin to some forms of the "naturalistic fallacy" in ethics, where some think, for example, that "good" is just what contributes to evolutionary progress, and that evolutionary progress is itself good.) If Pope meant what he said in the first line of his couplet, that "disorder" is only harmony not understood, the "partial evil" of the second line must, for consistency, mean "that which, taken in isolation, falsely appears to be evil," but it would more naturally mean "that which, in isolation, really is evil." The second line, in fact, hesitates between two views, that "partial evil." isn't really evil, since only the universal quality is real, and that "partial evil" is really an evil, but only a little one.

In addition, therefore, to adequate solutions, we must recognise unsatisfactory inconsistent solutions, in which there is only a half-hearted or temporary rejection of one of the propositions which together constitute the problem. In these, one of the constituent propositions is explicitly rejected, but it is covertly re-asserted or assumed elsewhere in the system.

Fallacious Solutions

Besides these half-hearted solutions, which explicitly reject but implicitly assert one of the constituent propositions, there are definitely fallacious solutions which explicitly maintain all the constituent propositions, but implicitly reject at least one of them in the course of the argument that explains away the problem of evil.

There are, in fact, many so-called solutions which purport to remove the contradiction without abandoning any of its constituent propositions. These must be fallacious, as we can see from the very statement of the problem, but it is not so easy to see in each case precisely where the fallacy lies. I suggest that in all cases the fallacy has the general form suggested above: in order to solve the problem one (or perhaps more) of its constituent propositions is given up, but in such a way that it appears to have been retained, and can therefore be asserted without qualification in other contexts. Sometimes there is a further complication: the supposed solution moves to and fro between, say, two of the constituent propositions, at one point asserting the first of these but covertly abandoning the second, at another point asserting the second but covertly abandoning the first. These fallacious solutions often turn upon some equivocation with the words "good" and "evil," or upon some vagueness about the way in which good and evil are opposed to one another, or about how much is meant by "omnipotence." I propose to examine some of these so-called solutions, and to exhibit their fallacies in detail. Incidentally, I shall also be considering whether an adequate solution could be reached by a minor modification of one or more of the constituent propositions, which would, however, still satisfy all the essential requirements of ordinary theism.

"Good Cannot Exist without Evil" or "Evil is Necessary as a Counterpart to Good"

It is sometimes suggested that evil is necessary as a counterpart to good, that if there were no evil there could be no good either, and that this solves the problem of evil. It is true that it points to an answer to the question "Why should there be evil?" But it does so only by qualifying some of the propositions that constitute the problem.

First, it sets a limit to what God can do, saying that God *cannot* create good without simultaneously creating evil, and this means either that God is not omnipotent or that there are *some* limits to what an omnipotent thing can do. It may be replied that these limits are always presupposed, that omnipotence has never meant the power to do what is logically impossible, and on the present view the existence of good without evil would be a logical impossibility. This interpretation of omnipotence may, indeed, be accepted as a modification of our original account which does not reject anything that is essential to theism, and I shall in general assume it in the subsequent discussion. It is, perhaps, the most common theistic view, but I think that some theists at least have maintained that God can do what is logically impossible. Many theists, at any rate, have held that logic itself is created or laid down by God, that logic is the way in which God arbitrarily chooses to think. (This is, of course, parallel to the ethical view that morally right actions are those which God arbitrarily chooses to command, and the two views encounter similar difficulties.) And *this* account of logic is clearly inconsistent with the view that God is bound by logical necessities—unless it is possible for an omnipotent being to bind himself, an issue which we shall consider later, when we come to the Paradox Omnipotence. This solution of the problem of evil cannot, therefore, be consistently adopted along with the view that logic is itself created by God.

But, secondly, this solution denies that evil is opposed to good in our original sense. If good and evil are counterparts, a good thing will not "eliminate evil as far as it can." Indeed, this view suggests that good and evil are not strictly qualities of things at all. Perhaps the suggestion is that good and evil are related in much the same way as great and small. Certainly, when the term "great" is used relatively as a condensation of "greater than so-and-so," and "small" is used correspondingly, greatness and smallness are counterparts and cannot exist without each other. But in this sense greatness is not a quality, not an intrinsic feature of anything; and it would be absurd to think of a movement in favor of greatness and against smallness in this sense. Such a movement would be self-defeating, since relative greatness can be promoted only by a simultaneous promotion of relative smallness. I feel sure that no theists would be content to regard God's goodness as analogous to this—as if what he supports were not the *good* but the *better*, and as if he had the paradoxical aim that all things should be better than other things.

This point is obscured by the fact that "great" and "small" seem to have an absolute as well as a relative sense. I cannot discuss here whether there is absolute magnitude or not, but if there is, there could be an absolute sense for "great," it could mean of at least a certain size, and it would make sense to speak of all things getting bigger, of a universe that was expanding all over, and therefore it would make sense to speak of promoting greatness. But in *this* sense great and small are not logically necessary counterparts: either quality could exist without the other. There would be no logical impossibility in everything's being small or in everything's being great.

Neither in the absolute nor in the relative sense, then, of "great" and "small" do these terms provide an analogy of the sort that would be needed to support this solution of the problem of evil. In neither case are greatness and smallness *both* necessary counterparts *and* mutually opposed forces or possible objects for support and attack.

It may be replied that good and evil are necessary counterparts in the same way as any quality and its logical opposite: redness can occur, it is suggested, only if non-redness also occurs. But unless evil is merely the privation of good, they are not logical opposites, and some further argument would be needed to show that they are counterparts in the same way as genuine logical opposites. Let us assume that this could be given. There is still doubt of the correctness of the metaphysical principle that a quality must have a real opposite: I suggest that it is not really impossible that everything should be, say, red, that the truth is merely that if everything were red we should not notice redness, and so we should have no word "red"; we observe and give names to qualities only if they have real opposites. If so, the principle that a term must have an opposite would belong only to our language or to our thought, and would not be an ontological principle, and, correspondingly, the rule that good cannot exist without evil would not state a logical necessity of a sort that God would just have to put up with. God might have made everything good, though *we* should not have noticed it if he had.

But, finally, even if we concede that this is an ontological principle, it will provide a solution for the problem of evil only if one is prepared to say, "Evil exists, but only just enough evil to serve as the counterpart of good." I doubt whether any theist will accept this. After all, the *ontological* requirement that non-redness should occur would be satisfied even if all the universe, except for a minute speck, were red, and, if there were a corresponding requirement for evil as a counterpart to good, a minute dose of evil would presumably do. But theists are not usually willing to say, in all contexts, that all the evil that occurs is a minute and necessary dose.

"Evil is Necessary as a Means to Good"

It is sometimes suggested that evil is necessary for good not as a counterpart but as a means. In its simple form this has little plausibility as a solution of the problem of evil, since it obviously implies a severe restriction of God's power. It would be a *causal* law that you cannot have a certain end without a certain means, so that if God has to introduce evil as a means to good, he must be subject to at least some causal laws. This certainly conflicts with what a theist normally means by omnipotence. This view of God as limited by causal laws also conflicts with the view that causal laws are themselves made by God, which is more widely held than the corresponding view about the laws of logic. This conflict, would, indeed, be resolved if it were possible for an omnipotent being to bind himself, and this possibility has still to be considered. Unless a favourable answer can be given to this question, the suggestion that evil is necessary as a means to good solves the problem of evil only by denying one of its constituent propositions, either that God is omnipotent or that "omnipotent" means what it says.

"The Universe Is Better with Some Evil in It Than It Could Be If There Were No Evil"

Much more important is a solution which at first seems to be a mere variant of the previous one, that evil may contribute to the goodness of a whole in which it is found, so that the universe as a whole is better as it is, with some evil in it, than it would be if there were no evil. This solution may be developed in either of two ways. It may be supported by an aesthetic analogy by the fact that contrasts heighten beauty, that in a musical work, for example, there may occur discords which somehow add to the beauty of the work as a whole. Alternatively, it may be worked out in connexion with the notion of progress, that the best possible organization of the universe will not be static, but progressive, that the gradual overcoming of evil by good is really a finer thing than would be the eternal unchallenged supremacy of good.

In either case, this solution usually starts from the assumption that the evil whose existence gives rise to the problem of evil is primarily what is called physical evil, that is to say, pain. In Hume's rather half-hearted presentation of the problem of evil, the evils that he stresses are pain and disease, and those who reply to him argue that the existence of pain and disease makes possible the existence of sympathy, benevolence, heroism, and the gradually successful struggle of doctors and reformers to overcome these evils. In fact, theists often seize the opportunity to accuse those who stress the problem of evil of taking a low, materialistic view of good and evil, equating these with pleasure and pain, and of ignoring the more spiritual goods which can arise in the struggle against evils.

But let us see exactly what is being done here. Let us call pain and misery "first order evil" or "evil (1)." What contrasts with this, namely, pleasure and happiness, will be called "first order good" or "good (1)."Distinct from this is "second order good" or "good (2)" which somehow emerges in a complex situation in which evil (1) is a necessary component—logically, not merely causally, necessary. (Exactly *how* it emerges does not matter: in the crudest version of this solution good (2) is simply the heightening of happiness by the contrast with misery, in other versions it includes sympathy with suffering, heroism in facing danger, and the gradual decrease of first order evil and increase of first order good.) It is also being assumed that second order good is more important than first order good or evil, in particular that it more than outweighs the first order evil it involves.

Now that is a particularly subtle attempt to solve the problem of evil. It defends God's goodness and omnipotence on the ground that (on a sufficiently long view) this is the best of all logically possible worlds, because it includes the important second order goods, and yet it admits that real evils, namely first order evils, exist. But does it still hold that good and evil are opposed? Not, clearly, in the sense that we set out originally: good does not tend to eliminate evil in general. Instead, we have a modified, a more complex pattern. First order good (e.g. happiness) *contrasts with* first order evil (e.g. misery): these two are opposed in a fairly mechanical way; some second order goods (e.g. benevolence) try to maximize first order good and minimize first order evil; but God's goodness is not this, it is rather the will to maximize second order good. We might, therefore, call God's goodness an example of a third order goodness, or good (3). While this account is different from our original one, it might well be held to be an improvement on it, to give a more accurate description of the way in which good is opposed to evil, and to be consistent with the essential theist position.

There might, however, be several objections to this solution.

First, some might argue that such qualities as benevolence—and a fortiori the third order goodness which promotes benevolence—have a merely derivative value, that they are not higher sorts of good, but merely means to good (1), that is, to happiness, so that it would be absurd for God to keep misery in existence in order to make possible the virtues of benevolence, heroism, etc. The theist who adopts the present solution must, of course, deny this, but he can do so with some plausibility, so I should not press this objection.

Secondly, it follows from this solution that God is not in our sense benevolent or sympathetic: he is not concerned to minimise evil (1), but only to promote good (2); and this might be a disturbing conclusion for some theists.

But, thirdly, the fatal objection is this. Our analysis shows clearly the possibility of the existence of a *second* order evil, an evil (2) contrasting with good (2) as evil (1) contrasts with good (1). This would include malevolence, cruelty, callousness, cowardice, and states in which good (1) is decreasing and evil (1) increasing. And just as good (2) is held to be the important kind of good, the kind that God is concerned to

480 • Part Six   Does God Exist?

promote, so evil (2) will, by analogy, be the important kind of evil, the kind which God, if he were wholly good and omnipotent, would eliminate. And yet evil (2) plainly exists, and indeed most theists (in other contexts) stress its existence more than that of evil (1). We should, therefore, state the problem of evil in terms of second order evil, and against this form of the problem the present solution is useless.

An attempt might be made to use this solution again, at a higher level, to explain the occurrence of evil (2): indeed the next main solution that we shall examine does just this, with the help of some new notions. Without any fresh notions, such a solution would have little plausibility: for example, we could hardly say that the really important good was a good (3), such as the increase of benevolence in proportion to cruelty, which logically required for its occurrence the occurrence of some second order evil. But even if evil (2) could be explained in this way, it is fairly clear that there would be third order evils contrasting with this third order good: and we should be well on the way to an infinite regress, where the solution of a problem of evil, stated in terms of evil (n), indicated the existence of an evil ($n + 1$), and a further problem to be solved.

"Evil Is Due to Human Freewill"

Perhaps the most important proposed solution of the problem of evil is that evil is not to be ascribed to God at all, but to the independent actions of human beings, supposed to have been endowed by God with freedom of the will. This solution may be combined with the preceding one: first order evil (e.g. pain) may be justified as a logically necessary component in second order good (e.g. sympathy) while second order evil (e.g. cruelty) is not *justified*, but is so ascribed to human beings that God cannot be held responsible for it. This combination evades my third criticism of the preceding solution.

The freewill solution also involves the preceding solution at a higher level. To explain why a wholly good God gave men free will although it would lead to some important evils, it must be argued that it is better on the whole that men should act freely, and sometimes err, than that they should be innocent automata, acting rightly in a wholly determined way. Freedom, that is to say, is now treated as a third order good, and as being more valuable than second order goods (such as sympathy and heroism) would be if they were deterministically produced, and it is being assumed that second order evils, such as cruelty, are logically necessary accompaniments of freedom, just as pain is a logically necessary precondition of sympathy.

I think that this solution is unsatisfactory primarily because of the incoherence of the notion of freedom of the will: but I cannot discuss this topic adequately here, although some of my criticisms will touch upon it.

First I should query the assumption that second order evils are logically necessary accompaniments of freedom. I should ask this: if God has made men such that in their free choices they sometimes prefer what is good and sometimes what is evil, why could He not have made men such that they always freely choose the good? If there is no logical impossibility in a man's freely choosing the good on one, or on several, occasions, there cannot be a logical impossibility in his freely choosing the good on every occasion. God was not, then, faced with a choice between making innocent automata and making beings who, in acting freely, would sometimes go wrong: there was open to him the obviously better possibility of making beings who would act freely but always go right. Clearly, his failure to avail himself of this possibility is inconsistent with his being both omnipotent and wholly good.

If it is replied that this objection is absurd, that the making of some wrong choices is logically necessary for freedom, it would seem that "freedom" must here mean complete randomness or indeterminacy, including randomness with regard to the alternatives good and evil, in other words that men's choices and consequent action can be "free" only if they are not determined by their characters. Only on this assumption can God escape the responsibility for men's actions; for if he made them as they are, but did not determine their wrong choices, this can only be because the wrong choices are not determined by men as they are. But then if freedom is randomness, how can it be a characteristic of *will*? And still more, how can it be the most important good? What value or merit would there be in free choices if these were random actions which were not determined by the nature of the agent?

I conclude that to make this solution plausible two different senses of "freedom" must be confused, one sense which will justify the view that freedom is third order good, more valuable than other goods would be without it, and another sense, sheer randomness, to prevent us from ascribing to God a decision to make men such that they sometimes go wrong when he might have made them such that they would always freely go right.

This criticism is sufficient to dispose of this solution. But besides this there is a fundamental difficulty in the notion of an omnipotent God creating men with free will, for if men's wills are really free this must mean that even God cannot control them, that is, that God is no longer omnipotent. It may be objected that God's gift of freedom to men does not mean that he *cannot* control their wills, but that he always *refrains* from controlling their wills. But why, we may ask, should God refrain from controlling evil wills? Why should he not leave men free to will rightly, but intervene when he sees them beginning to will wrongly? If God could do this, but does not, and if he is wholly good, the only explanation could be that even a wrong free act of will is not really evil, that its freedom is a value which outweighs its wrongness, so that there would be a loss of value if God took away the wrongness and the freedom together. But this is utterly opposed to what theists say about sin in other contexts. The present solution of the problem of evil, then, can be maintained only in the form that God has made men so free that he *cannot* control their wills.

This leads us to what I call the Paradox of Omnipotence: can an omnipotent being make things which he cannot subsequently control? Or, what is practically equivalent to this, can an omnipotent being make rules which then bind himself? (These are practically equivalent because any such rules could be regarded as setting certain things beyond his control, and vice versa.) The second of these formulations is relevant to the suggestions that we have already met, that an omnipotent God creates the rules of logic or causal laws, and is then bound by them.

It is clear that this is a paradox: the questions cannot be answered satisfactorily either in the affirmative or in the negative. If we answer "Yes," it follows that if God actually makes things which he cannot control, or makes rules which bind himself, he is not omnipotent once he has made them: there are *then* things which he cannot do. But if we answer "No," we are immediately asserting that there are things which he cannot do, that is to say that he is already not omnipotent.

It cannot be replied that the question which sets this paradox is not a proper question. It would make perfectly good sense to say that a human mechanic has made a machine which he cannot control: if there is any difficulty about the question it lies in the notion of omnipotence itself.

This, incidentally, shows that although we have approached this paradox from the free will theory, it is equally a problem for a theological determinist. No one thinks that machines have free will, yet they may be beyond the control of their makers. The determinist might reply that anyone who makes anything determines its ways of acting, and so determines its subsequent behaviour: even the human mechanic does this by his *choice* of materials and structure for his machine, though he does not know all about either of these: the mechanic thus determines, though he may not foresee, his machine's action. And since God is omniscient, and since his creation of things is total, he both determines and foresees the ways in which his creatures will act. We may grant this, but it is beside the point. The question is not whether God *originally* determined the future actions of his creatures, but whether he can *subsequently* control their actions, or whether he was able in his original creation to put things beyond his subsequent control. Even on determinist principles the answers "Yes" and "No" are equally irreconcilable with God's omnipotence.

Before suggesting a solution of this paradox, I would point out that there is a parallel Paradox of Sovereignty. Can a legal sovereign make a law restricting its own future legislative power? For example, could the British parliament make a law forbidding any future parliament to socialise banking, and also forbidding the future repeal of this law itself? Or could the British parliament, which was legally sovereign in Australia in, say, 1899, pass a valid law, or series of laws, which made it no longer sovereign in 1933? Again, neither the affirmative nor the negative answer is really satisfactory. If we were to answer "Yes," we should be admitting the validity of a law which, if it were actually made, would mean that parliament was no longer sovereign. If we were to answer "No," we should be admitting that there is a law, not logically absurd, which parliament cannot validly make, that is, that parliament is not now a legal sovereign. This paradox can be solved in the following way. We should distinguish between first order laws, that is laws governing the actions of individuals and bodies other than the legislature, and second order laws, that is laws about laws, laws governing the actions of the legislature itself. Correspondingly, we should distinguish two orders of sovereignty, first order sovereignty (sovereignty (1)) which is unlimited authority to make first order laws, and second order sovereignty (sovereignty (2)) which is unlimited authority to make second order laws. If we say that parliament is sovereign we might mean that any parliament at any time has sovereignty (1), or we might mean that parliament has both sovereignty (1) and sovereignty (2) at present, but we cannot without contradiction mean both that the present parliament has sovereignty (2) and that every parliament at every time has sovereignty (1), for if the present parliament has sovereignty (2) it may use it to take away the sovereignty (1) of later parliaments. What the paradox shows is that we cannot ascribe to any continuing institution legal sovereignty in an inclusive sense.

The analogy between omnipotence and sovereignty shows that the paradox of omnipotence can be solved in a similar way. We must distinguish between first order omnipotence (omnipotence (1)), that is unlimited power to act, and second order omnipotence (omnipotence

(2)), that is unlimited power to determine what powers to act things shall have. Then we could consistently say that God all the time has omnipotence (1), but if so no beings at any time have powers to act independently of God. Or we could say that God at one time had omnipotence (2), and used it to assign independent powers to act to certain things, so that God thereafter did not have omnipotence (1). But what the paradox shows is that we cannot consistently ascribe to any continuing being omnipotence is an inclusive sense.

An alternative solution of this paradox would be simply to deny that God is a continuing being, that any times can be assigned to his actions at all. But on this assumption (which also has difficulties of its own) no meaning can be given to the assertion that God made men with wills so free that he could not control them. The paradox of omnipotence can be avoided by putting God outside time, but the freewill solution of the problem of evil cannot be saved in this way, and equally it remains impossible to hold that an omnipotent God *binds himself* by causal or logical laws.

Conclusion

Of the proposed solution of the problem of evil which we have examined, none has stood up to criticism. There may be other solutions which require examination, but this study strongly suggests that there is no valid solution of the problem which does not modify at least one of the constituent propositions in a way which would seriously affect the essential core of the theistic position.

Quite apart from the problem of evil, the paradox of omnipotence has shown that God's omnipotence must in any case be restricted in one way or another, that unqualified omnipotence cannot be ascribed to any being that continues through time. And if God and his actions are not in time, can omnipotence, or power of any sort, be meaningfully ascribed to him?

Why God Allows Evil
Richard Swinburne

The world . . . contains much evil. An omnipotent God could have prevented this evil, and surely a perfectly good and omnipotent God would have done so. So why is there this evil? Is not its existence strong evidence against the existence of God? It would be unless we can construct what is known as a theodicy, an explanation of why God would allow such evil to occur. I believe that that can be done, and I shall outline a theodicy. . . . I emphasize that . . . in writing that God would do this or that, I am not taking for granted the existence of God, but merely claiming that, if there is a God, it is to be expected that he would do certain things, including allowing the occurrence of certain evils; and so, I am claiming, their occurrence is not evidence against his existence.

It is inevitable that any attempt by myself or any one else to construct a theodicy will sound callous, indeed totally insensitive to human suffering. Many theists, as well as atheists, have felt that any attempt to construct a theodicy evinces an immoral approach to suffering. I can only ask the reader to believe that I am not totally insensitive to human suffering, and that I do mind about the agony of poisoning, child abuse, bereavement, solitary imprisonment, and marital infidelity as much as anyone else. True, I would not in most cases recommend that a pastor give this chapter to victims of sudden distress at their worst moment to read for consolation. But this is not because its arguments are unsound; it is simply that most people in deep distress need comfort, not argument. Yet there is a problem about why God allows evil, and, if the theist does not have (in a cool moment) a satisfactory answer to it, then his belief in God is less than rational, and there is no reason why the atheist should share it. To appreciate the argument of this chapter, each of us needs to stand back a bit from the particular situation of his or her own life and that of close relatives and friends (which can so easily seem the only important thing in the world), and ask very generally what good things would a generous and everlasting God give to human beings in the course of a short earthly life. Of course thrills of pleasure and periods of contentment are good things, and—other things being equal—God would certainly seek to provide plenty of those. But a generous God will seek to give deeper good things than these. He will seek to give us great responsibility for ourselves, each other, and the world, and thus a share in his own creative activity of determining what sort of world it is to be. And he will seek to make our lives valuable, of great use to ourselves and each other. The problem is that God cannot give us these goods in full measure without allowing much evil on the way. . . .

[T]here are plenty of evils, positive bad states, which God could if he chose remove. I divide these into moral evils and natural evils. I understand by "natural evil" all evil which is not deliberately produced by human beings and which is not allowed by human beings to occur as a result of their negligence. Natural evil includes both physical suffering and mental suffering, of animals as well as humans; all the trial of suffering which disease, natural disasters, and accidents unpredictable by humans bring in their train. "Moral evil" I understand as including all evil caused deliberately by humans doing what they ought not to do (or allowed to occur by humans negligently failing to do what they ought to do) *and* also the evil constituted by such deliberate actions or negligent failure. It includes the sensory pain of the blow inflicted by the bad parent on his child, the mental pain of the parent depriving the child of love, the starvation allowed to occur in Africa because of negligence by members of foreign governments who could have prevented it, and also the evil of the parent or politician deliberately bringing about the pain or not trying to prevent the starvation.

Moral Evil

The central core of any theodicy must, I believe, be the "free-will defence," which deals—to start with—with moral evil, but can be extended to deal with much natural evil as well. The free-will defence claims that it is a great good that humans have a certain sort of free will which I shall call free and responsible choice, but that, if they do, then necessarily there will be the natural possibility of moral evil. (By the "natural possibility" I mean that it will not be determined in advance whether or not the evil will occur.) A God who gives humans such free will necessarily brings about the possibility, and puts outside his own control whether or not that evil occurs. It is not logically possible—that is, it would be self-contradictory to suppose—that God could give us such free will and yet ensure that we always use it in the right way.

Free and responsible choice is not just free will in the narrow sense of being able to choose between alternative actions, without our choice being causally necessitated by some prior cause. . . . [H]umans could have that kind of free will merely in virtue of being able to choose freely between two equally good and unimportant alternatives. Free and responsible choice is rather free will (of the kind discussed) to make significant choices between good and evil, which make a big difference to the agent, to others, and to the world.

Given that we have free will, we certainly have free and responsible choice. Let us remind ourselves of the difference that humans can make to themselves, others, and the world. Humans have opportunities to give themselves and others pleasurable sensations, and to pursue worthwhile activities—to play tennis or the piano, to acquire knowledge of history and science and philosophy, and to help others to do so, and thereby to build deep personal relations founded upon such sensations and activities. And humans are so made that they can form their characters. Aristotle famously remarked: "we become just by doing just acts, prudent by doing prudent acts, brave by doing brave acts." That is, by doing a just act when it is difficult—when it goes against our natural inclinations (which is what I understand by desires)—we make it easier to do a just act next time. We can gradually change our desires, so that—for example—doing just acts becomes natural. Thereby we can free ourselves from the power of the less good desires to which we are subject. And, by choosing to acquire knowledge and to use it to build machines of various sorts, humans can extend the range of the differences they can make to the world—they can build universities to last for centuries, or save energy for the next generation; and by cooperative effort over many decades they can eliminate poverty. The possibilities for free and responsible choice are enormous.

It is good that the free choices of humans should include *genuine* responsibility for other humans, and that involves the opportunity to benefit *or* harm them. God has the power to benefit or to harm humans. If other agents are to be given a share in his creative work, it is good that they have that power too (although perhaps to a lesser degree). A world in which agents can benefit each other but not do each other harm is one where they have only very limited responsibility for each other. If my responsibility for you is limited to whether or not to give you a camcorder, but I cannot cause you pain, stunt your growth, or limit your education, then I do not have a great deal of responsibility for you. A God who gave agents only such limited responsibilities for their fellows would not have given much. God would have reserved for himself the all-important choice of the kind of world it was to be, while simply allowing humans the minor choice of filling in the details. He would be like a father asking his elder son to look after the younger son, and adding that he would be watching the elder son's every move and would intervene the moment the elder son did a thing wrong. The elder son might justly retort that, while he would be happy to share his father's work, he could really do so only if he were left to make his own judgements as to what to do within a significant range of the options available to the father. A good God, like a good father, will delegate responsibility. In order to allow creatures a share in creation, he will allow them the choice of hurting and maiming, of frustrating the divine plan. Our world is one where creatures have just such deep responsibility for each other. I cannot only benefit my children, but harm them. One way in which I can harm them is that I can inflict physical pain on them. But there are much more damaging things which I can do to them. Above all I can stop them growing into creatures with significant knowledge, power, and freedom; I can determine whether they come to have the kind of free and responsible choice which I have. The possibility of humans bringing about significant evil is a logical consequence of their having this free and responsible choice. Not even God could give us this choice without the possibility of resulting evil.

Now . . . an action would not be intentional unless it was done for a reason—that is, seen as in some way a good thing (either in itself or because of its consequences). And, if reasons alone influence actions, that regarded by the subject as most important will determine what is done; an agent under the influence of reason alone will inevitably do the action which he regards as overall the best. If an agent does not do the action which he regards as overall the best, he must have allowed factors other than reason to exert an influence on him. In other words, he must have allowed desires for what he regards as good only in a certain respect, but not overall, to influence his conduct. So, in order to have a choice between good and evil, agents need already a certain depravity, in the sense of a system of desires for what they correctly believe to be evil. I need to *want* to overeat, get more than my fair share of money or power, indulge my sexual appetites even by deceiving my spouse or partner, want to see you hurt, if I am to have choice between good and evil. This depravity is itself an evil which is a necessary condition of a greater good. It makes possible a choice made seriously and deliberately, because [it is one] made in the face of a genuine alternative. I stress that, according to the free-will defence, it is the natural possibility of moral evil which is the necessary condition of the great good, not the actual evil itself. Whether that occurs is (through God's choice) outside God's control and up to us.

Note further and crucially that, if I suffer in consequence of your freely chosen bad action, that is not by any means pure loss for me. In a certain respect it is good for *me*. My suffering would be pure loss for me if the only good thing in life was sensory pleasure, and the only bad thing sensory pain; and it is because the modern world tends to think in those terms that the problem of evil seems so acute. If these were the only good and bad things, the occurrence of suffering would indeed be a conclusive objection to the existence of God. But we have already noted the great good of freely choosing and influencing our future, that of our fellows, and that of the world. And now note another great good—the good of our life serving a purpose, of being of use to ourselves and others. Recall the words of Christ, "it is more blessed to give than to receive" (as quoted by St. Paul (Acts 20: 35)). We tend to think, when the beggar appears on our doorstep and we feel obliged to give and do give, that that was lucky for him but not for us who happened to be at home. That is not what Christ's words say. They say that *we* are the lucky ones, not just because we have a lot, out of which we can give a little, but because we are privileged to contribute to the beggar's happiness—and that privilege is worth a lot more than money. And, just as it is a great good freely to choose to do good, so it is also a good to be used by someone else for a worthy purpose (so long, that is, that he or she has the right, the authority, to use us in this way). Being allowed to suffer to make possible a great good is a privilege, even if the privilege is forced upon you. Those who are allowed to die for their country and thereby save their country from foreign oppression are privileged. Cultures less obsessed than our own by the evil of purely physical pain have always recognized that. And they have recognized that it is still a blessing, even if the one who died had been conscripted to fight.

And even twentieth-century man can begin to see that—sometimes—when he seeks to help prisoners, not by giving them more comfortable quarters, but by letting them help the handicapped; or when he pities rather than envies the "poor little rich girl" who has everything and does nothing for anyone else. And one phenomenon prevalent in end-of-century Britain draws this especially to our attention—the evil of unemployment. Because of our system of Social Security, the unemployed on the whole have enough money to live without too much discomfort; certainly they are a lot better off than are many employed in Africa or Asia or Victorian Britain. What is evil about unemployment is not so much any resulting poverty but the uselessness of the unemployed. They often report feeling unvalued by society, of no use, "on the scrap heap." They rightly think it would be a good for them to contribute; but they cannot. Many of them would welcome a system where they were obliged to do useful work in preference to one where society has no use for them.

It follows from that fact that being of use is a benefit for him who is of use, and that those who suffer at the hands of others, and thereby make possible the good of those others who have free and responsible choice, are themselves benefited in this respect. I am fortunate if the natural possibility of my suffering if you choose to hurt me is the vehicle which makes your choice really matter. My vulnerability, my openness to suffering (which necessarily involves my actually suffering if you make the wrong choice), means that you are not just like a pilot in a simulator, where it does not matter if mistakes are made. That our choices matter tremendously, that we can make great differences to things for good or ill, is one of the greatest gifts a creator can give us. And if my suffering is the means by which he can give you that choice, I too am in this respect fortunate. Though of course suffering is in itself a bad thing, my good fortune is that the suffering is not random, pointless suffering. It is suffering which is a consequence of my vulnerability which makes me of such use.

Someone may object that the only good thing is not *being* of use (dying for one's country or being vulnerable to suffering at your hands), but *believing* that one is of use—believing that one is dying for one's country and that this is of use; the "feel-good" experience. But that cannot be correct. Having comforting beliefs is only a good thing if they are true beliefs. It is not a good thing to believe that things are going well when they are not, or that your life is of use when it is not. Getting pleasure out of a comforting falsehood is a cheat. But if I get pleasure out of a true belief, it must be that I regard the state of things which I believe to hold to be a good thing. If I get pleasure out of the true belief that my daughter is doing well at school, it must be that I regard it as a good thing that my daughter does well at school (whether or not I believe that she is doing well). If I did not think the latter, I would not get any pleasure out of believing that she is doing well. Likewise, the belief that I am vulnerable to suffering at your hands, and that that is a good thing, can only be a good thing if being vulnerable to suffering at your hands is itself a good thing (independently of whether I believe it or not). Certainly, when my life is of use and that is a good for me, it is even better if I believe it and get comfort therefrom; but it can only be even better if it is already a good for me whether I believe it or not.

But though suffering may in these ways serve good purposes, does God have the right to allow me to suffer for your benefit, without asking my permission? For surely, an objector will say, no one has the right to allow one person A to suffer for the benefit of another one B without A's consent. We judge that doctors who use patients as involuntary objects of experimentation in medical experiments which they hope will produce results which can be used to benefit others are doing something wrong. After all, if my arguments about the utility of suffering are sound, ought we not all to be causing suffering to others in order that those others may have the opportunity to react in the right way?

There are, however, crucial differences between God and the doctors. The first is that God as the author of our being has certain rights, a certain authority over us, which we do not have over our fellow humans. He is the cause of our existence at each moment of our existence and sustains the laws of nature which give us everything we are and have. To allow someone to suffer for his own good or that of others, one has to stand in some kind of parental relationship towards him. I do not have the right to let some stranger suffer for the sake of some good, when I could easily prevent this, but I do have *some* right of this kind in respect of my own children. I may let the younger son suffer *somewhat* for his own good or that of his brother. I have this right because in small part I am responsible for the younger son's existence, his beginning and continuance. If I have begotten him, nourished, and educated him, I have some limited rights over him in return; to a *very limited* extent I can use him for some worthy purpose. If this is correct, then a God who is so much more the author of our being than are our parents has so much more right in this respect. Doctors do have over us even the rights of parents.

But secondly and all-importantly, the doctors *could* have asked the patients for permission; and the patients, being free agents of some power and knowledge, could have made an informed choice of whether or not to allow themselves to be used. By contrast, God's choice is not about how to use already existing agents, but about the sort of agents to make and the sort of world into which to put them. In God's situation there are no agents to be asked. I am arguing that it is good that one agent A should have deep responsibility for another B (who in turn could have deep responsibility for another C). It is not logically possible for God to have asked B if he wanted things thus, for, if A is to be responsible for B's growth in freedom, knowledge, and power, there will not be a B with enough freedom and knowledge to make any choice, before God has to choose whether or not to give A responsibility for him. One cannot ask a baby into which sort of world he or she wishes to be born. The creator has to make the choice independently of his creatures. He will seek on balance to benefit them—all of them. And, in giving them the gift of life—whatever suffering goes with it—that is a substantial benefit. But when one suffers at the hands of another, often perhaps it is not enough of a benefit to outweigh the suffering. Here is the point to recall that it is an additional benefit to the sufferer that his suffering is the means whereby the one who hurt him had the opportunity to make a significant choice between good and evil which otherwise he would not have had.

Although for these reasons, as I have been urging, God has the right to allow humans to cause each other to suffer, there must be a limit to the amount of suffering which he has the right to allow a human being to suffer for the sake of a great good. A parent may allow an elder child to have the power to do some harm to a younger child for the sake of the responsibility given to the elder child; but there are limits. And there are limits even to the moral right of God, our creator and sustainer, to use free sentient beings as pawns in a greater game. Yet, if these limits were too narrow, God would be unable to give humans much real responsibility; he would be able to allow them only to play a toy game. Still, limits there must be to God's rights to allow humans to hurt each other; and limits there are in the world to the extent to which they can hurt each other, provided above all by the short finite life enjoyed by humans and other creatures—one human can hurt another for no more than eighty years or so. And there are a number of other safety-devices in-built into our physiology and psychology, limiting the amount of pain we can suffer. But the primary safety limit is that provided by the shortness of our finite life. Unending, unchosen suffering would indeed to my mind provide a very strong argument against the existence of God. But that is not the human situation.

So then God, without asking humans, has to choose for them between the kinds of world in which they can live—basically either a world in which there is very little opportunity for humans to benefit or harm each other, or a world in which there is considerable opportunity. How shall he choose? There are clearly reasons for both choices. But it seems to me (just, on balance) that his choosing to create the world in which we have considerable opportunity to benefit or harm each other is to bring about a good at least as great as the evil which he thereby allows to occur. *Of course* the suffering he allows is a bad thing; and, other things being equal, to be avoided. But having the natural possibility of causing suffering makes possible a greater God, in creating humans who (of logical necessity) cannot choose for themselves the kind of world into which they are to come, plausibly exhibits his goodness in making for them the heroic choice that they come into a risky world where they may have to suffer for the good of others.

Natural Evil

Natural evil is not to be accounted for along the same lines as moral evil. Its main role rather, I suggest, is to make it possible for humans to have the kind of choice which the free-will defence extols, and to make available to humans specially worthwhile kinds of choice.

There are two ways in which natural evil operates to give humans those choices. First, the operation of natural laws producing evils gives humans knowledge (if they choose to seek it) of how to bring about such evils themselves. Observing you catch some disease by the operation of natural processes gives me the power either to use those processes to give that disease to other people, or through negligence to allow others to catch it, or to take measures to prevent others from catching the disease. Study of the mechanisms of nature producing various evils (and goods) opens up for humans a wide range of choice. This is the way in which in fact we learn how to bring about (good and) evil. But could not God give us the requisite knowledge (of how to bring about good or evil) which we need in order to have free and responsible choice by a less costly means?

Could he not just whisper in our ears from time to time what are the different consequences of different actions of ours? Yes. But anyone who believed that an action of his would have some effect because he believed that God had told him so would see all his actions as done under the all-watchful eye of God. He would not merely believe strongly that there was a God, but would know it with real certainty. That knowledge would greatly inhibit his freedom of choice, would make it very difficult for him to choose to do evil. This is because we all have a natural inclination to wish to be thought well of by everyone, and above all by an all-good God; that we have such an inclination is a very good feature of humans, without which we would be less than human. Also, if we were directly informed of the consequences of our actions, we would be deprived of the choice whether to seek to discover what the consequences were through experiment and hard cooperative work. Knowledge would be available on tap. Natural processes alone give humans knowledge of the effects of their actions without inhibiting their freedom, and if evil is to be a possibility for them they must know how to allow it to occur.

The other way in which natural evil operates to give humans their freedom is that it makes possible certain kinds of action towards it between which agents can choose. It increases the range of significant choice. A particular natural evil, such as physical pain, gives to the sufferer a choice—whether to endure it with patience, or to bemoan his lot. His friend can choose whether to show compassion towards the sufferer, or to be callous. The pain makes possible these choices, which would not otherwise exist. There is no guarantee that our actions in response to the pain will be good ones, but the pain gives us the opportunity to perform good actions. The good or bad actions which we perform in the face of natural evil themselves provide opportunities for further choice—of good or evil stances towards the former actions. If I am patient with my suffering, you can choose whether to encourage or laugh at my patience; If I bemoan my lot, you can teach me by word and example what a good thing patience is. If you are sympathetic, I have then the opportunity to show gratitude for the sympathy; or to be so self-involved that I ignore it. If you are callous, I can choose whether to ignore this or to resent it for life. And so on. I do not think that there can be much doubt that natural evil, such as physical pain, makes available these sorts of choice. The actions which natural evil makes possible are ones which allow us to perform at our best and interact with our fellows at the deepest level.

It may, however, be suggested that adequate opportunity for these great good actions would be provided by the occurrence of moral evil without any need for suffering to be caused by natural processes. You can show courage when threatened by a gunman, as well as when threatened by cancer; and show sympathy to those likely to be killed by gunmen as well as to those likely to die of cancer. But just imagine all the suffering of mind and body caused by disease, earthquake, and accident unpreventable by humans removed at a stroke from our society. No sickness, no bereavement in consequence of the untimely death of the young. Many of us would then have such an easy life that we simply would not have much opportunity to show courage or, indeed, manifest much in the way of great goodness at all. We need those insidious processes of decay and dissolution which money and strength cannot ward off for long to give us the opportunities, so easy otherwise to avoid, to become heroes.

God has the right to allow natural evils to occur (for the same reason as he has the right to allow moral evils to occur)—up to a limit. It would, of course, be crazy for God to multiply evils more and more in order to give endless opportunity for heroism, but to have *some* significant opportunity for real heroism and consequent character formation is a benefit for the person to whom it is given. Natural evils give to us the knowledge to make a range of choices between good and evil, and the opportunity to perform actions of especially valuable kinds.

There is, however, no reason to suppose that animals have free will. So what about their suffering? Animals had been suffering for a long time before humans appeared on this planet—just how long depends on which animals are conscious beings. The first thing to take into account here is that, while the higher animals, at any rate the vertebrates, suffer, it is most unlikely that they suffer nearly as much as humans do. Given that suffering depends directly on brain events (in turn caused by events in other parts of the body), then, since the lower animals do not suffer at all and humans suffer a lot, animals of intermediate complexity (it is reasonable to suppose) suffer only a moderate amount. So, while one does need a theodicy to account for why God allows animals to suffer, one does not need as powerful a theodicy as one does in respect of humans. One only needs reasons adequate to account for God allowing an amount of suffering much less than that of humans. That said, there is, I believe, available for animals parts of the theodicy which I have outlined above for humans.

The good of animals, like that of humans, does not consist solely in thrills of pleasure. For animals, too, there are more worthwhile things, and in particular intentional actions, and among them serious significant intentional actions. The life of animals involves many serious significant intentional actions. Animals look for a mate, despite being tired and failing to find one. They take great trouble to build nests and feed their young, to decoy predators and explore. But all this inevitably involves pain (going on despite being tired) and danger. An animal cannot intentionally avoid forest fires, or take trouble to rescue its offspring from forest fires, unless there exists a serious danger of getting caught in a forest fire. The action of rescuing despite danger simply cannot be done unless the danger exists—and the danger will not exist unless there is a significant natural probability of being caught in the fire. Animals do not choose freely to do such actions, but the actions are nevertheless worthwhile. It is great that animals feed their young, not just themselves; that animals explore when they know it to be dangerous; that animals save each other from predators, and so on. These are the things that give the lives of animals their value. But they do often involve some suffering to some creature.

To return to the central case of humans—the reader will agree with me to the extent to which he or she values responsibility, free choice, and being of use very much more than thrills of pleasure or absence of pain. There is no other way to get the evils of this world into the right perspective, except to reflect at length on innumerable very detailed thought experiments (in addition to actual experiences of life) in which we postulate very different sorts of worlds from our own, and then ask ourselves whether the perfect goodness of God would require him to create one of these (or no world at all) rather than our own. But I conclude with a very small thought experiment, which may help to begin this process. Suppose that you exist in another world before your birth in this one, and are given a choice as to the sort of life you are to have in this one. You are told that you are to have only a short life, maybe of only a few minutes, although it will be an adult life in the sense that you will have the richness of sensation and belief characteristic of adults. You have a choice as to the sort of life you will have. You can have either a few minutes of very considerable pleasure, of the kind produced by some drug such as heroin, which you will experience by yourself and which will have no effects at all in the world (for example, no one else will know about it); or you can have a few minutes of considerable pain, such as the pain of childbirth, which will have (unknown to you at the time of pain) considerable good effects on others over a few years. You are told that, if you do not make the second choice, those others will never exist—and so you are under no moral obligation to make the second choice. But you seek to make the choice which will make *your* own life the best life for *you* to have led. How will you choose? The choice is, I hope, obvious. You should choose the second alternative.

For someone who remains unconvinced by my claims about the relative strengths of the good and evils involved—holding that, great though the goods are, they do not justify the evils which they involve—there is a fallback position. My arguments may have convinced you of the greatness of the goods involved sufficiently for you to allow that a perfectly good God would be justified in bringing about the evils for the sake of the good which they make possible, if and only if God also provided compensation in the form of happiness after death to the victims whose sufferings make possible the goods. . . . While believing that God does provide at any rate for many humans such life after death, I have expounded a theodicy without relying on this assumption. But I can understand someone thinking that the assumption is needed, especially when we are considering the worst evils. (This compensatory afterlife need not necessarily be the everlasting life of Heaven.)

It remains the case, however, that evil is evil, and there is a substantial price to pay for the goods of our world which it makes possible. God would not be less than perfectly good if he created instead a world without pain and suffering, and so without the particular goods which those evils make possible. Christian, Islamic, and much Jewish tradition claims that God has created worlds of both kinds—our world, and the Heaven of the blessed. The latter is a marvelous world with a vast range of possible deep goods, but it lacks a few goods which our world contains, including the good of being able to reject the good. A generous God might well choose to give some of us the choice of rejecting the good in a world like ours before giving to those who embrace it a wonderful world in which the former possibility no longer exists.

Male-Chauvinist Religion
Deborah Mathieu

Man for the field and woman for the hearth
Man for the sword and for the needle she
Man with the head and woman with the heart
Man to command and woman to obey
All else confusion.
ALFRED, LORD TENNYSON[1]

All functioning societies rely on a division of labor: some individuals raise children, some produce food, some construct roads, some adjudicate disputes, and so on. Occasionally these tasks overlap, but often they do not. How do societies decide who does what? How, in other words, are rights and responsibilities allocated?

There is no one universally accepted method of determining which people will perform which roles, and often a given society will employ several methods. One common distributive standard is age: no one over a certain age or under a certain age may perform certain functions. Another distributive standard is ability: an intelligent person with a sense of fairness may adjudicate disputes, for instance, while a brawny person willing to work hard may construct roads. Yet another common standard is gender: males perform one set of tasks while females perform another. There are other allocative standards as well: race, religion, family, class, education, and so on.

The United States has employed all of these (and more) to determine who does what. Most of the criteria are unfair most of the time: your family name, for instance, should be irrelevant to your career (unless you work in the family business), as should your theology (unless you work as a religious official). But I am not concerned with all unfair standards, just with one: gender. If positions are allocated according to gender, then no female—regardless of her talents, her education, her aspirations—may perform those tasks assigned to males.

During the many decades in which the United States used gender as a principle method of distribution, a woman could wash clothes but she could not shine shoes, she could be a barmaid but not a bartender, she could raise children but could not hold public office. Women could not be lawyers, serve on juries, operate elevators, or mine coal. Indeed, it was once illegal in this country for women to perform *most* jobs outside the home.[2] This type of occupational gender segregation, of course, is very common around the world. One result is that work traditionally performed by women—rearing children, cleaning house, teaching grammar school—though necessary and often arduous, is usually undervalued and underpaid.[3]

The separation of tasks according to gender typically means that males act in the public sphere of politics and paid work while females stay in the private sphere of the home. But why would an intelligent woman with a robust sense of fairness concede that she should spend her time cleaning house instead of refereeing disputes? Why would any woman acquiesce to any sort of gender stereotyping, especially when the results are harmful to her?

The answer is simple and somewhat frightening: she believes that only certain narrowly defined roles are appropriate for her. Why would she believe that? Because every facet of her society—the media, her schools, her books, her friends, her parents, even her toys—have conspired to convince her that it is so.

One of the most powerful tools in this respect is religion, for it tells people not only what is proper and good, but what is holy and unholy, natural and unnatural. Having certain activities branded by a sacred text as unholy or unnatural when performed by females certainly helps ensure that females will avoid those activities. Equally inhibiting are declarations from religious leaders. Public declarations by a few Islamic *ulama* that women may not drive automobiles, for instance, surely have more clout than the private remonstrations of a multitude of husbands. In short, when important distinctions are made along gender lines, religious doctrines and practices are valuable instruments of indoctrination.

Of the many male-chauvinist religions, three have been especially successful in relegating females to inferior positions: Christianity, Islam, and Judaism. In addition to the institutionalization of patriarchal, even misogynistic, mores and practices, these familiar religions have much in common: belief in one and only one supreme being, identification of one book as a record of its god's words and deeds, characterization of its god as male, emphasis on compassion, and status as a major world religion. The relationship among these factors is fascinating, especially the roles they have played in the subjugation of females.

Misogyny on High

The practices of Christianity, Islam, and Judaism originated when males and females were assigned different social roles in life: males in the public sphere, females in the private.[4] Because the males' role included designing the rules, they designed the rules to favor themselves. One of the most important rules, of course, was that only males could craft the rules.

This separation of roles extended to religion, so the males designed the rules there as well: they formulated the beliefs and practices, they created the institutions, they controlled the rituals. It should be no surprise, then, that the resulting religions explicitly reinforced the belief that males are superior to females and endorsed a set of social relations in which males controlled females.[5]

Religious practices demonstrated this message constantly. Females could not be religious leaders, and they could be religious participants only from a distance. They were not permitted near the holy sanctuaries, allowed to speak (or sing) in the church/mosque/synagogue, or even allowed to read the holy books. Of course the religious teachings were often harshly judgmental of females. A leader of the early Christian church, for instance, went so far as to blame human sin and suffering on females:

> The sentence of God on this sex of yours lives in this age: the guilt must of necessity live too. You are the Devil's gateway; you are the first deserter of the divine law; you are she who persuaded him whom the devil was not valiant enough to attack. You so carelessly destroyed man, God's image. On account of your desert, even the Son of God had to die.[6]

Indeed, all facets of the religions could be used to dishonor females, even prayer. Every morning, for instance, the Jewish man was expected to thank God: "Blessed art thou, O Lord our God, King of the Universe, who has not made me a woman."

And yet, despite their malice toward the female sex, these three religions flourished. How could this be? How could a theology that demeaned females become a significant religion throughout the world? How could something so blatantly one-sided and unfair gain such legitimacy? It is easy to imagine the existence of a few all-male cults built around the idea (and it is just an idea) of male superiority. But why would millions of sensible women support three worldwide religions based on that idea? How could reasonable women believe in these gods?

Co-opting Females

The first part of the explanation relates to the high value all three religions place on compassion and equality. All virtuous people are equal in the sight of God, the holy books proclaim. To honor each other is to honor God, the books declare, so be kind to each other, show concern for the vulnerable, help those less fortunate, be fair in all your dealings. No doubt females heard these words and believed them, despite the mountains of evidence to the contrary.

The second, and less comforting, reason females accepted these religions is related to the need of those who wield power to justify that status quo to themselves and to others. Men claiming such inordinate power needed to mollify any misgivings the advantaged might have and to gain the acquiescence of the disadvantaged. The benefits of this to those who make and enforce the rules are obvious: if people believe that the status quo is the best system, they will not fight against it, and the privileged can maintain their position (relatively) peacefully.

Therefore males used their religion to brainwash females into accepting the theory of male superiority as fact. The technique has been effective because of its multi-faceted approach: it appeals to the female's intellect as well as her emotions.

The crux of the male's argument for supremacy over females is inherent in all three religions: the contention that the one and only true god is male. Thus the very cores of all three theologies were deployed to subjugate females. The results were devastatingly successful, as well as successfully devastating.

The basic deductive argument is built around two simple syllogisms of the following classic form:

If P, Then Q.

P
_____
Therefore Q.

The first part of the argument goes like this:

If god is male, then human males are more like god than human females are.

God is male.
_____
Therefore human males are more like god than human females are.

The second part of the argument is:

If human males are more like god than human females are, then human males are superior to human females.

Human males are more like god than human females are.
_____
Therefore human males are superior to human females.

The argument is not a sound one. But it still has power, for if you accept the premises, then the conclusions follow inevitably and indisputably.

Those conclusions have led to the disenfranchisement of females, especially within the religions themselves. Why couldn't Christian women be priests? Because a priest impersonates (the male) Christ during Eucharist. Why must Jewish women sit behind a screen in the synagogue, away from the sanctuary? Because they are too flawed to be near the holy objects. Why must Islamic women cover their entire bodies even though Allah commanded only that they dress modestly? Because the (male) *ulama* interpret Allah otherwise, and they know better. Why were women prevented from conducting the religious ceremonies, setting the rules, designing the practices? Because of their inherent inferiority to the men who do. And why is a woman's labor rewarded less than a man's? Need we ask?

It is curious that the deductive arguments noted above could ever be persuasive, for under scrutiny they collapse. Both syllogisms suffer from the same flaw: they rely on premises that are open to dispute. The first shaky premise is the assertion that god is male. It need not be so.

Indeed, there are other, equally plausible alternatives: god may be female, or neither male nor female, or both male and female. In short, one may believe in the existence of god and yet deny that god is male.[7] This seems a sound approach for religious females to take, especially as it is to their advantage to do so.

Feminist theologians have staunchly advocated this approach. But this is a very recent development; for thousands of years women agreed that god was male, and many women still do. Why? Because that contention enjoys powerful support: the holy books of the three religions. According to the Jewish *Tenakh*, the Christian *Bible*, and the Islamic *Qur'an*, god is male. Yahweh, Christ, and Allah all have male attributes and male sobriquets: Lord of Hosts, God the Father, God the Son, King of the Universe, He who gives life and death, He who exalts. If you accept any of these books as literally true, then you are likely to view your god as male.

But if females believe that their god is male, and therefore refuse to challenge that part of the argument, they still may challenge another, equally shaky premise: the contention that, if human males are more like god than human females are, then human males are superior to human females. Other plausible options are available here, too. If the god is an inferior one, for instance, then being similar to him may not be an asset; perhaps being similar to god in some way makes one, not better than another, but more vulnerable. Perhaps being different (i.e., female) makes someone more, not less, fit to rule.

Of course the holy books can be used to rebut this challenge as well. God is magnificent, omnipotent, omniscient, wonderful in every way, the three books declare. To be like him, then, is to have positive attributes. And to be unlike him is to have negative attributes. It follows that because males are like god and females are not, males must be superior to females. And surely superior beings should rule inferior ones.

This argument could be broken down into a set of syllogisms, each of which would have at least one shaky premise. But the response would be the same as above: an appeal could be made to any of the three holy books to attest to the inevitability, the undeniability, the universality of female subordinancy. In short, if god is male, then females are in trouble. It is that simple.

This brings us to the second component of religious brainwashing: the appeal to emotions. The religious ceremonies and teachings were designed to make females feel both accepted (if they conform to certain standards) and unacceptable (because of their inherent unworthiness). They were designed, as well, to make the females doubt themselves.

Imagine how a woman might feel as she listened to St. Paul's Letter to the Ephesians read as part of the day's religious ceremony:

> Wives, submit yourselves unto your own husbands, as unto the Lord. For the husband is the head of the wife, even as Christ is the head of the church, and he is the savior of the body. Therefore, as the church is subject unto Christ, so let the wives be to their own husbands in every thing. (Eph 5:22–24)[8]

How would a female feel, seated in the back of the synagogue behind a screen during every religious service of her life? How would she feel when her presence in the synagogue is not even counted toward the quorum needed for a service? How would she feel, covered in black from head to foot in the blazing sun of a desert summer? Would she be angry? Would she be offended? Or might she instead feel inferior, inadequate?

And how might she feel when she realizes that all meaningful choices in life are denied to her? How might she feel when she is told—in school, at home, and in her place of worship—that males are superior to females? Might she come to believe that her want of options, as well as her lack of power, was natural? On what basis might she think otherwise?

And if she believes that everyone else accepts the proposition that she is second-rate, simply because she is female, is she likely to rebel? Is she even likely to question the system? Or is she more apt to question her own feelings, to distrust her ability to understand? If no one else believes that she is intelligent, or even rational, is she likely to presume it? If no one else believes she is capable of performing anything other than the most routine, mundane tasks, will she? Probably not.

So what is the result? Is she likely to be brimming with confidence and self-respect, eager to strike out on her own to make her way in the world? Is she likely to question the foundations of the dominant religion, to argue forcefully against the unfairness of the system? Or is she more likely to be someone who is fearful and insecure, someone who is subservient to others?

The answer is obvious: she behaves as you would expect someone who has been marginalized all her life would behave. She does what she is told, she acquiesces to the system, she accepts her fate. Perhaps she suffers from low self-esteem, perhaps she is passive and dependent and anxious. She behaves, in other words, like an unempowered female. After all, the whole system is designed to make her this way.

In short, males have heavy-handedly used these three religions to advance their own interests and to justify their having the upper hand.

It can even be argued that the basic features of the religions—belief in one and only one supreme being, identification of one book as a record of the god's words and deeds, and characterization of its god as male—were designed to augment male domination over female members of his species. Perhaps even the purported emphasis on compassion and equality was merely a smokescreen hiding the truth, a cruel hoax played on females to entice them to acquiesce in their own destruction.

Misogyny and Monotheism

The question is, then, how important is male chauvinism to these religions? Is the misogyny, in other words, as integral a part as the monotheism?

Four responses to this question merit discussion:

1. "anatomy is destiny"[9]
2. god is a male chauvinist
3. the religious images should be taken symbolically
4. sexism has always been superfluous to these religions.

I will explain each in turn and also offer a rebuttal to each.

1. Anatomy Is Destiny

The contention here is that the three religions accurately reflect the fact that males and females are different types of beings. Males are rational while females are emotional; males are rule-oriented while females are relationship-oriented; males are domineering while females are submissive; males are properly heads of households while females are their helpmates; males belong in the public sphere while females belong in the private sphere. It has been this way since time immemorial. It has been this way, not because males have unfairly dominated females, but because it is the natural course of life. This is the way the world was designed, it is the way the world works, and all reasonable people recognize it. To fight this natural order is to invite disaster.

We have heard declarations like these for centuries; but all of them are wrong, terribly, tragically wrong. A female is not by nature someone who stays home to raise children, wash clothes, and bake bread. Nor is she by nature subservient to males. She becomes that type of person by adopting a certain gender role, a view of what is acceptable for her to do/say/think as a female. Gender roles are social constructions that begin at birth, not biological determinates beginning at conception.

There is one question everyone asks when told of a birth: Is it a boy or a girl? We ask because it makes a difference to us; we need to know how to treat this new being. We dress a male differently from a female; we address a male differently from a female; we expect different behaviors from a male than from a female. The children, of course, internalize these differences, and behave accordingly. They tend to repeat behaviors we have rewarded and reinforced, just as they tend to avoid behaviors we have punished and discouraged. They learn gender differences in other ways as well: from observation, for instance, and by generalizing from one type of experience to another.

These patterns continue throughout their lives, as males and females adapt to the dissimilar social expectations and mores imposed on them. The interplay of their behaviors with variations in treatment by others creates different life experiences. And these different life experiences form different sorts of people—people with the characteristics of distinct genders—with different feelings, beliefs, and skills. This, then, is how gender is constructed. And because gender roles are social constructs, they vary from culture to culture, and may even vary within a culture over time.

This is not to say that there are no biological differences between male and female humans; of course there are. The contrasts are sometimes obvious (such as their dramatically dissimilar reproductive organs), sometimes less noticeable (the two X chromosomes of a typical female, versus the one X chromosome and one Y of a typical male). The point is, rather, that these biological differences are less significant than the cultural ones in determining the ways males and females operate in the world. In other words, in the nature/nurture debate, I am arguing that the evidence indicates that more weight should be given to nurture than nature when it comes to gender differences.[10]

It is difficult, though, to convince skeptics of the validity of an ambiguous stance like this: it is true that there are innate differences between males and females *and* that gender is a largely social construct. In contrast, positions on the outside boundaries of the debate offer the comfort of firm absolutes. At one end are the postmodernists, who reject grand explanatory theories in general and theories of innate human traits in particular; all of our options and preferences, they argue, are the result of cultural influences. And at the other end are their archenemies, the sociobiologists, who argue that myriad human traits are genetically based. I am suggesting, instead, that the truth lies somewhere between the two; that, while genes exert a probabalistic influence on human behavior, their influence is muted dramatically by the environment.

This is not the place, however, to engage at length in the contentious nature/nurture debate that has raged across disciplines for years (and which shows no signs of abating). Suffice it to say that it seems clear to me that anatomy is not destiny (at least with regard to most gender differences), that females are not inherently inferior to males, and that cultural conditioning shapes most gender roles.

2. God Is a Male Chauvinist

Nothing about the nature of god follows from my criticisms of these three religions. And I offer no propositions about the true nature of god, or even about the existence of god. Instead, let us assume for the sake of argument that these three religions are correct: god exists and he is a male chauvinist. In this case, it does not matter whether males and females are inherently different because god has designated separate social roles for them. And if we wish to obey god's will, then we will treat males and females as different. If one result is that the members of one gender wield most of the power, then so be it.

This position raises a fundamental question about the response of females to god. Would a male chauvinist god be likely to inspire love in females? Would a biased, unfair god inspire awe? Or devotion? Or would such a being inspire some other reaction in females: something closer to wrath, perhaps, or resentment?

When confronted with a god who consigns you to a drab, dull existence, wouldn't you be angry? When told during religious services that you are base and inferior, simply because of the design of your genitalia, wouldn't you be indignant? Or perhaps Nelle Morton illustrates the proper tone for a female to adopt:

> No one is wise enough to know why God made female reproductive organs compact and internal so that woman is physically free to move about unencumbered and take her natural place of leadership in the world of womankind. Or why God made a male's organs external and exposed, so that he would demand sheltering and protection from the outside in order that he may be kept for reproducing the race.[11]

Surely Morton is correct that the situation calls for at least a little irony. Maybe even a good dose of sarcasm. But not love, certainly not love. Fear might be appropriate perhaps, given the unsavory outcomes for females, but not love. And not awe. After all, there is nothing splendid about a sexist god. And should we even consider such a limited being to be a god?

But females did not spurn the gods of these three religions, at least not generally. Nor were anger, indignation, and irony the typical responses of females to these gods or their religions. Instead, Christianity, Islam, and Judaism became powerful in part because of their female adherents.

That is because attitudes such as irony and indignation are possible only if you are able to step back from the god, to view the religion clearly. Females were prevented from doing precisely that. One successful method was to deny them access to education (so they could not read the holy books themselves) as well as access to any decision-making processes. Another, equally effective method was to prey on their emotions, to make them believe they were somehow inadequate, even irrational.

But today these techniques are not nearly so widespread nor so effective. And misogyny is no longer so much in vogue. Eventually, as sexist social systems disappear, so will sexist religions. And as our mores change, so must our gods.

3. The Religious Images Should Be Taken Symbolically, Not Literally

One way to save these three religions from the charge of unfair sexism is to deny that the holy books are literally true. The religious images, it is argued, should be understood as metaphors, as devices for expounding profound truths too difficult for the average person to describe (or understand) in the abstract. And abstractions are too impersonal and cold to instill the deeply emotional responses that religious faith requires. It seems more natural, for instance, to love and honor the particularized image of Jesus—a god who became a man in order to die for all human sin—than an abstruse concept of forgiveness.

So religious stories use familiar objects to create images we can grasp and to which we are likely to react with reverence and awe. These images are so powerful that we often forget that they are mere symbols. But that is our failing, not the fault of the holy books. We need to remind ourselves that religious discourse was meant to be taken figuratively, that, for instance, Yahweh's promise in Genesis to deliver his chosen people into a "land flowing with milk and honey" is not a contract at all, and certainly not one guaranteeing a future awash in sweetened dairy products; it is, instead, a reassurance of a brighter future, an exhortation to be hopeful.

It should not be surprising, the argument continues, that some of these images are couched in misogynistic language, given the low status of women at the time the religious works were compiled. But this sexism is only a contingent feature of the religions; the religious tenets can be expressed in nonsexist, even nongendered, language. Thus God need not be seen as a male, but understood instead as a perfect nongendered being, "the being than whom a more perfect being cannot be conceived." In short, we should be able to see beyond these time-bound images to appreciate the deeper truths they contain; we should be able to proceed beyond the sexist language of these ancient works to understand the universalist metaphors they express.

As compelling as this argument appears, it is persuasive only if one is willing to deny reality. Among its many weaknesses, three are worth noting here. The first problem is that even the sophisticated have difficulty being abstract. Can you really imagine what it means to be "the being than whom a more perfect being cannot be conceived" or "a ground of all contingency"? Most people cannot. And that is why religious literature continues to maintain a gendered image of god. Even those who seek to expunge sexism from religious practices find it impossible to erase gender altogether. Take, for instance, the Society for the Promotion of Christian Knowledge, Britain's oldest publisher of religious books, which touts its new, nonsexist prayer book. In it, Christianity's most often recited prayer, the Lord's Prayer, has been cleansed of its male chauvinist overtones. Retitled the "Prayer of Jesus," it now appeals not to a male god or an ungendered god but to an androgynous god. Thus where the prayer once began, "Our father, who art in heaven, hallowed be thy name," it now begins: "Beloved, our father and mother, in whom is heaven, hallowed be your name."[12] The new prayer book has met, of course, with considerable resistance. "I think it's heretical," the Archdeacon of York recently said. "I would walk out of a service if that was read."[13] This attitude is reflected in many places, including the Catholic Mass, which still features the centuries-old Nicene Creed:

> We believe in one God, the Father, Almighty, maker of heaven and earth, of all that is seen and unseen. We believe in one Lord, Jesus Christ, the only Son of God, eternally begotten of the Father. . . .

It seems clear that, while change is coming, it is slow and halting, and leaves untouched millions of lives.

A second and related problem is that one may adopt the theoretical principle that religious images are to be taken symbolically yet fail to accept that precept on an emotional level. It often is the case that "images function powerfully long after they have been repudiated intellectually."[14] Thus we find ourselves making declarations on an intellectual level that we simply do not accept on an emotional level. With religious images tending to honor males and dishonor females, we may find ourselves unconsciously doing the same.

Finally, there is the woeful fact that for thousands of years these images were used to subjugate women. Suggesting that the interpretations may have been mistaken, or that we should understand them figuratively, is insufficient; the sexist language is there, and it has caused terrible harm by marginalizing generations of females. And it continues to do so.

4. Male Chauvinism Is and Always Has Been Superfluous to Christianity, Islam, and Judaism

The holy books of all three religions acknowledge the profound value of females: the account of creation in the *Qur'an* describes the common origin of men and women, as does one of the versions of creation in the *Tenakh*, while the Gospels of the *New Testament* indicate that Christ treated females with respect and compassion. Indeed, all of the holy books give the impression that, in ultimate spiritual terms, males and females are equal.[15] Thus the fact that these religions may have been used by males to subjugate females shows only that males will manipulate anything and everything in order to maintain power; it does not show that these religions are necessarily sexist.

This is both the strongest and the weakest of the countervailing considerations. It is the strongest because it is accurate: I have shown only that male chauvinism is a major part of these three religions, I have not demonstrated that it is an essential part. Nor could I. A few Christian sects (such as Christian Scientists and Quakers) have always treated females as the equals of males; the largest Islamic group, Sunni Muslims, believe that females are as competent as males to perform some religious rites; and there have been Jewish female (reform) rabbis since 1972. Surely these are powerful counterexamples to my arguments.

Yes and no. Yes, they demonstrate that these three religions can exist intact minus a certain degree of misogyny. But no, they are not powerful enough to do the job; the examples are too few, and are overwhelmed by the countless instances of raw sexism. Indeed, many religious sects remain robustly male chauvinist, continuing to justify their stance by reference to their sacred texts and customs. The Catholic Church, for instance, declared as recently as 1995 that women may not be priests, not now, not ever.[16] This is to be expected; in the traditional forms of these religions, men continue to keep most of the interesting and influential roles for themselves.

The contention that the male chauvinism of these religions is only contingently a part of them—that they could exist intact without it—is a serious indictment against those who are unwilling to relinquish it. To hold tight to tradition is to embrace patriarchy. And that is not a pretty picture: it conserves an unfair and damaging conception of what it means to be female; it supports a one-sided power grab, allowing males to monopolize key roles; and it may even, as Mary Daly charges, sustain a hoax, "a front for men's plans and a cover for inadequacy, ignorance, and evil."[17]

The traditional forms of these religions are opting, in short, to cast doubt on the nature and value of religion itself. They are opting, as well, to cast doubt on the existence of an infinitely powerful yet benevolent god, for their disgraceful treatment of females raises the same demanding question posed by all great evils: what kind of god would allow this to happen?

Notes

1. Alfred Lord Tennyson, *The Princess: A Medley.* William J. Rolfe, ed., Cambridge, MA: Riverside Press 1884, lines 437–441.
2. See D. M. Stetson, *Women's Rights in the U.S.A.*, Belmont, CA: Wadsworth, 1991; Carol Hymowitz and Michaele Weissman, *A History of Women in America*, N.Y.: Bantam Books, 1978.
3. See Pamela K. Brubaker, *Women Don't Count*, Atlanta: Scholars Press 1994; *The State of the World's Women, 1985*, Oxford: New International Publications, 1985.
4. For a thoughtful history of the evolution of these three religions, see Karen Armstrong, *A History of God*, N.Y.: Ballentine Books, 1993.
5. Rachel Biale, *Women and Jewish Law*, N.Y.: Schocken, 1986; Mary Daly, *Beyond God the Father*, Boston: Beacon Press, 1973; Alice L. Hageman, ed., *Sexist Religion and Women in the Church*, N.Y.: Association Press, 1974; John S. Hawley, *Fundamentalism and Gender*, N.Y.: Oxford University Press, 1994; Jean Holm, ed. *Women in Religion*, N.Y.: Pinter, 1994; Rosemary R. Ruether, ed. *Images of Women in the Jewish and Christian Traditions*, N.Y.: Simon and Schuster, 1973.
6. Tertullian, *On Female Dress*, I, i. Tertullian, a North African theologian, lived about a hundred years after the death of Christ.

   Note as well the male chauvinist writings of other well-known Christian writers: Augustine, Cyprian, Jerome, Aquinas, Karl Barth, Dietrich Bonhoeffer, and Reinhold Niebuhr.

7. You may also dispute the premise by claiming that there is no god, or at least not one that matters much. Two directions are then possible: you can reject all religious belief, or you can choose a system of spiritual thought, that the second alternative contains its own set of sexist elements. Consider, for instance, Buddhism, a non-theistic religion which emphasizes the human roots of suffering. Although the details of Buddhism change with every culture into which it is introduced, a core set of "Noble Truths" is embraced by nearly all Buddhists: suffering is universal, suffering is a result of desire, to eliminate suffering you must eliminate desire, a path can be followed to achieve freedom from desire and suffering. These tenets are gender-neutral and apply to all, without exception. Yet Buddhism is still tainted by misogyny. According to Buddha himself, for instance, the most senior nun must defer to the most junior monk. And in the system of reincarnation, rebirth as a female is generally considered unfortunate compared to rebirth as a male.

8. See also the words ascribed to Paul in 1 Tim. 2: 12: "But I suffer not a woman to teach, nor to usurp authority over the man, but to be in silence." Interestingly, many contemporary scholars agree that Paul never made any of these sexist remarks, that they were appended later to his letters. See e.g., Robin Scroggs, "Paul and the Eschatological Woman," *Journal of the American Academy of Religion* 40: 283–303, 1972.

9. Freud said this, earning the enmity of feminists. Sigmund Freud, *On Sexuality: Three Essays on the Theory of Sexuality and Other Works*, James Strachey, cn., London: Penguin, 1991.

10. For more on gender socialization see: Pierre Bourdieu, *The Logic of Practice*, Stanford, CA: Stanford University Press, 1990; R. W. Connell, *Gender and Power*, Stanford, CA: Stanford University Press, 1987; Michelle H. Garskof, ed. *Roles Women Play*, Belmont, CA: Belmont/Cole, 1971; Eleanor E. Maccoby, ed. *The Development of Sex Differences*, Stanford, CA: Stanford University Press, 1966; Dorothy E. Smith, *The Everyday World as Problematic*, Toronto: University of Toronto Press, 1987.

11. Nelle Morton, "Preaching the Word," in Alice L. Hageman, ed. *Sexist Religion and Women in the Church*, N.Y.: Association Press, 1974, pp. 30–31.

12. *Including Women: A Non-Sexist Prayer Book* is published by the Society for the Promotion of Christian Knowledge, and has been adopted by some Church of England congregations since 1991.

13. "Equal-opportunity Prayers." *Maclean's* August 5, 1991.

14. Morton, *op. cit.*, p. 32.

15. The *Qur'an* even gave women legal rights of inheritance and divorce, rights most Western women would not gain for over a thousand years.

16. Pope John Paul II issued an apostolic letter in 1994 declaring that the Catholic Church may not ordain women; in 1995 the Vatican's Congregation for the Doctrine of the Faith confirmed that this conclusion was infallible and irrevocable.

17. Mary Daly, *op. cit.*, p. 30.

PART SEVEN

WHAT IS MORAL?

Most people have a good idea of what is and what is not moral. We feel confident saying that we know that it is morally wrong to hurt others, take what is not ours, and be dishonest. Likewise, we know that, as moral agents, we ought to be kind to others, obey the laws, and help others pursue their interests. Still, very few people could say *why* some actions, motives, or character traits are morally good and others are morally bad. We seem to know that we are governed by certain norms or guidelines, and yet it is no easy task to explicitly state or justify those norms and guidelines.

Thus, one might think that, when it comes to morality, the only guidelines are those we impose on ourselves or those that our culture imposes on us. That is, one might think that because there seems to be a plethora of moral opinions, there is no one morality or there is no definite answer to the question *What is moral?* This skeptical view about morality is called *ethical relativism* and is juxtaposed to *ethical objectivism*—the view that, when it comes to morality, there *are* moral facts. In the first reading in this section, "A Defense of Ethical Objectivism," Louis Pojman examines several varieties of relativism and explains why each should be rejected. Morality, he argues, is not just a matter of opinion.

If morality is not a matter of opinion, one might think that morality is related to religion in some way—that moral values and ideas of right and wrong stem from religious beliefs. James Rachels' paper, "Must God's Commands Conform to Moral Standards?" reveals the dilemma one faces in answering the question, "Is conduct right because the gods command it, or do the gods command it because it is right?" He concludes that the view that God is the source of the moral law has unsavory consequences.

Given that there is reason to think that morality is not just a matter of opinion or some mandate from God, what is it? *Ethics* is the area of philosophy that seeks to answer this question. Ethics is the study of the standards that govern our moral lives; it is the study of *morality*.

The two main areas of ethics with which philosophers are concerned are *normative* (or *prescriptive*) *ethics* and *applied ethics*. The former is that area of ethics concerned with answering the question "What, morally speaking, ought we to do?" The latter is concerned with how we might go about resolving specific moral issues. A normative ethical theory provides a theory of what is morality, and thus it provides criteria by which we judge people, laws, actions, or intentions as moral or immoral, good or bad. In this way, normative ethics goes hand in hand with applied ethics—we want a theory that guides us in acting morally and making moral judgments.

John Stuart Mill, in the selection from *Utilitarianism*, defends a consequentialist theory. According to it, the morally best thing to do is that which produces the greatest amount of happiness for the greatest number of people. Thus, it is the *consequences* of one's actions that are morally significant. There is an objective fact of the matter as to whether one's action produces greater happiness than some alternative action may produce. So, there is an objective fact which to ground moral judgments.

Immanuel Kant rejects consequentialism. In the selection from his *Groundwork of the Metaphysics of Morals*, he argues it is not the results of one's action that determine the action's moral worth, but it is what motivates one to act in the first place—one's *reasons* or *intentions*—that determines whether one's actions are moral. Ultimately, Kant thinks that being moral amounts to being rational, and being immoral amounts to being irrational.

Aristotle's moral theory focuses on an agent's character—the kind of person one is—and how one acquires a virtuous character. The virtuous person is she who uses reason to govern her emotions, with the goal of being a good person and thus living the good life. In the selection from Aristotle's *Nicomachean Ethics*, Aristotle argues that moral virtue is a state of character that is a mean between two deficiencies.

In "Virtue Ethics in TV's *Seinfeld*," Aeon Skoble argues that the characters of Jerry and George in the TV sitcom *Seinfeld* exemplify this sort of Aristotelian character building. They do, after all, want to do what good people would do, or at least they want others to see them as good people. Aristotle would condone this sort of moral role-modeling because he thinks that we have to learn to be virtuous by engaging in virtuous behavior. Only when virtuous acts become second nature, or habit, are we really virtuous.

Marilyn Friedman, in "The Practice of Partiality," addresses a discrepancy that arises between what we take to be morally permissible, perhaps even morally mandatory, and what is morally justified on either utilitarian or Kantian grounds—namely, the practice of giving special moral consideration to those with whom we have special relationships. The practice of partiality seems to be inconsistent with the utilitarian's requirement that everyone's happiness count equally, as well as with the Kantian requirement that moral maxims be universalizable. Friedman argues that the commonsense moral intuition that we have certain special duties to those close to us can be justified on the basis of the moral value of the very relationships partiality serves. She offers a characterization of the nature of the relationships that ground these special duties but also recognizes an important pragmatic obstacle to the practice of partiality. Specifically, some people are in a better position than others to satisfy their moral obligations of partiality.

Because the primary reason for doing normative ethics is to discover how we ought to live, an essential component of ethical theory is its practical application to resolve genuine moral problems. In applied ethics, we examine ethical problems in light of what we understand about ethical theory. The final readings in this section fall under the heading of applied ethics. In them, the authors are defending a particular moral position by making appeals, either implicitly or explicitly, to certain fundamental moral principles. We have provided two sets of papers that each address a moral question from opposing moral positions.

The first set of papers addresses the issue of animal rights. In his paper, "The Moral Basis of Vegetarianism," Tom Regan examines a number of reasons one might give for denying rights to animals—arguments grounded on the ability to feel pain, to communicate, or to reason, but argues that none of these arguments are strong. He concludes by saying that the burden of proof falls on those who would deny animals have rights. Carl Cohen, in "Do Animals Have Rights?" argues that while we may have certain obligations to animals, it does not follow from this that animals have rights. Rights, he argues, are essentially human.

The final papers in this section address the moral controversy surrounding same-sex marriage. In "The Case for Gay Marriage," Michael Nava and Robert Dawidoff argue that exclusionary marriage laws not only violate the rights of gays and lesbians who would marry if they could, but they harm the institution of marriage, contribute to the instability of relationships, reinforce sexual inequality, and are ultimately unfair.

In "The Case Against Gay Marriage," Manuel Lopez argues that the institution of marriage is a fundamental part of our world and provides guidance that helps people live their lives. Lopez portrays marriage as we know it as bound up with natural sexual differentiation and the potential for reproduction. Marriage is an institution that developed over many centuries to meet the needs of heterosexuals. Gay marriage, on the other hand, would inevitably be a kind of imitation; it couldn't wholly succeed and would result in a self-conscious parody. Lopez argues that permitting gay marriage would therefore weaken the institution of marriage for everyone.

The Case for Moral Objectivism

Louis P. Pojman

There is a great uniformity among the actions of men, in all nations and ages, and that human nature remains still the same, in its principles and operations. The same events follow from the same causes. Ambition, avarice, self-love, vanity, friendship, generosity, public spirit; these passions, mixed in various degrees, and distributed through society, have been, from the beginning of the world, and still are, the source of all the actions and enterprises which have ever been observed among mankind. . . . [History's] chief use is only to discover the constant and universal principles of human nature, by showing men in all varieties of circumstances and situations, and furnishing us with materials, from which we may form our observations, and become acquainted with the regular springs of human action and behavior.

David Hume, *Essays, Moral, Political and Literary*

. . . Moral relativism is the thesis that moral principles gain their validity only via approval by the culture or the individual, and it is plagued with severe problems. But showing that relativism is loaded with liabilities is one thing; showing that moral principles have objective validity, independent of cultural acceptance, is quite another. If the objectivists are to make their case, they must offer a better explanation of cultural diversity and of why we should nevertheless adhere to moral objectivism. One kind of explanation is to appeal to a divine law and to human sin, which causes deviation from that law. Although I think that human greed, selfishness, pride, self-deception, and other maladies have a great deal to do with moral differences and that religion may lend great support to morality, I don't think that a religious justification is necessary to establish the validity of moral principles. Another kind of explanation is to appeal to the doctrine of **natural law,** which holds that morality is a function of human nature, meaning that reason can discover valid moral principles by looking at the nature of humanity and society. I will examine this position and distinguish a strong, or absolutist, version from a moderate, or nonabsolutist, version of natural law. I will defend this latter view, which may be called *modest objectivism*, first by appealing to our intuitions and second by giving a naturalist account of morality that transcends individual cultures.

First, let's distinguish between moral **absolutism** and moral **objectivism**. The absolutist believes there are nonoverridable moral principles that one ought never violate. The moral norms are *exceptionless*. Kant's system is a good example of this. One ought never break a promise, no matter what. *Act utilitarianism* also seems absolutist, for the principle "Do that act that has the most promise of yielding the most utility" is nonoverridable. In this chapter, we examine the strong view of natural law, which is also absolutist.

The objectivist, on the other hand, shares with the absolutist the notion that moral principles have universal, objective validity but denies that moral norms are necessarily exceptionless. The objectivist could believe that, although moral principles override all other considerations, no moral duty has absolute weight or strict priority; each moral principle must be weighed against other moral principles. There are many types of objectivism, ranging from the position that there are some absolutes and some nonabsolute objective principles to the position that there are no absolutes, some nonabsolute objective principles, and some principles that are valid through a society's acceptance.

We turn first to the absolutist position, natural law ethics.

Natural Law

The idea of natural law first appears among the Stoics (first century B.C.), who believed that human beings have within them a divine spark (*logos spermatikos*—"the rational seed or sperm") that enables them to discover the essential eternal laws necessary for individual happiness and social harmony.[1] The whole universe is governed by laws that exhibit rationality. Nature in general and animals in particular obey these laws by necessity, but humans have choice. Humans obey these laws because they can perceive the laws' inner reasonableness. This notion enabled the Stoics to be *cosmopolitans* ("people of the cosmos") who imposed a universal standard of righteousness (*jus naturale*) on all societies, evaluating various positive laws (*jus gentium*—"laws of the nations") by this higher bar of reason.

Thomas Aquinas (1225–1274) combined the sense of cosmic natural law with Aristotle's view that human beings, like every other natural object, have a specific nature, purpose, and function. A knife's function is to cut sharply, a chair's function is to support the body in a certain position, and a house's function is to provide shelter from the elements. Humanity's essence or proper function is to live the life of reason. As Aristotle put it,

Reason is the true self of every man, since it is the supreme and better part. It will be strange, then, if he should choose not his own life, but some other's. . . . What is naturally proper to every creature is the highest and pleasantest for him. And so, to man, this will be the life of Reason, since Reason is, in the highest sense, a man's self.[2]

Humanity's function is to exhibit rationality in all its forms: contemplation, deliberation, and action. For Aquinas, reason's deliberative processes discover the natural laws. They are universal rules, or "ordinances of reason for the common good, promulgated by him who has the care of the community":

To the natural law belong those things to which a man is inclined naturally; and among these it is proper to man to be inclined to act according to reason. . . . Hence this is the first precept of law, that *good is to be done and promoted, and evil is to be avoided*. All other precepts of the natural law are based upon this; so that all the things which the practical reason naturally apprehends as man's good belong to the precepts of the natural law under the form of things to be done or avoided.

Since, however, good has the nature of an end, and evil, the nature of the contrary, hence it is that all those things to which man has a natural inclination are naturally apprehended by reason as good, and consequently as objects of pursuit, and their contraries as evil, and objects of avoidance. Therefore, the order of the precepts of the natural law is according to the order of natural inclinations.[3]

Aquinas and other Christians who espoused natural law appealed to the Epistle to the Romans in the New Testament, where Paul wrote:

When the Gentiles, who have not the [Jewish-revealed] law, do by nature what the law requires, they are a law to themselves, even though they do not have the law. They show that what the law requires is written on their hearts, while their conscience also bears witness and their conflicting thoughts accuse or perhaps excuse them.

The key ideas of the natural law tradition are the following:

1. Human beings have an essential rational nature established by God, who designed us to live and flourish in prescribed ways (from Aristotle and the Stoics).
2. Even without knowledge of God, reason, as the essence of our nature, can discover the laws necessary for human flourishing (from Aristotle; developed by Aquinas).

3. The natural laws are universal and unchangeable, and one should use them to judge individual societies and their positive laws. Positive (or actual) laws of societies that are not in line with the natural law are not truly laws but counterfeits (from the Stoics).

Moral laws have objective validity. Reason can sort out which inclinations are part of our true nature and how we are to relate them to one another. Aquinas listed the desires for life and procreation as fundamental values without which other values could not even get established. Knowledge and friendship (or sociability) are two other intrinsic values. These values are not good because we desire them; rather, we desire them because they are good—they are absolutely necessary for human flourishing.

Aquinas's position and the natural law tradition are in general absolutist. Humanity has an essentially rational nature, and reason can discover the right action in every situation by following an appropriate, exceptionless principle. But sometimes we encounter moral conflicts, dilemmas in which we cannot do good without also bringing about evil consequences. To this end, the **doctrine of double effect** was devised—a doctrine that provides a neat algorithm for solving all moral disputes in which an act will have two effects, one good and the other bad. The doctrine says, roughly, that it is always wrong to do a bad act intentionally in order to bring about good consequences, but that it is sometimes permissible to do a good act despite knowing that it will bring about bad consequences. This doctrine consists in four conditions that must be satisfied before an act is morally permissible:

1. *The Nature-of-the-Act Condition*   The action must be either morally good or indifferent. Lying or intentionally killing an innocent person is never permissible.
2. *The Means-End Condition*   The bad effect must not be the means by which one achieves the good effect.
3. *The Right-Intention Condition*   The intention must be the achieving of only the good effect, with the bad effect being only an unintended side effect. If the bad effect is a means of obtaining the good effect, then the act is immoral. The bad effect may be foreseen but must not be intended.
4. *The Proportionality Condition*   The good effect must be at least equivalent in importance to the bad effect.

Let's illustrate this doctrine by applying it to a woman whose life is endangered by her pregnancy. Is it morally permissible for her to have an abortion in order to save her life? The DDE says that an abortion is not permissible. Since abortion kills an innocent human being and since intentionally killing innocent human beings is always wrong, it is always wrong to have an abortion—even to save the woman's life. Abortion also fails condition 2 (the means–end condition). Killing the innocent in order to bring about a good effect is never justified, not even to save a whole city—or the world. As the Stoics said, "Let justice be done, though the heavens fall." However, if the woman's uterus happens to be cancerous, then she may have a hysterectomy, even though it will result in the death of the fetus. This is because the act of removing a cancerous uterus is morally good (thus passing condition 1). The act of performing a hysterectomy also passes condition 3, since the death of the fetus is the unintended (though foreseen) effect of the hysterectomy. Condition 2 is passed, since the death of the fetus isn't the means of saving the woman's life—the hysterectomy is. Condition 4 is passed, since saving the woman's life is a great good, at least as good as saving the fetus. In this case, given the DDE, the woman is really lucky to have a cancerous uterus (rather than a pregnancy-related life-threatening condition).

On the other hand, if the doctor could save the woman's life only by changing the composition of the amniotic fluid (say, with saline solution), which in turn would kill the fetus, then this would not be morally permissible according to the DDE. In this case, the same result occurs as in the hysterectomy, but killing the fetus is *intended* as the means of saving the woman's life. Similarly, a craniotomy, or crushing the fetus's head in order to remove it and thus save the woman's life, would be disallowed, since this would violate conditions 2 and 3.

The Roman Catholic Church uses this doctrine to prohibit not only most abortions but also the use of contraceptives. Since the procreation of life is good and the frustration of life is bad and since the natural purpose of sexual intercourse is to produce new life, it is wrong to use devices that prevent intercourse from producing its natural result.

Or consider the trolley problem, first set forth by Philippa Foot. A trolley is speeding down a track, when Edward the driver notices that the brakes have failed. Five people are standing on the track a short distance ahead of the trolley and will be killed if something is not done. To the right is a sidetrack on which a single worker is working. Should Edward steer the trolley to the sidetrack, killing the single worker? Utilitarians and many others would say that Edward should turn the trolley to the sidetrack, for it is better to kill one man than allow five equally innocent men to die. The DDE would seem to prohibit this action, holding that it would violate conditions 2 and 3, or at least condition 2: doing a bad effect to bring about a good effect. It would seem to violate condition 3 since the effect of turning the trolley to the right sidetrack is so closely linked with the death of the worker. The idea is that killing is worse than letting die. So Edward should not turn the trolley to the sidetrack.

Consider another example. Suppose Sally's father has planted a nuclear bomb that will detonate in a half hour. Sally is the only person who knows where he hid it, and she has promised him that she will not reveal the location to anyone. Although she regrets his act, as a devoted daughter she refuses to break her promise and give away the secret. However, if we do not discover where the bomb is and dismantle it within the next half hour, it will blow up a city and kill a million people. Suppose we can torture Sally in order to get this information from her. According to the DDE, is this permissible? No, for the end does not justify the means. Condition 2 is violated. We are using a bad act to bring about a good effect.

On the other hand, suppose someone has tampered with the wires of my television set in such a way that turning it on will send an electrical signal to the next town, where it will detonate a bomb. Suppose I know that this will happen. Is it morally wrong, according to the DDE, to turn on my television to watch an edifying program? Yes it is, since condition 4 is violated. The unintended evil outweighs the good.

But if we interpret the proportionality principle in this way, then a lot of other seemingly innocent or good actions would also violate it. Suppose I am contemplating joining the true religion (I leave you to tell me which one that is) in order to save my eternal soul. However, I realize that, by doing so, I will create enormous resentment in my neighborhood over my act, resentment that will cause five neighbors to be damned. Or suppose my marrying the woman of my heart's desire generates such despair in five other fellows (who, we may imagine, would be reasonably happy as bachelors as long as no one married her) that they all commit suicide. We may suppose that the despair I cause these five fellows will make their free will nonoperational. I understand ahead of time that my act will have this result. Is my act morally justified?

There is also a problem with distinguishing unforeseen from unintended consequences. Could I not redescribe abortion in which the woman's health or life is in danger as *intending* to improve the woman's health (or save her life) and only foreseeing that removing the fetus will result in its (unintended) death? Or could I not steal some food from the grocery store, intending to feed the poor and foreseeing that the grocer will be slightly poorer?

Of course, the DDE must set limits to redescription; otherwise, almost any act can be justified by ingenious redescription (see if you can redescribe the craniotomy case to fit condition 3). Eric D'Arcy has attempted to set such limits. He quotes the jingle "Imperious Caesar, dead and turned to clay, might stop a hole to keep the wind away," but adds that it would be ridiculous to describe killing Caesar as intending to block a windy draft. His own solution to this problem is that "certain kinds of acts are of such significance that the terms which denote them may not, special contexts apart, be elided into terms which (a) denote their consequences, and (b) conceal, or even fail to reveal, the nature of the act itself."[4]

This explanation may lend plausibility to the DDE, but it is not always possible to identify the exact nature of the act itself—it may have various interpretations. Furthermore, the absolutism of the doctrine will make it counterintuitive to many of us. It would seem to prohibit lying in order to save a life or breaking a promise in order to spare someone great suffering. Why should we accept a system that allows the destruction of many innocent people simply because we may have to override a normal moral precept? Aren't morals made for the human good? And doesn't the strong natural law tradition get things reversed—requiring that humans serve rules for the rules' own sake? Furthermore, there may be more than a single right answer to every moral dilemma. The DDE seems **casuistic,** making hairsplitting distinctions that miss the point of morality. It gives us solutions to problems that seem to impose an artificial rigidity on human existence.

There is one other difficulty with the absolute version of natural law: It is tied closely to a teleological view of human nature, a view that sees humanity, and each individual, as having a plan designed by God or a godlike nature that any deviation from the norm is morally wrong. Hence, since the plan of humanity includes procreation and since sexuality is the means to that goal, only heterosexual intercourse (without artificial birth control devices) is morally permitted.

If Darwinian evolutionary theory is correct, there is no design. Human beings are animals who evolved from "lower" forms of life via the survival of the fittest. We are the product of chance in this struggle for existence. If this is so, then the ideas of a single human purpose and an absolute set of laws to serve that purpose are problematic. We may have many purposes, and our moral domain may include a certain relativity. For example, heterosexuality may serve one social purpose whereas homosexuality serves another, and both may be fulfilling for different types of individuals. Reason's task may not be to discover an essence of humanity or unchangeable laws, but, rather, simply to help us survive and fulfill our desires.

However, even if this nonreligious account of evolution is inaccurate and there is a God who has guided evolution, it's still not obvious that the absolutist's way of looking at the world and morality is the best one available. Nonetheless, the DDE may remind us of important moral truths: (1) Negative duties are typically more stringent than positive ones. Ordinarily, it is less wrong to allow an evil than to do evil—otherwise, a maniac, known to reliably execute his threats, could get us to kill someone, merely by threatening to kill five people unless we carried out the murder; (2) people have rights that must be respected, so we cannot simply decide what to do based on a crude utilitarian calculus.

Although I must say more on this subject, I now want to propose a more modest version of an objectivist ethics, one that is consistent with evolutionary theory but could be seen as a nonabsolutist version of the natural law theory.

Moderate Objectivism

If we give up the notion that a moral system must contain only absolute principles, duties that proceed out of a definite algorithm such as the doctrine of double effect, what can we put in its place?

The moderate objectivist's account of moral principles is what William Ross refers to as "prima facie principles"[5]—valid rules of action to which one should generally adhere but, in cases of moral conflict, may be overrideable by another moral principle. For example, even though a principle of justice may generally outweigh a principle of benevolence, there are times when one could do enormous good by sacrificing a small amount of justice; thus, an objectivist would be inclined to act according to the principle of benevolence. There may be some absolute or nonoverridable principles, but there need not be any (or many) for objectivism to be true.[6] Renford Bambrough states this point nicely:

> To suggest that there is a *right* answer to a moral problem is at once to be accused of or credited with a belief in moral absolutes. But it is no more necessary to believe in moral absolutes in order to believe in moral objectivity than it is to believe in the existence of absolute space or absolute time in order to believe in the objectivity of temporal and spatial relations and of judgments about them.[7]

If we can establish or show that it is reasonable to believe that there is, in some ideal sense, at least one objective moral principle that is binding on all people everywhere, then we shall have shown that relativism probably is false and that a limited objectivism is true. Actually, I believe that many qualified general ethical principles are binding on all rational beings, but one principle will suffice to refute relativism:

A. It is morally wrong to torture people for the fun of it.

I claim that this principle is binding on all rational agents, so that if some agent, S, rejects A, we should not let that affect our intuition that A is a true principle; rather, we should try to explain S's behavior as perverse, ignorant, or irrational instead. For example, suppose Adolf Hitler doesn't accept A. Should that affect our confidence in the truth of A? Is it not more reasonable to infer that Hitler is morally deficient, morally blind, ignorant, or irrational than to suppose that his noncompliance is evidence against the truth of A?

Suppose further there is a tribe of "Hitlerites" somewhere who enjoy torturing people. Their whole culture accepts torturing others for the fun of it. Suppose Mother Teresa or Mahatma Gandhi tries unsuccessfully to convince these sadists that they should stop torturing people altogether, and the sadists respond by torturing her or him. Should this affect our confidence in A? Would it not be more reasonable to look for some explanation of Hitlerite behavior? For example, we might hypothesize that this tribe lacks the developed sense of sympathetic imagination that is necessary for the moral life. Or we might theorize that this tribe is on a lower evolutionary level than most *Homo sapiens*. Or we might simply conclude that the tribe is closer to a Hobbesian state of nature than most societies and as such probably would not survive very long—or if it did, the lives of its people would be largely "solitary, poor, nasty, brutish and short," as in the Ik culture in northern Uganda, where the core morality has partly broken down.

But we need not know the correct answer about why the tribe is in such bad shape in order to maintain our confidence in A as a moral principle. If A is a basic or core belief for us, then we will be more likely to doubt the Hitlerites' sanity or ability to think morally than to doubt the validity of A.

We can perhaps produce other candidates for membership in our minimally basic objective moral set:

1. Do not kill innocent people.
2. Do not cause unnecessary pain or suffering.
3. Do not steal or cheat.
4. Keep your promises and honor your contracts.
5. Do not deprive another person of his or her freedom.

6. Tell the truth or, at least, don't lie.
7. Do justice, treating equals as equals and unequals as unequals.
8. Reciprocate. Show gratitude for services rendered.
9. Help other people, especially when the cost to oneself is minimal.
10. Obey just laws.

These ten principles are examples of the *core morality*, principles necessary for the good life within a flourishing human community. They are not arbitrary, for we can give reasons that explain why they are constitutive elements of a successful society, necessary to social cohesion and personal well-being. Principles like the Golden Rule, not killing innocent people, treating equals equally, truth telling, promise keeping, respecting liberty, and the like are central to the fluid progression of social interaction and the resolution of conflicts of interest that ethics bears on (at least minimal morality does, even though there may be more to morality than simply these concerns). For example, language itself depends on a general and implicit commitment to the principle of truth telling. Accuracy of expression is a primitive form of truthfulness. Hence, every time we use words correctly (e.g., "That is a book" or "My name is Sam"), we are telling the truth. Without a high degree of reliable matching between words and objects, language itself would be impossible. Likewise, without the practice of promise keeping we could not rely on one another's words when they inform us about future acts. We could have no reliable expectations about their behavior. But our lives are social, dependent on cooperation, so it is vital that when we make agreement (e.g., "I'll help you with your philosophy paper, if you'll help me install a new computer program"). We need to have confidence that the other party will reciprocate when we have done our part. Even chimpanzees follow the rule of reciprocity, *returning good for good* (*returning evil for evil* may not be as necessary for morality) and without a prohibition against stealing and cheating, we could not claim property—not even ownership of our very limbs, let alone external goods. Without the protection of innocent life and liberty, we could hardly attain our goals. Sometimes people question whether rule 7—"Do justice, treating equals as equals and unequals as unequals"—is valid. But this only specifies a formal condition of justice—act consistently. If a teacher gives Jack an A– for a certain quality of essay, she should give Jill the same grade if her essay is of the same quality. A stronger, more substantive principle of justice would be "Give people what they deserve," and you might want to substitute this for the purely formal principle. Of course, these principles are **prima facie,** not absolutes. They can be overridden when they come into conflict, but in general they should be adhered to in order to give maximal guarantee for the good life.

There may be other moral rules necessary or highly relevant to an objective core morality. A moral code would be adequate if it contained a requisite set of these objective principles, but there could be more than one adequate moral code that contained different rankings or different combinations of rules; there may be specific, necessary rules in different situations. Different specific rules may be required in different situations. For example, in a desert community, there may be a strict rule prohibiting the wasting of water, and in a community with a preponderance of females over males, there may be a rule permitting polygamy. Such moral plasticity does not entail moral relativism, but simply a recognition that social situations can determine which rules are relevant to the flourishing community. A society where birth control devices are available may differ from one that lacks such technology on the rule prescribing chastity. Nevertheless, an essential core morality, such as that described above, will be universally necessary.

The core moral rules are analogous to the set of vitamins necessary for a healthy diet. We need an adequate amount of each vitamin—some need more of one than another—but in prescribing a nutritional diet we needn't set forth recipes, specific foods, place settings, or culinary habits. Gourmets will meet the requirements differently than ascetics and vegetarians, but all may obtain the basic nutrients without rigid regimentation or an absolute set of recipes.

In more positive terms, an objectivist who bases his or her moral system on a common human nature with common needs and desires might argue for objectivism in the following manner:

1. Human nature is relatively similar in essential respects, having a common set of basic needs and interests.
2. Moral principles are functions of human needs and interests, instituted by reason in order to meet the needs and promote the most significant interests of human (or rational) beings.
3. Some moral principles will meet needs and promote human interests better than other principles will.
4. Principles that will meet essential human needs and promote the most significant interests in optimal ways are objectively valid moral principles.
5. Therefore, since there is a common human nature, there is an objectively valid set of moral principles, applicable to all humanity (or rational beings).

The argument assumes that there is a common human nature. In a sense, an objectivist accepts the *strong dependency thesis* discussed in the last chapter on relativism—morality does depend on some social reality for its authentication, only it is not the reality or cultural acceptance but the reality of our nature as rational beings, with needs, interests, and the ability to reason. there is only one large human framework to which all humans belong and to which all principles are relative.[8] The quotation from David Hume at the beginning of this chapter nicely describes such a thesis. Relativists, some calling themselves *postmodernists*, sometimes claim that the idea of a common human nature is an illusion, but our knowledge of human genetics, as well as anthropology and history, provides overwhelming evidence that we are all related by common needs, interests, and desires. We all generally prefer to survive, to be happy, to experience love and friendship rather than hatred and enmity, to be successful in reaching our goals, and the like. Still, even without the concept of a common human nature, we could construct a similar argument for objectivism:

1. Objectively moral principles are such that adherence to them meets the needs and promotes the most significant interests of persons.
2. Some principles are such that adherence to them meets the needs of and promotes the most significant interests of persons.
3. Therefore, there are some objectively valid moral principles.

Either argument would satisfy objectivism, but the first argument makes it clearer that our common human nature generates the need for common moral principles.[9] The second argument would provide a basis for morality even if we had different natures.

If this argument is sound, at least one ideal morality (not merely *adequate* ones) exists. There could be more than one ideal morality, which presumably an ideal observer (perhaps God) would choose under ideal conditions. The ideal observer may conclude that, out of an infinite set of moralities, two or three or more moralities would tie for first place. One would expect these to be relevantly similar, but there is reason to believe that all would contain the set of core moral principles.

Of course, we don't know exactly what an ideal observer would choose, but we can imagine that such an observer would choose under conditions of impartiality and maximal knowledge about the consequences of action types, second-order qualities that ensure that agents have the best chance of making optimal decisions. If this is so, then the more we learn to judge impartially and the more we know about possible forms of life, the better chance we have to approximate an ideal moral system. If ideal moral systems with an objective core and other objective components can be approximated, then ethical relativism is false, and ethical objectivism true.

Let me make the same point by appealing to your intuitions through relating a childhood dream. Deeply afraid that I, as a naughty child, would go to hell when I died, I would regularly be visited with nightmares of dying and descending into the abode of the damned. One night I dreamed that I had died and gone to the dark kingdom of hell. But it wasn't so dark, for I viewed the damned writhing in abject misery, contorting their faces and howling like wounded dogs. Why were they writhing and howling? What was their punishment? Well, they had eternal back itches that ebbed and flowed. But they were unable to scratch their backs because their arms were paralyzed in a frontal position, so they writhed with itchiness throughout eternity. But just as I began to feel my own back itch, I was transported to heaven. What do you think I saw in the kingdom of the blessed? People with eternal back itches who couldn't scratch their own backs. Nevertheless, they were all smiling ecstatically, not writhing. Why? Because everyone had stretched his or her arms forward to scratch someone else's back, and, so arranged in one big circle, they turned a hell of abject agony into a heaven of supreme bliss.

If we can imagine some states of affairs or cultures that are better than others in a way that depends on human action, we can ask what character traits make them so. In my dream, people in heaven, unlike those in hell, cooperate to ameliorate suffering and produce pleasure and happiness. These are very primitive goods, not sufficient for a full-blown morality, but they give us a hint about the objectivity of morality. Moral goodness has something to do with the amelioration of suffering, the resolution of conflicts, and the promotion of human flourishing. If a blissful heaven is rationally preferable, really better than the eternal itchiness of hell, then whatever makes it so is constitutively related to moral rightness.

An Explanation of the Attraction of Ethical Relativism

If one can make a reasonable case for a modest objectivism, why is there such a strong inclination toward ethical relativism? I think there are five reasons, which haven't been adequately emphasized. The first reason is that the operations are usually presented as though absolutism and relativism were the only alternatives, so conventionalism wins out against an implausible competitor. My student questionnaire reads: "Are there any ethical absolutes—moral duties binding on all persons at all times—

or are moral duties relative to culture? Is there any alternative to these two positions?" Less than 5 percent of my students suggest a third position, and very few of these identify objectivism. Granted, it takes a little philosophical sophistication to make the crucial distinctions, and it is precisely for the lack of this sophistication or reflection that relativism has achieved its enormous prestige. But, as Ross and others have shown and as I have argued in this chapter, one can have an objective morality without being absolutist.

The second reason for the inclination toward ethical relativism is similar to the first. Some philosophers and thoughtful people confuse objectivism with **realism,** the view that moral truths make up an independent reality, as scientific truths do. Plato is perhaps the classic realist; he believed in a separate and transcendental sphere of reality ("the really real") wherein ideal forms exist that all the things in our world more or less copy. Moral ideals and principles would have their existence in this sphere of reality. Most contemporary moral realists hold less extravagant views, but they believe, nevertheless, in an independent status for moral truths. Moral principles are synthetic a priori truths or necessary truths, valid for all possible worlds. But moral objectivists need not be realists. They may affirm the validity of moral principles only on the basis of common human nature and intersubjective agreement among people in favorable conditions.

A leading relativist, my teacher, J. L. Mackie, while attacking moral objectivism, admits that there is a great deal of intersubjectivity in ethics: "There could be agreement in valuing even if valuing is just something people do, even if this activity is not further validated. Subjective agreement would give intersubjective values, but intersubjectivity is not objectivity."[10] But Mackie fails to note that there are two kinds of intersubjectivity and that one of them gives all that the objectivist wants for a moral theory. Consider the following situations of intersubjective agreement:

A1. All the children in first grade at school S would agree that playing in the mud is preferable to learning arithmetic.
A2. All the youth in the district would rather take drugs than go to school.
A3. All the people in Jonestown, Guyana, agree that Reverend Jones is a prophet from God and love him dearly.
A4. Almost all the people in community C voted for Bill Clinton.

B1. All the thirsty desire water to quench their thirst.
B2. All humans (and animals) prefer pleasure to pain.

B3. Almost all people agree that living in society is more satisfying than living alone as hermits.

The naturalist contrasts these two sets of intersubjective agreements (A1–A4 and B1–B3) and says that the first set is accidental, not part of what it means to be a person, whereas the agreements in the second set are basic to being a person, basic to our nature. Agreement on the essence of morality, the core set, is the kind of intersubjective agreement that is more like the second set, not the first set. It is part of the essence of humans in community, part of what it means to flourish as a person, to agree with and adhere to the moral code.

The third reason is that our recent sensitivity to **cultural relativism** and the evils of ethnocentrism, which have plagued Europeans' and Americans' relations with people of other cultures, has made us conscious of the frailty of many aspects of our moral repertoire, so there is a tendency to wonder, "Who's to judge what's really right and wrong?" However, the move from a reasonable cultural relativisim, which rightly causes us to rethink our moral systems, to an ethical relativism, which causes us to give up the heart of morality altogether, exemplifies the fallacy of confusing factual or descriptive statements with normative ones. Cultural relativism doesn't entail ethical relativism. The very reason that we are against ethnocentrism constitutes the basis for our favoring an objective moral system: Impartial reason draws us to it.

We may well agree that cultures differ and that we ought to be cautious in condemning what we don't understand, but this in no way must imply that there are not better and worse ways of living. We can understand and excuse, to some degree at least, those who differ from our best notions of morality, without abdicating the notion that cultures that lack principles of justice, promise keeping, or protection of the innocent are morally poorer for these omissions.

The fourth reason, which has driven some to moral nihilism and others to relativism, is the decline of religion in Western society. As one of Dostoevsky's characters said, "If God is dead, all things are permitted." People who have lost religious faith feel a deep vacuum and understandably confuse it with a moral vacuum, or they finally become resigned to a form of secular conventionalism. Such people reason that, if there is no God to guarantee the validity of the moral order, then there must be no universal moral order—just radical cultural diversity and death at the end. I have tried to argue that, even without God, objective moral principles are valid.

The fifth reason, one that is influential with philosophers overimpressed with *metaethics*, is that many philosophers believe it is important to begin the study of ethics with a morally neutral definition. *Merriam Webster's Collegiate Dictionary* (tenth edition) defines *ethics* as "the principles of conduct governing an individual or a group." No judgment is made from the outset about the content of those principles, and since the diversity thesis is plausible, one can be led to think that a certain relativism follows.

Although this definition may be a fair one for sociology or anthropology, it is inadequate for philosophy. There is a narrower, more substantive definition of *ethics* that has to do with the good, with human flourishing (and, I believe, with animal flourishing as well). And this flourishing involves the amelioration of suffering, the resolution of conflicts of interest, and the promotion of happiness. Given this content-laden conception of morality, we can explain why we are loathe to call Hitler's actions or the torturing of little children morally right, regardless of whether a majority approves of such actions.

Conclusion

I have presented arguments for an objective morality—both the strong natural law version and the moderate objectivist (or moderate natural law) version. If either of these is correct, then society will not long survive, and individuals will not flourish, without adherence to a core set of moral principles. Reason can discover the correct principles, and it is in our interest to promote them.

Who's to judge what's right and wrong? The reply is, "We are—every rational being on Earth." And we are to judge on the basis of the best reasoning we can bring forth, in dialogue with one another, and with sympathy and understanding.

Notes

1. Arthur Kuflik, in his review of this book [from which this chapter is excerpted], has pointed out that one can find the idea of natural law in the early chapters of Genesis and in the Talmud. Kuflik writes:

   As long as we are looking for *early* manifestations of natural law thinking (and not insisting on a wholly nontheistic model for natural law), we can find very important elements of natural law thinking in the first chapters of *Genesis:* (1) when God approaches Cain about the whereabouts of Abel, Cain doesn't simply say he killed him (something he might well have said without guilt or fear if he had no sense of having behaved wrongly). On the contrary, Cain is afraid to answer God truthfully and he is awkwardly defensive in his denial that he knows what happened to Abel. But recall that

God had not previously laid down any law against murder nor made any explicit pronouncement on the wrongness of murder. Despite this, God punishes Cain. Cain and Able were the third and fourth human beings ever to walk the earth—universal human prototypes—living long before the revelations on Mount Sinai of an elaborate Divine Law. Hence implicit in this story is the idea that murder is a basic, naturally recognizable wrong that can be justly punished with *or without* a preexisting humanly legislated or Divinely stated prohibition; (2) when God sets out to destroy all the people on earth except Noah and his family—because the earth was "filled with violence"—the implication seems to be not only that those other people should have lived *much* less violent lives than they did, but that they should have, and could have, realized the badness of their ways; also (3) in Deuteronomy 30:11–14, Moses, speaking on behalf of God, claims that the commandment which God had commanded the people that day [to do what is good and refrain from what is evil] is not "far off"—"it is not in the heavens that you should say, who will go up and bring it down to us" but is "near to you . . . in your mouth and in your heart." Kuflik also points out that the Talmudic rabbis worked a theory called "the seven laws of the sons of Noah" that contained rules of conduct "that all the peoples of the world (descended after all from Noah) should be able to recognize and live by even though they were not audience to an explicit Divine Revelation such as took place at Mount Sinai."

2. Aristotle, *Nicomachean Ethics*, trans. W. D. Ross, Oxford University Press, 1925, bk. 10. p.7.

3. Thomas Aquinas, *Summa Theologica*, in *Basic Writings of St. Thomas Aquinas*, trans. A. C. Pegis, Random House, 1945, question 94. All references to Aquinas are from this volume.

4. Eric D'Arcy, *Human Acts*, Oxford University Press, 1963, ch. 4. Quoted in J. Glover, *Causing Deaths and Saving Lives* (Penguin Books, 1977), p. 91.

5. William Ross, *The Right and the Good*, Oxford University Press, 1932, p. 18 f.

6. See Marcus Singer's "The Idea of a Rational Morality" in *Proceedings of the American Philosophical Association* (September 1986), in which he argues that such principles as "It is always wrong to lie for lying's sake" are absolutely wrong. "Given any moral rule to the effect that some kind of action is generally wrong, it follows that it is always wrong to do an act of that kind just for the sake of doing it" (p. 28). An unqualified general principle would be of the form "Always do X" or "In general, do X," but a qualified general principle would be of the form "In general, do X except under condition C" or "Except under condition C, always do X." Suitably conditioned objective principles might turn out to be qualified absolutes. I am sympathetic to this approach and suspect that some absolutes are valid. Most objectively valid moral principles seem to be principles of prima facie duty rather than of absolute, unconditional duty.

7. Renford Bambrough, *Moral Skepticism and Moral Knowledge*, Routledge & Kegan Paul, 1979, p. 33.
8. In Gilbert Harman's essay "Moral Relativism," in Gilbert Harman and Judith Jarvis Thomson, *Moral Relativism and Moral Objectivity*, Blackwell, 1996, p. 5, he defines moral relativism as the claim that "there is no single true morality. There are many different moral frameworks, none of which is more correct than the others." I hold that morality has a function of serving the needs and interests of human beings, so some frameworks do this better than others. Essentially, all adequate theories will contain the principles I have identified in this essay.
9. I owe the reformulation of the argument to Bruce Russell.
10. J. L. Mackie, *Ethics: Inventing Right and Wrong*, Penguin, 1977, p. 22.

Must God's Commands Conform to Moral Standards?

James Rachels

In both the Jewish and Christian traditions, God is presented as a law-giver who has created us, and the world we live in, for a purpose. That purpose is not completely understood, but much has been revealed through the prophets, the Holy Scriptures, and the church. These sources teach that, to guide us in righteous living, God has promulgated rules that we are to obey. He does not compel us to obey them. We were created as free agents, so we may choose to accept or to reject his commandments. But if we are to live as we *should* live, we must follow God's laws. This, it is said, is the essence of morality.

This line of thought has been elaborated by some theologians into a theory about the nature of right and wrong, known as the *Divine Command Theory*. Essentially, this theory says that "morally right" means "commanded by God," and "morally wrong" means "forbidden by God."

From a theoretical point of view, this conception has a number of pleasing features. It immediately solves the old problem about the subjectivity/objectivity of ethics. According to this theory, ethics is not merely a matter of personal feelings or social custom. Whether something is right or wrong is a perfectly objective matter: it is right if God commands it, wrong if God forbids it. Moreover, the Divine Command Theory suggests an answer to the perennial question of why anyone should bother with morality. Why not just look out for one's own interests? If immorality is the violation of God's commandments, there is an easy answer: on the day of final reckoning, you will be held accountable.

There are, however, serious problems for the theory. Of course, atheists would not accept it, because they do not believe that God exists. But the problems that arise are not merely problems for atheists. There are difficulties even for believers. The main problem was first noted by Plato, the Greek philosopher who lived 400 years before the birth of Jesus.

Plato's writings were in the form of dialogues, usually between Socrates and one or more interlocutors. In one of these dialogues, the *Euthyphro*, there is a discussion concerning whether "right" can be defined as "that which the gods command." Socrates is skeptical and asks: *Is conduct right because the gods command it, or do the gods command it because it is right?* It is one of the most famous questions in the history of philosophy. The contemporary British philosopher Antony Flew suggests that "one good test of a person's aptitude for philosophy is to discover whether he can grasp its force and point."

The point is this. If we accept the theological conception of right and wrong, we are caught in a dilemma. Socrates's question asks us to clarify what we mean. There are two things we might mean, and both options lead to trouble.

1. First, we might mean that conduct is right *because God commands it.* For example, according to Exodus 20:16, God commands us to be truthful. On this option, the *reason* we should be truthful is simply that God requires it. Apart from the divine command, truth telling is neither good nor bad. It is God's command that *makes* truthfulness right.

But this leads to trouble, for it represents God's commands as arbitrary. It means that God could have given *different* commands just as easily. He could have commanded us to be liars, and then lying and not truthfulness, would be right. (You may be tempted to reply: "But God would never command us to be liars!" But why not? If he did endorse lying, God would not be commanding us to do wrong, because his command would make lying right.) Remember that on this view, honesty was not right *before* God commanded it. Therefore, he could have had no more reason to command it than its opposite; and so, from a moral point of view, his command is perfectly arbitrary.

Moreover, on this view, the doctrine of the goodness of God is reduced to nonsense. It is important to religious believers that God is not only all-powerful and all-knowing, but that he is also *good*; yet if we accept the idea that good and bad are defined by reference to God's will, this notion is deprived of any meaning. What could it mean to say that God's commands are good? If "X is good" simply means "X is commanded by God," then "God's commands are good" would mean only "God's commands are commanded by God"—an empty truism. In his *Discourse on Metaphysics* (1686) Leibniz put the point very clearly:

> So in saying that things are not good by any rule of goodness, but sheerly by the will of God, it seems to me that one destroys, without realizing it, all the love of God and all his glory. For why praise him for what he has done if he would be equally praiseworthy in doing exactly the contrary?

Thus if we choose the first of Socrates's two options, we are stuck with consequences that even the most religious people must find unacceptable.

2. There is a way to avoid these troublesome consequences. We can take the second of Socrates's options. We need not say that right conduct is right because God commands it. Instead, we may say that God commands right conduct *because it is right*. God, who is infinitely wise, realizes that truthfulness is far better than deceitfulness, and so he commands us to be truthful; he sees that killing is wrong, and so he commands us not to kill; and so on for all the commandments.

If we take this option, we avoid the troublesome consequences that plagued the first alternative. God's commands turn out to be not at all arbitrary; they are the result of his wisdom in knowing what is best. And the doctrine of the goodness of God is preserved: to say that his commands are good means that he commands only what, in perfect wisdom, he sees to be the best. But this option leads to a different problem, which is equally troublesome for the theological conception of right and wrong: indeed, in taking this option, we have virtually *abandoned* the theological conception of right and wrong.

If we say that God commands us to be truthful because truthfulness is right, then we are admitting that there is some standard of right and wrong that is independent of God's will. We are saying that God *sees* or *recognizes* that truthfulness is right: this is very different from his *making* it right. The rightness exists prior to and independent of God's command, and it is the reason for the command. Thus if we want to know why we should be truthful, the reply "Because God commands it" will not take us very far. We may still ask "But why does God command it?" and the answer to *that* question will provide the underlying reasons why truthfulness is a good thing.

All this may be summarized in the following argument:

1. Suppose God commands us to do what is right. Then *either* (a) the right actions are right because he commands them *or* (b) he commands them because they are right.
2. If we take option (a), then God's commands are, from a moral point of view, arbitrary; moreover, the doctrine of the goodness of God is rendered meaningless.
3. If we take option (b), then we have admitted there is a standard of right and wrong that is independent of God's will.
4. Therefore, we must *either* regard God's commands as arbitrary, and give up the doctrine of the goodness of God, *or* admit that there is a standard of right and wrong that is independent of his will, and give up the theological definitions of right and wrong.
5. From a religious point of view, it is undesirable to regard God's commands as arbitrary or to give up the doctrine of the goodness of God.
6. Therefore, even from a religious point of view, a standard of right and wrong that is independent of God's will must be accepted.

Many religious people believe that they should accept a theological conception of right and wrong because it would be impious not to do so. They feel, somehow, that if they believe in God, they *should* think that right and wrong are to be defined ultimately in terms of his will. But this argument suggests otherwise: it suggests that, on the contrary, the Divine Command Theory of right and wrong itself leads to impious results, so that a pious person should *not* accept it. And in fact, some of the greatest theologians, such as St. Thomas Aquinas (ca. 1225–1274), rejected the theory for just this reason.

Utilitarianism*
John Stuart Mill

Chapter I: General Remarks

There are few circumstances among those which make up the present condition of human knowledge more unlike what might have been expected, or more significant of the backward state in which specula-

*From *Utilitarianism*, Chapters I, II and IV. First published in 1863. Public domain.

tion on the most important subjects still lingers, than the little progress which has been made in the decision of the controversy respecting the criterion of right and wrong. From the dawn of philosophy, the question concerning the *summum bonum*, or, what is the same thing, concerning the foundation of morality, has been accounted the main problem in speculative thought, has occupied the most gifted intellects and divided them into sects and schools carrying on a vigorous warfare against one another. And after more than two thousand years the same discussions continue, philosophers are still ranged under the same contending banners, and neither thinkers nor mankind at large seem nearer to being unanimous on the subject than when the youth Socrates listened to the old Protagoras and asserted (if Plato's dialogue be grounded on a real conversation) the theory of utilitarianism against the popular morality of the so-called sophist.

It is true that similar confusion and uncertainty and, in some cases, similar discordance exist respecting the first principles of all the sciences, not excepting that which is deemed the most certain of them—mathematics, without much impairing, generally indeed without impairing at all, the trustworthiness of the conclusions of those sciences. An apparent anomaly, the explanation of which is that the detailed doctrines of a science are not usually deduced from, nor depend for their evidence upon, what are called its first principles. Were it not so, there would be no science more precarious, or whose conclusions were more insufficiently made out, than algebra, which derives none of its certainty from what are commonly taught to learners as its elements, since these, as laid down by some of its most eminent teachers, are as full of fictions as English law, and of mysteries as theology. The truths which are ultimately accepted as the first principles of a science are really the last results of metaphysical analysis practiced on the elementary notions with which the science is conversant; and their relation to the science is not that of foundations to an edifice, but of roots to a tree, which may perform their office equally well though they be never dug down to and exposed to light. But though in science the particular truths precede the general theory, the contrary might be expected to be the case with a practical art, such as morals or legislation. All action is for the sake of some end, and rules of action, it seems natural to suppose, must take their whole character and color from the end to which they are subservient. When we engage in a pursuit, a clear and precise conception of what we are pursuing would seem to be the first thing we need, instead of the last we are to look forward to. A test of right and wrong must be the means, one would think, or ascertaining what is right or wrong, and not a consequence of having already ascertained it.

The difficulty is not avoided by having recourse to the popular theory of a natural, faculty, a sense of instinct, informing us of right and wrong. For—besides that the existence of such a moral instinct is itself one of the matters in dispute—those believers in it who have any pretensions to philosophy have been obliged to abandon the idea that it discerns what is right or wrong in the particular case in hand, as our other senses discern the sight or sound actually present. Our moral faculty, according to all those of its interpreters who are entitled to the name of thinkers, supplies us only with the general principles of moral judgments; it is a branch of our reason, not of our sensitive faculty, and must be looked to for the abstract doctrines of morality, not for perception of it in the concrete. The intuitive, no less than what may be termed the inductive, school of ethics insists on the necessity of general laws. They both agree that the morality of an individual action is not a question of direct perception, but of the application of a law to an individual case. They recognize also, to a great extent, the same moral laws, but differ as to their evidence and the source from which they derive their authority. According to the one opinion, the principles of morals are evident a priori, requiring nothing to command assent except that the meaning of the terms be understood. According to the other doctrine, right and wrong, as well as truth and falsehood, are questions of observation and experience. But both hold equally that morality must be deduced from principles; and the intuitive school affirm as strongly as the inductive that there is a science of morals. Yet they seldom attempt to make out a list of the a priori principles which are to serve as the premises of the science; still more rarely do they make any effort to reduce those various principles to one first principle or common ground of obligation. They either assume the ordinary precepts of morals as of a priori authority, or they lay down as the common groundwork of those maxims some generality much less obviously authoritative than the maxims themselves, and which has never succeeded in gaining popular acceptance. Yet to support their pretensions there ought either to be some one fundamental principle or law at the root of all morality, or, if there be several, there should be a determinate order of precedence among them; and the one principle, or the rule for deciding between the various principles when they conflict, ought to be self-evident.

To inquire how far the bad effects of this deficiency have been mitigated in practice, or to what extent the moral beliefs of mankind have been vitiated or made uncertain by the absence of any distinct recognition of an ultimate standard, would imply a complete survey and criticism of past and present ethical doctrine. It would, however, be easy to show that whatever steadiness or consistency these moral beliefs have

attained has been mainly due to the tacit influence of a standard not recognized. Although the non-existence of an acknowledged first principle
has made ethics not so much a guide as a consecration of men's actual
sentiments, still, as men's sentiments, both of favor and of aversion, are
greatly influenced by what they suppose to be the effects of things upon
their happiness, the principle of utility, or, as Bentham latterly called
it, the greatest happiness principle, has had a large share in forming the
moral doctrines even of those who most scornfully reject its authority. Nor
is there any school of thought which refuses to admit that the influence
of actions on happiness is a most material and even predominant consideration in many of the details of morals, however unwilling to
acknowledge it as the fundamental principle of morality and the source
of moral obligation. I might go much further and say that to all those a
priori moralists who deem it necessary to argue at all, utilitarian arguments are indispensable. It is not my present purpose to criticize these
thinkers; but I cannot help referring, for illustration, to a systematic treatise by one of the most illustrious of them, the *Metaphysics of Ethics* by
Kant. This remarkable man, whose system of thought will long remain
one of the landmarks in the history of philosophical speculation, does,
in the treatise in question, lay down a universal first principle as the
origin and ground of moral obligation; it is this: "So act that the rule
on which thou actest would admit of being adopted as a law by all rational beings." But when he begins to deduce from this precept any of the
actual duties of morality, he fails, almost grotesquely, to show that there
would be any contradiction, any logical (not to say physical) impossibility, in the adoption by all rational beings of the most outrageously
immoral rules of conduct. All he shows is that the *consequences* of their
universal adoption would be such as no one would choose to incur.

On the present occasion, I shall, without further discussion of the
other theories, attempt to contribute something toward the understanding and appreciation of the "utilitarian" or "happiness" theory, and
toward such proof as it is susceptible of. It is evident that this cannot
be proof in the ordinary and popular meaning of the term. Questions
of ultimate ends are not amenable to direct proof. Whatever can be
proved to be good must be so by being shown to be a means to something
admitted to be good without proof. The medical art is proved to be good
by its conducing to health; but how is it possible to prove that health is
good? The art of music is good, for the reason, among others, that it produces pleasure; but what proof is it possible to give that pleasure is good?
If, then, it is asserted that there is a comprehensive formula, including all
things which are in themselves good, and that whatever else is good is not

so as an end but as a means, the formula may be accepted or rejected, but is not a subject of what is commonly understood by proof. We are not, however, to infer that its acceptance or rejection must depend on blind impulse or arbitrary choice. There is a large meaning of the word "proof," in which this question is as amenable to it as any other of the disputed questions of philosophy. The subject is within the cognizance of the rational faculty; and neither does that faculty deal with it solely in the way of intuition. Considerations may be presented capable of determining the intellect either to give or withhold its assent to the doctrine; and this is equivalent to proof.

We shall examine presently of what nature are these considerations; in what manner they apply to the case, and what rational grounds, therefore, can be given for accepting or rejecting the utilitarian formula. But it is a preliminary condition of rational acceptance or rejection that the formula should be correctly understood. I believe that the very imperfect notion ordinarily formed of its meaning is the chief obstacle which impedes its reception, and that, could it be cleared even from only the grosser misconceptions, the question would be greatly simplified and a large proportion of its difficulties removed. Before, therefore, I attempt to enter into the philosophical grounds which can be given for assenting to the utilitarian standard, I shall offer some illustrations of the doctrine itself, with the view of showing more clearly what it is, distinguishing it from what it is not, and disposing of such of the practical objections to it as either originate in, or are closely connected with, mistaken interpretations of its meaning. Having thus prepared the ground, I shall afterwards endeavor to throw such light as I can call upon the question considered as one of philosophical theory.

Chapter II: What Utilitarianism Is

A passing remark is all that needs be given to the ignorant blunder of supposing that those who stand up for utility as the test of right and wrong use the term in that restricted and merely colloquial sense in which utility is opposed to pleasure. An apology is due to the philosophical opponents of utilitarianism for even the momentary appearance of confounding them with anyone capable of so absurd a misconception; which is the more extraordinary, inasmuch as the contrary accusation, of referring everything to pleasure, and that, too, in its grossest form, is another of the common charges against utilitarianism: and, as has been pointedly remarked by an able writer, the same sort of persons, and often the very same persons, denounce the theory "as impracticably dry when the word 'utility' precedes the word 'pleasure,' and as too practically voluptuous when the word 'pleasure' precedes the word 'utility.'" Those who know anything about the matter are aware that every writer, from Epicurus to Bentham, who maintained the theory of utility meant by it, not something to be contradistinguished from pleasure, but pleasure itself, together with exemption from pain; and instead of opposing the useful to the agreeable or the ornamental, have always declared that the useful means these, among other things. Yet the common herd, including the herd of writers, not only in newspapers and periodicals, but in books of weight and pretension, are perpetually falling into this shallow mistake. Having caught up the word "utilitarian," while knowing nothing whatever about it but its sound, they habitually express by it the rejection or the neglect of pleasure in some of its forms: of beauty, of ornament, or of amusement. Nor is the term thus ignorantly misapplied solely in disparagement, but occasionally in compliment, as though it implied superiority to frivolity and the mere pleasures of the moment. And this perverted use is the only one in which the word is popularly known, and the one from which the new generation are acquiring their sole notion of its meaning. Those who introduced the word, but who had for many years discontinued it as a distinctive appellation, may well feel themselves called upon to resume it if by doing so they can hope to contribute anything toward rescuing it from this utter degradation.[1]

The creed which accepts as the foundation of morals "utility" or the "greatest happiness principle" holds that actions are right in proportion as they tend to promote happiness; wrong as they tend to produce the reverse of happiness. By happiness is intended pleasure and the absence of pain; by unhappiness, pain and the privation of pleasure. To give a clear view of the moral standard set up by the theory, much more requires to be said; in particular, what things it includes in the ideas of pain and pleasure, and to what extent this is left an open question. But these supplementary explanations do not affect the theory of life on which this theory of morality is grounded—namely, that pleasure and freedom from pain are the only things desirable as ends; and that all desirable things (which are as numerous in the utilitarian as in any other scheme) are desirable either for pleasure inherent in themselves or as means to the promotion of pleasure and the prevention of pain.

Now such a theory of life excites in many minds, and among them in some of the most estimable in feeling and purpose, inveterate dislike. To suppose that life has (as they express it) no higher end than pleasure—no better and nobler object of desire and pursuit—they designate as utterly mean and groveling, as a doctrine worthy only of swine, to whom the followers of Epicurus were, at a very early period, contemptuously likened; and modern holders of the doctrine are occasionally made the subject of equally polite comparisons by its German, French, and English assailants.

When thus attacked, the Epicureans have always answered that it is not they, but their accusers, who represent human nature in a degrading light, since the accusation supposes human beings to be capable of no pleasures except those of which swine are capable. If this supposition were true, the charge could not be gainsaid, but would then be no longer an imputation; for if the sources of pleasure were precisely the same to human beings and to swine, the rule of life which is good enough for the one would be good enough for the other. The comparison of the Epicurean life to that of beasts is felt as degrading, precisely because a beast's pleasures do not satisfy a human being's conceptions of happiness. Human beings have faculties more elevated than the animal appetites and, when once made conscious of them, do not regard anything as happiness which does not include their gratification. I do not, indeed, consider the Epicureans to have been by any means faultless in drawing out their scheme of consequences from the utilitarian principle. To do this in any sufficient manner, many Stoic, as well as Christian, elements require to be included. But there is no known Epicurean theory of life which does not assign to the pleasures of the intellect, of the feelings and imagination, and of the moral sentiments a much higher value as pleasures than to those of mere sensation. It must be admitted, however, that utilitarian writers in general have placed the superiority of mental over bodily pleasures chiefly in the greater permanency, safety, uncostliness, etc., of the former—that is, in their circumstantial advantages rather than in their intrinsic nature. And on all these points utilitarians have fully proved their case; but they might have taken the other and, as it may be called, higher ground with entire consistency. It is quite compatible with the principle of utility to recognize the fact that some kinds of pleasure are more desirable and more valuable than others. It would be absurd that, while in estimating all other things quality is considered as well as quantity, the estimation of pleasure should be supposed to depend on quantity alone.

If I am asked what I mean by difference of quality in pleasures, or what makes one pleasure more valuable than another, merely as a pleasure, except its being greater in amount, there is but one possible answer. Of two pleasures, if there be one to which all or almost all who have experience of both give a decided preference, irrespective of any feeling of moral obligation to prefer it, that is the more desirable pleasure. If one of the two is, by those who are competently acquainted with both, placed so far above the other that they prefer it, even though knowing it to be

attended with a greater amount of discontent, and would not resign it for
any quantity of the other pleasure which their nature is capable of, we
are justified in ascribing to the preferred enjoyment a superiority in quality so far outweighing quantity as to render it, in comparison, of small
account.

Now it is an unquestionable fact that those who are equally
acquainted with and equally capable of appreciating and enjoying both
do give a most marked preference to the manner of existence which
employs their higher faculties. Few human creatures would consent to be
changed into any of the lower animals for a promise of the fullest
allowance of a beast's pleasures; no intelligent human being would consent to be a fool, no instructed person would be an ignoramus, no person of feeling and conscience would be selfish and base, even though they
should be persuaded that the fool, the dunce, or the rascal is better satisfied with his lot than they are with theirs. They would not resign what
they possess more than he for the most complete satisfaction of all of
the desires which they have in common with him. If they ever fancy
they would, it is only in cases of unhappiness so extreme that to escape
from it they would exchange their lot for almost any other, however undesirable in their own eyes. A being of higher faculties requires more to
make him happy, is capable probably of more acute suffering, and certainly accessible to it at more points, than one of an inferior type; but
in spite of these liabilities, he can never really wish to sink into what
he feels to be a lower grade of existence. We may give what explanation
we please of this unwillingness; we may attribute it to pride, a name
which is given indiscriminately to some of the most and to some of the
least estimable feelings of which mankind are capable; we may refer it
to the love of liberty and personal independence, an appeal to which
was with the Stoics one of the most effective means for the inculcation
of it; to the love of power or to the love of excitement, both of which do
really enter into and contribute to it; but its most appropriate appellation is a sense of dignity, which all human beings possess in one form
or other, and in some, though by no means in exact, proportion to their
higher faculties, and which is so essential a part of the happiness of those
in whom it is strong that nothing which conflicts with it could be otherwise than momentarily an object of desire to them. Whoever supposes
that this preference takes place at a sacrifice of happiness—that the superior being, in anything like equal circumstances, is not happier than the
inferior—confounds the two very different ideas of happiness and content. It is indisputable that the being whose capacities of enjoyment are
low has the greatest chance of having them fully satisfied; and a highly
endowed being will always feel that any happiness which he can look for,

as the world is constituted, is imperfect. But he can learn to bear its imperfections, if they are at all bearable; and they will not make him envy the being who is indeed conscious of the imperfections, but only because he feels not at all the good which those imperfections qualify. It is better to be a human being dissatisfied than a pig satisfied; better to be Socrates dissatisfied than a fool satisfied. And if the fool, or the pig, are of a different opinion, it is because they only know their own side of the question. The other party to the comparison knows both sides.

It may be objected that many who are capable of the higher pleasures occasionally, under the influence of temptation, postpone them to the lower. But this is quite compatible with a full appreciation of the intrinsic superiority of the higher. Men often, from infirmity of character, make their election for the nearer good, though they know it to be the less valuable; and this no less when the choice is between two bodily pleasures than when it is between bodily and mental. They pursue sensual indulgences to the injury of health, though perfectly aware that health is the greater good. It may be further objected that many who begin with youthful enthusiasm for everything noble, as they advance in years, sink into indolence and selfishness. But I do not believe that those who undergo this very common change voluntarily choose the lower description of pleasures in preference to the higher. I believe they devote themselves exclusively to the one, they have already become incapable of the other. Capacity for the nobler feelings is in most natures a very tender plant, easily killed, not only by hostile influences, but by mere want of sustenance; and in the majority of young persons it speedily dies away if the occupations to which their position in life has devoted them, and the society into which it has thrown them, are not favorable to keeping that higher capacity in exercise. Men lose their high aspirations as they lose their intellectual tastes, because they have not time or opportunity for indulging them; and they addict themselves to inferior pleasures, not because they deliberately prefer them, but because they are either the only ones to which they have access or the only ones which they are any longer capable of enjoying. It may be questioned whether anyone who has remained equally susceptible to both classes of pleasures ever knowingly and calmly preferred the lower, though many, in all ages, have broken down in an ineffectual attempt to combine both.

From this verdict of the only competent judges, I apprehend there can be no appeal. On a question which is the best worth having of two pleasures, or which of two modes of existence is the most grateful to the feelings, apart from its moral attributes and from its consequences, the judgment of those who are qualified by knowledge of both, or, if they differ, that of the majority among them, must be admitted as final. And there needs be the less hesitation to accept this judgment respecting the quality of pleasures, since there is no other tribunal to be referred to even on the question of quantity. What means are there of determining which is the acutest of two pains, or the intensest of two pleasurable sensations, except the general suffrage of those who are familiar with both? Neither pains nor pleasures are homogeneous, and pain is always heterogeneous with pleasure. What is there to decide whether a particular pleasure is worth purchasing at the cost of a particular pain, except the feelings and judgment of the experienced? When, therefore, those feelings and judgment declare the pleasures derived from the higher faculties to be preferable *in kind*, apart from the question of intensity, to those of which the animal nature, disjoined from the higher faculties, is susceptible, they are entitled on this subject to the same regard.

I have dwelt on this point as being a necessary part of a perfectly just conception of utility or happiness considered as the directive rule of human conduct. But it is by no means an indispensable condition to the acceptance of the utilitarian standard; for that standard is not the agent's own greatest happiness, but the greatest amount of happiness altogether; and if it may possibly be doubted whether a noble character is always the happier for its nobleness, there can be no doubt that it makes other people happier, and that the world in general is immensely a gainer by it. Utilitarianism, therefore, could only attain its end by the general cultivation of nobleness of character, even if each individual were only benefited by the nobleness of others, and his own, so far as happiness is concerned, were a sheer deduction from the benefit. But the bare enunciation of such an absurdity as this last renders refutation superfluous.

According to the greatest happiness principle, as above explained, the ultimate end, with reference to and for the sake of which all other things are desirable—whether we are considering our own good or that of other people—is an existence exempt as far as possible from pain, and as rich as possible in enjoyments, both in point of quantity and quality; the test of quality and the rule for measuring it against quantity being the preference felt by those who, in their opportunities of experience, to which must be added their habits of self-consciousness and self-observation, are best furnished with the means of comparison. This, being according to the utilitarian opinion the end of human action, is necessarily also the standard of morality, which may accordingly be defined "the rules and precepts for human conduct," by the observance of which an existence such as has been described might be, to the greatest extent possible, secured to all mankind; and not to them only, but, so far as the nature of things admits, to the whole sentient creation. . . .

Unquestionably it is possible to do without happiness; it is done involuntarily by nineteen-twentieths of mankind, even in those parts of our present world which are least deep in barbarism; and it often has to be done voluntarily by the hero or the martyr, for the sake of something which he prizes more than his individual happiness. But this something, what is it, unless the happiness of others or some of the requisites of happiness? It is noble to be capable of resigning entirely one's own portion of happiness, or chances of it; but, after all, this self-sacrifice must be for some end; it is not its own end; and if we are told that its end is not happiness but virtue, which is better than happiness, I ask, would the sacrifice be made if the hero or martyr did not believe that it would earn for others immunity from similar sacrifices? Would it be made if he thought that his renunciation of happiness for himself would produce no fruit for any of his fellow creatures, but to make their lot like his and place them also in the condition of persons who have renounced happiness? All honor to those who can abnegate for themselves the personal enjoyment of life when by such renunciation they contribute worthily to increase the amount of happiness in the world; but he who does it or professes to do it for any other purpose is no more deserving of admiration than the ascetic mounted on his pillar. He may be an inspiriting proof of what men *can* do, but assuredly not an example of what they *should*.

Though it is only in a very imperfect state of the world's arrangements that anyone can best serve the happiness of others by the absolute sacrifice of his own, yet, so long as the world is in that imperfect state, I fully acknowledge that the readiness to make such a sacrifice is the highest virtue which can be found in man. I will add that in this condition of the world, paradoxical as the assertion may be, the conscious ability to do without happiness gives the best prospect of realizing such happiness as is attainable. For nothing except that consciousness can raise a person above the chances of life by making him feel that, let fate and fortune do their worst, they have not power to subdue him; which, once felt, frees him from excess of anxiety concerning the evils of life and enables him, like many a Stoic in the worst times of the Roman Empire, to cultivate in tranquility the sources of satisfaction accessible to him, without concerning himself about the uncertainty of their duration any more than about their inevitable end.

Meanwhile, let utilitarians never cease to claim the morality of self-devotion as a possession which belongs by as good a right to them as either to the Stoic or to the Transcendentalist. The utilitarian morality does recognize in human beings the power of sacrificing their own greatest good for the good of others. It only refuses to admit that the sacrifice is itself a good. A sacrifice which does not increase or tend to increase the sum total of happiness, it considers as wasted. The only self-renunciation which it applauds is devotion to the happiness, or to some of the means of happiness, of others, either of mankind collectively or of individuals within the limits imposed by the collective interests of mankind.

I must again repeat what the assailants of utilitarianism seldom have the justice to acknowledge, that the happiness which forms the utilitarian standard of what is right in conduct is not the agent's own happiness but that of all concerned. As between his own happiness and that of others, utilitarianism requires him to be as strictly impartial as a disinterested and benevolent spectator. In the golden rule of Jesus of Nazareth, we read the complete spirit of the ethics of utility. "To do as you would be done by," and "to love your neighbor as yourself," constitute the ideal perfection of utilitarian morality. As the means of making the nearest approach to this ideal, utility would enjoin, first, that laws and social arrangements should place the happiness or (as, speaking practically, it may be called) the interest of every individual as nearly as possible in harmony with the interest of the whole; and, secondly, that education and opinion, which have so vast a power over human character, should so use that power as to establish in the mind of every individual an indissoluble association between his own happiness and the good of the whole, especially between his own happiness and the practice of such modes of conduct, negative and positive, as regard for the universal happiness prescribes; so that not only he may be unable to conceive the possibility of happiness to himself, consistently with conduct opposed to the general good, but also that a direct impulse to promote the general good may be in every individual one of the habitual motives of action, and the sentiments connected therewith may fill a large and prominent place in every human being's existence. If the impugners of the utilitarian morality represented it to their own minds in this its true character, I know not what recommendation possessed by any other morality they could possibly affirm to be wanting to it; what more beautiful or more exalted developments of human nature any other ethical system can be supposed to foster, or what springs of action, not accessible to the utilitarian, such systems rely on for giving effect to their mandates.

The objectors to utilitarianism cannot always be charged with representing it in a discreditable light. On the contrary, those among them who entertain anything like a just idea of its disinterested character sometimes find fault with its standard as being too high for humanity. They say it is exacting too much to require that people shall always act from the inducement of promoting the general interests of society. But this is to mistake the very meaning of a standard of morals and confound the rule of action with the motive of it. It is the business of ethics to tell us what are our duties, or by what test we may know them; but no system of ethics requires that the sole motive of all we do shall be a feeling of duty; on the contrary, ninety-nine hundredths of all our actions are done from other motives, and rightly so done if the rule of duty does not condemn them. It is the more unjust to utilitarianism that this particular misapprehension should be made a ground of objection to it, inasmuch as utilitarian moralists have gone beyond almost all others in affirming that the motive has nothing to do with the morality of the action, though much with the worth of the agent. He who saves a fellow creature from drowning does what is morally right, whether his motive be duty or the hope of being paid for his trouble; he who betrays the friend that trusts him to guilty of a crime, even if his object be to serve another friend to whom he is under greater obligations.[2] But to speak only of actions done from the motive of duty, and in direct obedience to principle: it is a misapprehension of the utilitarian mode of though to conceive it as implying that people should fix their minds upon so wide a generality as the world, or society at large. The great majority of good actions are intended not for the benefit of the world, but for that of individuals, of which the good of the world is made up; and the thoughts of the most virtuous man need not on these occasions travel beyond the particular persons concerned, except so far as is necessary to assure himself that in benefiting them he is not violating the rights, that is, the legitimate and authorized expectations, of anyone else. The multiplication of happiness is, according to the utilitarian ethics, the object of virtue: the occasions on which any person (except one in a thousand) has it in his power to do this on an extended scale—in other words, to be a public benefactor— are but exceptional; and on these occasions alone is he called on to consider public utility; in every other case, private utility, the interest or happiness of some few persons, is all he has to attend to. Those alone the influence of whose actions extends to society in general need concern themselves habitually about so large an object. In the case of abstinences indeed—of things which people forbear to do from moral considerations, though the consequences in the particular case might be beneficial—it would be unworthy of an intelligent agent not to be consciously aware that the action is of a class which, if practiced generally, would be generally injurious, and that this is the ground of the obligation to abstain from it. The amount of regard for the public interest implied in this recognition is no greater than is demanded by every system of morals, for they all enjoin to abstain from whatever is manifestly pernicious to society. . . .

It may not be superfluous to notice a few more of the common mis-apprehensions of utilitarian ethics, even those which are so obvious and gross that it might appear impossible for any person of candor and intelligence to fall into them; since persons, even of considerable mental endowment, often give themselves so little trouble to understand the bearings of any opinion against which they entertain a prejudice, and men are in general so little conscious of this voluntary ignorance as a defect that the vulgarest misunderstandings of ethical doctrines are continually met with in the deliberate writings of persons of the greatest pretensions both to high principle and to philosophy. We not uncommonly hear the doctrine of utility inveighed against as a *godless* doctrine. If it be necessary to say anything at all against to mere as assumption, we may say that the question depends upon what idea we have formed of the moral character of the Deity. If it be a true belief that God desires, above all things, the happiness of his creatures, and that this was his purpose in their creation, utility is not only not a godless doctrine, but more profoundly religious than any other. If it be meant that utilitarianism does not recognize the revealed will of God as the supreme law of morals, I answer that a utilitarian who believes in the perfect goodness and wisdom of *God* necessarily believes that whatever God has thought fit to reveal on the subject of morals must fulfill the requirements of utility in a supreme degree. But others besides utilitarians have been of opinion that the Christian revelation was intended, and is fitted, to inform the hearts and minds of mankind with a spirit which should enable them to find for themselves what is right, and incline them to do it when found, rather than to tell them, except in very general way, what it is; and that we need a doctrine of ethics, carefully followed out, to *interpret* to us the will of God. Whether this opinion is correct or not, it is superfluous here to discuss; since whatever aid religion, either natural or revealed, can afford to ethical investigation is as open to the utilitarian moralist as to any other. He can use it as the testimony of God to the usefulness or hurtfulness of any given course of action by as good a right as others can use it for the indication of a transcendental law having no connection with usefulness or with happiness. . . .

Again, defenders of utility often find themselves called upon to reply to such objections as this—that there is not time, previous to action, for calculating and weighting the effects of any line of conduct on the general happiness. This is exactly as if anyone were to say that it is impossible to guide our conduct by Christianity because there is not time, on every occasion on which anything has to be done, to read through the Old and New Testaments. The answer to the onjection is that there has been ample time, namely, the whole past duration of the human species. During all that time mankind have been learning by experience the tendencies of actions; on which experience all the prudence as well as all the morality of life are dependent. People talk as if the commencement of this course of experience has hitherto been put off, and as if, at the moment when some man feels tempted to meddle with the property or life of another, he had to begin considering for the first time whether murder and theft are injurious to human happiness. Even then I do not think that he would find the question very puzzling; but, at all events, the matter is now done to his hand. It is truly a whimsical supposition that, if mankind were agreed in considering utility to be the test of morality, they would remain without any agreement as to what *is* useful, and would take no measures for having their notions on the subject taught to the young and enforced by law and opinion. There is no difficulty in proving any ethical standard whatever to work ill if we suppose universal idiocy to be conjoined with it; but on any hypothesis short of that, mankind must by this time have acquired positive beliefs as to the effects of some actions on their happiness; and the beliefs which have thus come down are the rules of morality for the multitude, and for the philosopher until he has succeeded in finding better. That philosophers might easily do this even now, on many subjects; that the received code of ethics is by no means of divine right; and that mankind have still much to learn as to the effects of actions on the general happiness, I admit or rather earnestly maintain. The corollaries from the principle of utility, like the precepts of every practical art, admit of indefinite improvement, and, in a progressive state of the human mind, their improvement is prepetually going on. But to consider the rules of morality as improvable is one thing; to pass over the intermediate generalization entirely and endeavor to test each individual action directly by the first principle is another. It is a strange notion that the acknowledgement of a first principle is inconsistent with the admission of secondary ones. To inform a traveler respecting the place of his ultimate destination is not to forbid the use of landmarks and direction-posts on the way. The proposition that happiness is the end and aim of morality does not mean that no road ought to be laid down to that goal, or that persons going thither should not be advised to take one direction rather than another. Men really ought to leave off talking a kind of nonsense on this subject, which they would neither talk nor listen to on other matters of practical concernment. Nobody argues that the art of navigation is not founded on astronomy because sailors cannot wait to calculate the Nautical Almanac. Being rational creatures, they go to sea with it ready calculated; and all rational creatures go out upon the sea of life with their minds made up on the common questions of right and wrong, as well as on many of the far more difficult questions of wise and foolish. And this, as long as foresight is a human quality, it is to be presumed they will continue to do. Whatever we adopt as the fundamental principle of morality, we require subordinate principles to apply it by; the impossibility of doing without them, being common to all systems, can afford no argument against any one in particular; but gravely to argue as if no such secondary principles could be had, and as if mankind had remained till now, and always must remain, without drawing any general conclusions from the experience of human life is as high a pitch, I think, as absurdity has ever reached in philosophical controversy.

The remainder of the stock arguments against utilitarianism mostly consist in laying to its charge the common infirmities of human nature, and the general difficulties which embarrass conscientious persons in shaping their course through life. We are told that a utilitarian will be apt to make his own particular case an exception to moral rules, and, when under temptation, will see a utility in the breach of a rule, greater than he will see in its observance. But is utility the only creed which is able to furnish us with excuses for evil-doing and means of cheating our own conscience? They are afforded in abundance by all doctrines which recognize as a fact in morals the existence of conflicting considerations, which all doctrines do that have been believed by sane persons. It is not the fault of any creed, but of the complicated nature of human affairs, that rules of conduct cannot be so framed as to require no exceptions, and that hardly any kind of action can safely be laid down as either always obligatory or always condemnable. There is no ethical creed which does not temper the rigidity of its laws by giving a certain latitude, under the moral responsibility of the agent, for accommodation to peculiarities of circumstances; and under every creed, at the opening thus made, self-deception and dishonest casuistry get in. There exists no moral system under which there do not arise unequivocal cases of conflicting obligation. These are the real difficulties, the knotty points both in the theory of ethics and in the conscientious guidance of personal conduct. They are overcome practically, with greater or with less success, according to the intellect and virtue of the individual; but it can hardly be pretended that anyone will be the less qualified for dealing with them, from possessing an ultimate standard to which conflicting rights and duties can be referred. If utility is the ultimate source of moral obligations, utility may be invoked to decide between them when their demands are incompatible. Though the application of the standard may be difficult, it is better than none at all; while in other systems, the moral laws all claiming independent authority, there is no common umpire entitled to interfere between them; their claims of precedence one over another rest on little better than sophistry, and unless determined, as they generally are, by the unacknowledged influence of consideration of utility, afford a free scope for the action of personal desires and partialities. We must remember that only in these cases of conflict between secondary principles is it requisite that first principles should be appealed to. There is no case of moral obligation in which some secondary principle is not involved; and if only one, there can seldom be any real doubt which one it is, in the mind of any person by whom the principle itself is recognized. . . .

Chapter IV: Of What Sort of Proof the Principle of Utility Is Susceptible

It has already been remarked that questions of ultimate ends do not admit of proof, in the ordinary acceptation of the term. To be incapable of proof by reasoning is common to all first principles; to the first premises of our knowledge, as well as to those of our conduct. But the former, being matters of fact, may be the subject of a direct appeal to the faculties which judge of fact—namely, our senses and our internal consciousness. Can an appeal be made, to the same faculties on questions of practical ends? Or by what other faculty is cognizance taken of them?

Questions about ends are, in other words, questions about what things are desirable. The utilitarian doctrine is that happiness is desirable, and the only thing desirable, as an end; all other things being only desirable as means to that end. What ought to be required of this doctrine—what conditions is it requisite that the doctrine should fulfill—to make good its claim to be believed?

The only proof capable of being given that an object is visible, is that people actually see it. The only proof that a sound is audible, is that people hear it: and so of the other sources of our experience. In like manner, I apprehend, the sole evidence it is possible to produce that anything is desirable, is that people do actually desire it. If the end which the utilitarian doctrine proposes to itself were not, in theory and in practice, acknowledged to be an end, nothing could ever convince any person that it was so. No reason can be given why the general happiness is desirable, except that each person, so far as he believes it to be attainable, desires his own happiness. This, however, being a fact, we have not only all the proof which the case admits of, but all which it is possible to require, that happiness is a good: that each person's happiness is a good to that person, and the general happiness, therefore, a good to the aggregate of all persons. Happiness has made out its title as *one* of the ends of conduct, and consequently one of the criteria of morality.

But it has not, by this alone, proved itself to be the sole criterion. To do that, it would seem, by the same rule, necessary to show, not only that people desire happiness, but that they never desire anything else. Now it is palpable that they do desire things which, in common language, are decidedly distinguished from happiness. They desire, for example, virtue, and the absence of vice, no less really than pleasure and the absence of pain. The desire of virtue is not as universal; but it is as authentic a fact, as the desire of happiness. And hence the opponents of the utilitarian standard deem that they have a right to infer that there are other ends of human action besides happiness, and that happiness is not the standard of approbation and disapprobation.

But does the utilitarian doctrine deny that people desire virtue, or maintain that virtue is not a thing to be desired? The very reverse. It maintains not only that virtue is to be desired, but that it is to be desired disinterestedly, for itself. Whatever may be the opinion of utilitarian moralists as to the original conditions by which virtue is made virtue; however they may believe (as they do) that actions and dispositions are only virtuous because they promote another end than virtue; yet this being granted, and it having been decided, from considerations of this description, what *is* virtuous, they not only place virtue at the very head of the things which are good as means to the ultimate end, but they also recognize as a psychological fact the possibility of its being, to the individual, a good in itself, without looking to any end beyond it; and hold, that the mind is not in a right state, not in a state conformable to utility, not in the state most conducive to the general happiness, unless it does love virtue in this manner—as a thing desirable in itself, even although, in the individual instance, it should not produce those other desirable consequences which it tends to produce and on account of which it is held to be virtue. This opinion is not, in the smallest degree, a departure from the happiness principle. The ingredients of happiness are very various, and each of them is desirable in itself, and not merely when considered as swelling an aggregate. The principle of utility does not mean that any given pleasure, as music for instance, or any given exemption from pain, as for example health, are to be looked upon as a means to a collective something termed happiness, and to be desired on that account. They are desired and desirable in and for themselves; besides being means, they are part of the end. Virtue, according to the utilitarian doctrine, is not naturally and originally part of the end, but it is capable of becoming so; and in those who love it disinterestedly it has become so, and is desired and cherished, not as a means to happiness, but as a part of their happiness.

To illustrate this farther, we may remember that virtue is not the only thing, originally a means, and which if it were not a means to anything else, would be and remain indifferent, but which by association with what it is a means to, comes to be desired for itself, and that too with the utmost intensity. What, for example, shall we say of the love of money? There is nothing originally more desirable about money than about any heap of glittering pebbles. Its worth is solely that of the things which it will buy; the desires for other things than itself, which it is a means of gratifying. Yet the love of money is not only one of the strongest moving forces of human life, but money is, in many cases, desired in and for itself; the desire to possess it is often stronger than the desire to use it, and goes on increasing when all the desires which point to ends beyond it, to be encompassed by it, are falling off. It may be then said truly, that money is desired not for the sake of an end, but as part of the end. From being a means to happiness, it has come to be itself a principal ingredient of the individual's conception of happiness. The same may be said of the majority of the great objects of human life—power, for example, or fame; except that to each of these there is a certain amount of immediate pleasure annexed, which has at least the semblance of being naturally inherent in them; a thing which cannot be said of money. Still, however, the strongest natural attraction, both of power and of fame, is the immense aid they give to the attainment of our other wishes; and it is the strong association thus generated between them and all our objects of desire, which gives to the direct desire of them the intensity it often assumes, so as in some characters to surpass in strength all other desires. In these cases the means have become a part of the end, and a more important part of it than any of the things which they are means to. What was once desired as an instrument of the attainment of happiness, has come to be desired for its own sake. In being desired for its own sake it is, however, desired as *part* of happiness. The person is made, or thinks he would be made, happy by its mere possession; and is made unhappy by failure to obtain it. The desire of it is not a different thing from the desire of happiness, any more than the love of music or the desire of health. They are included in happiness. They are some of the elements of which the desire of happiness is made up. Happiness is not an abstract idea, but a concrete whole; and these are some of its parts. And the utilitarian standard sanctions and approves there being so. Life would be a poor thing, very ill provided with sources of happiness, if there were not this provision of nature, by which things originally indifferent, but conducive to, or otherwise associated with, the satisfaction of our primitive desires, become in themselves sources of pleasure more valuable than the primitive pleasures, both in permanency, in the space of human existence than they are capable of covering, and even in intensity.

Virtue, according to the utilitarian conception, is a good of this description. There was no original desire of it, or motive to it, save its conduciveness to pleasure, and especially to protection from pain. But through the association thus formed, it may he felt a good in itself, and desired as such with as great intensity as any other good; and with this difference between it and the love of money, of power, or of fame, that all of these may, and often do, render the individual noxious to the other members of the society to which he belongs, whereas there is nothing which makes him so much a blessing to them as the cultivation of the disinterested love of virtue. And consequently, the utilitarian standard, when it tolerates and approves those other acquired desires, up to the point beyond which they would be more injurious to the general happiness than promotive of it, enjoins and requires the cultivation of the love of virtue up to the greatest strength possible, as being above all things important to the general happiness.

It results from the preceding considerations, that there is in reality nothing desired except happiness. Whatever is desired otherwise than as a means to some end beyond itself, and ultimately to happiness, is desired as itself a part of happiness, and is not desired for itself until it has become so. Those who desire virtue for its own sake, desire it either because the consciousness of it is a pleasure, or because the consciousness of being without it is a pain, or for both reasons united; as in truth the pleasure and pain seldom exist separately, but almost always together, the same person feeling pleasure in the degree of virtue attained, and pain in not having attained more. If one of these gave him no pleasure, and the other no pain, he would not love or desire virtue, or would desire it only for the other benefits which it might produce to himself or to persons whom he cared for.

We have now, then, an answer to the question, of what sort of proof the principle of utility is susceptible. If the opinion which I have now stated is psychologically true—if human nature is so constituted as to desire nothing which is not either a part of happiness or a means of happiness, we can have no other proof, and we require no other, that these are the only things desirable. If so, happiness is the sole end of human action, and the promotion of it the rest by which to judge of all human conduct; from whence it necessarily follows that it must be the criterion of morality, since a part is included in the whole.

And now to decide whether this is really so; whether mankind do desire nothing for itself but that which is a pleasure to them, or of which the absence is a pain; we have evidently arrived at a question of fact and experience, dependent like all similar questions, upon evidence. It can only be determined by practiced self-consciousness and self-observation, assisted by observation of others. I believe that these sources of evidence, impartially consulted, will declare that desiring a thing and finding it pleasant, aversion to it and thinking of it as painful, are phenomena entirely inseparable, or rather two parts of the same phenomenon; in strictness of language, two different modes of naming the same psychological fact: that to think of an object as desirable (unless for the sake of its consequences), and to think of it as pleasant, are one and the same thing; and that to desire anything, except in proportion as the idea of it is pleasant, is a physical and metaphysical impossibility.

So obvious does this appear to me, that I expect it will hardly be disputed: and the objection made will be, not that desire can possibly be directed to anything ultimately except pleasure and exemption from pain, but that the will is a different thing from desire; that a person of confirmed virtue, or any other person whose purposes are fixed, carries out his purposes without any thought of the pleasure he has in contemplating them, or expects to derive from their fulfillment; and persists in acting on them, even though these pleasures are much diminished, by changes in his character or decay of his passive sensibilities, or are outweighed by the pains which the pursuit of the purposes may bring upon him. All this I fully admit, and have stated it elsewhere, as positively and emphatically as any one. Will, the active phenomenon, is a different thing from desire, the state of passive sensibility, and though originally an offshoot from it, may in time take root and detach itself from the parent stock; so much so that in the case of an habitual propose, instead of willing the thing because we desire it, we often desire it only because we will it. This, however, is but an instance of that familiar fact, the power of habit, and is nowise confined to the case of virtuous actions. Many indifferent things, which men originally did from a motive of some sort, they continue to do from habit. Sometimes this is done unconsciously, the consciousness coming only after the action: at other times with conscious volition, but volition which has become habitual, and is put into operation by the force of habit, in opposition perhaps to the deliberate preference, as often happens with those who have contracted habits of vicious or hurtful indulgence. Third and last comes the case in which the habitual act of will in the individual instance is not in contradiction to the general intention prevailing at other times, but in fulfillment of it; as in the case of the person of confirmed virtue, and of all who pursue deliberately and consistently any determinate end. The distinction between will and desire thus understood, is an authentic and highly important psychological fact; but the fact consists solely in this—that will, like all other parts of our constitution, is amenable to habit, and that we may will from habit what we no longer desire for itself, or desire only because we will it. It is not the less true that will, in the beginning, is entirely produced by desire; including in that term the repelling influence of pain as well as the attractive one of pleasure. Let us take into consideration, no longer the person who has a firmed will to do right, but him in whom that virtuous will is still feeble, conquerable by temptation, and not to be fully relied on; by what means can it be strengthened? How can the will to be virtuous, where it does not exist in sufficient force, be implanted or awakened? Only by making the person *desire* virtue—by making him think of it in a pleasurable light, or of its absence in a painful one. It is by associating the doing right with pleasure, or the doing wrong with pain, or by eliciting and impressing and bringing home to the person's experience the pleasure naturally involved in the one or the pain in the other, that it is possible to call for forth that will to be virtuous, which, when confirmed, acts without any thought of either pleasure or pain. Will is the child of desire, and passes out of habit. That which is the result of habit affords no presumption of being intrinsically good; and there would be no reason for wishing that the purpose of virtue should become independent of pleasure and pain, were it not that the influence of the pleasurable and painful associations which prompt to virtue is not sufficiently to be depended on for unerring constancy of action until it has acquired the support of habit. Both in feeling and in conduct, habit is the only thing which imparts certainty; and it is because of the importance to others of being able to rely absolutely on one's feelings and conduct, and to oneself of being able to rely on one's own, that the will to do right ought to be cultivated into this habitual independence. In other words, this state of the will is a means to good, not intrinsically a good; and does not contradict the doctrine that nothing is a good to human beings but in so far as it is either itself pleasurable, or a means of attaining pleasure of averting pain.

But if this doctrine be true, the principle of utility is proved. Whether it is so or not, must now be left to the consideration of the thoughtful reader.

Notes

1. The author of this essay has reason for believing himself to be the first person who brought the word "utilitarian" into use. He did not invent it, but adopted it from a passing expression in Mr [John] Galt's *Annals of the Parish*. After using it as a designation for several years, he and others abandoned it from a growing dislike to anything resembling a badge or watchwood of sectarian distinction. But as a name for one single opinion,— not a set of opinions—to denote the recognition of utility as a standard, not any particular way of applying it—the term supplies a want in the language, and offers, in many cases, a convenient mode of avoiding tiresome circumlocution.

2. An opponent, whose intellectual and moral fairness it is a pleasure to acknowledge (the Revd. J. Llewellyn Davies), has objected to this passage, saying, "Surely the rightness or wrongness of saving a man from drowning does depend very much upon the motive with which it is done. Suppose that a tyrant, when his enemy jumped into the sea to escape from him, saved him from drowning simply in order that he might inflict upon him more exquisite tortures, would it tend to clearness to speak of that rescue as 'a morally right action'? Or suppose again, according to one of the stock illustrations of ethical inquiries, that a man betrayed a trust received from a friend, because the discharge of it would fatally injure that friend himself or someone belonging to him, would utilitarianism compel one to call the betrayal 'a crime' as much as if it had been done from the meanest motive?"

   I submit that he who saves another from drowning in order to kill him by torture afterwards does not differ only in motive from him who does that same thing from duty or benevolence; the act itself is different. The rescue of the man is, in the case supposed, only the necessary first step of an act far more atrocious than leaving him to drown would have been. Had Mr Davies said, "The rightness or wrongness of saving a man from drowning does depend very much"—not upon the motive, but—"upon the *intention*," no utilitarian would have differed from him. Mr Davies, by an oversight too common not to be quite venial, has in this case confounded the very different ideas of Motive and Intention. There is no point which utilitarian thinkers (and Bentham pre-eminently) have taken more pains to illustrate than this. The morality of the action depends entirely upon the intention—that is, upon what the agent *wills to do*. But the motive, that is, the feeling which makes him will so to do, if it makes no difference in the act, makes none in the morality: though it makes a great difference in our moral estimation of the agent, especially if it indicates a good or a bad habitual *disposition*—a bent of character from which useful, or from which hurtful actions are likely to arise.

Groundwork of the Metaphysics of Morals

Immanuel Kant   *(Translated by James Ellington)*

. . . . Everything in nature works according to laws. Only a rational being has the power to act according to his conception of laws, i.e., according to principles, and thereby has he a will. Since the derivation of actions from laws requires reason, the will is nothing but practical reason. If reason infallibly determines the will, then in the case of such a being actions which are recognized to be objectively necessary are also subjectively necessary, i.e., the will is a faculty of choosing only that which reason, independently of inclination, recognizes as being practically necessary, i.e., as good. But if reason of itself does not sufficiently determine the will, and if the will submits also to subjective conditions (certain incentives) which do not always agree with objective conditions; in a word, if the will does not in itself completely accord with reason (as is actually the case with men), then actions which are recognized as objectively necessary are subjectively contingent, and the determination of such a will according to objective laws is necessitation. That is to say that the relation of objective laws to a will not thoroughly good is represented as the determination of the will of a rational being by principles of reason which the will does not necessarily follow because of its own nature.

The representation of an objective principle insofar as it necessitates the will is called a command (of reason), and the formula of the command is called an imperative.

All imperatives are expressed by an *ought* and thereby indicate the relation of an objective law of reason to a will that is not necessarily determined by this law because of its subjective constitution (the relation of necessitation). Imperatives say that something would be good to do or to refrain from doing, but they say it to a will that does not always therefore do something simply because it has been represented to the will as something good to do. That is practically good which determines the will by means of representations of reason and hence not by subjective causes, but objectively, i.e., on grounds valid for every rational being us such. It is distinguished from the pleasant as that which influences the will only by means of sensation from merely subjective causes, which hold only for this or that person's senses but do not hold as a principle of reason valid for everyone.[1]

A perfectly good will would thus be quite as much subject to objective laws (of the good), but could not be conceived as thereby necessitated to act in conformity with law, inasmuch as it can of itself, according to its subjective constitution, be determined only by the representation of the good. Therefore no imperatives hold for the divine will, and in general for a holy will; the *ought* is here out of place, because the *would* is already of itself necessarily in agreement with the law. Consequently, imperatives are only formulas for expressing the relation of objective laws of willing in general to the subjective imperfection of the will of this or that rational being, e.g., the human will.

Now all imperatives command either hypothetically or categorically. The former represent the practical necessity of a possible action as a means for attaining something else that one wants (or may possibly want). The categorical imperative would be one which represented an action as objectively necessary in itself, without reference to another end.

Every practical law represents a possible action as good and hence as necessary for a subject who is practically determinable by reason; therefore all imperatives are formulas for determining an action which is necessary according to the principle of a will that is good in some way. Now if the action would be good merely us a means to something else, so is the imperative hypothetical. But if the action is represented as good in itself, and hence as necessary in a will which of itself conforms to reason as the principle of the will, then the imperative is categorical.

An imperative thus says what action possible by me would be good, and it presents the practical rule in relation to a will which does not forthwith perform an action simply because it is good, partly because the subject does not always know that the action is good and partly because

---

[1]The dependence of the faculty of desire on sensations is called inclination, which accordingly always indicates a need. The dependence of a contingently determinable will on principles of reason, however, is called interest. Therefore an interest is found only in a dependent will which is not of itself always in accord with reason; in the divine will no interest can be thought. But even the human will can take an interest in something without thereby acting from interest. The former signifies practical interest in the action, while the latter signifies pathological interest in the object of the action. The former indicates only dependence of the will on principles of reason by itself, while the latter indicates the will's dependence on principles of reason for the sake of inclination, i.e., reason merely gives the practical rule for meeting the need of inclination. It the former case the action interests me, while in the latter case what interests me is the object of the action (so far as this subject is pleasant for me).

(even if he does know it is good) his maxims might yet be opposed to the objective principles of practical reason.

A hypothetical imperative thus says only that an action is good for some purpose, either possible or actual. In the first case it is a problematic practical principle; in the second case an assertoric one. A categorical imperative, which declares an action to be of itself objectively necessary without reference to any purpose, i.e., without any other end, holds as an apodeictic practical principle.

Whatever is possible only through the powers of some rational being can be thought of as a possible purpose of some will. Consequently, there are in fact infinitely many principles of action insofar as they are represented as necessary for attaining a possible purpose achievable by them. All sciences have a practical part consisting of problems saying that some end is possible for us and of imperatives telling us how it can be attained. These can, therefore, be called in general imperatives of skill. Here there is no question at all whether the end is reasonable and good, but there is only a question as to what must be done to attain it. The prescriptions needed by a doctor in order to make his patient thoroughly healthy and by a poisoner in order to make sure of killing his victim are of equal value so far as each serves to bring about its purpose perfectly. Since there cannot be known in early youth what ends may be presented to us in the course of life, parents especially seek to have their children learn many different kinds of things, and they provide for skill in the use of means to all sorts of arbitrary ends, among which they cannot determine whether any one of them could in the future become an actual purpose for their ward, though there is always the possibility that he might adopt it. Their concern is so great that they commonly neglect to form and correct their children's judgment regarding the worth of things which might be chosen as ends.

There is, however, one end that can be presupposed as actual for all rational beings (so far as they are dependent beings to whom imperatives apply); and thus there is one purpose which they not merely can have but which can certainly be assumed to be such that they all do have by a natural necessity, and this is happiness. A hypothetical imperative which represents the practical necessity of an action as means for the promotion of happiness is assertoric. It may be expounded not simply as necessary to an uncertain, merely possible purpose, but as necessary to a purpose which can be presupposed a priori and with certainty as being present in everyone because it belongs to his essence. Now skill in the choice of means to one's own greatest well-being can be called prudence[2] in the narrowest sense. And thus the imperative that refers to the choice of means to one's own happiness, i.e., the precept of prudence, still remains hypothetical; the action is commanded not absolutely but only as a means to a further purpose.

Finally, there is one imperative which immediately commands a certain conduct without having as its condition any other purpose to be attained by it. This imperative is categorical. It is not concerned with the matter of the action and its intended result, but rather with the form of the action and the principle from which it follows; what is essentially good in the action consists in the mental disposition, let the consequences be what they may. This imperative may be called that of morality.

Willing according to these three kinds of principles is also clearly distinguished by dissimilarity in the necessitation of the will. To make this dissimilarity clear I think that they are most suitably named in their order when they are said to be either *rules of skill, counsels of prudence,* or *commands (laws) of morality*. For law alone involves the concept of a necessity that is unconditioned and indeed objective and hence universally valid, and commands are laws which must be obeyed, i.e., must be followed even in opposition to inclination. Counsel does indeed involve necessity, but involves such necessity as is valid only under a subjectively contingent condition, viz., whether this or that man counts this or that as belonging to his happiness. On the other hand, the categorical imperative is limited by no condition, and can quite properly be called a command since it is absolutely, though practically, necessary. The first kind of imperatives might also be called technical (belonging to art), the second kind pragmatic[3] (belonging to welfare), the third kind moral (belonging to free conduct us such, i.e., to morals).

The question now arises: how are all of these imperatives possible?[4] This question does not seek to know how the fulfillment of the action

---

[2]The word "prudence" is used in a double sense: firstly, it can mean worldly wisdom, and, secondly, private wisdom. The former is the skill of someone in influencing others so as to use them for his own purposes. The latter is the sagacity to combine all these purposes for his own lasting advantage. The value of the former is properly reduced to the latter, and it might better be said of one who is prudent in the former sense but not in the latter that he is clever and cunning, but on the whole imprudent.

[3]It seems to me that the proper meaning of the word "pragmatic" could be defined most accurately in this way. For those sanctions are called pragmatic which properly flow not from the law of states as necessury enactments but from provision for the general welfare. A history is pragmatically written when it teaches prudence, i.e., instructs the world how it can provide for its interests better than, or at least as well as, has been done in former times.

[4][That is, why should one let his actions be determined at various times by one of the other of these three kinds of imperatives?]

commanded by the imperative can be conceived, but merely how the necessitation of the will expressed by the imperative in setting a task can be conceived. How an imperative of skill is possible requires no special discussion. Whoever wills the end, wills (so far as reason has decisive influence on his actions) also the means that are indispensably necessary to his actions and that lie in his power. This proposition, as far as willing is concerned, is analytic. For in willing an object as my effect there is already thought the causality of myself as an acting cause, i.e., the use of means. The imperative derives the concept of actions necessary to this end form the concept of willing this end. (Synthetic propositions are indeed required for determining the means to a proposed end; but such propositions are concerned not with the ground, i.e., the act of the will, but only with the way to realize the object of the will.) Mathematics teaches by nothing but synthetic propositions that in order to bisect a line according to a sure principle I must from each of its extremities draw arcs such that they intersect. But when I know that the proposed result can come about only by means of such an action, then the proposition (if I fully will the effect, then I also will the action required for it) is analytic. For it is one and the same thing to conceive of something as an effect that is possible in a certain way through me and to conceive of my self as acting in the same way with regard to the aforesaid effect.

If it were only as easy to give a determinate concept of happiness, then the imperatives of prudence would exactly correspond to those of skill and would be likewise analytic. For there could be said in this case just as in the former that whoever wills the end also wills (necessarily according to reason) the sole means thereto which are in his power. But, unfortunately, the concept of happiness is such an indeterminate one that even though everyone wishes to attain happiness, yet he can never say definitely and consistently what it is that he really wishes and wills. The reason for this is that all the elements belonging to the concept of happiness are unexceptionally empirical, i.e., they must be borrowed from experience, while for the idea of happiness there is required an absolute whole, a maximum of well-being in my present and in every future condition. Now it is impossible for the most insightful and at the same time most powerful, but nonetheless finite, being to frame here a determinate concept of what it is that he really wills. Does he want riches? How much anxiety, envy, and intrigue might he not thereby bring down upon his own head! Or knowledge and insight? Perhaps these might only give him an eye that much sharper for revealing that much more dreadfully evils which are at present hidden but are yet unavoidable, or such an eye might burden him with still further needs for the desires which already concern him enough. Or long life? Who guarantees that it would not be a long misery? Or health at least? How often has infirmity of the body kept one from excesses into which perfect health would have allowed him to fall, and so on? In brief, he is not able on any principle to determine with complete certainty what will make him truly happy, because to do so would require omniscience. Therefore, one cannot act according to determinate principles in order to be happy, but only according to empirical counsels, e.g., of diet, frugality, politeness, reserve, etc., which are shown by experience to contribute on the average the most to well-being. There follows from this that imperatives of prudence, strictly speaking cannot command at all, i.e., present actions objectively as practically necessary. They are to be taken as counsels (*consilia*) rather than as commands (*praecepta*) of reason. The problem of determining certainly and universally what action will promote the happiness of a rational being is completely insoluble. Therefore, regarding such action no imperative that in the strictest sense could command what is to be done to make one happy is possible, inasmuch as happiness is not an ideal of reason but of imagination. Such an ideal rests merely on empirical grounds; in vain can there be expected that such grounds should determine an action whereby the totality of an infinite series of consequences could be attained. This imperative of prudence would, nevertheless, be an analytic practical proposition if one assumes that the means to happiness could with certainty be assigned; for it differs from the imperative of skill only in that for it the end is given while for the latter the end is merely possible. Since both, however, command only the means to what is assumed to be willed as an end, the imperative commanding him who wills the end to will likewise the means thereto is in both cases analytic. Hence there is also no difficulty regarding the possibility of an imperative of prudence.

On the other hand, the question as to how the imperative of morality is possible is undoubtedly the only one requiring a solution. For it is not at all hypothetical; and hence the objective necessity which it presents cannot be based on any presupposition, as was the case with the hypothetical imperatives. Only there must never here be forgotten that no example can show, i.e., empirically, whether there is any such imperative at all. Rather, care must be taken lest all imperatives which are seemingly categorical may nevertheless be covertly hypothetical. For instance, when it is said that you should not make a false promise, the assumption is that the necessity of this avoidance is no mere advice for escaping some other evil, so that is might be said that you should not make a false promise lest you ruin your credit when the falsity comes to light. But when it is asserted that an action of this kind must be regarded as bad in itself, then the imperative of prohibition is therefore categorical. Nevertheless, it cannot with certainty be shown by means of an example that the will is here determined solely by the law without any other incentive, even though such may seem to be the case. For it is always possible that secretly there is fear of disgrace and perhaps also obscure dread of other dangers; such fear and dread may have influenced the will. Who can prove by experience that a cause is not present? Experience only shows that a cause is not perceived. But in such a case the so-called moral imperative, which as such appears to be categorical and unconditioned, would actually be only a pragmatic precept which makes us pay attention to our own advantage and merely teaches us to take such advantage into consideration.

We shall, therefore, have to investigate the possibility of a categorical imperative entirely a priori, inasmuch as we do not here have the advantage of having its reality given in experience and consequently of thus being obligated merely to explain its possibility rather than to establish it. In the meantime so much can be seen for now: the categorical imperative alone purports to be a practical law, while all the others may be called principles of the will but not laws. The reason for this is that whatever is necessary merely in order to attain some arbitrary purpose can be regarded as in itself contingent, and the precept can always be ignored once the purpose is abandoned. Contrariwise, an unconditioned command does not leave the will free to choose the opposite at its own liking. Consequently, only such a command carries with it that necessity which is demanded from a law.

Secondly, in the case of this categorical imperative, or law of morality, the reason for the difficulty (of discerning its possibility) is quite serious. The categorical imperative is an a priori synthetic practical proposition,[5] and since discerning the possibility of propositions of this sort involves so much difficulty in theoretic knowledge, there may readily be gathered that there will be no less difficulty in practical knowledge.

In solving this problem, we want first to inquire whether perhaps the mere concept of a categorical imperative may not also supply us

[5]I connect a priori, and therefore necessarily, the act with the will without presupposing any condition taken from some inclination (though I make such a connection only objectively, i.e., under the idea of a reason having full power over all subjective motives). Hence this is a practical proposition which does not analytically derive the willing of an action from some other willing already presupposed (for we possess no such perfect will) but which connects the willing of an action immediately with the concept of the will of a rational being as something which is not contained in this concept.

with the formula containing the proposition that can alone be a categorical imperative. For even when we know the purport of such an absolute command, the question as to how it is possible will still require a special and difficult effort, which we postpone to the last section.[6]

If I think of a hypothetical imperative in general, I do not know beforehand what it will contain until its condition is given. But if I think of a categorical imperative, I know immediately what it contains. For since, besides the law, the imperative contains only the necessity that the maxim[7] should accord with this law, while the law contains no condition to restrict it, there remains nothing but the universality of a law as such with which the maxim of the action should conform. This conformity alone is properly what is represented as necessary by the imperative.

Hence there is only one categorical imperative and it is this: Act only according to that maxim whereby you can at the same time will that it should become a universal law.[8]

Now if all imperatives of duty can be derived from this one imperative as their principle, then there can at least be shown what is understood by the concept of duty and what it means, even though there is left undecided whether what is called duty may not be an empty concept.

The universality of law according to which effects are produced constitutes what is properly called nature in the most general sense (as to form), i.e., the existence of things as far as determined by universal laws. Accordingly, the universal imperative of duty may be expressed thus: Act as if the maxim of your action were to become through your will a universal law of nature.[9]

We shall now enumerate some duties, following the usual division of them into duties to ourselves and to others and into perfect and imperfect duties.[10]

---

[6][See below Ak. 446–63.]

[7]A maxim is the subjective principle of acting and must be distinguished from the objective principle, viz., the practical law. A maxim contains the practical rule which reason determines in accordance with the conditions of the subject (often his ignorance or his inclinations) and is thus the principle according to which the subject does act. But the law is the objective principle valid for every rational being, and it is the principle according to which he ought to act, i.e., an imperative.

[8][This formulation of the categorical imperative is often referred to as the formula of universal law.]

[9][This is often called the formula of the law of nature.]

[10]There should be noted here that I reserve the division of duties for a future *Metaphysics of Morals* [in Part II of the *Metaphysics of Morals*, entitled *The Metaphysical Principles of Virtue*, Ak. 417–474]. The division presented here stands as merely an arbitrary one (in order to arrange my examples). For the rest, I understand here by a perfect duty one which permits no exception in the interest of inclination. Accordingly, I have perfect duties which are external [to others], while other ones are internal [to oneself]. This classification runs contrary to the accepted usage of the schools, but I do not intend to justify it here, since there is no difference for my purpose whether this classification is accepted or not.

1. A man reduced to despair by a series of misfortunes feels sick of life but is still so far in possession of his reason that he can ask himself whether taking his own life would not be contrary to his duty to himself.[11] Now he asks whether the maxim of his action could become a universal law of nature. But his maxim is this: from self-love I make as my principle to shorten my life when its continued duration threatens more evil than it promises satisfaction. There only remains the question as to whether this principle of self-love can become a universal law of nature. One sees at once a contradiction in a system of nature whose law would destroy life by means of the very same feeling that acts so as to stimulate the furtherance of life, and hence there could be no existence as a system of nature. Therefore, such a maxim cannot possibly hold as a universal law of nature and is, consequently, wholly opposed to the supreme principle of all duty.

2. Another man in need finds himself forced to borrow money. He knows well that he won't be able to repay it, but he sees also that he will not get any loan unless he firmly promises to repay it within a fixed time. He wants to make such a promise, but he still has conscience enough to ask himself whether it is not permissible and is contrary to duty to get out of difficulty in this way. Suppose, however, that he decides to do so. The maxim of his action would then be expressed as follows: when I believe myself to be in need of money, I will borrow money and promise to pay it back, although I know that I can never do so. Now this principle of self-love or personal advantage may perhaps be quite compatible with one's entire future welfare, but the question is now whether it is right.[12] I then transform the requirement of self-love into a universal law and put the question thus: how would things stand if my maxim were to become a universal law? He then sees at once that such a maxim could never hold as a universal law of nature and be consistent with itself, but must necessarily be self-contradictory. For the universality of a law which says that anyone believing himself to be in difficulty could promise whatever he pleases with the intention of not keeping it would make promising itself and the end to be attained thereby quite impossible, inasmuch as no one would believe what was promised him but would merely laugh at all such utterances as being vain pretenses.

---

[11][Not committing suicide is an example of a perfect duty of oneself. See *Metaphysical Principles of Virtue*, Ak. 422-24.]

[12][Keeping promises is an example of a perfect duty to others. See *ibid.*, Ak. 423-31.]

3. A third finds in himself a talent whose cultivation could make him a man useful in many respects. But he finds himself in comfortable circumstances and prefers to indulge in pleasure rather than to bother himself about broadening and improving his fortunate natural aptitudes. But he asks himself further whether his maxim of neglecting his natural gifts, besides agreeing of itself with his propensity to indulgence, might agree also with what is called duty.¹³ He then sees that a system of nature could indeed always subsist according to such a universal law, even though every man (like South Sea Islanders) should let his talents rust and resolve to devote his life entirely to idleness, indulgence, propagation, and, in a word, to enjoyment. But he cannot possibly will that this should become a universal law of nature or be implanted in us as such a law by a natural instinct. For as a rational being he necessarily wills that all his faculties should be developed, inasmuch as they are given him for all sorts of possible purposes.

4. A fourth man finds things going well for himself but sees others (whom he could help) struggling with great hardships; and he thinks: what does it matter to me? Let everybody be as happy as Heaven wills or as he can make himself; I shall take nothing from him nor even envy him; but I have no desire to contribute anything to his well-being or to his assistance when in need. If such a way of thinking were to become a universal law of nature, the human race admittedly could very well subsist and doubtless could subsist even better than when everyone prates about sympathy and benevolence and even on occasion exerts himself to practice them but, on the other hand, also cheats when he can, betrays the rights of man, or otherwise violates them. But even though it is possible that a universal law of nature could subsist in accordance with that maxim, still it is impossible to will that such a principle should hold everywhere as a law of nature.¹⁴ For a will which resolved in this way would contradict itself, inasmuch as cases might often arise in which one would have need of the love and sympathy of others and in which he would deprive himself, by such a law of nature springing from his own will, of all hope of the aid he wants for himself.

These are some of the many actual duties, or at least what are taken to be such, whose derivation from the single principle cited above is clear. We must be able to will that a maxim of our action become a universal

---

¹³[Cultivating one's talents is an example of an imperfect duty to oneself. See *ibid.*, Ak. 444–46.]

¹⁴[Benefiting others is an example of an imperfect duty to others. See *ibid.*, Ak. 452–54.]

law; this is the canon for morally estimating any of our actions. Some actions are so constituted that their maxims cannot without contradiction even by thought as a universal law of nature, much less be willed as what should become one. In the case of others this internal impossibility is indeed not found, but there is still no possibility of willing that their maxim should be raised to the universality of a law of nature, because such a will would contradict itself. There is no difficulty in seeing that the former kind of action conflicts with strict or narrow [perfect] (irremissible) duty, while the second kind conflicts only with broad [imperfect] (meritorious) duty.[15] By means of these examples there has thus been fully set forth how all duties depend as regards the kind of obligation (not the object of their action) upon the one principle.

If we now attend to ourselves in any transgression of a duty, we find that we actually do not will that our maxim should become a universal law—because this is impossible for us—but rather that the opposite of this maxim should remain a law universally.[16] We only take the liberty of making an exception to the law for ourselves (or just for this one time) to the advantage of our inclination. Consequently, if we weighed up everything from one and the same standpoint, namely, that of reason, we would find a contradiction in our own will, viz., that a certain principle be objectively necessary as a universal law and yet subjectively not hold universally but should admit of exceptions. But since we at one moment regard our action from the standpoint of a will wholly in accord with reason and then at another moment regard the very same action from the standpoint of a will affected by inclination, there is really no contradiction here. Rather, there is an opposition (*antagonismus*) of inclination to the precept of reason, whereby the universality (*universalitas*) of the principle is changed into a mere generality (*generalitas*) so that the practical principle of reason may meet the maxim halfway. Although this procedure cannot be justified in out own impartial judgment, yet it does show that we actually acknowledge the validity of the categorical imperative and (with all respect for it) merely allow ourselves a few exceptions which, as they seem to us, are unimportant and forced upon us.

We have thus at least shown that if duty is a concept which is to have significance and real legislative authority for our actions, then such

---

[15][Compare *ibid.*, Ak. 390–94, 410–11, 421–51.]

[16][This is to say, for example, that when you tell a lie, you do so on the condition that others are truthful and believe that what you are saying is true, because otherwise your lie will never work to get you what you want. When you tell a lie, you simply take exception to the general rule that says everyone should always tell the truth.]

duty can be expressed only in categorical imperatives but not at all in hypothetical ones. We have also—and this is already a great deal—exhibited clearly and definitely for every application what is the content of the categorical imperative, which must contain the principle of all duty (if there is such a thing at all). But we have not yet advanced far enough to prove a priori that there actually is an imperative of this kind, that there is a practical law which of itself commands absolutely and without any incentives, and that following this law is duty.

Nicomachean Ethics
Aristotle

Book I

To understand what moral goodness is we must study the soul of man

. . . Since happiness is an activity of the soul in accordance with perfect virtue, we must examine the nature of virtue; for perhaps in this way we shall be better able to form a view about happiness too. Besides, the true statesman is thought of as a man who has taken special pains to study this subject; for he wants to make his fellow-citizens good and law-abiding people (we have an example of this in the law-givers of Crete and Sparta, and any others who have shown similar qualities). And if this investigation is a part of political science, clearly our inquiry will be in keeping with the plan that we adopted at the outset.

The goodness that we have to consider is human goodness, obviously; for it was the good *for man* or happiness *for man* that we set out to discover. But by human goodness is meant goodness not of the body but of the soul, and happiness also we define as an activity of the soul. This being so, it is evident that the statesman ought to have some acquaintance with psychology, just as, a doctor who intends to treat the eye must have a knowledge of the body as a whole. Indeed the statesman's need is greater than the doctor's, inasmuch as politics is a better and more honourable science than medicine. But the best kind of doctors take a good deal of trouble to acquire a knowledge of the body; so the statesman too must study the soul, but with a view to politics, and only so far as is sufficient for the questions that we are investigating; for to explore its nature in greater detail would presumably be too laborious for our present purpose.

The several faculties of the soul distinguished

Some aspects of psychology are adequately treated in discourses elsewhere, and we should make use of the results: e.g. that the soul is part rational and part irrational (whether these are separate like the parts of the body or anything else that is physically divisible, or whether like the convex and concave aspects of the circumference of a circle they are distinguishable as two only in definition and thought, and are by nature inseparable, makes no difference for our present purpose). Of the irrational soul one part seems to be common, viz. the vegetative: I mean the cause of nutrition and growth; because one can assume such a faculty of soul in everything that receives nourishment, even in embryos; and this same faculty too in the fully developed creature, because this is more reasonable than to suppose that the latter has a different one. Thus the excellence of this faculty is evidently common and not confined to man; because this part or faculty seems to be most active in sleep, when the good and the bad are least easy to distinguish (hence the saying 'for half their lives the happy are no different from the wretched'). This is a natural consequence, because sleep is a suspension of that function of the soul by which it is distinguished as good and bad—except that to a certain limited extent some of the stimuli reach the soul; this is what makes the dreams of decent people better than those of the ordinary man. But enough of this subject; we may dismiss the nutritive soul, because of its very nature it has no part in human goodness.

But there seems to be another element of the soul which, while irrational, is in a sense receptive of reason. Take the types of man which we call continent and incontinent. They have a principle—a rational element in their souls—which we commend, because it urges them in the right direction and encourages them to take the best course; but there is also observable in them another element, by nature irrational, which struggles and strains against the rational. Just as in the case of the body paralysed limbs, when the subject chooses to move them to the right, swing away in the contrary direction to the left, so exactly the same happens in the case of the soul; for the impulses of the incontinent take them in the contrary direction. 'But in bodies we see what swings away, whereas in the case of the soul we do not.' Probably we should believe nevertheless that the soul too contains an irrational element which opposes and runs counter to reason—in what sense it is a separate element does not matter at all. But this too, as we said seems to be receptive of reason; at any rate in the continent man it is obedient to reason, and is presumably still more amenable in the temperate and in the brave man, because in them it is in complete harmony with the rational principle.

Evidently, then, the irrational part of the soul also consists of two parts. The vegetative has no association at all with reason, but the desiderative and generally appetitive part does in a way participate in reason, in the sense that it is submissive and obedient to it (this is the sense of *logon echein* in which we speak of 'taking account' of one's father or friends, not that in which we speak of 'having an account' of mathematical propositions). That the irrational part is in some way persuaded by reason is indicated by our use of admonition, and of reproof and encouragement of all kinds. If, however, one should speak of the appetitive part of the soul as rational too, it will be the rational part that is divided in two: one rational in the proper sense of the word and in itself, the other in the sense that a child pays attention to its father.

Virtue, too, is divided into classes in accordance with this differentiation of the soul. Some virtues are called intellectual and others moral; Wisdom and Understanding and Prudence are intellectual, Liberality and Temperance are moral virtues. When we are speaking of a man's character we do not describe him as wise or understanding, but as patient or temperate. We do, however, praise a wise man on the ground of his state of mind; and those states that are praiseworthy we call virtues.

Book II

Moral virtues, like crafts, are acquired by practice and habituation

Virtue, then, is of two kinds, intellectual and moral. Intellectual virtue owes both its inception and its growth chiefly to instruction, and for this very reason needs time and experience. Moral goodness, on the other hand, is the result of habit, from which it has actually got its name, being a slight modification of the word *ethos*. This fact makes it obvious that none of the moral virtues is engendered in us by nature, since nothing that is what it is by nature can be made to behave differently by habituation. For instance, a stone, which has a natural tendency downwards, cannot be habituated to rise, however often you try to train it by throwing it into the air; nor can you train fire to burn downwards; nor can anything else that has any other natural tendency be trained to depart from it. The moral virtues, then, are engendered in us neither *by* nor *contrary to* nature; we are constituted by nature to receive them, but their full development in us is due to habit.

Again, of all those faculties with which nature endows us we first acquire the potentialities, and only later effect their actualization. (This is evident in the case of the senses. It was not from repeated acts of seeing or hearing that we acquired the senses but the other way round: we had these senses before we used them; we did not acquire them as the result of using them.) But the virtues we do acquire by first exercising them, just as happens in the arts. Anything that we have to learn to do we learn by the actual doing of it: people become builders by building and instrumentalists by playing instruments. Similarly we become just by performing just acts, temperate by performing temperate ones, brave by performing brave ones. This view is supported by what happens in city-states. Legislators make their citizens good by habituation; this is the intention of every legislator, and those who do not carry it out fail of their object. This is what makes the difference between a good constitution and a bad one.

Again, the causes or means that bring about any form of excellence are the same as those that destroy it, and similarly with art; for it is as a result of playing the harp that people become good and bad harpists. The same principle applies to builders and all other craftsmen. Men will become good builders as a result of building well, and bad ones as a result of building badly. Otherwise there would be no need of anyone to teach them: they would all be *born* either good or bad. Now this holds good also of the virtues. It is the way that we behave in our dealings with other people that makes us just or unjust, and the way that we behave in the face of danger, accustoming ourselves to be timid or confident, that makes us brave or cowardly. Similarly with situations involving desires and angry feelings: some people become temperate and patient from one kind of conduct in such situations, others licentious and choleric from another. In a word, then, like activities produce like dispositions. Hence we must give our activities a certain quality, because it is their characteristics that determine the resulting dispositions. So it is a matter of no little importance what sort of habits we form from the earliest age—it makes a vast difference, or rather all the difference in the world.

In a practical science, so much depends on particular circumstances that only general rules can be given

Since the branch of philosophy on which we are at present engaged is not, like the others, theoretical in its aim—because we are studying not to know what goodness is, but how to become good men, since otherwise it would be useless—we must apply our minds to the problem of how our actions should be performed, because, as we have just said, it is these that actually determine our dispositions.

Now that we should act according to the right principle is common ground and may be assumed as a basis for discussion (the point will be discussed later, both what 'the right principle' is, and how it is related to the other virtues). But we must first agree that any account of conduct must be stated in outline and not in precise detail, just as we said at the beginning that accounts are to be required only in such a form as befits their subject-matter. Now questions of conduct and expedience have as little fixity about them as questions of what is healthful; and if this is true of the general rule, it is still more true that its application to particular problems admits of no precision. For they do not fall under any art or professional tradition, but the agents are compelled at every step to think out for themselves what the circumstances demand, just as happens in the arts of medicine and navigation. However, although our present account is of this kind, we must try to support it.

A cardinal rule: right conduct is incompatible with excess or deficiency in feelings and actions

First, then, we must consider this fact: that it is in the nature of moral qualities that they are destroyed by deficiency and excess, just as we can see (since we have to use the evidence of visible facts to throw light on those that are invisible) in the case of <bodily> health and strength. For both excessive and insufficient exercise destroy one's strength, and both eating and drinking too much or too little destroy health, whereas the right quantity produces, increases and preserves it. So it is the same with temperance, courage and the other virtues. The man who shuns and fears everything and stands up to nothing becomes a coward; the man who is afraid of nothing at all, but marches up to every danger, becomes foolhardy. Similarly the man who indulges in every pleasure and refrains from none becomes licentious; but if a man behaves like a boor and turns his back on every pleasure, he is a case of insensibility. Thus temperance and courage are destroyed by excess and deficiency and preserved by the mean.

574 • *Part Seven What Is Moral?*

Our virtues are exercised in the same kinds of action as gave rise to them

But besides the fact that the virtues are induced and fostered as a result, and by the agency, of the same sort of actions as cause their destruction, the activities that flow from them will also consist in the same sort of actions. This is so in all the other more observable instances, e.g. in that of <bodily> strength. This results from taking plenty of nourishment and undergoing severe training, and it is the strong man that will be best able to carry out this programme. So with the virtues. It is by refraining from pleasures that we become temperate, and it is when we have become temperate that we are most able to abstain from pleasures. Similarly with courage; it is by habituating ourselves to make light of alarming situations and to face them that we become brave, and it is when we have become brave that we shall be most able to face an alarming situation.

The pleasure or pain that actions cause the agent may serve as an index of moral progress, since good conduct consists in a proper attitude towards pleasure and pain

The pleasure or pain that accompanies people's acts should be taken as a sign of their dispositions. A man who abstains from bodily pleasures and enjoys the very fact of so doing is temperate; if he finds it irksome he is licentious. Again, the man who faces danger gladly, or at least without distress, is brave; the one who feels distressed is a coward. For it is with pleasures and pains that moral goodness is concerned. Pleasure induces us to behave badly, and pain to shrink from fine actions. Hence the importance (as Plato says) of having been trained in some way from infancy to feel joy and grief at the right things: true education is precisely this. If the virtues are concerned with actions and feelings, and every feeling and every action is always accompanied by pleasure or pain, on this ground too virtue will be concerned with pleasures and pains. The fact that punishments are effected by their means is further evidence, because punishment is a kind of remedial treatment and such treatment is naturally effected by contraries. Again, as we said above, every state of the soul attains its natural development in relation to, and in the sphere of, those conditions by which it is naturally made better or worse. Now when people become bad it is because of pleasures and pains, through seeking (or shunning) the wrong ones, or at the wrong time, or in the wrong way, or in any other manner in which such offences are distinguished by principle. This is why some thinkers actually define the virtues as forms of impassivity or tranquillity. But they are wrong in speaking absolutely instead of adding 'in the right (or wrong) manner and at the right time' and any other due qualifications.

We have decided, then, that this kind of virtue disposes us to act in the best way with regard to pleasures and pains, and contrariwise with the corresponding vice. But we may obtain further light on the same point from the following considerations.

There are three factors that make for choice, and three that make for avoidance: the fine, the advantageous, and the pleasant, and their contraries, the base, the harmful, and the painful. Now with regard to all these the good man tends to go right and the bad man to go wrong, especially about pleasure. This is common to all animals, and accompanies all objects of choice, for clearly the fine and the advantageous are pleasant too. Consciousness of pleasure has grown up with all of us from our infancy, and therefore our life is so deeply imbued with this feeling that it is hard to remove all trace of it. Pleasure and pain are also the standards by which—to a greater or lesser extent—we regulate our actions. Since to feel pleasure and pain rightly or wrongly has no little effect upon conduct, it follows that our whole inquiry must be concerned with these sensations. Heraclitus says that it is hard to fight against emotion, but harder still to fight against pleasure; and the harder course is always the concern of both art and virtue, because success is better in the face of difficulty. Thus on this ground too the whole concern of both morality and political science must be with pleasures and pains, since the man who treats them rightly will be good and the one who treats them wrongly will be bad.

We may take this as a sufficient statement that virtue is concerned with pains and pleasures; that the actions that produce it also increase it, or if differently performed, destroy it; and that the actions that produce it also constitute the sphere of its activity.

Acts that are incidentally virtuous distinguished from those that are done knowingly, of choice, and from a virtuous disposition

A difficulty, however, may be raised as to how we can say that people must perform just actions if they are to become just, and temperate ones if they are to become temperate; because if they do what is just and temperate, they are just and temperate already, in the same way that if they use words or play music correctly they are already literate or musical. But surely this is not true even of the arts. It is possible to put a few words together correctly by accident, or at the prompting of another person; so the agent will only be literate if he does a literate act in a literate way, viz. in virtue of his own literacy. Nor, again, is there an analogy between the arts and the virtues. Works of art have their merit in themselves; so it is enough for them to be turned out with a certain quality of their own. But virtuous acts are not done in a just or temperate way merely because *they* have a certain quality, but only if the agent also acts in a certain state, viz. (1) if he knows what he is doing, (2) if he chooses it, and chooses it for its own sake, and (3) if he does it from a fixed and permanent disposition. Now these—knowledge excepted—are not reckoned as necessary qualifications for the arts as well. For the acquisition of virtues, on the other hand, knowledge has little or no force; but the other requirements are not of little but of supreme importance, granted that it is from the repeated performance of just and temperate acts that we acquire virtues. Acts, to be sure, are called just and temperate when they are such as a just or temperate man would do; but what makes the agent just or temperate is not merely the fact that he does such things, but the fact that he does them in the way that just and temperate men do. It is therefore right to say that a man becomes just by the performance of just, and temperate by the performance of temperate, acts; nor is there the smallest likelihood of any man's becoming good by not doing them. This is not, however, the course that most people follow: they have recourse to their principle, and imagine that they are being philosophical and that in this way they will become serious-minded—behaving rather like invalids who listen carefully to their doctor, but carry out none of his instructions. Just as the bodies of the latter will get no benefit from such treatment, so the souls of the former will get none from such philosophy.

In order to define virtue we must decide to what class or genus it belongs. It is not a feeling or a faculty, but a disposition

We must now consider what virtue is. Since there are three kinds of modification that are found in the soul, viz. feelings, faculties and dispositions, virtue must be one of these three. By feelings I mean desire, anger, fear, daring, envy, joy, friendliness, hatred, longing, jealousy, pity, and in general all conditions that are attended by pleasure or pain. By faculties I mean those susceptibilities in virtue of which we are said to be capable of the feelings in question, e.g. capable of anger or sorrow or pity. By dispositions I mean conditions in virtue of which we are well or ill disposed in respect of the feelings concerned. We have, for instance, a bad disposition towards anger if our tendency is too strong or too weak, and a good one if our tendency is moderate. Similarly with the other feelings.

Now neither the virtues nor the vices are feelings, because we are not called good or bad on the ground of our feelings, but we are so called on the ground of our virtues and vices; nor are we either praised or blamed for our feelings (a man is not praised for being frightened or angry, nor is he blamed just for being angry; it is for being angry in a particular way); but we are praised and blamed for our virtues and vices. Again, when we are angry or frightened it is not by our choice; but our virtues are expressions of our choice, or at any rate imply choice. Besides, we are said to be moved in respect of our feelings, but in respect of our virtues and vices we are said to be not moved but disposed in a particular way. By the same line of reasoning they are not faculties either. We are not called good or bad, nor are we praised or blamed, merely because we are capable of feeling. Again, what faculties we have, we have by nature; but it is not nature that makes us good or bad (we mentioned this point above). So if the virtues are neither feelings nor faculties, it remains that they are dispositions.

We have now stated what virtue is generically.

But what is its differentia? Any excellence enables its possessor to function; therefore this is true of human excellence, i.e. virtue

But we must not only make the simple statement that it is a disposition; we must also say what *kind* of disposition. Let us assert, then, that any kind of excellence renders that of which it is the excellence *good*, and makes it perform its function *well*. For example, the excellence of the eye makes both the eye and its function good (because it is through the excellence of the eye that we see well). Similarly the excellence of a horse makes him both a fine horse and good at running and carrying his rider and facing the enemy. If this rule holds good for all cases, then *human* excellence will be the disposition that makes one a good man and causes him to perform his function well. We have already explained how this will be; but it will also become clear in another way if we consider what is the specific nature of virtue.

This is confirmed by the doctrine of the Mean

In anything continuous and divisible it is possible to take a part which is greater or less than, or equal to, the remainder; and that in relation either to the thing divided or to us. The equal part is a sort of mean between excess and deficiency; and I call mean in relation to the *thing* whatever is equidistant from the extremes, which is one and the same for everybody; but I call mean in relation to us that which is neither excessive nor deficient, and this is *not* one and the same for all. For example, if ten is 'many' and two 'few' of some quantity, six is the mean if one takes it in relation to the thing, because it exceeds the one number and is exceeded by the other by the same amount; and this is the mean by arithmetical reckoning. But the mean in relation to us is not to be obtained in this way. Supposing that ten pounds of food is a large and two pounds a small allowance for an athlete, it does not follow that the trainer will prescribe six pounds; for even this is perhaps too much or too little for the person who is to receive it—too little for Milo but too much for one who is only beginning to train. Similarly in the case of running and wrestling. In this way, then, every knowledgeable person avoids excess and deficiency, but looks for the mean and chooses it—not the mean of the thing, but the mean relative to us.

If, then, every science performs its function well only when it observes the mean and refers its products to it (which is why it is customary to say of well-executed works that nothing can be added to them or taken away, the implication being that excess and deficiency alike destroy perfection, while the mean preserves it)—if good craftsmen, as we hold, work with the mean in view; and if virtue, like nature, is more exact and more efficient than any art, it follows that virtue aims to hit the mean. By virtue I mean moral virtue since it is this that is concerned with feelings and actions, and these involve excess, deficiency and a mean. It is possible, for example, to feel fear, confidence, desire, anger, pity, and pleasure and pain generally, too much or too little; and both of these are wrong. But to have these feelings at the right times on the right grounds towards the right people for the right motive and in the right way is to feel them to an intermediate, that is to the best, degree; and this is the mark of virtue. Similarly there are excess and deficiency and a mean in the case of actions. But it is in the field of actions and feelings that virtue operates; and in them excess and deficiency are failings, whereas the mean is praised and recognized as a success: and these are both marks of virtue. Virtue, then, is a mean condition, inasmuch as it aims at hitting the mean.

Again, failure is possible in many ways (for evil, as the Pythagoreans represented it, is a form of the Unlimited, and good of the Limited), but success is only one. That is why the one is easy and the other difficult; it is easy to miss the target and difficult to hit it. Here, then, is another reason why excess and deficiency fall under evil, and the mean state under good;

For men are bad in countless ways, but good in only one.

A provisional definition of virtue

So virtue is a purposive disposition, lying in a mean that is relative to us and determined by a rational principle, and by that which a prudent man would use to determine it. It is a mean between two kinds of vice, one of excess and the other of deficiency; and also for this reason, that whereas these vices fall short of or exceed the right measure in both feelings and actions, virtue discovers the mean and chooses it. Thus from the point of view of its essence and the definition of its real nature, virtue is a mean; but in respect of what is right and best, it is an extreme.

But the rule of choosing the mean cannot be applied to some actions and feelings, which are essentially evil

But not every action or feeling admits of a mean; because some have names that directly connote depravity, such as malice, shamelessness and envy, and among actions adultery, theft and murder. All these, and more like them, are so called as being evil in themselves; it is not the excess or deficiency of them that is evil. In their case, then, it is impossible to act rightly; one is always wrong. Nor does acting rightly or wrongly in such cases depend upon circumstances—whether a man commits adultery with the right woman or at the right time or in the right way, because to do anything of that kind is simply wrong. One might as well claim that there is a mean and excess and deficiency even in unjust or cowardly or intemperate actions. On that basis there must be a mean of excess, a mean of deficiency, an excess of excess and a deficiency of deficiency. But just as in temperance and courage there can be no mean or excess or deficiency, because the mean is in a sense an extreme, so there can be no mean or excess or deficiency in the vices that we mentioned; however done, they are wrong. For in general neither excess nor deficiency admits of a mean, nor does a mean admit of excess and deficiency.

The doctrine of the mean applied to particular virtues

But a generalization of this kind is not enough; we must apply it to particular cases. When we are discussing actions, although general state-

TABLE OF VIRTUES AND VICES

Sphere of Action or Feeling	Excess	Mean	Deficiency
Fear and Confidence	Rashness *thrasutēs*	Courage *andreia*	Cowardice *deilia*
Pleasure and Pain	Licentiousness *akolasia*	Temperance *sōphrosunē*	Insensibility *anaisthēsia*
Getting and Spending (minor)	Prodigality *asōtia*	Liberality *eleutheriotēs*	Illiberality *aneleutheria*
Getting and Spending (major)	Vulgarity *aperiokalia, banausia*	Magnificence *megaloprepeia*	Pettiness *mikroprepeia*
Honour and Dishonour (major)	Vanity *chaunotēs*	Magnanimity *megalopsūchia*	Pusillanimity *mikropsūchia*
Honour and Dishonour (minor)	Ambition *philotīmia*	Proper ambition	Unambitiousness *aphilotīmia*
Anger	Irascibility *orgilotēs*	Patience *prāotēs*	Lack of spirit *aorgēsia*
Self-expression	Boastfulness *alazoneia*	Truthfulness *alētheia*	Understatement *eirōneia*
Conversation	Buffoonery *bōmolochia*	Wittiness *eutrapelia*	Boorishness *agroikia*
Social Conduct	Obsequiousness *areskeia* Flattery *kolakeia*	Friendliness *philia*(?)	Cantankerousness *duskolia* (*duseris*)
Shame	Shyness *kataplēxis*	Modesty *aidōs*	Shamelessness *anaischuntia*
Indignation	Envy *phthonos*	Righteous indignation *nemesis*	Malicious enjoyment *epichairekakia*

ments have a wider application, particular statements are closer to the truth. This is because actions are concerned with particular facts, and theories must be brought into harmony with these. Let us, then, take these instances from the diagram.

In the field of Fear and Confidence the mean is Courage; and of those who go to extremes the man who exceeds in fearlessness has no name to describe him (there are many nameless cases), the one who exceeds in confidence is called Rash, and the one who shows an excess of fear and a deficiency of confidence is called Cowardly. In the field of Pleasures and Pains—not in all, especially not in all pains—the mean is Temperance, the excess Licentiousness; cases of defective response to pleasures scarcely occur, and therefore people of this sort too have no name to describe them, but let us class them as Insensible. In the field of Giving and Receiving Money the mean is Liberality, the excess and deficiency are Prodigality and Illiberality; but these show excess and deficiency in contrary ways to one another: the prodigal man goes too far in spending and not far enough in getting, while the illiberal man goes too far in getting money and not far enough in spending it. This present account is in outline and summary, which is all that we need at this stage; we shall give a more accurate analysis later.

But there are other dispositions too that are concerned with money. There is a mean called Magnificence (because the magnificent is not the same as the liberal man: the one deals in large and the other in small outlays); the excess is Tastelessness and Vulgarity, the deficiency Pettiness. These are different from the extremes between which liberality lies; how they differ will be discussed later. In the field of Public Honour and Dishonour the mean is Magnanimity, the excess is called a sort of Vanity, and the deficiency Pusillanimity. And just as liberality differs, as we said, from magnificence in being concerned with small outlays, so there is a state related to Magnanimity in the same way, being concerned with small honours, while magnanimity is concerned with great ones; because it is possible to aspire to <small> honours in the right way, or to a greater or less degree than is right. The man who goes too far in his aspirations is called Ambitious, the one who falls short, Unambitious; the one who is a mean between them has no name. This is true also of the corresponding dispositions, except that the ambitious man's is called Ambitiousness. This is why the extremes lay claim to the intermediate territory. We ourselves sometimes call the intermediate man ambitious and sometimes unambitious; that is, we sometimes commend the ambitious and sometimes the unambitious. Why it is that we do this will be explained in our later remarks. Meanwhile let us continue our discussion of the remaining virtues and vices, following the method already laid down.

In the field of Anger, too, there is excess, deficiency and the mean. They do not really possess names, but we may call the intermediate man Patient and the mean Patience; and of the extremes the one who exceeds can be Irascible and his vice Irascibility, while the one who is deficient can be Spiritless and the deficiency Lack of Spirit.

There are also three other means which, though different, somewhat resemble each other. They are all concerned with what we do and say in social intercourse, but they differ in this respect, that one is concerned with truthfulness in such intercourse, the other two with pleasantness— one with pleasantness in entertainment, the other with pleasantness in every department of life. We must therefore say something about these too, in order that we may better discern that in all things the mean is to be commended, while the extremes are neither commendable nor right, but reprehensible. Most of these too have no names; but, as in the other cases, we must try to coin names for them in the interest of clarity and to make it easy to follow the argument.

Well, then, as regards Truth the intermediate man may be called Truthful and the mean Truthfulness; pretension that goes too far may be Boastfulness and the man who is disposed to it a Boaster, while that which is deficient may be called Irony and its exponent Ironical. As for Pleasantness in Social Entertainment, the intermediate man is Witty, and the disposition Wit; the excess is Buffoonery and the indulger in it a Buffoon; the man who is deficient is a kind of Boor and his disposition Boorishness. In the rest of the sphere of the Pleasant—life in general— the person who is pleasant in the right way is Friendly and the mean is Friendliness; the person who goes too far, if he has no motive, is Obse- quious; if his motive is self-interest, he is a Flatterer. The man who is defi- cient and is unpleasant in all circumstances is Cantankerous and Ill-tempered.

There are mean states also in the sphere of feelings and emotions. Modesty is not a virtue, but the modest man too is praised. Here too one person is called intermediate and another excessive—like the Shy man who is overawed at anything. The man who feels too little shame or none at all is Shameless, and the intermediate man is Modest. Right- eous Indignation is a mean between Envy and Spite, and they are all con- cerned with feelings of pain or pleasure at the experiences of our neighbours. The man who feels righteous indignation is distressed at instances of undeserved good fortune, but the envious man goes further and is distressed at *any* good fortune, while the spiteful man is so far from feeling distress that he actually rejoices.

However, we shall have occasion to continue this discussion elsewhere. After that we shall treat of Justice, distinguishing its two kinds—because the word is used in more senses than one—and explain in what way each of them is a mean. [We shall also treat similarly of the rational virtues.]

The mean is often nearer to one extreme than to the other, or seems nearer because of our natural tendencies

Thus there are three dispositions, two of them vicious (one by way of excess, the other of deficiency), and one good, the mean. They are all in some way opposed to one another: the extremes are contrary both to the mean and to each other, and the mean to the extremes. For just as the equal is greater compared with the less, and less compared with the greater, so the mean states (in both feelings and actions) are excessive compared with the deficient and deficient compared with the excessive. A brave man appears rash compared with a coward, and cowardly compared with a rash man; similarly a temperate man appears licentious compared with an insensible one and insensible compared with a licentious one, and a liberal man prodigal compared with an illiberal one and illiberal compared with a prodigal one. This is the reason why each extreme type tries to push the mean nearer to the other: the coward calls the brave man rash, the rash man calls him a coward; and similarly in all other cases. But while all these dispositions are opposed to one another in this way, the greatest degree of contrariety is that which is found between the two extremes. For they are separated by a greater interval from one another than from the mean, just as the great is further from the small, and the small from the great, than either is from the equal. Again, some extremes seem to bear a resemblance to a mean; e.g. rashness seems like courage, and prodigality like liberality; but between the extremes there is always the maximum dissimilarity. Now contraries are by definition as far distant as possible from one another; hence the further apart things are, the more contrary they will be. In some cases it is the deficiency, in others the excess, that is more opposed to the mean; for instance, the more direct opposite of courage is not the excess, rashness, but the deficiency, cowardice; and that of temperance is not the deficiency, insensibility, but the excess, licentiousness. This result is due to two causes. One lies in the nature of the thing itself. When one extreme has a closer affinity and resemblance to the mean, we tend to oppose to the mean not that extreme but the other. For instance, since rashness is held to be nearer to courage and more like it than cowardice is, it is cowardice that we tend to oppose to courage, because the extremes that are further from the mean are thought to be more opposed to it. This is one cause, the one that lies in the *thing*. The other lies in ourselves. It is the things towards which we have the stronger natural inclination that seem to us more opposed to the mean. For example, we are naturally more inclined towards pleasures, and this makes us more prone towards licentiousness than towards temperance; so we describe as more contrary to the mean those things towards which we have the stronger tendency. This is why licentiousness, the excess, is more contrary to temperance.

Summing up of the foregoing discussion, together with three practical rules for good conduct

We have now said enough to show that moral virtue is a mean, and in what sense it is so: that it is a mean between two vices, one of excess and the other of deficiency, and that it is such because it aims at hitting the mean point in feelings and actions. For this reason it is a difficult business to be good; because in any given case it is difficult to find the midpoint—for instance, not everyone can find the centre of a circle; only the man who knows how. So too it is easy to get angry—anyone can do that—or to give and spend money; but to feel or act towards the right person to the right extent at the right time for the right reason in the right way—that is not easy, and it is not everyone that can do it. Hence to do these things well is a rare, laudable and fine achievement.

For this reason anyone who is aiming at the mean should (1) keep away from that extreme which is more contrary to the mean, just as Calypso advises:

Far from this surf and surge keep thou thy ship.

For one of the extremes is always more erroneous than the other; and since it is extremely difficult to hit the mean, we must take the next best course, as they say, and choose the lesser of the evils; and this will be most readily done in the way that we are suggesting. (2) We must notice the errors into which we ourselves are liable to fall (because we all have different natural tendencies—we shall find out what ours are from the pleasure and pain that they give us), and we must drag ourselves in the contrary direction; for we shall arrive at the mean by pressing well away from our failing—just like somebody straightening a warped piece of wood. (3) In every situation one must guard especially against pleasure and pleasant things, because we are not impartial judges of pleasure. So we should adopt the same attitude towards it as the Trojan elders did towards Helen, and constantly repeat their pronouncement; because if in this way we relieve ourselves of the attraction, we shall be less likely to go wrong.

To sum up: by following these rules we shall have the best chance of hitting the mean. But this is presumably difficult, especially in particular cases; because it is not easy to determine what is the right way to be angry, and with whom, and on what grounds, and for how long. Indeed we sometimes praise those who show deficiency, and call them patient, and sometimes those who display temper, calling them manly. However, the man who deviates only a little from the right degree, either in excess or in deficiency, is not censured—only the one who goes too far, because he is noticeable. Yet it is not easy to define by rule for how long, and how much, a man may go wrong before he incurs blame; no easier than it is to define any other object of perception. Such questions of degree occur in particular cases, and the decision lies with our perception.

This much, then, is clear: in all our conduct it is the mean that is to be commended. But one should incline sometimes towards excess and sometimes towards deficiency, because in this way we shall most easily hit upon the mean, that is, the right course. . . .

Virtue Ethics in TV's *Seinfeld*

Aeon J. Skoble

Contemporary moral philosophy is in a troubled state. Kantians, utilitarians, and other theoretical camps continue to quarrel while being beset by growing challenges from subjectivists and cultural relativists. To make matters worse, contemporary society seems to be in the thrall of an incoherent value system, wherein marijuana use often engenders longer jail time than murder, smokers are seen as more heinous than liars, and many people maintain, simultaneously, that they believe in God *and* that there is no such thing as right and wrong. What would it take to resolve the disputes within the academy and also enlighten a confused public? To do the former would require a splendid moral theory. To do the latter would require that powerful tool of mass learning, television. Not a documentary, not a high-band cable channel, but a popular program which reaches millions each week, one which can educate people even when they are intent on not learning anything. The moral theory which can best address our concerns is Aristotle's virtue ethics. The television program is NBC's popular comedy *Seinfeld*.

Aristotle's Virtue Ethics

Seinfeld has often been described as a comedy of manners, but it can actually be understood as an explication of Aristotelian moral theory. First, then, what is Aristotle's moral theory, and why is it a helpful one? Aristotle's *Nicomachean Ethics* is an example, indeed the *locus classicus*, of virtue ethics. In this moral paradigm, the important question is not so much "which acts are right and wrong?", but "what sort of character should I develop?"

Competing alternative theories are less satisfying in many respects. Utilitarianism, for example, is the view that the proper course is that which produces the greatest overall benefit for the greatest number of people—*act so as to produce the greatest good for the greatest number.* One common objection to this theory is that it seems to entail results which are so counterintuitive as to be unacceptable. For example, in its simplest form, the theory would allow us to inflict great suffering on a single innocent if it could benefit a larger number in a manner that outweighs that suffering. As a consequentialist theory, one which judges the moral acceptability of an action based on its consequences, utilitarianism holds that the end justifies the means, but our moral intuitions tell us that this is not always so. Utilitarianism is problematic, but, in any case, *Seinfeld*'s main characters can hardly be said to be exemplars of promoting the greatest good for the greatest number. The duty-based theory of Immanuel Kant, which exhorts us to follow the categorical imperative—*act so that you could will that the maxim of your action would become universal law*—is also problematic. Kant's theory implies that we have certain duties, but when we are faced with conflicting duties, it seems as though the only way to resolve them is to appeal to consequences. Because duty-based theories try to avoid the obvious problems with consequentialist theories, this is an unhappy turn. In any case, for a Kantian, right actions must proceed from a sense of duty, but while Jerry and his friends are often curious as to how to act, they seldom seem to be concerned with absolute moral duties.

Virtue ethics, in contrast to utilitarian and Kantian theories, is concerned with how to act, but focuses the inquiry on the character from which the actions proceed. This seems closer to the concerns of Jerry and George. The question "What is the right thing to do in this situation?" is often examined via a consideration of "what sort of person acts in such-and-such ways?" and "what would the wise person do in this situation?" These questions are the hallmarks of the Aristotelian approach, which is why the characters Jerry and George, in particular, can actually be understood as lessons in virtue ethics. While they sometimes seem to be concerned with "the rules," chiefly when they inquire into "protocol" or etiquette, closer investigation reveals that their primary concern is their character, what sort of person they should be. Of course, they are not perfect representatives of virtue ethics, but they nevertheless give us lessons in Greek wisdom.

For Aristotle, moral virtues are states of character one develops which, as they become more integral to one's being, help one to lead a happier, more fulfilled life. To acquire virtues, one needs to do three things: develop practical wisdom, discover and emulate positive role models, and practice acting well. Let us examine each of these in turn.

In Aristotle's theory, reason operates in more than one way. Reason tells me how to achieve a value or accomplish a goal efficiently, given any goal I might have. But reason can also tell me whether I should have the goals I have in the first place. For example, if I desire to eat cereal frequently, reason can tell me that I ought to have many bowls, much cereal, and ample milk in the house. But reason can also judge whether the desire for cereal is one which helps me live a better life overall, which, using skim milk, it does. Reason can judge the worthiness of a goal only with reference to a predominant goal. In other words, this-or-that value is good-for-me-to-have if and only if the pursuit of that value is conducive to my overall predominant value. On the Aristotelian view, there is such an overall predominant value, life, or more specifically, a flourishing or good life. One *naturally* desires to live a good life, and other desires must be shown to aid, not hinder, that larger goal.

Reason is also operative in deducing the proper course of action in a given situation. Aristotle recommends striving for the mean between extremes. Courage, for example, is said to be not only different from cowardice, but also from a rash faux-bravery. In other words, while cowardice is a vice, so is total fearlessness. The person who claims to be unafraid of *anything* is surely mistaken about the way the world works. One has ample reason to fear, say, angry grizzly bears, cannibalistic serial killers, or Crazy Joe Davola. Also, one must temper one's bravery with a consideration of circumstance—taking a foolish risk may look brave, but if it makes the situation worse, it's hardly virtuous. Now, this is no armchair philosophy. Aristotle says that one must learn how to be virtuous by practicing: by living through situations, and learning from experience.

Reason also leads us to the emulation of proper role models. The *phronemos*, or man of practical wisdom, is someone to be observed and learned from. The *phronemos* is not the same thing as a teacher, for one cannot teach virtues the way one teaches the alphabet. No one, for example, could "teach" Kramer to play golf, not even the caddy. To learn the game of golf, he had to study the fundamentals (such as angles, and body mechanics), observe good golfers, and practice, practice, practice. To learn virtue, one must study the fundamentals (such as the need for moderation between extremes), observe those who live well, and practice, practice, practice.

Jerry, George, and Aristotle?

Jerry and George frequently attempt to use reason to realize a goal, though sometimes not a terribly lofty goal. What is the best way to switch from dating one roommate to the other? When can I ask out someone who has just ended a relationship? How can I do as little work as possible without getting fired? But more to the point, they are often also concerned with how these short-term goals contribute to their overall well-being. For instance, when Jerry has an opportunity to have sex with multiple partners, he reflects not on the momentary pleasure such an experience would bring, but rather on what sort of person he would thus become: "I don't want to be an 'orgy guy,'" he realizes. Note the emphasis is not on rule-following, as in rule based ethics. A Kantian, for example, would ask whether he could rationally will it to be universal law that everyone have multiple sex partners. The emphasis is not on consequences either. A utilitarian, for example, would ask whether the greater number of people would be made happy by this act (which, in this case, they would). Jerry's emphasis, however, is not on the act itself at all; rather, the focus of his self-examination is what sort of person he would be were he to engage in this practice. What sort of character produces this action? Jerry does not want to be that kind of person, an "orgy guy." That lifestyle, with its bathrobes and cigarette holders, is not a lifestyle that Jerry sees as conducive to his long-term happiness.

In the episode entitled "The Lip Reader," Jerry decides to simply approach and ask out a beautiful woman, rather than engage in any subterfuge. George cautions against this, on the grounds that Jerry would therefore become a different sort of person, one of "*those* guys," as George articulately describes it. Note that George is not concerned here with the objective rightness or wrongness of the act, nor with the outcome of the act, but rather with what sort of person Jerry would thus become.

Of course, George is extrapolating from his own fear of not being one of "those guys" that Jerry should not try to "cross over," but Jerry, judging that state to be one which would be conducive to his long-term well-being, chooses to ignore George's objection, correctly perceiving that the objection is not rational.

In addition to using reason to determine how to act, Aristotle says we ought to consider how a person of practical wisdom (a *phronemos*) would act in similar circumstances. The *phronemos* is supposed to be the role model for correct behavior. Here we can see another way virtue ethics manifests its influence in *Seinfeld*. For Jerry, of course, the primary role model is Superman. On occasion, Jerry seeks George's advice, typically on matters George might know better than Superman would, such as how to dump a girlfriend. But many times Jerry simply looks to and considers Superman. (The character Superman was, ironically, created by a person named Jerry, and the character Jerry was created by the real Jerry, perhaps suggesting that we are meant to see this connection.)

For George, who realizes he is "king of the idiots," the *phronemos* must be he who does the exact opposite of what George's instinct is to do. George comes to this realization in an episode entitled "The Opposite," and he is exactly right. George may refer to himself as king of the idiots, but paradoxically, his recognition of his idiocy is what enables him to create his own *phronemos* by doing the opposite. This, of course, is a good update of the parable of Socrates and the Oracle. Socrates, who claimed to know nothing, was said by the Oracle at Delphi to be, in fact, the wisest man in Greece. After much searching and pestering of politicians, playwrights, and craftsmen, Socrates surmised that this could only mean that only those who *recognize* their own ignorance are in a position to acquire wisdom and hence virtue. This is precisely analogous to George's deduction in "The Opposite." If everything his instinct tells him is wrong, the opposite must be right. Jerry aids in the deductive process here, applying the logical axiom known as the Law of Excluded Middle. George had suggested the connection, but was unsure as to its logical validity. Jerry steps in and assures him that it is indeed correct, thus assuming the role of Oracle, or perhaps Socrates. This is appropriate, for on many occasions, Jerry is actually George's role model, his *phronemos*. But Jerry cannot be a complete role model, as he is often confused himself. But the opposite-of-George would be a perfect source of guidance, given that George has had everything wrong to that point.

We see the proof of George's strategy immediately. He approaches a beautiful woman, and wins her affection. He refuses to be intimidated by obnoxious thugs in a theater, and instead intimidates them. He gets an

590 • Part Seven   What Is Moral?

interview with the New York Yankees, and when introduced to the owner of the team, George Steinbrenner, he proceeds to upbraid "the Boss" rather than kowtow to him. Steinbrenner rewards this bold candor by offering him a job. Of course, George does not continue this strategy, and frequently lapses into error as a result, confirming the theory.

Elaine, Kramer, and Newman: Not Wise

Elaine sometimes adopts a character-oriented approach, but she is less committed to it than George and Jerry, and frequently winds up in a jam as a result. For example, in "The Sponge," she tries to consider the character of her potential sex partners, surely a wise move (although she is actually motivated less by selectivity in her choice of men than by conservation of contraceptives). Other times, in fact more frequently, she does not consider the wise course, trying, for instance, to assassinate a noisy dog. She is often concerned with rules or "etiquette," suggesting that she may be thought of as a foil, an example of *not* using the Aristotelian approach. The trouble she gets into is often the result of sticking with rule-based approaches, which, as we have seen, often fail to account for the nuances which distinguish one situation from another. Elaine suffers accordingly. When she is guided by rules, she winds up dating the wrong man or stuck buying presents for people she doesn't like. When she tries to follow utilitarian strategies, this also backfires. She deduces that stopping to purchase Jujyfruits will only delay her trip to the hospital by a couple of minutes. But since this infuriates her injured boyfriend, he dumps her.

Kramer does not seem to participate in virtue ethics either. He lives so far outside the rest of the culture that, despite his friendship with Jerry and the others, he cannot take advantage of the social dialectic which helps produce virtue. He is more a figure of the Sartrean self-made self. On Aristotle's account, the virtuous soul requires interaction with other virtuous souls for its development. The price Kramer pays is that he ends up friends with Newman, and even FDR (Franklin Delano Romanowski), who tries to kill him.

Although Newman clearly is not a *phronemos*, he is sometimes ironically invoked as one. When Elaine and Kramer have a dispute over ownership of a bicycle, they both defer to Newman's judgment. When there is some dispute as to whether Elaine's nipple is visible on a Christmas card photograph, they call in Newman to confirm. These appeals are clearly ironical because it is only Elaine and Kramer who appeal to Newman's alleged wisdom. George admits when pressed that Newman is "merry," but has no real use for him. Jerry regards Newman only as his nemesis. Since we can interpret both Jerry and George as participating in a Socratic investigation in search of Aristotelian virtue, Newman's role as nemesis serves to demonstrate one difficulty of virtue ethics. The *phronemos* must be chosen wisely, which is paradoxical in the sense that if we were wise enough to choose the right role-model, perhaps we would be wise enough not to need one. George is generally unimpressed by Newman; Jerry is wise enough to hold Newman in contempt; Kramer and Elaine actually defer to his judgment, indicating perhaps that they are less wise than Jerry and even George.

It is clear that Aristotelian virtue ethics presents a coherent moral theory, and a satisfactory alternative to utilitarian and Kantian theories. It stresses the use of both reason and experience in the development of character, producing the actions which lead one to flourish. What is less clear is whether Jerry and George can be seen as having learned as much as they might from their participation in this Socratic partnership in the search for virtue. That is, are they friends in the Aristotelian sense, augmenting and improving the virtues in one another? If the show were to have realized its full potential for moral education on the Aristotelian model, we ought to have seen a finale in which the characters translated their social dialectic into the good and happy life, rather than ending up in prison. But, perhaps this is a further subtlety. Recall that Socrates also ended up in prison (and was actually executed), and that Plato and Aristotle argued that happiness is a state of the soul, regardless of the political conditions in which one finds oneself. In the last hours of his life, Socrates persisted in philosophizing. When we last see the group in prison, Jerry is his usual self, doing his observational comedy routine. Perhaps we've made something out of nothing here, or perhaps there is a useful parallel to Greek wisdom, but one which was too subtle for the television audience.

The Practice of Partiality
Marilyn Friedman

Hardly any moral philosopher, these days, would deny that we are each entitled to favor our loved ones. Some would say, even more strongly, that we ought to favor them, that it is not simply a moral option. This notion of partiality toward loved ones is lately gaining wide philosophical acclaim. (Ordinary people, fortunately, have held this view for quite some time.)

It seems indisputable that intimacy and close relationships require partiality, that is, require special attentiveness, responsiveness, and favoritism between or among those who are to be close.[1] Close relationships, in turn, are among what Bernard Williams has called the "ground projects" that are essential for character, integrity, and flourishing in a human life.[2] Partiality, accordingly, seems instrumentally essential to integrity and the good life. There seems, in addition, to be sheer intrinsic value in the very benefiting of friends and loved ones.[3]

While the appropriateness of partiality toward loved ones is itself uncontested, its theoretical justification is the subject of a lively contemporary debate. The hottest question in this debate is whether partiality can adequately be justified by any of the dominant theoretical traditions of modern moral philosophy, utilitarian consequentialism, or Kantian deontology. The feature of these theories that seems to threaten the legitimacy of partiality is their requirement of moral impartiality— the requirement to be unbiased and to show equal consideration, in some sense, for all persons.[4]

According to critics, impartialist moral theories are not able to account for the moral value of close personal relationships.[5] The impartial standpoint calls for detachment from personal concerns and loyalties, an attitude which Lawrence Blum considers to be inimical to the loving concern and particularized responsiveness that are essential to successful close relationships.[6] The impartial perspective aimed at equal concern for all persons, in John Cottingham's view, radically diminishes or

---

[1]See Lawrence Blum, *Friendship, Altruism, and Morality* (London: Routledge & Kegan Paul, 1980), chap. 3; and John Kekes, "Morality and Impartiality," *American Philosophical Quarterly* 18 (October 1981): 299.

[2]"Persons, Character, and Morality," in his *Moral Luck* (Cambridge: Cambridge University Press, 1981), p. 13. On the contribution of partiality to integrity and fulfillment, see also John Cottingham, "Ethics and Impartiality," *Philosophical Studies* 43 (1983): 83–99.

[3]See Blum, *Friendship, Altruism, and Morality*; and Charles Fried, *Right and Wrong* (Cambridge: Harvard University Press, 1978), pp. 170, 179.

[4]Of course, the two traditions define very differently the morally relevant interests of persons that are to be considered. In Chapter 1 of my book *What Are Friends For?* (Cornell University, 1993), I characterized impartiality as an absence of bias. Here I switch to construing it as the equal consideration of all persons. This conceptualization is the one most commonly found in the context of the contemporary debates over partiality. For my purposes, there is no significant difference between the two formulations. The two notions diverge in the areas of animal rights and environmental concerns, but those issues are beyond the scope of this essay.

[5]Some partialists also defend partiality in special relationships other than close personal relationships, for example, relationships among members of the same community, city, or nation. However, there is less agreement about the legitimacy of the partiality shown in these cases. [Here I] concentrate only on partiality in close personal relationships, such as those with parents, children, siblings, friends, and lovers.

[6]See Blum, *Friendship, Altruism, and Morality*, p. 56.

altogether eliminates a person's opportunity to show special attention and concern to her own loved ones.[7]

Each impartialist ethical tradition has its own additional short-comings, from the partialist perspective. Bernard Williams charges utilitarianism with failing to recognize the separateness of persons and, therefore, giving no special moral status to personal integrity or to the essential contribution made to personal integrity by relationships and projects which are the agent's own, in some important sense.[8] Kantian deontology, according to Michael Stocker, fails to accord moral value to the motivations, such as loving concern and affectionate inclination, that are necessary ingredients in successful personal relationships, and counts only a depersonalized sense of duty as a genuinely moral motivation.[9]

The recent challenges to impartiality range even more widely. Andrew Oldenquist contends that impartiality calls for equal concern for the whole of humanity, a sentiment which is, in any case, too weak to be effective as moral motivation.[10] Perhaps, the final coup de grace is the claim that genuine impartiality is humanly unachievable, a charge with which I myself concur.[11] In her defense of this view, Iris Young urges, further, that the rhetoric of impartiality[12] be distrusted because it has been used in practice by dominant social groups to disguise their de facto political and cultural hegemony.[13]

Defenders of impartialist moral theories have responded by trying to show that those theories do indeed warrant partiality in special relationships. These rejoinders treat partiality as morally permissible, even obligatory, so long as there is *some* way in which this behavior or the deliberation that justifies it exemplifies an equal consideration of the interests of all. A clarified notion of impartiality has, thus, emerged from these defenses.

Thomas E. Hill, Jr., for example, argues that an impartial perspective is required only when considering basic moral principles, but not when

---

[7]See Cottingham, "Ethics and Impartiality," pp. 89–90.

[8]See Williams, *Moral Luck*, p. 3 and passim.

[9]See Michael Stocker, "The Schizophrenia of Modern Ethical Theories," *Journal of Philosophy* 63 (August 12, 1976): 453–66; and Williams, *Moral Luck*, pp. 3, 15–19.

[10]See Andrew Oldenquist, "Loyalties," *Journal of Philosophy* 79 (April 1982): 181.

[11]See Alasdair MacIntyre, *After Virtue* (Notre Dame, Ind.: University of Notre Dame Press, 1981); and Iris Young, "Impartiality and the Civic Public: Some Implications of Feminist Critiques of Moral and Political Theory," *Praxis International* 5 (January 1986): 384–85.

[12]The rhetorical dimension of uses of the notion of impartiality is insightfully explored by Margaret Walker in "Partial Consideration," *Ethics* 101 (July 1991): 758–74.

[13]Young, "Impartiality and the Civic Public," p. 389.

judging the specific moral matters of daily life.[14] Peter Railton draws a distinction between procedures for moral decision making by particular persons in particular situations and the truth conditions of a moral theory: impartiality is part of the latter but need not be part of the former.[15] On Alan Gewirth's view, partiality may be permitted in individual behavior so long as that behavior is regulated by social institutions which themselves give equal consideration to the interests of all persons.[16] Contemporary Kantians, such as Barbara Herman and Marcia Baron, further contend that a sense of duty is necessary only as a second-order limiting condition on our primary, first-order motivations and that partial sentiments are permissible as first-order motivations so long as they do not violate those second-order constraints.[17]

In nearly all of these discussions, both those that favor and those that oppose impartialist defenses of partiality, controversy centers on the notion of *im*partiality and on whether it supports or repudiates the favoring of loved ones. Partialists have generally been on the offensive and impartialists have been compelled to clarify what impartiality really means and what it actually requires. By contrast, the notion of partiality has not been subjected to vigorous critical investigation, except in a few discussions of its unjustified forms.[18]

In this [reading] I counteract that trend by taking a closer than usual look at the moral complexity of our social practices of partiality. My adoption of this approach does not represent an endorsement of current notions of impartiality. . . . [The] concept of impartiality must be substantially reformulated if it is to survive as a practicable ideal of moral thinking. That the concept of impartiality needs reexamination, however, does not mean that the concept of partiality is transparently defensible. In this discussion, I focus on aspects of partiality that complicate the philosophical defense of it.[19]

---

[14]See Thomas E. Hill, Jr., "The Importance of Autonomy," in Eva Feder Kittay and Diana T. Meyers, eds., *Women and Moral Theory* (Totowa, N.J.: Rowman & Littlefield, 1987), pp. 131–32.

[15]See Peter Railton, "Alienation, Consequentialism, and the Demands of Morality," *Philosophy and Public Affairs* 13 (Spring 1984): 153–55.

[16]See Alan Gewirth, "Ethical Universalism and Particularism," *Journal of Philosophy* 85, no. 6 (1988): 292–93.

[17]See Barbara Herman, "On the Value of Acting from the Motive of Duty," *Philosophical Review* 67 (July 1981): 233–50; and Marcia Baron, "The Alleged Moral Repugnance of Acting from Duty," *Journal of Philosophy* 81 (April 1984): 197–220.

[18]See Blum, *Friendship, Altruism, and Morality*, pp. 46–47; Marcia Baron, *The Moral Status of Loyalty* (Dubuque, Iowa: Kendall Hunt. 1984): John Cottingham, "Partiality, Favouritism, and Morality," *Philosophical Quarterly* 36, no. 144 (1986): 357–73; and Gewirth, "Ethical Universalism," pp. 295–98.

[19]This focus continues in Chapter 3 [of *What Are Friends For?*] (Cornell University, 1993)] where I contrast feminist and nonfeminist defenses of partiality. That chapter begins with its own somewhat varied sketch of the partiality debates.

In the first section of this [reading], I argue that the moral value of partiality depends partly on the moral value of the relationships that it helps to sustain. It matters to the philosophical issues at stake that personal relationships can be abusive, exploitative, and oppressive. I survey some considerations that are relevant to the critical assessment of personal relationships. In section 2 I consider the vastly unequal social distribution of the material means for favoring loved ones. Because many people have inadequate resources for caring for their loved ones, our conventional relationship practices of partiality—practices by which we each care only for our "own"—can be disastrous for many people. This observation seriously complicates the defense of partiality.

1. Partiality and the Value of Relationships

Partiality varies widely. It appears in numerous sorts of relationships, is expressed in many forms, and has a correspondingly varied moral status. Devoted attention to one's children is a matter of moral duty; loyalty to a distant relative under criminal indictment is morally permissible but not required; white supremacist cults are morally prohibited. Partiality comprises an area of daily moral life about which most people have deeply held convictions.

When partiality is morally required, this is often (if not always) because of what it contributes to the personal relationships of which it is a part. I favor my children, my friends, and so on because such favoring expresses the love I feel for them, promotes their well-being which is of special concern to me (and which, in some cases, is also my personal responsibility), differentiates my close relationships from relationships to people I do not particularly love, and respects the uniqueness of those I love by the specifically appropriate responsiveness I show to them.[20] To the extent that personal relationships are necessary for integrity and fulfillment in life, then, to that extent partiality is instrumentally required as a means to achieving those morally valuable ends.

Even if integrity and fulfillment require close relationships, however, this does not entail that every close relationship contributes to integrity or fulfillment. It depends on the nature of the relationship in question. Personal relationships vary widely in their moral value. The quality of a particular relationship is profoundly important in determining the moral worth of any partiality which is necessary for sustain-

---

[20]On the importance of respect for uniqueness in a caring relationship, see Robin Dillon, "Care and Respect," in Eve Browning Cole and Susan Coultrap-McQuin, eds., *Explorations in Feminist Ethics* (Bloomington, Ind.: Indiana University Press, 1992), pp. 69–81.

ing that relationship. To the extent that partiality is a duty in close personal relationships, it is a prima facie duty only, to be fully assessed, among other things, in light of the moral worth of the particular relationships it helps to preserve.

Discussions of partiality have, heretofore, largely overlooked the differing moral value of the varied sorts of personal relationships that commonly manifest partiality. Some of these discussions do acknowledge that partiality may be shown in an inappropriate manner, but this is a different issue.[21] Partiality toward loved ones, for example, is wrong on the part of someone who holds a public office that calls for impartial treatment of some large number of persons extending beyond the official's loved ones. Also wrong are partial attitudes toward a particular group which unjustly advantage members of that group over other groups, for example, racism and sexism.[22] When partiality is judged to be wrong in those discussions, its wrongness is linked to circumstances other than the nature of the relationship itself. The issue that concerns me, by contrast, is the partialist's apparent underlying presumption that mere relationship with someone who is, in some sense, "one's own" is, all things considered, always morally worth promoting.

In the most general terms, relationships are morally wrong to the extent that they harm people, especially one or more of the participants in the relationship. The relationship between master and slave is the paradigm of a wrongful relationship, and slavery epitomizes immoral relationship practices. Slavery is an extreme form of harmful relationship but by no means the only such form. Even in intimate, "consensual" relationships, people can be subjected to emotional duress, assault and battery, sexual abuse, and economic exploitation.[23] Anything that sustains relationships such as these, including whatever partiality is shown within them, is prima facie morally improper.

Just how bad these sustaining conditions are in any particular case depends partly on the prospects for ending that relationship. If a battered woman, for instance, cannot leave an abusive relationship because she has no viable economic alternative for herself and her dependent chil-

---

[21]See the references in note 18.

[22]The key phrase is "unjustly advantage." Sometimes it is just to favor members of certain groups, most especially in attempts to overcome the persistent untoward effects of their history of unjust treatment and the lingering, unjustified biases against them. This, of course, is the familiar notion of "affirmative action," a topic far afield of the present discussion.

[23]Among female homicide victims in the United States, about one-third are slain by a family member or male friend; see Deborah Rhode, *Gender and Justice* (Cambridge: Harvard University Press, 1989), p. 237. See her chapter 7, "Sex and Violence," for a wide-ranging discussion of the abuses to which women in particular are vulnerable in personal relationships.

dren, then, in that case, it is good for her partner to show the sort of partiality in caring and support that would counterbalance or offset the abuse. To the extent, however, that his partiality diminishes her capacity to recognize her situation for what it is and to pursue any nonoppressive alternatives that are genuinely accessible to her, to the extent that the partiality binds her the more strongly to her still-abusive partner when she could free herself of that tie, then, to that extent, the partiality is insidious and more than simply prima facie bad. In case a troubled relationship can be brought to an end to the betterment of the abused member and her dependents, the morally best option is its dissolution. Sometimes "this marriage" should not be "saved." The current approach to partiality is, thus, incomplete. It fails to take account of the differing moral value of different personal relationships, and it mistakenly presumes that whatever sustains any personal relationship is a moral good without qualification.

Assessing the harm that is done in personal relationships is a complex matter. Intimates and close affiliates can harm each other in a great variety of ways. The harms of a relationship might be a function of its own particularities, or they might be a function of the social conventions for relationships of that sort. A relationship can harm both those who are participants in the relationship and those who are nonparticipants. Nonparticipants can be harmed, for example, if they are unjustifiably excluded from relationship practices which afford some positive value to their participants.[24] My present concern, however, is with the harms to which the participants in a relationship are vulnerable.

Roughly speaking, we may distinguish four levels at which the practice of any particular relationship can be morally evaluated. First, there is the most generic level for defining relationships of a certain sort. The most prominent dictionary definition of "marriage" is wedlock, that is, the relationship between wife and husband; and, by dictionary definition, wives are women while husbands are men. This simple generic meaning covers a variety of actual practices in different cultures, for example, monogamy, polyandry, and polygyny.

Second, relationships can be evaluated at the level of the specific cultural formalization of a relationship practice. Historically, American case law considered husbands to be responsible for the economic support of the marriage household while wives were held responsible for child care,

[24]Here I have in mind such examples as the legal and religious bans against lesbian and gay marriage.

domestic work, and the sexual service of their husbands.[25] Any aspect of a relationship on which the law must, at some time or other, pronounce judgment may become a part of its formal social arrangements. Marriage law, in the past, has condoned wife battering by husbands, misconstruing it under a legitimating description: corrective chastisement.[26] Such tolerance made wife battering formally permissible social practice.

Third, there may be informal practices associated with a relationship tradition which are neither formally codified nor legally enforced, yet which are culturally normative. In our culture, a woman who marries a man is still widely expected to drop her own last name and adopt that of her husband and sometimes to submerge herself entirely under his name ("Mrs. John Doe"). Fourth, and finally, any relationship may have its own specific particularities which do not derive from the generic nature of the relationship or from its formal or informal social conventions. The particular emotional abuse heaped upon one spouse by her partner may be quite idiosyncratic to their interaction.

Marital relationships can be evaluated at all of these levels, from particular marriages on up to the most generic level of marriage practice—and similarly for other relationships. A challenge to the generic notion of marriage as a relationship between a woman and a man may well rely on a related, but even more generic, meaning of marriage, namely, that of a close or intimate union. Close and intimate unions may form between women and between men. Some lesbian and gay couples are now seeking, for their own close and intimate unions, the formal imprimatur of legally or religiously sanctioned marriage, an innovation which most religious and legal authorities continue to obstruct. Nevertheless, this example reminds us that evaluation of marriage practice can occur even at its most generic level.

In order to decide which close relationships are morally wrong at any level of assessment, we need to consider more than simply the obvious harms its participants inflict on each other. We need as well some sense of what it is that makes close relationships morally right, what it is that determines the moral worth that they have as relationships. Evaluating the worth of relationships in part requires knowing something about the underlying moral basis of the duties of partiality they gener-

[25]See Sara Ann Ketchum, "Liberalism and Marriage Law," in Mary Vetterling-Braggin, Frederick A. Elliston, and Jane English, eds., *Feminism and Philosophy* (Totowa, N.J.: Littlefield, Adams, 1977), pp. 264–76.
[26]See Dorie Klein, "The Dark Side of Marriage: Battered Wives and the Domination of Women," in Nicole Hahn Rafter and Elizabeth A. Stanko, eds., *Judge, Lawyer, Victim, Thief: Gender Roles and Criminal Justice* (Boston: Northeastern University Press, 1982), pp. 83–107.

ate. Robert Goodin has theorized that partiality is morally required in a relationship to the extent that it contributes to the protection of those who are vulnerable.[27] Social conventions assign responsibilities for the care of those who need it to particular others who are (presumed to be) best situated to render care effectively. Such conventions are sensible to the extent that they ensure genuine protection for all at dependent stages of their lives and that, in emergencies, there are guidelines which promote effective help to those in danger.[28]

People are typically held responsible for the well-being of those to whom they are connected in some identifiable way, such as by kinship. Our close friends and relations are especially well placed to offer protection to each of us in virtue of the familiarity, concern, and frequency of interaction which are commonly greater in those relationships than in others. Immediate family relationships are among our most important social relationships for providing care, nurturance, protection, and support. They are keystones in the social arrangements by which children, in particular, are cared for, and are also centrally important for care of the elderly and of infirm persons at any age. In such relationships, the circumstances of being the one uniquely situated to answer to someone's need derives from an ongoing, publicly recognized connection with her in virtue of which one is held responsible for her well-being.

Goodin recognizes the need to evaluate social conventions themselves. Relationship conventions, on his view, are morally justified to the extent that they are genuinely successful in promoting the protection of the vulnerable.[29] For instance, it is because most people care well enough for their own biological offspring that our social arrangements should and do hold them accountable, as a rule, for that care.[30] Given arrangements of these sorts, the vulnerability of the one who is cared for is especially a vulnerability with regard to the behavior of those persons who are held responsible for her care. A parent's disregard of the needs of her own young child nearly always constitutes neglect; not so someone else's disregard.

---

[27]*Protecting the Vulnerable* (Chicago: University of Chicago Press, 1985). It is noteworthy that Goodin is particularly concerned to show that the best theoretical account of our responsibilities to loved ones also grounds general duties to strangers, duties that are stronger than is usually allowed by partialists (pp. 9–11). Another perspective on what it is that grounds duties of partiality in personal relationships is offered in Lawrence C. Becker, *Reciprocity* (London: Routledge & Kegan Paul, 1986).

[28]Goodin, *Protecting the Vulnerable*, pp. 109–25.

[29]Ibid., pp. 124–25.

[30]In Chapter 6 [of *What Are Friends for?*] I qualify this view by exploring the gender asymmetry in these practices, particularly the far heavier burden of parental caretaking accountability demanded of women than of men.

On Goodin's view, once caretaking conventions are in place, even if they are not justifiable as the best arrangements for ensuring care of certain sorts of persons (children, the elderly, etc.), they may still create caretaking obligations, since the existence of conventions almost guarantees that no one else will do the required caretaking in any particular case.[31] Knowing that I am related to someone in a specific and close way alerts me to the fact that other people will not likely attend to her needs. On Goodin's view, my duty to care for someone follows from being the one who is conventionally expected to care for her and, because of that expectation, the only one who is likely to do so.

Following Goodin's account, we may thus view partiality in close personal relationships as prima facie morally required to the extent that it safeguards those who are vulnerable and to the extent that it accords with social conventions that assign responsibilities for the care of vulnerable persons to certain others who are related to them in particular ways. These responsibilities, to emphasize, constitute prima facie duties only. Their overall moral merit depends on the extent to which the relationships in question really do protect those who are vulnerable without exacting too high a price for such care.

One additional qualification merits special emphasis. Goodin contends that one of the deeper factors which determine whether or not the prima facie duties of partiality constitute duties all things considered is the nature of the vulnerability in question and, in particular, its origin. As Goodin recognizes, some vulnerabilities are socially created. Illness, for example, may result from socially created conditions and be exacerbated by societal hindrances to access to health care. Many socially created vulnerabilities can be directly tied to income levels and employment status, themselves substantially a function of market practices.[32] These reflections on the nature of vulnerability extend Goodin's account in crucially important directions.

It is part of Goodin's enriched account of our responsibilities to protect the vulnerable that we should also be striving to change those alterable social arrangements that foster and perpetuate undesirable human vulnerabilities and dependencies.[33] Susan Moller Okin develops this strand of Goodin's thought into a comprehensive critique of marital practices. In Okin's view, "gender-structured marriage *involves women in a cycle of socially caused and distinctly asymmetric vulnerability.*"[34] The

[31]Goodin, *Protecting the Vulnerable*, p. 125.
[32]Ibid., pp. 190–91.
[33]Ibid., chapter 7.
[34]Susan Moller Okin, *Justice, Gender, and the Family* (New York: Basic Books, 1989), p. 138.

social determinants begin early in a woman's life. Okin's findings are worth quoting at length. In her view, women are:

> first set up for vulnerability during their developing years by their per-
> sonal (and socially reinforced) expectations that they will be the primary
> caretakers of children, and that in fulfilling this role they will need to
> try to attract and to keep the economic support of a man, to whose work
> life they will be expected to give priority. They are rendered vulnerable
> by the actual division of labor within almost all current marriages. They
> are disadvantaged at work by the fact that the world of wage work,
> including the professions, is still largely structured around the assump-
> tion that "workers" have wives at home. They are rendered far more vul-
> nerable if they become the primary caretakers of children, and their
> vulnerability peaks if their marriages dissolve and they become single
> parents.[35]

The details that support Okin's account are convincing, yet they are not likely to persuade everyone. The moral value of close personal rela-tionships is a hotly contested matter. In our time, the debates over the nature and value of marital and family relationships are often particu-larly vitriolic. Many of us have a stake in believing that our family rela-tionships are personally fulfilling. We might, otherwise, feel required to change them—often a daunting prospect. Our evaluations of these rela-tionships may, accordingly, take on idealized and mythic dimensions.

To complicate matters further, family relationships, especially under comfortable material circumstances, are culturally invested with the function of providing emotional nurturance as well as material protec-tion for both their more vulnerable and their less vulnerable members. The modern nuclear family is supposed to be a refuge, a "haven in a heartless world."[36] Such norms are widely appealing. How much bet-ter it is to love than to hate one's parents, siblings, and so on. Family members who share mutual affection will care, nurture, help, and sup-port one another out of spontaneous inclination and enthusiasm and will probably do so more attentively and wisely than if the care is begrudged.

Tangentially, let us recall that some critics of impartiality, with an eye toward the partiality they champion for close relationships, have chal-lenged the Kantian view that the only specifically moral motivation is a

[35]Ibid., pp. 138–39. See her chapter 7 for the ample data and persuasive arguments that support her conclusions.

[36]The familiar phrase, of course, is the title of Christopher Lasch's book, *Haven in a Heartless World: The Family Besieged* (New York: Basic Books, 1977), a book that bemoans the decline of patriarchal authority in contemporary families.

sense of duty.[37] Such a motivation, so the criticism goes, excludes the loving concern that is due to our intimates. The critics suppose that it is the impartialist dimension of Kantianism which leads to the motivational emphasis on duty. If a sense of duty is troubling as a moral motive among loved ones, however, this problem is not limited to theories that ground relational duties on impartial considerations. The problem arises for any (deontological) view that holds there to be moral duties of partiality in close personal relationships,[38] whether these duties are accounted for in impartial or in partialist terms.

For certain particular relationships, and for many relationships on occasion, a sense of duty may be the only attitude available to motivate the required caretaking. A sense of duty may well be necessary in relationships based on some permanent tie, such as biological kinship, which endures independently of how the participants feel about each other. If one lacks affection for an elderly and infirm parent, then caring for her out of a sense of duty is surely preferable to neglecting her altogether. The lack of spontaneous compassion of concern does not diminish the caretaking responsibility and may engender additional responsibilities of self-control so that one's behavior does not reveal the lack of affection.[39]

Attitudes of loving concern, thus, are not necessarily owed to all our intimates at all times. A duty to be partial to family members and other intimates is a duty to treat them in certain ways, to favor them with care, protection, and so forth, over other persons whom one could also attend. Duties to favor certain particular persons in certain ways are, in the first instance, duties of behavior; they are not necessarily duties to undertake the required behavior from certain motives. To be sure, (mutual) loving concern shared with those close to us is one of life's greatest joys, an ideal truly worth seeking to the extent that its realization lies within our power. In troubled relationships, however, this attitude may simply surpass our emotional capacities and lie beyond our abilities to control. It is not uncommon, in daily life, for people to care for those close to them primarily out of a sense of duty, given the vicissitudes of human affections.

Nonmarital family relationships, to return to the question of evaluating close relationships, persist independently of how we feel about the partner—indeed, they persist independently of whether or not the care-

---

[37]See the references in note 9 and the text at that point.

[38]I am inclined to agree with Herman and Baron that the problems can be resolved; see the references in note 17.

[39]For a similar point, see Baron, "The Alleged Moral Repugnance of Acting from Duty," pp. 204–5.

taking responsibilities are neglected. (Marital relationships can linger on in a similar manner.) My brother (supposing I had one) will remain my brother whether or not I am partial to him, emotionally or materially. As adults, he and I may choose to avoid each other's company, but our formal relationship continues. Being related in those ways is compatible with feelings of disrespect, spite, jealousy, contempt, hatred, or simple indifference. Partners in such relationships may loathe and mistreat each other, yet remain profoundly involved in each other's lives.

Perhaps it is because family relationships are so permanent that we place such a high premium on the emotional concern family members *could* provide for one another if such relationships functioned at their best. Our relationship conventions and practices, thus, include numerous rituals and occasions that serve, among other things, to promote affection and concern among loved ones: Mother's Day, Father's Day, celebrations of wedding anniversaries, family-oriented religious holiday traditions, and so on. A heavy suffusion of myths, clichés, and cultural idealizations permeate marriage and family relationship practices. In virtue of these myths and idealizations, our feelings about our own family relationships (like many aspects of our emotional lives) are subject to a good deal of social manipulation and dissemblance. Rituals, such as gift giving, may disguise the lack of affection among family members by simulating the manifestation of love. An accompanying set of clichés may blindly assert the existence of love regardless of the facts in a particular case. How often a young child, despondent over a parent's anger or neglect, is told, "of *course*, your father loves you; he simply doesn't know how to show it," by someone who, resorting to a stock cliché, has never even met the father in question.

These myths and idealizations can easily mystify our understandings of how it really is with us in our relationships, and, thereby, further complicate the already monumental task of assessing relationships. Philosophers, it seems, have a special responsibility to assist in the critical assessment of relationships by avoiding further mystification. One way to help penetrate through the mythic and idealized understanding of relationships is to resist arguments that sound like nothing more than appeals to unreflective opinions.[40]

---

[40]For an essay that violates this stricture, see Christina Hoff Sommers, "Philosophers against the Family," in George Graham and Hugh LaFollette, eds., *Person to Person* (Philadelphia: Temple University Press, 1989), pp. 82–105. My critical discussion of this and other essays by Sommers appears in my "'They Lived Happily Ever After': Sommers on Women and Marriage," *Journal of Social Philosophy* 21 (Fall/Winter 1990): 57–65. A commentary by Sommers and my rejoinder to her commentary follow in the same journal issue, with a further response by Sommers in the following issue of the journal.

Unreflective opinions about values and practices, however popular those opinions may be, are not decisively authoritative for critical moral reflection or moral theory. Such opinions are, to be sure, important starting points of such reflection. They certainly belong in the cultural dialogue about marital and family relationships, a type of dialogue which, as I urged in the previous chapter, should supplant an abstract, monological ideal of impartiality in the human quest for moral wisdom. Unreflective opinions, however (this is part of my own contribution to the dialogue), cannot constitute conclusive defenses of conventional practices because they simply exhibit (and confirm) the conventionality of those practices. The moral worth of particular relationship practices must be assessed, among other things, in terms of the daily reality of those relationships rather than in terms of the hopes or idealistic aspirations that mystify those practices. Real marriages, for example, usually fall far short of their fairy-tale counterparts, which fade "happily ever after" into the sunset.

Even if unreflective opinions are not decisively authoritative for moral theory, it is nevertheless important to understand those opinions carefully. In this regard, the champions of traditional marriage and family who invoke popular support on behalf of these institutions usually make an additional mistake. A familiar adage tells us that actions speak louder than words. What people, in general, actually think about marriage is probably better revealed by the recent rise in the divorce rate than by idealistic popular pronouncements on the topic of marriage.

Some philosophers and social commentators, seeking a populist defense of traditional marriage and family, try to discount what the divorce rate reveals about popular views of marriage by finding culprits to blame for the "breakdown of the traditional family." Feminists, in particular, are frequent scapegoats for this alleged social disintegration.[41] Such an accusation misses an obvious point. Critics of the institution of marriage do not break into people's homes to serve them with mandatory divorce decrees. If feminism, for example, has anything to do with the rising divorce rate, it must be in virtue of the increasing plausibility, to more and more people, of feminist critiques of marriage.[42]

---

[41]See Sommers, "Philosophers against the Family," pp. 82–83.

[42]A growing divorce rate suggests that many people find their marriages to be unsatisfactory. By shifting responsibility for the rising divorce rate away from the divorcing parties and toward marriage critics, such as feminists (ibid., pp. 82–83, 99, and passim), Sommers, in effect, treats this widespread dissatisfaction as if it were merely the result of the manipulation of popular opinion by marriage critics. Such a low regard for popular opinion is curiously inconsistent with Sommers's insistence that philosophers heed the "opinions of the community" (p. 103). It appears that Sommers herself ignores popular opinion when it inconveniently does not support her views (in this case, about marriage).

Feminist criticisms of marriage are not the only analyses of marriage available for public consumption; there is no dearth of published apologetics on behalf of traditional marriage.[43] The inability of such marital defenses to stem the tide of divorces provides invaluable information about what people really think about the daily reality of their married lives.

The declining durability of marriages in general may be due to their frequent inability to provide, without undue personal costs, the protection and care needed by their participants. The context of changing economic circumstances is also significant. As Okin has well shown, when decent economic alternatives to marriage are available to a woman, her economic dependence on her husband diminishes, thus providing her with otherwise unavailable options to leave the relationship should it prove unsatisfactory.[44] Whether the current divorce trends, in themselves, reveal problems with marriage at the generic level, the formal conventional level, the informal conventional level, or merely in a substantially large number of instances is a matter for further investigation.

In the first part of this discussion, I suggested, following Robert Goodin, that duties of partiality in close relationships are based, in part, on the various vulnerabilities of persons in those relationships and, in part, on social conventions that assign responsibilities for the care of the vulnerable to others who stand in certain relationships to them. I cautioned, however, that the duties based on those conventions should be viewed as prima facie duties only, pending a deep evaluation of those conventional practices and the vulnerabilities to which they answer. I then outlined some difficulties in the crucial project of assessing those relationship practices.

In the next section, I turn to a different sort of problem with our practices of partiality in close relationships, namely, that many people lack sufficient resources for favoring their loved ones effectively.

2. Partiality and Inadequate Resources

Derek Parfit poses an argument that challenges the simple notion that I should help my child rather than a stranger when they each face roughly equivalent dangers and when I cannot help both. Parfit asks and answers the following questions: "When I try to protect my child, what should my

---

[43]George Gilder's defenses of traditional marriage and family were especially prominent during the Reagan presidency; see his *Sexual Suicide* (New York: Quadrangle, 1973).

[44]Okin, *Justice, Gender, and the Family*, pp. 137–38, 167–68.

aim be? Should it simply be that he is not harmed? Or should it rather be that he is saved from harm *by me*? If you would have a better chance of saving him from harm, I would be wrong to insist that the attempt be made by me. This shows that my aim should take the simpler form."[45] Parfit later extends this point to cover any sort of benefiting of loved ones, not simply the saving of them from harm. Parfit subsequently qualifies his argument, as I note below. First, however, let us consider the position in its original form. Stated in this way, the argument is both right and wrong. Certainly, on a particular occasion when my child is threatened, I should want her to be saved from danger no matter who saves her.

Relationships, however, are long-term interpersonal involvements. Partialists do not generally defend partiality for its own sake. Their defenses always refer to some further value to be served by partiality, for example, the maintenance of close relationships (which might, in turn, derive their value from what they contribute to integrity or the good life). A relationship, as it endures, is at its best if its participants both feel that they derive something special from their partner and have something special to offer their partner.[46] This is part of the sense of uniqueness and irreplaceability that people feel about loved ones and about themselves in relation to their loved ones, when relationships are flourishing. This recognition of, and responsiveness to, uniqueness itself seems to require that people be able to do special things for each other, things which cannot be done by others or for others.[47]

Thus, wanting to have a close personal relationship with someone is more than simply wishing well for her; it also involves wanting to make a distinctive contribution to her well-being, wanting to be an irreplaceably valuable part of her life. Parfit does acknowledge this point. He subsequently amends his statement of the argument by nothing the there may be some kinds of benefit "that my child should receive *from me*."[48]

Parfit's initial argument, however, is not completely wrong. It remains true that in emergencies one should want loved ones to be saved, no matter by whom. This point can be extended as well to the whole of a relationship. Love for someone over the long haul should include not only a concern to be an irreplaceably valuable part of her life but also the simple concern for her well-being. Because I care for my loved ones, I should

[45]Derek Parfit, *Reasons and Persons* (Oxford: Clarendon Press, 1984), p. 96.

[46]This point is made by Williams, "Persons, Character and Morality," p. 15; and by John Hardwig, "In Search of an Ethics of Personal Relationships," in George Graham and Hugh LaFollette, eds., *Person to Person* (Philadelphia: Temple University Press, 1989), p. 67.

[47]Blum extensively discusses this aspect of close relationships in *Friendship, Altruism, and Morality*.

[48]Parfit, *Reasons and Persons*, p. 96.

want them both to be cared for or benefited by me and to do well, to flourish. Both concerns blend in a loving relationship with someone.

Close personal relationships in any society, as noted earlier, are highly conventionalized by a variety of practices.[49] Those practices organize and normalize partiality, making it legitimate, even required, toward certain persons rather than others, and in certain forms. (If friends do not provide the special care, support, and assistance we think of as appropriate for friendship, then hardly anyone can be expected to do so. After all, what are friends for?) Substantial partiality is expected in close relationships and is normative for them.

The relationship practices by which I justify preferentially saving my child from a danger equally facing several other children (when I can only save one) are the same practices that justify another parent in abandoning my child and saving solely her own when she herself is able to save only one. That is, the practices in question may sometimes be detrimental to my own child, whose welfare is of overriding partial concern to me. Remember that love does (or should) involve not only wanting to benefit one's beloved oneself but also wanting to see the loved one do well. It should matter to the partialist whether or not actual practices of partiality, the conventions determining when and to what extent we should favor loved ones, really do promote overall the well-being of our loved ones. If particular conventions of partiality reduce the well-being of some of those we love, then they diminish the extent to which we together find fulfillment and integrity through close relationships.

A partialist might not be troubled by the fact that the same practices which lead me to favor my child will also lead others to disfavor my child. From the partialist's standpoint, some child or other is being favored on each occasion by someone who loves her. The result does not seem to involve a net loss of integrity or fulfillment and so should not worry the partialist. To ferret out the worrisome feature of unqualified partiality, we must think about conditions in the "real world" that are relevant to the partial ways in which we practice close personal relationships.

It is common among philosophers to think that extant relationship conventions are operative because people in general benefit from them.[50]

---

[49]For Parfit's discussion of the role played by social convention in our relationship practices, see ibid., pp. 96–110.

[50]R. M. Hare's view, for example, that strong maternal partiality promotes good care for children seems typical; see *Moral Thinking* (Oxford: Clarendon Press, 1981), p. 137.

Even if people in general do benefit from certain relationship conventions, this does not entail that each and every person benefits. Relationship norms do not take account of the varying social and economic conditions of people's lives. Whether someone benefits from certain conventions may have a lot to do with her "social location," her share in that all-important dispersion, the distribution of the benefits and burdens of social cooperation. Because of limited resources, some people, vulnerable children and elderly persons among them, do not derive from their close personal relationships the values we think those relationships ought to serve.

An indirect line of thought may best help us to approach this problem. Consider John Cottingham's 1983 attack on what he (in that essay) presents as a close cousin of the impartiality requirement, the Christian maxim "love thy neighbor as thyself."[51] Passages in the Bible indicate that "neighbor" here refers to anyone in need, not simply the person next door.[52] For the sake of argument, however, let us think about the meaning of this directive in the narrower sense, an approach taken also by Cottingham in 1983. Doing so will afford us a vehicle with which to explore some limits to the partialist's perspective. Cottingham ridicules the maxim, in its narrow sense, for demanding that one give the "same importance" to the interests of the person next door that one gives to one's own interests. Cottingham's attack on the narrowly interpreted maxim has something to it, but his reasons miss a key point.

Whether my neighbor needs any special moral attention from me depends, both literally and metaphorically, on where we live. Until recently, I lived next door to a retired engineering professor from Purdue. He spent every summer at his condominium in Colorado. For his months away, he hired a lawn service to maintain the grounds around his home, including the dozen or so tomato plants that he would install in his garden every spring. Each summer, before leaving for Colorado, he would invite me to help myself to his homegrown, professionally watered tomatoes when they started ripening in August, since he would not return from

---

[51]Cottingham, *Partiality, Favoritism, and Morality,* p. 87.

[52]According to the New Testament parable of the Good Samaritan (Luke 10:29–37), the "neighbor" is anyone in need. I am grateful to Cynthia Read for bringing this passage to my (non-Christian) attention. Cottingham, as well, has recently emphasized that the maxim to love thy neighbor as thyself applies to any human being; see his "Ethics of Self-Concern," *Ethics* 101 (July 1991): 799, n. 5. Referring to an earlier draft of this chapter, Cottingham, in his footnote, suggests that my discussion of the maxim is "off the mark" because I interpret "neighbor" narrowly. Pace Cottingham, my narrow (mis)interpretation is not a mistake; instead, it is designed to afford a useful vehicle for making a point about resource differences between neighborhoods. Certainly, Cottingham's own earlier, more literal reading of "neighbor" also served a rhetorical purpose and was not a distortion of Christian doctrine.

Colorado until September. My former neighbor deserves my deepest gratitude, but he hardly needs my special moral concern.

The same cannot be said about those people across town who have no condominiums in Colorado, no homes of their own anywhere, no lawn services, no tomato plants, and little else. It is not really the neighbor as such who needs the special concern of others. The one who really needs special attention is the person without resources whose friends and family are equally lacking. She would not be adequately cared for even if all her friends and family were as partial toward her as they could be. There are radical disparities among different "neighborhoods" in the distribution of the resources for caring and protecting others. Those of us who live in comfortable middle-class neighborhoods (or better) need a metaphor other than "love thy neighbor" to express what impartiality really calls for.

Interpreted narrowly, "love thy neighbor as thyself" is itself a statement of one form of partiality: it is *thy* neighbor whom you are exhorted to love, not neighbors in general or neighbors everywhere. Cottingham well knows that it is not the person next door but all inhabitants of the planet who matter to the impartiality thesis.[53] This means that Cottingham's (and my own) attack on the narrow meaning of the injunction to love by neighbor is actually a criticism of a certain form of partiality and not an attack on the impartiality thesis at all. It is no argument against impartiality that I need not have paid any special moral regard to my engineer neighbor, since he was doing splendidly without me.

Not so for the numerous others who live in dire need. Of course, fulfilling relationships are logically—and empirically—possible under conditions of extreme material need, but they are certainly also severely threatened by such conditions. It is difficult to find fulfillment or integrity, that is, wholeness, in life if those I love are starving. If they continue to starve no matter how much favoritism I show them, because my resources are so meager, then partiality, while it might be necessary for my integrity and fulfillment, is hardly sufficient. In many cases, this insufficiency is profound.

There are, to be sure, some reasons on behalf of favoring the interests of neighbors and acquaintances, even those with resources, over the interests of unknown strangers. When one is acquainted with someone, then one knows something, however minimal, about her. One may be familiar with her needs, wants, situation, or the like. Knowing something about someone's particular circumstances makes it easier to help

[53]"Ethics and Impartiality," pp. 90–91.

or care for her effectively than if one knows nothing in particular about her. In such cases of greater familiarity, the risk is lessened that the help or care one renders will be ineffective or, worse yet, detrimental to the recipient.

These considerations modify, but they do not override or even substantially diminish, the moral importance of social and economic conditions in determining how practices of partiality should be organized society-wide. Relationship norms, to reiterate, are silent about those conditions. It matters to the partialist's theoretical stance, however, that large numbers of people do not have adequate resources to favor their loved ones. (This is the point that I have approached indirectly.)[54] As a result, whether or not, and to what extent, someone benefits from certain partialist relationship conventions has a lot to do with her socioeconomic location. It hinges heavily on the sort of luck she had in being born to, adopted by, or linked by marriage to relations with adequate resources for her care, nurturance, and protection.

When many families are substantially impoverished, then practices of partiality further diminish the number of people who can achieve well-being, integrity, and fulfillment through close relationships. If we each tend to our own loved ones only, then some of those loved ones will flourish while others languish. Those who can care for their loved ones well, materially, emotionally, and so on, will enhance the well-being and life prospects of their loved ones and will thereby realize some measure of the sort of personal integrity and fulfillment that is attained through close relationships. Those who cannot take good care of their loved ones will not realize integrity or fulfillment through such relationships because they can do little to enhance the well-being of those they love. Partiality, if practiced by all, untempered by any redistribution of wealth or resources, would appear to lead to the integrity and fulfillment of only some persons, but not all.

The implications of this line of thought are particularly relevant to the defenses of partiality that appeal to its role in furthering human integrity and fulfillment, an approach taken by Williams and Cottingham.[55] On such a view, partiality is not intrinsically valuable but derives its value largely from being a necessary ingredient in relationships that themselves realize integrity and fulfillment in someone's life because they

[54]For a related argument, see James Rachels, "Morality, Parents, and Children," in Graham and LaFollette, *Person to Person*, pp. 46–62.

[55]Other defenses of partiality, such as Fried's libertarian account, are not so clearly challenged by these considerations, although they might be if we could substitute freedom for integrity and fulfillment, mutatis mutandis.

are her relationships, connections through which she herself strives to promote the well-being of those she loves. As Cottingham puts it, "to be a person, to have a sense of identity and personal integrity, implies the possession of plans, projects and desires which have a *special status* in your scale of values precisely because they are yours."[56]

Recall the significance of Parfit's argument: in loving my loved ones, my aim is not simply that they be cared for by me, but that they be cared for *well*. If someone cannot care effectively for her loved ones, then her aims remain unrealized, putting her own integrity and fulfillment at risk along with the (to her) all-important well-being of her loved ones. Were the unqualified practice of partiality to lead to less integrity or fulfillment than is possible under other social arrangements, then, on this partialist account, there would be something wrong with the unqualified practice of partiality.

If the defense of partiality is predicated on the importance of human integrity and fulfillment in general, then the numbers must count theoretically.[57] It should matter to what call the "fulfillment defense" of partiality that some people live in circumstances which critically compromise the care they can show to loved ones and which, accordingly, diminish their chances of achieving integrity and fulfillment through close personal relationships. If partiality is everyone's moral prerogative, and, more so, if it is everyone's responsibility, then, on certain partialist grounds alone, there ought to be a distribution of the resources for protecting, caring for, and otherwise favoring loved ones that permits as many of us as possible to do so in a fulfilling and integrity-conferring manner.

A defense of partiality toward loved ones is incomplete without a defense of the social conventions by which such partiality would be realized in practice and turned into a set of legitimated expectations for a society. Surely Bernard Williams is not merely trying to convince us that it is all right for him to favor members of the Williams clan, John Cottingham is not simply trying to justify his own partiality toward his loved ones, and so on. If partiality, as such, is to be justified, then the defense must be in general terms. If the very practices of partiality are not defensible, then particular instances of it lose one of their primary justifications.

---

[56]Cottingham, "Ethics and Impartiality," p. 87.

[57]A similar point is raised by David O. Brink against William's well-known hypothetical counterexample to utilitarianism involving the case of Jim and the nineteen villagers sentenced to death; "Utilitarianism and the Personal Point of View," *Journal of Philosophy* 83 (August 1986): 432.

The justification of practices, however, often taken a decidedly different form from the justification of actions that exemplify or fall under those practices.[58] If partiality is to be defended in virtue of the integrity and fulfillment it makes possible for *all* those who practice it, then we must consider the effects of practices of partiality on all who together engage in them, including those who lack the minimum resources for showing partiality effectively. The justification of practices requires us to consider people who are not our friends or relations, for whom we feel no particular affection, and whom we may not even know.

On a fulfillment defense of partiality, social institutions should be structured so that partiality, as practiced in close relationships, contributes to the well-being, integrity, and fulfillment of as many people as possible. I do not pretend to have a blueprint for thus restructuring our institutions. I have no formula for modifying our practices of partiality so as to alleviate the worldwide scarcity of caretaking resources while still preserving the values afforded by partiality itself. The best solution, in my view, will arise out of a sort of public dialogue, a dialogue that its current participants should restructure so as to include in particular the voices of those who lack adequate means for favoring their loved ones effectively.

This conclusion, which appears to show consideration for all persons, is derived from certain partialist concerns. Thus, by viewing partiality as morally valuable because of what it ultimately contributes to human well-being, integrity, and fulfillment in life, and by considering the reality of inadequate resources for some, we are led to a notion that sounds suspiciously like my proposed method for promoting a modified, practicable moral impartiality.

In this [reading], I sketched the partiality debate and highlighted features of the practice of partiality that complicate its philosophical defense. First, I proposed that the moral value of partiality depends partly on the moral worth of the particular relationships in which it appears. Second, I suggested that practices of partiality must be tempered by the recognition that many persons lack adequate resources for favoring their loved ones effectively. . . .

---

[58]This point has long been recognized. For what is, by now, a classic discussion and application of it, see John Rawls, "Two Concepts of Rules," *Philosophical Review* 64 (1955).

The Moral Basis of Vegetarianism

Tom Regan

My initial interest in vegetarianism grew out of my study of the life and writings of Mahatma Gandhi. Gandhi, as is well known, was an advocate of nonviolence (ahimsā), not only in political affairs but in the conduct of one's life generally. The extreme pacifistic position he advocated, from which he derived the obligatoriness of vegetarianism, struck me as inadequate, and I sought a less radical moral basis for vegetarianism, one that those of us in the Western world would find more hospitable. Since the leading theories were (and remain) one or another version of utilitarianism, on the one hand, and, on the other, theories that proclaim basic moral rights, it seemed to me that the moral basis of vegetarianism would have to be found somewhere among these options. That such a basis may be provided by a rights-based theory is what "The Moral Basis of Vegetarianism" attempts to show. Both the moral right not to be caused gratuitous suffering and the right to life, I argue, are possessed by the animals we eat if they are possessed by the humans we do not. To cause animals to suffer cannot be defended merely on the grounds that we like the taste of their flesh, and even if animals were raised so that they led generally pleasant lives and were "humanely" slaughtered that would not insure that their rights, including their right to life, were not violated. Despite the Western custom of supposing that vegetarians must defend their "eccentric" way of life, the essay attempts to shift the burden of proof onto the shoulders of those who should bear it—the nonvegetarians.

Now, there can be no doubt that animals sometimes appear to be in pain. On this point, even Descartes would agree. In order for us to be rationally entitled to abandon the belief that they actually do experience pain, therefore, especially in view of the close physiological resemblances that often exist between them and us, we are in need of some rationally compelling argument that would demonstrate that this belief is erroneous. Descartes's principle argument in this regard fails to present a compelling case for his view. Essentially, it consists in the claim that, since animals cannot speak or use a language, they do not think and since they do not think, they have no minds: lacking in these respects, therefore, they have no consciousness either. Thus, since a necessary condition of a creature's being able to experience pain is that it be a conscious being, it follows, given Descartes's reasoning, that animals do not experience pain. . . .

Imagine a person whose vocal chords have been damaged to such an extent that he no longer has the ability to utter words or even make inarticulate sounds, and whose arms have been paralyzed so that he cannot write, but who, when his tooth abscesses, twists and turns on his bed, grimaces and sobs. We do not say, "Ah, if only he could still speak, we could give him something for his pain. As it is, since he cannot speak, there's nothing we need give him. For he feels no pain." We say he is in pain, despite his loss of the ability to say so.

Whether or not a person is experiencing pain, in short, does not depend on his being able to perform one or another linguistic feat. Why, then, should it be any different in the case of animals? It would seem to be the height of human arrogance, rather than of . . . "superstition," to erect a double standard here, requiring that animals meet a standard not set for humans. If humans can experience pain without being logically required to be able to say so or in any other ways to use a language, then the same standard should apply to animals as well. . . .

Now, an essential part of any enlightened morality is the principle of noninjury. What this principle declares is that we are not to inflict pain on, or otherwise bring about or contribute to the pain in, any being capable of experiencing it. This principle, moreover, is derivable from the more general principle of nonmaleficence, which declares that we are not to do or cause evil, together with the value judgment that pain, considered in itself, is intrinsically evil. . . .

Given the intrinsic evil of pain, and assuming further that pleasure is intrinsically good, it is clear that cases can arise in which the evil (pain) caused to animals is not compensated for by the good (pleasure) caused humans. The classical utilitarians—Bentham, Mill, and Sidgwick—all were aware of this . . .

It has already been pointed out that the pain an animal feels is just as much pain, and just as much an intrinsic evil, as a comparable pain felt by a human being. So, if there is any rational basis for rendering conflicting judgments about the two practices, it must be looked for in some other direction.

The most likely and, on the face of it, the most plausible direction in which to look is in the direction of rights. "Humans," this line of reasoning goes, "have certain natural rights that animals lack, and that is what makes the two practices differ in a morally significant way. For in the case of the practice involving humans, their equal natural right to be spared undeserved pain is being violated, while in the case of the practice involving animals, since animals can have no rights, *their* rights are not being ignored. That is what makes the two cases differ. And that is what makes the practice involving humans an immoral one, while the practice involving animals is not."

Natural though this line of argument is, I do not think it justifies the differential treatment of the animals and humans in question. For on what grounds might it be claimed that the humans, but not the animals have an equal natural right to be spared undeserved pain? Well, it cannot be, as it is sometimes alleged, that all and only human beings have this right because all and only humans reason, make free choices, or have a concept of their identity. These grounds will not justify the ascription of rights to all humans because some humans—infants and the severely mentally defective, for example—do not meet these conditions. Moreover, even if these conditions did form the grounds for the possession of rights; and even if it were true that all human beings met them; it still would not follow that *only* human beings have them. For on what grounds, precisely, might it be claimed that no animals can reason, make free choices, or form a concept of themselves? What one would want here are detailed analyses of these operative concepts together with rationally compelling empirical data and other arguments that support the view that all non-human animals are deficient in these respects. It would be the height of prejudice merely to assume that man is unique in being able to reason. To the extent that these beliefs are not examined in the light of what we know about animals and animal intelligence, the supposition and *only* human beings have these capacities in just that—a supposition, and one that could hardly bear the moral weight placed upon it by the differential treatment of animals and humans. . . .

Two objections should be addressed before proceeding. Both involve difficulties that are supposed to attend the attribution of rights to animals. The first declares that animals cannot have rights because they lack the capacity to *claim* them. Now, this objection seems to be a variant of the view that animals cannot have rights because they cannot speak, and, like this more general view, this one too will not withstand a moment's serious reflection. For there are many human beings who cannot speak or claim their rights—tiny infants, for example—and yet who would not be denied the right in question, assuming, as we are, that it is supposed to be a right possessed by *all* human beings. Thus, if a human being can possess this (or any other right) without being able to demand it, it cannot be reasonable to require that animals be able to do so, if they are to possess this (or any other) right. The second objection is different. It declares that the attribution of rights to animals leads to absurdity. For if, say, a lamb has the natural right to be spared undeserved pain, then the wolf, who devours it unmercifully, without the benefit of anesthetic, should be said to violate the lamb's right. This, it is alleged, is absurd, and so, then, is the attribution of rights to animals. Well, absurd it may be to say that the wolf violates the lamb's right. But even supposing that it is, nothing said here implies that such deeds on the part of the wolf violate the lamb's rights. For the lamb can have rights only against those beings who are capable of taking the interests of the lamb into account and [are] trying to determine, on the basis of its interests, as well as other relevant considerations, what, morally speaking, ought to be done. In other words, the only kind of being against which another being can have rights is a being that can be held to be morally responsible for its actions. Thus, the lamb can have rights against, say, most adult human beings. But a wolf, I think it would be agreed, is not capable of making decisions from the moral point of view; nor is a wolf the kind of being that can be held morally responsible; neither, then, can it make sense to say that the lamb has any rights against the wolf. This situation has its counterpart in human affairs. The severely mentally feeble, for example, lack the requisite powers to act morally; thus, *they* cannot be expected to recognize our rights, nor can *they* be said to violate our rights, even if, for example, they should happen to cause us undeserved pain. For as they are not the kind of being that can be held responsible for what they do, neither can they be said to violate anyone's rights by what they do. . . .

Animals who are raised to be eaten by human beings very often are made to suffer. Nor is it simply that they suffer only when they are being shipped to the slaughterhouse or actually being slaughtered. For what is happening is this: The human appetite for meat has become so great that new methods of raising animals have come into being. Called intensive rearing methods, these methods seek to insure that the largest amount of meat can be produced in the shortest amount of time with the least possible expense. In ever increasing numbers, animals are being subjected to the rigors of these methods. Many are being forced to live in incredibly crowded conditions. Moreover, as a result of these methods, the natural desires of many animals often are being frustrated. In short, both in terms of the physical pain these animals must endure, and in terms of the psychological pain that attends the frustration of their natural inclinations, there can be no reasonable doubt that animals who are raised according to intensive rearing methods experience much nontrivial, undeserved pain. Add to this the gruesome realities of "humane" slaughter and we have, I think, an amount and intensity of suffering that can, with propriety, be called "great."

To the extent, therefore, that we eat the flesh of animals that have been raised under such circumstances, we help create the demand for meat that farmers who use intensive rearing methods endeavor to satisfy. Thus, to the extent that it is known that such methods will bring about much undeserved, nontrivial pain on the part of the animals raised according to these methods, anyone who purchases meat that is a product of these methods—and almost everyone who buys meat at a typical supermarket or restaurant does this—is *causally implicated* in a practice that causes pain that is both nontrivial and undeserved for the animals in question. On this point too, I think there can be no doubt. . . .

Now, there are, as I mentioned earlier two further objections that might be raised, both of which, I think, uncover important limitations in the argument of this section. The first is that a meat eater might be able to escape the thrust of my argument by the simple expedient of buying meat from farms where the animals are not raised according to intensive rearing methods a difficult but not impossible task at the present time. For despite the widespread use of these methods, it remains true that there are farms where animals are raised in clean, comfortable quarters, and where the pain they experience is the natural result of the exigencies of animal existence rather than, to use an expression of Hume's, of "human art and contrivance." . . .

The [second] objection that reads thus: "Granted, the amount of pain animals experience in intensive rearing units is deplorable and ought to be eliminated as far as is possible; still, it does not follow that we ought to give up meat altogether or to go to the trouble of hunting or buying it from other farmers. After all, all we need do is get rid of the pain and our moral worries will be over. So, what we should do is this; we should try to figure out how to *desensitize* animals so that they do not feel any pain, even in the most barbarous surroundings. Then, if this could be worked out, there would not be any grounds for worrying about the 'morality' of eating meat. Remove the animals' capacity for feeling pain and you thereby remove the possibility of their experiencing any pain that is gratuitous."

Now, I think it is obvious that nothing that I have said thus far can form a basis for responding to this objection, and though I think there are alternative ways in which one might try to respond to it, the case I try to make against it evolves out of my response to the first objection; I try to show, in other words, that an adequate response to this objection can be based upon the thesis that *it is the killing of animals, and not just their pain, that matters morally*.

Let us begin, then, with the idea that all humans possess an equal natural right to life. And let us notice, once again, that it is an *equal natural* right that we are speaking of, one that we cannot acquire or have granted to us, and one that we all are supposed to have just because we are human beings. On what basis, then, might it be alleged that all and only human beings possess this right to an equal extent? Well, several familiar possibilities come immediately to mind. It might be argued that all and only human beings have an equal right to life because either (*a*) all and only human beings have the capacity to reason, or (*b*) all and only human beings have the capacity to make free choices, or (*c*) all and only human beings have a concept of "self," or (*d*) all and only human beings have all or some combination of the previously mentioned capacities. And it is easy to imagine how someone might argue that, since animals do not have any of these capacities, *they* do not possess a right to life, least of all one that is equal to the one possessed by humans.

I have already touched upon some of the difficulties such views must inevitably encounter. Briefly, it is not clear, first, that no nonhuman animals satisfy any one (or all) of these conditions, and, second, it is reasonably clear that not all human beings satisfy them. The severely mentally feeble, for example, fail to satisfy them. Accordingly, *if* we want to insist that they have a right to life, then we cannot also maintain that they have it because they satisfy one or another of these conditions. Thus, *if* we want to insist that they have an equal right to life, despite their failure to satisfy these conditions, we cannot consistently maintain that animals, because they fail to satisfy these conditions, therefore lack this right.

Another possible ground is that of sentience, by which I understand the capacity to experience pleasure and pain. But this view, too, must encounter a familiar difficulty—namely, that it could not justify restricting the right *only* to human beings. . . .

The onus of justification lies not on the shoulders of those who are vegetarians but on the shoulders of those who are not. If the argument of the present section is sound, it is the nonvegetarian who must show us how he can be justified in eating meat, when he knows that, to do so, an animal has had to be killed. It is the nonvegetarian who must show us how his manner of life does not contribute to practices that systematically ignore the right to life which animals possess, if humans are supposed to possess it on the basis of the most plausible argument considered here. And it is the nonvegetarian who must do all this while being fully cognizant that he cannot defend his way of life merely by summing up the intrinsic goods—the delicious taste of meat, for example—that come into being as a result of the slaughter of animals.

This is not to say that practices that involve taking the lives of animals cannot possibly be justified. . . . For example, perhaps they are satisfied in the case of the Eskimo's killing of animals and in the case of having a restricted hunting season for such animals as deer. But to say that this is (or may be) true of *some* cases is not to say that it is true of all, and it will remain the task of the nonvegetarian to show that what is true in these cases, assuming that it is true, is also true of any practice that involves killing animals which, by his actions, he supports. . . .

Even if it should turn out that there are no natural rights, that would not put an end to many of the problems discussed here. For even if we do not possess natural rights, we would still object to practices that caused nontrivial, undeserved pain for some human beings if their "justification" was that they brought about this or that amount of pleasure or other forms of intrinsic good for this or that number of people; . . . and we would still object to any practice that involved the killing of human beings, even if killed painlessly, if the practice was supposed to be justified in the same way. But this being so, what clearly would be needed, if we cease to invoke the idea of rights, is some explanation of why practices that are not right, when they involve the treatment of people, can be right (or at least permissible) when they involve the treatment of animals. What clearly would be needed, in short, is what we have found to be needed and wanting all along—namely, the specification of some morally relevant feature of being human which is possessed by *all* human beings and *only* by those beings who are human. Unless or until some such feature can be pointed out, I do not see how the differential treatment of humans and animals can be rationally defended, natural rights or no.

Do Animals Have Rights?
Carl Cohen

Whether animals have rights is a question of great importance because if they do, those rights must be respected, even at the cost of great burdens for human beings. A right (unlike an interest) is a valid claim, or potential claim, made by a moral agent, under principles that govern both the claimant and the target of the claim. Rights are precious; they are dispositive; they count.

You have a right to the return of money you lent me; we both understand that. It may be very convenient for me to keep the money, and you may have no need of it whatever; but my convenience and your needs are not to the point. You have a *right* to it, and we have courts of law partly to ensure that such rights will be respected.

If you make me a promise, I have a moral right to its fulfillment—even though there may be no law to enforce my right. It may be very much in your interest to break that promise, but your great interests and the silence of the law cut no mustard when your solemn promise—which we both well understood—had been given. Likewise, those holding power may have a great and benevolent interest in denying my rights to travel or to speak freely—but their interests are overridden by my rights.

A great deal was learned about hypothermia by some Nazi doctors who advanced their learning by soaking Jews in cold water and putting them in refrigerators to learn how hypothermia proceeds. We have no difficulty in seeing that they may not advance medicine in that way; the subjects of those atrocious experiments had rights that demanded respect. For those who ignored their rights we have nothing but moral loathing.

Some persons believe that animals have rights as surely as those Jews had rights, and they therefore look on the uses of animals in medical investigations just as we look at the Nazi use of the Jews, with moral loathing. They are consistent in doing so. If animals have rights they certainly have the right not to be killed, even to advance our important interests.

Some may say, "Well, they have rights, but we have rights too, and our rights override theirs." They may be true in some cases, but it will not solve the problem because, although we may have a weighty *interest* in learning, say, how to vaccinate against polio or other diseases, we do not have a *right* to learn such things. Nor could we honestly claim that we kill research animals in self-defense; they did not attack us. If animals have rights, they certainly have the right not to be killed to advance the interests of others, whatever rights those others may have.

In 1952 there were about 58,000 cases of polio reported in the United States, and 3,000 polio deaths; my parents, parents everywhere, trembled in fear for their children at camp or away from home. Polio vaccination became routine in 1955, and cases dropped to about a dozen a year; today polio has been eradicated completely from the Western Hemisphere. The vaccine that achieved this, party developed and tested only blocks from where I live in Ann Arbor, could have been developed *only* with the substantial use of animals. Polio vaccines had been tried many times earlier, but from those earlier vaccines children had contracted the diseases; investigators had become, understandably, exceedingly cautious.

The killer disease for which a vaccine now is needed most desperately is malaria, which kills about 2 million people each year, most of them children. Many vaccines have been tried—not on children, thank God— and have failed. But very recently, after decades of effort, we learned how to make a vaccine that does, with complete success, inoculate mice against malaria. A safe vaccine for humans we do not yet have—but soon we will have it, thanks to the use of those mice, many of whom will have died in the process. To test that vaccine first on children would be an outrage, as it would have been an outrage to do so with the Salk and Sabin polio vaccines years ago. We use mice or monkeys *because there is no other way.* And there never will be another way because untested vaccines are very dangerous; their use on a living organism is inescapably experimental; there is and will be no way to determine the reliability and safety of new vaccines without repeated tests on live organisms. Therefore, because we certainly may not use human children to test them, we will use mice (or as we develop an AIDS vaccine, primates) *or we will never have such vaccines.*

But if those animals we use in such tests have rights as human children do, what we did and are doing to them is as profoundly wrong as what the Nazis did to those Jews not long ago. Defenders of animal rights need not hold that medical scientists are vicious; they simply believe that what medical investigators are doing with animals is morally wrong. Most biomedical investigations involving animal subjects use rodents; mice and rats. The rat is the animal appropriately considered (and used by the critic) as the exemplar whose moral stature is in dispute here. Tom Regan is a leading defender of the view that rats do have such rights, and may not be used in biomedical investigations. He is an honest man. He sees the consequences of his view and accepts them forthrightly. In *The Case for Animal Rights* (Regan, 1983) he wrote,

> The harms others might face as a result of the dissolution of [some] practice or institution is no defense of allowing it to continue. . . . No one has a right to be protected against being harmed if the protection in question involves violating the rights of others. . . . No one has a right to be protected by the continuation of an unjust practice, one that violates the rights of others. . . . Justice *must* be done, though the . . . heavens fall. (pp. 346–347)

That last line echoes Kant, who borrowed it from an older tradition. Believing that rats have rights as humans do, Regan (1983) was convinced that killing them in medical research was morally intolerable. He wrote,

On the rights view, [he means, of course, the Regan rights view] we cannot justify harming a single rat *merely* by aggregating "the many human and humane benefits" that flow from doing it. . . . Not even a single rat is to be treated as if that animal's value were reducible to his *possible utility* relative to the interests of others. (p. 384)

If there are some things that we cannot learn because animals have rights, well, as Regan (1983) put it, so be it.

This is the conclusion to which one certainly is driven if one holds that animals have rights. If Regan is correct about the moral standing of rats, we humans can have no right, ever, to kill them—unless perchance a rat attacks a person or a human baby, as rats sometimes do; then our right of self-defense may enter, I suppose. But medical investigations cannot honestly be described as self-defense, and medical investigations commonly require that many mice and rats be killed. Therefore, all medical investigations relying on them, or any other animal subjects—which includes most studies and all the most important studies of certain kinds—will have to stop. Bear in mind that the replacement of animal subjects by computer simulations, or tissue samples, and so on, is in most research a phantasm, a fantasy. Biomedical investigations using animal subjects (and of course all uses of animals as food) will have to stop.

This extraordinary consequence has no argumentative force for Regan and his followers; they are not consequentialists. For Regan the *interests* of humans, their desire to be freed of disease or relieved of pain, simply cannot outweigh the *rights* of a single rat. For him the issue is one of justice, and the use of animals in medical experiments (he believes) is simply not just. But the consequences of his view will give most of us, I submit, good reason to weigh very carefully the arguments he offers to support such far-reaching claims. Do you believe that the work of Drs. Salk and Sabin was morally right? Would you support it now, or support work just like it saving tens of thousands of human children from diphtheria, hepatitis, measles, rabies, rubella, and tetanus (all of which relied essentially on animal subjects)—as well as, now, AIDS, Lyme disease, and malaria? I surely do. If you would join me in this support we must conclude that the defense of animal rights is a gigantic mistake. I next aim to explain why animals *cannot* possess rights.

Why Animals Do Not Have Rights

Many obligations are owed by humans to animals; few will deny that. But it certainly does not follow from this that animals have rights because it is certainly not true that every obligation of ours arises from the rights of another. Not at all. We need to be clear and careful here. Rights entail obligations. If you have a right to the return of the money I borrowed, I have an obligation to repay it. No issue. If we have the right to speak freely on public policy matters, the community has the obligation to respect out right to do so. But the proposition *all rights entail obligations* does not convert simply, as the logicians say. From the true proposition that all trees are plants, it does not follow that all plants are trees. Similarly, not all obligations are entailed by rights. Some obligations, like mine to repay the money I borrowed from you, do arise out of rights. But many obligations are owed to persons or other beings who have no rights whatever in the matter.

Obligations may arise from commitments freely made: As a college professor I accept the obligation to comment at length on the papers my students submit, and I do so; but they have not the right to *demand* that I do so. Civil servants and elected officials surely ought to be courteous to members of the public, but that obligation certainly is not grounded in citizens' rights.

Special relations often give rise to obligations: Hosts have the obligation to be cordial to their guests, but the guest has not the right to demand cordiality. Shepherds have obligations to their dogs, and cowboys to their horses, which do not flow from the rights of those dogs or horses. My son, now 5, may someday wish to study veterinary medicine as my father did; I will then have the obligation to help him as I can, and with pride I shall—but he has not the authority to demand such help as a matter of right. My dog has no right to daily exercise and veterinary care, but I do have the obligation to provide those things for her.

One may be obliged to another for a special act of kindness done; one may be obliged to put an animal out of its misery in view of its condition—but neither the beneficiary of that kindness nor that dying animal may have had a claim of right.

Beauchamp and Childress (1994) addressed what they called the "correlativity of rights and obligations" and wrote that they would defend an "untidy" (pp. 73–75) variety of that principle. It would be very untidy indeed. Some of our most important obligations—to members of our family, to the needy, to neighbors, and to sentient creatures of every sort—have no foundation in rights at all. Correlativity appears critical from the perspective of one who holds a right; your right correlates with my obligation to respect it. But the claim that rights and obligations are *reciprocals*, that *every* obligation flows from another's right, is false, plainly inconsistent with our general understanding of the differences between what we think we ought to do, and what others can justly *demand* that we do.

I emphasize this because, although animals have no rights, it surely does not follow from this that one is free to treat them with callous disregard. Animals are not stones; they feel. A rat may suffer; surely we have the obligation not to torture it gratuitously, even though it be true that the concept of a right could not possibly apply to it. We humans are obliged to act humanely, that is, being aware of their sentience, to apply to animals the moral principles that govern us regarding the gratuitous imposition of pain and suffering; which is not, of course, to treat animals as the possessors of rights.

Animals cannot be the bearers of rights because the concept of rights is essentially *human*; it is rooted in, and has force within, a human moral world. Humans must deal with rats—all too frequently in some parts of the world—and must be moral in their dealing with them; but a rat can no more be said to have rights than a table can be said to have ambition. To say of a rat that it has rights is to confuse categories, to apply to its world a moral category that has content only in the human moral world.

Try this thought experiment. Imagine, on the Serengeti Plain in East Africa, a lioness hunting for her cubs. A baby zebra, momentarily left unattended by its mother, is the prey; the lioness snatches it, rips open its throat, tears out chunks of its flesh, and departs. The mother zebra is driven nearly out of her wits when she cannot locate her baby; finding its carcass she will not even leave the remains for days. The scene my be thought unpleasant, but it is entirely natural, of course, and extremely common. If the zebra has a right to live, if the prey is just but the predator unjust, we ought to intervene, if we can, on behalf of right. But we do not intervene, of course—as we surely would intervene if we saw the lioness about to attack an unprotected human baby or you. What accounts for the moral difference? We justify different responses to humans and to zebras on the ground (implicit or explicit) that their moral stature is very different. The human has a right not to be eaten alive; it is, after all, a human being. Do you believe the baby zebra has the *right* not to be slaughtered by that lioness? That the lioness has the *right* to kill that baby zebra for her cubs? If you are inclined to say, confronted by such natural rapacity—duplicated with untold variety millions of times each day on planet earth—that neither is right or wrong, that neither has a *right* against the other, I am on your side. Rights are of the highest moral consequence, yes; but zebras and lions and rats are totally amoral; there is no morality for them; they do no wrong, ever. In their world there are no rights.

A contemporary philosopher who has thought a good deal about animals, referring to them as "moral patients," put it this way:

A moral patient lacks the ability to formulate, let alone bring to bear, moral principles in deliberating about which one among a number of possible acts it would be right or proper to perform. Moral patients, in a word, cannot do what is right, nor can they do what is wrong. . . . Even when a moral patient causes significant harm to another, the moral patient has not done what is wrong. Only moral agents can do what is wrong. (Regan, 1983, pp. 152–153)

Just so. The concepts of wrong and right are totally foreign to animals, not conceivably within their ken or applicable to them, as the author of that passage clearly understands.

When using animals in our research, therefore, we ought indeed be humane—but we can never violate the rights of those animals because, to be blunt, they have none. Rights do not *apply* to them.

But humans do have rights. Where do our rights come from? Why are we not crudely natural creatures like rats and zebras? This question philosophers have struggled to answer from earliest times. A definitive account of the human moral condition I cannot here present, of course. But reflect for a moment on the kinds of answers that have been widely given:

- Some think our moral understanding, with its attendant duties, to be a divine gift. So St. Thomas said: The moral law is binding, and humans have the power, given by God, to grasp it binding character, and must therefore respect the rights that other humans possess. God makes us (Saint Augustine said before him) in his own image, and therefore with a will that is free, and gives us the power to recognize that, and therefore, unlike other creatures, we must choose between good and evil, between right and wrong.

- Many philosophers, distrusting theological justifications of rights and duties, sought the ground of human morality in the membership, by all humans, in a moral community. The English idealist, Bradley, called it an organic moral community; the German idealist, Hegel, called it an objective ethical order. These and like accounts commonly center on human interrelations, on a moral *fabric* within which human agents always act, and within which animals never act and never can possibly act.

- The highly abstract reasoning from which such views emerge has dissatisfied many; you may find more nearly true the convictions of ethical intuitionists and realists who said, as H. A. Prichard, Sir David Ross, and my friend and teacher C. D. Broad, of happy memory, used to say, that there is a direct, underivative, intuitive cognition of rights as possessed by other humans but not by animals.

- Or perhaps in the end we will return to Kant, and say with him that critical reason reveals at the core of human action a uniquely moral will, and the unique ability to grasp and to lay down moral laws for oneself and for others—an ability that is not conceivably within the capacity of any nonhuman animal whatever.

To be a moral agent (on this view) is to be able to grasp the generality of moral restrictions on our will. Humans understand that some things, which may be in our interest, *must not be willed*; we lay down moral laws for ourselves, and thus exhibit, as no other animal can exhibit, moral autonomy. My dog knows that there are certain things she must not do—but she knows this only as the outcome of her learning about her interests, the pains she may suffer if she does what had been taught forbidden. She does not know, cannot know (as Regan agrees) that any conduct is wrong. The proposition *It would be highly advantageous to act in such-and-such a way, but I may not because it would be wrong* is one that no dog or mouse or rabbit, however sweet and endearing; however loyal or attentive to its young, can ever entertain, or intend, or begin to grasp. Right is not in their world. But right and wrong are the very stuff of human moral life, the ever-present awareness of human beings who can do wrong, and who by seeking (often) to avoid wrong conduct prove themselves members of a moral community in which rights may be exercised and must be respected.

Some respond by saying, "This can't be correct, for human infants (and the comatose and senile, etc.) surely have rights, but they make no moral claims or judgments and can make none—and any view entailing that children can have no rights must be absurd." Objections of this kind miss the point badly. It is not individual persons who qualify (or are disqualified) for the possession of rights because of the presence or absence in them of some special capacity, thus resulting in the award or rights to some but not to others. Rights are universally human; they arise in a *human moral world*, in a moral *sphere*. In the human world moral judgments are pervasive; it is the fact that all humans including infants and the senile are members of that moral community—not the fact that as individuals they have or do not have certain special capacities, or merits—that makes humans bearers of rights. Therefore, it is beside the point to insist that animals have remarkable capacities, that they really have a consciousness of self, or of the future, or make plans, and so on. And the tired response that because infants plainly cannot make moral claims they must have no rights at all, or rats must have them too, we ought forever put aside. Responses like these arise out of a misconception of right itself. They mistakenly suppose that rights are tied to some identifiable individual abilities or sensibilities, and they fail to see that rights arise only in a community of moral beings, and that therefore there are spheres in which rights do apply and spheres in which they do not.

Rationality is not at issue; the capacity to communicate is not at issue. My dog can reason, if rather weakly, and she certainly can communicate. Cognitive criteria for the possession of rights, Beauchamp said, are morally perilous. Indeed they are. Nor is the capacity to suffer here at issue. And, if *autonomy* be understood only as the capacity to choose this course rather than that, autonomy is not to the point either. But *moral autonomy*—that is, *moral selflegislation*—is to the point, because moral autonomy is uniquely human and is for animals out of the question, as we have seen, and as Regan and I agree. In talking about autonomy, therefore, we must be careful and precise.

Because humans do have rights, and these rights can be violated by other humans, we say that some humans commit *crimes*. But whether a crime has been committed depends utterly on the moral state of mind of the actor. If I take your coat, or your book, honestly thinking it was mine, I do not steal it. The *actus reus* (the guilty deed) must be accompanied, in a genuine crime, by a guilty mind, a *mens rea*. That recognition, not just of possible punishment for an act, but of moral duties that govern us, no rat or cow ever can posses. In primitive times humans did sometimes bring cows and horses to the bar of human justice. We chuckle at that practice now, realizing that accusing cows of crimes marks the primitive moral view as inane. Animals never can be criminals because they have no moral state of mind.

Mistakes parallel to this in other spheres may be helpful to think about. In the Third Part of *The Critique of Pure Reason*, Immanuel Kant explained with care the metaphysical blunders into which we are led when we misapply concepts of great human import. In our human experience, for example, the concepts of time and space, the relations of cause and effect, of subject and attribute, and others, are essential, fundamental. But, forgetting that these are concepts arising only within the world of our human experience, we sometimes are misled into asking: Was the world caused, or is it uncaused? Did the world have a beginning in time, or did it not? Kant explained—in one of the most brilliant long passages in all philosophical literature—why *it makes no sense to ask such questions.* Cause applies to phenomena we humans encounter *in* the world, it is a category of our experience and cannot apply to the world as a whole. Time is the condition of our experience, not an absolute container in which the world could have begun. The antinomies of pure reason, and after those the paralogisms of pure reason, Kant patiently exhibited as confusions arising from the misapplication of the categories of experience. His lesson is powerful and deep. The misapplication of concepts leads to error and, some time to nonsense. So it is with rights also. To say that rats have rights is to apply to the world of rats a concept that makes good sense when applied to humans, but which makes no sense at all when applied to rats.

Why Animals Are Mistakenly Believed to Have Rights

From the foregoing discussion it follows that, if some philosophers believe that they have proved that animals have rights, they must have erred in the alleged proof. Regan is a leader among those who claim to *argue* in defense of the rights of rats; he contends that the best arguments are on his side. I aim next to show how he and others with like views go astray. Bear in mind that Regan's book is long, its argument tortuous and at times convoluted. In what follows I must compress the report of his views, obviously; but I promise to be fair and to hold Regan responsible for nothing that he does not clearly say. We know—if we are agreed that rats are not the holders of rights—that Regan must have got off the track. Examining *The Case for Animal Rights*, let us see if we can find the faulty switch.

Much of Regan's (1983) book is devoted to a general treatment of the nature of ethical thinking and theory, to discussions of animal consciousness and animal awareness, and to detailed critiques of the views of others whom he thinks in error. Regan sought to show, patiently and laboriously, that the common belief that we do have obligations to animals, although they have no rights, has not been defended satisfactorily. That belief cannot be justified, he contended, by direct duty views of which he finds two categories: those depending on the obligation to be kind or not to be cruel, and those depending on any kind of utilitarian calculation.

None of this counterargument could possibly establish his conclusion that animals do have rights, unless Regan had proved that his listing of all alternative conflicting views was exhaustive, which it was not, and unless he had proved conclusively that every such candidate is untenable, which he did not do. . . .

The case is built entirely on the principle that allegedly *carries over* almost everything earlier claimed about human rights to rats and other animals. What principle is that? It is the principle, put in italics but given no name, that equates moral agents with moral patients:

> *The validity of the claim to respectful treatment, and thus the case for the recognition of the right to such treatment, cannot be any stranger or weaker in the case of moral patients than it is in the case of moral agents.* (Regan, p. 279)

But hold on. Why in the world should anyone think this principle to be true? Back where Regan first recounted his view of moral patients, he allowed that some of them are, although capable of experiencing pleasure and pain, lacking in other capacities. But he is interested, he told us there, in those moral patients—those animals—that are like humans in having *inherent value*. This is the key to the argument for animal rights, the possession of inherent value. How that concept functions in the argument becomes absolutely critical. I will say first briefly what will be shown more carefully later: *Inherent value* is an expression used by Regan (and many like him) with two very different senses—in one of which it is reasonable to conclude that those who have inherent value have rights, and in another sense in which that inference is wholly unwarranted. But the phrase *inherent value* has some plausibility in both contexts, and thus by sliding from one sense of inherent value to the other Regan appears to succeed . . . in making the case for animal rights.

The concept of inherent value first entered the discussion in the seventh chapter of Regan's (1983) book, at which point his principle object is to fault and defeat utilitarian arguments. It is not (he argued there) the pleasures or pains that go "into the cup" of humanity that give value, but the "cups" themselves; humans are equal in value because they are humans, having inherent value. So we are, all of us, equal—equal in being moral agents who have this inherent value. This approach to the moral stature of humans is likely to be found quite plausible. Regan called it the "postulate of inherent value"; all humans, "The lonely, forsaken, unwanted, and unloved are no more nor less inherently valuable then those who enjoy a more hospitable relationship with others" (p. 237). And Regan went on to argue for the proposition that all moral agents are "equal in inherent value." Holding some such views we are likely to say, with Kant, that all humans are beyond price. Their inherent value gives them moral dignity, a unique role in the moral world, as agents having the capacity to act morally and make moral judgments. This is inherent value in Sense 1.

The expression *inherent value* has another sense, however, also common and also plausible. My dog has inherent value, and so does every wild animal, every lion and zebra, which is why the senseless killing of animals is so repugnant. Each animal is unique, not replaceable in itself by another animal or by any rocks or clay. Animals, like humans, are not just things; they live, and as unique living creatures they have inherent value. This is an important point, and again likely to be thought plausible; but here, in Sense 2, the phrase *inherent value* means something quite distinct from what was meant in its earlier uses.

Inherent value in Sense 1, possessed by all humans but not by all animals, which warrants the claim of human rights, is very different from inherent value in Sense 2, which warrants no such claim. The uniqueness of animals, their intrinsic worthiness as individual living things, does not ground the possession of rights, has nothing to do with the moral condition in which rights arise. Regan's argument reached its critical objective with almost magical speed because, having argued that beings with inherent value (Sense 1) have rights that must be respected, he quickly asserted (putting it in italics lest the reader be inclined to express doubt) that rats and rabbits also have rights because they, too, have inherent value (Sense 2).

This is an egregious example of the fallacy of equivocation: the informal fallacy in which two or more meanings of the same word or phrase have been confused in the several premises of an argument (Cohen & Copi, 1994, pp. 143–144). Why is this slippage not seen at once? Partly because we know the phrase *inherent value* often is used loosely, so the reader is not prone to quibble about its introduction; partly because the two uses of the phrase relied on are both common, so neither signals danger; partly because inherent value in Sense 2 is indeed shared by those who have it in Sense 1; and partly because the phrase *inherent value* is woven into accounts of what Regan (1983) elsewhere called the *subject-of-a-life criterion*, a phrase of his own devising for which he can stipulate any meaning he pleases, of course, and which also slides back and forth between the sphere of genuine moral agency and the sphere of animal experience. But perhaps the chief reason the equivocation between these two uses of the phrase *inherent value* is obscured (from the author, I believe, as well as from the reader) is the fact that the assertion that animals have rights appears only indirectly, as the outcome of the application of the principle that moral patients are entitled to the same respect as moral agents—a principle introduced at a point in the book long after the important moral differences between moral patients and moral agents have been recognized, with a good deal of tangled philosophical argument having been injected in between.

I invite readers to trace out this equivocation in detail; my limited space here precludes more extended quotation. But this assurance I will give: there is no argument or set of arguments in *The Case for Animal Rights* that successfully makes the case for animal rights. Indeed, there *could* not be, any more than any book, however long and convoluted, could make the case for the emotions of oak trees, or the criminality of snakes.

Animals do not have rights. 'Right' does not apply in their world. We do have many obligations to animals, of course, and I honor Regan's appreciation of their sensitivities. I also honor his seriousness of purpose, and his always civil and always rational spirit. But he is, I submit, profoundly mistaken. I conclude with the observation that, had his mistaken views about the rights of animals long been accepted, most successful medical therapies recently devised—antibiotics, vaccines, prosthetic devices, and other compounds and instruments on which we now rely for saving and improving human lives and for the protection of our children—could not have been developed; and were his views to become general now (an outcome that is unlikely but possible) the consequences for medical science and for human well-being in the years ahead would be nothing less than catastrophic.

Advances in medicine absolutely require experiments, many of which are dangerous. Dangerous experiments absolutely require living organisms as subjects. Those living organisms (we now agree) certainly may not be human beings. Therefore, most advances in medicine will continue to rely on the use of nonhuman animals, or they will stop. Regan is free to say in response, as he does, "so be it." The rest of us must ask if the argument he presents is so compelling as to force us to accept that dreadful result.

References

Beauchamp, T. L., & Childress, J. F. (1994). *Principles of Biomedical Ethics* (4th ed.), New York: Oxford University Press.

Cohen, C., & Copi, I. M. (1994). *Introduction to Logic* (9th ed.). New York: Macmillan.

Regan, T. (1983). *The Case for Animal Rights*. Berkeley: University of California Press.

The Case for Gay Marriage
Michael Nava and Robert Dawidoff

. . . Marriage is how society recognizes the intimate and lasting bond between two people and, in turn, it has become the cornerstone of the American family. Curiously, the American family as we know it is not "traditional" but innovative. Instead of inherited property or bloodlines or unquestioned patriarchal authority, the American family early on developed the view of marriage as a partnership between two consenting adults, not an agreement on their account by their parents or families. The churches that bless the marriage sacrament took their cue from secular, individualist America and, in general, endorse marriage as something entered into by the participants, if they are of age to contract, because they choose to make that commitment.

In the United States marriage is understood to be the decision of two people to live together and be a partnership, a unit, a family. Neither family nor church participates in the legal ceremony, and the religious wedding acquires legal force by the power vested in the officiant by the civil society, the religious ceremony confirms the civil arrangement. Marriage is not conditioned on the intention or the capacity to have children. Nothing in marriage, except custom, mandates partners of different genders. For example, John Boswell notes that in ancient Rome "marriages between males and between females were legal and familiar among the upper classes."[1] The institution of marriage in our society appears to be one that encourages monogamy as the basis for stable personal lives and as one aspect of the family. If we think about what marriage is for, it becomes clear that it is for people to find ways to live ordered, shared lives; it is intended to be the stablest possible unit of family life and a stable structure of intimacy.

Marriage is part of the formal and informal network of extended family, kinship, and friendship, and it is acknowledged in law as society's preferred way for consenting adults to connect their lives. Society recognizes that people have the right and the desire to have those connections solemnized according to their own beliefs; thus, religious ceremonies of all sorts, established or homemade, are encouraged as adjuncts to the civil bond. But it is the civil bond that the law acknowledges and that society encourages in all sorts of ways. No wonder many gay and lesbian Americans see marriage as their equal right. Marriage is society's way of making things easier and better for people who want to form permanent relationships, share their lives and property, and form families.

Marriage is not mere form. society recognizes its importance not only rhetorically but with such benefits as preferential tax treatment, spousal Social Security and veteran's benefits, favorable immigration laws, property and support rights upon divorce, and intestate succession. In addition, according to Alissa Friedman, "both state and federal governments allocate a great many rights on the basis of marital status and have created powerful incentives for an individual to marry. Furthermore, private entities like insurance companies often provide special benefits and lower rates for married couples and legally recognized couples. Restrictions on the right to marry, therefore, affect both associational rights and a variety of societal entitlements."[2] . . .

Gays and lesbians want the right to marry for the same reasons other Americans do: to gain the moral, legal, social, and spiritual benefits conferred on the marrying couple and especially on their family unit. The material benefits of marriage are considerable, but it is the moral benefit that is especially attractive to many couples, including gay and lesbian ones. Marriage is, or can be, a moral commitment that two people make to one another. The marriage vow enshrines love, honor, respect, and mutual support and gives people access to resources and community acknowledgment that serve to strengthen their bond. Brought up and socialized as most Americans are, gays and lesbians also regard the prospect of marriage as reverently and respectfully as heterosexuals do. To mock and deny them is ultimately to mock and deny the institution of marriage. The impulse to marry, among gays, is essentially the same as it is among heterosexuals, and the capacity to do it well is probably the same. The only real difference is in the identity of the people who want to get married.

What is drastically different, of course, is that gay and lesbian unions get none of the support, encouragement, and benefits society regularly gives to heterosexual unions, however ill-advised. Instead, gays and lesbians are reviled for their "inability" to form permanent attachments. Of course, relationships between people that have to remain clandestine or have no foundations in law or social convention are just that much harder to maintain. Gay relationships can succeed, but always against heavy odds, odds not of the participants' making; heterosexual marriages fail all too often in spite of every conceivable social, familial, legal, and moral support.

The journal *Demography* recently published the results of a twenty-three-year study of the relationship of cohabitation to marriage; they suggest "the possibility that cohabitation weakens commitment to marriage as an institution." The authors of the study concluded that living together before marriage may not strengthen marriage; on the contrary, living together before marriage commonly produces "attitudes and values which increase the probability of divorce."[3] . . . If, as the *Demography* study indicates, marriage is a key ingredient in the longevity and solidity of intimate relationships, then denial of that most important advantage to one class of citizens on account of sexual orientation is cruelly unfair.

One of the ironies of our situation is that the American marriage that is so celebrated actually borrows from the historical character of gay relationships to describe itself. Far from being unnatural, gay and lesbian ways of living have played important roles in every human society. One almost universal function of those relationships has been to pioneer the more equal relations between the sexes. Long-standing relationships between men and between women are well known to history. Antiquity celebrated the bonds of friendship and loyalty between men, bonds that scholars tell us commonly included the sexual. The relationships among Greek soldiers and philosophers, which have played so critical a role in the traditional Western understanding of noble human relations (including the cohesion of the military unit), were modeled on love between men that regularly included sex.

The lifelong partnerships between middle-class or upper-class women in American history—the famous "Boston marriages"—also influenced decisively the understanding of marriage that American women derived from their colleges and their genteel upbringings. Female friendships played a critical role in the creation of the American institution of marriage as a partnership within which the woman was not owned but respected, not a human beast of burden and procreation but an equal source of authority and values for the family that marriage creates. . . .

The distinctive quality of modern American marriage and family is the equal and respectful, relations between husband and wife as partners, friends, and co-parents, in the place of the economic, procreative, and kinship unit of traditional societies. Men and women are learning to treat one another as they more habitually treat favored members of their own gender—with confidence, trust, equality, respect, and sensitivity. Gays and lesbians are as capable of forming such relationships and making them work as heterosexual men and women are . . . .

Two main obstacles appear to gay marriage: legal definitions of marriage and the claim that marriage is chiefly for procreation or child-rearing. The legal argument boils down to the following: Marriage is a union of man and woman because it's always been that way. The civil law that governs marriage has its roots in ecclesiastrical law, which reflects the biblical proscription of homosexuality. The statutes say that marriage is the union of man and woman, so that is what marriage must be. . . .

Even if we accept parenting as one important reason for the institution of marriage, shifting the model of marriage to include common if untraditional parenting units makes sense. Whatever was the case in the past, it is now common for gays and lesbians to be parents, not just to have fathered or borne children in heterosexual unions, but to be raising children as open gays and lesbians. In a survey of gay couples, Mary Mendola looked at gays and lesbians involved in a "gay marriage relationship," as she put it. She found that a quarter of the women and 17 percent of the men reported that they or their partners had children. Nearly 60 percent of the women reported that their children lived with them and their partners most of the time, while 39 percent reported that their children regularly visited. While only 3 percent of the men reported that their children lived with them and their partners, 53 percent reported that their children regularly visited them.[4] Mendola's report is a dozen years old; if anything the numbers have probably increased as more gays and lesbians are producing children by using artificial insemination (the so-called gayby boom) or adopting them or winning custody of them. If society is serious in its claim that marriage produces the best environment for raising children, then marriage must be extended to gays and lesbians who, in increasing numbers, are becoming parents.

Moreover, the studies available on gay parenting demonstrate that gays and lesbians make good parents; the children of gay families appear to do as well as the children of heterosexual ones. If, as it is sometimes argued, these children face difficulties among their peers because of negative attitudes toward homosexuality, the clear solution is to change those attitudes through education. Allowing same-sex marriage would be an important part of that change and would also promote family stability. If, in fact, that kind of stability is one of the reasons that marriage exists, it makes no sense to promote it in some families but not others by restricting marriage to heterosexuals.

Opponents of gay marriage finally arrive at the bedrock of their argument when they assert that allowing gays and lesbians to marry would encourage illegal sexual activity in the face of sodomy laws. . . . [This] implies a moral judgment against that activity (even in places where there are no sodomy laws), then allowing gays and lesbians to marry is contrary to acceptable morality. Of course, the whole point of gay and lesbian activism is to expose the underlying premise of immorality for the bigotry it is. Making an act illegal doesn't mean the act is inherently criminal. . . .

The quarter century of gay and lesbian political activism and openness has not resulted in a dramatic increase in the homosexual population (although it has dramatically increased the awareness of homosexuality and has also increased the numbers of lesbians and gays living openly). The points to the conclusion that this population is relatively stable and will always be a minority. Thus, punitive laws accomplish nothing but to intimidate a class of American citizens and deny them their constitutional rights. Denying gay and lesbian marriage will not eliminate gay and lesbian relationships; it will just make those relationships harder to sustain. If creating unnecessary suffering in the cause of popular prejudice is a permissible goal of legislation, then not only gay Americans are in for a bad time of it. . . .

Far from harming heterosexuals, gay marriage would give family-inclined gay men and lesbians the chance to fulfill this aspiration in conformity with their own natures. The legitimacy of gay marriage would save lives by creating the kind of respect for gays and lesbians that will work as a counterweight to bigotry and bashing. . . .

What We Want

What do gays and lesbians want? What does any person want? Enough to live; basic protections; love, family, freedom. Beyond the basics, in the case of gays and lesbians, would be equal protection of the law, representation along with taxation. And what lies beyond that, it is the individual's place to say. We do not think there is a shared agenda among gays and lesbians that goes much beyond equality and freedom. But there are some other things that we imagine as human counterparts to legal protections.

It would be wonderful if families could see in their children the full range of the affectional possibilities that life in fact holds out. If girlish boys and boyish girls, who do not constitute the full range of homosexuality but who are often the ones targeted, could receive encouragement and praise and the love they deserve instead of derision, intimidation, and disappointment, their lives would be much improved. And it would improve the quality of the culture if these children could grow into adults who, because they were loved and valued, made rich contributions to the culture instead of expending that energy on overcoming the wounds that were inflicted on them.

It would also be wonderful if friends and colleagues of gay people would be as interested in their lives as they are in their company and counsel, if the walls came down and revealed each other's essential humanity. And it would be wonderful to see gay and lesbian judges, mayors, kindergarten teachers, construction workers, actors, fathers, brothers, mothers, sisters, musicians and clerics, all of them acknowledged and honored. In this utopia, little would appear changed, but there would be an addition rather than a diminution of freedom and well-being. . . .

Notes

1. John Boswell, *Christianity, Social Tolerance and Homosexuality,* Chicago: University of Chicago Press, 1980, p. 82.
2. Alissa Friedman, "The Necessity for State Recognition of Same-Sex Marriage: Constitutional Requirements and Evolving Notions of Family," 3 *Berkeley Women's Law Journal* (1988), pp. 134–70.
3. William G. Axinn and Arland Thorton, "The Relationship Between Cohabitation and Divorce: Selectivity or Casual Influence?" *Demography* 29 (August 1992) 3:357, 361.
4. Mary Mendola, *The Mendola Report: A New Look at Gay Couples* (1980), p. 254.

The Case Against Gay Marriage
Manuel A. Lopez

While opinion polls have consistently shown most Americans in favor of maintaining current marriage laws, two-thirds of high school seniors and a majority of those in their twenties favor gay marriage. The reason for this divergence is clear. There was been less public argument against gay marriage than in favor of it. While older people nonetheless tend to retain an older view of marriage, many young people have concluded that opposition to change merely reflects prejudice or squeamishness. Moreover, the case for gay marriage largely boils down to the simple claim that everybody should be treated the same way. This is always a powerful claim in a democracy, especially among the young.

The problem in the debate so far has been the failure to grasp what marriage means in most people's lives. Marriage is so much a part of our world that we have trouble imagining how things would look without it. Some people say marriage is "by definition" between a man and a woman, but that by itself tells us nothing. We have to seriously consider what stands *behind* this definition, and why people are so attached to it.

It seems to me undeniable that the potential for reproduction constitutes something unique about the union of one man and one woman. Science may eventually change that, but sexual reproduction is sure to remain the easiest and manifestly most natural way. Even if some marriages are childless, it surely makes a difference that all marriages are between men and women. Marriages as we know it is bound up with, even a product of, natural sexual differentiation, whose most massive and undeniable feature is the potential for reproduction. This gives rise to a feeling that marriage is part of the natural order, an order bigger than ourselves and our desires. To be sure, widespread divorce has weakened this feeling over the past thirty years; but it remains a powerful force in people's lives, one that we perhaps take for granted precisely because of its ubiquity. Permitting marriage between people of the same sex would make marriage a *different* thing—and not a better one.

More than any other institution, marriage provides guidance that helps people live their lives. One need only think of the times in one's youth when one wondered whom one would eventually marry. (I can attest that even young homosexuals wonder about this—though with a certain ambivalence.) Those youthful daydreams, which are so important in shaping and coloring the rest of one's life, would not be possible in a world without marriage, and would not be easy in a world where marriage was merely one choice among many. Our youthful (and not so youthful) daydreams presuppose marriage as a touchstone, a choice which isn't simply *a* choice but is somehow *the* choice.

Unlike some conservatives, I don't think allowing gays to marry would cause many people to view marriage as "just another contract," similar to buying a car or taking a job. Most people feel that an intimate connection to one other person is an indispensable part of a good life, and I don't think gay marriage would change that. (Legalized polygamy might be another story, at least after several generations.)

However, disconnecting marriage from procreation would make it seem less bound up with a world larger than we are. Marriage would seem more like a commitment we make, an act of the will, and less like an acceptance of or conformity to the fundamental order of things. Perhaps such a change would, to some extent, constitute greater realism. However, I don't think it would produce greater happiness, either in itself or in its consequences, which would include people taking their marriages less seriously, considering alternatives more readily when the going gets rough, and seeking guidance more often in desire, whim, and fashion.

Moreover, true conservatives are wary of fundamental changes in laws and institutions, even when those changes are in themselves improvements. Humans are not so rational that we can dispense with awe or the sense that some things are greater than human enactment. Any major change in marriage laws would weaken people's sense of marriage as something slightly awesome that must be accepted or rejected on its own terms. Any such change would encourage us to pay less attention to the demands of marriage and more attention to ourselves, to consider how we might gratify the desires we feel, even to look within ourselves to see what desires we find.

We humans are ambiguous creatures. We are of course unhappy if our desires are thwarted; but we are also unhappy if we have no guidance apart from desire. Our desires themselves need to be guided or informed by a view of what is good, what constitutes happiness. Some desires can lead to happiness, others cannot; distinguishing between the two is sometimes a delicate task, one at which we all need help, especially when we're young. No institution informs the desires of most human beings in as profound and salutary a manner as marriage.

Of course marriage in its current form fails to provide such guidance for those who are homosexual. Now there are some people who believe homosexuality to be a mere perversion, akin to bestiality or taking drugs, which can in no way lead to a good life. To such people I can only say that this attraction is at the core of what gays are. (The experience of lesbian women seems somewhat different; their sexuality is perhaps more fluid or socially determined.) Whether or not scientists have "proven" that homosexuality has a natural or genetic basis, those who oppose gay marriage are unwise to base their case on an insistence that it doesn't. I suppose it's possible that some subtle observer might understand gay men better than we understand ourselves; but so far this superior understanding has not made itself apparent. Freudian accounts of the emergence of homosexuality offered by self-styled "reparative therapists" are even more convoluted and unconvincing than Freudian accounts of other things.

In my view instituting homosexual marriage would indeed provide guidance to some young homosexuals, and would thereby improve some people's lives. This is a serious argument; however, I don't think marriage could be as crucial to gays as it is to other people. Marriage has developed over many centuries to meet the needs of heterosexuals. Gay marriage would inevitably be a kind of limitation. Like most imitations, it couldn't wholly succeed, and would therefore result in more or less self-conscious parody.

Many gays want the right to marry, without actually wanting to marry. This boils down to a form of "me-too"-ism, a desire to have whatever rights heterosexuals have. Regarding marriage, however, gays already have the rights that heterosexuals have: A gay man can marry a woman, a lesbian woman can marry a man. That such marriages would not be satisfying is unfortunate, but also beside the point. The state can go no further without fundamentally changing marriage. Widening marriage to include people of the same sex means stripping it of much of its meaning and diminishing it for everybody. This would have a relatively small effect on the lives of people who are already married, and whose notion of marriage is already largely settled; but it would have a profound effect on future generations of Americans.

This, it seems to me, is the most important argument against same-sex marriage. However, I must add that there is also legitimate reason for concern on the empirical question of how married gays would behave, with serious consequences for the upbringing of children.

No sensible observer can deny that gay men are, in general, more promiscuous than heterosexual men. (Believe me, I come to this conclusion reluctantly.) If allowed to marry, gay men will, I predict, be more adulterous, and more openly adulterous, than heterosexual couples. Gays will separate and divorce more often. Adultery and divorce will become more common than they already are; and in some subtle way the institution of marriage will be further weakened.

There is already evidence that should give cause for concern. In Sweden for example, demographers Gunnar Andersson and Turid Noack report that male same-sex partnerships have a 50% higher divorce rate than heterosexual marriages. Female same-sex partnerships have a 170% higher divorce rate. This remains true after controlling for age, education, and other factors. Keep in mind that we're looking at those most committed to making it succeed, a very small fraction of gays. At any rate, the damage that gay marriage might do in this respect probably won't occur in the first decade or two. It is precisely once marriage becomes a normal part of gay life that gays will adapt the institution to their own tastes and beliefs. I have nothing against that, except that their example will inevitably influence how marriage is seen by the heterosexual majority.

To be sure, gay marriage wouldn't be as harmful as polygamous or group marriage. While gay marriage should be opposed on its own terms, it's hard to see how polygamy won't eventually follow if gay marriage is established. I realize this suggestion has a ridiculous sound to it (as did gay marriage not long ago); but there are already groups in America supporting polygamy and group marriage, including the American Civil Liberties Union. Believe it or not, since 1991 the position of the ACLU has been quote: "criminal and civil laws prohibiting or penalizing the practice of plural marriage violate constitutional protections." In other words, the state must treat "plural marriage" no differently than marriage as we know it.

Supporters of polygamy or "plural" marriage view their position as the logical conclusion of supporting gay marriage; and there is evidently something to that. If marriage has no intrinsic connection to procreation, but simply means two people who love each other, then why not three, or four? On what principled basis does the state reject a definition of marriage embraced by consenting adult citizens, and deny them what their hearts desire? (Similar arguments might also be made on behalf of incestuous marriages.)

To be sure, there are arguments against polygamy apart from those against gay marriage. Feminists oppose it as tending to exploit women, and people who genuinely care about marriage feel that "plural" marriage is a travesty of the core meaning of the institution. If same-sex marriage becomes the law of the land, however, arguments like the latter one will already have taken a beating. On the other side will be the right of individuals to make their own decisions in life, the importance of consent as the bedrock of our democracy, and above all the illegitimacy of judging or discriminating against people who harm nobody and simply wish to pursue happiness where they believe it lies. One can even imagine proponents of polygamy claiming to hold the true conservative position: Polygamy will mean a lower divorce rate and fewer single-parent homes, since many married people (notably mothers with children) will prefer allowing their spouses an additional spouse to seeking divorce, and so on.

My guess is that if gay marriage comes, polygamy will eventually follow. If it does, American life will take a giant step towards the restless and unhappy hedonism that characterized the Roman Empire. Gay marriage by itself would be a smaller step in the same direction.

Congressman Barney Frank has asked what harm it does if he is allowed to marry his boyfriend. This is a reasonable question; the answer is that it would do little harm to those who are already married, but considerable harm to future generations of Americans.

Credits

Aristotle, "Nicomachean Ethics." From *The Ethics of Aristotle*, translated by J. A. K. Thomson, revised by Hugh Tredennick (Penguin, 1976): 87–110. Revised translation © Hugh Tredennick, 1976. Reproduced by permission of Penguin Books Ltd.

David Armstrong, "The Nature of Mind." From David Armstrong, "The Nature of Mind" (University of Queensland Press, 1980).

A. J. Ayer, "Freedom and Necessity." From A. J. Ayer, *Philosophical Essays* (Macmillan, 1954). Reproduced with permission of Palgrave Macmillan.

A. J. Ayer, "Philosophy and Knowledge." From *The Problem of Knowledge* by A. J. Ayer (Penguin Books, 1956): 24–35. Copyright © A.J. Ayer, 1956. Reproduced by permission of Penguin Books Ltd.

Micheal J. Behe, "Molecular Machines: Experimental Support for the Design Inference." © 1997 by Michael J. Behe. Reprinted by permission of the author.

Roderick Chrisholm, "Human Freedom and the Self." From Roderick Chisholm, "Human Freedom and the Self" in the 1964 E. H. Lindley Lecture (© University of Kansas Lindley Lecture). Reprinted by permission of the University of Kansas.

Paul Churchland, "Dualism." From Paul Churchland, *Matter and Consciousness, Revised Edition* (MIT Press, 1988, 1997). Used by permission of the MIT Press.

Carl Cohen, "Do Animals Have Rights? (1997). *Ethics and Behavior*, 7, 103–111. Reprinted by permission of Lawrence Erlbaum Associates, Inc.

Daniel Dennett, "The Mythical Threat of Genetic Determinism." From Daniel C. Dennett, *Chronicle of Higher Education*, vol. 49, issue 21 (2003). By permission of the author.

Daniel Dennett, "Where Am I?" From Daniel C. Dennett, *Brainstorms: Philosophical Essays on Mind and Psychology* (MIT Press, 1980). Used by permission of the MIT Press.

René Descartes, "Meditations 1 and 2." From *Discourse on Method and the Meditations* by Descartes, translated by F. E. Sutcliffe (Penguin Classics, 1968): 95–113. Copyright © F. E. Sutcliffe, 1968. Reproduced by permission of Penguin Books, Ltd.

Dennis Earl, "Classical Conceptual Analysis." Published with permission of the author.

Harry Frankfurt, "Alternate Possibilities and Moral Responsibility." From Harry Frankfurt, *Journal of Philosophy* LXVI, 23 (December 4, 1969). Reprinted by permission of the author and publisher.

Marilyn Friedman, "The Practice of Partiality." © 1991 by Marilyn Friedman. Used by kind permission of the author.

Edmund L. Gettier, "Is Justified True Belief Knowledge?" From Edmond L. Gettier, *Analysis 23* (1963). Reprinted with permission of the author.

Christopher Grau, "Brain in a Vat Skepticism." Printed with permission of the author.

John Heil, "Philosophical Behaviorism." From John Heil, *Philosophy of Mind* (Routledge, 1998). Reprinted by permission of author and Taylor and Francis Books Ltd.

Terry Horgan, "Functionalism, Qualia, and the Inverted Spectrum." From Terry Horgan, *Philosophy and Pheno-*

menological Research, vol. 44 (International Phenomenological Society, 1984).

Frank Jackson, "Epiphenomenal Qualia." From Frank Jackson, *Philosophical Quarterly*, vol. 32 (Blackwell Publishing, 1982).

William James, "The Will to Believe" reprinted by permission of the publisher from *The Works of William James: The Will to Believe*, Frederick Berkhardt, General Editor and Fredson Bowers, Textual Editor, pp. 13–33, Cambridge, Mass.: Harvard University Press, copyright © 1979 by the President and Fellows of Harvard College.

Howard Kahane and Paul Tidman, "The Problem of Induction—Old and New." From *Logic & Philosophy; A Modern Introduction* 7th edition by Kahane / Tidman. © 1995. Reprinted with permission of Wadsworth, a division of Thomson Learning: www.thomsonrights.com. Fax 800 730-2215.

Immanuel Kant, "Groundwork of the Metaphysics of Morals." From *Groundwork of the Metaphysics of Morals*, trans. James Ellington (Hackett 1993), pp. 7–8, 9–14, 23–33. Reprinted by permission of Hackett Publishing Company, Inc. All rights reserved.

Immanuel Kant, "What Is Enlightenment?" *Perpetual Peace and Other Essays*, trans. Ted Humphrey (Hackett 1983), pp. 41–48 ("An Answer to the Question: What Is Enlightenment?"). Reprinted by permission of Hackett Publishing Company, Inc. All rights reserved.

Philip Kitcher, "Born-Again Creationism." From Robert T. Pennock, *Intelligent Design Creationism and Its Critics* (MIT Press, 2001). Used by permission of the MIT Press.

Serge-Christophe Kolm, "The Buddhist Theory of 'No-self'." From John Elster, *The Multiple Self* (Cambridge University Press, 1985). Reprinted with the permission of Cambridge University Press.

David Lewis, "Mad Pain and Martian Pain." From Ned Block, D. Terence Langendoen, and Jerrold J. Katz, *Readings in Philosophy of Psychology* (Harvard University Press, 1980). Used by kind permission of Stephanie Lewis.

Manuel Lopez, "The Case Against Gay Marriage." © by Louis Manuel Lopez. Used by kind permission of the author.

Deborah Mathieu, "Male-Chauvinist Religion." © by Deborah Mathieu. Used by kind permission of the author.

Alfred Mele, "Philosophy, a Bus Ride and Dumb Luck." From *Falling in Love with Wisdom: American Philosophers Talk About Their Calling*, edited by David D. Karnos & Robert Shoemaker, copyright 1993 by Oxford University Press, Inc. Used by permission of Oxford University Press, Inc.

Diana Meyers, "Feminist Perspectives on the Self." © Diana Tietjens Meyers from "Feminist Perspectives on the Self," by Diana Tietjens Meyers and Edward N. Zalta, ed. from *The Stanford Encyclopedia of Philosophy* (Spring 2004 Edition). Reprinted by permission of the author and publisher.

Marvin Minsky, "Why People Think Computers Can't." © 1982 by Marvin Minsky. Used by kind permission of the author.

G. E. Moore, "Proof of an External World." From "Proof of an External World" by G. E. Moore in G. E. Moore *Selected Writings*, edited by Thomas Baldwin, copyright 1993 by Thomson Publishing Services. Reprinted by permission of editor and publisher.

Michael Nava and Robert Dawidoff, "The Case for Gay Marriage." Copyright © 1994 by Michael Nava and Robert Dawidoff. From *Created Equal: Why Gay Rights Matter to America* by Michael Nava with Robert Dawidoff. Reprinted by permission of St. Martin's Press, LLC.

John Perry, "A Dialogue on Personal Identity and Immortality." From John Perry, *A Dialogue on Personal Identity and Immortality* (Hackett 1978), pp. 1–18. Reprinted by permission of Hackett Publishing Company, Inc. All rights reserved.

Plato, "Apology." From *The Last Days of Socrates* by Plato, translated by Hugh Tredennick and Harold Tarrant (Penguin 1954) Copyright © Hugh Tredennick, 1954, 1959, 1969. Copyright © Harold Tarrant, 1993.

Louis P. Pojman, "The Case for Moral Objectivism." © 2002 by Louis Pojman. Used by kind permission of the author.

James Rachels, "Must God's Commands Conform to Moral Standards." From *Questions About God: Today's Philosophers Ponder the Divine*, edited by Steven M. Cahn, David Shatz, copyright 2002 by Oxford University Press, Inc. Used by permission of Oxford University Press, Inc.

Tom Regan, "The Moral Basis of Vegetarianism." From Tom Regan, "The Moral Basis of Vegetarianism" in *Canadian Journal of Philosophy* (Published by the University of Calgary Press, O 75:5): 181–214. Reprinted by permission of the University of Calgary Press.

William L. Rowe, "Why the Ontological Argument Fails." From *Philosophy of Religion: An Introduction*, 3rd Edition. © 2001. Reprinted with permission of Wadsworth, a division of Thomson Learning: www.thomsonrights.com. Fax 800 730-2215

George Schlesinger, "Pascal's Wager." From Jeff Jordan, *Gambling on God: Essays on Pascal's Wager* (Roman and Littlefield, 1994). Reprinted by permission of the publisher.

John Searle, "Minds, Brains and Programs." From John Searle, *The Behavioral and Brain Sciences III*, vol. 3 (Cambridge University Press, September 1980): 417–24. Reprinted with the permission of Cambridge University Press.

Aeon Skoble, "Virtue Ethics in TV's *Seinfeld*." Reprinted by permission of Open Court Publishing Company, a division of Carus Publishing Company, Peru, IL, from *Seinfeld and Philosophy* by William Irwin, copyright © 2000 by Open Court Publishing Company.

Baruch Spinoza, "Excerpt from Treatise on the Emendation of the Intellect." From Baruch Spinoza, *Ethics, Treatise on the Emendation of the Intellect, and Selected Letters*, trans. Samuel Shirley, ed. Seymour Feldman (Hackett 1992), pp. 233–236. Reprinted by permission of Hackett Publishing Company, Inc. All rights reserved.

W. T. Stace, "Science and the Physical World." From *Man Against Darkness*, by W. T. Stace, © 1967 by University Pittsburgh Press. Reprinted by permission of the University of Pittsburgh Press.

Richard Swinburne, "Why Does God Allow Evil?" From *Questions About God: Today's Philosophers Ponder the Divine*, edited by Steven M. Cahn, David Shatz, copyright 2002 by Oxford University Press, Inc. Used by permission of Oxford University Press, Inc.

Peter van Inwagen, "The Incompatibility of Free Will and Determinism." From Peter Van Inwagen, "The Incompatibility of Free Will and Determinism" in *Philosophical Studies*, vol. 27 (Kluwer Academic Publishers, 1975): 185–99. With kind permission of Kluwer Academic Publishers.

Announcing . . .
The Longman Publishers and Penguin Books Partnership in Philosophy

Note to Instructors: Bundle any of the titles listed below with *Readings on the Ultimate Questions: An Introduction to Philosophy* and your students will receive up to 60% off the price of the Penguin book! Contact your local Allyn & Bacon/Longman sales representative for details on how to create a Penguin-Longman Value Package.

Early Socratic Dialogues
Plato
Edited by Trevor J. Saunders
Penguin Classic

Meditations and Other Metaphysical Writings
René Descartes
Translated and Introduced by Desmond M. Clarke
Penguin Classic

The Penguin Dictionary of Philosophy
Edited by Thomas Mautner
Penguin

The Last Days of Socrates: Euthyphro, The Apology, Crito, Phaedo
Plato
Translated by Hugh Tredennick
Introduction and Notes by Harold Tarrant
Penguin Classic

Ten Great Works of Philosophy
Edited by Robert Paul Wolff
Signet Classic

The Varieties of Religious Experience: A Study in Human Nature
William James
Edited and Introduced by Martin E. Marty
Penguin Classic